Second Edition

# The Structure of
# Canadian History

**Second Edition**

# The Structure of Canadian History

**J. L. Finlay/D. N. Sprague**

University of Manitoba

Maps by
Victor Lytwyn

Prentice-Hall Canada Inc.

*Scarborough, Ontario*

Canadian Cataloguing in Publication Data

Finlay, John L., 1939-
  The structure of Canadian history

Includes index.
ISBN 0-13-854364-X

1. Canada-History.        I. Sprague, Douglas N.,
1944-    II. Title.

FC164.F55          971          C79-094086-8
F1026.F55

Prentice-Hall, Inc., Englewood Cliffs, New Jersey
Prentice-Hall International, Inc., London
Prentice-Hall of Australia, Pty., Ltd., Sydney
Prentice-Hall of India, Pvt., Ltd., New Delhi
Prentice-Hall of Japan, Inc., Tokyo
Prentice-Hall of Southeast Asia (Pte.) Ltd., Singapore
Editora Prentice-Hall do Brasil Ltda., Rio de Janeiro

Production Editor: Linda Findlay
Design: Gail Ferreira
Production: Monika Heike
Composition: Howarth & Smith Limited

ISBN 0-13-854364-X

        4    5        87    86

Printed and bound in Canada

*For Mary and*
*For Lawrence and David*

---

# Contents

# Preface

The "structure" on which this volume focuses is the story of power: who held it, how, and for what purposes. In our view, the study of history as a whole requires due attention to society's rulers, the more fully to appreciate the means and purposes by which society itself is organized. But, since politics does not develop in a vacuum, social and economic themes are developed as well.

For the most part, the work is based on other published materials, monographs, and articles appearing within the last fifteen years. Such sources are acknowledged in several ways. In the body of the text, bold interpretations are mentioned by author and long quotations are cited by volume and page. At the end of each chapter, bibliographical essays are offered to give readers an appreciation of the wider debate — and alternate points of view — on the many issues that are covered all too briefly in the pages that follow. But acknowledging our sources in this manner in no way acknowledges in full the debt we owe to past historians and above all to the latest generation without whose careful archival research the present study would have been quite impossible. Moreover, we realize that we owe the same scholars an apology for the simplification of complex arguments and reduction of detail that has occurred in condensation for grafting onto a larger story in ways that no scholar may originally have intended. Still, in this revised and expanded edition — as with our first attempt at synthesis written some years ago — we hope that the work will spark interest as well as criticism, and continue to be of some use to students in the classroom.

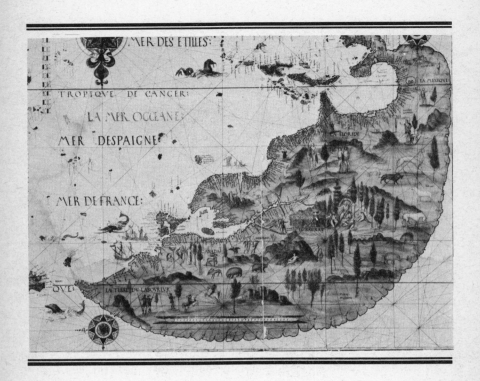

"Discovery . . . does not lead necessarily or immediately to settlement."

# CHAPTER 1

# The Invention of the New World

## I    Old World Background to New World History

The background to Canadian history does not lie in voyages of discovery, in those, say, of Jacques Cartier. For that matter, the wider background to New World history is not to be sought in the voyages of Columbus or even in those of his predecessors. Discovery is but a first step, a prerequisite, a beginning that does not lead necessarily or immediately to settlement. It is salutary for those living in the Americas today to realize how uninterested, in fact, fifteenth- and sixteenth-century Europe was in what its sea captains had stumbled across. For instance, there were seven reprintings of a world geography reference book in France between 1539 and 1558 (a time that spans France's own early interest in the New World and Cartier's voyages) and in not one of these was any mention made of the New World. The real background, then, to Canadian and New World history after 1492 must be sought in the *invention* of the Americas, that is, in imagining that something could be made out of mere discovery; something so attractive that Europeans would undertake the costly and dangerous task of crossing the Atlantic Ocean and conquering new territory. The nature of the invention may be understood from an examination of European society in the fifteenth century. At the same time, that examination will indicate why, initially at least, the Americas were so small a part of the European consciousness.

The fifteenth century was a time both of contraction and expansion in Europe — or, more precisely, of contraction in the East and expansion in the West. This pattern was to be seen, for instance, in the fortunes of that age-old Christian imperative to go forth and convert the heathen. In the earlier Middle Ages, during the twelfth and thirteenth centuries, Christen-

1

dom had expanded into the Middle East, successfully taking Jerusalem and the Holy Land. Since then, however, the Islamic enemy had counter-attacked and with their thrusts, especially into the area of present-day Turkey, Christendom had been forced onto the defensive. A singular set-back occurred when Constantinople, the headquarters of Orthodox Christianity, fell to Islam in 1453. Such developments contributed significantly to the diminution of missionary activity in the East. However, the impulse was not completely dead, and it found its outlet in the West in the Iberian peninsula. There the work of centuries was coming to fruition: the Christian reconquest of that area was capped in 1492 when Granada, the last stronghold of the Islamic Moors in Spain, was captured. The period and movement known in Spanish history as the *Reconquista* was now complete.

The pattern of withdrawal in the East and expansion in the West had mundane yet important consequences. Long-established trade routes to the Far East, especially for the all-important spices that made the foul, stinking living conditions and the food of the wealthy slightly more tolerable than they would otherwise have been, were disrupted by these new developments in the Middle East. Western Europeans began to seek to outflank these obstacles; and throughout the fifteenth century the Portuguese in particular were at the forefront of voyages of discovery aimed at finding an all-water route to the wealth of Asia. It was a venture that finally succeeded in 1486 when Bartholemew Diaz sailed beyond the Cape of Good Hope into the Indian Ocean, and in 1498 when Vasco da Gama reached India itself.

Accompanying this Western European search for new trade routes was a psychological development which intensified that search and gave to the discovery, and exploitation of new wealth, a cutting edge never before experienced. The early Middle Ages had known wealthy individuals, of course. There is, for example, record of one William of Duvenwoorde (1290-1353) who was said to have enjoyed an annual income of some 70 000 *livres*, perhaps the equivalent of $1 million today. But William and others like him were not esteemed for their wealth. Indeed, they were distrusted. Wealth was something to be wary of, an exposure to sin in its getting and spending. Predictably, the watchdog of society's morals, the Church, was outspoken in its condemnation of the lust for gain as leading to "damnable avarice, sensuality and pride." In particular, the lending of money with a charge of interest, the very basis of a modern, capitalist economy, was denounced by the Church in the harshest terms. But increasingly in the fifteenth century such attitudes were changing, and the old prohibitions were losing their force. The idea that economics was at most a branch of theology was breaking down, and gradually the more modern idea that economics was an autonomous discipline with methods and ends of its own was taking its place. Wealth was pursued with fewer reservations deriving from other-worldly or countervailing considerations. And while the common people might never dream of becoming as wealthy as kings or princes, they began in an unprecedented way to see themselves as worthy of riches.

This intensified interest in trading for wealth, and the search for new routes to that wealth, were directed to Asia. When Columbus sailed due west from Spain in 1492 it was with the determination of avoiding the Portuguese sphere of influence and finding a shorter route to the Spice Islands, China, and Japan. The Americas were not thought to exist; to this day, the name of the islands where he made his first landfalls, the West Indies, serves to underline the fact that Columbus and Europe had made a gigantic miscalculation and had hit upon an unexpected world that was truly new.

The Europeans' miscalculation, of course, did not remain a liability for long. It became apparent that the New World might yield immense wealth of all kinds and became a legitimate alternative to Asia. At the same time, there were millions of souls to be converted to Christianity there by Christian missionary activity. Here, then, were two possible inventions of America. But a third kind of invention took precedence, the background for which is also found in the development of late medieval European society.

Fifteenth-century Europe was changing not only physically and intellectually, but politically, too. Just as early economists had broken free from medieval constraints in order to direct men's minds to the question of how to acquire wealth, so, too, observers of politics had broken free from earlier approaches to statecraft. In place of theologically-structured discussions of the rights and duties of rulers and the ruled, intellectuals increasingly went back to history and sought to show *how* notable rulers had conducted themselves to use their power effectively. At a time when Europe was plagued by a general breakdown of law and order (in England this was the time of the Wars of the Roses, in France the aftermath of the Hundred Years War and a situation where the French Crown controlled only about one fourth of the kingdom) the appeal of political writers such as Machiavelli was enormous. *The Prince*, which he published early in the sixteenth century, is a superb example of a "how to" book. Any medieval discussion of the Christian duty owed by the Prince to his subjects is completely absent; everywhere is advice on how to gain and hold on to power.

The rulers of the late fifteenth and early sixteenth centuries showed themselves to be outstanding Machiavellians. Ruthless, scheming and despotic, they centralized their power and strengthened the royal courts and procedures. Their concentration of power was helped by the technological developments of weapons because the new key to victory in battle was the possession of artillery and professional infantry. Both were costly investments that only kings and princes could afford. Both developments helped spell the end of the feudal lord on horseback, who could, with his armed retainers defy the ruler and defend himself in his castle. In this new period the feudal noble was transformed into a courtier and the castle gave way to the country house or chateau.

There were those among the nobility who made the transition to the new order of things with relative ease. They made their peace with the king, were rewarded with courtly handouts, and concentrated upon a methodical exploitation of their lands, ceasing to see them as the means of supporting potential troops. But there were many who could not make the adjustment. For them, the newly emerging Europe, increasingly dominated by absolutist kings and merchant princes, was anathema. Their ideals, their glorification of military skills, courage and honor, all built upon a servile base of obedient peasants, had no place in Europe. It became necessary to invent a new world where such ideals could be accommodated.

Spain was the country best placed to invent this new world. There the missionary drive was most vital and the far western search for new trade routes was strongly marked. With Spain the leader in the production of wool and metal wares, the new psychology of wealth was well developed. But the appeal of the feudal *hidalgo*, the knight on horseback, was also deeply entrenched because the *Reconquista* had kept these values to the fore, and the triumphant conclusion of that Holy War had seemed to confirm them.

How could the centralizing kings of Spain tolerate the *hidalgo?* Was there room in a country suddenly at peace for the soldier of fortune? Just at the moment when the reconquest was completed the doors to the New World opened in the minds of those who identified with the life of the fighting nobleman and who imagined ennoblement as legitimate even if it came by conquest of exotic people in a strange new world. If he remained in Europe, the soldier of fortune might be nothing more than a superfluous anachronism; but in the Indies this man — any man — might become a lord of land, of Indians, and of gold. So, the first invention of the New World was not by merchants or kings. The first invention was by Spaniards who envisioned the Indies as a place for advancing themselves by exporting feudalism after it had begun to decline in Europe.

## II    The Spanish Prototype of Colonization by Conquest

The islands of the Caribbean did not, however, provide the Spaniards with an ideal setting for enacting their invention of America. A generation later, after first landing in the West Indies, they undertook the conquest of Mexico in 1519 and in so doing established the prototype of New World occupation. Later, other Spaniards would apply the formula to Peru and the English and French would attempt the same project further north. Everyone came to accept this first invention of the New World as the most plausible. The salient features of the Spanish subjugation of Mexico are therefore important to Canadian history because it is the Spanish precedent that makes intelligible Jacques Cartier's apparently foolhardy quest for the Kingdom of the Saguenay twenty years later. Cartier and the others were not fools. Emulating the Spanish example of colonization by conquest, they came away with less, quite simply, because in the north there was less to take.

The great attraction of Mexico was that it was organized as an advanced civilization under Aztec rule in such a way as to satisfy the three needs of European expansion. The need for missionary work was pointed up by the nature of the Aztec religion, calling for human sacrifice on a massive scale. Then there was Aztec wealth. The Aztecs lacked metal tools and any domesticated animals other than poultry, but they did practice horticulture, and farming was a technological advance that made others possible. Their capital, Tenochtitlan, on the site of present-day Mexico City, was a metropolis with more than a quarter of a million inhabitants (contemporary London had some 50 000). Not only was it impressive in scale, it was also built of stone, the dominant structure being a huge pyramid at the center, crowned with a sacrificial altar. Here was every sign of wealth with an apparent abundance of gold and silver. Finally, since the Aztec empire was a complex hierarchical ordering of peoples, it could be taken over in its existing form. All the Spaniards had to do was to take the place of the Aztec overlords. The *hidalgo* would have his peasantry ready-made.

What increased the attractiveness of Mexico was the fact that the appetizing prize was sufficiently flawed internally that its ability to withstand external aggression was limited. The technological deficiencies hinted at above meant that the Spaniards enjoyed immense military advantages. The invaders possessed artillery and horses, which together gave them a mobility and a power infinitely superior to their enemy's. Also, the Aztec empire embraced recently conquered people who would be eager to rally to the Spaniards as a means of gaining revenge. Above all, Aztec society was psychologically unprepared to confront invasion because Aztec religion had become self-defeating. Human sacrifice had been practised on such a massive scale (the coronation of a new emperor might be marked by as many as 80 000 sacrifices) that the population could not have been expected to defend the regime spontaneously. More important, perhaps, was the fact that the population had been conditioned to be extraordinarily obedient and passive, since one principle of selection for sacrifice was criminality, often of a minor kind. For such a people, the substitution of one ruling class for another would be largely a matter of indifference. Then, too, Aztec society was assailed by fears of imminent destruction. There had been three successive crop failures between 1505 and 1507 and in this frightening setting rumors of doom circulated widely. Prophecy had foretold that the world would end one day; now signs and omens from various sources pointed to fulfillment. In 1511 a comet confirmed the worst fears of many.

By 1515 garbled tales of the sighting of strange, bearded men with fair skins began to filter through to Tenochtitlan. In that year a trunk that was washed ashore provided confirmation for the rumors. When the Emperor Montezuma opened it he found, in addition to unusual jewelry and trinkets, clothing abnormally large and a frightening weapon. This last was clearly a sword, but it was not carved of wood and set with obsidian chips; instead it was made entirely of an unknown substance.

Everything that supported the mood of doubt and vague apprehension served also to rejuvenate the myth of Quetzacoatl, the god who would come in the fullness of time to slay the emperor and forbid human sacrifice. The prophecy foretold that "when the world is become oppressed, when it is the end of the world, at the time of its ending, he will come to bring it to an end."

Given these various factors, the march of the Spaniards from the coast to Tenochtitlan was easily accomplished in less than six months under their leader, Cortés. The emperor Montezuma was convinced that Cortés was Quetzacoatl, and when the invading force reached the capital he abdicated and surrendered his empire. Even when the Aztec nobility repudiated Montezuma's act and attacked the Spanish, the new order was not seriously imperiled. Cortés and a small remnant of his orginal force escaped to the territory of Indians hostile to the Aztecs. In the following year, thanks to clever tactical maneuvering, superior weaponry, and the backing of his Indian allies, Cortés successfully defeated the nobles' rebellion.

By 1521, in a mere two years, a force of some six hundred men had defeated and entirely subdued an empire of over twenty million people. After subjugation came serfdom and baptism. Individual Spaniards received lordship over villages of Indians; they became *encomenderos*. Cortés himself became a feudal lord with supreme authority over his vassals and their serfs. The conquest had succeeded brilliantly. These invaders, the *conquistadores*, were enriched and ennobled. The New World had proved worthwhile; in particular, a handful of Europeans had invented it as their opportunity to revitalize a way of life which was slipping away in Europe. Soon others would attempt the same adventure farther north.

## III    French Attempts to Seize a Northern Mexico

Not surprisingly, the conquerors of Mexico published their exploits, and found an eager audience in Europe. In time their works were translated into other languages (two Englishmen, Richard Hakluyt and Robert Eden, were leading translators). In this way, a large following learned of the fabulous wealth and opportunities of the New World, now portrayed as a paradise densely populated with guileless and loving people who lived on the produce of a bountiful nature. Since they were no match for artillery and muskets, Europeans had nothing to do but to move to America, master the people, and enjoy sumptuous leisure by putting their Indian serfs to work for them. Englishmen, Frenchmen, and others resolved to imitate the Spanish example in those parts of the New World not yet effectively occupied by Spain or Portugal.

First, there were scouting ventures. For instance, Henry VII of England sent John Cabot to Newfoundland in 1497 and Francis I of France sent Verrazano to explore the North Atlantic coast in 1524; but more ambitious undertakings began only after the additional incentive of more Spanish conquests in the manner of Cortés. After news of Pizarro's conquest of Peru in 1530, the French decided it was time that they broke Spain's monopoly in the New World. Pizarro had succeeded with only two hundred men (more proof that Cortés' feat had not been simply a lucky accident). As a result, in 1534 Francis I commissioned a decayed squire from Brittany, Jacques Cartier, to "discover ... countries where it is said that he should find great quantity of gold and other valuable things." It should be added that Cartier also believed he might find a northwest passage to Asia and the Spice Islands.

Cartier's expedition reached North America too late in the summer of 1534 to do more than stake a claim to the territory. North of what is now called Anticosti Island, Cartier encountered a tremendous current which led him to believe that the channel leading west might be a river running out of northern Asia. He also made contact with the native people, enough to dismiss them as "the sorriest folk there can be in the world." Unlike the Indians Cortés and Pizarro had plundered, the northerners "had not anything above the value of five sous, their canoes and fishing nets excepted." Since the season was turning cold and provisions were running low, Cartier decided to return to France with two captive natives, train them as interpreters, and persuade his patron to support a second voyage. Columbus had used such means to gain further support from his patrons after his first voyage. Cartier hoped that the tactic would also be sufficient to maintain the interest of his king.

Cartier's hope was confirmed. Even though he returned with nothing more than two unhappy Indians and the unsolved mystery of what lay beyond the Gulf of St. Lawrence, Francis I agreed to support another expedition with sufficient provisions to stay over the winter. On the voyage of 1535, Cartier commanded three ships rather than the two of 1534 and he arrived in the Gulf early enough for extensive exploration. At the spot where the sea narrowed to what was evidently the mouth of a river, he found a village, Stadacona (the site of what was later called Quebec). The place was the home of the two Indians, now interpreters. All were welcomed. Then, with roughly one third of his men, he continued up river as far as was navigable. Stopped by rapids, he found himself at a town site called Hochelaga. Like Stadacona, the village was no more than a collection of bark longhouses surrounded by corn fields. The appearance of the place — and the people — was hardly encouraging. But Cartier climbed a hill above Hochelaga, a promontory he named Mount Royal (or Montreal) and, from this vantage point, the explorer beheld a panaroma that was awe-inspiring in comparison with the village below or with the rocky coast of Labrador, which he had decribed as "the land God gave Cain" on his previous visit. From Mount Royal, Cartier said that he could see "for more than thirty leagues round about." Between the Laurentian and the northern Adirondack mountains he saw "the finest land it is possible to see." The valley before him looked "arable, level, and flat." And in the midst was the river, "large, wide and broad." He was disappointed that it was not navigable any farther; still, he found himself imagining the St. Lawrence Valley as a land hospitable to farming, and he saw the site of Hochelaga as the location of an entrepôt for the whole continent. Here at Mount Royal he was already about a thousand miles from the Atlantic Coast (see map 1.1) and according to his guides, this water highway could take a traveler another thousand miles inland. What of the interior though?

With gestures and signs, his guides from Hochelaga gave information that the explorer had almost abandoned hope of obtaining. "Without our asking any questions or making any sign, they seized the chain of the Captain's whistle and a dagger-handle of yellow copper-gilt like gold ... and gave us to understand that both came from up that river." The waterway to which they pointed was the Ottawa River. But they could not venture further. It was too late in the summer and, without benefit of appropriate boats, the traveling would have been doubly difficult. So Cartier descended the St. Lawrence to Stadacona and rejoined the rest of his company encamped there.

Over the long winter the French learned more about the interior. They learned it was well populated and the people were wealthy. The chieftain in Stadacona, Donnacona, was eager to please the French by telling them whatever they wanted to hear. Thus, Cartier determined to return to France to win command of an adequate expeditionary force to take the

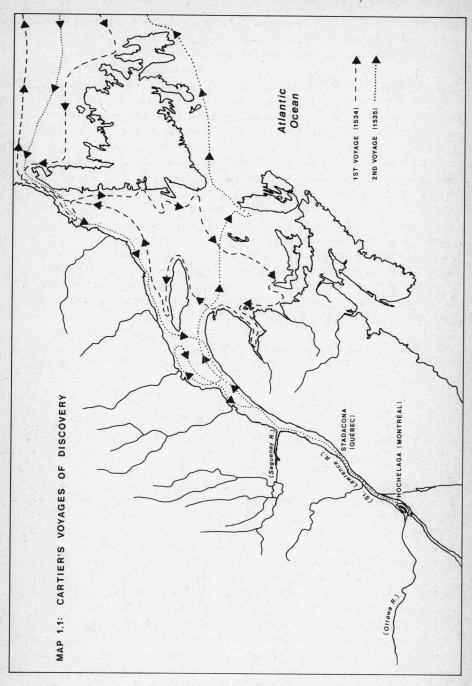

MAP 1.1: CARTIER'S VOYAGES OF DISCOVERY

Atlantic Ocean

1ST VOYAGE (1534)

2ND VOYAGE (1535)

(Saguenay R.)

STADACONA
(QUÉBEC)

(St. Lawrence R.)

HOCHELAGA (MONTRÉAL)

(Ottawa R.)

kingdom. As soon as the ice was out of the river he set sail for home, having seized Donnacona and others with him.

The old chief realized that if he wanted to return to his people he would have to give a convincing performance for Francis I. Learning of the European desire for spices, he added to his tales of gold, silver, and jewels stories about cinnamon, cloves, and oranges that grew in the fabulous Kingdom of the Saguenay. In time Donnaconas's stories had their effect, and a little later a Spanish spy at the French court reported to his king that "the King of France says the Indian king told him there is a large city called the Sagana, where there are many mines of gold and silver in great abundance, and men who dress and wear shoes as we do; and that there is abundance of cloves, nutmeg, and pepper." But more than five years passed before Francis I could bring himself to finance another expedition. By this time Donnacona had despaired, sickened, and died of smallpox.

Finally, in 1541 an expedition was launched, modeled on the Spanish plan, with about the same number of men Cortés had used to conquer the Aztecs. There was support staff including stonemasons, carpenters, plowmen, and even women, but fighting men predominated, including seven hundred soldiers and sailors to operate from twenty small boats complete with artillery. The plan called for the establishment of a stronghold near the mouth of the entrance to the Gulf of St. Lawrence, then a move inland to the interior to find the Kingdom of the Saguenay and subdue it by playing off one Indian population against another. After the conquest, the conquerors were to divide the spoils and the people in accordance with the system used to subdue the Aztecs. "In order to encourage ... those who will undertake the expedition" the King promised a division of booty (one third for himself, one third for the commander, and one third for the men). He also promised baronial social status for the French *conquistadores:* "We grant to our Lieutenant full power and authority in the lands ... to grant in fief and seigniory ... ." Thus, the Indians were to be looted and then made into Christian serfs. Their conquerors — largely nobodies in France — would become nobility by virtue of their migration to the New World and by their conquest of the Kingdom of the Saguenay.

The expedition was to be under dual leadership. The King's lieutenant, Jean-François de la Rocque, sieur de Roberval, a nobleman and a soldier, was to have the supreme command on land and, at sea, immediate command over five ships, half of the force that was assembled. Jacques Cartier, the man with precedence by virtue of his experience, was the junior commander because of his lack of military experience and inferior social position. Perhaps he would rise in status by conquest. For this reason he may have been the more anxious to embark. Impatient with delays, Cartier set out first with his five ships with Roberval's permission; the sieur was to follow as soon as he assembled his artillery.

When Cartier arrived in the Gulf of St. Lawrence in late summer of

1541, he promptly set to work constructing the base in accordance with the plan. From this time onward everything went badly, however. The Indians were suspicious of Cartier's failure to return with Donnacona and were not soothed by his story that the captive Indians taken in 1535 were great lords in France now and refused to return to their homeland. Consequently, over the winter, friction increased. Roberval did not arrive in the early spring, and Cartier began to suspect that the Kingdom of the Saguenay was only a myth. In the meantime, the soldiers under his command were acting as if they had no need to go further in search of their treasure, and occupied themselves by gathering "precious stones" that lay conveniently all about. If Cartier suspected that such gems were less than they seemed, his doubts did not prevent him from allowing his men to barrel them up and load the cargo on board ship. With nearly a dozen barrels of "treasure", he then set sail for France.

Before Cartier reached the open sea, however, he happened to encounter Roberval with the other half of the expedition. But Cartier had no intention of lingering any longer in this land God gave Cain. Disobeying orders from Roberval to return to the St. Lawrence, he slipped into a fog bank and sailed to France. Roberval was left to see for himself the poverty of the native people, the harshness of the climate, and the barrenness of the land once he and his men ventured up river to explore the country and complete their mission. At Cap Rouge they spent the winter — five months of incredible misery. Then they, too, returned to France as quickly as they could. Roberval had found nothing of value, and the barrels of treasure Cartier had carried home proved to be nothing more than quartz crystals. Thus, the only tangible prize from the expedition was the enrichment of the language. Henceforth, anyone wanting to convey the idea of utter worthlessness in an object had only to call it a Canadian diamond: "Voilà un diamant du Canada."

## IV   The English Attempt to Imitate New Spain

The Cartier-Roberval expedition of 1541-43 had proven that the territory in the vicinity of the Gulf of the St. Lawrence did not support a people with wealth like the Aztecs'. Sixty years later, the English proved that territory to the south was similarly barren. English involvement was delayed this long because England was less centralized than Portugal, Spain, or France. Also, insofar as the English were prepared for such activity earlier, they were involved in colonization closer to home in the attempt to subdue Ireland. The energy devoted to this project intensified after the completion of the final chapter of the English war between competing nobles that made Henry Tudor king of England in 1485. Subsequently, he directed new attention to Ireland at the same time that he attempted to centralize the administration of England. Later, his son, Henry VIII, split the English church from the Roman (over legal and ecclesiastical issues arising from the first of his many divorces). The younger Henry thus gained a new reason to subdue Ireland: it was a potential backdoor to England accessible to his country's Roman Catholic enemies, France and Spain.

An important turning point came in the 1560s. In this decade, Sir Henry Sidney proposed occupation of Ireland in much the same way that the Spaniards had taken over Mexico and Peru. His plan was to conquer Ireland by colonizing it with English soldier-settlers in key areas. The proposal circulated by Sidney (with royal approval, of course) appealed greatly to adventurous younger sons in England, English equivalents of Cortés and his men.

The English experience in Ireland differed from the Spanish occupation of Mexico, however, in the mission aspect because in Ireland the native people were not anxious to abandon the old church. With increasing fervor, the Irish turned to their Catholicism as a badge of their resistance to and difference from the English. The English, for their part, redoubled their efforts to obliterate all traces of Gallic tribalism. Since English missionary zeal was thus as much national as religious, the English colonizers of Ireland were not willing to accept Irishmen for a "peasantry" as they found them. The Irish were required to become English or to perish. They were expected to build houses, make townships, and "manure or improve their land as it ought to be" or to make way for those who would. Resistors were killed. As a result, one English official boasted that in one month of the year 1573 he had killed "of the rebels and their riders about the number of eight hundred persons." Two years later, Francis Drake (better known, perhaps, as the navigator who was knighted for his expoits against the Spaniards), massacred six hundred children, women, and men on Rathlin Island for the crime of allowing a "good and fruitful country to lie waste like a wilderness."

The Irish adventure was a preparation for later exploits that exhibited the same peculiar kind of missionary zeal. When English colonizers stated that it was a "goodly deed" to have attempted to eradicate "so wicked a race" as the Irish, they were indicating the extent to which they had conditioned themselves to see native peoples as devils rather than fellow human beings. Upon subduing them, therefore, the English were less inclined to incorporate aboriginal people into the social hierarchy of the new society — even on the bottom level.

Encouraged by their Irish adventures, the English felt ready to probe beyond Ireland to America by the 1580s, and many of those involved in the next ventures had gained their first experience in Ireland. What they hoped to find in the New World, however, were the kinds of empires the Spaniards had taken. Moreover, since the English state was quite impoverished, the English colonizers sought the assistance of private subscribers rather than the Crown. In 1606, a joint-stock company was formed to recruit soldiers and artisans with orders to make contact with docile Indians and train them in the arts appropriate to the exotic resources imagined to be abundant in the New World — goldsmiths, perfumers, and glass-blowers, for example.

In accordance with this general plan, some 100 employees of the company boarded three ships in December of 1606 and set out for Virginia (a southern portion of North America, renamed at this time in honor of the late "Virgin Queen" of England, Elizabeth I). Four months after departure, they arrived in what is now called Chesapeake Bay and selected a spot on a low-lying peninsula forty miles up a river they called the James, in honor of their new monarch. The site seemed militarily defensible. On the river side, the water was deep enough to serve as an anchorage, and, on the land side, the area could be barricaded against Indians should they prove hostile. The problem was that the natives were neither troublesome nor easily subdued. In this area, they were under a government at once powerful and well regarded. Their leader, Powhatan, did have his enemies, but they were considerably inland and Powhatan felt entirely competent to deal with them without English assistance. Since Powhatan's enemies were too far away to serve as alternate allies for the Company, the English invaders were kept at a distance by Powhatan, and were not assisted by their potential allies. Weakened by malaria and poor diet, the invasion force languished in the swamp they named Jamestown.

But the Company had invested too much to give up after only one year. In the following spring, despite the attrition of their force in Virginia from 120 people to just 40, the survivors were resupplied, reinforced, and given more time to fulfill their mission. By the spring of 1609, there was still no sign of improvement. Still, too much had been committed to abandon the project. As a result, the men in Virginia were ordered to hold their ground — in fact, to cultivate it.

Normally, soldiers were expected to fight and to die, to go hungry and perhaps even to starve, but military men — especially those of "gentle" birth — were never expected to do the work of plain farmers. For this reason, the directors of the company had to subject their employees to a discipline even harsher than standard military custom. The managers sought and found a disciplinarian equal to the task in Sir Thomas Dale, recruited in the Netherlands to go to Virginia to make the party self-sufficient in food. He imposed the death penalty for idleness as well as for insubordination, for swearing as well as for failure to attend church. By 1612, Virginia's "starving time" was ending.

The Virginia Company could whip its employees into growing their own food, but survival did not spell profit. If the expedition was able to feed itself after 1612, it had still failed to make money for the Virginia Company. The region of Chesapeake Bay had been proved to be no more fit for conquest than the area around the Gulf of St. Lawrence. It seemed only a matter of time before the stockholders would recognize reality and abandon Virginia entirely.

Yet abandonment did not occur. Between 1612 and 1614, one of the employee-settlers, John Rolfe, began growing tobacco and, by using a better curing process, he was able to produce a "sotweed" superior to that which was already imported to Europe from the Spanish colonies. As nearly everyone began to grow tobacco, Virginia took on a new meaning and value, especially to the Company. King James disapproved of the development and denounced tobacco-smoking as "A custom loathsome to the eye, hateful to the nose, harmful to the brain, dangerous to the lungs, and in the black stinking fume thereof, nearest resembling the horrible Stigian smoke of the pit that is bottomless." But the habit continued to grow in popularity among the people who could afford such an expensive novelty. Naturally, the Virginia Company was only too happy to provide that for which European aristocrats were willing to pay so dearly. Over one ton of tobacco was produced for export from the colony in 1616. Two years later, production soared to 50 000 pounds. In this way, Jamestown became North America's first boom town. In the rush to grow tobacco, the "streets and all other spare places" were planted. Soon the colony dispersed from the town to the countryside, and to satisfy the demand for vacant land, one entire tribe of Indians was invited to a feast celebrating the new prosperity. All were deliberately poisoned, and new farms sprang up on the land thus vacated.

The lure of wealth to be gained from growing tobacco on land free for the taking preserved the English interest in the New World after their other illusions had been lost. In 1612, William Simmonds had announced that Virginia as they found it was "ill peopled" and poor. There was "only an idle, improvident people, ignorant of the knowledge of gold and silver" to be found in the place. The Indians themselves were thus not an exploitable resource — but their land was. Ralph Homer, writing from Virginia two years after Simmonds, also reported that there was no easy gold to be found, "nor will the deer come when they are called." But Homer suggested that any man who doubted the "goodness of the ground" would find comfort in the "cheapness of it." Still, the Virginia tobacco boom could not be expanded into every region of North America, certainly not to the coast of Labrador. It remained to be seen if some other European invention was suitable for the more northerly part of the New World; or, whether it would remain undisturbed as a homeland for the people the Europeans now dismissed as too poor to plunder.

# Bibliography

One of the most useful general surveys of the history of Canada is the projected eighteen-volume Canadian Centenary Series, in which collection the work that covers the period of the age of discovery is *Early Voyages and Northern Approaches, 1000-1632* (1959) by T.J. Olesson. Another book generally on the same subject is S.E. Morison, *The European Discovery of America* (1971). Works that are more concerned with the European reaction to discovery are J.H. Elliott, *The Old World and the New, 1492-1650* (1972) and Edmundo O'Gorman, *The Invention of America* (1961).

The background to Spain's leadership in New World expansion is interpreted provocatively by Eric Wolf in the early parts of his analysis of Spanish exploitation of Central America in *Sons of the Shaking Earth* (1959). A fascinating account of Cortés and his conquest of Mexico is *The Hummingbird and the Hawk: Conquest and Sovereignty in the Valley of Mexico, 1503-1541* (1967) by R.C. Padden. An account of the French and English attempts to conquer empires north of the Aztec's is found in J.B. Brebner, *The Explorers of North America, 1492 to 1806* (1933). The special case of the relationship between the English experience in Ireland and what was attempted in Virginia is covered by essays in K.R. Andrews, *et al., The Westward Enterprise: English Activities in Ireland, the Atlantic, and America, 1480-1650* (1979). For an account of the transition from colonization by conquest to agricultural bonanza in Virginia, see E.S. Morgan, "The Labor Problem at Jamestown, 1607-18," *American Historical Review* (1971).

"The colony . . . was the focal point in a trading system
requiring only enough clerks and warehousemen to
handle the volume of the fur trade."

# CHAPTER 2

# The Canadian Fur Rush

## I    Retreat to Fishing, Advance to Fur Trade

The original invention of America as a refuge for a rejuvenated feudalism had been abandoned by the French in failure and disillusionment in 1543. After the Kingdom of the Saguenay had proved illusory, there was no incentive to return to the region of the St. Lawrence on a permanent basis. The use of North America by Europeans, therefore, reverted to an earlier form of exploitation that in fact predated Cartier. This was the cod fishery which had flourished since the early 1500s off the Newfoundland Banks. It was reported that the sea in this vicinity was "swarming with fish which can be taken not only with the net, but in buckets let down with a stone." But what was incentive enough to draw fishermen across the Atlantic was not sufficient to make them go there to live. For these French, Basque, English, and Portuguese fishermen, the Banks were inviting as a resource base, but home was in Europe, and to their homelands they always returned.

No matter how casual the contacts of these fishing expeditions with the territory of the New World, they did provide European mariners with a growing body of knowledge about the water approaches to the new land. Thus, long before Cartier made his first voyage as a potential conqueror, he had been to America as a commercial fisherman. As he and other Europeans came to know the land and its people through the cod fishery, so, too, did the native peoples become acquainted with the Europeans and value the trade potential of the new association. On Cartier's arrival in 1534, for example, they "made frequent signs" for him to come on shore, suggesting that trading had been taking place between native and visitor long before this date.

At first, no doubt, only curios were exchanged. But very quickly it became clear that the Indians had special interests. Cartier reported that

17

they had particularly "great pleasure in possessing and obtaining ... iron wares ... ." Iron and copper kettles were the special marvel because until European trading contact, the Indians had been obliged to cook their food by the clumsy and time-consuming method of heating stones and then dropping them into wooden bowls, thus boiling the ingredients. "Iron wares" could be placed over an open flame.

For their part, the Europeans were happy to trade for furs. In signalling to Cartier in 1534, Indians lured his party to shore with pelts "held up ... on sticks." Here was one of the few commodities possessed by the native people that was highly valued in Europe. Consequently, Cartier's men eagerly traded for everything on hand — including the Indians' wearing apparel (They "went back naked without any skins on them"). The scene of laughing, naked Indians with arm loads of kettles might have been comic to the Europeans, but the Indians knew what they wanted, and, since the appearance of the newcomers was so unpredictable, they realized that they had to seize every trading opportunity to the fullest.

By the mid-sixteenth century, however, ships completely laden with pots and pans would sail occasionally to the St. Lawrence area for the express purpose of trading in furs, usually the luxury pelts of ermine and marten used to trim the robes of superior state officials, higher ecclesiastics, and others of the very loftiest positions in European society. The demand for such furs was still not great enough to call into existence anything more than infrequent trading, but about the end of the 1500s a change in men's fashion led to a large-scale demand for a kind of fur that was abundant in North America but nearly extinct in Europe. It had suddenly become *de rigueur* for every gentleman and nobleman to sport a broad brimmed felt hat. Given the tendency of felt fabricated from the hair of rabbits and sheep to droop, a more suitable fiber for hats was sought and found in the soft undercoat of the beaver. Scandinavian and Russian supplies were soon depleted, but in the northern parts of the New World there seemed to be an unlimited stock. On this basis, it became possible to transform the occasional fur trade into a steady rush for beaver skins.

Enormous profits could be realized. For one iron kettle a trader could obtain an Indian's beaver robe consisting of five to eight skins. The older the robe, the better it was for felting because it was worn with the fur-side next to the wearer and after a period of constant wearing, the beaver guard hairs would fall away leaving only the soft and greasy undercoat, ready to be removed from the skin and matted into felt. The Indians would gladly trade what was becoming a worn-out robe for a new kettle. Once in Paris, one "greasy beaver" robe (sufficient for six to eight hats) could be sold by the trader, at times, for enough to buy one hundred kettles. The costs of venturing to the vicinity of the St. Lawrence were indeed high, but the return was so handsome that it was worthwhile. Here was an incentive to make the French think seriously again of permanent settlement in the St. Lawrence area.

## II    Fur Trade Outpost

In 1588 the King of France, Henry III, granted the fur trade of Canada as a monopoly to two nephews of Jacques Cartier in compensation for the expenses claimed by the Cartier family for the explorer's three voyages of discovery. But it soon proved impossible for them to enforce their rights. By 1603, the need for establishing a permanent outpost to exclude interlopers was fully evident. Consequently, the monopoly passed to Pierre du Gua, sieur de Monts, who then took the initiative to plant a settlement in Canada to protect his exclusive rights.

The site chosen by de Monts to protect his fur trade was on the Bay of Fundy, a location close enough to the open Atlantic to maintain easy contact with the fisheries and France, yet close enough to fur stocks to serve as a base for the more profitable operation. The location failed, however, in the primary requirement of serving as a strategic obstacle to interlopers trading near the mouth of the St. Lawrence. Accordingly, the base was moved from Port Royal to a location which, in the opinion of the company's cartographer and soon-to-be manager, Samuel de Champlain, was more suitable. The site he selected in 1608 was at the head of the Gulf of St. Lawrence, formerly the Indian village of Stadacona, named *Québec Habitation* by Champlain. Here, a company of some twenty employees was able to enforce the trade monopoly. At the same time, Champlain was able to improve trading relations with the Indians — a critical point because the native people found and killed the beaver, and prepared the pelts for sale to the traders. Without Indian goodwill there could be no rush, not even a sparse trade.

In developing the trade, the French did not deal with diverse groups of different Indians. One group, the Huron, emerged early as their primary suppliers because they were the Indians with an already well-established trading network of their own. The Huron were the northernmost farmers of America and usually produced abundant crops of tobacco and corn. On the basis of their surplus, they had established far-flung lines of communication trading for shells and other luxuries with their Indian neighbors. The Huron opportunity to trade over an even greater territory was at hand when an apparently mutually profitable relationship was sealed in 1609 by Champlain's joining Huron warriors in an invasion of the territory of their inveterate enemies, the Iroquois. By participating in this season's unusually successful blood sport (given the use of firearms on the French-Huron side) Champlain won the undying friendship of the Huron.

Even though the prosperity of the fur trade was assured by the alliance with the Huron, *Québec Habitation* did not subsequently attract a large influx of newcomers from France. What the French established was neither a conquest culture (a new society modeled after the Spanish subjugation of Mexico) nor an agricultural frontier (the invention the English were then developing in Virginia). The colony established on the St. Lawrence was the focal point in a trading system requiring only enough clerks and warehousemen to handle the volume of the fur trade. Consequently, even though the French did enjoy hegemony over almost the entire area of present-day Quebec and Ontario through their alliance with the Huron, the colonial foundation established by 1627 consisted of just one hundred traders and one farmer. With this modest establishment, the monopolists in France were content. The government of France, however, was developing a more grandiose conception of overseas expansion.

## III    Fur Trade Outpost to Overseas Settlement

In the development of the French state, the seventeenth century was a critical period. The preceding century had been a time of chaos, with the country violently divided between Catholic and Protestant (Huguenot) armies. In addition, the Spanish-Austrian house of Hapsburg was taking advantage of the internal weakness of France to strengthen its own position. But the slide into anarchy was arrested at the end of the 1500s and the turning of the tide was symbolized by the accession to the throne of a new dynasty, the Bourbon, in the person of Henry IV who became king in 1589. It was under the Bourbons that the monarchy became the principal agent for overcoming the country's divisions by a centralizing administration. In the 1620s and 1630s this Bourbon policy was fostered by the leading minister of the day, Cardinal Richelieu.

Two elements in his policy were of special relevance to the French presence in North America. Richelieu observed that the increasingly powerful countries of Europe (Spain, England, and Holland) were building up their strength by paying attention to trade and overseas settlement. Openly basing his plans on those of England and Holland, Richelieu tried to initiate vast schemes for colonization companies in which private initiative would be encouraged by state backing and investment. North America had its due place in his scheme. Consequently, he revoked all previous monopolies and launched the Company of One Hundred Associates in 1627. In return for the monopoly of the fur trade, the Associates had to support the migration to Canada of two hundred colonists per year because Richelieu feared that twenty years of expanding fur trade had established a claim to wide territory without securing it by effective occupation. Settling a large population would consolidate the claim and serve as insurance against embarrassment by invasion and overseas defeat.

The second element was Richelieu's determination to make Canada an exclusively Roman Catholic colony. Internal division was to be avoided by insisting upon religious uniformity — no Protestants. The total exclusion of Huguenots was consistent with a general repression of Protestantism which Richelieu saw as a necessary precondition for bringing political peace to France. Much of the trouble of his century he could attribute to the experiment in religious toleration that was established by Henry IV in 1598 through the Edict of Nantes. Since then the Huguenots had been in retreat, however. One by one the Protestant enclaves that had flourished previously were reduced to submission. By 1627, only one last Huguenot stronghold remained — La Rochelle — and this place was under siege. In fact, it was before the very walls of La Rochelle that the charter for Richelieu's New France with its stipulation of Protestant exclusion was sealed between the French government and the One Hundred Associates. Richelieu wanted to avoid exporting the conflicts to the new land where a peaceful and prosperous New France was expected.

From the start, however, the company found it easier to make promises than to fulfil the bargain. They ran into one problem after another even though they did make a sincere effort to keep their part of the contract. In 1628 alone, four ships with four hundred settlers set sail for the St. Lawrence, but the entire expedition fell prey to British privateers, the Kirke brothers. Then, the same enemies continued up the Gulf, sacked *Québec Habitation* and took possession of the area for the King of England. It is true that by the peace treaty of St. Germain-en-Laye, 1632, the territory was returned to France, but the Company of One Hundred Associates had been hit so heavily that the promotion of settlement was subsequently regarded as an expendable frill. After 1633, when there were profits from the fur trade they were diverted to recoup old losses. As a result, the population that ought to have been approaching two thousand by 1633 was but a few hundred. Finally, since the government of France was fully preoccupied with war in Europe until the late 1640s, a vacuum of authority was created in New France, a void that was temporarily more than filled from a source very different from company or state. Where the fur rush had pioneered and the state had briefly followed, the Catholic Church moved in to reap the harvest — not of empire or of profit, but of souls.


## IV    Overseas Settlement as Missionary Ordeal

The first half of the seventeenth century was a vibrant period in the history of the Catholic Church, especially in France. The drive of the Counter-Reformation, the Church's response to the challenges of Luther, Calvin, and the other reformers of the preceding century, had reached its full momentum. Inevitably, French involvement in the New World would draw on this religious dimension sooner if not later.

An important aspect of French religiosity was a harshness in morality that resembled the puritanism that was struggling for control of the English Church at the same time. It was to be seen, for instance, in the various religious societies formed to cater to the narrow piety of those who believed that the mainstream of the Church had become much too lax, the most extreme example of which was the powerful *Compagnie de Saint Sacrement*, a secret society founded in 1627 and which included numerous highly placed state officials. Its outlook and influence may be judged by the widespread assumption that it was they who were behind a highly organized and effective crusade against the playwright Molière, whose only crime was satirizing overzealous Catholics. This same fanaticism was to be seen in another tendency that burst out openly about 1640 as Jansenism, stressing the limited, sinful nature of man, his total dependence upon God, and insisting upon predestination in salvation. Jansenism was eventually condemned by the Church, but Jansenist tendencies were prominent throughout the seventeenth century.

A very different form for French Catholic loyalties was provided by the Jesuits. This order had been founded in the mid-sixteenth century by an ex-soldier and immediately became the leading example of Counter-Reformation zeal. By the 1620s the Jesuits had achieved particular note for educational and missionary work in which the order displayed a suave flexibility in both dogma and methods. Indeed, it was resentment against this flexibility that had given the narrow Jansenists such a following. Although they were always in conflict, in an odd way, Jansenist and Jesuit converged. From their military origin, the Jesuits had developed a fanatical conception of duty and self-sacrifice, just as the Jansenists had developed a sense of moral superiority if not invulnerability out of their narrow and rigorous beliefs. In the New World setting the bickering between these two styles of Catholicism continued; but, as will soon be apparent, in their zeal they had something important in common.

The zealous fanaticism of the Jesuits was revealed in their *Relations* (annual reports between 1632 and 1673 in which the Order's missionaries in North America reported to their superiors). They, in turn, edited and published these accounts for wide circulation among pious members of the French gentry and aristocracy in the hope of attracting financial support. For this reason, the *Relations* included full accounts of the terrible suffering and ghoulish martyrdoms to increase sympathy for their work. At the same time, since the *Relations* were also published with a view to attracting additional recruits to the missionary field, there is some basis for interpreting their gruesome detail as an indication of a subliminal longing for such treatment. (It is worth comparing this aspect of North American experience with that of Mexico, for example, where the main missionary activity was carried on not by Jesuits but by the Pre-Reformation Franciscans. There, martyrdom was viewed merely as a remote possibility; in Canada, it was actually sought, and frequently found.)

The initial Jesuit experience of suffering in Canada was gained among migratory groups of Indians along the Gulf of St. Lawrence. Without agriculture, they also lacked villages and surplus food. Forced to hunt continually, they wandered nonstop in pursuit of game, feasting some days and starving on others. They simply endured the cold and the snows of winter without erecting permanent shelter. Bringing Christianity to these nomads was therefore an incredible ordeal. In his first week among the Montagnais, for example, one missionary, Father Le Jeune, found himself overcome by a violent fever. "Being cured," he said he "tried to follow them during the winter, and … was ill the greater part of the time." Le Jeune concluded in 1634 that "not much ought to be hoped for from the savages as long as they are wanderers; you will instruct them today, tomorrow hunger snatches your hearers away, forcing them to go and seek their food in the rivers and woods." The result was there were very few converts indeed.

The futility of the project on the Gulf led missionaries to conclude that the Huron would be superior prospective converts since they were already farmers and sedentary. According to Father Garnier, writing in 1636: "the country of the Hurons is the *sancta sanctorum*. It is of all the country where we are, the field where our fathers hope to establish the most beautiful mission because they are a stable nation and not vagabonds like most of the others." One additional reason for concentrating on the Huron was their middleman position in the fur trade: the fur rush had made them too dependent upon the French market to refuse to accept a few French missionaries.

It was not long before Huronia (the territory between Lake Simcoe and Georgian Bay) was the area of most intense Jesuit missionary activity. Missions were established in four of the largest villages, and at a location near today's Midland they built a fifth village that they named Ste. Marie, intending it as a missionary capital, the nerve center for the entire project.

Still, even in Huronia, conversion took place only slowly. In part, the difficulty was in communication, in translating theology from French to Huron in ways that would compel belief as well as comprehension. But equally obstructive was a contradiction that the Indians perceived in Europeans themselves. On one side, the Jesuits were attempting to impose self-denial and chastity, while on the other, their trade compatriots pursued profits and satisfied human appetites in the same promiscuous way as the Huron men and women.

Between 1635 and 1640, however, a series of devastating smallpox epidemics struck Huronia, and the people were ill-prepared to cope with either avoidance of or recovery from the disease. There was no separation of the sick from the healthy so smallpox passed easily from one person to another either by vectors such as lice or from mothers to infants because of the custom of parental mastication of the food for teething children. Moreover, the native diet was so low in liquids such as soups, fruit juices, or plain water, that the virulence of the disease was not thus diluted and passed from the body in the period of potential recovery. The result was that morbidity (the prevalence of the disease) was almost total, and mortality was also devastatingly high. A conservative estimate places the death toll at 70 percent between 1635 and 1640.

As the Indians lay dying, the Jesuits would baptise them and receive them into the Church. Under the circumstances, little chance of apostasy existed. To people believing that this life was but a vale of tears — a preparation for the glory to come — such conversion was as successful, as wonderful, as any other. In this light, the epidemic was as providential to the missionaries as it was disastrous to the Huron. The Indians, however, regarded death by smallpox as unspeakably vile and identified the Jesuits as the source of their misery. In 1640, an old Huron woman (with reference to the missionaries) asserted that "if we do not put them to death promptly they will ruin the whole country." Her reasoning was that "as soon as they were established everyone except three or four died" in a village that was previously entirely healthy. They moved and the same thing happened "only those into which they did not enter have been exempted from illness or death." Had it not been for the need to maintain peace with the French to continue the trading connection, it is highly likely that the Huron would have granted the Jesuits the martyrdom many seemed so fervently to have desired. But the epidemic did not kill everyone, and since the fur trade had become the new mainstay of the economy, there were simply fewer people to receive the limited luxuries derived from contact with the French. Consequently, the fur rush continued and the Jesuits maintained their presence accordingly.

By 1647 there were eighteen priests and twenty-four laymen in the missions to the Huron, whose own population had shrunk from about 30 000 to less than 10 000, and the marvel of what was happening in Huronia encouraged other zealots to enter this earthly purgatory. In 1639, two women's orders, the Ursulines and the *Hospitalières de la Miséricorde de Jésus de l'ordre de Saint Augustin* arrived. But an even more significant reinforcement was the contingent sent by the *Compagnie de Saint Sacrement*. Under the command of Paul de Chomédy, sieur de Maisonneuve, forty *dévots* arrived at Quebec in 1642 with the intention of establishing a mission near the hostile Iroquois whose tortures had made such grisly reading in the Jesuit *Relations*. But this did not deter Maisonneuve and his company of men and women from going up river to establish a settlement at the gates of hell itself on the island with the promontory Cartier had called Montreal. The Iroquois failed completely to anticipate their daring maneuvre and the newcomers spent their first year in complete peace.

Initial good luck, and the conviction of the settlers that they had been preserved by divine providence, eased Montreal over the year of its greatest vulnerability. By the time it was discovered by the Iroquois, the settlement was well fortified. The strategic value of the site also ensured that these beginnings would not be abandoned. Lying at the confluence of the Ottawa and St. Lawrence rivers, Montreal was ideally situated to become the headquarters of the fur trade. For this reason, it was profits, not piety, that would determine Montreal's growth and significance. But this was still in the future. In the period of company and government neglect — from the 1630s through the 1650s — it was evangelism that mattered for Montreal as it did for Huronia. During this generation, the evangelical conception of America dominated the commercial. In the St. Lawrence region, the most active agency of colonization was the Church. Eventually, the original extremism of intentional martyrdom softened, but even then, the influence of the Church did not weaken. Rather, it shifted from an emphasis on bringing Christianity to the Indians to building a truly religious society of newcomers in North America.

## V    The Dangers of Inter-Imperial Rivalry

Meanwhile the Company of One Hundred Associates was struggling to meet its obligations. As has been indicated, the setbacks of the early years meant that trading profits were not spared for settlement. The business of bringing over colonists and establishing them on the land was simply too expensive. It was also unnecessary, from the standpoint of the fur trade, since commerce could expand over large territory through Indian alliances. The land did not have to be occupied to realize large profits in the fur rush. And yet, the legal obligations of the company to promote settlement could not be completely ignored.

To subcontract its land settlement obligation, the Company tried the expedient of making seigneurial grants. Large blocks of territory along the St. Lawrence were granted to individuals as fiefs. For their part, the seigneurs were obliged to recruit settlers from France in order to realize the privileges of a nobility over a peasantry in Canada. Predictably, it was easier to obtain would-be barons than would-be serfs. Consequently, although nearly seventy such fiefs were conceded by 1660 (twenty going to the Church), such concessions resulted in little settlement. Still, it would be a mistake to call the early seigneurial system a complete failure. Between 1642 and 1663, population increased from under 300 persons to more than 3000. Since deaths exceeded births in this period, the population grew more by immigration than by natural increase. Moreover, since the clerical population in 1663 was only five percent of the total, the growing numbers of people cannot be attributed just to missionary activity. But compared to other colonies in North America at the same time, the population of New France was insignificant — less than one third of the Dutch, and less than one-twentieth the number of the English.

The most important obstacle to population growth was the menace of the Iroquois Confederacy. Ever since the time of Champlain there had been enmity with them, and with the Mohawk nation in particular. Beginning in 1640, at just the time Maisonneuve was on the point of establishing Montreal, the violence escalated to a higher level. The Iroquois had been trading with France's commercial rival, the Dutch, who had been established at Fort Orange (later Albany) since 1624. Soon the Iroquois had exhausted the supply of beaver within their own territory, and were obliged to seek supplies by making peace with the Huron. But the French had very naturally moved to prevent such a development; in 1624 and again in 1633 they had effectively blocked Iroquois bids for division of the trade. The French and Huron preferred monopoly even though it meant collapse of the Iroquois economy. In desperation, supported by the Dutch, the Mohawk Indians planned a war of unprecedented aggressiveness and the limited blood sport of an earlier period gave way to unlimited war. In the next ten years (judging by what happened at Trois-Rivières), only ten out of any forty colonists were likely to survive. The wrath of the Iroquois fell with tremendous fury.

The first to feel the full force of the Iroquois offensive were the Huron. In March of 1649, a thousand Iroquois warriors fell upon Huronia and killed everyone they could find. They captured Fathers Brébeuf and Lalement, carried them to their camp, and tortured them to death. The surviving remnant of the Huron was completely demoralized. Father Ragueneau attempted to lead them to Manitoulin Island because it was defensible and bountiful. But the Huron insisted upon taking more immediate refuge at nearby Christian Island. Throughout the rest of the winter they starved. Some who did not succumb joined other Indian bands and were assimilated by them. The remainder — barely five hundred in number — limped into Quebec to tell the story of the destruction of their nation. Between 1635 and 1640 they had been decimated by smallpox; in 1649 they were ravaged by war; then they starved. Epidemic, war, and starvation was a sequence that would recur again and again as Europeans traded, invaded, allied, and oversaw the destruction of the Indians.

The Iroquois had hoped that once the Huron had been broken, they would inherit their trading empire. But quite unexpectedly the elimination of the Huron proved to be the opportunity for the Ottawa Indians trading with the French at Montreal. Naturally, the Iroquois concluded that the French themselves would have to be driven out of the St. Lawrence Valley. If the Huron could be destroyed as a people even though only one quarter had actually been killed in battle, they reasoned that the same kind of terrifying, lightning attacks would have a similar effect on the French and make them lose their will to persist in the region.

Subsequent fierce onslaughts were not without the expected effect. Years later, an Iroquois chief boasted that their war against the French settlements was so effective that his five hundred warriors were able to keep a much larger force of the French confined almost entirely to their fortifications. As there were now more deaths in New France than births, old settlers began to lose hope and returned home. Newcomers began to dwindle. Even the steely Jesuits began to rethink their earlier zeal for martyrdom and appealed to France for military protection. Thus, the "mystical age" began to crumble. In 1658 François de Laval became Vicar Apostolic of New France — though as yet Quebec was not a bishopric. No sooner was he established in his new office than Laval began to press for assistance from the mother country. In this plea, the ecclesiastical authorities were joined by the civil. Since help was not forthcoming in the 1650s, many officials began to wonder if abandonment of the region was the only rational course. By 1660, it seemed that the French presence in the St. Lawrence area was coming to an end. New France, like Huronia, appeared to be moving toward extinction — an invention that had failed.

## Bibliography

The volume in the Canadian Centenary Series that covers the earliest development of New France is Marcel Trudel, *The Beginnings of New France, 1524-1663* (1973). Briefer — but equally useful for general readers — are the first two chapters of W.J. Eccles, *The Canadian Frontier, 1534-1760* (1969) and the first part of the introduction to Yves F. Zoltvany, ed., *The French Tradition in North America* (1972).

For the economics of Europeans' first contact with North America, two books by Harold Innis, *The Cod Fisheries: The History of an International Economy*, revised edition (1954) and *The Fur Trade in Canada: An Introduction to Canadian Economic History*, revised edition (1956) are classics. But the fur trade volume should be reconsidered in light of W.J. Eccles, "A Belated Review of Harold Adam Innis, *The Fur Trade in Canada*," CHR (1979) and readers with a background in economics should consider the theoretical material on "Early Staples" in W.L. Marr and D.G. Paterson, *Canada: An Economic History* (1980).

The subject of the Huron, their relations with the French, and their destruction by the Iroquois has received exhaustive attention in recent scholarship. Bruce Trigger, *The Huron: Farmers of the North* (1969) and his two volume expansion of this work into *The Children of Aataentsic: A History of the Huron People to 1660* (1976) are regarded as ethnographic masterpieces. Works that focus more generally on cultural interaction are A.G. Bailey, *The Conflict of European and Eastern Algonkian Cultures, 1504-1700* (second edition, 1969) and C.J. Jaenen, *Friend and Foe: Aspects of French-Amerindian Cultural Contact in the Sixteenth and Seventeenth Centuries* (1976). The disastrous impact of the early fur trade upon the Indians is treated by George T. Hunt, *The Wars of the Iroquois: A Study of Intertribal Trade Relations* (1970), Conrad Heidenreich, *Huronia: A History and Geography of the Huron Indians* (1971), and Calvin Martin, *Keepers of the Game: Indian-Animal Relationships and the Fur Trade* (1978).

"The lord of the manor might demand respect and rents, but the peasants owed service to no one but the state."

# CHAPTER 3

# *Trading Post to Planned Society*

## I   Small and Vulnerable Colony

Richelieu's attempt to transform the fur rush into a venture in colonization had begun as an enticing dream, but within a generation it had turned into a nightmare. Admittedly, a French presence in North America did continue despite the attacks of the Iroquois — primarily because of the lure of the fur trade. Even though Iroquois interruptions had made it unpredictable and caused it to develop along new lines (merchants were employing French *coureurs de bois* as middlemen between themselves and the Indian trappers to replace the Huron), the fur trade was occasionally still rewarding. But a commerce that functioned by fits and starts was not an adequate base for long-term growth. As a result, the tiny colony began to lose its will to withstand further attacks.

Discouragement did not arise from the fact that New France was out-numbered by the Indians. Of the nearly three thousand total population in the colony in 1660 at least one thousand were able-bodied men who — had they still been in France — would have been liable for conscription into the army. Against this potential force, the Iroquois confederacy could have mobilized twice as many warriors, but only if all nations fought together at once. In practice, no such Iroquois army existed. Rather, it was but one Iroquois nation, the Mohawk, with about 500 warriors, that was the main and long-standing threat. On the score of manpower, then, New France had no reason to despair.

More significant than numbers was the nature of the war. The struggle was one of continuing and terrifying ambush. Here, the French superiority in weaponry and numbers was no match against Iroquois patience and skill. One of the first historians of New France, Dollier de Casson, indicated precisely how such combat was a war of nerves which the French were losing. According to de Casson, incidents such as the following were too typical. A group of settlers working in a field posted one of their number as a sentry to keep watch from atop a large stump. In the shadow of another stump, an Indian lay hidden and waiting. By stages, the lone Iroquois warrior drew closer to the guard without being seen. "Finally, the fox got so near to the badly perched bird that he leaped up all at once on to him, seized him ... and dashed off with his load much as a thief would carry off a sheep." The victim and the others were all too shocked to do anything more than to cry out in surprise and anger. Later, the captive sentinel suffered torture and death in an Iroquois bonfire and the others found a more prolonged anguish in the terror of the example.

Such demoralization was intensified by the apparent inability of New France to organize effective militia units for their own defense. On paper, the colony was organized around a local nobility, the *seigneur*, historically the class that had taken the lead in military matters in France. But in New France, the seigneurs did not exercise any such power. At most, they were land settlement agents, responsible for recruiting peasants and getting them established on the land. In this they had been somewhat successful: sixty-nine (of whom seven were religious orders) had made 708 concessions of land between Quebec and Montreal before 1655. Thus, the distinctive pattern of long and narrow river-front farms had begun to emerge. There was nothing in this that contributed to defense, however. Moreover, when the persons charged with civil administration of the colony attempted to organize the population into an effective militia, the peasantry, in large part, seems simply to have ignored the effort. The result was inadequate, unorganized defense, and a request for help from home rather than meeting the need from resources in the colony itself.

The apparent inertia evident in military matters extended to the affairs of the colony more generally as well. A council consisting of the governors of each of the three areas of most concentrated settlement (Quebec, Trois-Rivières, and Montreal), the Superior of the Jesuits, and several other colonial notables, did meet regularly, but bickered constantly. In the issue of the use of brandy in the fur trade, for example, spokesmen for the Church demanded a total ban while the secular arm insisted that liquor had to be traded or commerce would flow to the Dutch and English who had no such scruples. Each side asserted its position with equal certainty and claimed superior authority. Stalemate followed. The deadlock on the brandy question pointed to a fatal flaw in the structure of the organization of the colony itself. In matters of church and state there was no clear supremacy of one side over another. New France lacked a controlling center.

But even while the fatal shortcomings of the colony were becoming only too painfully evident, developments in the mother country were reaching a conclusion that would highlight what was lacking in New France and therefore what might be added to enhance the colony's chances of survival.

## II   Modernizing Mother Country

The overhaul of the French state by the Bourbon monarchs was described in the last chapter simply as a program of centralization. For the purpose of more detailed analysis here, that centralization may be divided into two main components. The first was an innovation in government known as *absolutism*, a term that draws attention to the part played by the Crown in the modernization process since this agent was to rule absolutely over all sections of society on the basis of divine right (the notion that the legitimacy of a king was dependent ultimately upon the will of God). Any rival to the authority of the Crown was not to be tolerated. Thus, the ostensibly very Catholic Louis XIV did not hesitate to quarrel with the Pope, even to the point of instigating street-fighting in Rome, in order to uphold what he saw as his — or French — national rights as opposed to those of the international church. (For this reason Bourbon policy in ecclesiastical matters is referred to as *Gallican* to contrast it with the Papal alternative known as *Ultramontanism*).

Just as the Church was subordinated, so also was the judiciary made to realize that its function was not to act apart from the Crown, nor to review or check it, but rather to facilitate the royal will. To prevent competition from a legislative branch, the French Parliament, the Estates General of France, was simply not summoned. For 175 years after 1614 France did without any national representative institution at all, a condition which was changed only by the shock of the French Revolution. This placing of the Estates General in suspension is the clearest indicator of the successful taming of the nobility. But it did not happen without a struggle. As Bourbon centralism became ever more effective, the feudal class staged a last resistance; from 1648 to 1653, France — especially Paris — was convulsed by an uprising of the nobility known as the *Fronde*. But the failure of the revolt of the aristocracy exposed the weakness of the old feudal regime and intensified the Bourbons in their determination to humble the mighty.

Louis XIV dealt the nobility a death blow later when he built Versailles and made it into the cultural capital not only of France but of Europe as well. (It was so attractive that anyone who claimed to be anyone had to be there in full-time residence.) In this way, members of the nobility were cut off from their local roots, robbed of their independence, and reduced to mere courtiers, creatures of the king. As a class, they were emasculated.

Having disposed of rivals, the way was open for the Crown to extend its bureaucratic control over the country at large. The civil service was expanded, its personnel promoted — so much so that the late seventeenth century unfolded as a golden age for social ascendancy by public service. In the Church, the army, the navy, and in the civil service generally middle-class functionaries rose to prominence as never before. In this process, a key official was the *intendant*, a high ranking bureaucrat, recruited and appointed on the basis of merit, who was sent as the king's personal representative to oversee the provinces, and to report directly to him on their administration. Under such coordination, the business of the kingdom was conducted with unprecedented efficiency.

After absolutism, the second component in centralization was the central planning of the economy in accordance with a doctrine known as *mercantilism*. The basis for this idea was the belief that since the amount of wealth in the world was limited, for any state to increase its prosperity, and hence power, another would have to lose that much. It was possible to increase a country's wealth by war, of course, and although nations showed themselves ready to go to war, advancement by conquest was regarded increasingly as distinctly old-fashioned. Empire by trade was coming to be regarded as more appropriate. But trading empires were not supposed to arise without state encouragement. By means of government bounties, producers were encouraged to export goods abroad (and bring home the wealth of competitor countries). At the same time, tariffs discouraged imports (preventing a loss of specie to competitor nations). Thus, state intervention in directing the flow of trade was one requirement of mercantilism. Another was *imperialism* since no self-sufficient power in Europe could exist on the basis of the resources within its own boundaries. Any important country would acquire colonies to provide the mother country with raw materials unavailable at home. Thus, in Richelieu's reorganization of New France in 1627, the St. Lawrence was to provide fur and naval stores, eliminating the country's reliance upon Scandinavia. At the same time, French possessions in North America would deprive the British of both staples. The same strategy applied to sugar and the French presence in the West Indies.

And yet it is important to note that French pursuit of mercantilist ends was vitiated by a flaw in French society. In her mode of modernization,

France had not managed to break sufficiently with the older ways. The nobility might have been tamed, but an aristocratic ethos persisted to impede the full working out of meritocratic bureaucracy. Versailles domesticated the nobility, but at an enormous expense. Moreover, the *intendant* was never completely supreme in the provinces, for the office of the aristocratic governor was not abolished, merely pushed somewhat aside by the new creation. The old order had not been eliminated, and so modernization was only partly achieved. This was especially the case in trade since the whole business of merchandising was regarded as work for inferiors. No aristocrat could take part in retail trade without losing status: that is, without being derogated and becoming a commoner. Louis XIV wanted to break this old prejudice, but even he could not bring himself to go further than making exceptions for certain key trades to which *dérogeance* would not apply.

The fact was that a business outlook was foreign to the upper levels of French society, a weakness that was reinforced further by venality, the practice that permitted the wealthy to buy offices, including judgeships, and treat them like property to be bought, rented, and sold much like real estate. Since such positions carried noble status, and since nobility was valued in the extreme, the practice of too many successful merchants was to accumulate a fortune, only to leave business after buying status. Since so many *bourgeois* bought themselves out of trade and commerce and into the aristocracy, capital did not remain in private hands, and economic development depended excessively upon the king (usually at war). In this way, a gap opened between the French and their competitors, the Dutch and the English. There was little nobility in Holland; it was a nation of bourgeois. In England, although there was a hereditary nobility, *dérogeance* had never been an inhibiting factor since the participation of the aristocracy in trade and commerce had long been a marked feature of its economy. By taking a personal interest in their acres and sinking large amounts of capital in the hope of boosting yields, English lords of the manor had become capitalist landlords while their French counterparts preferred exploitation of their feudal rights and dues to augment their income. At a time when feudalism seemed fated to die a death of obsolescence, the old nobility of France *(noblesse d'épée)* assisted by an army of aspiring pettifogging lawyers (would-be entrants to the *noblesse de robe*) revived feudal customs for their cash value to the aristocracy.

The relevance to Canada of these impediments to the modernization of France can be exaggerated, however, because the mid-seventeenth century was still the early period of the process in France, and the shortcomings of the French pattern were not to show up fully until the eighteenth century.

In fact, in the 1660s, the time was ideal for Richelieu's failed invention of New France to be resurrected and implemented again, this time with success, thanks to the intervention of a modernizing mother country.

## III    Colbert's New France

One way of summing up absolutism and of explaining its initial superiority over what went before is to draw attention to its creation of a controlling center. Where feudalism had been decentralized and diffused, absolutism was centralized and concentrated. New France was not a feudal society but authority was dangerously diffuse, and the colony did suffer from a glaring lack of cohesion. Was the colony a trading outpost, a missionary frontier, or an agricultural settlement? Was the civil government sovereign or did it share power with the Church? What liberty did the individual settler enjoy? Was he free to decline the government's order that he enroll in militia companies? What was the status of the colony itself? Was it to be closely tied to France or self-reliant and therefore granted a good deal of autonomy? Answers to all these questions were lacking in the colony. In the mother country, answers to all were ready for export.

Given the problem of defense, civil and church authorities both invited any initiative from the metropolis that would guarantee security. In 1661, there was a change in France that gave them reason to think the mother country would be unusually receptive to their appeals for help. Louis XIV, having inherited the crown in 1643 as a child, now came of age and took over the personal direction of state affairs. Eager to capitalize on the advances made by his Bourbon predecessors, he was aided by his leading minister, Jean-Baptiste Colbert, the ideal bureaucrat under whose direction the caliber of the civil service was improving daily. Together, monarch and minister turned to New France and were delighted to discover the very formlessness of the colony. It meant that they could treat it as an experiment in which they might build the sort of community that stubborn tradition was preventing them from creating in France itself.

The appeal for aid carried by Pierre Boucher to France in 1661 came at just the right moment. Had an urgent request for assistance come earlier the French government might have been too preoccupied with foreign wars to spend time and trouble upon the tiny settlement, and the disheartened settlers would have abandoned the St. Lawrence. Had it come later, France would once again have been involved in European affairs. The 1660s was the perfect decade, free from pressing concerns in Europe, and a time when the bureaucracy was approaching its creative zenith. In this brief interval New France was transformed.

In 1663 Company rule was abolished and the colony became, in effect, another province of the motherland, essentially no different from, say, Normandy, or Saintonge. But there were some differences, and these are signficant in showing the goals of absolutism freed from tradition. A Sovereign Council was established as the counterpart to a *Parlement* in a region of France. But in the colony, the individuals who filled its positions served at the pleasure of the king; they were not people who bought title to governmental posts with cash. In a *Parlement* of France, by contrast, one could, for example, buy judgeships; this is the venality that was not exported to the colony. Then, too,the legal profession was excluded from New France. And no shadow of representative government was permitted. The absolutism — that is, the control — was intended to be complete.

But even more significant than making New France a province was the drive and organization which this decision implied. The mood in 1661 had been one of defeat, indeed demoralization; the new royal initiative convinced the settlers that the resources of the metropolis would be put behind them, that it was worth continuing. In this sense, initially, Louis XIV provided a boost to morale. As the developments of the period between 1661 and 1672 are considered, it becomes clear that materially nearly as much already existed in New France as was contributed afresh. The qualification is true even of the psychological boost since the royal initiative was so slow to manifest itself. In 1661 Colbert was still consolidating his authority over his department. Consequently he had to move cautiously with New France, for he had enemies who would seize upon any indication of incompetence. And the King himself, remembering the *Fronde*, had similar fears. The delay between the decision to plan a New France and its implementation therefore seems unnecessarily drawn out unless this fact is kept in mind. Although civil and clerical authorities were assured in 1661 that the new monarch would take an unprecedented interest in protecting and promoting the colony, it was not until 1663 that the company rule was formally suspended. A military campaign against the Iroquois did not come until 1666. And economic development did not receive much attention until after 1667. Then, in 1672, European war diverted the attention of the French government away from Canada and it was never to be redirected to the colony with quite the same intensity as in the nine years following royal assumption of formal responsibility in 1663. Therefore, if New France is described as a planned society, this must refer to the colony primarily between 1663-72 and to the activities of one planner, Jean-Baptiste Colbert.

Colbert's first move was to rationalize power, to declare who was in charge and by what authority. He accomplished this by creating a Sovereign Council consisting of a figurehead governor, circumscribed bishop, and an *intendant* of justice, finance and administration. In other words, his first move was to invest sovereignty in an official in charge of practically everything, to surround him with the majesty of the royal symbol, and aid him by the bureaucrat in charge of religious affairs. He did this in 1663, but without filling the office of *intendant* immediately. It took Colbert two years to find the appropriate candidate for the all-important administrative office. When the search was only half completed he despaired that all who seemed qualified "lack the mettle" and those who were willing to undertake the long voyage and rude conditions "lack the intelligence, integrity and ability needed to be of some use there." His solution was to create a kind of caretaker government for the interim. But to boost the morale of the settlers immediately he did send some soldiers with the promise of more to follow.

Then, in February of 1665, Colbert found his man to fill the office of *intendant*, Jean Talon, a candidate with intelligence and equal amounts of courage and integrity. In the summer of that year, Talon departed for New France agreeing to serve two years. Actually, Talon stayed through the dynamic formative years, to 1672. His arrival at Quebec coincided with that of Alexandre de Prouville, sieur de Tracy, commander of the long awaited regiment to fight the Iroquois. Then with Tracy's one thousand soldiers, and the Sovereign Council with its *intendant*, the new regime was launched with all the pomp and excitement of people in small communities who hope they are on the threshold of great things to come.

But it was not until 1666 that Tracy and his men took the war to the Iroquois in their own territory. Then, the conflict was anticlimactic. Colbert had expected pitched battles between French soldiers and the Iroquois warriors. For this reason, the men who were ordered to the colony were veterans of the Carignan-Salières regiment. The fighting that was anticipated did not occur, however, even though in one of three campaigns the regiment did march into the very heartland of the Mohawk nation. But the Indians fled without engaging their enemy. The French destroyed the Indians' food supply stored in the abandoned villages in the autumn of 1666. In the following year, having suffered more by hunger than from fighting, the Mohawk sought a truce in the long war that had raged intermittently since 1609. What followed were nearly twenty years of peace.

By 1667 the security of New France from attacks by the Indians was thus assured and the administration of the colony was established on lines of centralized efficiency. It was then possible to implement more comprehensive plans of social and economic development. In the next five years, steps were taken accordingly to augment the population, to integrate the

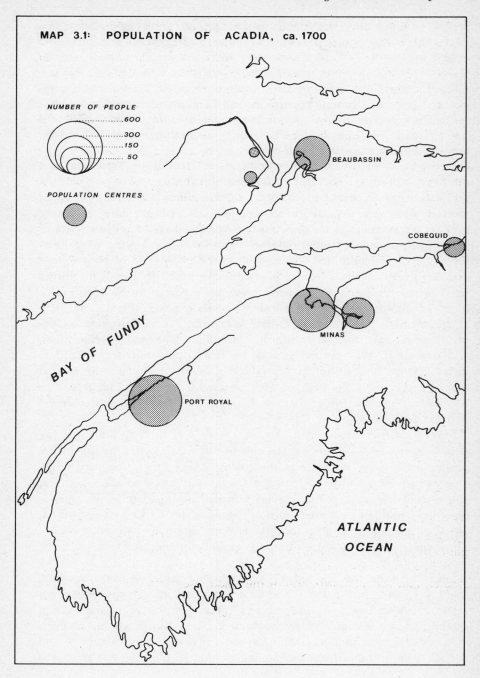

MAP 3.1:  POPULATION  OF  ACADIA, ca. 1700

NUMBER OF PEOPLE
.................600
.........300
......150
.....50

POPULATION CENTRES

BEAUBASSIN

COBEQUID

MINAS

BAY OF FUNDY

PORT ROYAL

ATLANTIC
OCEAN

central administration with local institutions, and to promote self-sufficiency and diversity in the economy. Here, however, all emphasis was placed on the St. Lawrence area, even though a French population persisted at several locations around the Bay of Fundy (see map 3.1). No significant attempt was made to foster the growth of Acadia further. Consequently, the small groups of farmers and fishermen, scattered in sparse settlements, remained small in number for the next fifty years. Acadia did have its own governor, but the isolated population of barely 500 in 1660 totaled no more than 1000 a half-century later.

In the St. Lawrence region, by contrast, the growth of population was dramatic, and encouraged by every means. Incentives were provided by the state to encourage a high birth rate, for example. Parents of ten or more children were awarded handsome annuities; people marrying young (under 20 for males, 16 for females) received royal wedding dowries; and fathers whose children grew older at home without marrying were fined for each year of continued celibacy. Since the population of New France doubled every twenty years, it is readily concluded that cash incentives were successful, but since the same tendency occurred in the British colonies without such a system of bounties a better conclusion is that the state encouragement to population growth was simply a reinforcement of the real determinants of rapid natural increase (abundant food, plentiful fuel, and free land). Wherever such was the case, population was bound to increase at the limit of human reproductory capacity. The more important difference between New France and the English colonies with regard to population development is that the French state sponsored settlement of persons deemed to be desirable colonists.

More than four thousand immigrants were sent to New France in the decade after 1666 — entirely at the expense of the Crown. One third were soldiers encouraged to retire in the colony. Many others were marriageable women recruited to balance the sex ratio upset by so many retiring, single males. Moreover, the women recruited by the state were carefully screened candidates selected from orphanages, for as Colbert explained, "in the establishment of a country it is important to sow good seed." Thus, the colony was not a dumping ground for the undesirables of the mother country.

Since the state was the agency for recruiting settlers and transporting them to Canada in the 1660s, the Crown also assumed responsibility for their orderly settlement upon the land. To this end, the seigneurial system established by the company was continued. Under its extension, however, it was even more evident that it would convey all the formalities and almost none of the functions of feudalism; that is, the seigneur after 1663 (as before) was a high status landlord but no commander of troops. The lord of the manor might demand respect and rents, but the peasants owed service to no one but the state. This was made plain once the able-bodied men of the colony were organized into militia companies in 1669. The colonial militia had its captains, but they were not seigneurs. The *capitaines de milice* were appointed from the ranks of ordinary inhabitants because they were persons with apparent leadership qualities that the government was willing to recognize to a limited extent for a limited period. Consequently, the *capitaine de milice* was also the intermediary between the Crown and the local population. The seigneur, by contrast, was the local land settlement agent. His role was to subdivide a fief into eighty-acre concessions as rapidly as he might find peasants or *censitaires* to take them. His reward, initially, was of status rather than money or power since the local squires received only nominal rents and no military position.

Here, then, were the main elements in the foundations of Colbert's colony: a sovereign council with dominant *intendant* had been defined as the controlling center; French military power insured peace with the Iroquois; the state recruited and transported a substantial "seed" population; and orderly settlement without weakening the centralized authority of the colony was achieved by perpetuating a remodeled version of the seigneurial system. On such social foundations, a program of economic development followed after 1667 with two strategic objectives. One was self-sufficiency in the production of food, clothing, and shelter. The other goal was economic diversification to encourage the production of naval stores, and a shipbuilding industry to support a merchant marine for carrying foodstuffs to the French West Indies, the sugar islands that provided the most lucrative staple to France from the New World. But shipbuilding encouraged by the skillful managerial talent of Talon and the capital investment of the Crown did not flourish because it continued to be cheaper to build ships in France. Similarly, the encouragement of the colonists to develop a fishery and produce an exportable agricultural surplus also failed because the Caribbean was relatively inaccessible from the St. Lawrence. When the river was open for safe navigation to the French West Indies, the Caribbean was dangerous because of the hurricane season there. Consequently, the Dutch and the British, already providing the French sugar producers with their slaves, enjoyed the provision of much of the rest as well. The most thriving intercolonial coastal trade was that between the Acadians and New England (because the Bay of Fundy was ice-free the year round and so near the English colonies). But even this commerce developed fitfully because the English and French were usually at war.

Beyond subsistence agriculture, the economic activity that continued to thrive in New France was the fur trade, even though Colbert attempted to discourage it. He had hoped that the original invention of New France would wither. Consequently, Colbert attempted to restrict access to the fur economy by renting it to monopolists for a sum equal to the annual cost of the civil administration, or about one-fifth the amount annually invested to develop such industries as shipbuilding. But the lure of the fur trade continued to be overwhelming since a few good seasons in the hinterland could yield phenomenal returns. Here, however, the individuals who led in the accumulation of fortunes by this means did not invest their profits in shipbuilding or tanneries (enterprises with mercantilist legitimacy); they spent what they made as fast as they earned it or invested their fortunes like so many *bourgeois* in France: they bought status. They accumulated *gloire* rather than wealth or power. Such behavior was consistent with the absolutist design of the colony, but it spelled defeat for the program of economic diversification. Yet the colony did prosper from the standpoint of its growing population and agricultural prosperity. The population of the colony on the St. Lawrence doubled every twenty years and because of the fur trade it expanded phenomenally in territory south to the Gulf of Mexico, north to Hudson Bay, and west as far as the Rocky Mountains — and all this before the English had penetrated beyond the Appalachian Mountains. Half of Colbert's plan for New France, the mercantilist scheme, was thus a partial failure. But the other half, the plan pertaining to social organizaton and control, did unfold more or less as Colbert had hoped. Moreover, the colony seems to have developed thus to the satisfaction of most of the inhabitants as an examination of relations between individuals and the state will soon make apparent.

## Bibliography

Two volumes in the Canadian Centenary Series cover the transition from company rule to the creation of Colbert's New France. One is *The Beginnings of New France, 1524-1663* (1973) by Marcel Trudel. The other is *Canada Under Louis XIV, 1663-1701* (1964) by W.J. Eccles. Other general works, one by Eccles, *The Canadian Frontier, 1534-1760* (1969) and another, the introduction to a selection of source material edited by Y.F. Zoltvany, *The French Tradition in North America* (1972) introduce the general reader to the same material in fewer pages. For additional background on absolutism, the relevant chapters in Barrington Moore, *Social Origins of Dictatorship and Democracy: Lord and Peasant in the Making of the Modern World* (1966) are provocative. A more detailed discussion of Colbert and his policies is found in C.W. Cole, *Colbert and a Century of French Mercantilism*, 2 vols. (1939).

"The people tended to be crowded into small houses, enjoyed little cash income, and their seigneurial rents were at least potentially burdensome."

# CHAPTER 4

# State and Individual in New France

## I    Absolutism vs. Liberty

In one decisively important aspect, the colony of New France deviated very little from its social and institutional model invented by Colbert: for nearly one hundred years, the colonists lived under authoritarian government. From 1663 to 1760, the very stability of the colony's absolutism tended to confirm outsiders in their opinion that the government was despotic. There were no newspapers, and therefore no effective focus for public opinion. There was no parliament, and therefore no politics or even a belief that government should be based on the consent of the governed. There was no toleration of dissent, and therefore no religious pluralism or legitimate political factions. And since there was no freehold land tenure, and therefore no truly private property, the possibility of an effectively independent landed interest in opposition to the Crown was minimal. What had been planted and perpetuated, in the eighteenth-century English view of it, was a "perfect system of French despotism".

In addition to being authoritarian, however, the government of New France was paternalistic; the king governed in the colony through agents by the same kind of legitimacy that (until recently) used to justify a father in the governing of his family. The head of a family who only disciplined its members was a despot or a tyrant; the good father was a good provider as well as a stern disciplinarian. So also in matters of state, the good king in being a father to his subjects was a provider as well as a law giver. Thus, Louis XIV, expressing his intention of being a good king, indicated that he thought he ought to "pay heed to all the inhabitants' complaints and their needs, and attend to them as much as he possibly can ... ."

The king's good intentions were fulfilled to a limited extent at home but were more fully realized in the case of New France. There was no freehold land tenure, but there were no landless poor. Every man was assured a minimum of about eighty acres for himself and his heirs conditional upon the payment of nothing more than allegiance and an annual token offering to him who held the land in the king's name. Similarly, there was no representative government, but neither were there direct taxes. And, although there was no toleration of religious or political dissent, there was little indication of a sense of deprivation on this account, that is, laws were obeyed remarkably well without compulsion. Finally, although there was no vehicle such as voting or a newspaper for articulating public opinion, the means for collecting individual opinions were diverse and constantly in operation. It was Colbert's instruction that no person would assume to speak with any authority greater than his own voice. He said, it is "a good thing that each man speak for himself and that no one speaks for all." His intention was to prevent anything that would "give a corporate form to the inhabitants of Canada" but this did not mean an individual might not register requests or grievances that the appropriate agent ought to consider seriously. The government of New France was thus benevolent as well as authoritarian because it was paternalistic as well as absolutist. A more succinct way of making the same general point is simply to report that in the eighteenth century the government of France usually spent about six times more in the colony than it derived in revenue from indirect taxation upon imports and exports. And there is another effective clue to the well-being of the colony in the surprised comment by a new *intendant* that more children had died in the preceding year by drowning than from any other cause. He did not mean that drownings were unusually high, but that the tremendous infant mortality of old France and of Europe in general was unknown on the St. Lawrence.

Returning to the perspective of the eighteenth-century Englishman, however, the benevolence of a despotism would only make it more bearable. The "yoke of tyranny" would seem less burdensome but even this was unforgivable because paternalism was supposed to encourage lethargy and stagnation. In the eighteenth and nineteenth centuries, Englishmen (and Americans) were quite smug in their general agreement that starvation was nature's way of teaching self-reliance and individual initiative. English critics who would denounce New France first as a "perfect system of French despotism" would, therefore, simply change the target of denunciation upon learning of its paternalism. Thus, Francis Parkman (the first writer in English to be fully acquainted with the history of New France), admitted in the late nineteenth century that the government of the colony was benevolent, saying of the king that "not only did he give money to support parish priests, build churches, and aid the seminary, the Ursulines, the missions, and the hospitals; but he established a fund destined, among other objects, to relieve indigent persons ... ." All such actions were mistaken in Parkman's view because the state "did for the colonists what they would far better have learned to do for themselves." The colonists were denied a school for learning the virtues of self-reliance, thrift, and industry. Population doubled every twenty years, but economic development lagged far behind New England's. Here, for Parkman, was the ultimate proof of the superiority of Anglo-Saxon social values, government, and institutions.

The superior economic performance of the English colonies was also Parkman's proof of the superiority of the broader differences between English and French civilization. In the English world, by the last quarter of the eighteenth century, it was assumed generally that the good of society was served best by leaving each individual as free as possible to pursue his own self-interest. The heavy hand of government, restraining and regulating mankind, was to be withdrawn. "The sovereign is completely discharged" and it was the "invisible hand" of nature that was to govern details of wages, prices, the pace and direction of economic development. According to this view, government had only three legitimate functions; three simple operations to pursue with the consent of the governed in a frugal and self-denying way. The first was military defense, protecting society from invasion. The second was justice, protecting innocent individuals from other oppressive individuals. The third was "creating and maintaining certain public works and certain public institutions which," in the words of Adam Smith (whose championing of this point of view appeared as *The Wealth of Nations* in 1776), "can never be for the interest of any individual, or small number of individuals, to erect and maintain, because the profit could never repay the expense ... ." In other words, if investors were not motivated to pool their capital to provide a service to extinguish fires, for example, then a government might create a fire department if it were demonstrated that such an institution was indispensable to the public good.

In France and New France, by contrast, it was far more common for individuals to assume that government should be active, not passive, because individuals — far from being free and equal — were recipients by birth of positions in an organic community of structured inequality. Here, the good king, in his role of good father, would intervene continually in the minutest details of life not only to maintain order but also to guarantee a minimum level of social welfare. In this sense, absolutism was an adminstrative response to ensure the security of a system of social relationships based on status, where the libertarian alternative, Smith's "system of natural liberty", found its justification in its stimulation of economic development by disavowing all notions that a person in some sense belonged to a community by the mere fact of survival.

In attempting to weigh English libertarianism against French absolutism, those who prefer size-growth of an economy will be forever troubled by the comparatively unimpressive economic development of New France and will conclude that absolutism rather than climate or geography limited the colony's growth because New England — nearly as impossible in its endowment of natural resources — was a libertarian, economic success story. Those who place human development above property rights, on the other hand, will forever defend the statism of New France and denounce the New Englanders because although they were successful economically, the Yankees were said to be notoriously compulsive strivers, and extraordinarily litigious toward one another — a society that had lost its soul in comparison with New France. For this reason, those who prefer human development to material progress will point forever to New France for the availability of its justice, the balance of its authorities, the *joie de vivre* of its citizenry, and the adventure of its clandestine economy, all of which will now be discussed. Here, the problem is not to determine whether New France was governed by a paternalistic regime or comparatively stunted in its economic development. The issue is to assess the significance of these facts.

## II    The Administration of Justice

Perhaps nothing illustrates better the day-to-day significance of paternalism in Colbert's planned society than the administration of justice. In England and colonial America, justice — like fire extinction — was dispensed in accordance with the principles of the free market rather than according to notions of *noblesse oblige*. Under the Anglo-Saxon adversary system, competing lawyers were hired to tell a story in an open court and a panel of jurors decided which agent performed more credibly. Justice therefore depended upon three variables: money (competent lawyers who knew their law and had the rhetorical skills to do good service with that knowledge were expensive), the competence of the jurors (it was this panel that had to decide between the conflicting accounts presented to them), and the judge (who controlled the presentation of evidence and summed up the conflicting stories). Under the adversarial model, justice could be painfully slow and even more painfully expensive. But in New France, justice depended upon one variable only: the competence of the judges charged with dispensing it.

Under the inquisitional system of New France, there were no lawyers and no juries and the accused man was considered guilty until he proved himself innocent — in his own words, by himself. To facilitate the process, torture was permitted but infrequently used. In fact, there were less than twenty such instances of "extraordinary questioning" in the whole history of New France. Furthermore, torture did not always spell conviction because nearly one third of the accused persons questioned under duress established their innocence. Still, all was up to the judges to decide. It was they who heard the accused person's testimony and that of the witnesses for the prosecution or defense. The judges heard them all individually and in private. Consequently, no one contributing evidence for or against was exactly certain of the other witnesses' testimony. When the judges thought that they had heard enough to come to a decision, they rendered a verdict and sentence at once. The penalties were arbitrary, that is, at the judge's discretion. If conviction meant execution, it was carried out quickly, frequently on the same day as the verdict. Sometimes, in accordance with the custom in Europe — in order to create an especially strong example — the condemned person would suffer the severance of the right hand just before hanging. And after the sentence was carried out, again for the assumed deterrent value, a victim's head and hands might be displayed in public as a reminder of the fate of convicted robbers, rapists, and murderers.

Since the inquisitional system depended so much upon the discretion of individual judges it could be called a government of men rather than the rule of law. Clearly, the system was vulnerable on this account because it was only as good as the officials who made it work. But judgeships were not for sale as in France itself. Moreover, the judicial system was subject to the continual scrutiny of the *intendant*, and in all instances save one (Bigot, the last) they were competent civil servants who filled their positions with intelligence and integrity. Then, too, there was a liberal right of appeal. There was a hierarchy of officials through whom a case might be appealed, even to the *intendant* himself.

But from the ghoulish cruelty of the punishments imposed by inquisitional justice, the system could be criticized for its brutality. Accused persons who were tortured or condemned offenders who had their hands severed just prior to execution by hanging would certainly have felt that this was a system which dispensed retribution, that is, revenge, rather than relief for victims or rehabilitation for criminals. Yet this criticism applied to any system in which punishment was regarded as the most appropriate response to social deviancy. Thus, in eighteenth-century England, for instance, petty theft was a problem and hanging offenders was the solution.

What was remarkable about the administration of justice in New France was how swiftly and impartially it seems to have been dispensed. Despite the lack of lawyers and trial by jury what was lost was primarily the expensive court costs and lawyers' fees. What was gained was swift, inexpensive justice for all. The evidence for the alleged superiority of the inquisitional system over the adversary system employed at the same time in England and the British colonies is varied. Close examination of the record of a small but random assortment of criminal cases tends to substantiate the claim of swiftness and impartiality. The low rate of capital convictions (only 67 executions for the whole period of one hundred years) might suggest a low incidence of crimes such as robbery, rape and murder (the capital offenses), or that officials were simply lax in enforcing the law. But since the government of the colony extended to the minutest affairs, including the standards of quality and prices of merchandise and the regulation of children's playing in the streets of Quebec, it seems ludicrous to contend that a blind eye was turned to murder. At the same time, it might also be said that the interventionist government that regulated the quality of prices of goods for sale provided protection to consumers and the ban on snowballing in the streets of the towns prevented injury to children and pedestrians alike. Such detailed interference with day-to-day living and the arbitrary nature of the inquisitional judicial system horrified critics of "French despotism" but later observers would suggest that swift justice and close regulation were simply good government.

## III    Competing Authority in Administration

Vigorous government might have weighed more heavily upon the shoulders of individual citizens had the power of civil administration not been divided by competition between individual administrators, or had the vigorous Church not operated as an even more tangible competing authority. In the secular realm, the competition was between governor and *intendant*, ostensibly co-operators, not rivals. But the Governor General was invariably chosen from the old military nobility (the *noblesse d'épée*) and the *intendant* was always an official selected from the new nobility of the civil service *(noblesse de robe)*. There was inherent competition in this dichotomy of social positions since the governor's status was superior to the intendant's, but the inferior noble was the official whose class was on the rise; conflict was therefore inevitable, and the structure of the administration served to accentuate the tendancy. Nominally, the governor was superior to the *intendant* in authority as well as social rank; he was, after all, the personification of the monarchy. But the *intendant* exercised more power in his day-to-day management of finance, justice, police, and civil administration. He did more than the governor and therefore counted for more. Louis de Buade, Comte de Frontenac, governor of New France from the year of the departure of the first (and perhaps best) *intendant*, Jean Talon, tried to amend this. From the moment of his arrival, Frontenac attempted to inflate his office with the regal majesty befitting a king's representative. His court became the focal point of the colonial status hierarchy, but this did not alter the fact that the center of power was the office of the *intendant*. In a confrontation, the governor was supposed to be supreme but he could not not override his *intendant's* judgments in the areas of his responsibility without showing good cause. This was usually difficult, and therefore the two officials wrangled constantly with each complaining of the other in reports home to the minister, who replied — just as monotonously — that they ought to learn harmony and good will.

The Crown had not intended to create a system of checks and balances at the pinnacle of colonial society; but this, very nearly, is how the separate offices of governor and *intendant* related to one another in practice. The problem was that the governor seemed to have status more than power, and the *intendant* to have more power than majesty. Their relative economic positions were even more anomalous since the richer in money might be the poorer in status. Wealth, power, and status are normally congruent, however. In most societies, the wealthiest individuals are also the most powerful and therefore the ones who enjoy the most prestige as well. But in New France, the social pyramid came to an apex at two locations. The governor, as the king's viceroy, enjoyed a higher status than anyone in the colony. This alone was enough for him to command the highest respect of the seigneurial class. Thus, when the governor made his annual progress from Quebec to Montreal it was a matter of high honor among the seigneurs to have him stay on their particular seigneuries, to afford him the ceremony due to his office. But when the inhabitants of that place were instructed to leave whatever they were doing and appear at the manor house, in their best clothes, hats in hand, although they did appear, they did so without enthusiasm. In their view, the *intendant* was the most powerful person in the colony, therefore such obeisance to the governor was a ceremony that seemed superfluous to say the least.

At the same time, it should be noted that the seigneur-governor and *habitant-intendant* identifications were neither very clear nor well fixed. Both classes and all individuals in the colony could take advantage of the fact that authority was not monolithic in order to appeal, or more effectively to threaten to appeal, to the rival hierarchy whenever the other appeared to act harshly in the certainty that each hierarchy would be only too happy to take up a complaint, forwarding it if necessary to their common superior in France.

This same principle of competing authority applied to relations between the populace and the church. Here the fate of the tithe Bishop Laval sought is the clearest illustration of the colonists' winning the freedom they wanted by playing one authority against another.

Laval attempted to obtain a tithe for the support of the secular clergy, the parish priests. The original proposal was, as in France, for one thirteenth of the value of the produce of the land. When the colonists objected to the civil authorities that this was outrageously high, the Bishop was persuaded to reduce his demand to one twentieth. The colonists objected again. Finally, Bishop Laval had to settle for half his original demand. But the colonists calculated this portion at one twenty-sixth of the wheat alone rather than of the entire produce of the land, and the civil administration sustained them in their interpretation.

The reality of competing authority created degrees of freedom in practice that were never recognized in theory. It was simply what happened in the course of establishing authoritarian government while consciously avoiding the imposition of tyranny, the fruit of the recognition that "Canadians are difficult to govern" and in their governance, finesse was preferable to force. Authoritarian government was thus diluted in competition. So also was the authoritarian Church made less capable of pursuing its every whim. In New France the Church was privileged and established, of course, but it was not free to establish the theocracy Bishop Laval had intended. It was subsidized by the civil administration and well attended by the colonists but not recognized as having any coercive power of its own. When it became fashionable for women to wear blouses with plunging necklines the bishop denounced such "scandalous nudities" and ordered the women to change their fashion. They ignored him. When the Bishop ordered the priests to withhold the sacraments from all such women until they covered their charms more completely they appealed to the *intendant* and the governor to intervene on their behalf. The state responded and the women were saved their fashion. But when the men attempted to launch the custom of bringing their dogs with them inside the church for Sunday mass and of getting up and going out for a smoke during the sermon, the state intervened to uphold decorum.

Such disputes were so frequent in the eighteenth century that they draw attention to the clarity of the dynamics of competing authority. They also point to the importance of another theme: the status consciousness in New France.

## IV    Status Consciousness

Traditional societies were extremely status conscious by modern standards. Even persons low in the social hierarchy were concerned with prestige in ways that seem far more intense than their economic circumstances would justify because in one sense people were more secure: those who survived belonged somewhere. But inherited belonging produced keen competition for fine gradations of prestige within particular social ranks. Then, too, there was the stimulus of the exceptional case of social mobility. There were those individuals — most frequently by distinction in war or marriage — who gained promotion from one large stratum to the next. With modernization social mobility accelerated but the means shifted to ascent by acquisition of wealth. Thus, in France, as has been shown, the system of inherited statuses was overlaid by another system of achieved status that resulted in two nobilities appearing at the top of the social hierary as the new *noblesse de robe* in addition to the old *noblesse d'épée*. In New France, all such tendencies were even more pronounced and the inclination to display whatever status material prosperity made possible extended even to the peasantry.

Legally and technically, the ordinary inhabitants of New France were peasants, mere concession holders, only *censitaires*. But the relatively greater abundance in Canada made them more worthy in practice than they were in law, hence the name *habitants* replaced the more official label for their place in the social hierarchy. By way of illustration, consider the circumstances of two farmers, one an inhabitant of New France and the other a French peasant. The Canadian, Jean C., was typical in the sense that he held a concession of average size — the usual farm about 150 yards wide and 2500 yards long. About one quarter of the land was tillable soil, so the area he farmed was just over twenty acres. He had some livestock, implements, a house, a barn, and stables. Altogether, the farm cost him two bushels of wheat, a live capon, and — in 1968 Canadian dollars — about 20 cents per year in rent to his *seigneur*. Back in France, by contrast, Pierre B. held roughly the same acreage, livestock and building accommodations but he paid rents in Normandy equal to about 600 1968 Canadian dollars. Pierre B. also had taxes to pay while Jean C. and his Canadian neighbors enjoyed an exemption from all direct taxes (except the one twenty-sixth tithe on the wheat grown). Relative to their cousins in France, the farmers of the colony were privileged gentry with respect to rent and taxation.

But in New France the peasantry was still poor in absolute terms. The people tended to be crowded into small houses, enjoyed little cash income, and their seigneurial rents were at least potentially burdensome. Despite these facts, the *habitants* were said to have developed preoccupations with fashionable clothing and other simple luxuries rather than turning whatever surplus they did accumulate into the development of their agricultural estate. Such alleged practices were a source of continual consternation to officers of the government who — admittedly with all the bias characteristic of the "better sort" looking down on social inferiors — claimed that the ordinary people of the colony were too well clothed and kept too many horses rather than dressing plainly and developing their stock of cattle and oxen. The explanation was that horsepower could pull a sleigh on social occasions, or carry individuals riding for pleasure, while cattle and oxen were draft animals or merely food. Officials could hardly bear the contrast between the supposedly social-conscious *habitants* and the thrifty farmers of New England. Father Charlevoix complained that "The English colonist amasses means and makes no superfluous expense; the French enjoys what he has and often parades what he has not."

Other officials put the same complaint even more bluntly. Champigny, an *intendant*, claimed that "The men are all strong and vigorous but have no liking for work; the women love display and are excessively lazy, those of the country districts just as much as the towns' people." Poor but pretentious, this is the version of the *habitant* that comes through in the testimony of officials and travelers through the colony. If such accounts are accurate even by half, they raise the problem of attempting to account for preoccupations with luxuries and leisure among people who, by modern standards, were economically still very poor. Why was the populace apparently comfortable with so little that they did not discipline themselves to underconsumption in the expectation of developing a larger estate for the future? The possible reasons for such a preference are varied. In the first place, if it is recognized that satisfaction with economic attainment (the decision to say *this is enough* after the barest subsistence is met) is a function of expectations as much as — perhaps more than — actual income, then it becomes clear how the *habitant* had arrived at a level of economic security unknown to the peasants of France. Here was a genuine economic and social incentive for a work ethic oriented to consumption rather than to production, even though other economic realities dictated that what W.J. Eccles calls the "aristocratic ethos" would have to be gratified by simple pleasures. Continual idleness was not possible, but there were five months of winter during which time the *habitant* was relieved from much of the drudgery of farming and more free to enjoy leisure. But this line of analysis only accounts for the material basis of status consciousness, not its continuation.

The relatively greater abundance of New France does not explain why the colony failed to go beyond status consciousness (and passive consumption) into career consciousness (and active commercial agriculture, for example). In New England, on the other hand, the colonists started like the *habitants* in the sense that they were aware from the beginning that they were materially better off than their cousins in England, but they felt compelled to improve this marginal difference and developed a commercial culture. Perhaps the religious difference accounts for their different motivational response. Maybe there was something about the social isolation of the lone Protestant (saved individually by faith alone) that made such a person a compulsive striver. In this view, profit was only the carrot, anxiety about worthiness in the sight of God was a mighty stick. Each Protestant had to earn his salvation alone, whereas Catholicism provided a curative intermediary, the priest, and sacraments such as confession that militated against the discharge of productive energy for the simple reason that one did not feel quite so despised and rejected by God. To feel in touch with salvation, a Catholic had only to maintain communication with God through the miracle of the sacraments. It was worthiness in the sight of man that was more troublesome; hence the excruciating status consciousness. This sort of speculation is hypothetical, but the fact remains that surprisingly few colonists in New France seem to have been motivated by what Max Weber called the "spirit of capitalism".

Beyond culture, however, there were important factors in the structure of the situation that would discourage all but an exceptional few from attempting to become the commercial producers Colbert hoped to develop as the model *habitants*. The Jean C. who sold his horses and replaced them with cattle to produce beef and dairy products for cash ultimately to build up his eighty-acre concession into an expanding cash crop farm, faced several severe obstacles to his success.

One was the lack of attractive and accessible markets. Ships' captains who brought cargoes of manufactured goods from Europe were not interested in hauling agricultural produce back with them. Anything grown in New France — even before shipping charges — was more expensive in the colony than in the mother country. Sometimes French merchants accepted grain as payment for debts, but the price was always about half what the Canadian farmer believed it was worth. Occasionally, especially in the later years, ships would sail in ballast to the Caribbean for sugar as their return cargo to France. It might seem that such vessels would have been a usable transportation link between Canada and an alternative market for their agricultural surplus. But the ships attempting to reach the Caribbean from the St. Lawrence were few because the voyage was so hazardous (owing to tropical storms the months that Canada was accessible from France). Moreover, the items most in demand in the French West Indies were "refuse" fish as food for the slaves and white oak as material for making sugar barrels. The New Englanders provided both at prices that were difficult to beat. Thus, the French West Indies were hardly any more attractive or accessible than the markets of the mother country.

Still, the colonists might have gained entry to the home market by doing as the Virginians had done; that is, by producing an agricultural staple such as tobacco which was of high value relative to bulk, and therefore able to sustain the high cost of transoceanic shipping. If not tobacco then perhaps some other staple, such as hemp, could have been the commodity to solve the problem of the market. But then there was another obstacle, another impediment to commercial agriculture that would have frustrated the would-be capitalist farmer. This was the immobility of land; that is, the extreme difficulty of buying and selling acreage in order to consolidate small farms into large commercial operations. The *Coutume de Paris*, the system of precedents and traditions that applied to the legal development of the colony, placed a number of brakes upon real estate transactions. It imposed, for example, a tax known as a *quint* amounting to a fifth of the sum that a person received as his compensation for rights to a *seigneurie* (or a concession on one). The same code also defined a *retrait lignager* by which any relative of the seller could buy the holding back within one year by refunding the sale price, or the similar *légitime* by which sales were voided if a lawful heir appeared to claim the acreage as his legitimate inheritance. Clearly, these safeguards could stabilize land tenure and inhibit land speculation. In most of the English colonies, there were no such safeguards (some observed the custom of primogeniture which functioned vaguely like *légitime)* but more characteristic of the English pattern was the province of Connecticut where land titles circulated on a great carousel of speculation with any given acre likely to change hands frequently. In New France, by contrast, there were concessions that remained in the same family for generations. If what happened in the parish of St. Famille on the Ile d'Orléans was typical, concessions were usually subdivided just to accommodate succeeding generations of the original *censitaire.* Of more than 70 farms in the sample, only ten absorbed others between 1670 and 1725. Since consolidation is an indicator of a developing commercial agriculture, the absence of such a trend in New France is a fair guide to its limitations in the colony and a hint to the relevance of the *quint, retrait lignager,* and *légitime* as obstacles to the development of commercial agriculture. Still, a determined producer of a cash crop eager to take his profits and "increase his estate" (as the English called acquisitive individualism) might still have done so with patience but then he would have faced the social stigma of producing for its own sake, the apparent meaning of the capitalist work ethic in New France. Benjamin Franklin in mid-eighteenth century America rationalized the virtues of thrift and industry as leading to health, wealth, and wisdom, but in New France it always seemed more sensible to enjoy today on the chance that there might not even be a tomorrow. People worked to produce that which they would consume or for living "nobly" rather than frugally. Thrift or business for its own sake was regarded as degrading.

Finally, even if our Jean C. ignored his neighbors' whispers behind his back for his plunge into commerce; even if he overcame the marketing difficulties or the frustrations of consolidating his holdings for economy of scale; even if he were to double his capital every ten years (as certain planters in South Carolina did in the eightenth century), what would he gain that he did not already have? Here we return to the realities of the structure of authority in New France, because here, in contrast to the English pattern in which status followed power and that came after wealth, power was the monopoly of the king. To be sure, there were small groups of colonists who gathered about the governor for social and economic favors, but there was no assembly, no system for recognizing and rewarding colonial bigwigs by bestowing upon these wealthy entrepreneurs the rights of running the colony because they had demonstrated their ability in economic success. Consequently, no myth of success developed as a dynamic of early French Canadian society. Comfortable with quite little, and satisfied with what they could appear to be, the *habitants* of New France developed status consciousness rather than capitalism.

## V    Easy Money

French-Canadian status consciousness sustained the anomaly of great ostentation on small wealth, especially at the top echelon of society with the seigneurial class. They held the greatest rank, displayed the greatest ostentation; but as seigneurs, they were quite poor. The revenues from tenants were too low to support them. How, then, did they maintain that style which led one military officer newly arrived in the colony around 1750 to exclaim that "Quebec is more full of pagaentry than is the court of France"? The answer is the fur trade. By their connections with the governor they gained licenses to trade at the western posts. But even the most ambitious gamblers in the fur trade did not control the economy which continued to be dominated by merchants based in La Rochelle or Bordeaux. The prices paid the Canadian participants were usually enough to maintain local notables in style but only by spending their cash receipts as fast as they received them or by living on credit from their French buyers. Aubert de la Chesnaye, for example, was active in the fur trade and accumulated more *seigneuries* on this basis than anyone ever did. But when he died, he was so heavily in debt that all his holdings were divided among creditors — merchants in France.

In New France the fur trade did expand and it did maintain its primacy in the economy, consistently accounting for more than 70 percent of the value of exports. But the economy did not develop. The size of the fur-trade hinterland increased enormously but the essential hinterland-metropolitan relationship between the colony and the mother country did not alter. Thus, the fur trade does not appear to have led to the development of an indigenous commercial class (although a furious debate on this particular point still continues among historians). It seems that when the exceptional Canadian did appear to contradict the general rule and attempted to displace the French merchants from their primacy in the trade, he soon discovered that his inferior connections in France left him at a fatal disadvantage and eventually he, too, would fall victim to the excessive consumption of working capital, and then emerge from the encounter poorer for the experience but perhaps richer in status for the attempt.

The use of the fur trade to sustain high status rather than as a springboard for capital accumulation was not restricted to the seigneurs or would-be merchants, either. For just as the seigneurial elite participated in the fur trade for the *gloire* it sustained, so also did a few of the *habitants* (precisely how many, however, is another point of contentious debate between historians). Perhaps it is safe to suggest that the main sequence in the life of the most adventuresome colonist was establishment of a concession, marriage, and family life. Then, with the first of the children old enough to run the farm and feed the stock, he and a friend would acquire a canoe-load of trade goods and venture out to the area of the Great Lakes, thus participating clandestinely in the fur trade as *coureurs de bois*, ultimately returning home to gain a little money and the esteem of having been places beyond the rapids. In this pattern as well, the lure of the trade was more than economic, more than the attractions of the Indian way of life, more than a desire to escape the tedium of the regulated existence in the settlements on the St. Lawerence. Here, too, the reward was primarily one of status, the prestige one gained as a person who ventured west despite the dangers or the rules against trading without a license.

New France thus developed as a world of broad horizons. Its economy was a scene of constantly expanding adventure in the fur trade rather than the pursuit of profits in other forms of commerce. And, although there was no legislative assembly or trial by jury, social justice was guaranteed by a plethora of competing authorities. Its history was not impressive for its economic development, but the harsh land sustained a tolerably good life for its colonists and the social existence was even more satisfactory. New France was not the economic success story of the New World, but for the people to whom it was home the land was doubtless no less precious than was New England to the New Englanders. By 1750, there had been invented in North America two colonial systems — each a new nationality in its own right, yet both were attached to empires in conflict. In this struggle, the French and the English soon encountered changes neither expected nor desired.

# Bibliography

No volume in the Canadian Centenary Series is limited solely to the subject of state-individual relations in New France between 1663 and 1760.

Several general works do contain a wealth of material on the subject, however. Y.F. Zoltvany, *The Government of New France: Royal, Clerical, or Class Rule?* (1971) is an excellent introduction to the issues, but now, unfortunately, somewhat dated. Raymond Douville and Jacques Casanova, *Daily Life in Early Canada* (1967) offers interesting comparisons of conditions in the colony with those of the mother country. More analytical, particularly on the theme of "the aristocratic welfare state" is W.J. Eccles, *Canadian Society During the French Regime* (1968). The idea of an all-pervading aristocratic ethos, developed elsewhere by Eccles, for instance, in the "Social, Economic, and Political Significance of the Military Establishment in New France," CHR (1971) has come under criticism recently, however, by Louise Dechêne, in *Habitants et marchands de Montréal au XVIIe siècle* (1974). She argues that the *habitant* of New France lived much like the peasantry of France itself and the alleged "consumer ethic" postulated by Eccles applied only to a very few of the wealthiest colonists. Dechêne also contends that the seigneurial system was at least potentially quite burdensome and very few *habitants* found any alternative opportunities in the fur trade. Since Dechêne's conclusions are based on an unusually systematic study of Montreal Island (from the late seventeenth to the early eighteenth centuries) her statements cannot be ignored. However, since Montreal contained but one quarter of the population and since Dechêne's study is also limited in chronological scope, the interpretations she dismisses so completely are perhaps abandoned too readily.

Works addressed to other aspects of the society of New France that are also at odds with Dechêne are E.R. Adair, "The French-Canadian Seigneury," CHR (1954), Richard Colebrook Harris, *The Seigneurial System in Early Canada: A Geographical Study* (1968), C.J. Jaenen, *The Role of the Church in New France* (1976), and André Lachance, *La Justice criminelle du roi au Canada au XVIIIe siècle* (1978). Adair and Harris argue that the seigneurial system bore so lightly on the habitants that no seigneur could live on his rents alone; Jaenen offers an overview showing how the clerical establishment was subordinate to the purposes of the state; and Lachance advances conclusions that suggest the administration of criminal law in the colony was extraordinarily humane by eighteenth-century standards.

For the counterexample of New England, readers should consult Charles S. Grant, *Democracy in the Connecticut Frontier Town of Kent* (1972). The classic by Max Weber, *The Protestant Ethic and the Spirit of Capitalism* (1904) is also still instructive.

"The British acquisition of New France was something
of an accident in the fortunes of war and the diplomacy
of peace."

# CHAPTER 5

# Imperial Adjustments and Colonial Reactions

## I   Conflict of Empires

Two inventions had inspired the migration of the French to North America. One, the fur rush, was economic. The other, the vision of a New France, was a social and religious ideal. The first entailed a frontier that was far-flung and ever-expanding as it followed new sources of supply always further west and north. The second invention called for a mode of settlement that was less a moving frontier and more a recreation of the metropolis itself within the limits defined by the arable land along the St. Lawrence River and to some extent on the Bay of Fundy in Acadia. In this way, the history of the French presence in North America to 1760 was divided: the quest for fur led to claims of continental proportions; the advance of settlement effectively occupied but one river valley.

Division entailed a fatal weakness that Colbert had foreseen as early as the 1660's. He appreciated that the economics of the fur trade dictated continual expansion, but he foresaw a time when France would be claiming the heart of the continent by virtue of the alliances between a few fur traders and Indian nations. But while the fur frontier could claim the territory, it would not be able to maintain that claim as only settlement could. In Colbert's opinion, it was wiser to restrict the colony to settled territory than to embrace indefensible claims to the whole continent. In his words, if "too vast an area" were claimed, "one would perhaps one day be obliged to abandon a part with some reduction of the prestige of His Majesty and state."

Perceiving the dual character of, if not the conflict between, the fur trade and settlement, Colbert preferred to reduce the fur rush and to develop the settlement on the St. Lawrence by diversifying its economy.

He preferred a compact colony with an economic future in agriculture, lumbering, shipbuilding, and the fisheries to a settlement that was a mere adjunct of the beaver bonanza and certain to lead France into future embarrassment by expanding into far more territory than French numbers could defend.

From the first, however, Colbert's compact colony policy was frustrated. Although he instituted a system of limited licenses, every year more traders ventured out without them. Furthermore, such *coureurs de bois* were encouraged by the officials in the colony, sometimes by even the governor and *intendant* themselves. By 1700, the result was communication with an enormous hinterland, an empire built on fur rather than by settlement. Its influence extended as far north as Hudson Bay, west to the Saskatchewan River, and south through the Mississippi all the way to the Gulf of Mexico. The expanding presence of France in North America was based on control of the Indians in trade, not occupation by colonists tilling the soil. Even the food for the handful of persons at the few posts in the hinterland was usually brought in from the St. Lawrence rather than produced on the spot.

Officially, the metropolis opposed such expansion, but the lure of profits and imaginative interpretation of the regulations sustained it nevertheless. Then, after 1700, there arose a new motive to claim the continent, a reason not only to establish ever-widening trading alliances with the native peoples but to fortify their land at strategic points as well. The King of Spain died in 1700 and left his vast empire to a grandson of Louis XIV. The potential power that such an inheritance conferred upon the Bourbons was frightening to Europe, especially to a maritime power like Britain which feared the colonial and trading challenge of a combined French-Spanish empire. Accordingly, in 1702, Britain joined the war against Louis XIV to maintain the balance of power. And the French king, in his turn, decided to fortify his holdings bordering on the British in North America. Later, if Louis emerged the victor, he would dominate all of Europe and most of the Western Hemisphere. Should the war go badly, North American holdings could be used as sacrificial pawns to divert the enemy from more valuable holdings in Europe or the Caribbean.

Eleven years later, sacrifice was demanded. Defeated in the old world and the new (Acadia, for instance, had been seized by the British in 1710), France was forced to negotiate concessions. By the Treaty of Utrecht, 1713, the French gave up Hudson Bay, Acadia, Newfoundland, and the fur lands south of the Great Lakes. The year 1713 thus marked an important turning point in the history of New France. Henceforth, the colony was limited as never before, bounded by two long river corridors, the St. Lawrence and the Mississippi. The traders were deprived, apparently, of the rich fur reserve draining into Hudson Bay, and the colonists lost the security of the approaches to the St. Lawrence by British occupation of New-foundland and Acadia.

From 1713, the history of the colony focused on resistance as officials concentrated their efforts to nullify the effects of the Treaty of Utrecht. They built a chain of posts from Lake Superior out through Lake of the Woods and Lake Winnipeg to the Saskatchewan River to intercept the trade in furs before they could reach the British on Hudson Bay. Similarly, a chain of posts was built in the upper Mississippi region to protect the commercial flank to the southwest. To compensate for the loss of Acadia and Newfoundland, Cape Breton Island was fortified by the building of Louisbourg, and in the St. Lawrence Valley itself, the *intendant* Gilles Hoc-quart, resurrected the old economic program of state-sponsored immigra-tion and diversification of the economy. Almost two thousand settlers (most of them soldiers) were recruited for service and subsequent retire-ment in the colonies and new industries (shipyards and ironworks) were established at Quebec and Trois Rivières. In short, from 1713, New France prepared for war with the British, a war to decide whether the future of the northern half of the continent (see map 5.1) would be merged with that of the British colonies to the south or continue on a course of its own.

Nearly thirty years of preparation seemed justified when war resumed between the two mother countries in 1741. Although none of the fighting touched the St. Lawrence valley, Louisbourg, the fortress on Cape Breton Island, was taken in 1745 by an expedition of New Englanders under the command of the governor of Massachusetts. By the Treaty of Aix-la-Cha-pelle, in 1748, the stronghold was returned to France. But the peace that followed could not be final because the British had not yet tested the new defenses at Quebec and Montreal. Until they had done so, they would never accept the fact of a French presence in the north. Every year after 1748, therefore, war threatened to resume. Finally it flared over control of the Ohio River valley in 1754. In preparation for the fighting that was expected for control of the St. Lawrence, the British launched a massive round-up of the entire French-speaking population in Acadia in 1755. Everyone caught was deported and dumped in the English colonies to the south. Refusing assimilation, many eventually made their way to Louisia-na, the other French province in North America. Thus, more than 5000 persons were displaced after capture. Approximately 8000 others escaped to territory in the north that was still under the control of France. In the meantime, the British destroyed or sold off everything that had been left behind in Acadia (the northeastern arm of the Bay of Fundy), and extinguished a distinctive pattern of diked farmsteads that had developed over the previous century to make use of the marshlands near the sea. With the Acadian landscape thus cleared for occupancy by British settlers from New England, and war once again upon New France, the colonists on the St. Lawrence might have wondered if a similar fate awaited them.

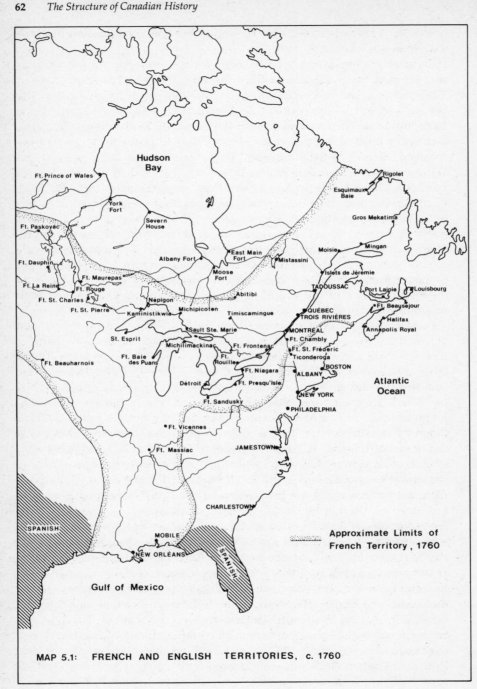

Hudson Bay

Ft. Prince of Wales

York Fort

Ft. Paskoyac

Severn House

Ft. Dauphin

Albany Fort

East Main Fort

Rigolet

Esquimaux Baie

Gros Mekatima

Moisie

Mingan

Ft. Maurepas

Ft. La Reine

Ft. Rouge

Ft. St. Charles

Nepigon

Moose Fort

Mistassini

Abitibi

Islets de Jérémie

TADOUSSAC

Port Lajoie

Louisbourg

Ft. St. Pierre

Kaministikwia

Michipicoten

Timiscamingue

QUÉBEC

TROIS RIVIÈRES

Ft. Beausejour

St. Esprit

Sault Ste. Marie

MONTRÉAL

Ft. Chambly

Halifax

Annapolis Royal

Michilimackinac

Ft. Frontenac

Ft. St. Fréderic

Ticonderoga

Ft. Beauharnois

Ft. Baie des Puans

Ft. Rouillé

Ft. Niagara

BOSTON

Détroit

Ft. Presqu'Isle

ALBANY

Atlantic Ocean

Ft. Sandusky

NEW YORK

PHILADELPHIA

Ft. Vicennes

Ft. Massiac

JAMESTOWN

CHARLESTOWN

SPANISH

MOBILE

NEW ORLEANS

SPANISH

·········  Approximate Limits of French Territory, 1760

Gulf of Mexico

**MAP 5.1:   FRENCH AND ENGLISH   TERRITORIES,  c. 1760**

At the beginning of the war, the mood in New France was not one of despondence, however. Although the population of the colony was only about 60 000 people in 1750 (far less than one-tenth of the British non-slave population to the south) there was some basis for confidence on the French side despite the apparent disparity of numbers. Unlike the British colonists, those of New France had a well organized militia, and more importantly, regular troops from the mother country were stationed at strategic points throughout the territory claimed by France. The command was unified and ties with the allied native peoples were also close. In the British colonies, by contrast, the militia was poorly organized and there were few British regulars in America or fortifications on the frontiers. Command was divided colony by colony and working alliances with the Indians were almost nonexistent. Consequently, a better accounting of numbers on the two sides would be the population of any one British colony against the whole of New France rather than that of all British colonies together since division was so complete on the British side. The English colonists could not even agree in principle on a common plan for defense. The one conference convened by Britain to discuss the problem in 1754 ended at Albany in bickering and recrimination.

In the meantime, the open conflict that had developed in the Ohio valley to determine whether the territory was a French fur reserve or land clear for British land speculators and farmers, led to instructions from Great Britain that the Americans would have to defend themselves. Subsequently, everything went in favor of the French. Defeat followed humiliating defeat and these fortunes did not begin to turn until the war came under the energetic coordination of the British minister, William Pitt the Elder, after 1757. Now British regulars were sent to North America and the navy was used to bottle up the French fleet in its home ports. By the strategy of blockade, Louisbourg fell in 1758, Quebec fell to Wolfe's seaborn force in September of the following year, and the conquest of the remainder of the region occurred in the next twelve months. Thus ended the American phase of the struggle that is known in European history as the Seven Years' War because fighting continued elsewhere for several more seasons. It was not until 1763 that a treaty, the Peace of Paris, concluded hostilities between France and Britain. Once again, as in 1713, France used the holdings in North America as sacrificial pawns in the game of global diplomacy. This time, however, France was forced to sacrifice everything in the north, all territory except two small islands in the Gulf of St. Lawrence (St. Pierre and Miquelon), in order to prevent the British from advancing additional claims against French possessions in the Caribbean.

## II    Immediate Consequences of Conquest

The British acquisition of New France was something of an accident in the fortunes of war and the diplomacy of peace. But the change itself was monumental in the sense that the people of an entire colony ceased legally to be French and were reduced at once merely to *canadiens*, residents of a place known as Canada (which the British now renamed Quebec). Still, the change of names and monarchs does not seem to have been intolerable to the vast majority of the population. The Acadians did suffer a second deportation (after the fall of Louisbourg) to clear the territory that the British named Prince Edward Island. But no dispersal of the vastly more numerous population on the St. Lawrence was attempted. Nor did many people voluntarily return to France rather than take their chances under British rule. Just three percent of the population returned to the former mother country. To those remaining, the church advised loyalty to the new authority saying that the British ought to receive "what we owed the French when they ruled." These and other indications of a relatively smooth transition to British rule have been cited by a long succession of historians to "prove" that the conquest and cession of the colony were far from tragic events in the history of New France. More recently, however, it has been suggested that the sequence of events that began in 1759 led to colossal retardation the *canadien* nation's development.

Michel Brunet has suggested that the emigration "home" of the three percent was significant beyond the numbers of persons involved because these were "Canadians of the upper class who refused to submit." According to Brunet, the 97 percent left behind were easily forced into a pattern of childlike "subordination" having lost their "natural leaders" by "social decapitation". But Jean Hamelin denies that there was anything novel about the process of return migration. In his view, such outmigration was "merely the repetition of a recurrent phenomenon". Where Brunet has argued that there was a French-Canadian commercial class who might have played a leading role in the development of the *canadien* nation had they not been displaced by the British, Hamelin contends that New France itself was locked into an "anemic collective survival" because the persons who controlled the fur trade were metropolitan by origin and destination.

Both historians may have exaggerated the importance of the commercial class. According to W.J. Eccles, military preferment conveyed more status, and therefore leadership, than success in trade. In his view, capitalism arrived with the British and at the time of its arrival, the *canadiens* were no more inclined to respect these merchants than those from France. Moreover, since the local militia captains tended to remain in the colony and to retain their old offices even under the British, the remarkable phenomenon immediately was not social decapitation but accommodation as British officials embraced a pattern of administration that was consistent with that recommended by the *canadien* squierarchy and officials of the Church.

The accommodation of the *canadiens* by the military governors — Haldimand, Murray, and Carleton — was contrary to the policy declared by Great Britain after the cession, however. Originally, the British had hoped to turn Quebec into a normal English colony. A program of assimilation was announced accordingly in 1763 by Royal Proclamation. Official status was to be withdrawn from the Catholic Church, French civil law and the seignuerial sytem of land distribution were both to be discouraged, and a massive influx of English settlers was expected by inviting British soldiers to retire in the colony on land to be granted in freehold. As soon as a substantial number of these newcomers were settled in Quebec, the governor was instructed to call a General Assembly of their representatives "to make, constitute, and ordain Laws ... agreeable to the laws of England." In this way, by stages, Quebec was expected to become a truly British colony. Eventually the *canadiens* were supposed to become English colonists in their own right — even their Catholic Church would be incorporated into the Church of England.

But such a design never materialized. And in this failure, a distorted version of absolutism was continued by default, largely because the expected influx of English immigrants failed to materialize. Since the British part of the population did not increase according to plan, James Murray, the governor at the time, did not call an Assembly. Instead, he governed with the assistance of an appointed council consisting primarily of *seigneurs* and Catholic clergy. Then the governor even gave his backing to establishing Jean Briand as a Roman Catholic bishop, a position to which Briand was consecrated in 1766. In this way, the administration of Quebec under the British was even more absolutist than in the years of the French regime. The supreme authority then had been shared by at least two officials, the *intendant* and the governor. Now the governor alone was supreme.

The irony of British absolutism did not end with the departure of Murray in 1765. His successor, Guy Carleton, went further in preserving Quebec as Murray had left it. Carleton soon came to know the province as a colony which was accustomed to government from the top. More particularly, he saw Quebec as a society of peasants, dutifully deferential to their superiors and betters, the *seigneurs* and the clergy. Here was "perfect subordination" too valuable to throw away. Consequently, in 1769, Carleton recommended statutory recognition of Quebec's institutional and social life as he imagined it had always been. The clergy and the *canadien* squirearchy of the province cooperated in Carleton's project formally to institutionalize absolutism since they saw their opportunity to gain more influence than they had exercised previously. At first, British officials balked at the proposal. But then came the threat of open rebellion in the colonies to the south. In 1774, by the Quebec Act, the seigneurial system was confirmed, the Church regained its tithe, French civil law was recognized, and authoritarian government was endorsed by dropping any reference to representative institutions for the present or the future. Naturally, the ascendant clergy and *seigneurs* were pleased.

Criticism of the Quebec Act in Canada came from another source. There was a small but significant group in the province which felt that the retreat from anglicization was a betrayal of promises made in 1760-1763. This was an English-speaking mercantile community in Montreal that had begun to replace the French traders with the change of mother countries. Since 1760 opportunists had been arriving in Quebec to enter into trade or speculate in land. From the first, they were not farmers or frontiersmen, but profiteers with connections in London who arrived to draw the promise of the northern economy into their own pockets. As a social group the English-speaking merchants were self-assertive and purposeful; soon they were the most outspoken segment of the population. By 1770 they numbered about one hundred and fifty, but their behavior betrayed an expectation that government and society existed to serve their private ends.

From the beginning of British rule, the English-speaking mercantile clique showed themselves critical of the governors — but not from any expressed animosity to the French-speaking majority. Indeed, they established close relations with the French whose cooperation in the fur trade, especially as *voyageurs*, they needed, and they sealed this working arrangement by social interaction such as the camaraderie of the newly founded Beaver Club and by taking French Canadian wives. Their animosity was directed against British policy and British governors as it pertained to the fur trade.

In the first place, they opposed provisions of the Royal Proclamation that discouraged ventures into Indian country; more particularly, they objected to a licensing system and to the stipulation that trading could only occur at designated posts. Murray was expected to relax or ignore these rules. Since he had used discretionary power to avoid calling an Assembly, why could he not use similar discretion in this case?

The result of the merchants' criticism was a two-year power struggle between the governor, allied with the clergy and the squirearchy, on the one side, and the merchants, unassisted, on the other. Ultimately, the traders emerged victorious by appealing to the mother country on the twin grounds of constitutionalism and mercantilism. They had a right, they claimed, to an Assembly, and London had an interest in expanding trade. Governor Murray was recalled.

The new governor, Guy Carleton, at first seemed the true champion of the merchants' cause. Carleton vigorously supported their wish to see the trade restrictions relaxed. In 1768 control of the fur trade was transferred to the colony and previous handicaps were thus removed. The competitive edge was now — as in the days before the Conquest — with Montreal. Soon merchants in New York were conceding as much by relocating to Quebec.

In 1774, with the passage of the Quebec Act, fur traders had further cause to rejoice. Although the statute institutionalized Murray's and Carleton's version of royal absolutism by sanctioning government by appointed (rather than elected) representatives, the same statute also restored the pre-Proclamation boundaries of the province. The lack of representative institutions that they might dominate was disappointing. But this was an object of criticism rather than rage. The reaction was otherwise with British colonists to the south of Quebec in 1774.

## III    American Reactions to Postwar Reforms

The rationale for Britain's empire, as for that of France, was the mercantilism that has already been described in connection with Richelieu's and Colbert's reorganization of New France after 1627. Mercantilism, a system of closed commerce with mother country and colonies bound together by a tight network of Navigation Acts to keep trade out of the hands of foreigners, used tariffs as a major mechanism of control. Thus, in the eighteenth century, New England distillers of rum were allowed to import their raw product (molasses) duty-free from the British West Indies; if they chose to import from the French West Indies a tariff of six pence per gallon, considered prohibitively high, had to be paid. But if tariffs were useful in shaping trading patterns, they were also useful in raising a revenue. And, after 1763, when Britain was economically pinched due to the burden of war-debt, it seemed reasonable to expect that the yields of the North American customs should pay for the cost of the mercantilist bureaucracy there at least. But here the expectations of British politicians were disappointed.

By and large, the colonists in North America had accepted the mercantilist framework and willingly acquiesced in their allotted place in the system. That is, the Navigation Acts were obeyed tolerably well without compulsion because, usually, it was good for the colonists' economic self-interest to sell their raw materials and buy their manufactures in accordance with the law. By 1760 the British Empire was very much in fact what it was supposed to be in theory. The colonies enriched the mother country and the rate of return to themselves was high enough that, in material terms, the ordinary people — including slaves — were better off in America than their counterparts in England.

But to this general pattern there were exceptions. The colonists balked when it came to paying the taxes on molasses and tea, and they smuggled both with impunity. Earlier governments had been able to ignore these evasions, preferring to let sleeping dogs lie. But by 1763 the government of George Grenville could not afford to be so lax. In 1764 he confronted Parliament with the astonishing fact that over the years the average cost of maintaining the American customs service was 8000 sterling. The average annual collection was 2000. To remedy this problem, Grenville brought in the Sugar Act by which the tax on molasses was halved and its enforcement made much more strict. No matter how reasonable this measure seemed to Grenville and Parliament, it caused resentment in America, however, for as it was pointed out in Britain itself, "the beginning to execute the laws afresh made them have the appearance of new laws."

Within a year, resentment increased to a frenzy of opposition as Americans protested Grenville's next reform, a suggestion that the colonial assemblies provide revenue to pay for an army which was now needed to police the frontier separating the old colonies from the *canadiens* and the Indians. With the acquisition of Quebec, British North America had become a mixture of diverse — and antagonistic — ethnic groups. In addition to the Protestant-Catholic tension exacerbated by the inclusion of the people in the St. Lawrence region, the inclusion of the fur-trading frontier sharpened the antagonism between farmer-settlers and those who wished to keep the west as a fur reserve. This conflict widened into one between Indians and whites in 1763 when native peoples south of the Great Lakes united in "Pontiac's Conspiracy" to halt the threat of advancing settlement from the east. The difficulty — and expense — of suppressing this rebellion dramatized the need for keeping the three populations of North Aemrica separate and for arming the boundary between them at strategic points. It was the cost of stationing British regulars which became Grenville's first concern because the North American deficit was now expected to rise to about £300 000 per annum.

Grenville warned that if the Americans failed to devise acceptable means for "defraying the expenses of defending, protecting and securing" the expanded empire on their own, he would impose a kind of colonial sales tax after one year. When the colonists failed to comply, Grenville brought in the Stamp Act of 1765. After November 1, all licenses, land titles, private contracts, bills of lading, almanacs, and newspapers were required to carry a revenue stamp. This tax would not generate a large revenue (only about £60 000 per year), but it would establish the principle that the cost of colonial administration was a responsibility of the colonists themselves rather than of the mother country. At the time, the 1.5 million inhabitants of North America were virtually free of taxes, whereas the eight million people of Britain were laboring under a national debt so large that merely to service it each year cost almost one hundred times the yield of the proposed Stamp Act. It seemed, therefore, a reasonable beginning; as Charles Townshend (soon to be Chancellor of the Exchequer) asked, "Will they grudge to contribute their mite to relieve us from the heavy weight of that burden which we lie under?" It seemed especially sensible to anyone who paused to consider that a large amount of the debt had been incurred by fighting a war in which the Americans were the chief beneficiaries.

## IV   Rebellion

Events immediately showed, however, that to the colonists the raising of an American revenue was not at all reasonable. In every colony from New Hampshire to Georgia riots and organized opposition prevented the law's implementation. The Stamp Act was nullified for the very simple reason that no one was permitted to fill the office of Stamp Master. Without stamps, there was no tax, and this was not all. The colonists demanded repeal, enforcing their demand with vigilante groups to coerce merchants into canceling orders of goods from Britain until Parliament changed its mind about taxing the self-governing colonies of British America. Finally, they succeeded. In the spring of 1766 the hated tax was repealed. However, at the same time that it was admitted to be inexpedient in practice, the law was affirmed to be fully legitimate in theory by another measure, the Decaratory Act, passed right after the Stamp Act's demise.

Here the American question might have remained — for generations, perhaps. But the new Chancellor of the Exchequer, Charles Townshend, reopened the issue one year later with a scheme the colonists were bound to accept, he said. Townshend indicated that the colonists objected to the Stamp Act because they claimed it was beyond the jurisdiction of Parliament. The colonists maintained that only their legislatures had the power to tax them, and they reconciled this view of the constitution with membership in the British Empire by drawing a distinction between internal and external taxation. An internal tax was a levy upon property by a local legislature elected by the taxpayers to defray the cost of government in its limited business of providing security for liberty and property. External taxes were tariffs which incidentally generated a revenue, but were imposed by the imperial legislature primarily to regulate trade in the imperial interest. Townshend regarded the distinction as utterly false since it seemed to him that Parliament's power extended, in the words of the

Declaratory Act, to all cases whatsoever. Still, to demonstrate his leadership as well as to establish the supremacy of Great Britain over the colonies, he proposed some external taxes, import duties, for the purpose of generating American revenue. In May of 1767, taxes were imposed on tea, paper, glass, and paint pigments. Once again the colonists from New Hampshire to Georgia complained bitterly. Once again they organized a boycott.

With the death of Charles Townshend in 1767, and after several other changes of government, the new ministry of Lord North decided upon repealing the Townshend program in the spring of 1770 because by then it was clearly no more than a continuing source of discontent in the relations between the colonies and mother country. Lord North preferred to drop the American question and get on with more important matters in the nation's business. Therefore, on April 12, 1770, Parliament repealed all the hated Townshend duties, all but the small tax on tea (retained to save something of the principle of Parliamentary supremacy). The important point was North's obvious acceptance of the probability that colonial administration was always going to be run at a deficit. Never again would Parliament attempt anything like a Stamp Act or the Townshend Duties. Great Britain would be satisfied with the formal or informal advantages derived from overseas empire. There would be no attempt to generate imperial tribute, particularly if the colonists denounced it as such.

Ironically, this concession was a disappointment to many of the colonists who had grown accustomed to expecting the worst from British ministeries since 1764. The escalation of their resentment, an almost paranoid pessimism, is the major signficance of the American Revolution as it pertains to Canada because the colonists who were most afraid were the ones who called themselves Patriots. It was they who distinctively affirmed that the British constitution was safe only in their hands, because in England, public virtue was supposedly corrupted by private greed and false principles. Effeminacy, luxury, and sin were rampant there, especially in the circles of government where wicked men pursued the public business for private gain. In Great Britain, the constitution was out of balance. The king, lords, and commons were no longer independent of one another and so in a position to check one another's tendency to tyranny; they were increasingly united in one vast conspiracy for personal aggrandizement with the arch-conspirators going under the name of *king's ministers*. Now Lord North, the king's first minister, had withdrawn the Townshend scheme. True Patriots in America were not pleased and their disappointment was double-pronged. On the one hand, the ministry's retreat was interpreted as a strategic withdrawal to plot subtler means of subverting American liberty. On the other hand, the retreat had a more personal signficance. In all of the leading urban areas of America (in Boston, New York, Philadelphia, and Charleston, South Carolina), obscure political hacks such as Sam Adams of Boston had achieved public renown and personal success for the first time in their lives by denouncing the threat of British tyranny from the moment of the Stamp Act. No new dish of outrage from Britain meant lean days or bad home-cooking. As the months passed into years, the stature of politicians whose popularity depended upon British tyranny diminished progressively. They knew there was a ministerial plot to subvert American liberty. They despaired for their colonies and themselves. Their influence faded inexorably.

Then in 1773, Parliament passed a law with American implications. In the course of regulating the affairs of the East India Company the House of Commons legislated some provisions that would make British tea, legitimately imported, cheaper and therefore competitive with that smuggled into the colonies from Holland. Ardent Patriots like Sam Adams interpreted cheap tea as the means of seducing the Sons of Liberty into paying the tea tax remnant of the Townshend scheme. Thus, the ministery had paused for three years "not to repent their evil deeds, but rather to collect themselves, and devise some measures more effectual. For so far from giving over the execrable design, the plan of oppression is renewed." Adams and the others decided to "venture upon a desperate remedy" to prevent the tea even from being landed. On December 16, 1773, one hundred and fifty Sons of Liberty disguised as Indians boarded three ships in Boston harbor and "in a very little time," according to Sam Adams, "every one of the teas ... was immersed in the bay, without the least injury to private property."

Of course the East India Company regarded their tea as of some value; in fact, by their accounting, £10 000 worth of private property had been wantonly and publicly destroyed. In the weeks that followed, tea parties occurred elsewhere. There was even a second one in Boston and the ministry decided to make an example of Massachusetts. A bill to close the port until Boston's town meeting voted restitution to the company passed the British House of Commons without division on March 25. Although the innocent as well as the guilty would suffer thereby, the innocent shared responsibility in North's view because they had failed to act on their own to punish vandals acting under the guise of patriotism. This was not all. Three other bills were passed to ensure that the first would not be nullified. A Port Bill shut down Boston's commerce, the other measures suspended the constitution and brought Massachusetts under martial law until order was restored.

The rest of the thirteen colonies that had spawned protest movements since 1764 viewed Lord North's program of coercion as "Intolerable Acts". To them, the Quebec Act (which passed Parliament at the same time as the "Coercive Acts") was widely regarded as the model of government intended eventually for every colony. Consequently, the thirteen protesting colonies except Georgia sent delegates to Philadelphia for a "Continental Congress" meeting in September of 1774. There they agreed to make common cause. The delegates drafted a Bill of Rights in which George Grenville, Charles Townshend, and Lord North were characterized as vultures picking over the carcass of a dying empire rather than as administrators who intended no ill but found themselves in a difficult constitutional situation nonetheless. Finally, the Congress approved yet another boycott upon British imports until Parliament relented. Then they agreed to meet again in May of 1775 "unless the redress of grievances, which we have desired, be obtained before that time." But when they reconvened, it was to plan a war rather than a continuation of the protest because skirmishing had broken out between British soldiers and colonial militia just outside Boston in April. In this way, the rebellion began more than a year before the colonies formally declared their independence in 1776 and the fighting went on for seven years after that. Finally, weary of the contest and divided at home, Great Britain agreed in 1783 to recognize the united colonies as independent states. Except for the settlement of the displaced persons in the revolution, the struggle was over.

## V    The Loyalists

Not everyone, perhaps not even a majority of the population in the rebellious colonies welcomed independence. Nor was it a majority of the colonies in the British Empire that united to separate from the old arrangement. By 1763 there were nearly thirty distinct provinces that together made up the English possessions in the Western Hemisphere. They varied from the sugar islands of the West Indies to the fur trading stations on Hudson Bay. Only thirteen joined the War for Independence. The others remained aloof, either passively neutral, unreceptive to American requests to join, or actively hostile to the rebels' attempts to force acquiescence. Thus, there were two kinds of loyalism. The first was that which occurred beyond the context of the American Revolution, that is, one phenomenon was the loyalism of whole provinces. The other was the loyalty of individuals resident in colonies that did rebel. The first loyalism was quiet and situational; the other was tumultuous, painfully personal, and frequently ended in persecution or exile.

Consider particular cases. There was no independence movement in the British West Indies, for instance, the most conspicuous example of situational loyalty. The islands produced but one product, sugar, and it was produced by slave labor. Soil exhaustion determined that the cost of West Indian sugar exceeded the world price. As a matter of course, the owners of the land and slaves had requested and received a protected market under mercantilism. An Act of Parliament was passed to guarantee their profits. The plantation owners were more than deferential to the mother country. Most of them actually lived there. As the West India lobby, they were one of the most powerful interest groups pressuring Parliament. More influential than the North American interest, they were nearly equal to the East India lobby. Abolition of slavery would occur to them sooner than rebellion against the authority of Great Britain.

The newly arrived businessmen in Quebec were another group that illustrated the phenomenon of situational loyalty. Interested in realizing maximum profits from the northern fur trade, their economic interests isolated them from the thirteen colonies as much as sugar set the West India lobby apart from the Americans. As for the *canadiens*, it has already been shown that the clergy and squirearchy had more to gain from British than American affiliation since the Patriots expressed real hostility to any idea of established religion and hereditary aristocracy. The increased seigneurial rents implied by the new power and prosperity of the seigneurial elite should have operated as a powerful incentive to make the *habitants* join the American army which invaded Quebec over the winter of 1775-76. In some areas, such as the upper Richelieu River valley — where profiteers had moved in as *seigneurs* and had begun to exploit feudal dues with unprecedented ruthlessness — they did. But elsewhere the overwhelming majority knew the Americans as enemies rather than liberators and remained aloof accordingly.

The same combination of situational factors led to neutrality in Nova Scotia, Ile St. Jean (later Prince Edward Island), and Newfoundland. In the latter example, the colony was a fishing station; in fact, the bulk of Newfoundlanders maintained their permanent residences in Great Britain since settlement on the island was prohibited. The prohibition notwithstanding, there were thousands of permanent residents on the eastern tip of the island between Trinity and Placentia Bays. Their orientation was completely eastward to Britain. It never occurred to them to join the rebellion.

Similarly, on Ile St. John the population was small — only about one thousand in 1776 (having expelled almost five thousand Acadians in 1758). Moreover, the newcomers had only recently arrived from the British Isles, since 1765. For this reason, their orientation was also still completely toward the metropolis. As recent immigrants, the people showed little willingness to jeopardize their stake in the rich soil on which they had just settled. If the issues of the dispute reached many of the settlers at all, they had a greater desire to build on their dream of security and prosperity in the New World than to choose ephemeral political issues agitated in other colonies by persons none of them knew.

Similar isolation operated in Nova Scotia but this case was complicated by the fact that half of the population had recently arrived from New England. Some definitely leaned in the direction their cousins were moving, but since so much of the rest of the population was British-born, and since nearly everyone had settled within one generation, society and politics had not yet crystalized. To the extent that the events of the period were a source of anxiety, that psychological energy was discharged in religious revival fostered by Henry Alline rather than in political slogan-shouting from the south. Then, too, it should be mentioned that Halifax was a naval base. Besides the economic hold this had upon the hinterland, the daily presence of British warships served most certainly as a sober reinforcement of the already firm British orientation of these early Nova Scotians.

Loyalty in these areas was therefore a function of the configuration of circumstances. These provinces were Loyalist because any other position was simply unthinkable. The Loyalism in the colonies from New Hampshire to Georgia was different, however. Following the tide there meant joining the revolt, reluctantly perhaps, but still this was the best way to safeguard one's life and property. Loyalism was the risky option. From the outbreak of fighting in 1775 but especially after Britain's recognition of American independence in 1783, Loyalists were a hopeless minority who found themselves expelled from their homes. The wealthy could afford to move to Great Britain; but the vast majority were of the "middle sort" and these had to find their refuge in what remained of British North America. The great bulk of them, nearly 30 000, sailed for Nova Scotia. There, for the most part, they settled in what had formerly been Acadia. Thus, they found themselves quite apart from the other Nova Scotians upon whom they looked down with disdain for having been but lukewarm in support of Britain in the late war. Not surprisingly, the Loyalist newcomers on the Bay of Fundy wanted their own province and were accommodated in 1784 with the creation of New Brunswick as a political jurisdiction separate from Nova Scotia. The imperial authorities, believing that small separate colonies were preferable to single large regions complied here as elsewhere because they hoped that a policy of divide and rule might prevent future wars of independence. For the same reason, barely populated Cape Breton Island was raised to the dignity of separate provincial status and kept it until 1820 when the island was reunited with Nova Scotia.

The settlement of the Loyalists in the Atlantic region was thus hardly more complicated than rearranging the political geography for the newcomers. It was otherwise in Quebec where some 10 000 colonists arrived expecting to find the kind of political environment they had known in the provinces of their birth: freehold land tenure, English laws, a Protestant religious establishment, and representative government. All were, of course, lacking. Consequently, a potential clash of cultures obliged the British legislators to amend the Quebec Act in the attempt to avoid such trouble. By the Constitutional Act of 1791, Quebec was divided into two distinct provinces: an upriver portion west of Montreal to be known as Upper Canada and the downriver part to the east to be called Lower Canada.

As far as Upper Canada was concerned, the solution was simply the Nova Scotia formula carried west because there was no prior French settlement in the sense of *seigneuries* — only mile after mile of unoccupied waterfront. For this reason, Upper Canada was the part of Quebec that attracted most of the Loyalists who did not seek homes in the Atlantic region, and the transition to provincial status in Upper Canada was taken with the same comparative ease as in New Brunswick. Elective institutions were established, English civil and criminal law were instituted, land was granted by the Crown in freehold, and the established religion was understood by most to be the Church of England.

The eastern portion of Quebec presented the difficult problem. Here, the population was still overwhelmingly *canadien*. Nevertheless, English institutions of law and government were established for the benefit of the incoming minority of approximately 3000 Loyalists. Land lying outside the *seigneuries* was to be granted in freehold while the existing seigneurial system was preserved; English criminal law was instituted alongside French civil law; and elective government was to be established while continuing the privileged positon of the Catholic church. Thus, although there were some important changes designed to accommodate the British, in several ways the distinctive French character of the province was to be maintained. In other words, the Constitutional Act of 1791 provided a legal framework for two societies in a single state. But since it soon beame clear that the *canadiens* were at a disadvantage in using the newcomers' institutions, representative government and the free economy were at first instruments of subordination.

In the first years after the fall of Quebec in 1759, the mass of the ordinary inhabitants retained their possessions, continued to make their customary living, spoke the familiar language, observed the old laws, and maintained the traditional religion. The slight British presence before 1783 was probably no more unsettling to most than an abrupt change of administration. Common people did not feel conquered until their way of life was submerged under a set of parallel institutions established for the benefit of an incoming minority. It would appear that this is the major signficance of the Loyalist migrations to Quebec after 1783. The English part of the colony was crucially strengthened in numbers and attitude, and although they were a minority, they felt themselves to be in possession of everything substantial. The French were left with everything the British regarded as ephemeral — the foreign language, the quaint legal system, and the "Romish" church. In this dualism there was also the basis for a system of social stratification, a conquest culture with a superior minority subjugating the majority.

For the other colonies, the significance of the Loyalist migrations is less clear. On the Bay of Fundy and west of the Ottawa River they did indeed set up the society they knew. Here the problem is assessing the character of these new provinces in comparison with the country they left behind. The complication is finding a synonym for *Loyalism*. The labels from the right-left political continuum have not been particularly instructive since there is little evidence that the Loyalist-migrants were less *liberal* or notably more *conservative* than the Americans they left behind. For this reason, the interesting speculation of historians such as David Bell and H.A. Morton is that the opposing sides in the American Revolution are more intelligible from the standpoint of their different temperaments than from the content of their ideology. In the context of the rebellion, the people had to decide whether the imperial legislature was behaving ill-advisedly or tyrannically. To be a Patriot — in the American sense — one had to be ready to believe that there was a plot to enslave the colonies, and believing this, to deduce with such as Josiah Quincy that "Britons are our oppressors: WE ARE SLAVES." But anyone unable to see intentional tyranny in the Stamp Act would probably regard the Patriots' deduction as "enthusiastic". In this sense, the Loyalists were inclined to see themselves as members of a political community that had local and metropolitan dimensions. They realized the colonists were not represented in the central legislature and for this reason most of the Loyalists considered the attempt to raise an American revenue to be ill-advised. But Samuel Seabury, after arguing that it was more reasonable to concede the planning of imperial defense to the central leglislature, went on to assert that Parliament's right to do the reasonable thing of imposing a small tax for imperial defense implied no right to impose large and more burdensome taxes without resolving the representation issue. The Patriots, however, were uncompromising and prepared to believe the worst. According to Loyalists such as Peter Oliver, if the leaders of the rebellion had "told their deluded Followers that an Army of 30 000 Men were crossing the Atlantic in Egg shells, with a Design to roast the Inhabitants alive and eat them afterwards, the People would have first stared, and swallowed down the Tale, whole."

The Loyalist denunciation was of "enthusiasm", of the crazy willingness to believe that evil men in Britain were plotting the overthrow of Anglo-American liberties. The Loyalists were thus the skeptics of the revolution. They did not believe the British Parliament was trying to enslave America. Nor were they inclined to believe the American pretensions — rampant after 1775 — that the United States, on an independent course, would be a better, freer England. This skepticism is what made the Loyalists "un-American" and that is why they left or were forced to leave.

There was nothing in Loyalist skepticism that conflicted with the attitudes of the English-speaking colonists already in the northern remnant of the shattered empire. For this reason, the impact of their arrival outside the settled portions of Quebec (immediately, and perhaps also for the long term) was simply to reinforce the British hold on the regions to which they fled. In the case of Lower Canada, however, the Loyalist migration may have had the more profound significance that has already been described: after 1783, the *canadiens* continued to be the numerically superior group but with the establishment of parallel British institutions the majority of the population began to be treated as exceptional and of lesser importance. Here was a conquest that was more tangible than the change of governors, and a change in the life of the *canadiens* that was more revolutionary than the American War of Independence had been for either the Americans or the Loyalists.

# Bibliography

No single volume of the Canadian Centenary Series covers the subject of the conflict of empires and the imperial adjustments that led to the division of the continent into the United States and British North America. G.F.G. Stanley, *New France, 1744-1760* (1968) and H. Neatby, *Quebec, 1760-1791* (1966) treat the subject of the conflict for the continent and the cession to Britain. The concluding chapters of Neatby's work and the early chapters of the Centenary History volumes by W.S. MacNutt, *The Atlantic Provinces, 1712-1857* (1965), and *Upper Canada, 1784-1841* (1963) by Gerald M. Craig, deal with the migration of the Loyalists.

More specialized works considering the struggle that led to the cession of New France to Britain include the old but readable history by Francis

Parkman, *Half-Century of Conflict* (1892). Two books by Naomi Griffiths, *The Acadian Deportation* (1969) and *The Acadians: Creation of a People* (1973) cover the opening round of the conquest. Errol Sharpe, *A People's History of Prince Edward Island* (1976) includes a chapter on the remarkable "second expulsion". C.P. Stacey, *Quebec, 1759: The Seige and the Battle* (1959) is a masterful description of the final action.

For the debate on the significance of the cession, Dale Miquelon, *Society and Conquest: The Debate on the Bourgeoisie and Social Class in French Canada, 1700-1850* (1977) provides a valuable selection and translation of material from historians such as Brunet and Hamelin, otherwise available only in French. H. Neatby, *The Quebec Act: Protest and Policy* (1972) considers the statute that is usually interpreted as the French-Canadian blueprint for cultural survival.

In the English colonies, the Quebec Act was another of the "intolerable acts" of Britain, of course. For background to the violent protests that began in 1765 see Bernard Bailyn, *The Origins of American Politics* (1965), an analysis of eighteenth-century political culture. Thomas Barrow, *Trade and Empire: The British Customs Service in Colonial America, 1660-1775* (1960) describes the administation of the Navigation Acts and argues that in nearly all cases they were obeyed without compulsion because it was usually in the economic interest of the colonists to do so. In 1765, however, the colonists perceived a "new departure" in policy. Edmund S. and Helen M. Morgan, *The Stamp Act Crisis: Prologue to Revolution* (1953) describes the results. Gary B. Nash, *The Urban Crucible: Social Change, Political Consciousness and the Origins of the American Revolution* (1979) attempts to explain why centers such as Boston and Philadelphia were so important in the development of the revolution. Benjamin Woods Labaree, *The Boston Tea Party* (1964) shows how the protest movement reached a point of inevitability that led to the American War for Independence.

On the subject of the loyal colonies, Gordon Stewart and George Rawlyk offer insight into the case of Nova Scotia in *A People Highly Favoured of God: The Nova Scotia Yankees and the American Revolution* (1972). A small but valuable bit of material on the reaction of Quebeckers to their possible "liberation" by the Americans is found in Allan S. Everest, *Moses Hazen and the Canadian Refugees in the American Revolution* (1976). The same subject is covered in greater detail by G.F.G. Stanley, *Canada Invaded, 1775-1776* (1973).

For the study of Loyalist individuals, Mary Beth Norton has provided a full account in *The Loyalist Exiles in England, 1774-1789* (1972). L.F.S. Upton has focused on those in Canada, first in a biography of a New Yorker in Quebec, *William Smith, The Loyal Whig* (1969), and secondly in an edition of selections from other works, *The United Empire Loyalists: Men and Myths* (1967).

Two essays offering provocative interpretations of the significance of the Loyalist migrations for later development of Canadian political culture are David V.J. Bell, "The Loyalist Tradition in Canada," *JCS* (1970), and H.A. Morton, "The American Revolution: A View from the North," *JCS* (1972).

"Such rafts . . . were fabricated without any metal
fasteners . . . entirely by hand."

# CHAPTER 6

# *Expansion*

## I Old Staples

At the conclusion of the American Revolution, the British peace negotiators might have been expected to insist upon a border between their possessions and the United States that reflected the existing limit of effective American occupation: the Appalachian Mountains. But at the negotiations, the diplomats representing Great Britain showed themselves to be more interested in appeasing the late enemy. Consequently, the boundary was drawn through the Great Lakes at the north and with the Mississippi River at the west. The old Canadian southwest was thus lost.

Montreal fur traders adjusted by expanding their operations into the region north and west of Lake Superior. To facilitate the enormously long lines of supply that this required, an association of Montreal partners formed and called itself the North West Company. Through the employment of technological innovations such as the steel trap and organizational novelty such as the idea of the wintering partner (employees in the hinterland who received rapid promotion and a large share of the profits), these "Montreal Pedlars" built a successful transcontinental trading system. By 1800 the North West Company was garnering more than four times the amount of fur as the Hudson's Bay Company and all other Canadian rivals combined.

At the same time, farmers in the Canadas enjoyed prosperity exporting grain to the British market, a fact which was particularly important in Lower Canada. Here, rather than spending their profits in the approved American manner of expanding their base of production, the most prosperous *canadiens* appear to have spent their income as consumers. One taste that was indulged with special enthusiasm was education for farmers' sons, thus promoting a family's social ascent by the entry of one of its members to the learned professions of medicine and law.

Here were economic and social tendencies that deepened the lines of conquest culture, however. To the duality of institutions (representative government, freehold land tenure, Protestant religion for the English; political quiescence, seigneurial system and Catholicism for the French) was added a duality of life expectations (commercial agriculture, trade and dominance for the English; consumer farming, the professions and acquiescence for the French). Yet, this pattern of duality does not appear to have been condemned in the 1790s.

Prosperity was one support of *canadien* quiescence. Another reinforcement was the French Revolution. By 1792, the upheaval of France had given rise to a regime that was militantly exporting republicanism and anticlericalism to the horror of the clergy and *seigneurs* of Lower Canada. Both groups responded by transferring an allegiance from a France that was rapidly disappearing to the British institutions that were just then arriving. The Church and the French-Canadian squirearchy heaped mountains of praise upon Great Britain for the leadership that country provided in the counterrevolution. Then, as England emerged as the refuge and the fortress of European conservatism, the Catholic clergy of Lower Canada responded with a sort of  permanent witch hunt to eradicate what few signs of sympathy there were with the French Revolution among the *habitants*.

Given the enjoyment of prosperity and revulsion at the French Revolution, there was more cause for indifference than for activism among the mass of the citizenry in the 1790s. This and the French-Canadian unfamiliarity with respresentative government enabled the English minority to dominate public affairs without protest. They filled only sixteen of the fifty seats in the Assembly, but since they were the one politically self-conscious group whose private interests were articulated in terms to suggest a public purpose, representative government worked to the advantage of the English despite their minority position. *Canadiens* did not challenge their predominance in the control of provincial affairs for another decade.

Dissent began to develop with the beginnings of a period of profound economic dislocation. One reason was declining agriculture. In part this was due to methods that resulted in the soil being mined rather than worked. Crop rotation, and the other aspects of conscientious horticulture appear not to have been practised in Lower Canada (or many other parts of North America). But because the arable land of the *seigneuries* had been worked longer, and also because increasing population placed prior demands on a crop, cash income declined after 1800. Another factor in the dislocation of the economy was a dwindling participation of the *canadiens* in the fur trade since the exploitable fur was becoming relatively more accessible to traders from Hudson Bay, to the detriment of the North West Company.

Of course, economic change affected the Montreal English-speaking elite as well. Their major alternatives were land speculation and forwarding

Upper Canadian and American grain to Britain. Initially, land speculation was more attractive. Consequently, the brisk market in acreage that had been such a conspicuous aspect of the English colonies from the beginning of their settlement developed in Canada as well. But the land the merchants bought first was purely speculative because the Crown was the primary land-settlement promoter between 1783 and 1792. The people to be settled in these years were the displaced persons, the refugees from the American Revolution, rewarded by a grateful mother country. Every Loyalist was provided land free of charge, along with the implements necessary for farming. Moreover, each newcomer was guaranteed subsistance for up to three years after his arrival. But these extraordinary gifts were not continued for long.

After 1791, the Americans who emigrated to Canada and received only land were less likely to be motivated by political loyalty. It was also hoped by land speculators such as John Richardson that they would be less likely to take what the Crown offered free and instead purchase retail the land which he and his friends acquired wholesale. They would not charge a great deal for the privilege of settling on land more strategically located than were the Crown grants. But then how much did one need to ask for land which was acquired for less than one penny an acre?

Here it might be wondered how the Crown could be a land settlement agency dealing directly with immigrants for "wasteland" but indirectly through speculators in the more desirable acreage. The answer is that no such pattern was ever intended. Technically, land speculation was illegal. No individual could purchase more acreage than he was likely to use, no one could acquire land directly from the Crown for the sole purpose of selling it in the future. No individual could claim more than 1200 acres for his own freehold. Speculators such as Richardson evaded the law, however, by promoting deals through a system of so-called leaders and associates. The leader, that is the speculator, would obtain a vast tract of land for the mere payment of survey and registration fees, ostensibly because he represented a group of settlers, the associates who either did not exist or were individuals giving their name for a price and too poor to care how it was used. The real associates were recruited, one by one, as they became purchasers of the land the Richardsons of Canada had received virtually free.

The relationship of leader to associate did not end with the settler buying his potential farm. Since the big speculators were also the established merchants, they found it expedient to plant branch stores wherever settlement proceeded. Having sold pioneers their land, they subsequently provided them with the calicoes, broadaxes, and other necessities of pioneering. The terms of credit were fairly generous as the merchants awaited the farmers' first cash crop, potash (the result of leaching lye from the ashes of the settlers' felled trees). In time, the other marketable crops of grain, salt beef, and pork would follow. The mercantile firms centered in Montreal which branched out into the expanding agricultural frontiers of the Canadas were thus the farmers' access to the markets of the world, and the settlers, in turn, were the consumers of imported goods shipped into the hinterland by those same businessmen.

To facilitate their new commerce, the English-speaking elite proposed a program of modernization and internal improvements early in the 1800s. Their main purpose was to make Lower Canada more commercial and to link it more closely with the relatively more dynamic economic development of Upper Canada and the United States. To this end, they sought the dissolution of the seigneurial system as a first step toward the development of capitalist agriculture in Lower Canada; to develop roads and canals linking the lower St. Lawrence with the American and British Great Lakes region; and the linking of financial institutions with the public purse in advancing the program of development. But the businessmen's economic ambitions also required social change, changes as radical as the abolition of the *seigneuries*. They wanted to shift the burden of taxation, for instance, from commerce to agriculture, from excise taxes to land taxes, and they wanted modernization of legal procedures as well as land tenures.

The merchants' program of modernization could also be interpreted as a plan to move Lower Canada from a conquest culture to a unitary capitalist state by eradicating all the many dualisms that had developed in the years since 1760. Of course, unity implied assimilation. From the point of view of English-speaking colonists, the advocacy of such change was neither sinister nor chauvinistic since the reward to the *canadiens* would be greater economic opportunity — full participation in the the enterprise of social ascent by economic acquisition.

Given their economic difficulties, the *canadiens* might have been expected to have been somewhat receptive to a program that was supposed to improve their material prospects. But to the young lawyers educated in the 1790s, the commercialism advocated by the "transient" English-speaking merchants was not for the general good; it was only to advance a few private interests. The real impediment to social happiness, in their opinion, was a failure to recognize that the majority ought to determine the shape of administration. The problem they saw was the governor's allowing the British to govern Lower Canada as if the majority did not count and as if they deserved no better fate than subordination.

Between 1805 and 1810 English and *canadien* parties thus wrangled over the issue of the future destiny of Lower Canada: was the province to be commercial and British, or traditionally — yet democratically — *canadien*? The year 1805 marked the beginning of the open conflict when the Assembly approved a bill to build jails at Quebec and Montreal but refused to shift the cost away from commerce by imposing a land tax to pay for them. The same Assembly also refused to enact legislation for the gradual abolition of the seigneurial system. The business elite which dominated the legislative and executive councils took these actions as an open assault upon commerce and progress, and urged the governor to exercise his veto. Failing here, they took their case to the imperial authorities and failed there as well.

Meanwhile, the British party thundered denunciations of the *canadiens* publicly and privately. At a dinner to honor the valiant English minority in the Assembly, a toast was offered "To Our Representatives in the Provincial Parliament who proposed a Constitutional and proper mode of Taxation for the building of Gaols and who opposed a Tax on Commerce for that purpose as contrary to the sound practice of the Parent State." Then came another toast, more a prayer: "May the Commercial Interest of this Province have its due influence in the administration of its Government." After these proceedings were reported with emotional embellishment in the English press, the *canadien*-dominated Assembly called the editors to the house to apologize for the libels they had printed, and the battle was on.

Ultimately victory fell to the English party. By 1854 they had won almost everything they had demanded in the way of banks, canals, and institutional changes such as the abolition of the seigneurial system. Thus, they gained full security for profits from land, grain, and imports. But such local enterprises were not as rewarding as a new staple, timber, whose exploitation began in the first decade of the new century and almost immediately dwarfed everything else in importance.

## II　The Timber Rush

War was the reason the timber industry expanded so rapidly. In 1807 Napoleon blocked Britain's access to traditional sources in northern Europe. Naturally, the British looked to Canada as an alternate supplier and found the stock more than ample. As a result, the importations of wood from the colonies grew from practically nothing to impressive levels almost immediately. By 1810 timber was the most important trade of both Canadas and New Brunswick, and for the next thirty years wood, by itself, consistently accounted for roughly half the value of all exports from British North America.

The crisis of 1807 was the immediate cause for the new staple but the long-term factor that sustained the Canadian timber trade was a heavy tariff imposed upon the Baltic product, a tax that was continued long after the Napoleonic wars for the mercantilist encouragement it gave to British merchants to obtain their wood in Canada. The tax on foreign wood was increased by stages to more than one hundred percent by 1815, but colonial timber was never taxed. So long as the duty on Baltic timber amounted to more than its whole value, conditions were exceedingly favorable to maintain Canada as "Great Britain's woodyard". The colonial commodity could bear the high cost of transportation and still return a handsome profit. Of course, another result was that timber was artificially expensive in England. But the shippers and dealers were content with their profits from the trade and exerted pressure on Parliament to maintain the tariff long after the crisis brought on by Napoleon was passed and the only justification for its continuation was the doctrine of mercantilism.

In the operation of the trade, British firms accustomed to buying their timber in the Baltic opened branch offices in Saint John, New Brunswick, and Quebec City where they underwrote the cutting operations performed by the colonists. It appears that Canadians only rarely moved into the middleman role, perhaps for the same reasons that the people of New France appear to have deferred to metropolitan merchants in the organization of the trade of an earlier era. For one reason, the local population lacked the business connections in the metropolis; for another, they tended to regard transoceanic business as risky in itself. Consequently, in the new century — as earlier — local money apparently went to local purposes. Except in the new era, the monied colonists did appear to invest their surplus rather than to consume it. But they invested cautiously, in freehold land, for instance, because real property never vanished, whereas timber (carried on the oldest, least seaworthy vessels), failed to reach its destination so frequently it was an uninsurable cargo. Even if wood had been transported in more reliable vessels (impossible from an economic standpoint since timber was of so little value relative to bulk) there was still the difficulty of predicting the market, as unpredictable as the Atlantic Ocean to inexperienced colonists. For both reasons, colonial businessmen tended to regard the timber trade as suitable for no one but those with great backing, capable of absorbing heavy losses. It was not until the 1830s that colonial firms began to appear. Then, of necessity, they opened offices in Liverpool or Glasgow, the chief ports of entry for timber in Britain. If successful, the branch at the metropolis naturally grew into the main trunk of the operation and another metropolitan business would thus emerge. Only the origins of the relatively new company would differentiate it from the other, older firms.

The risks of timber marketing that dampened Canadian enthusiasm to enter the business on the middleman level were real, but according to A.R.M. Lower they were too frequently exaggerated. In Lower's view, the stability of the roll of the firms engaged in the trade is evidence that while timber dealing was inherently speculative, it was a remarkably stable kind of speculation. Some two dozen companies were among the first to exploit the staple in Canada. These same companies continued to operate until the timber was "done" or until economics attracted them elsewhere (back to the Baltic area, for instance, once the imperial preference diminished between 1840 and 1860). Only at the end of the period did colonial companies join in the trade. For the main period of its dominance, the fortunes made by the timber middlemen were thus usually acquired by Englishmen and spent in England. This is the important point to which it will be necessary to return later: although timber dwarfed every other aspect of the Canadian economy, the entrepreneurial role ordinarily was played by foreigners, not Canadians. In the timber trade, the colonists were quite literally the hewers of wood and the drawers of water.

## III    Lumbering as a Primitive Technology

The lumber the English merchants bought was either hand-hewn timbers or precisely cut planks no thinner than three inches. Since the sawn product required precise milling and was still subject to warping in transit, the dominant export was squared timber, produced in the bush with hand tools. No matter what squared timber went over or through on its course to Quebec or Saint John it was still as saleable as when it was squared where it fell.

The pre-eminence of the squared log as the unit of production meant that the logging that occurred was incredibly wasteful. In the red and white pine forests of New Brunswick and the Ottawa River valley only about one tenth of the trees were good for squaring, but nearly everything else was ravaged in the process of felling the largest trees.

An outline of the actual cutting and squaring operations clarifies why the early lumbering was so wasteful. To begin, the smaller trees in the path of the large pines had themselves to be felled, and arranged so as to provide a bed for the falling giant. Then, once the selected pine had been brought down, it had to be examined for any sign of rot that had previously escaped notice; the slightest discoloration of the heartwood would disqualify any tree that was otherwise superior. Rejects were abandoned where they fell. Only the sound at heart were squared, then removed. In the squaring process, the first step was topping and limbing. Then a workman called a *liner* whisked the bark from two sides and drew lines to indicate the size of the finished timber. Another worker, the *scorer*, would then use his axe to cut a row of notches to the line about every three feet. The first squaring began as he split away slabs of wood between notches, working as close as possible to the line. Finally came the *hewer*, hewing just to the line, working a "broadaxe" with its twelve-inch blade to make the surface perfectly smooth. Upon completing the second side, the half-completed timber would be rolled ninety degrees and the same sequence of scoring and hewing would be repeated to finish the timber perhaps one or two feet on each side.

Over a winter, a gang of six men could produce nearly six hundred timbers. But to obtain this amount of exportable lumber they had lay waste to the choicest trees of an entire forest. And to make matters worse, the other dead trees, and the slabs and chips produced in the squaring, provided tinder for wild fires ignited by lightning or human carelessness in the summer. Then the destruction would be complete.

In the meantime, the lumbermen would have rafted their exportable timber to market. The construction of the rafts occurred in the spring, while the waterways of the forest were at full flood. The object was to join the whole winter's work into one body to be rowed and sailed to market. An average size St. Lawrence raft actually covered about the same area as a modern football field. Obviously, a craft of such size would be far too unwieldy to run the small rivers draining the areas where the timber was cut. Consequently, in the first miles of their transit to market, the squared trees might be borne by streams so narrow that the timber would be floated as individual sticks, but this posed the danger of enormous jams of individual timbers forming at the many small falls or rapids in a stream. As soon as depth of water permitted, the timbers were therefore gathered into *cribs* or *drams* and it was these units that made up the rafts, even the very largest, so they had to be built with ingenuity and craftsmanship. Otherwise the raft would disintegrate in the rapids and a winter's work would scatter in the great river like so many snowflakes.

A St. Lawrence dram was a frame of timbers defining a rectangle about ten yards wide and thirty long. The frame went over a layer of side-by-side timbers arrayed in the area defined by the frame. A second layer of timber rode on top. In part, it was simply the weight of the top layer and the buoyancy of the bottom that held it all together. To maintain the integrity of the basic structure, the frame was pegged at intervals. But protection against the destructive power of rapids was guaranteed by lashing the whole assembly together with *withes*, a kind of cable made from twisted saplings the thickness of a man's thumb. To make the large rafts, one dram was simply lashed to the end of another. On the St. Lawrence, ten drams (each containing about four hundred timbers) were not uncommon. Such rafts, the largest handcrafted structures of the day, were fabricated without any metal fasteners. As the enormous weight of the thousands of squared timbers heaved and groaned through the largest of the rivers of British North America, their motion to market must have been a source of great pride for the half-dozen timberers who tended the oars and sails of the craft they themselves had created — entirely by hand.

From the standpoint of the craftsmanship involved, the timber trade offered an occupation that was easy to romanticize. But for the most part, the timber trade offered only backbreaking manual labor and — with due regard to the waste involved in the utter destruction of the natural environment — was, quite simply, primitive. There is also evidence to suggest that the trade was socially disruptive. Once the lumbermen and raftsmen tied up in the coves of the merchants of Saint John or Quebec, they stepped ashore as men who had lived months in the bush without amenities or the company of women. Ordinarily they worked in isolation from September through June and usually when they were paid they received their year's wages in one lump sum. Consequently, the months of July and August were days of violent roistering wherever lumbermen gathered. At times, the violence was purely recreational. On other occasions the conflicts reflected animosity between *canadiens* and immigrant Irish in competition for employment in the bush, a competition at which the newcomers were ordinarily at a disadvantage because of their lack of skill. Between the two types of social disruption, the recreational sort appears to have been the most common since most observers contended that the lumbermen were a transient lot, ill-disposed to save their earnings or moderate their passions in the idle period of summer. But this view of the lumbermen may reflect nothing more than social prejudice. It is possible that the population that worked in the bush was distinct from and despised by the numerically superior agricultural community. It is also possible that some newcomers found that a few seasons in the timber trade was their best means of accumulating a surplus to become farmers themselves later. But judging by newspaper accounts of lumbermen on holiday, the savers seem to have been a distinct minority.

## IV    The Timber Staple and Economic Development

The suggestion that workers in the timber trade normally labored all winter for nothing more than a summer spree implies that they worked without advancement. The same criticism may apply even more broadly, beyond the individuals who worked in the bush, to British North America as a whole. In fact, it may be reasonable to suggest that despite the staple's dominance, it provided but weak encouragement to economic growth in the sense of development.

In one respect, the simple "mining" of resources was an unvarying characteristic of modern colonization. All the colonies of Europe began by producing exportable staples. Under the conditions of initial settlement newcomers invariably exploited some commodity — gold, tobacco, fur, fish, timber — readily available in the new land and in heavy demand at home. A marketable staple insured the growth of the colony, and colonies became states in their own right as they invested the profits from the staple trades to create a more intricate industrial structure. But in the colonies of the nineteenth century that grew into the underdeveloped countries of the twentieth, development did not take place since the profits from their staples were siphoned away from the hinterland, or invested merely to increase the production of the raw material rather than to industrialize. All European colonies began as nothing more than supply bases. Some still are.

In the Canadian case, to the extent that the timber trade dominated, so also did it retard industrialization since the evidence is fairly clear that the bulk of the profits went to British shippers and timber importers, such firms as Pollock, Gilmour and Company based in Glasgow. To be sure, the colonists who managed the gangs of laborers who did the actual cutting and rafting of the wood amassed considerable personal fortunes, but relative to the amount of money that was generated in the overall wrecking of the forests of the Canadas and New Brunswick, these were merely "the crumbs of a harvest feast", according to A.R.M. Lower.

Not only did comparatively few of the profits fall to Canadian producers, those Canadians who made their money in the production of square timber were disinclined to invest their capital in anything other than more of the same. They might have invested in sawmills and exported sawn lumber, for example, but until the ties to Britain began to diminish in the 1840s, their market connections were entirely transoceanic. For reasons previously cited, to the timber middlemen in Glasgow and Liverpool, wood was not wood if it were not handhewn timber. Some colonists attempted to defy this reality and suffered losses early and bitterly. In 1806 Philemon Wright, for example, experimented with a scheme for sawing logs into inchboards and scantlings to sell for export. That year he spent over a month rafting a winter's work of sawn lumber from Ottawa to Quebec but when he arrived at his destination he could not find a buyer. Naturally, he returned to the production of square timbers and to the task of making their supply cheaper and more efficient (slides around water falls for instance). Thus, the dynamics of the timber trade militated against the rise of Canadian industries using logs as a raw material in manufacturing for export. Like the fur trade, the new staple held its predominance but it did not develop the economy. The timber trade, thus, was a kind of mining operation that recklessly depleted the natural bounty and left only a desert behind.

Occasionally, individuals condemned the timber trade for the great waste and small return to the colonies. One such observer was Peter Fisher, the first historian of New Brunswick, writing in 1825. According to Fisher, the trade that generated "great riches" was not yielding any improvement to the colony. On the contrary,

> The persons principally engaged in shipping the timber have been strangers who have taken no interest in the welfare of the country; but have merely occupied a spot to make what they could in the shortest possible time. Some have done well, and others have had to quit the trade; but whether they won or lost, the capital of the country has been wasted, and no improvement of any consequence made to compensate for it, or to secure a source of trade when the lumber shall fail. Instead of seeing towns built, farms improved and the country cleared and stocked with the reasonable returns of so great a trade; the forests are stripped and nothing left in prospect, but the gloomy apprehension when the timber is gone, of sinking into insignificance and poverty. (Quoted in Lower, *Great Britain's Woodyard* [1973], pp. 32-33.)

Recent studies of the economic development of the two Canadas have tended to confirm Fisher's rather dismal assessment of the impact of the trade upon the colonies. According to John McCallum, "wood and wheat varied markedly in their effects on industrial development. Viewed as a staple product, wood, whether in the form of square timber or lumber, was much less effective than wheat as an initiator of urban and industrial growth."

The fundamentally exploitative nature of nineteenth-century timber cutting might have been blunted somewhat if it were compatible with agriculture. Indeed, such a relationship has been traditionally asserted by apologists for the industry. W.L. Marr and D.G. Paterson, for example, have asserted in their otherwise excellent recent general account of Canadian economic history that the destruction of the forests left "cleared land... well suited for agriculture" and "many farmers supplemented their incomes by engaging in the timber industry during the winter months...." On this account, they assert that "the rapid depletion of much of the forests ... may have been not only the most reasonable alternative in a frontier society but also the most efficient method of promoting economic develoment." But A.R.M. Lower has attempted to demonstrate that both contentions are false by showing that the pine forests normally grew in soils that were too sandy or rocky to support commercial agriculture, and where the timber cutters did happen to work through potentially fertile farm land, what they left was an enormous amount of inflammable litter, not half cleared land that invited conversion into family farms. In this sense, the "rapid depletion" ruined arable land as well as the rest. But the adverse effects of lumbering upon agriculture did not end here. Lower also contends that the attractive wages of timber cutting drew countless thousands of young men from farms without releasing them in time for planting the following spring, and Michael Cross has shown that the competition for employment in such winter work led to social disorder in the Ottawa River Valley that approached civil war.

The growth of the timber trade at the expense of agricultural development might have been a harmless, even beneficial, trade-off if the industry had been organized in other hands. But profits concentrated in the firms of foreigners, and Canada was capital poor throughout the period that timber-making was the predominant enterprise. Consequently, the population grew, the volume and value of exports increased, but the pace of development (especially in Lower Canada and New Brunswick) was slow, frustrated at every turn by a lack of investment capital in Canada.

Nothing illustrated the scarcity of capital better than the difficulties in launching Canada's first transportation revolution. Since the 1790s there was an awareness of a need to make the St. Lawrence navigable by ship to the Great Lakes. This meant canals around a half dozen cataracts in the St. Lawrence and at the Niagara escarpment, but there was always too little money in Canada. Consequently, the capital had to be recruited abroad or taken from the public purse. The latter expedient encouraged a tradition, not peculiar to Canada, but Canadian in its justification: the practice of funding private projects with public money on grounds that geography rather than colonialism limited the amount of capital that was otherwise available.

It is probably too much to say categorically that the timber trade was an unmitigated disaster in the development of British North America. But it is reasonable to suggest that its benefits were more ephemeral than tangible. Thus, critics such as Lower and Cross, seeking something positive in the timber trade, have suggested that the production of the staple was "picturesque and romantic in itself" and lumbering "gave to this country a technique of broadaxe and raft that has permanently enriched its cultural heritage." When the industry was launched in 1807, however, no one speculated about what might be contributed to Canadian culture or even the economic consequences. In that early year, the new trade appeared beneficial because it supplied a vital commodity for the British then in a death struggle with Napoleon. Incidentally, Canadian workers received good wages as they assisted Great Britain in the distant but desperate war. Soon that war would embroil British North America in other ways as well.

# Bibliography

Several volumes in the Canadian Centenary Series cover the period during which agriculture began to decline in Lower Canada, and found its earliest commercial beginnings in Upper Canada. However, Fernand Ouellet, *Lower Canada, 1791-1840* (1980), W.S. MacNutt, *The Atlantic Provinces, 1712-1857* (1965), and Gerald Craig, *Upper Canada, 1784-1841* (1963) all focus more on political issues that culminated in the crises of the 1830s, than on the economic issues that are emphasized in this chapter.

On the subject of the old staples of fur and wheat, E.E. Rich, *The Fur Trade and the North West to 1857* (1967) provides the standard account of changes in the fur trade and Donald Creighton's *Commercial Empire of the St. Lawrence* (1937) is the classic account of the English-speaking merchants' adaptations to new circumstances. Creighton tends to ignore the French-speaking population, however, and to lavish far too much sympathy on the English elite than is fashionable at present. More recent accounts, most notably the work by Ouellet (cited above), have attempted to tell the story of the French-Canadians and the political consequences of their declining position. But here a controversy has developed over the timing of the decline. A middle position espoused by T.J.A. LeGoff in "The Agricultural Crisis in Lower Canada, 1802-12: A Review of a Controversy," *CHR* (1974) is the interpretive stance taken here.

On the subject of the timber staple, the most comprehensive general history is A.R.M. Lower's, *Great Britain's Woodyard: British America and the Timber Trade, 1763-1867* (1973). Less critical of lumbering in Canada's development is the local history of the trade by Graeme Wynn, *Timber Colony: A Historical Geography of Early Nineteenth Century New Brunswick* (1981). D.L. Marr and D.G. Paterson provide an interesting theory on staples in general and the exploitation of timber in comparison with fur and fish in their chapter on "Renewable-Natural-Resource Exploitation" in *Canada: An Economic History* (1980). A view of the timber trade by an economic historian that is more in accord with Lower's is found in John McCallum, *Unequal Beginnings: Agriculture and Economic Development in Quebec and Ontario until 1870* (1980). Other relevant works by economic historians are M.H. Watkins, "A Staple Theory of Economic Growth," *Canadian Journal of Economics and Political Science* (1963), and C. Pentland, "The Role of Capital in Canadian Economic Development before 1875," same journal (1950).

The social historian of the timber trade is Michael Cross. His "Lumber Community of Upper Canada, 1815-1867," *Ontario History* (1960), advances the thesis that the lumberman was distinct from the farmer — raucous and prodigal — but still "the true pioneer of British North America." Another article by Cross, "The Shiner's War: Social Violence in the Ottawa Valley in the 1830s," *CHR* (1973), discusses the disorders that arose from the competition between the French-Canadians and immigrant Irish for employment in lumbering.

"For most Americans, just declaring war had been enough."

# CHAPTER 7

# *War Returns to British North America*

## I    "Mr. Madison's War"

The wars in which Great Britain participated after 1793 had significant impact upon British North America for economic reasons, but throughout most of the fighting, the colonists could regard the struggle with something of the philosophical detachment that is normally reserved for the suffering of others. They themselves were protected by the greatest naval power in the world, and the British in North America also enjoyed privileged access to a seller's market in the metropolis. The timber boom, in the short term, provided ready money and attractive wages. Thus, the hardship of war seemed even more remote. But early in the second decade of the nineteenth century, British North America itself faced the threat of war. In these circumstances, the old complacency was no longer tenable.

The first hint that the colonies might be drawn into the conflicts of the mother country came in 1807. For the last four years British warships had been stopping and boarding merchant vessels of the United States to recover deserters from the royal navy because the British had been losing four to five thousand seamen per year through desertions. It appears that most of the fugitives sought refuge in America where they enjoyed better pay and the security of peace. Since the British denied that a man could shed his citizenship as easily as his shirt, they paid little heed to the certificates deserters received from American magistrates making them citizens of the United States. Consequently, a program of impressment began in 1803 as British ships started boarding American vessels at sea to restore Britons to what was deemed to be their rightful service. Naturally, the Americans considered such action a national humiliation, and serious trouble flared in 1807 when the *Chesapeake*, an American naval ship, refused to recognize the signal of the *Leopard*, a British frigate. The English ship fired on the American and twenty-one Americans were killed in the subsequent chase. Finally the *Chesapeake* was boarded and four of her crew were taken into custody.

"War Hawks" in the American Congress denounced the "*Chesapeake* affair" as a cause for war and demanded an immediate invasion of Canada to punish the British. Expecting attack, Britain reinforced the colonies. But the American president, Thomas Jefferson, preferred what he called "peaceful coercion" and persuaded Congress to impose an embargo on all American shipping. After December 1807, it was illegal for any vessel of the United States to venture into transatlantic commerce. Thus, Jefferson attempted to solve the problem of impressment by avoiding it. The embargo also eliminated the other source of conflict with the British — their refusal to recognize the neutrality of American vessels and their right to trade with either side in the Napoleonic wars.

In practice, American shippers were far more distressed by the embargo than either Britain or France. Despite its unpopularity in the New England maritime section of the United States, a form of embargo continued after 1808, beyond the presidency of Thomas Jefferson. His successor, James Madison, persuaded Congress to continue the "peaceful coercion" by continuing the boycott in a somewhat less rigorous form. Still, both belligerents continued to ignore the Americans' neutrality: the French seized vessels in Europe if they had stopped first to trade with the English; the British seized vessels that did business with Napoleon. Finally, in the summer of 1812, Madison addressed Congress to announce that economic sanctions had failed. He said both belligerents refused to treat the United States with the respect due to a sovereign country, and he asked for war. Since the belligerent that insulted the national honor more often was Great Britain, the official enemy would be the old mother country in what Madison and other Americans now called the second war for independence.

New Englanders were horrified, preferring to run the embargo and taking their chances with impressment or confiscation to a total interruption of trade, particularly by declaring war on the world's foremost sea power. But westerners were pleased with the prospects for success in "Mr. Madison's War". Andrew Jackson, the future President (then a general), announced with pride and confidence that "We are going to fight for the re-establishment of our national character, misunderstood and vilified at home and abroad ... to seek some indemnity for past injuries ... by the conquest of all the British dominions upon the continent of North America." Surely this would follow even without the enthusiasm of the New England states. There were seven million Americans and only seven hundred thousand residents of the "British dominions". How could the people of six disunited colonies resist invasion when they were outnumbered ten to one by the invader and when the forces of Great Britain were totally engaged elsewhere?

## II   Lower Canada: The Crisis of War Resolves a Crisis in Politics

Ironically, in Lower Canada the threat of American invasion had a unifying effect by interrupting the conflict between agrarian and commercial interests (described in the previous chapter). In 1806 the controversy over the "proper mode of taxation" led the French-Canadian farmers to establish their own newspaper, *Le Canadien*, to publicize their cause. Here they exalted the traditional laws, customs, and religion of the colony to cultivate strong national feelings around a distinctive way of life. In propagating the idea that the issue was whether Lower Canada was to be commercial and British or traditionally (yet democratically) *canadien* they asserted that the latter choice was the only guarantee for the survival of the *nation canadienne*.

Inevitably, this escalation of the controversy brought the writers for *Le Canadien* into open conflict with the *seigneurs* as well as the British business elite. The landowners were particularly angered by the threat of majority rule. They pined for the *ancien régime* under their leadership. But the seigneurs constituted a class in deep decline. The more important opponents of the young *canadien* professionals were the merchants and, after 1807, the governor, Sir James Craig.

Governor Craig was a military man of considerable experience who arrived in the colony when the mother country was engaged to the fullest against Napoleon, and just as the United States was beginning to make threatening noises about its right to be neutral. At first, Craig attempted to remain aloof from the factional wrangling in the colony. But his Protestant respect for middle-class ideals of enterprise impelled him into an alliance with the "most respectable" merchants. Then, after a setback in the election of 1808, his contempt for *canadien* aspirations for majority rule only increased. He dissolved the House in 1809. After the re-election of a similar group he dissolved the Assembly yet another time less than one year from its election.

The second dissolution precipitated such a crisis, such vituperation in the press, that Craig felt justified in taking emergency measures in 1810. In the midst of the third election campaign since his arrival just three years before, he rounded up the editors and chief contributors to *Le Canadien*. In all, more than twenty of the most ardent young nationalists were jailed on charges of seditious libel. In the election that followed, their side, the *Parti Canadien*, came back stronger than ever.

The crisis demonstrated to the British party that the institutions of representative government were unworkable in Lower Canada so long as the colony was not "unfrenchified". The Chief Justice, Jonathan Sewall, recommended assimilation by encouraging a large immigration from the United States and by a union of the two Canadas. But Craig knew that any thorough assimilation of *canadien* "habits, religion and laws" would require many years, perhaps generations. He preferred a remedy that would be immediate and found it in a proposal to revoke the Constitutional Act of 1791, thus suspending representative government altogether.

Authorities in London, involved in the final, most desperate phase of the struggle against Napoleon, wanted no trouble in Canada. Since suspension of the constitution was certain to be troublesome, instead of acquiescing in Craig's repressive proposal, Sir James was recalled in 1811 and replaced with a new governor instructed to moderate the situation. Sir George Prevost subsequently fulfilled his mandate by dissociating himself from extremists of both sides and promoting the moderates of the two leading parties. Then, just as his program of moderation was beginning to have some visible effect, the colony faced the crisis of threatened invasion by the United States.

If the *canadiens* disliked the English-speaking merchants for their crass commercialism, their religion, and their smug arrogance, all such qualities were found even more abundantly in the Americans. In fact, since 1807, the *canadiens* had been denouncing the British "transients" as no better than "Yenkés". Consequently, in 1812, as the British party said they were as eager to drub the invaders as any of the others, mutual hostility directed toward the common enemy united the former enemies, and the Assembly of Lower Canada — recently denounced by Craig for its domination by "traitorous demagogues" — voted more financial support for the war than any other colony in British North America. In this way, one crisis negated another.

## III    Upper Canada: The Crisis of Invasion Threatens Civil War

The same could not be said of Upper Canada where the settlers between the Niagara Peninsula and Detroit were notable for their lack of enthusiasm and for their increasing division as the war crisis came upon them. If there were to be invasions of Canada from the United States, it was their farms that were most likely to become battlegrounds. The Atlantic colonies were more than adequately protected by British seapower and friendly trade relations with the New Englanders. Lower Canada was relatively well protected by natural barriers. But Upper Canada was little more than an extension of the State of New York from one side and Michigan Territory from the other.

Upper Canada could be looked upon as an extension of the United States demographically as well. Since 1792 Americans had been pouring into the province along with a tide of settlers that rolled into the Ohio River valley to the south in search of free land. When the northerly settlers left the United States, none of them had foreseen a second war with Britain, nor was there anything political in their migration. American officials therefore expected them to welcome an invasion as a liberation from monarchy and a reunion with republicanism. Ironically, their origins only made them more vulnerable to attack by their fellow Americans.

The settlers recognized that fighting in defense of British North America would embroil them with their relatives to the south, but they also knew that taking the American side would jeopardize their new homes in Canada. Neutrality, therefore, seemed the most sensible solution to their predicament. To Governor Isaac Brock, however, such an easy escape from their responsibility to aid the Crown was only treason by another name. When he called out the militia, some refused to muster, others mustered but could not be relied upon in battle. The Legislative Assembly of the province was also uncooperative in putting the province on a wartime footing by refusing Brock's request for special war measures. Thus, Upper Canada prepared for conquest: the militia was at half strength, individuals openly encouraged surrender before the fighting began, and the lawmakers refused any action that would compromise the citizens' full enjoyment of peacetime civil liberties. General Brock had 1600 British regulars with which to defend the colony. He reported the situation as "critical".

Fortunately for Canada, the Americans appear to have been true to their stated purpose of declaring war just to vindicate national honor. Had they sought more, surely nothing would have prevented the fulfillment of Henry Clay's boast to his fellow senators that "the militia of Kentucky are alone competent to place Montreal and Upper Canada at your feet." But as it turned out, the militia of Kentucky did not even leave the state, nor did that of any other. (New York's militia intended to conquer Lower Canada but thought better of it after initial skirmishing.) For most Americans, just declaring the war had been enough. Nearly all of the actual fighting was left to the ill-equipped and ill-prepared federal troops.

The result of weak American commitment was that a plan for invasion on three fronts failed from the start. A mixed force of militia and regulars under General William Hull did cross into British territory, but the amateur soldiers proved incompetent in the face of a joint British-Indian threat, and they withdrew back to Detroit where an invading Brock compelled them to surrender. Shortly thereafter, a second force performed less disgracefully in the east, having crossed the Niagara River. The battle that followed at Queenston Heights went badly for the British regulars and colonial militia, and Brock himself was slain. Eventually, however, British reinforcements turned the tide, and when the New York militia refused to leave their state by crossing the river to join the struggle, the battle became a British triumph. The third force, a militia attack upon Montreal, likewise fizzled when the troops proved reluctant to leave their base. Thus, at the end of the first year of the war, all three attempts of the United States to conquer British North America had failed. In fact, the British held American soil in Michigan Territory.

In 1813 the Americans aimed to recover by water that which they had lost on land. A naval victory on Lake Erie isolated the British in Detroit and when they attempted a retreat the troops were almost completely destroyed at Moraviantown. Another American naval force moving across Lake Ontario landed at the capital of Upper Canada. York (later renamed Toronto) was looted and then burned. But the successes on the lakes were not followed by successful invasions over land. Thus, once again, the Americans made bold strokes that looked better in dispatches than in fact. After two years of war, British North America was still neither defeated nor occupied.

In the third year of the affair, selective use of British seapower humiliated the United States. A force entered Chesapeake Bay and proceeded up the Potomac River to the capital whose defenses were commanded by none other than the President himself. More humiliation followed when British forces dealt Washington, D.C. what American forces had given to York the year before and Madison's own home was scorched. As even the War Hawks' enthusiasm for continuing the war declined, peace negotiations between representatives of Great Britain and the United States began late in the summer.

In negotiating a settlement, Great Britain held the best cards. It was American, not British territory that was then occupied by invading troops. Napoleon had just abdicated, and, while the English were certainly warweary in Europe they were anything but weak. In fact, at the very moment negotiations began, veteran forces of British regulars were on their way to America. But the American spokesmen affirmed with great clarity that their country would continue the war forever rather than sacrifice any of the ground so recently hallowed by their new generation of Patriots. This bluff carried the game and the British negotiators withdrew their demands for territorial concessions. Consequently, the Treaty of Ghent emerged simply as the instrument for ending the fighting and returning to the status quo before the war.

Hoping to recover the land south of the Great Lakes between the Ohio and the Mississippi Rivers, the English businessmen of Montreal had seen the resumption of war as an ideal opportunity to amend the boundary settlement of 1783. Naturally, they were disappointed when the British negotiators proved no more forthright in 1814 than in the earlier negotiations. But for the British the War of 1812 had been an unpleasant distraction from which they wanted escape. Their last interest was the dream of a few traders for a commercial empire of the St. Lawrence. It mattered little to the diplomats that the war was a three-year waste. The important objective was simply ending it and the treaty did just that. Appropriately, the last battle — at New Orleans — was a needless encounter that occurred two weeks after the Treaty had been signed because there was no way to notify the players that the game was over.

## IV    Consequences of War and the Return to Peace

In many ways, then, the War of 1812 had been a fiasco. But its impact was not unimportant. First, it had been shown that no one power could dominate the entire Great Lakes drainage basin. On their side, the Americans saw that British sea power would prevent their attempts to conquer Britain's colonies. On the other, the Montreal merchants finally realized that their dreams of recovering the old North West were delusions. In other words, the war established a balance of power that led to a boundary which could be regarded as permanent, a reality that was cemented more firmly in 1818 when the United States and Great Britain agreed to the 49th parallel from the Lake of the Woods to the Rocky Mountains as the boundary in the west. And in the east, the Americans were compelled to accept permanent exclusion from the inshore fisheries of New Brunswick and Nova Scotia.

The new balance of power led to the notion of an "undefended" border. By the Rush-Bagot agreement of 1817 Great Britain and the United States agreed to limit their armed naval vessels on the Great Lakes. This was not the end of war scares between Britain and the United States over British North America, nor did it prevent the construction of land fortifications, but the Rush-Bagot agreement was a crucial step in the emergence of the myth of the undefended border.

A second way in which the war had significant impact was in its effect upon the view of Americans as potential settlers. Anti-Americanism (briefly strong after the American Revolution) emerged more durably after the War of 1812. Since 1792, the Upper Canadian authorities had been keen to attract Americans as potential settlers. Farmers were needed to fill up the vast expanses, and Americans who knew how to clear land and to bear the privations of pioneer farming were to be preferred to British immigrants for whom the axe was simply an unfamiliar hammer. After 1816, new laws aimed at discouraging American immigration went into force. One postwar governor said as much himself when he declared that "the speedy settlement of the Colony, however desirable, is a secondary object compared to its settlement in such a manner as shall best secure its attachment to British Laws and Government."

Governor Gore's comment reflected heightened sensitivity to another lesson of the war. The Americans had been beaten back, it is true, but few could fail to recognize that had they been more purposeful in their invasions they could not have failed. Consequently, if British North America were to remain British, it was especially important for inland Upper Canada (not defensible by the Royal Navy) to have a population on the spot who would not hesitate to fight off the Americans should they invade again.

Entirely in keeping with the new policy of increasing the population from loyal stock were the steps taken by authorities to encourage British soldiers to settle in Upper Canada close to the American border. Also, assisted passages were provided for immigrants from Britain and settlements of Scots appeared. But as it happened, the authorities did not have to persist for long with such schemes because the tide of unassisted British immigration was soon running so fully that official encouragement became unnecessary. British North America loomed as a promised land on a scale that was without precedent.

New World prosperity exerted an extraordinary pull because Old World famine, industrial squalor, and political unrest began to push Britons out as never before. During the twenty years of the previous wars there was no manpower to spare for colonization, but after 1815 people appeared superfluous by the thousands. In the new circumstances, emigration was viewed as the safest, most expedient means of coping with the potentially explosive problem of overpopulation. Between 1815 and 1850 nearly three million people were drawn to North America. About two million landed in time to participate in the industrialization of the United States. The British Colonies, one tenth as large, and not yet industrializing, received one third of the flow of this great migration.

One reason British North America received so many immigrants was because Quebec was the cheapest New World destination owing to the number and kind of ships that engaged in the timber trade. By 1815, nearly 600 ships per year called at Quebec alone. They were the oldest, least seaworthy vessels of the British merchant marine, leaking far too badly to carry outbound cargo of any value (nothing more than coal perhaps), but with the installation of a few bunks and some crude provision for cooking, the holds easily converted into areas for hauling the poorest class of passengers. Thus, the timber ship emerged as the most inexpensive means for an impoverished Scot or Irishman to get to America.

The immigrants who volunteered as the paying ballast to the shipowners were treated little differently from the cargoes of coal or cobblestones they replaced, however. The ships were so crowded there were usually more passengers than sleeping quarters. There was no comfort or privacy, and the people usually ran low on food and sometimes even on water. But there was never a shortage of vermin and disease. In one year, about one third of the season's immigrants died within five months of their arrival. Of those immigrants who did survive, three fourths moved from Quebec to the northeastern United States after recovering from the ordeal of the crossing. Three times the British Parliament passed legislation to ameliorate conditions for passengers but on every occasion the shipowners simply found new ways of evading the laws pertaining to such basic matters as crowding and provisions. According to A.R.M. Lower, until steam replaced sail, conditions on the passenger-carrying timber ships were more abominable than upon the slave ships of the previous century: "Every slave thrown overboard meant so much money lost; every emigrant less decreased the ship's liability to have to feed him, and more room for those that were left."

Of course there were better ships for those who emigrated with a little money. For this "better class" of newcomer (usually English, perhaps Scottish, but almost never Irish) there was a group of speculators who perfected the leader and associate system of land speculation. In 1823 they formed the Canada Land Company, purchased one million acres of Crown land, and proceeded to sell half their total acreage over the next ten years. The farmers who bought their land from them produced cash crops such as wheat. But the merchants who anticipated great profits from exporting grain abroad were not immediately gratified. In fact, in 1830 they exported less wheat than in 1800. It was not until the 1840s that agricultural exports through the St. Lawrence increased dramatically, so much was devoured by the timber-makers working their way north and west up the Ottawa River Valley.

# V    Postwar Expansion and Conflict in Rupert's Land

As far as British North America was concerned, the impact of war was felt most signficantly in the more settled areas. But there was also a part of the British Empire in North America that was not yet colonized, which did experience the effects of war, and if at the time the impact seemed slight in comparison to what has just been described, later the consequences would loom large indeed. For this peripheral area of the empire was the land held by the Hudson's Bay Company, Rupert's Land, the crossroads of the continent and in the opening years of the nineteenth century the last haven of the fur trade.

By 1812 the fur trade was in deep decline, a trend that had been accelerated by the war and the closing of the continent of Europe. In reaction, the Montreal traders reorganized the North West Company with some effect. The less flexible Hudson's Bay Company fell behind again, handling only two fourteenths of the fur trade — eleven fourteenths being in the hands of their Montreal rivals. In the first decade of the new century, it seemed that the Canadians might buy out the English competition.

But toward the end of the Napoleonic wars a dramatic change took place in the fortunes of the HBC. A major factor in its rejuvenation was the entry into the Company's direction of a group of men headed by the Earl of Selkirk, a Scottish peer appalled at the destitution of many Britons, especially the Scots-Irish. He decided that assisted emigration was the key to improving their condition. After trying without success on Prince Edward Island and in Upper Canada he chose to concentrate upon that uncolonized part of the New World that was accessible from Hudson Bay by way of the Nelson River and Lake Winnipeg. This is why he decided to buy into the Company and why Selkirk and his associates worked for a preponderant voice in the Company's affairs.

Selkirk's colonization scheme could be seen as incompatible with the fur trade, however. Insofar as the "Montreal peddlars" thought so, it meant certain conflict, perhaps even war between the two firms. From the first, the North West Company did take this view because as they had expanded operations west to the Rockies the Montrealers had used the area Selkirk intended to colonize as their base of supply. Since the 1790s their wintering partners had been provisioned by employing the Métis (mixed blood natives born of *voyageur* fathers and Indian mothers) in the Red River region as buffalo hunters. Twice annually hundreds of the bison were slaughtered. The women cut the meat into large thin slabs, dried it in the sun, and then tied the meat in bales. The final processing involved shredding the large, dried pieces, mixing them in a kettle of fat with berries, and pouring the mixture of grease, meat, and fruit into buffalo-hide bags. This was pemmican. One pound equaled roughly four pounds of fresh meat. It was not altogether unappetizing and properly cured and cared for, pemmican could keep for years. Pemmican is what fed the wintering partners. Without it, Montreal could not have been the springboard for a transcontinental fur trade. For this reason, the Montreal traders took great offense at the Hudson's Bay Company's plans to launch an agricultural settlement for impoverished Scots, and retired employees of the HBC, precisely in the center of their pemmican supply area. Quite simply, the survival of their trade depended upon the failure of Selkirk's settlement scheme.

Should the North West Company go under, however, Hudson's Bay Company officials would enjoy the lost competition that tended to drive up the cost of trade goods wherever Indians had access to both firms. In this sense, philanthropy made good economic sense, so the HBC blessed Selkirk in his settlement scheme and the "lord proprietor" proceeded in exactly the same fashion that colonies were launched by other British adventurers in the seventeenth century. By virtue of royal charter the company claimed sovereignty over the land and its people. The person named to be governor was an employee of the firm. Each colonist, in his own turn, was also signed on as a company servant. But there was one distinguishing characteristic between this venture and that of, say, the Virginia Company. Unlike the merchants who attempted to colonize Virginia, those who backed settlement south of Lake Winnipeg were intending to plant a colony where another commercial company was already active. Consequently, conflict to the point of war between the two firms was inevitable.

The Nor'westers reacted immediately. As soon as they learned of the HBC's intentions they began a newspaper campaign in Scotland to frustrate the recruitment of settlers. The Indians and climate were both depicted in terms to arouse terror and discouragement. Thus, Simon McGillivray under the name of "Highlander" wrote in the *Inverness Journal* that "Even if [the colonists] escape the scalping knife ... they will find it impossible to exist in the country."

Lord Selkirk's agents were able to recruit only one hundred and five servants to embark on the colonizing adventure. They left Scotland in 1811 too late to reach Lake Winnipeg before freeze-up. And in the following spring their journey upriver to Lake Winnipeg (see map 7.1) was arduous indeed. The northerly route to the heartland of North America had advantages for fur traders (since it was so much shorter than the route over the Great Lakes) but the trek of Governor Miles Macdonell and the Selkirk settlers proved that the northerly access was inappropriate for settlers because it was nearly impossible for colonists to arrive at the destination inland during the same summer as their arrival on the Bay. Nevertheless, Macdonell and his group did arrive in 1812 and were succeeded by a second company of settlers who set out in 1813. Neither natural obstacles nor North West Company hostility had killed the project. A confrontation was likely.

The first occasion for direct conflict was an edict proclaimed by Governor Macdonell in January 1814 forbidding the exportation of any provisions produced by anyone within the territory of his jurisdiction. The so-called "Pemmican Proclamation" was not issued merely to frustrate the

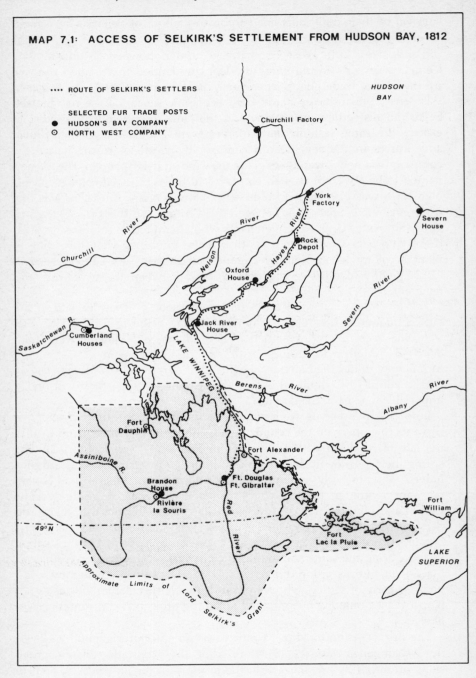

MAP 7.1:  ACCESS OF SELKIRK'S SETTLEMENT FROM HUDSON BAY, 1812

competing company. Macdonell was worried about a real threat of starvation since all efforts at farming had failed.

The Métis led the opposition to Macdonell in his gesture to control the pemmican trade. For one reason, their ties were almost entirely to the North West Company. For another, they resented the HBC's presumption that they owned Rupert's Land. Consequently, when the first brigades of North West Company canoes came down Lake Winnipeg expecting to be resupplied, the Métis obliged. Macdonell agreed to compromise his previous proclamation, and a clash was avoided for the moment.

The directors of the North West Company were insulted at the very idea of compromise, however. When they heard of the proceedings at Red River they sent a commander of their own, Duncan Cameron, to organize the Métis for the purpose of dispersing the Hudson's Bay Company settlers. When Cameron arrived on the scene, Macdonell was out of the colony recovering his health at York Factory, giving Cameron the opportunity to rule with all the imperiousness so recently displayed by the HBC's commander. Learning that better land and weather awaited the newcomers in Upper Canada, over 150 of the colonists were transported by North West Company canoe to the alternate promised land in June 1815. All that remained were a group of about sixty settlers, harassed through the summer of 1815 by the Métis until they were reinforced in November by more HBC settlers and a new governor, Robert Semple.

Governor Semple, like Macdonell, believed himself to be the supreme authority in the territory. Also like his predecessor, he did nothing to win the allegiance of the Métis. The harrassment of the previous year grew more serious in 1816 as Semple aimed to impose the order and respect that the Métis would not willingly give. The climactic moment came on June 19, 1816 when a group of about thirty-five armed Métis led by Cuthbert Grant approached Semple's fortress. Semple rode out to meet them with twenty-six volunteers and began to talk to the half-breeds like a schoolmaster attempting to discipline a gang of unruly children. In the course of his speaking, Semple reached for someone's gun, a shot was fired, then the shooting became general. In the melee that followed, Semple himself and twenty-one of his fellows were struck dead, mutilated, and stripped naked. Since all the casualties were on the side of "civilization", the affair of June 19, 1816 is usually called the Seven Oaks *massacre*, not the battle of Seven Oaks.

Whether the first action was a battle or a massacre, the contest between the two companies was a war nonetheless. To be sure, a great deal of the fighting took place in British courts, but before the litigation and the other more overt hostilities ended in 1821, Lord Selkirk himself came over from Scotland to command Swiss and German mercenaries in the fight to beat the half-breeds and Canadians who presumed to act as if Rupert's Land belonged to them rather than to the Hudson's Bay Company. The British firm had the legality of royal charter and resources of a growing number of stockholders to support them. The North West Company and the Métis were less well advantaged. Finally, in 1821, the North West Company partners agreed to a merger and settled for stockholder status in the HBC themselves. Thus, Montreal ceased to be the springboard to the Prairies. Henceforth, the organization of the fur trade normally took place in London and trade goods moved by ship to York Factory, then by small boat up the rivers that fed into the Bay. A fragment of the colony of Lord Selkirk survived as a kind of fur trade company town, inhabited mainly by the Métis, providing pemmican or their labor to the HBC. From 1821, the region of Rupert's Land thus ceased to be a hinterland of Canada. The first transcontinental trading system of North America was broken, and left the *canadiens* of Lower Canada still more isolated in their homeland of the valley of the St. Lawrence.

# Bibliography

Several volumes in the Canadian Centenary Series cover the period of the War of 1812 and its immediate aftermath, each focusing on a particular region. But Fernand Ouellet, *Lower Canada, 1791-1840* (1980), W.S. Macnutt, *The Atlantic Provinces, 1712-1857* (1965), and Gerald Craig, *Upper Canada, 1784-1841* (1963), do not consider the war years as anything more than a minor step in the larger political evolution of the provinces.

There is no lack, however, of more specialized works that consider the War of 1812 to be of monumental importance. Pierre Berton, *The Invasion of Canada, 1812-1813* (1980) emphasizes colorful characters and the seriousness of the fighting in contrast to those who would interpret the war as a series of minor skirmishes with neither belligerent taking the conflict completely seriously. Less prone to sensationalism (despite its title) is J.M. Hitsman, *The Incredible War of 1812* (1965). On the American side, Roger Brown, *The Republic in Peril: 1812* (1964) imagines that serious interference with independence led the United States to go to war to defend a "unique" form of government. Bradford Perkins, *Prologue to War: England and the United States, 1805-1812* (1963) also blames Britain, while Julius W. Pratt, *Expansionists of 1812* (1965) claims western "War Hawks" wanted a war to gratify their territorial ambitions.

On postwar matters, C.P. Stacey, *The Undefended Border: The Myth and the Reality* (1967), offers a brief but comprehensive accounting of the basis for the balance of power that was recognized in diplomacy. Norman Macdonald, *Canada, 1763-1841: Immigration and Settlement* (1939), Helen I. Cowan, *British Emigration to British North America: The First Hundred Years* (1961), and Kenneth Duncan, "Irish Famine Immigration and the Social Structure of Canada West" in Michiel Horn and Ronald Sabourin, eds., *Studies in Canadian Social History* (1974), discuss postwar migrations of population. Excellent material on the relation between immigration and the timber trade is found in A.R.M. Lower, *Great Britain's Woodyard: British America and the Timber Trade, 1763-1867* (1973). C. Karr, *The Canada Land Company: The Early Years* (1974) describes the land settlement business to 1843.

On the conflict of trading empires in the west, E.E. Rich, *The Fur Trade and the North West to 1857* (1967) is a useful general account. W.A. Macleod and W.L. Morton, *Cuthbert Grant of Grantown: Warden of the Plains of Red River* (1963) is more detailed on the conflicts that culminated in the deaths of Semple and his associates in 1816. For the subsequent struggle leading to the merger of the two companies, John S. Galbraith, *The Little Emperor: Governor Simpson of the Hudson's Bay Company* (1976) is informative. On business relations between the HBC and Indians, Arthur J. Ray, *Indians in the Fur Trade: Their Role as Hunters, Trappers, and Middlemen in the Lands Southwest of Hudson Bay, 1660-1870* (1974) is indispensable.

". . . it was only too easy for small disagreements to
intensify quickly, assume cosmic proportions; and end
in allegations of disloyalty both to empire and to
colony."

# CHAPTER 8

# *Political Wrangles*

## I    The Transatlantic Interest in Reform

With the end of a generation of war so widespread that it had repercussions as far away as Rupert's Land, people at all levels of society enjoyed release from the hardships war conditions had imposed. In individual terms, peacetime meant an open invitation for everyone to indulge rising expectations. For the governing classes in Britain, this meant preserving their monopoly of political power in order to increase their economic advantage by such devices as mercantilist privilege. But for the British middle and lower classes such were precisely the obstacles they hoped to have removed. Similarly, in the United States in the same postwar period, the general scramble encouraged by prosperity was also the occasion for great political wrangling and demands for reform. The precise issues varied, of course, but everywhere there was a remarkable questioning of oligarchic exclusiveness.

For a variety of local reasons, British North America was not immune from polarization either. Thus, even if there had been no influence exercised from Britain and the United States there would have been controversy along lines that divided the upwardly mobile colonists from those already privileged. But there were influences from immigration. Even though it was actively discouraged, there was continued immigration of Americans who brought populist slogans demanding government by the "real people". The British immigrants, far more significant both in numbers and the strength of their influence after 1816, contributed an outlook conveniently summarized by the slogan that the one legitimate object of government was providing for "the greatest happiness of the greatest number".

But even without utilitarian radicalism from Britain or republican influences from the United States, oligarchy throughout British North America was vulnerable to attack because in these colonies the tendency

toward oligarchic dominance was especially pronounced. The fact of existing oligarchies in the first place had not emerged by accident. The pattern
was imposed deliberately by the imperial authorities in their reorganization of the colonies after 1783. It was commonly agreed that the thirteen
rebellious colonies had strayed because in their earlier history they had
upset the traditional balance between monarchical, aristocratic, and democratic elements. There was too much democracy, too little monarchy, a
pale aristocracy, and no established church at all. As a result, no provincial nobles or bishops sat in a colonial equivalent of the House of Lords
governing by hereditary right. There had been governors' councils and
upper chambers of the legislatures in America, but these bodies had been
filled by wealthy colonists for short terms, in some colonies for no more
than one year and by election of the members of the lower house rather
than by appointment from the Crown. Other royal prerogatives such as
appointing the judiciary and assenting to legislation were compromised in
practice by governors who strove to avoid arousing popular indignation.
Thus, the effective pivot of every British colony before the American Revolution was the popular will. And since it was then axiomatic that democracy was the prelude to anarchy, eighteenth-century Englishmen understood the American Revolution accordingly.

The remedy for the British colonies after 1790 was strengthening the
aristocratic and monarchical elements of the constitution. Ordinary freeholders would elect whomever they chose for the Legislative Assembly,
but the governor would determine the membership of the upper house,
the Legislative Council. Also, he would have complete freedom in choosing his circle of ministers and advisors, the Executive Council. Since councillors — whether legislative or executive — would always come from the
upper class with its "more refinements, more elegance and fashion," and
since appointments ordinarily would run for life, a colonial aristocracy
would thus emerge with a stronger voice than had been the case in the
British colonies that separated from the Empire in 1776.

The essential element in the second British empire was to be the freedom of the executive, the ability of the governor and his friends to govern
with but minimal check from the people. As long as the costs of government were low, and so long as the imperial authorities were prepared to
support the civil administration by revenues other than those generated
by local taxes (therefore beyond the control of a local legislature), the prospects for continuing oligarchy remained bright. With this hope in mind, a
major provision of the Constitutional Act of 1791 was the reservation of
land for the maintenance of independent administration. The Anglican
Church was to be supportd by a Clergy Reserve of one seventh of the land
of Upper Canada. So, too, was the governor to be aided by a Crown
Reserve of equal size. The income from these lands, as they were rented
or sold off over the years, was to defray in large part the salaries of the

whole civil service and in this way to maintain the oligarchy's freedom from legislative control exercised through their power of the purse. In time, the scheme tended to break down because the costs of government went up and the yields from the Crown Reserves and other executive-controlled revenue failed to keep pace. Consequently, legislative grants began to play a larger role in provincial finance; in the case of Upper Canada, for instance, the process began after the War of 1812. But even so, the executive, thanks to various payments from sources beyond the control of the Assembly, enjoyed a good measure of independence.

Such executives were extremely powerful, and it was soon realized that the enjoyment of the more lucrative economic opportunities depended upon allegiance to them. Thus, in New Brunswick, leading lumber interests allied with the governor and his circle, and in this way secured access to timber land. In Upper Canada, promoters eager to profit from land settlement or local improvement schemes also adhered to the government. In British North America, the association between high office and valuable economic privilege was especially strong. For others — particularly those rising colonists near enough to smell the aroma but too far away to taste the feast — a feeling that privileges flowed more readily to those already privileged led to resentment and demands for change. As they developed a following, the demand for reform focused particularly sharply upon the oligarchy's main strength: its lack of accountability to the electorate.


## II    The Reform Impulse in the Maritimes

The challenge to oligarchy was general, occurring everywhere throughout settled British North America. However, in those areas where population was sparsely established the problems just alluded to did not, and could not, arise. Thus, the Red River Colony was not yet affected by such development. Nor was Newfoundland, for that island was still an anomaly within the empire.

Newfoundland's anomalous status did not mean the island was unimportant. From a very early period, Newfoundland had played a key role in imperial strategy. As early as 1583, Newfoundland had been claimed for England by Sir Humphrey Gilbert, and a settlement charter had been granted as early as 1610. Although the early venture was virtually a failure, settlement on the island did slowly increase, and by the end of the eighteenth century population had reached about 20 000. But such growth was offset by the peculiar perception of the place which persisted in the minds of authorities in England. Imperial interest lay in the cod fishery, which meant the land was to be a vast platform for drying the catch and repairing the fishing fleet. Officially, legally, there was no settlement in the sense of year-round residency. What elementary law and government existed was dispensed by the naval commanders of the fleet in the area. Consequently, a society developed over a period of centuries but without any of the normal accompaniments of British colonial tradition. By 1820 there were still no political institutions established — representative or otherwise.

It was only in 1825 that London began to move Newfoundland closer to the norm. In that year the island finally moved up to colonial status. But even then, with a population approaching 60 000 there was no willingness to grant representative government. That concession was not made until 1832. However, as London conferred the forms of government, the local population did not exhibit a willingness to make them work at once. The long traditon of informal government was difficult to break and economic difficulties in the 1830s further retarded advancement. The school system in particular lagged far behind other colonies. The result was that political life in Newfoundland was marred by extraordinary violence with political divisions along lines of religion, that is, Catholics versus Protestants. This meant that the change which brought Newfoundland representative government also brought election days that were so riotous the constitution was changed again in 1842 to make nearly half the seats in the Assembly appointive rather than elective. In Newfoundland, reform meant more oligarchy not less.

But it is important to bear in mind that Newfoundland was an anomaly, for her three Maritime neighbors all became less oligarchic in the same period. In one way this was surprising since Prince Edward Island, Nova Scotia, and New Brunswick all had oligarchies that had been particularly powerful. In all three colonies the Executive Council and the Legislative Council were one body, unlike the two Canadas. And in financial matters, the executive could be even more independent given lucrative timber limits — even on Prince Edward Island. But despite the compactness of executive authority and the oligarchies' independence in finance, there were changes that occurred, tending to make administration more open and responsible to the electorate. Moreover, they occurred relatively easily and without that acrimony characteristic of the political life of Newfoundland and the Canadas at the same time.

It was New Brunswick that pioneered in reform, and the reason for this lead was the colony's booming timber trade. So avid were the timber dealers for access to crown land that the executive was able to sell large amounts, thereby building up a vast treasury beyond the control of the Assembly. So vast did these sums become that the interest alone threatened to keep the executive in funds for all time. Still, the executive's control of the timber lands antagonized those who were outside the charmed inner circle, and these disappointed outsiders began to agitate through the Assembly for limitations upon the executive. Eventually in 1837 a deputation to the Colonial Office in London produced a compromise whereby the Assembly was given control of all revenue, including that produced from the sale of crown lands, in return for the granting of a civil list to the executive from which judges and civil servants were to be paid — automatically and without appropriation. At the same time, the imperial authorities instructed the governor of New Brunswick to integrate government more closely with popular demand by bringing members of the Assembly into the Executive Council. Subsequently the new head of the Executive Council was Charles Simonds, the man who first rallied the Assembly to fight for control of the revenue.

Much the same process of compromise unfolded in Nova Scotia. There the popular party's champion was Joseph Howe who made his reputation first as a newspaper editor. Fresh from a triumphant acquittal on a charge of having libeled the colonial oligarchy, he entered the Assembly in 1836 and quickly rose to prominence in his new role. Under Howe's leadership the House passed *Twelve Resolutions* in 1837 claiming sweeping powers for the Assembly, going so far as to call for election of the members of the Executive Council. London responded with the New Brunswick compromise. Subsequently, members of the Assembly did join the Executive Council, and, for a time, this was enough even for Joseph Howe since he, too, accepted promotion on these terms.

Soon the New Brunswick formula of trading a civil list for greater contol of the executive extended to Prince Edward Island as well. There, the oligarchy consisted of a narrow clique of absentee landlords who controlled gigantic estates. The tenant-settlers, for their part, argued that they could not pay and that their landlords should be dispossessed. The popular forces began to make headway in the late thirties, and like Howe (who was open to more American notions) began to agitate for an elective legislative council as a means of breaking the proprietors' power. But for PEI as elsewhere, the Colonial Office refused to sanction republicanism. Instead, they imposed the New Brunswick formula and successfully stifled further agitation. In 1839 the Council was split into legislative and executive sections, and two Assemblymen were taken into the Executive Council. For the moment, this was enough. Like Nova Scotia and New Brunswick, there arose in Prince Edward Island popular forces which first found their salvation in the elective principle but readily compromised when offered something less. Meanwhile, in the two Canadas, the popular parties had embraced republicanism as a doctrine too sacred to compromise.

The basic explanation for the contrast would appear to be found in the fact that in each Maritime colony (except Newfoundland), society was extremely homogenous by class and ethnicity. The vast majority of the population of New Brunswick and Nova Scotia still consisted of a people with a shared experience and purpose. Loyalists and their children still predominated. The result was that it was impossible to discredit reformers on the basis of their suspect origins. Elsewhere, society was more divided by religion, language, and social position. There, it was only too easy for small disagreements to intensify quickly, assume cosmic proportions, and end in allegations of disloyalty both to empire and to colony — precisely what happened in the two Canadas.

## III    Ethnic Conflict in Lower Canada

It has already been shown that conflict between an aroused electorate and an entrenched oligarchy in Lower Canada flared in 1807 but reached a point of unity and calm by the conciliatory gestures of Governor Prevost and the War of 1812. Such harmony was only temporary, however. In 1820 Prevost left the colony and was succeeded as governor by the Earl of Dalhousie, fresh from governing Nova Scotia and unable to accept Lower Canada as a colony unlike the others. Almost immediately, he found himself embroiled in a bitter struggle with the Speaker of the Assembly, Louis-Joseph Papineau.

Dalhousie's contempt for Papineau and *canadiens* in general led him into alliance with the merchant group that shared his prejudices. In 1822, Dalhousie followed their advice in recommending that the mother country unite the two Canadas for the commercial and political advantages that would follow to the British. Union would join the progressive mercantile elite of one region with that of the other. Together they might promote improvement of the navigation of the St. Lawrence with canals to the benefit of both. Papineau and the Assembly of Lower Canada consistently opposed public support for such undertakings. Here was the political attraction of union to the English-speaking mercantile elite of Montreal since their union with colonists of the same social character in the upper province appeared to promise easy subordination of the "unenterprising" French in Lower Canada. Papineau appreciated this as well and therefore went to London personally to lobby against the proposal on grounds that union was inspired by nothing more than extravagance and bigotry. When he was successful the antipathy between him and Dalhousie increased enormously.

In 1827 the governor dissolved the Assembly and plunged the province into a bitter election contest for the expressed purpose of ridding himself and his friends of Papineau. But the new House was still loyal to Papineau's volatile leadership and re-elected him speaker accordingly. Dalhousie responded by proroguing the Assembly and quitting the province in a fury.

What Lower Canada needed after Dalhousie's departure was a new governor to serve as conciliator between the embittered *canadiens* in the Assembly and the English entrenched in the Legislative and Executive Councils. The Colonial Office obligingly provided such a mediator in Sir James Kempt, who demonstrated the importance of the office of governor by successfully conciliating the French without infuriating the English. Thus, democracy and oligarchy came to a truce by 1830 when the governor retired.

Still, the conflict in Lower Canada was more general and fundamental than the periodic intransigence of its governors or the hotheadedness of leaders in the Assembly. Kempt's replacement, Lord Aylmer, was not nearly as bigoted as Dalhousie. Yet he found his administration even more deadlocked than Dalhousie's was in 1827, and Aylmer accomplished this in two rather than in eight years. By 1832 the government of Lower Canada was at a complete impasse and the general population was far more aroused than ever before. Since the objects of denunciation were the cholera imported by the timber ships carrying immigrants out from the British Isles and the favoritism which meant most offices of honor and profit went to English rather than to *canadiens*, the proposed remedies sounded like appropriate innovations. Popular spokesmen demanded close regulation if not a total ban on immigration and complete control of crown patronage. Such uncompromising majoritarianism was widely publicized as the medicine that would cure the ills of the poor farmers of the province who responded enthusiastically, even though the politicians' formula provided scapegoats more clearly than direct remedies for the growing agricultural crisis.

The harsh reality in Lower Canada was repeated crop failure. Crops failed because of soil exhaustion and outmoded agricultural practices. Rather than popularize the need for technical improvements, the politicians informed uneducated farmers that their crisis would be less severe if only there were no more immigrants coming into the province by the thousands bringing disease, competing for the vacant land, and threatening the purity of French Canadian customs and institutions by their unfamilar ways. Moreover, the politicians continued, if *seigneurs* were not rack-renters, if all the good offices did not go to the English, then government and authority would be closer to the people, rather than in the hands of those who would restore prosperity by fostering a commercialism that promised to erode further the character of the French-Canadian nation.

As Papineau's followers gained more support from the people but failed to win concessions from the government they became increasingly radical; that is, nationalist. Soon their nationalism was running in a republican course.

In February 1834 the Legislative Assembly went so far as to petition the British Colonial Office for a republican constitution in a list of grievances that was no less than *Ninety-two Resolutions*. Here, the Legislative Council was denounced as "the most active principle of evil and discontent" because the Council consistently frustrated the elected Assembly. The upper house was therefore "the servile tool of the authority which creates, composes and decomposes it." The cure was to make the Council an elective body like the Assembly. Only then would it "conform to the wishes, manners and social state of the Inhabitants of this continent." The same republicanism was also supposed to be the appropriate remedy for the "scandalous favoritism of the governors" who preferred to appoint English over French. In Resolution number 75 it was pointed out that of the total population of the province, "those of French origin are about 525 000, and those of British or other origin 75 000", but nearly 80 percent of the 204 government appointments were distributed to people "apparently of British or Foreign origin." There were only 47 government appointees who were "apparently natives of the Country, of French origin." On the basis of such resentments as these, for the second year running, the Assembly refused to vote supplies to the government.

Governor Aylmer responded by dissolving the House and hoping for improvement after the election. But the electorate returned a legislature even more republican than its predecessor. Twenty-four members previously had refused to assent to the *Ninety-two Resolutions*. All but three were defeated in their bids for re-election. With the colony thus locked in struggle between the popular forces and the royal prerogative, and without either side proposing a compromise acceptable to the other, it appeared that the only alternative remaining for the proponents of republicanism was agitation for independence. Of course, Great Britain hoped to prevent it. In the spring of 1835, Aylmer was recalled and a Commission of Inquiry under his successor, Lord Gosford, was instructed to investigate the whole range of grievances that was apparently bringing not only Lower Canada but also other provinces, even havens of Loyalism, to advocate open republicanism.

## IV    Reform as Sectarian Conflict in Upper Canada

By 1834 it seemed that Upper Canada was nearly as close to rebellion as was the lower province. In December, the Assembly adopted a critque of the status quo called the *Seventh Report on Grievances* that was every bit as republican as the *Ninety-two Resolutions* in advocating the "elective principle" as a cure-all. Less than fifty years after its founding, the province of Upper Canada thus seemed to have forsaken its Loyalist destiny.

Previous chapters have described the various steps taken by the authorities, both in Britain and in the colony, to preserve Upper Canada from the taint of American republicanism. Such institutional safeguards as the Clergy Reserves for Anglicans, or such governmental measures as the 1816 ban on American immigration, could do much toward this end, but there was one deviant phenomenon which the province's British-oriented Anglican oligarchy seemed incapable of eradicating. That was the extraordinary popularity of "enthusiastic" religion.

The early immigrants had been overwhelmingly evangelical; Presbyterians and Baptists, together with their near relations, the Methodists, had flooded Upper Canada, and later waves from Britain had not stemmed the tide. Nor was this surprising. Evangelical religion fostered by itinerent preachers was the primary, perhaps the only possible and effective, social cement in such a vast and thinly settled territory where there were few neighbors, hardly any villages, and not even the rudiments for Anglican parish organization. Upper Canada west of York (later Toronto) was only a geographical expression but the preacher, the meeting house, and emotional exhortation were tangible evidence that people might draw together occasionally and for such moments feel slightly less alone than they actually were. If there were officials at York who denounced this as "noxious", it only revealed the depth of their misunderstanding. The sectarians did not see themselves as particularly American or British. Their one clear identification was with their particular Protestant sect.

It was inevitable that social conflict would develop eventually between the two social models, the Family Compact's pro-British, Anglican elite and the sectarians with their backwoods evangelicalism. But it was not until 1820 that trouble flared openly, and even then the struggle opened rather inadvertently, after one Robert Gourlay, a newcomer from Scotland, had circulated a questionnaire among the pioneer population. His object in 1817 was to collect information for a book to be published in Great Britain promoting emigration. But some of his questions implied evaluation more than description. Thus, he asked, "What, in your opinion, retards the improvement of your township in particular, or the province in general; and what would most contribute to the same?" A storm of controversy soon developed over Gourlay's findings. In addition to poor roads, and a general lack of internal improvements, his respondents explained the extreme dispersal of settlers as arising in the first place from large tracts of land being held back from settlement by speculators and the government in the form of Clergy and Crown reserves. Gourlay called for a commission of inquiry. The government ignored his demand. Then Gourlay called for basic reform, particularly of the governor's power to dispense patronage, "to give away land at pleasure ... to grant licences, pardons and I know not what ... ." Then the government acted: Gourlay was arrested, prosecuted for writing "scurrilous and seditious libels", and ultimately expelled from the province.

In the 1820 election, protesters calling themselves "Gourlayites" were elected to the Assembly for the expressed purpose of opposing the government. They, no less than he, were dismissed as republican and denounced as traitors. Polarizing opinion seized upon the question of nationality as a means of highlighting this initial split. The oligarchy tended to claim that post-1792 immigrants from the United States were not to be treated as British, and that accordingly their citizenship rights were forfeited. This "alien question", which centered upon the prominent Reformers, the Bidwells (father and son), continued to dominate the 1820s.

The alien question was accompanied by a host of other contentious issues (the validity of the reserves, the question of church-state links, patronage, the argument over open or secret voting). In each case the tendency was to couch the debate in terms of British or American alternatives. Since Upper Canada was a British community, for the elite and any who automatically accepted an institution if it were English, the preferred alternative was plain at every point. They opposed the notion accepted by Americans that the state was purely secular. In their view, "There should be in every Christian country an established religion, otherwise it is not a Christian but an Infidel country." Similarly, they opposed American notions of democracy on grounds that "something like an aristocracy" was "essential to the happiness and good government of any people." But what the leading spokesman for this point of view — John Strachan, John Beverley Robinson, and Christopher Hagerman — failed to take sufficiently into account was that their opponents could advocate separation of church and state or curtailment of aristocratic power without being distinctively "Yankee".

The people of Upper Canada, especially in the western part of the province, did have many attitudes and patterns of speech in common with the Americans on the other side of the lakes. In fact European travelers who toured the United States as well as Upper Canada remarked often that on the British side of the line the feeling was "totally Yankee". Moreover, to a degree, the critics of the government were consciously imitating American patterns. This was certainly true of the government's most outspoken critic, William Lyon Mackenzie, Scottish-born editor of the wildly scurrilous newspaper, *The Colonial Advocate*. But Egerton Ryerson, equally critical of the idea of an established church, was no less Loyalist than his father, the "Yankee" who brought his family to Canada after the American Revolution in the first instance.

Since the only unvarying constant of the highly charged and changeable political climate of Upper Canada after 1824 was opposition to state-sponsored religion, the Ryersons of the colony proved far more typical of the population generally than the Mackenzies. But typicality was difficult to judge in the decade after 1824 since the voters constantly vacillated from one side to another. The province had not made up its mind on many matters other than the Clergy Reserves, but within the Assembly in 1834, by the *Seventh Report on Grievances*, the representatives then sitting did formally adopt the republican model as the means to defeat the governor and the "corruptionists" who gathered around him for his favors.

## V    The Failure of Rebellion in Lower Canada

The adoption of the *Seventh Report of Grievances* in Upper Canada and the *Ninety-two Resolutions* in Lower Canada created the impression at the Colonial Office that both Canadas were on the brink of rebellion. The British response in 1835 was to appoint a commission under Lord Gosford to look into the affairs of both provinces. Since Gosford was also to be the governor of Lower Canada, the commission's presence was felt more directly in the one province than the other.

Initially Gosford's manner was conciliatory but within months he found himself as deadlocked with the Assembly as any of his predecessors. The reason was that the full disclosure of his instructions from the colonial secretary made it clear that Gosford was not empowered to recommend any basic changes in the constitution. The Assembly responded by withholding supply. And the Gosford commission retaliated by reporting that conciliation would avail nothing. The governor as commissioner recommended that a show of force was needed.

The imperial government in which Lord John Russell was a dominant figure obliged by putting Gosford's recommendation before Parliament as the *Ten Resolutions* early in the spring of 1837. Two points were primary: there would be no structural change in the constitutions of the colonies agitating for it, and in the event that legislatures fought governors on this point by withholding supply, governors were authorized to remove funds from provincial treasuries without legislative appropriation.

As far as the *Patriotes* of Lower Canada were concerned, this was the end. On April 14, 1837, in the *Vindicator*, one of their most outspoken newspapers, they warned their readers that

> the die is cast; the British ministry have resolved to set the seal of degradation and slavery on this Province, and to render it actually, what it was only in repute — the 'IRELAND' of NORTH AMERICA.... One duty alone remains for the people of Lower Canada. Let them study the HISTORY OF THE AMERICAN REVOLUTION.... (Quoted in J.M.S. Careless, ed., *Colonists and Canadiens, 1760-1867* [1971], p. 187.)

Thus, the drive for constitutional change gained momentum as an independence movement. In May, a public meeting of delegates convened to denounce British "lying" and "oppression" and all the bonds to Great Britain were said to be those of force rather than of friendship. It was said that their "true friends and natural allies were on the other side of the 45th parallel." Louis Papineau was proclaimed national leader and steps were taken to repeat what the Americans had done between 1774 and 1776. An association to end trade with Great Britain reminiscent of the American Association of 1774 emerged. And after this step, an extra-legal government — the Assembly of Six Counties — appeared to administer the affairs of the province despite the continued existence of the legally constituted administration under the British.

The English party, and some *canadiens* holding appointments to various public offices, counterattacked in a newspaper campaign that was extraordinary for its verbal abuse. The Montreal *Gazette*, for instance, denounced Russell's *Ten Resolutions* as far too mild to meet "the thraldom of a FRENCHIFIED revolutionary faction" and demanded military action to break up "the treasonable designs" of Papineau and his "faction".

The *Patriotes* responded by moving against the dissident minority with a program of harassment similar to the American Patriots' treatment of Loyalists in their revolution. The idea was to discourage and terrorize them so completely that they would either abandon their opposition or quit the province altogether. *Fils de la liberté* (Sons of Liberty) shaved the manes and tails of Englishmen's horses. Groups of young *Patriotes* stamped through the streets of English neighborhoods shouting threats and singing bawdy songs.

While Loyalists and *Patriotes* prepared for civil war, Lord Gosford attempted to restore respect for regular government. To conciliate those who wanted to see strong measures taken against the radicals, he purged the militia and judiciary of anyone who was taking any part in the attempt to set up the extra-legal institutions. To conciliate those who wanted to see the establishment of majoritarian government, he called a session of the Assembly. Neither action was effective. Less than one week after legislative proceedings began, the members of the house started wrangling against the government with as much vehemence as ever, and the purge of the civil service (staffed primarily with English anyway) did not affect the radicals the British party wanted to see gibbetted. Thus, the governor and his authority became an irrelevance as the crisis was taken up again in the streets of Montreal between gangs of Loyalists organized as the Doric Club and the other side, the *Fils de la liberté*.

Suddenly the hierarchy of the Catholic Church took a stand behind the governor to stem the drift toward rebellion and civil war. The Bishops were in full sympathy with the nationalism of the radicals but they had no enthusiasm for rebellion against Britain. Early in November, the Bishop of Montreal, Monseigneur Lartigue, issued an order unequivocally condemning the radicals who would seek to destroy duly constituted authority and bring the province to the brink of war. They, for their part, disclaimed any intention of launching rebellion. The *Patriote* leaders said they merely wanted to bring about the disintegration of arbitrary government. At the same time, a few denounced the church authority as a force of tyranny as bad as the British insofar as it did not share their same dedication to national security by liberation from Britain.

The quarrel between clerical and lay leaders flared at a critical moment. On November 6, a street fight between political gangs resulted in property damage and Lord Gosford gave in to the demands to restore law and order. He called out the British garrison to patrol the streets and prevent public meetings. The governor also ordered the arrest of leading *Patriotes* whom he now intended to hold responsible for recent events.

On November 22, Charles Perrault, Jean Chenier, and Louis-Joseph Papineau withdrew from Montreal to the security of nearby towns. The government assumed they were retreating to mobilize the *canadiens* in open rebellion and pursued them in force accordingly, but the *Patriote* leaders were not yet ready for war. At St. Denis and (most notably) at St. Eustache there was fighting that resulted in total defeat. Perrault and Chenier were fairly effective commanders of rather unprepared followings. But Papineau had no intention of fighting a rebellion or of being captured and hanged as a rebel. Disguised in women's clothing he fled for security to the United States and thus ended the first rebellion of 1837.

## VI    The Failure of Rebellion in Upper Canada

Even more than military unpreparedness or incompetence, it was ambivalence that was the most probable reason for the failure of the independence movement in Lower Canada after it reached the point of armed struggle. In other words, the mass of the people were probably confused by the conflict that broke out between the clergy and lay leaders just as the fighting with the British reached its critical point. The Church said it was everyone's duty to obey. The radicals urged everyone to resist. Yet both kinds of leaders were advocates of national survival in their different ways. What divided them from one another was means more than ends. Thus, the ambivalence of the mass of the people could only have been made stronger.

A similar kind of ambivalence worked against the radicals in Upper Canada where the division among reformers had occurred earlier and the confusion therefore had more time for resolution. Unfortunately for the rebels, the decision was on the side of loyalty to Britain.

As early as 1834 there was a division among the leaders for reform. One group, around William Lyon Mackenzie, was concerned with rights and wrongs. They were dogmatic republicans, very much like those Patriots in the old empire, so wrapped up in protest that they seemed to be more concerned with the principles of government than its processes. The other faction, around Egerton Ryerson out of the Assembly and Robert Baldwin within, was only slightly less critical of the "Family Compact" than Mackenzie and his friends, but it was quite unlike the radicals since this group was more interested in the practice of government and its projects than they were preoccupied with moral purity for its own sake.

It is not difficult to see how divided leadership slowed the drift to revolution by confusing individual followers. It has already been mentioned that the electorate shifted its support continually between opposing and supporting the governor and his friends. Even the politicians were confused. The electorate as a political body was truly an unformed mass as far as attitudes toward basic reform were concerned. But then in 1836 they reached what might be regarded as a point of decision.

In some respects the election of 1836 in Upper Canada was a sordid, drunken, violent spree that is best forgotten. But in another way the election was important as no other because it was a confrontation between politicians, people, and issues that determined the course of decades to follow. The factor that added special color to the contest was the province's new governor, Sir Francis Bond Head, and his decision to involve himself directly with the electorate, face to face, in the campaigning.

Head had been governor of Upper Canada since 1835 (at the same time Gosford was charged with pacifying Lower Canada). Somewhat predictably, from the moment of Head's arrival, he was convinced that "a good feeling pervaded a majority of the people" since he believed that the "strong republican principles" of the Assembly were unrepresentative of true public opinion. Thus, his first impulse was to be conciliatory to the Assembly by promoting moderate reformers to his Council. When it seemed that nothing short of republican reform would satisfy the Assembly a year later, however, he dissolved the House. Then followed his two months of electioneering in May 1836.

Just two years before, a general meeting in Toronto established an organization called the Canadian Alliance to "enter into close alliance with any similar association that may be formed in Lower Canada or the other colonies, having for its object 'the Greatest happiness of the greatest number.'" By the summer of 1836 such happiness meant specific projects rather than reform rhetoric because a similar meeting of like-minded people called for a legislature to direct its attention "to the improvement of the land we live in, rather than to the consideration of abstract questions of Government." This Sir Francis promised to deliver. In a tour of speechmaking he constantly returned to the same basic point: "Can you do as much for yourselves as I can do for you? If you choose to dispute with me, and live on bad terms with the mother country, you will, to use a homely phrase, only quarrel with your own bread and butter." Then, too, he played on Loyalist sympathy and anti-American sentiment, and there were liberal quantities of liquor and bullies at the polls. The reformers were routed.

After the election it was the opinion of Mackenzie and his friends that the voting was no valid expression of public opinion. Yet how wrong was his judgment is illustrated best by the failure of his rebellion, the "revolution" that was called and in which few participated — not even Loyalists, to give their rebel enemies a good beating. In its one battle, the march down Yonge Street on December 5, 1837, just one person was killed.

The significance of the rebellion's failure was not that the people could not be relied upon. Their failure to respond to Mackenzie's call to seize the government, "declare the province free" and "call a convention together, to frame a suitable constitution... without shedding blood" only meant that the quiescent colonists interpreted reform in different terms. Head convinced them to judge a politician by the projects he proposed rather than by the constitutional principles he proclaimed. In this way, the political style that called voters to project their personal frustrations as public problems which was then and continued to be such a conspicuous feature of the American tradition, the style which the Loyalists rejected in the eighteenth century, the "late" Loyalists appeared finally to reject in their turn as well. By 1838, there was no sign that anyone in Upper Canada thought less well of himself for having failed to launch a "manly resistance" against the "poor deluded miserable ductile dupes of the dirty tools of arbitrary power," as Mackenzie had invited the year before. But people were talking a great deal about vast new internal improvement schemes the government would underwrite. They also began to talk about reform again, and while the new scheme was not republican it still held out the promise of improving the promotion of "the greatest happiness for the greatest number."

# Bibliography

Political developments leading to reform in the Maritimes and rebellion in the two Canadian provinces are surveyed well in the several relevant volumes of the Canadian Centenary Series: W.S. MacNutt, *The Atlantic Provinces, 1712-1857* (1965), Fernand Ouellet, *Lower Canada, 1791-1810* (1980), and Gerald Craig, *Upper Canada, 1784-1841* (1963). Excellent material on the same subjects is also found in J.M.S. Careless, ed., *Colonists and Canadiens, 1760-1867* (1971), in the chapters contributed by Michael Cross on "The 1820s" and G.M. Craig covering "The 1830s".

The persistent failure of British attempts at conciliation is described by Peter Burroughs, *The Canadian Crisis and British Colonial Policy* (1972). For more detailed treatments of the rebellions, H.T. Manning, *Revolt of French Canada: A Chapter in the History of the British Commonwealth* (1962), and A. Dunham, *Political Unrest in Upper Canada, 1815-1836* (1927), are the standard histories. More recent accounts are Joseph Schull, *Rebellion: The Rising of French Canada* (1971) emphasizing colorful events, and Fred Landon,

*Western Ontario and the American Frontier* (1967), emphasizing sectarian conflict. The one historian who chooses to interpret the rebellions as risings of the proletariat is Stanley B. Ryerson in *Unequal Union: Confederation and the Roots of Conflict in the Canadas, 1815-1873* (1968).

". . . radicals believed Radical Jack's heart was with the real people."

# CHAPTER 9

# *The Durham Solution*

## I   British Radicalism Discovers Canadian Majoritarianism

The news of rebellions in both Canadas shocked Great Britain. The government of Lord Melbourne, not a particularly strong one in 1838, suffered scorching criticism with the opposition suggesting administrative neglect and petty tyrannies were at fault. So successful was their assault that by the beginning of 1838 the fall of Melbourne, a latter-day Lord North, was being widely predicted.

But what was to be done? The rebellions were over almost before they had begun. In this sense there was not even a crisis to face. Still, the support for the rebels in Lower Canada was strong. At least an appearance of action was necessary for what had taken place in the other Canada. Melbourne's first response, therefore, was to strike a commission to investigate the origins of the turmoil and to recommend changes for the future. In forming such an investigative body, Melbourne recruited the undisputed champion of the cause of liberal reform in England to take the post of High Commissioner, visit British North America, and establish the truth on the spot.

The darling of British "radicalism" (the cause that championed, among other innovations, voting by ballot, extending the franchise to all male taxpayers, and legislative reapportionment) was John "Radical Jack" Lambton, the first Earl of Durham and "King of the Coal Country". Durham's appointment silenced critics of Melbourne because radicals believed Radical Jack's heart was with the real people. He would not hesitate to name the nabobs who brought disorder to the colonies. Since Melbourne believed such revelations could not distress the ministry in Great Britain, he was delighted with Durham's acceptance of the commission if only because it quieted the opposition and temporarily removed one of the most vocal troublemakers from England.

True to his reputation, Lord Durham prepared himself for his duties weeks before his departure. He talked to merchants who conducted their business in the colonies. He read documents including such items as the *Ninety-two Resolutions* and the *Seventh Report on Grievances*. In this way, he gained a preview (and preconception) of what awaited him in the two Canadas. Then, Durham set out early in the spring of 1838 with a retinue that included two especially trusted associates, Charles Buller and Edward Gibbon Wakefield.

The emissaries of inquiry arrived in Quebec on a beautiful day in May. Since Durham's reputation as a reformer had preceded him, people welcomed his arrival like warm sunshine after a long winter. Recently there had been two political executions in Upper Canada. More were expected in the lower province and the jails of both were filled with hundreds of accused rebels awaiting trial and possible execution. The constitution of Lower Canada was suspended. (In fact, the colony was under martial law more stringent in 1838 than in the years immediately after the Conquest). Upper Canada was less under a lid of repression but the people were no less desperate — for economic reasons. The Loyalist Assembly elected in 1836 had enacted a series of internal improvement schemes in keeping with their promise of promoting economic development rather than disputing abstract principles of government. Then, one of those recurring "panics" that periodically interrupted the rapid growth of the United States and Great Britain in the nineteenth century hit in 1837. As a result, Upper Canada was severely shaken and the public treasury nearly bankrupt.

Since Durham was the Governor General of all of British North America as well as the High Commissioner to investigate the disturbances in the Canadas, and since he was given extraordinary powers to cope with the emergency situation, it was generally expected that the governor would deal boldly with the matters at hand. He put his associates, Wakefield and Buller, at work heading committees to examine land questions — particularly how the Clergy and Crown Reserves affected economic development in Upper Canada — and occupied himself with the investigation of the causes of the rebellions, seeking long-term remedies as well as a way out of the immediate problem of the disposition of accused rebels. Clemency seemed the best way to handle would-be martyrs. Nearly all were pardoned. The exceptions (most in self-imposed exile already) were banished, but eight rebels jailed in Canada suffered banishment by deportation to Bermuda.

After disposing of the punishment issue, Durham held private audiences to deal with the question of appropriate reforms to prevent future rebellions. He talked to delegations from the Maritimes, for instance, to determine their reaction to a pet solution that had occurred to him even before he left England: the federation of all the provinces in one legislative union. From the perspective he acquired before leaving Britain, this seemed an attractive solution since it would create a structure too large for the petty oligarchy of any one colony to dominate. Equally important, a federal unit would have a revenue base large enough to handle internal improvement schemes on a much greater scale than any one province could undertake by itself. The one thing wrong with federalism, Durham discovered to his surprise, was that no one wanted it. The Maritimers were especially adamant. In the summer of 1838 their representatives told him that they would suffer almost any fate before they would willingly allow themselves to be dragged into a union with the obstreperous Canadians.

Thus, Durham abandoned his hope for a federation. But other schemes attracted him in its place. During an eleven-day visit to Upper Canada, Durham had occasion to talk with William and Robert Baldwin who proposed a reform acceptable to the people of the Maritimes but less all-embracing than union in its scope. The Baldwins suggested that the most useful reform would be recognition of the principle that a colonial governor should choose his closest advisors, the members of his Executive Council, entirely from the leadership of the majority group in the Assembly and, moreover, the representative of the Crown should be governed by their advice in all matters that could be construed as "domestic concerns". Such an innovation would break the deadlock between levels of government as effectively as by the "elective principle" but without, in fact, transforming the colonies into autonomous "republics". Here, also, was the means of making "a permanent connection between the colonies and the Mother Country" since an administration accountable to the popular Assembly would be freed from the criticism that it was an oligarchy supported only by foreigners.

The logic of the Baldwins' proposal was so attractive to Durham he was prepared to recommend its concession to every colony in British North America, except Lower Canada. The *canadiens*, as a "race", were an enormous disappointment to Lord Durham. Before leaving England, his informants had warned him that they were reactionary defenders of tradition and used their majority power in the Assembly to obstruct "the progressive intrusion of the English race." After seeing for himself that the Tory clique appeared to be the real progressives, Durham became even more convinced that the concession of self-government to the French-speaking majority would pose even greater impediments to the economic development of Lower Canada.

In the midst of pondering the larger issues of reform, Durham was interrupted early in the autumn when the Melbourne ministry informed him that his banishment of the political prisoners was illegal because the authority of his commission did not extend as far as Bermuda. He might have banished the worst of the rebels to Newfoundland or Cape Breton Island — territories that were part of British North America — but not to Bermuda, an island beyond his jurisdiction. Durham was furious since Melbourne's narrow legalism belied the promises of firm support the government had extended along with Durham's commission. Consequently, Durham resigned and quit the province after less than six months in office.

On Durham's departure, the administration of Lower Canada reverted to the martial law of Sir John Colborne. With such a sudden interruption of *canadiens'* hopes that there might be structural change without a war of independence, the *Patriotes* rose a second time in November 1838 and the second rebellion was suppressed with far greater force than the first. In the wake of the recriminations that followed the far more stringent reimposition of martial law, twelve people were executed and fifty-eight were exiled — this time to Australia and with the full approval of the imperial authorities.

## II    The Durham Report

As the *Patriotes* staged their second rebellion, Durham was on his way to England. Shortly after he arrived home he heard of the renewed "troubles", and Durham, along with his assistants, set to work writing a report to reveal for all what they supposed was the significance of the recent history of the two Canadas. The highly controversial recommendations, which appeared in 1839, made the *Report on Canada* immensely readable and refreshed Radical Jack's image in the conservative press. Thus, the influential London *Times* promptly identified its author as the "Lord High Seditioner".

Durham's advocacy of greater self-government was offensive to imperialists, but there was nothing in Durham's report to suggest that the "British possessions in North Amercia" existed as anything other than an appendage of Britain to aid "the suffering classes of the mother country" by offering them territory for migration without needing to abandon their British manners or citizenship. To encourage such transfer of population, Durham advocated the removal of supposed impediments to settlement.

One was a system of land distribution that seemed to help "land jobbers" more than emigrants. Accordingly, Durham recommended a reform of the system to abolish the Crown and Clergy reserves and large grants of land to speculators. Both were prerequisites to establishing a "sound system of colonization," he said.

The other flaw Durham identified was the constitutional arrangement that impeded the provision of "good government." However, in recommending that "the colonial Governor ... be instructed to secure the co-operation of the Assembly in his policy by entrusting its administration to such men as could command a majority," Durham contemplated an extremely narrow range of matters in which self-government might be exercised. Responsibility would cover domestic concerns but fall short of anything pertaining to relations with the mother country or economic development. Four such forbidden jurisdictions were enumerated: "the constitution of the form of government, the regulation of foreign relations and trade ... and the disposal of the public lands." Since such matters covered most of the areas in which colonial legislation was enacted, the autonomy Lord Durham proposed was very limited indeed. Moreover, the limited home rule advocated by Durham was proposed only for the "British" colonies.

Lower Canada was a special case qualified by what Durham thought he had learned of the struggle there. Expressing contrived surprise, Durham said that he "expected to find a contest between a government and a people." Instead, he "found two nations warring in the bosom of a single state: I found a struggle, not of principles, but of races ... ." Since Durham regarded such duality as anomalous to say the least, and since he also assumed that the French part was inferior to the English, he advocated a program of education to bring the "stationary French race" up to the level of the progressive minority. In the meantime, he considered it an enormous mistake to entrust the government of the colony to the backward majority. The solution, in Durham's opinion, was the legislative union of the two Canadas, at the same time placing the *canadiens* in a minority position. Durham believed this would be the most expedient means of discouraging *canadien* nationalism, and "hastening the process of assimilation," Durham's "first object." He wrote that "the alteration of the character of the province ought to be immediately entered on, and firmly, though cautiously followed up; that in any plan ... with this in view, the asendancy should never again be placed in any hands but those of an English population."

Naturally, the *canadiens* were not pleased to learn that Durham believed "There can hardly be conceived a nationality more destitute of all that can invigorate and elevate a people, than that which is exhibited by the descendants of the French of Lower Canada, owing to their retaining their peculiar language and manners." Still, the Durham report did interest those who read it in translation and by installments in Etienne Parent's newspaper, *Le Canadien*.

The people of the rest of British North America were no less interested but the reformers of Upper Canada were unqualifiedly enthusiastic about Durham's recommendation that a governor should be bound by the policy of advisors chosen only from among the leaders of the elected majority in the Assembly because the advocates of constitutional change were extremely vulnerable to accusations of disloyalty from the moment of Mackenzie's rebellion. With no less than a peer of the realm advocating the overthrow of the old oligarchy, "Durham Meetings" sprang up all over Upper Canada in 1839 to show support for the scheme.

The elite of the province was less enthusiastic about change that might broaden the base of privilege, but in one aspect of the report they too found something to praise. They supported Durham's proposal to restore the economic unity of the two provinces, a pet idea of business men in Lower Canada since it was first proposed in 1822. Still, it was difficult for the elite of Upper Canada to be enthusiastic about the scathing language with which Durham attacked them for their "monopoly of power having ... acquired nearly the whole of the wastelands of the Province, ... the chartered banks, and till lately, shared among themselves almost exclusively all offices of trust and profit." Durham believed that by making the Executive Council "responsible to the people" the monopoly would be broken and the happiness of the colony, if not the "Family Compact", would prevail.

But whether any of Durham's recommendations would go into effect depended upon the still shaky government of Lord Melbourne which found the idea of ministerial responsibility a "logical absurdity" for a colony. The other recommendations (the proposals pertaining to crown lands, the unification of the Canadas, and the gradual assimilation of the descendants of the French) were less repugnant in principle, but the government was reluctant to act on any of them immediately.


### III    The Union of Upper and Lower Canada

While Great Britain hesitated, reformers and *canadiens* speculated about the implementation of all or part of the major recommendations. To Etienne Parent, union and the risk of assimilation were tolerable if these changes were accompanied by responsible government. For Parent, writing in April 1839, the defeat of the oligarchy was more important than cultural purity. But the editor of *Le Canadien* changed his mind as soon as it became clear that subjection and subordination were the only aims of the union's English proponents. In the English newspapers of Lower Canada, union was advertised as the best way to punish the *Patriotes* for their rebellions of 1837 and 1838. The Montreal *Herald*, for instance, proposed that the representation in an eventually united province should be 103 seats to 25 in favor of the English. The *Gazette*, another Montreal paper, suggested that literacy in English, rather than property, ought to be the prerequisite for a man's having the right to vote. Soon only *vendus* (the name given to *canadiens* who had sold out for government salaries while claiming eagerly to serve the people) continued to support the idea of union.

Foremost among the unions's opponents was Bishop Lartigue, the cleric who figured so prominently in the opposition to rebellion. The man who so staunchly upheld the British government in 1837 spoke out in 1839 as an arch defender of local nationalism to save the existing system of Church-run schools.Durham had proposed a program of universal education to foster the anglification process. Since Lartigue imagined that a single system of schools would inevitably follow the unification of the two Canadas, he opposed union as well.

Confused by the many recent reversals of their clerical and lay leaders, the ordinary people of Lower Canada grew apathetic to the turns in the history of their province. Consequently, once the British decided to implement what Peter Burroughs has called the "cultural chauvinism" of the Durham *Report* by enacting the union scheme, it was possible to do so with all leaders (except *vendus*) protesting and the mass of the *canadiens* not rebelling a third time.

In November 1839, after receiving instructions from the Colonial Office to promote legislative union by diplomacy, the new Governor General, Charles Poulett Thomson, simply summoned the tribunal Colborne had used to maintain a semblance of civil administration and outlined the probable terms as follows: equal representation (there were then about 650 000 people in Lower Canada, to be called Canada East, and only 450 000 in the Upper Province, Canada West), assumption of the debts of both as one (the public debt in Upper Canada was £1.2 million, Lower Canada owed a mere £95 000), and no responsibility of the provincial ministry to the Assembly. Then the tribunal was instructed to vote its assent without discussion and the union proposal carried.

Flattering himself that the exercise secured the "deliberate wishes" of the people of Lower Canada, Thomson took the terms next to Toronto. But in Upper Canada the governor had to meet an Assembly since civil government had not been suspended there after the one feeble rebellion of 1837. The approval Thomson needed to obtain by persuasion required no genius on his part, however, since the Assembly was already favorably disposed to union for its economic advantages. As for the constitutional terms, there were too few reformers in the Assembly to push for "independent responsible government". The members of the Assembly then sitting insisted on only two additional points: Kingston should be the capital of the United Province and English should be the sole language of record.

Thus, with one province apathetic and the other enthusiastic, Thomson secured ready approval of the scheme soon after his arrival in Canada, and enabled the British to enact the union in 1840. At the last stage of the process, the terms were modified further in London by adding a civil list to make the salaries of civil servants independent of legislative debate. To bring the province into line with the practice at Westminster it was arranged that money bills were to be introduced by the executive only, not by private members (thus eliminating the opportunity for temporary combinations of legislators to vote supplies for extravagant schemes of local improvement).

Passed by the Parliament of Great Britian in 1840, the Act of Union was proclaimed in Canada in 1841. Representation and liability for past debts were equal even though on both scores Canada West gained disproportionately. And there was to be no responsible government as Durham had recommended and some reformers demanded. Indeed, the constitutional arrangement in 1841 was even more "despotic" than in 1837 (given the new powers that were formally assigned to the executive). Radicals predicted trouble; but there was none. There were no riots until the first elections took place. But riotous elections were quite normal in a time when men voted publicly by voice rather than in seclusion by ballot. By 1841 it appeared that anglification and pacification would proceed without difficulty. The rebellions had more than failed. The rebels had been routed.

# IV   The Concession of Responsible Government

The failure of the rebellions and the adoption of only the unification rec-ommendations of the Durham Report placed Canadian Toryism in the most privileged position that it had enjoyed to date. The Loyalist-refugees from the American Revolution were not nearly so privileged in the 1790s as the Tory-victors appeared to be in the 1840s. Yet the reform movement was so encouraged by Durham that its resurgence outlasted his report's official rejection. Before the rebellions it was easy and common to label all reformers as "republican" and disloyal for their advocacy of doctrines inimical to the British constitution. Indeed, the "elective principle" did conform to an American prototype. But after the rebellions, as reformers identified themselves with Durham and "responsible government", it was impossible to stigmatize their proposal as a Yankee import. Consequently, there is irony in the Tory ascendancy after the rebellions since they lost all their ammunition to fight the opponents of the old oligarchies once the reformers aimed for nothing more than adoption of the British constitution in its "latest form".

In the half-century from the time the right of the Assembly to impeach the Executive Council of Lower Canada was demanded in 1807 to the conces-sion of responsible government in 1848, the chief opponents of the inno-vation were in Britain, at the Colonial Office. It was they who rejected the suggestion of Dr. W.W. Baldwin of Upper Canada who wrote to the Colo-nial Office in 1828 to suggest that they permit establishment of

> a Provincial Ministry, if I may be allowed use of the term, responsible to the Provincial Parliament, and removeable from office ... when they lose the con-fidence of the people as expressed by the voice of their representatives in the Assembly ... . (Quoted in W.L. Morton, *The Kingdom of Canada* [1963], p. 241.)

As late as 1840, the Colonial Secretary, Lord John Russell, still believed the proposal was "absurd". To him, it was "impossible for a Governor to be responsible to his Sovereign and a local legislature both at the same time."

Because a colonial governor would have to ignore the advice of a "pro-vincial ministry" (should it run counter to his instructions from the Colo-nial Office), Russell found the concept of ministerial responsibility "inad-missable" as well as "impossible". From the late 1830s, however, the Colonial Office instructed its governors to choose their ministers only from the group in the Assembly that was capable of controlling a legislative majority since it was clear that any other practice would lead to rebellion.

Thus, in 1839 Lord John Russell informed the governor of New Brunswick that henceforward a new policy would govern the tenure of office. Earlier, government officials had held office "during good behaviour," that is, as long as they did not warrant dismissal for pernicious conduct. Under the new policy, they were to hold office "during pleasure," while the executive found it useful to retain them (meaning the period during which they enjoyed the support of the Assembly). In the Canadas, too, Charles Thomson (Baron Sydenham after 1840) selected his staff for the Executive Council from among the politicians who led the Assembly. To be sure, Sydenham set policy, disposed of the patronage, and did what he could to manage the legislature. But since there were no true parties in the sense of disciplined organizations of politicians dividing over policies as well as over spoils, and since he did not push policies repugnant to the majority of the members, Governor Sydenham did, in fact, head a responsible government in everything but its inadmissable sense. In other words, after 1839 British North America enjoyed administrations "responsive, if not responsible, to popular control."

After Sydenham was killed by a fall from his horse in the autumn of 1841, he was succeeded by a governor who appreciated even more frankly that popularity with the legislature was a prerequisite for ministerial office. Although the governor, Sir Charles Bagot, supervised the dispensation of patronage and reviewed legislation, actual leadership fell to colonists who commanded the confidence of the House. Thus, Bagot was governor but Francis Hincks, Louis LaFontaine, and Robert Baldwin were the government's leaders. Although responsible government was still not conceded in principle — a defect Hincks, LaFontaine, and Baldwin all regretted — still, in 1843 Bagot informed the Colonial Secretary that "whether the doctrine of responsible government is openly acknowledged, or is only tacitly acquiesced in, virtually it exists."

Such an admission was too frank for Lord Stanley, the new Colonial Secretary. Although expediency seemed to dictate good will between a governor and a local legislature, the strength of empire still called for official rejection of the doctrine by Lord Stanley. So when Bagot resigned in 1843 (to retire and subsequently succumb to terminal illness), Stanley chose a successor to hold the line where it was meant to be held. Stanley's choice was Sir Charles Metcalfe, a hardened veteran of thirty-seven years of military service in India and most recently the governor of Jamaica.

Predictably there was trouble between Metcalfe and the reform leaders almost from the moment of the governor's arrival. Since they controlled the majority, they wanted control of the patronage, to set policy, and to operate independently of the governor's interference. But this was responsible government in its inadmissable sense. Metcalfe therefore refused the reformers' demands, dissolved the House, and in 1844 he plunged the province into an election very much like that of 1836 when Sir Francis Bond Head also campaigned for a cooperative majority. As earlier, the governor's supporters outshouted his opponents, and Metcalfe subsequently filled the council with more compliant ministers. This might have led to trouble as serious as anything in 1837; but developments in Britain were leading to revisions in the old theory of empire.

In 1846 the British government repealed the most important of the mercantilist statutes — the old pillars of the old empire. The Parliament of Great Britain embraced free trade, and thus, in effect, the British declared the whole world their own, since the areas that were officially colonies were no longer the only suppliers of raw materials and buyers of manufactured goods. From an economic standpoint, there was no longer any sense in which responsible government was inadmissable.

In the new government which took office in 1846, Lord Grey, the Earl of Durham's brother-in-law, became Colonial Secretary; at the same time, Lord Elgin, Durham's son-in-law, became Governor General of Canada. Dispatches made it plain that as soon as circumstances permitted, responsible government was to be established. Early in 1848 full responsible government came into effect first in Nova Scotia and two months later in Canada. When the Nova Scotia legislature met in January it became clear that the recent election the opposition forces had defeated the incumbent majority and the old government leader, James W. Johnston. Within a few days, Johnston submitted his government to a vote of confidence, and when he lost, he resigned. The governor then invited the new majority to form a government in which Joseph Howe was prominent. Soon similar proceedings unfolded in Canada as well. After a January election it became clear that the incumbent government could not win a vote of confidence (the Reformers defeated it 54-20), the Executive Council resigned, and Elgin called upon the Reform majority, led by Robert Baldwin and Louis LaFontaine, to form the new council, dispense the patronage, and set policy. Thus, responsible government arrived in Canada in March of 1848.

The principle of responsible government was conceded in 1848 but it was years before the reality of the autonomy that was admitted in principle became fully established in practice. It was one matter for the British to hand over the patronage and the right to set policy. It was another for Great Britain to accept powerlessness in the face of statutes "repugnant to the laws of England." Here was the real test of autonomy versus colonial status.

In 1849 the Parliament of the United Province of Canada first tested its autonomy by passing a controversial statute to compensate those who had suffered losses in the Lower Canadian rebellions of 1837 and 1838. The controversy was that many of the people to receive compensation were in fact former rebels, and the opposition regarded the bill as a subsidy to treason. Elgin shared their displeasure with the bill. The question was whether he would disallow its passage. He signed.

Of course, the Rebellion Losses Bill was primarily of local significance. It did not directly contradict any established policy or statute of Great Britain. Responsible government was not fully tested until a provincial ministry chose to pursue a course directly contrary to that of the mother country. The second precedent was set in 1859 when the government of the United Province of Canada imposed a 20 percent duty upon imports to generate revenue for public works projects. English industrialists pointed out that such a measure also served to encourage the development of Canadian manufacturing at the expense of the British and they petitioned the Colonial Office to disallow the Canadian tariff on grounds that the law was directly contrary to Parliament's policy of free trade. The Colonial Secretary obliged the manufacturers by informing the colonial ministry of their grave concern and dangled the threat of disallowance should Canada not change her policy voluntarily. Politely, yet forthrightly, the ministry reminded the British that Canada was in certain respects independent: "Self-government would be utterly annihilated," they said,

> if the views of the imperial government were to be preferred to those of the people of Canada. It is therefore the duty of the present government distinctly to affirm the rights of the Canadian legislature to adjust taxation of the people in the way they deem best, even if it should unfortunately happen to meet the disapproval of the imperial ministry. (Quoted in W.P.M. Kennedy, *The Constitution of Canada* 1922 , p. 275.)

The Colonial Office backed down.

## V    The Significance of Responsible Government

The establishment of Canadian autonomy without repudiating the imperial connection was an achievement that inevitably bulked large in histories of Canada, sometimes in terms more mythical than real. In this respect, the story is usually related as a struggle for reform, a long fight but one that ended happily without war because the rebellions were digressions from which cool heads turned away, ultimately to be rewarded for their greater patience later. Certainly, there were groups in British North America who actively pursued reform objectives over a period of many years. It must be added, however, that the impetus for change was metropolitan as well as indigenous. Great Britain grew out of mercantilism at the same time that the pressure for greater independence reached critical proportions in the colonies. Thus, the colonists were able to gain their fuller autonomy without severing the imperial tie.

A second misapprehension about responsible government is that it was a change that necessarily brought government closer to the people by giving their elected representatives control over the executive. To be sure, the old base of oligarchy was broadened but in another sense the legislative process was removed even further from the people because the need to join independent members of legislative assemblies into effective voting blocks required discipline that transformed legislators into party members from constituency delegates. After the 1840s, stubbornly independent members — those who strove to serve constituencies above party — would be regarded by the others somewhat contemptuously as "loose fish". Elgin succinctly observed as much when he referred to responsible government as a procedure rather than a principle, "not a measure but a method". He meant that the majority grouping in the legislature had to act cohesively to retain its grip on power. Between elections, the only check on the majority was the opposition, and as events were to show this was usually but a feeble check indeed.

The major real significance of the achievement of responsible government may have been in the political culture it excluded than in the victory for democracy or quiet diplomacy it was supposed to signify. Here, the emphasis is upon the clear preference for British over American models that the innovation implied. Under the American form of "republican" government, "the government which governs best governs least." But the traditions of the colonists and *canadiens* that made British "responsible" government acceptable, allowed for much more vigorous adminstration than the checked and balanced republican constitution of the United States. In that country, legislative and executive branches were kept separate as insurance against tyranny. In the Maritime and Canadian versions of the British constitution, by contrast, power was concentrated in the Legislative Assembly. In British North America, wherever responsible government existed, the provincial ministers were free to confront the needs of their developing communities quickly and vigorously, unimpeded by competition between executive and legislative branches once the vice regal governors had lost their constitutional basis for interference. After 1850, the legislatures of British North America were free to plot their own courses just as forthrightly or evasively as they chose.

# Bibliography

Since the Canadian Centenary Series approaches early Canadian history regionally (and with diverse terminal points chronologically), readers who seek a more detailed treatment of the subject of the Durham mission, the union of the Canadas, and the subsequent achievement of responsible government must consult four different volumes. Fernand Ouellet, *Lower Canada, 1791-1840* (1980) and Gerald Craig, *Upper Canada, 1784-1841* (1963) cover the aftermath of the rebellions and events leading to union. W.S. McNutt, *The Atlantic Provinces, 1712-1857* (1965) and J.M.S. Careless, *The Union of the Canadas, 1841-1857* (1967) describe the concession of responsible government.

More detailed accounts of the Durham mission and the controversial report are found in Chester New, *Lord Durham: A Biography of John George Lambton, First Earl of Durham* (1929) and G.M. Craig, ed., *Lord Durham's Report: An Abridgement with Introduction* (1963). New's biography, although somewhat dated in interpretation, is still regarded as the definitive study of Durham's public career. The concluding pages of Peter Burroughs, *The Canadian Crisis and British Colonial Policy* (1972) are useful for a brief but lucid interpretation of Durham's "cultural chauvinism". A more detailed analysis of the impact of the same subject on French-speaking Canada is found in Jacques Monet, *The Last Canon Shot: A Study of French Canadian Nationalism, 1837-1850* (1969) and W. Ormsby, "Lord Durham and the Assimilation of French Canada" in N. Penlington, ed., *On Canada: Essays in Honour of Frank H. Underhill* (1971).

For the imperialism of Britain's move to free trade (and its implications for the concession of home rule to British North America) readers should consult the debate reflected in the essays introduced skillfully by A.G.L. Shaw, ed., *Great Britain and the Colonies, 1815-1865* (1970). Responsible government in its more domestic implications is surveyed provocatively by Graeme Patterson in "Whiggery, Nationality, and the Upper Canadian Reform Tradition," CHR (1975) and "An Enduring Canadian Myth: Responsible Government and the Family Compact," JCS (1977). Also relevant is the first part of *Canada Views the United States: Nineteenth Century Political Attitudes* (1967) edited by S.F. Wise and R.C. Brown. The link between ministerial responsibility and party discipline is traced by P.G. Cornell, *The Alignment of Political Groups in Canada, 1841-1867* (1962).

". . . every cove and inlet with a suitable upstream
stock of timber began to produce sailing vessels . . ."

# CHAPTER 10

# *The Price of Autonomy*

I     Transportation, Tariffs, and Visions of Imperial Grandeur

More relevant to businessmen than constitutional changes in the 1840s were the economic transformations. At first businessmen were optimistic about the profits inherent in the union of the Canadas after 1841. Canadian businessmen — especially the mercantile clique in Montreal — were among those who were more pleased than chagrined over the terms of union. In fact they had been active promoters of the idea since 1822, the year a bill to unify the two Canadas had almost passed the British House of Commons. Then, as later, the attraction was economic.

At the time of the Union's proclamation, it was disclosed that a loan of £1.5 million had been guaranteed by Britain to assist in paying off the public debt of the United Province, thus making new, additional projects possible. On this basis, it seemed that the transportation improvements Montreal businessmen had desired since the 1790s were at hand.

There was some question, however, whether the time had already passed for Canadian canals. The Americans' Erie Canal, in operation since 1825, served roughly the same hinterland as those proposed for the St. Lawrence, and New York had already surpassed Boston, Philadelphia, and New Orleans as the commercial center of the United States. The gamble was whether Montreal, with a better waterway in the improved St. Lawrence, and trading advantages in the British imperial preference, might still catch up and so establish the Canadian city as the entrepot for North America. This had always been the rationale for the visions of commercial empire in Montreal; in 1841 it finally seemed to have some chance of realization.

By 1841 there were still major obstacles to overcome in the river because insufficient progress had been made toward developing its transportation potential earlier. At this late date only one canal was operational on the St. Lawrence itself. The Lachine Canal gave access to the Ottawa˙ River (see map 10.1) but left the rest of the "aorta of the north" unnavigable beyond. The five cataracts of the Long Sault were still impassable, and the only water-connection with lake Ontario was the roundabout route to Kingston, built by the British for strategic reasons after the War of 1812.

In the 1820s the British government had responded to the strident demands for internal improvements by agreeing to build a canal at their expense, but nowhere on the St. Lawrence (too near the American border). The canal recommended by British military engineers would link Montreal with Lake Ontario by connecting the rivers and lakes between Kingston and Ottawa (originally named Bytown). When the 47 stone locks of the Rideau Canal were completed in 1832, schooners and steamers wishing to haul freight between Montreal and the Upper Lakes could do so, but only by sailing from Montreal to Bytown then slowly down to Kingston. Bulky cargoes could not bear the cost of transportation. Consequently, the Welland Canal around Niagara Falls, finished in 1829 with support from the province of Upper Canada (having been started privately by William Hamilton Merritt), connected Lake Ontario with Lake Erie and gave better access to the Americans' canal at Buffalo. Thus, the Welland served New York more than Montreal.

After the union, the merchants of Montreal looked forward to a change. St. Lawrence canals with locks one hundred feet long and nine feet deep (and the Welland Canal improved to the same standard) would give the Canadian metropolis a water transportation system at least 30 percent better than New York's. In 1848 it would cost fifteen dollars to move a ton of cargo to New York City from Lake Ontario, but over the first St. Lawrence seaway the cost would amount to a mere ten dollars.

Even though shipping costs from New York to Europe were lower than from Montreal, the merchants counted on imperial preference, the pattern of tariffs that defined the old colonial system as an economic trading community with preferred status for participating members. After the Americans' secession from the empire they were excluded entirely. Later, after 1815, they gained but limited entry while British North Americans enjoyed a distinct preference culminating in 1843. By the last of the mercantilist measures ("corn laws" when they applied to grain), Canadians gained their most privileged position ever. The Canada Corn Act of 1843 imposed a five shilling per bushel tariff on all grain imported to Britain from foreign places such as the United States. The duty on Canadian wheat was only three shillings. Moreover, American wheat milled into flour in Canada

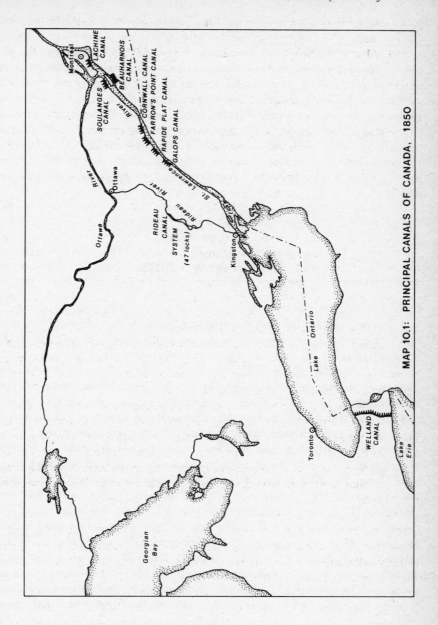

MAP 10.1: PRINCIPAL CANALS OF CANADA, 1850

could enter Great Britain as Canadian. To the business class of Montreal the last aspect of the arrangement was ideal. Since the seaway improvements were underway and expected to be fully completed before the end of the decade, Canadian businessmen cheerfully predicted that "We are destined to become a wealthy and powerful country at no remote period."

Then the bubble burst. The set of changes that gave victory to political reformers dashed the hopes for commercial empire. Down came the Corn Laws and other Navigation Acts (including the protection of colonial timber). With the repudiation of the old basis for empire, the colonies of British North America were free to exercise full powers of self-government, but they were also left more alone. Especially so were the business class.

## II   A New Strategy

In 1846, Montreal businessmen's vision of empire tumbled and the problem was worse than losing their privileged market and having to adjust to world competition, for the merchants found themselves facing the further humiliation of witnessing their oldest competitors seeming to thrive on the change. As Britain moved to free trade, the United States adjusted to take maximum advantage of the temporarily buoyant British market. They removed their duty on Canadian wheat for re-export and the grain dealers of Canada West rushed to take advantage of the lower freight rates from New York. Canadian merchants despaired: "The glory is departed."

Canadians had been mistaken in placing such blind faith in imperial preference. First, they were wrong to assume that a tariff in Great Britain could have the effect of funneling the produce of a continent to one warehousing point for transhipment to the world at large. Secondly, with respect to the limited market in which the colonists were protected, Canadians were mistaken in assuming that British consumers would tolerate artificially expensive bread and wood indefinitely for the sake of business interests overseas. To Canadians, though, imperial preference was only a small favor a grateful mother country extended in return for the continued loyalty of the colonists. To Britons, on the other hand, preference was a subsidy that enriched shippers and merchants and the reason why bread and wood cost more than they should. The Anti-Corn Law League, led by Richard Cobden, was more concerned with the price of bread than empire. Mercantilism was Goliath. Cobden was David. When free trade slew the tariffs, virtue triumphed.

Traders dependent upon protection had to adapt or go under. Apparently, few businessmen in Montreal turned to commercial alternatives quickly enough because Lord Elgin estimated that at least half of the trading firms of Montreal went bankrupt in the recession that began after 1846. Of course the general move to free trade affected lumbermen and timber merchants as well as grain dealers. But the British firms in Quebec and Saint John could return to Liverpool or Glasgow; the Montreal forwarders had no other home to which they might retire. Thus, they became a singularly desperate group by 1849. In that year, the price of flour was half what it had been five years earlier, and oats were selling for one third of their 1847 value.

As the worst seemed continually to worsen the business community sought relief in panaceas. The first was free trade with the United States. But since northeastern manufacturing interests feared that Canada's close relations with Great Britain might lead to merchants dumping cheap British manufactured goods in the American West via the Great Lakes, New England businessmen were opposed to any such arrangement. Nevertheless, a free trade bill did pass the House of Representatives before it was killed in the Senate in 1848. Governor Elgin despaired: "the conviction that they would be better off if annexed is almost universal among the commercial classes at present."

Indeed, many traders did actively push for political union with the United States as their next best salvation. In part, annexationism also resulted from political frustration. In April 1849 the Parliament of the United Province of Canada seemed to repudiate loyalty to Britain even more thoroughly than the British had dissolved their colonial preference. In 1849 the Canadian Parliament passed the bill appropriating £100 000 to indemnify sufferers in the rebellions (described in the previous chapter for its significance in Canada's constitutional evolution). Since the recipients of the appropriation included some of the most notorious rebels, Loyalists went on a rampage. They set fire to the Parliament building, and destroyed the homes of the most prominent members of the government. The Thistle Curling Club went so far as to strike the Governor, Lord Elgin, from its roll of honorary members because the hapless representative of the now limited royal prerogative had given royal assent to this most unroyal measure.

The violence lasted several days and the returning quiet did not bring back the rioters' loyalty. Many felt that if Great Britain were no longer interested in preferring them they might as well follow their economic self-interest into the United States. Thus, an annexation movement developed over the summer of 1849.

On October 11 "An Address to the People of Canada" appeared in the streets of Montreal as the manifesto of the annexationists. The document was short and surprisingly matter-of-fact given the extremity of its purposes. "The reversal of the ancient policy of Great Britain, whereby she withdrew from the Colonies their wonted protection in her markets" was identified as the cause of the crisis which "has produced the most disastrous effects upon Canada. In surveying the actual condition of the country, what but ruin or rapid decay meets the eye?" The evidence was impressive:

> Our Provincial Government and Civic Corporations, embarrassed; our banking and other securities greatly depreciated; our mercantile and agricultural interests alike unprosperous; real estate scarcely saleable upon any terms; our unrivalled rivers, lakes and canals almost unused; whilst commerce abandons our shores, the circulating capital amassed under a more favourable system is dissipated, with none from any quarter to replace it. (Reprinted in A.G. Doughty, ed., *The Elgin-Grey Papers, vol. 4* [1937], p. 1488.)

The "Address" posed six alternatives for Canadians to extricate themselves from such a dreadful situation. The first was "revival of protection in the markets of the United Kingdom." But the restoration of mercantilism was ruled out on grounds that the British would eventually stray back to free trade and "cheap food; and a second change from protection to free trade would complete that ruin which the first has done much to achieve." The second alternative was a Canadian tariff to "encourage the growth of a manufacturing interest in Canada." But the stated drawback to this policy was doubt that anybody outside Canada would buy such goods and "from want of consumers, manufactures could not survive on the home market alone." A commercial union of the "British American provinces" was the third proposal but the people in the "sister provinces" were said to have the same surpluses as the Canadians so this would only enlarge the scene of the suffering. On this account, a wider union was "no remedy." Nor was "the independence of the British North American colonies as a Federal Republic." This fourth alternative, with all that it entailed in the "acquirement of a name and character among the nations, would, we fear, prove an overmatch for the strength of the new republic." Apparently, since the creation would be entirely artificial, the entity would be no more than a non-nation and no such association could last for long on the basis of mere pretence. "Reciprocal free trade with the United States" was therefore attractive. But this had been proposed already and was rejected by the Americans. Thus, only one alternative was left. "This remedy consists of a friendly and peaceful separation from the British connection and a union upon equitable terms with the North American Confederacy of Sovereign states."

Then followed a long list of supposed benefits to the citizens of the State of Canada. First, "union would render Canada a field for American capital, into which it would enter as freely ... as into any of the present states." Annexationists predicted that real estate values would rise, "prob-

ably doubling at once the entire present value of property in Canada ...."
The St. Lawrence would be alive with commercial shipping once again.
And manufacturers would arise in "Lower Canada especially, where
water power and labour are abundant and cheap." Above all, the production of raw materials would increase "enhanced by free access to the
American market." On it rolled, the long list of economic benefits that
were supposed to follow from annexation.

Not one principle, not one moral intention was cited. Annexation arose
from material self-interest pure and simple. Equally striking was the utter
lack of self-confidence that the "Address" betrayed. The whole document
(usually cited as the *Annexation Manifesto* of 1849) was set in a tone of frank
acceptance of failure: the mother country had failed her colonies, thus, the
empire of the St. Lawrence had failed in its bid for commercial grandeur;
without a substitute for Britain, the proponents of annexation believed
their province could not succeed independently either. They were not
only saying that British North America consisted of colonies that had not
grown up; their stated conviction was that geography, climate, and a small
population precluded any national possibility in the future. Canada had
always been a dependency. The choice for the future was dependence
elsewhere or die.

The pessimism of the *Annexation Manifesto* was thus remarkable; but it
was also remarkable how prevalent the mood seems to have been among
the city's business population. The day the document appeared, almost
400 people signified their agreement by signing their names to the accompanying petition. By October 18, one week after the "Address" made its
first appearance, another 600 names were attached. The first 1000 signers
included many of the financial and political leaders of Montreal: John and
William Molson (the brewers), D.L. Macpherson (a future Lieutenant-Gov-
ernor of Ontario), and numerous other people even more prominent later
(such as J.J.C. Abbott, the Prime Minister of Canada in 1891-92).

As an Annexation Association took form, a plan emerged to establish
local committees beyond the city and build up strength with the electorate
to take control of the Assembly in the next election. Then, since it was
constitutionally permissable given responsible government, an annex-
ationist government would set policy on a course for union with the
United States.

It soon became evident, however, that the French-speaking population
of Canada East was distinctly cool to the scheme. (To the defenders of
cultural nationalism, that which was endangered by the present union
would be placed in even greater jeopardy following submergence in the
wider association of Yankee Protestants to the south). Similarly, in Canada
West, plain farmers were turned away from the scheme by such spokesmen as Robert Baldwin who appealed to their British loyalty and sense of
gratitude, saying "The mother country has now ... been leaving to us

powers of self-government, more ample than ever we asked ... ." On this account, Baldwin thought it "a most impious return to select such a time for asking for a separation." Here the cause foundered. The businessmen-annexationists were nearly alone.

## III    Unexpected Prosperity

At its peak, the annexation movement probably did not attract more than 2000 active adherents. Yet the discontent and uncertainty that gave rise to such defeatism was not limited to one colony nor was economic disappointment the only source of gloom. The immigration of the day was also distressing since the last great inflow of newcomers by timber ship arrived just as economic prospects dimmed, and the immigrants who landed then were the most destitute yet seen. They were refugees from the Irish potato famine of 1845-48. More than 60 000 people, "penniless and in rags," appeared in one year at Quebec, the major port of entry, and nearly one third perished soon after their arrival.

The diseases which killed the immigrants spread to the colonists as well, of course. In 1847 there were epidemics of typhoid fever from Saint John to Toronto and perhaps as many as 16 000 people died. In 1849 cholera again caused thousands of deaths. Many responded to the crisis with compassion and useful service; as Lord Elgin himself reported, "Nothing can exceed the devotion of the nuns and Roman Catholic priests and the conduct of the clergy and many of the laity of other denominations has been most exemplary." But far more responded with the baser reflexes of prejudice and panic. To discourage immigration, a head tax, a kind of entry fee, came into effect. And to prevent the spread of disease, stricter quarantine was imposed which meant prolonging the agony of immigrants in "foetid infections". Confinement of the apparently well with the obviously dying meant that newcomers could not spread infection among the established colonists who considered their own lives more important than the immigrants. Yet it also reflected virulent prejudice. Thus, Elgin reported that the prospective employers of immigrants in Canada West were "unwilling to hire even the healthy immigrants" after their quarantine period had passed. Unable to find work in British North America, many moved on to try their luck elsewhere — chiefly in the United States.

The recent immigrants were not alone in deserting British North America. United States immigration figures for the period are incomplete, but if the numbers in the records that do survive are taken as a sample, rather than as a complete enumeration, it is possible to suggest trends over time.

On this basis, it appears that twice as many residents of British North America emigrated to the United States in 1846 (the year the abandonment of British protection began) as in 1843 (the heyday of mercantilism, given the Canada Corn Act and the relatively unimpaired continuation of the protective tariff on timber). After the shift to free trade, however, the sharp increase for 1846 continued through the 1850s. In 1849 emigration to the United States was three times that of 1843. And in 1850 the tendency peaked with about five times the number leaving British North America then as in 1843. But later in the 1850s, the outmigration began to dwindle, falling dramatically in 1861, the year the War Between the States erupted. Then emigration fell back to the 1843 level. Thus, while some colonists registered their panic about lost protection by launching an annexation movement, many more expressed similar pessimism by abandoning their homeland altogether. Ironically, the developments that lured colonists south (the California gold rush of 1849, for example), had a beneficial impact on economic conditions in the colonies left behind.

Economic conditions began to improve after 1850 with an unexpected yet welcomed rise in the world price of the prime staples — grain and wood. A wonderful psychological boost was also won with the achievement of a substitute for imperial preference. At the height of the crisis over Britain's transition to free trade, William Hamilton Merritt (the Canadian entrepreneur of Welland Canal fame) persuaded New Brunswick to initiate the calling of an intercolonial conference at Halifax. What followed in 1849 was the first meeting between Canadian leaders and representatives of the Atlantic region to exchange views on matters of mutual concern. They discussed trade, of course, and more particularly what they might offer as enticement to the United States to win a reciprocity agreement which had been impossible to achieve by Canada alone. It was agreed that their best bargaining counter for free admission of Canadian staples would be unlimited access of the Americans to the inshore fisheries of New Brunswick, Nova Scotia, and Prince Edward Island. Although Nova Scotia was unenthusiastic and Newfoundland initially refused to discuss the proposal at all (St. John's merchants felt they had everything to lose and absolutely nothing to gain from any free trade deal with the Yankees), nevertheless, reciprocity, basically on the terms of the Halifax conference, was in fact secured in 1854 by the Governor General, Lord Elgin. The British agreed to share the inshore fisheries. The Americans conceded free entry of natural products including Newfoundland fish, Nova Scotia coal, New Brunswick lumber, and Canadian flour. Such access to a market of 34 million people appeared to amplify an already encouraging high-level of prosperity. The arrangement was not quite imperial preference, but to colonists who yearned for the supposed economic benefits of a mother country, the treaty was the comforting surrogate they desired.

The growth of trade with the United States did not depend on formal diplomatic sanctions, however. Reciprocity did not create American demand for Canadian staples, nor did it end a period of protectionist exclusion. The sale of fish, lumber, and grain was already expanding. But the new emphasis of the United States market, confirmed by reciprocity, induced significant structural changes in the economies of British North America because old commodities were sold in new forms. Prior dependence upon the British — a dependence encouraged by mercantilist protection — biased exports toward handhewn square timber rather than sawn lumber, and grain rather than flour. Prior to the late 1840s, the colonial economies had expanded along lines of primitive technology but they had shown remarkably little development in the sense of building more intricate industrial structures. After 1850 the growing trade with the closer neighbor encouraged development, though with different effects region by region.

In the Maritimes, the new volume of old staples in new forms stimulated both shipbuilding and lumber milling since the quantity of wood exported to the United States from British North America appears to have increased about 800 percent between 1850 and 1870 and most of this expansion was in sawn lumber. Figures for the sales of fish in the same market are not readily available but there is some reason to assume that the export of that commodity underwent similar increases in the same period because of the expansion of the fishing fleet on roughly the same scale as schooners engaged in the new coastal trade. The overall result was that every cove and inlet with a suitable upstream stock of timber began to produce sailing vessels, particularly schooners of approximately sixty tons burden. Here was industrialization, of a sort, that sustained a widely dispersed work force employed in farming and fishing when it was not assisting the local shipwrights. Perhaps for this reason, the linkages between boatbuilding and the wider economy have been extremely difficult to measure, but the resulting numbers of vessels and the pattern of continuing population dispersion (rather than urban concentration) are both unmistakeably clear (see map 10.2).

Unfortunately for the subsequent development of the Maritimes, the wooden schooner or square-rigged ship gradually replaced the imperial market as the invincible economic pivot. Just as the St. Lawrence merchants had once attributed omnipotence to their superior trading system, so later did the Maritime investors think that the superiority of their schooners and barques assured a future of unchanging profit. As the rest of the world was turning to iron ships and steam propulsion, Maritimers continued to invest their future in wooden sailing vessels. And when a Maritimer did go with the trend prevailing elsewhere he was soon drawn

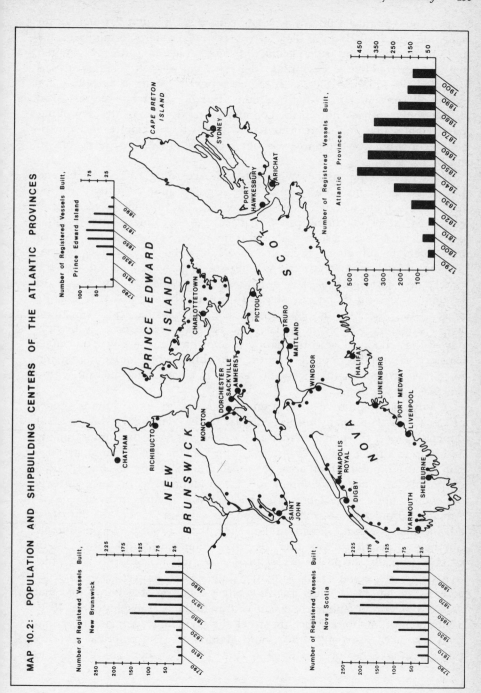

MAP 10.2: POPULATION AND SHIPBUILDING CENTERS OF THE ATLANTIC PROVINCES

away. Thus, Samuel Cunard, a Nova Scotian, set his first "steamship on schedule" in 1840. But in 1845 he moved the western terminus of his transatlantic operation from Halifax to Boston. A similar outcome emerged with another potential beginning, that of "coal oil" after kerosene was invented by Abraham Gesner in Nova Scotia to obtain a substitute for whale-oil lamp fuel from hydrocarbons. But he could not interest local businessmen to back him in the commercial production of the new luminant. Halifax investors were quite happy with whale-oil lamps and a maritime economy. Consequently, Gesner took his process to New York in 1853.

What other opportunities were missed? According to Eric Sager and Lewis Fischer, there were precious few. Arguing quite correctly that "the hypothesis that wooden ships were an unfortunate diversion of resources" depends upon proof that "better investment opportunities existed ... and that these better opportunities were rejected in favour of investment in shipping," their silence on the subject of suitable alternatives is offered as an argument that no suitable choices existed. But the undisputed fact remains that by the 1880s, wooden shipbuilding had become a sick and dying industry with nothing having arisen to take its place. Thus, the Atlantic region, especially New Brunswick, was caught with a single-industry economy later just as it had been earlier. In the heyday of the schooner, as in the happy time of timber, there was too much satisfaction with the 15 percent return from shipbuilding and shipping and too little recognition that wooden vessels involved a technology whose day was already done.

A remarkably different pattern emerged in the growth of the economy of Canada East, in many respects similar to the Maritimes given its prior dependence on the timber trade, and a new emphasis on lumber milling and shipbuilding after 1850. But in Lower Canada broader industrialization occurred in two urban areas, especially Montreal. By its concentration of population and development of a considerable work force entirely dependent upon wage labor, Canada East was unique in British North America. Ironically, a major reason for Lower Canada's industrial advancement was its agricultural decline that encouraged considerable numbers of people to seek alternate employment in Montreal and also in Quebec City. By the 1850s, a vast pool of seemingly superfluous population emerged as one of the province's greatest resources, noticeable as early as the late l840s. Thus, the *Annexation Manifesto* of 1849 asserted that "water power and labour are cheap" but regrettably unexploited. In 1856, a Montreal promotional brochure struck the same note again asserting that both resources were still "cheap and abundant". The potential laboring population was the special attraction, however: "Nowhere are there found people better adapted for factory hands, more intelligent, docile and giving less trouble to their employers, than in Lower Canada."

The result was enclave industrialization, meaning investment by foreigners to refine materials from abroad to be sold as manufactures in external markets. More than 25 such firms were established in Montreal in the 1850s. The largest, the Victoria Iron Works, employed 120 workers for wages that were the lowest in British North America. They made nails, enough for the entire Canadian market, using pig iron imported from Scotland and coal brought in from New York State. In the case of Canada East, therefore, the adjustment to the new environment of free trade led to concentration of population in what was emerging as Canada's largest industrial city and a proletarianization of labor that was equally singular.

In Canada West, by contrast, the development sequence more closely resembled that of the Maritimes in the sense that it was based on locally generated, organic growth, dispersed across many points of capital accumulation. But in the case of Upper Canada, the development was further and more striking because the region's staple was wheat, vastly more profitable than either fish or lumber. Each farming district had its own commercial center, with its own entrepreneurs profiting from the marketing of grain and investing in additional enterprise that was linked backed to

**Table 10.1** Early Urbanization of the Two Canadas, 1850s

1. Number of Towns

|  |  | Lower Canada | | Upper Canada | |
|---|---|---|---|---|---|
|  |  | 1850 | 1860 | 1850 | 1860 |
| Town Size: |  |  |  |  |  |
| I. | 1 000–5 000 | 14 | 18 | 33 | 50 |
| II. | 5 000–25 000 | 0 | 1 | 4 | 8 |
| III. | 25 000 + | 2 | 2 | 2 | 2 |
|  | TOTAL | 16 | 21 | 39 | 60 |

2. Urban-rural Population (thousands)

|  |  | Lower Canada | | Upper Canada | |
|---|---|---|---|---|---|
|  |  | 1850 | 1860 | 1850 | 1860 |
| Rural |  | 759 | 925 | 813 | 1 160 |
| Urban | I. | 31 | 39 | 67 | 108 |
|  | II. | — | 6 | 41 | 83 |
|  | III. | 100 | 141 | 31 | 45 |
|  | TOTAL | 890 | 1 112 | 952 | 1 396 |

SOURCE: Adapted from data in J. McCallum, *Unequal Beginnings* (Toronto, 1980), p. 55.

wheat production or forward to industrialization. But the investment in milling and implement works was relatively small-scale and dispersed through many different towns. Some places such as Toronto and Hamilton edged ahead of the others, but the remarkable phenomenon in Canada West (relative to Canada East) was the factor of dispersal and the smaller scale of industrial organization. There was nothing like the Victoria Iron Works even in Hamilton, the most heavily industrialized town of Upper Canada in the 1850s. Typically, the firms of Hamilton were small workshops employing less than ten workers rather than factories employing wage earners by the hundred, as was the case in a number of establishments in Montreal by 1860.

The different patterns of industrialization and urbanization are clearly evident in the data on the growth of towns in the two Canadas. While both saw only a two percent shift in the rural-urban balance in the 1850s, in Lower Canada migration was born of hard times and concentrated in two places, while in Upper Canada prosperity pushed villages ahead to the status of towns.

To John McCallum, the different pattern of urbanization is the evidence of the "organic, locally generated, industrial growth" based on profits from the wheat staple that gave Upper Canada an overall competitive edge. In the same decade as the wheat boom, however, the same region was also the chief recipient of investment from abroad for a new marvel in transportation, the railway.

## IV    The Railway Mania

In part, the railways were attractive because they could be made to run almost anywhere and in winter as well as in summer. They were also a faster means of transport than steamships or sailing vessels. For the farmer more than twenty miles from navigable water, or the merchant on a waterway who had to maintain a large inventory (owing to the impossibility of resupply after freeze up), a railway was highly attractive even as an alternative to other forms of land transportation. Thomas Keefer, a Canadian civil engineer, went further, however, in his estimation of their economic importance. Writing in 1849, he said they were "indispensible". Keefer asserted that "as a people we may as well in the present age attempt to live without books or newspapers, as without Railroads. A continuous Railway from tide water to Huron upon the north side of the St.

Lawrence, we *must* have, and as it will be the work of years we should lose no time in commencing it." By the late 1840s, however, the United Province of Canada had one of the finest systems of internal navigation in the world and it was employed at no more than 30 percent capacity. One measure of the optimism born of the unexpected prosperity of the 1850s was such writing as Keefer's — seriously asserting that the first St. Lawrence seaway needed to be paralleled by rail before Canada would have even the minimum transportation improvements. The railway mania affected Maritimers no less than Canadians. To the merchants of Halifax, for example, commercial empire seemed possible if they could but link their generally ice-free port overland by rail to the interior. Merchants of Saint John shared similar ambitions.

But railways were exciting for reasons that went far beyond their apparent economic benefits. Indeed, nearly all of the railway projects of the 1850s were undertaken despite financial failure initially. The waterways continued to carry most of the bulky cargo but receded in popular attention because the railway carried popular appeal. They seemed to abolish the cruelties of topography and climate that dealt British North America vast expanses of territory too rugged for agriculture and winters so severe that commerce slowed to a snail's pace from December through March. Overcoming the handicap of winter appears to have been the chief benefit from Keefer's point of view. "Old winter is once more upon us," he wrote, "our inland seas are 'dreary and inhospitable wastes' to the merchant and to the traveller; — our rivers are sealed fountains — and an embargo which no human power can remove is laid on our ports." With a railway to the "most neglected districts" there could be "the daily scream of the steam whistle" of a locomotive serving both as an "iron civilizer" and as a means of "escape". Keefer warned, "we can no longer afford to loiter away our winter months ... ."

Because the sense of urgency voiced by Thomas Keefer was shared by many others, the 1850s was a decade of vast beginnings in railway construction. In 1850, there was virtually nothing in commercial railway transport. By 1860, almost 2000 miles of track were put in operation (mainly in Canada West, see map 10.3). The first signficant line was launched and completed between 1850 and 1853. Once in service, the St. Lawrence and Atlantic Railway linked Montreal with Portland, Maine, giving Canada access to an ice-free but American port.

A rival to Canada's first railway was an intercolonial scheme. Rather than connecting Montreal with the United States, the proposed Intercolonial Railway would run through a much longer distance over virtually uninhabited territory ultimately to connect Canada's metropolis with Halifax. But the Intercolonial was stillborn late in the 1840s because too many

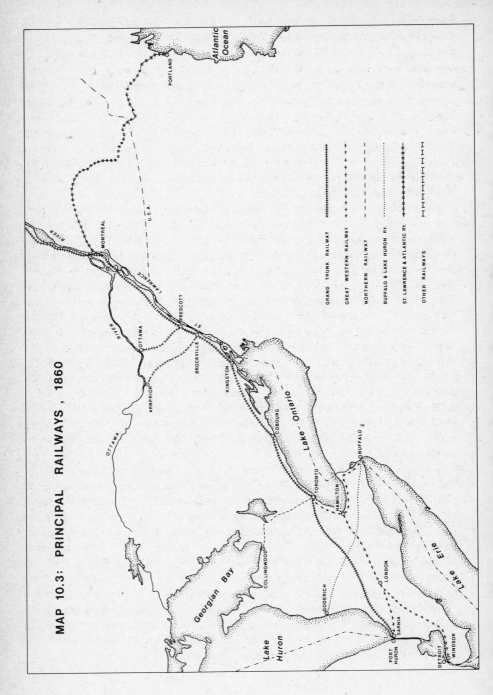

MAP 10.3: PRINCIPAL RAILWAYS, 1860

GRAND TRUNK RAILWAY
GREAT WESTERN RAILWAY
NORTHERN RAILWAY
BUFFALO & LAKE HURON RY.
ST. LAWRENCE & ATLANTIC RY.
OTHER RAILWAYS

difficulties were encountered in the interprovincial cooperation the scheme demanded. For this reason, the British championed the proposal in the new decade. But representatives from Nova Scotia, New Brunswick, and Canada meeting in London in 1851 were unable to agree on a route or the apportionment of costs. One of the Canadian representatives, Francis Hincks, returned from the conference hopeful that he might persuade his province to promote at least a trans-Canada line. Thus the Grand Trunk Railway was born in 1852. As originally chartered, the company was entirely private with an authorized capitalization of £9.5 million. Peto, Brassey, Jackson, and Betts were supposed to be the prime contractors in construction. Baring Brothers were to handle finance. Since both were reputable English firms, the railway was expected to succeed.

After seven years of feverish promotion and construction the Grand Trunk was indeed operational with more than one thousand miles of track laid by 1859. But the railway proved so unattractive to private investors, and generated so little revenue from its own operations, the Government of Canada emerged as the chief guarantor of the railway's solvency. In this way, the Grand Trunk failed as a business but since it worked the psychological magic required of a railway and paid some speculators handsomely, historians have tended to agree with J.M.S. Careless that, "Despite its costs in political scandals and bankrupt investors one could hardly imagine what the country would have been without the Grand Trunk." It was corrupt, it was extravagant, but it was thought to be indispensable. Most of all, the Grand Trunk Railway was typical of the others undertaken in the decade. It did not pay. The one solvent railway was the Great Western which ran from Hamilton to Detroit by 1855 and soon extended east as far as Toronto. The key to the Great Western's success appears to have been its route through heavily populated territory that was not already well served by water transport (three quarters of the Grand Trunk, by contrast, paralleled the waterway of the St. Lawrence). But all the railways, the colossal failures as well as the one success, had something in common: their building and their inauguration was the occasion of enormous enthusiasm. The railway boom and the optimism of their advertising thus joined British North America physically as no one had dreamed that it might be unified before. But this was a unity of proximity, not of national feeling because each autonomous colony was its own nation with its own sense of a separate past and little awareness of future cooperation with the others.

# Bibliography

The volumes in the Canadian Centenary Series that cover the period of the transition to conditions of free trade and economic growth in the 1850s are W.S. McNutt, *The Atlantic Provinces, 1712-1857* (1965) and J.M.S. Careless, *The Union of the Canadas, 1841-1857* (1967). Other general works with summaries of both themes are *Colonists and Canadiens* (1971) edited by J.M.S. Careless and *Canada: An Economic History* (1980) by W.L. Marr and D.G. Peterson.

More specialized accounts of the loss of the system of preferential tariffs and the consequences for British North America are the older but still readable works by G.N. Tucker, *The Canadian Commercial Revolution* (1936) and D.G. Creighton, *The Commercial Empire of the St. Lawrence, 1760-1850* (1937). C.D. Allin and G.M. Jones, *Annexation, Preferential Trade and Reciprocity* (1912) and D.F. Warner, *The Idea of Continental Union: Agitation for Annexation to the United States* (1960) are two lively accounts of the annexation movement of 1849. On reciprocity with the United States, D.C. Masters, *The Reciprocity Treaty of 1854* (1961) argues that it encouraged positive developments in Canadian-American trade. L.H. Officer and L.B. Smith, "The Canadian-American Reciprocity Treaty of 1855-1866," *Journal of Economic History* (1968) suggest that "where the trade effect was large, the impact on welfare was small."

Accounts of economic growth region by region include David Sutherland, "Halifax Merchants and the Pursuit of Development, 1783-1850," CHR (1978) and E.W. Sager and L.R. Fischer, "Atlantic Canada and the Age of Sail Revisited," CHR (1982) on the Maritimes. Sutherland describes merchants' aversion to landward enterprise. Sager and Fischer defend the emphasis that was placed on the building and sailing of wooden boats and ships. For the two Canadas, a most remarkable and brilliant synthesis is *Unequal Beginnings: Agriculture and Economic Development in Quebec and Ontario until 1870* (1980) by John McCallum, but D. McCalla, in "The Wheat Staple and Upper Canadian Development," CHR (1978) denies that the wheat boom generated as much capital as foreign investment.

A number of works on diverse themes in mid-nineteenth century Canadian social history add color and a human dimension to the economic history. H.V. Nelles, ed, *Philosophy of Railroads and Other Essays by T.C. Keefer* (1972) covers the railway mania. Judith Fingard describes voluntarism and public welfare in "The Relief of the Unemployed Poor in Saint John, Halifax, and St. John's, 1815-1860" *Acadiensis* (1975). Susan Houston suggests the middle class developed its enthusiasm for mass education at mid-century in "Politics, Schools, and Social Change in Upper Canada," CHR

(1972). Geoffrey Bilson describes the panic that developed over the spread of dread disease in *A Darkened House: Cholera in Nineteenth-Century Canada* (1980). And Michael Katz shows that the "two great themes of nine-teenth-century urban history ... are transiency and inequality" in "The People of a Canadian City: 1851-2," CHR (1972).

"... Maritimers agreed to have a meeting at which the
Canadians might attend."

# CHAPTER 11

# *Federal Union*

## I From Expected Assimilation to Quasi-Federalism in Canada

When the imperial authorities decided upon a union of the Canadas in 1840, they determined that harmony should prevail at almost any cost between the mother country and the colony, more specifically, between the governor and the Assembly. Lord John Russell, the Colonial Secretary at the time, had instructed the governor not to oppose the wishes of the local legislature except when "the honour of the Crown or the interests of the Empire were jeopardized." And this policy of harmony was continued by Russell's successor, Lord Stanley. Here was the imperial context for the emergence of "responsive" if not fully "responsible" government.

Ironically, the harmony principle was decisively important in the defeat of the program of planned assimilation that was the prime justification for the union in the first place. The two goals of harmony and assimilation proved irreconcilable primarily because of the equal representation that was accorded each section despite the fact that Canada West (Upper Canada) had but 450 000 population to Canada East's (Lower Canada's) 650 000 in 1841. The architects of union had thought that the "English" representatives from the upper half, together with those from the lower part, would be sufficient to "swamp the French". But the immediate result was dualism, rather than majoritarianism and the disappearance of French patterns in one common British mold.

The first governor, Charles Thomson (made Lord Sydenham in 1840 for his work in engineering the merger of the two Canadas) presided over not one but two systems for administering justice. Thus, there were two Attorneys General. The arrangement was considered a temporary expedient, essential for the moment because there were two systems of law then in use. Chaos would have resulted from an overly abrupt transition to one. Still, assimilation was expected, and in fact legal provision had been made to abolish French civil law — it only remained to be proclaimed by the governor.

But no assimilationist policies were implemented initially or later. After Sydenham's untimely death in the second year of his administration, his successor, Sir Charles Bagot (the official noted previously for his failure to hold the line against responsible government in its inadmissable sense), failed to advance the course of assimilation either. Within weeks of his assumption of office in 1842, Bagot recognized a need for dual administration of the different systems of instruction. Thus, he created two superintendents of education. At the same time, additional French-Canadian members of the legislature were promoted to the provincial executive. Simultaneously, Bagot realized that the developing dualism implied federalism rather than fusion and he informed the Colonial Secretary that assimilation was no more feasible than refusing responsible government. Lord Stanley was not pleased — on either account.

But Charles Metcalfe, Bagot's successor and the governor chosen to turn around the drift toward responsible government in 1843, emphatically agreed with Bagot that assimilation was entirely incompatible with a policy of harmony. "If the French Canadians are to be ruled to their satisfaction," he said, "every attempt to metamorphose them systematically into English must be abandoned ... ." As a case in point, Metcalfe cited the discrimination against the French language that was a part of the Act of Union itself. The clause in question stipulated that French could be used in debate, but not in record. Such a denial of official status was a cause for considerable resentment, Metcalfe reported, because it was perceived as a brutal attempt "to destroy their nationality and anglify them by Force." If such a rudimentary step by the imperial government toward assimilation were met by this hostility, Metcalfe reasoned, the attempt by one half of the province overtly to change the culture of the other would excite much greater "bad feeling" and "be made use of by designing Men for that purpose." Given Metcalfe's conservative inclinations, further concessions to the fact of dualism looked wiser than radical steps toward assimilation: "The course which I would recommend would be to leave the French Race no pretext for complaint ... ." Such appeasement meant recognizing official use of French and "equal" promotion of representatives from both sections to the Executive Council. Equality at the executive level became even more apparent after the attainment of responsible government. Then, and later, the ministries went by double, rather than single prime ministerial names (the first, for instance, was the LaFontaine-Baldwin government) and the precedent stuck. This was dualism at its starkest, revealing the full quasi-federal basis for the union. Ironically, in less than a decade from launching the "experiment" to assimilate the French by wedding them with a "normal" province, federalism rather than anglification had resulted. Metcalfe was the first to recognize and to accept the fact. Eventually even Stanley (who had instructed Metcalfe to resist and "play the game which we recommended to Sir Charles Bagot") realized that nothing else was consistent with Russell's policy of harmony. Thus, nobody chose federalism in this, its earliest stage. But the alternative was brutal repression, perhaps even civil war.


## II    From Quasi-Federalism to Legislative Deadlock in Canada

The Colonial Office hoped for harmony between governors and colonial legislators but the Canadian Members of Parliament had no such hopes concerning relations among themselves. Primarily, conflict arose from allegations that one section of the province interfered with the internal affairs of the other. From 1844 to 1846, for example, Louis LaFontaine complained that there were no fewer than seventeen votes on matters pertaining exclusively to Lower Canada (such items as elections in Montreal, schools, Jesuits' estates) and on each such matter the issue was decided by a majority consisting chiefly of members representing Upper Canada. Later, in the 1850s, the tendency moved in the other direction and Upper Canadian members began to complain of French domination. By then the balance of population had shifted to Canada West and an increasing number of politicians began to complain that equal representation was no longer satisfactory. Conflict intensified, ultimately reaching political stalemate.

The beginning of the processes that led to deadlock could be dated with the appearance of a census of 1851 that disclosed that the population of the two sections, in round numbers, was 890 000 to 952 000, with Upper Canada being the more heavily populated section. Once the disparity of equal representation pinched an English-speaking majority, it was they who began to resent others imposing their will from outside.

Public support for church-run schools was the particularly controversial issue. In 1850, Canada East appeared to have meddled in the affairs of Canada West when a School Act of that year increased state aid to Roman Catholic schools in Upper Canada. The Irish, who wanted the arrangement, were delighted at the assistance they had received from their Catholic allies in Lower Canada. But the Protestants of Canada West were furious and their outrage was expressed most eloquently in the pages of the Toronto *Globe*, the paper of George Brown, a Scottish-born Presbyterian who was especially skilled in formulating denunciations of the "entering wedge" of "priestly encroachment". Brown asserted that "We can never have peace in Canada until the principle is acknowledged that every church must stand on its own foundation without aid from government or legislature." In this way, Brown revived the old controversy over religious voluntarism, the idea that the state is completely secular and without any ties to religion, all churches being strictly voluntary associations supported exclusively by the cash contributions of their consenting members.

In the mid-1850s, however, following Brown's election to the Provincial Parliament on his cry of "no sectarian schools", he and his fellow "voluntaryists" moved for legislative reapportionment demanding representation on the basis of population rather than equality. Since it was well known that there were more people in Canada West, "rep by pop" emerged as the rallying point for Protestants and a new line for political division between themselves and the old-fashioned "reformers".

After 1848 the old division between "Tories" and "Reformers" had become practically meaningless because the reforms of the Reformers were achieved and their spirit was spent. Nothing divided them from the old Tories after the concession of responsible government except their historical animosities and these were soon forgotten in the face of the new, more bitter ethnic and religious conflicts in the 1850s. Consequently, the old Reformers and Tories joined in common cause against their new enemies. In 1854, Augustin-Norbert Morin (one-time republican and author of the *Ninety-Two Resolutions)* joined with Sir Allan MacNab (one-time member of the old oligarchy of Upper Canada) as joint premiers to head off dogmatics of every hue. With MacNab declaring "My politics now are railways," the Canadian "Liberal-Conservatives", an all-embracing center party, was born.

The MacNab-Morin alliance was not followed immediately by a united radical opposition, however. Basically, there were three such parties that would have to join. In addition to Brown's Voluntaryists there was an Upper Canadian republican party known as the "Clear Grits" for their uncompromising advocacy of full-blown democracy (reforms such as universal manhood suffrage, voting by ballot, and elections of new parliaments automatically every two years). The third group pursued similar objectives but in a narrowly French-Canadian context which meant that their democracy was as anti-British and anti-Protestant as it was anti-oligarchy. They were known as the *Parti Rouge*. Clearly, pragmatism could lead Brown to work with the Grits, even though he had originally denounced them as "bunkum talking cormorants" but nothing except the near total repudiation of his ultra-Protestant voluntaryism could induce him to work with the *Rouges*. Thus, Brown emerged as the grittiest champion of reform in Upper Canada. But in Canada East, the reform party led by A.A. Dorion remained distinctly separate from the western reform impulse gaining momentum in Upper Canada through the 1850s.

The division that united conservatives in both sections and left reformers fighting one another was harmless as long as reform itself continued to be relatively unpopular. But if the Grits swept Canada West, and if some crisis of circumstances led to significant desertions from the conservative group in Lower Canada (known as the *Parti Bleu*), then complete legislative paralysis would follow. The results of the election of 1854 hinted that deadlock might be forthcoming. The results of 1857 repeated the message. After that of 1854, MacNab and Morin were able to manage a sadly divided parliament by deft compromises and skillful use of patronage and the Grand Trunk Railway. Junior members of the government who were included in such operations — young opportunists such as John A. Macdonald and George Cartier — learned that the safest path through the legislative thicket was day-to-day coalition-formation and thoughtful, short-term expedients. The Conservatives did have principles, but it became clear that they believed the key to governing Canada was a willingness to compromise anything, a little. In 1857, however, the election returned a House that was impossible to manage.

Economic crisis (a severe "panic" in international capitalism) and local scandals increased the stock of reformers in Canada West. In fact, the Grits beat the Conservatives and took more than half of the representation accorded Upper Canada. But in Canada East, the *Rouges* won less than 15 percent of the section's representation. Thus the Conservatives of the two sections together continued to hold an overall majority. But sectional jealousy soon proved stronger than the leaders of the two Conservative parties. Macnab and Morin had both recently retired, to be succeeded by Macdonald and Cartier who had to confront an issue so thorny they were temporarily defeated.

The problem was locating a new seat of government, having lost the old one in the rioting of 1849. Since the destruction of the old parliament buildings the legislature had been "perambulating" between Quebec City and Toronto, session by session. After years of inconclusive debate concerning a suitable permanent site, the matter had been submitted to royal arbitration and Queen Victoria indicated her preference in 1858, choosing Ottawa, in Canada West. *Rouge* members moved for flat rejection of the Queen's selection and *Bleus* bolted their coalition to support their compatriots. Thus, the Macdonald-Cartier government was defeated 64 votes to 50 and they resigned on July 29. But this was not the end of the episode.

When the Governor General invited George Brown to form a government in coalition with A.A. Dorion, Brown seized his opportunity and the impossible alliance between Grits and *Rouges* emerged as the Government of Canada on Monday morning, August 2, 1858. Several hours later, one of the members of the opposition moved no confidence in the ministry because everyone knew Brown and Dorion were irreconcilable enemies. The debate dragged on until after midnight; then in the first hour of

August 3, the Brown-Dorion government was defeated seventy-one votes to fifty. The Governor General might have granted Brown's subsequent request for a dissolution, but the province had just had an election. Instead, he called back Macdonald who reformed the old government, with one complication. Under the rules governing Parliament in the 1850s, a cabinet minister had to refrain from voting in the new House until going through the ceremony of resigning and gaining confirmation of his promotion in a by-election. But if a minister simply changed from one position to another, the rule did not apply. Consequently, when the old government reformed on August 6, all the old faces sat in new places and the next day everyone resumed the positions from which they had resigned previously. Because of the rule that permitted changes in cabinet without by-elections, Macdonald argued that each minister was a Member of Parliament with full voting rights. George Brown claimed otherwise and denounced the chicanery of what he called the "Double Shuffle". But Macdonald prevailed even through a lengthy court battle and thus proved that he was no novice politician. At the same time, he seemed to demonstrate that the best devices for keeping the United Province of Canada out of deadlock were legal tricks rather than normal politics. People of all political hues began to wonder how workable was a union that depended upon trickery for its continuation.

## III    Frustrated Visions of Expansion

Another impossibility for the existing union was territorial expansion. By 1857, the best of the agricultural land in Upper Canada was either settled or available only from speculators. There was little inviting soil in the remaining "wild" land. Thus, the farmers of the region found themselves against the Precambrian Shield, that mantle of rock, lakes, and bush, picturesque and rich in mineral reserves but useless for farming. George Brown reported that his countrymen were ready for "new worlds to conquer". Naturally they looked to the country west of Lake Superior, the British West. Especially did they gaze westward when gold was discovered on the Fraser River in 1856.

Prior to the 1850s, the whole western country received little notice from Upper Canada, and the Canadians were largely indifferent to the region's continuing in the hands of the Hudson's Bay Company as its fief and fur reserve. After the part of British Columbia the Americans called Oregon was lost to the United States (in 1846 because Americans were first in occupying the land as settlers), the HBC decided to stake a settlement outpost on Vancouver Island in order to secure what remained of the region. Because of Upper Canada's indifference at the time, the people the company recruited were a handful of farmer-settlers obtained directly from Britain. Soon, however, the gold rush of 1856 brought a flood of Americans to the area around the Fraser River across the Strait of Georgia from the little colony named Victoria. James Douglas, the Hudson's Bay Company Governor on Vancouver Island, proclaimed his authority over the prospectors and was subsequently supported in his action by the British government. In this way, the remainder of British Columbia narrowly missed absorption by the United States.

The same company in charge of the west coast also had authority over the western interior. Periodically, however, the firm had to defend its use of the territory. Such an occasion occurred in 1857 when the British held hearings in London on the possible agricultural potential of the HBC's lands west of the Great Lakes, south of fifty-four degrees latitude. Since Canada was beginning to experience a sense of confinement within its own boundaries, the province sent Chief Justice William Draper to London to represent Canada's interest in expansion and a Toronto geology professor, Henry Hind, was sent west to view the land for himself and report on its potential for farming from firsthand observation. To Upper Canada's delight, Hind reported that there was a vast arc of terrain between land too dry and the region too cold that was itself ideal for agriculture (see map 11.1). His mapping of a "Fertile Belt" and its confirmation by a separate expedition sponsored by the British under Captain John Palliser banked high the embers of enthusiasm for expansion. But in the 1850s, the people of Upper Canada could only lobby, look, and hope. Even if the government of Great Britain had been willing to transfer the bounty that was described in such glowing terms in Hind's report, Canada was unable to accept its annexation in 1857 because only half the province wanted expansion and lustily demanded it. The other half, Canada East, resisted. The Members of Parliament representing Lower Canada knew that annexation of the West would end forever the equality that then existed, and since they were half the power of the House under the current arrangement, annexation of the West to the United Province of Canada was simply impossible.

In the late 1850s, Canada was thus restricted to internal, not western lines of expansion. The Grand Trunk Railway, for instance, was pursued with reinvigorated enthusiasm; that is, in proportion to which other projects were impossible, the Grand Trunk received increased attention, and all the knavery and speculation that might have found an outlet in a west-

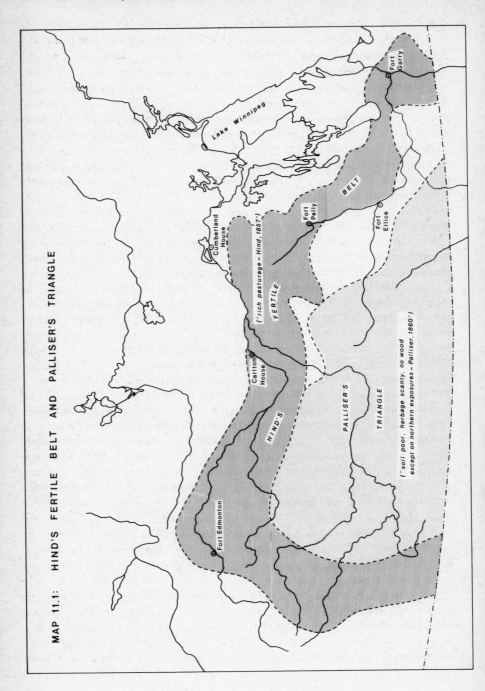

MAP 11.1: HIND'S FERTILE BELT AND PALLISER'S TRIANGLE

ern frontier experience had it begun in 1857 went into the Canadian railway instead. The result was extravagance and corruption, the full extent
of which may never be completely known, but individual incidents are
suggestive. At Sarnia, for instance, a certain acreage belonging to the British War Office was acquired for railway purposes for $825. However, for
some reason, the purchaser was not the Grand Trunk but the Canadian
contractors, Gzowski, Macpherson and Co. and by the time the $800
worth of land passed from them to the railway the price had risen to
$120 000. From the welter of such bargains the indebtedness of the firm
rose to $72 million by 1860 and receipts from operations were not enough
even to pay interest charges, not to mention a dividend to private investors who, of course, expected one. Appalled by written reports, one such
disappointd investor from Britain came out to Canada to inspect the railway himself. On-the-spot inspection only convinced him of what he had
feared earlier: "the Grand Trunk had not begun to be managed as a commercial carrying company ... ." The railway was a political patronage
machine.

But in 1861 a dramatic episode seemed to demonstrate the need for
another line even less commercial than the Grand Trunk. The reason was
defense. The problem was a crisis in the relations between the United
States and Great Britain arising from the Americans' failure to observe
Britain's freedom of the sea. The Civil War had just begun, and representatives of the separatist confederacy of the South were on board the British
mail steamer, *Trent*, bound for England to negotiate aid for the war. Naturally, the Union forces were anxious to prevent such an alliance. What
outraged the British was their stopping the *Trent* in international waters
and taking the Confederate ambassadors into custody at gunpoint. Some
British officials regarded the "Trent affair" as a cause for war and were
prepared to act accordingly. Others advocated moderation but everyone
could agree it was wise to strengthen the defenses of British North America should war with the United States prove unavoidable. Fourteen thousand troops were rushed to the colonies late in 1861 but they arrived too
late in the year to steam up to the eastern terminus of the Grand Trunk on
the St. Lawrence. Obviously the army could not disembark at the alternate
terminus of the railway at Portland, Maine, so the men were unloaded at
Saint John, and made their way overland through 700 miles of hip-deep
snow. If the Intercolonial Railway, proposed even before the Grand
Trunk, had been undertaken with the same energy (and less waste), the
whole trek would have been unnecessary.

But the Intercolonial required interprovincial cooperation. Moreover, it
was difficult to see the transportation of 10 or 20 000 troops from Halifax
or Saint John to Quebec on those rare occasions when there was a winter

war scare as sufficient justification, and defense against the United States would have to be the sole rationale; if the Grand Trunk could barely hope for enough revenue to pay operating expenses and some of the interest charges on its outstanding indebtedness, a railway through the most sparsely settled parts of New Brunswick and Nova Scotia could be expected to fare even worse. Still, the enthusiasm of Saint John and Halifax businessmen for railways was almost limitless, and for some Canadian politicians railway finance was the only interesting political problem. For a while, therefore, it appeared in 1862 that the legislatures of the three provinces directly involved would cooperate with the imperial authorities in building the Intercolonial Railway as an entirely public project. Then Canada backed out, having just increased taxation to bolster the still faltering Grand Trunk Railway.

In the autumn of 1863, Maritimers learned with anger that the Canadians would only commit themselves to sharing survey costs of the proposed venture. Saint John merchants sought solace by pursuing an alternate scheme that was attractive because it seemed more economic. But since their alternative involved nothing more than the extension of a rail line to the State of Maine it failed to spark the same enthusiasm or sense of British patriotism. Nor did "western extension" please the Nova Scotians. They proposed a solution more patriotic, and more thoroughly political. The Nova Scotians attempted to sell the idea of a Maritime union.

The concept of maritime union was not new in 1863. It had been actively pursued several times before, and history did seem naturally to erode the artificial division of the region into many different provinces. Cape Breton Island joined Nova Sotia in 1820. New Brunswick contemplated the same prospect in the early 1860s once the railway age came upon them and they could attempt nothing grander than "western extension" by themselves. United with the other Atlantic provinces, grander schemes were possible. One united "Acadia" was not ludicrous, perhaps only premature in 1863. Still, the first reactions were interesting in the sense that the several provinces concerned at least debated the idea seriously in their provincial parliaments.

Then two events occurred in 1864 to sidetrack the Maritime union development. One was a revival of the Intercolonial Railway proposal when Canada announced its intention of beginning the project on its own to the extent of paying all the costs of surveying the route. The other event was deadlock in the Canadian legislature and the formation of a coalition to seek a solution in a more general union, one that included all the provinces of British North America. Thus, the Canadians decided to take over the maritime union movement for their own purposes. But the drive for

Maritime union had not developed even to the extent of setting a date for a meeting of the relevant provinces. Undeterred, the Canadians persisted and begged for an invitation to the unset conference. Encouraged by the revival of the Intercolonial Railway project and by some of the attractions of a wider union, Maritimers agreed to have a meeting at which the Canadians might attend. The date was set for September 1, 1864. The place was Charlottetown, Prince Edward Island.

## IV   The Scheme for a Wider Union

The Charlottetown conference, which lasted only six days, was an enormously significant encounter primarily for the nationalism the Canadian delegates defeated. The Canadians fought nationalism in the sense that they talked representatives of autonomous provinces out of local patriotism in favour of continentalism. Surprisingly, the other delegates were receptive to their arguments even though the Maritime provinces were entitled to see themselves as nations with their own boundaries, autonomy, and a sense of pride in the prosperity they enjoyed. By the end of the meeting, however, Charles Tupper of Nova Scota was deriding his country as a "little province" and "nation by itself". Nor was he alone in this attitude, so successful were the Canadians in persuading those at Charlottetown that their best future lay in a transcontinental British North America.

The Canadians were desperate. Ironically, their's was the one province in all of British North America that lacked any national integrity of its own in present circumstances. Canada, East and West, was an artificial entity and deadlocked. The alternatives were complete separation (two "little provinces"), a federal union of the two (with the prospect of deadlock between equals still likely), or a wider merger on the supposition that every interest in the diverse agglomeration might enter a majority coalition enough of the time to make the alliance more or less permanent; that is, no one faction or ethnic group would be the predictable winner of everything, nor any one group the inevitable loser of all.

These political prospects — which appealed to the delegates as politicians — were still not as attractive to the Charlottetown delegates as the other impulse, the belief that British North America had a common "destiny". Thus, to Charles Tupper, it was a perversion of history that the "little provinces" of British North America had their own legislatures, borders, and customs officers. For him, it was far grander to contemplate a unity of one "race" united from sea to sea. They, the "Anglo-Norman" people of North America might then realize their proper cosmic purpose. In this way, the delegates heard and made great speeches about their "moral courage" and agreed to discuss the more mechanical aspects of union later in the year, at Quebec City.

After the Charlottetown meeting, the good feeling seemed to persist. Thus, in Halifax for example, the *Witness* reported on September 24 that "a very manifest change has been creeping over the spirit of our leading politicians, and we believe of the people generally. There is less aversion to Canada. Indeed, there seems to be a positive desire for union."

What P.B. Waite has called an "authentic national spirit" persisted through the follow-up conference at Quebec in the last two weeks of October, 1864. At the later event more conspicuous than romance, however, was the hard bargaining over the actual terms of the union. After all, the Quebec conference was a constitutional convention, the first in Canadian history (all previous such developments — 1774, 1791, and 1840 — were initiated, drafted, and passed by the outside influence of British official-dom and the Parliament of Great Britain). The 1864 meeting was the first time colonists themselves determined that a change in constitution was due and what form it should take. Every colony except the western fiefs of the Hudson's Bay Company sent delegates. Even more remarkably, in *Seventy-two Resolutions*, they agreed upon a pattern. They decided there would be a legislative union with a central government modeled after the form that already existed in the autonomous provinces. That is, rather than imitating the American union with its system of controls balancing executive and legislative branches, in the proposed central goverment of British North America there was to be a House of Commons (with representation according to population) led by an executive responsible to that body itself. Such potentially vigorous government was attractive to delegates who, fearful of the looser American system, sought to create the closest approximation possible to a unitary state. Moreover, the representation-by-population aspect was pleasing to the reformers from Canada West. But vigorous central government and "rep by pop" were both compromised to meet the objections of delegates who welcomed neither.

To pacify those who feared representation by population (because it seemed too populist or prejudicial to the provinces with small populations), an upper house, the Senate, was conceded. Here, representation was to be equal, not proportional; that is, each region was promised the same number of senators regardless of population considerations. Upper and Lower Canada (becoming separate provinces once again) were each to have 24 Senators with an additional 24 to be apportioned among Prince Edward Island, Nova Scotia and New Brunswick (the Maritime region). The more remote appendages of Newfoundland and the West were each to receive four. Since no act of the House of Commons could receive royal assent before receiving the confirmation of the Senate, small provinces were assured considerable influence in the chamber of "sober second thought". But there were two problems with the compromise. One was the obvious fact that Upper and Lower Canada were economically one region (the empire of the St. Lawrence), not two (as was established for senatorial representation). Consequently, on economic questions that would bring the interests of the maritime region into conflict with the St. Lawrence area, the Maritimers were going to be outvoted in the Senate as well as in the House. To be sure, there was the possibility that Lower Canada and the Maritimes might gang up on Upper Canada in the Senate on other matters, but if they were to do so such action would almost certainly be troublesome because the second problem with the idea of the Senate was that the provinces of British North America had indicated growing hostility to the very idea of bicameralism. With the concession of responsible government, an appointive upper house had no more freedom to kill legislation emanating from an elected legislature than a governor had free rein to veto acts of the Assembly. This was supposed to be the nub of responsible government: the power of the Crown and the "aristocracy" had become nice legal fictions, symbolic more than substantive. Perhaps the delegates from Canada West agreed to the compromise because they suspected that the Senate would always defer to the House. But why would the the delegates from small provinces such as Prince Edward Island accept such a proposal if they for their part also suspected it was meaningless?

Similar contradictions arose from another compromise. Since it was agreed that the central government would not supersede the provinces entirely, the basis of union would be federalism. Some principle for the division of sovereignty had to be devised. The agreement on the division of powers was that the provinces would have full autonomy over matters of a "merely local or private nature" with the word *merely* implying that the provinces would retain their distinctiveness only on matters of little consequence. If this were so it would have been more efficient to have abolished the provinces altogether and substituted something like *départements* in France or the counties in England. But the fact then — and later — was the impossibility of such a reduction. The provinces were to continue because they were not guardians of trivial particularisms. The proposed division of sovereignty was problematic in the sense that the provincial governments were to continue autonomous in areas even the weakest central government would envy. The way around the paradox was to dismiss the sphere of the provinces as unimportant, but such dismissal was self-deception.

The problems notwithstanding, bicameralism and federalism were the major aspects of compromise that emerged in the two weeks of bargaining at Quebec. All that remained was for each delegation to return to its home province and persuade the legislature that it was in their interest to compromise local pride and seek grandeur in the larger context. Each Assembly was to adopt an address to the Queen praying for an Act of Union on the agreed terms. Since the conference was over before the end of October 1864, it was possible that a united British North America could come into existence within the year. But in the weeks and months that followed, the *Seventy-two Resolutions* of the Quebec conference only sparked the enthusiasm of the western half of one province, Canada West alone. In Canada East the English-speaking elite was at first completely skeptical, and some persons — such as the Principal of McGill University — were actively opposed to a change that would restore the autonomy of Lower Canada. What they feared was isolation and subordination as a despised minority. McGill's J.W. Dawson said the "English dominion will be destroyed beyond redemption." Proponents of the union successfully allayed that anxiety by pointing out that the powers to the provinces were nothing compared with those to the central government. A.T. Galt dismissed the provinces as mere "municipalities of larger growth". But Galt's assertion served to support *Rouge* spokesmen who denounced the union as simply another attempt to suppress the *canadiens*, the Durham scheme all over again. That accusation prompted the *Bleus* to reply that the autonomy which was retained was in all the areas most precious: "*sociale, civile et religieuse*". Thus, they won over the Catholic hierarchy without offending the elites Galt had courted. Consequently, with the commercial elite looking to the central authority and the clerical elite interested in local sovereignty, there was little enthusiasm for the union, but the anti-union forces were at least neutralized.

It was not Canada East that struck the death blow to confederation in 1864; that deed was done in the Atlantic provinces. One by one, every autonomous colony in the Atlantic region rejected the change for a variety of reasons but local nationalism was primary. Prince Edward Island was perhaps the best example in this regard. Out of the union, PEI was a community of self-sufficient farmers and boat-builders all within "a day's drive" of the capital. They had unhappy experiences in the past from absentee directors. The legislators liked having the "independent powers" they enjoyed. Why surrender or even compromise? they asked. Or, as a Nova Scotian put the same idea, emphasizing economic independence: "We have the trade of the world now open to us on nearly equal terms and why should we allow Canada to hamper us?" The reply that "We seek Union because we are, in reality, one people and ought to be one nationality ... ." was at best a pious wish, at worst a dangerous delusion. Joseph Howe pointed to the obvious duality of the United Province and said that division was the primary basis for the dangerous federalism in the proposed arrangement. Suggesting that it was a structure of competing authority that invited disaster, Howe pointed to the Civil War that was even then still raging in the United States and asked: "Have we not seen enough of federations ...? Shall we not draw wisdom from the errors of others?"

## V    The Enactment of Confederation

Although the courtship of the Atlantic governments by the Canadian cabinet was extraordinarily successful at the Charlottetown and the Quebec conferences, the romance failed to last. One year after drafting the Quebec Resolutions, only Canada had approved them. The simple truth was that the specific terms of the proposed union could not stand the close scrutiny of persons whose importance would be diminished by the change. Local politicians and individual citizens, of Prince Edward Island for instance, could see themselves as significant parts of a community complete unto itself. Each Islander was one eighty-seven thousandth of a country. In confederation each such subject would be just one person in an artificial community of three million. What power ordained that bigger nations were inherently better? On such reasoning, the confederation scheme foundered. Were it not for two external factors, Great Britain and the United States, the cause of the confederates would have remained becalmed indefinitely.

Intervention arose from the incredible fact that at the very moment the delegates were drafting resolutions of confederation at Quebec, soldiers of the southern Confederacy were robbing banks in the little town of St. Albans, Vermont, and making good their theft by seeking safety across the border in Canada. Most of the robbers and some of the money were subsequently apprehended at Montreal but a judge dismissed all charges against them and Canada hesitated to comply with the American demand for their extradition. As the Confederate agents went free, the American government registered its displeasure by closing the border to everyone but passport holders and a movement developed in the United States Senate to abrogate the Reciprocity Treaty that was up for renewal. Ultimately Senate vindictives succeeded just as the Atlantic provinces rejected Canada by turning their back on the confederation scheme. Moreover, American leaders such as the Secretary of State, William Seward, and the senatorial leader, Charles Sumner, suggested that additional reprisal for the St. Alban's raid and other alleged injuries might be appropriate.

Britain's principal offense was providing armaments to the South, including naval ships such as the highly effective commerce raider, the *Alabama*. For Seward and Summer, reprisal was in order unless appropriate compensation were paid. One reasonable award, in the Americans' view, was the western land under the control of the Hudson's Bay Company.

The British took the American anger deadly seriously. They saw the North's ultimate victory over the South in 1865 as an indication not only of the triumph of one section over another, but also of the emergence of a bolder power in North America. The British felt that they had to concede American supremacy and gracefully withdraw their forces from the continent or to reinforce them sufficiently to restore the balance. Since their interests in British North America no longer warranted such enormous expenditure, withdrawal appeared the more prudent alternative. Thus, Great Britain developed a deepening commitment to confederation: a united British North America could be expected to shift for itself, and Britain might withdraw its own forces from the new nation without losing face to the world at large.

After 1865, Britain not only encouraged Canada in the confederation proposal, officials in England simmered with anger over the Atlantic region's reluctance to join. In this spirit, William Gladstone, a leading British politician and soon to become Prime Minister, blustered that since "John Bull pays the piper in the matter of defense for the Lower Provinces, there is something almost ridiculous in the idea of their standing upon an opinion of their own in such a matter against ours, and against that of Canada with five or six times their population." The result was British intervention to break the resistance of Nova Scotia and New Brunswick, the two Maritime provinces indispensible to the union (Prince Edward Island and Newfoundland, out at sea in any event, could be left there indefinitely and picked up later; much later as it turned out in the case of Newfoundland which did not join until 1949). For Nova Scotia, the British provided a new governor, for New Brunswick, a new set of instructions to the royal representative. Finesse was required, but in 1865 results were demanded. The colonists must join.

The governors' opportunity came with an exploitable crisis in 1866. The Fenian Order, an Irish patriotic society formed in 1858 to secure Ireland's independence from Great Britain, became a serious threat to British North America when the Order began to recruit immigrant Irish from the American army disbanding after the surrender of the South the year before. In such cities as Boston and New York, immigrant Irish caught the vision of freeing their homeland by waging a successful flank attack upon Britain in North America, made all the more attractive by the knowledge that one third to one half of the colonists were of Irish descent, presumably sympathetic to the cause of an independent Ireland. Although such sympathy was largely imaginary, the governments of the autonomous colonies grew increasingly anxious through the spring and summer of 1866. The Fenians gathered men and arms without active opposition from the United States, and in June actually invaded Canada with nearly one thousand men. Since Great Britain remained steadfastly determined to withdraw British defense forces, the Fenian threat was an exploitable crisis indeed.

In the face of the Fenian menace, mutual defense could be cited as a justification for confederation. At the precise moment that the threat was most critical in New Brunswick, the governor, Arthur Gordon, maneuvered local politicians into an election only one year after a previous appeal to the electorate. In the earlier contest, candidates associated with the confederation scheme had been defeated. The anti-confederate victors had won thirty seats to the pro-confederates' eleven members. But the earlier vote in New Brunswick had been extremely close: 15 556 pro-confederates to 15 949 anti-confederates. In the face of the Fenian crisis (and with generous cash support from Canada) Leonard Tilley's pro-confederation party was able to tip the scale for victory. In June, 1866, Tilley was back in power with 31 seats in the Assembly and a resolution affirming support for confederation. A similar resolve revived in Nova Scotia even though the life of the legislature had almost expired. But Charles Tupper did not dare to call an election, for confederation was still too odious for many voters. Still, the governor incited him to action and Tupper moved the all-important resolution in the Nova Scotia Assembly. Dormant since 1864, the confederation scheme was stirred back to life.

Once the threatened and actual Fenian invasions had subsided with the protection of winter, delegates from Canada, New Brunswick, and Nova Scotia met in London to draft the Quebec Resolutions into a bill for submission to Parliament. There the act was presented as a treaty to be accepted or rejected without alteration. Since rejection was unthinkable, passage was rapid. On March 29, 1867, The British North America Act received royal assent and "one Dominion under the name of Canada" remained only to be proclaimed on July 1. Then Great Britain could formally recognize the United States as the supreme power in the Western Hemisphere and prepare for the withdrawal of her own forces. But it remained to be seen how the Americans would regard the forced marriage of the former colonies. The *Alabama* claims were still not settled, and the American government believed it was their "destiny" to expand from pole to pole in the Western Hemisphere. On the same day the British North America Act received royal assent, the United States purchased Alaska from Russia, thus defining its northern frontier. Was confederation merely a preparation for annexation? The question was germane in 1867 — and later.

# Bibliography

The volumes in the Canadian Centenary Series that cover the subject of Canadian politics in the 1850s, subsequent deadlock, and the quest for a wider union are J.M.S. Careless, *The Union of the Canadas, 1841-1857* (1967) and W.L. Morton, *The Critical Years: The Union of British North America, 1867-1873* (1964). Another excellent general work that covers the same developments, more briefly but with similar interpretive skill, is "The 1850s" by J.M.S. Careless and "The 1860s" by P.B. Waite in J.M.S. Careless, ed., *Colonists and Canadiens, 1760-1867* (1971).

More specialized, relevant works on developments that led to the initiatives for confederation by Canada are W.G. Ormsby, *The Emergence of the Federal Concept in Canada, 1839-1845* (1969); David Gagan, "Land, Population, and Social Change: The 'Critical Years' in Rural Canada West," CHR (1978), and Doug Owram, *Promise of Eden: The Canadian Expansionist Movement and the Idea of the West, 1856-1900* (1980). Ormsby describes the fact of continuing dualism, despite the original assimilationist intent of the Act of Union. Gagan and Owram consider the theme of developing "confinement" in Canada West.

The political difficulties and frustrated expansionism that led to confederation between 1864 and 1867 are described in several important works that treat the subject from remarkably different perspectives. P.B. Waite follows reactions to the scheme region by region in *The Life and Times of Confederation, 1864-1867* (1962) and finds that there were legitimate grounds for opposition as well as promotion of the change. But D.G. Creighton considers the union unqualifiedly heroic with the great men — those with broad visions for a wider country — ultimately prevailing on their *Road to Confederation: The Emergence of Canada, 1863-1867* (1964). Less interested in the details of politics or the role of personalities is S.B. Ryerson in *Unequal Union: Confederation and the Roots of Conflict, 1815-1873*, second edition (1975). He sees confederation as a triumph of capitalism over more democratic forces.

For the imperial context that provided the essential extra pressure on New Brunswick and Nova Scotia, Robin Winks, *Canada and the United States: The Civil War Years* (1960) is comprehensive. W.S. Neidhardt focuses on the critical invasions in *Fenianism in North America* (1975).

". . . it was not a principle or a philosophy that united
his group but a program . . ."

# CHAPTER 12

# *Their Program Was Their Politics*

## I    The Unpopularity of Confederation

Complex problems had driven representatives of all parties in the two Canadas to form a coalition in 1864 for the pursuit of a legislative union of all British North America. Such a creation would immediately solve the problem of legislative deadlock in the old union by dissolving it. The larger entity might then proceed to acquire the Prairie West and begin to satisfy Upper Canada's expansionist ambitions. The material attraction offered to the Maritimes was the Intercolonial Railway. On this basis, the Canadians achieved a remarkable measure of success in 1864, first at Charlottetown and later with the *Seventy-two Resolutions* drafted at Quebec City.

In 1865, however, the terms of union did not bear the scrutiny of the legislatures and newspapers of the Atlantic provinces. Thus, the Confederation movement faltered. At this point, tension in the relations between the United States and Great Britain played a decisive role in revitalizing the local initiatives that had lost their force. In 1865, as in the 1840s, the British opted for a less formal version of imperialism and decided to withdraw their garrisons from North America, as earlier they had decided to reduce the role of local governors from constant intervention to a largely symbolic presence. Before withdrawing, however, it was necesary to have a more independent British North America from which they might logically retreat. For this reason, Britain insisted upon the change that Maritimers had previously rejected. Intervention brought pro-Confederate resolutions from New Brunswick and Nova Scotia in the summer of 1866 and Confederation itself was proclaimed on July 1, 1867. Although achieved by Act of Parliament as a constitutional development, the federation remained as unpopular as ever in the Maritimes. Newfoundland and Prince Edward Island remained aloof. Nova Scotians sought escape.

At the time of the enactment of the union, the people of Nova Scotia petitioned against it. Failing in that effort, they mourned the loss of their autonomy on the day of the Act's proclamation. Then, in September of 1867 there were elections to the provincial and federal legislatures, and in both contests the anti-confederation faction won sweeping victories. In the contests for the local legislature, 36 of the 38 seats were won by separatist candidates called *repealers*. Similarly, nearly all of the Nova Scotians elected to go to Ottawa were also dedicated to the dissolution of the union. Eighteen of the 19 Nova Scotia Members of Parliament were repealers.

When the anti-confederate legislature of Nova Scotia began its first session in January of 1868, the provincial Treasurer presented no budget, the leader of the assembly presented no program. Led by Martin Wilkins, the Attorney General, the government presented repeal resolutions, simultaneously presented and approved by public meetings of repealers in every county. Wilkins asserted that Charles Tupper had exceeded his authority in arranging confederation in London and the British Parliament had also exceeded its power by passing the act. According to Wilkins, the fundamental law of Nova Scotia derived from a compact between the Crown and the people; therefore, the province could not be confederated without their consent, for instance by plebiscite.

In the context of the pre-Civil War United States, such developments would have been considered plausible steps for "nullification". There, an elaborate ratifying procedure had been employed to legitimize the American union by collecting the voices of white, male freeholders — the "people" of each state. Electoral ratification had made their constitution more popular, but what the majority had a right to create, they might also claim to destroy. Separatism was thus endemic to the United States, threatened repeatedly, and finally achieved, briefly, until the Civil War solidified the union by establishing whose people were at least mightier. In the Canadian case, Nova Scotians believed that without British sanction, "secession" would be illegal in their circumstances. On this account, the legislature appointed a committee, which included Wilkins, to go to London in order to persuade the Imperial Parliament to exempt Nova Scotia from the provisions of the BNA Act. Not surprisingly, the Colonial Secretary refused to accept Wilkins' argument, approving instead the defense of Confederation written by Charles Tupper. Lord Granville declared that the "Confederation Act ... took place in accordance with the expressed desire of the people of all the Provinces expressed in the only known constitutional mode — through their respective legislatures." In this argument, it did not matter that there had been no election in Nova Scotia between 1864 and the time of the enactment of the union scheme, just as it was of no account that there had recently been elections and public meetings in which the pro-confederation position had been repudiated. At this point, in June 1868, the choice for repealers was submission or repudiation of British authority. Since the latter course was equivalent to rebellion, nearly all repealers eventually chose submission.

The decline of the Nova Scotia repeal movement over the summer and autumn of 1868 demonstrated that the British connection in Nova Scotia was still potent even though it was becoming ever more patently symbolic. The alternative republicanism with its inherent instability conjured up images of constitutional revolving doors, perhaps civil war. What one government would accomplish constitutionally, another could unmake until force would ultimately decide the issue. The horror of the prospect turned around Joseph Howe who proved to be a more important leader than Martin Wilkins. Howe met John A. Macdonald in Halifax early in August 1868 and later launched a series of newspaper articles diverting the repealers from separatism to the cause of "better terms" within Confederation.

By January 1869, other important leaders of the Nova Scotia repeal movement were, in Macdonald's words, "about to take the shilling and enlist." The enlistment bounty included tariff adjustments, and an additional $80 000 per year subsidy for the province. For Joseph Howe, there was a position in the cabinet. Wilkins continued to grumble in the Assembly that the terms were not nearly adequate and came close to joining the repealer minority which advocated annexation of Nova Scotia to the United States as a last resort. In the end, however, Wilkins also took his shilling, but as John A. Macdonald himself admitted, Nova Scotia would "consider itself for some time, a conscript rather than a volunteer" because the unity which arose from the pacification of Nova Scotia arose more from an acceptance of defeat than positive affirmation. In 1869, the union was still a political creation, no less so than in 1867.

## II   Macdonald and Company Acquire Rupert's Land

That the BNA Act provided a constitutional structure which was an offical imposition rather than a spontaneous outgrowth from the will of the people was illustrated by the Nova Scotia repeal movement between 1867 and 1869. The business merger aspect of national consolidation was also emphasized by the first projects embarked upon by the government. Building railways, territorial expansion, and the recruitment of a national revenue all indicated that Confederation was unfolding with about the same excitement as the incorporation and growth of a joint-stock company. Moreover, since the earliest acts of national activity had the character of simply extending the actions of the old Province of Canada, there was no doubt either as to which party to the merger had seniority. There were some 500 employees in the first federal offices in Ottawa and 490 were Canadians even though Nova Scotia and New Brunswick together had enough population to expect at least one fourth of the federal patronage. Similarly, the first tariff was also merely an extension of that which had been previous Canadian policy, completely disregarding the interests of the Atlantic region.

Nova Scotia repealers had worked to remedy the more discriminatory aspects of the tariff and the disparities of patronage with their quest for "better terms" while other persons struggled to remedy the defect that the country was yet to be defined in heroic or even poetic terms. A tiny group of self-appointed guardians of the public spirit came together in Ottawa to look after the creation of the nation's mythology. The motto of the group became "Canada First" in order to convey the idea that they were united to put the cause of nationalism above all others. They felt Confederation was incomplete until a strong outpouring of "national sentiment" cemented the country into "one nation of brothers." Such an attitude was to be expected to arise from some group in some part of the Dominion to the extent that Confederation had arisen from any "national spirit" at all. But the union had not emerged from the same kind of struggles which had raged — were raging — in Europe and America to make nations out of the principalities of Italy and Germany and the federation that was the United States. In those countries a bevy of poets, demagogues, and other national myth-makers had attended the actions of the generals and the politicians to attribute cosmic significance to the bloodshed and political changes that were taking place.

In Canada, the only material to celebrate poetically was the action of the "Fathers of Confederation", commemorated by the politicians themselves. Thus, D'Arcy McGee emerged as the "orator and prophet" of the union. As the delegates emerged from drafting the *Seventy-two Resolutions* in Quebec, for instance, everyone wanted to hear a little oratory to punctuate the great moment. According to P.B. Waite, this is what "deserves to be remembered" from McGee's speech that followed:

> they had not gone into the Chamber to invent any new system of Government, but had entered it in a reverent spirit to consult the oracles of the history of their race. They had gone there to build, if they had to build, upon the old foundation — (Cheers) — not a showy edifice for themselves, with a stucco front, and a lath and plaster continuation — (Laughter) — but a piece of solid British masonry, as solid as the foundations of Eddystone, which would bear the whole force of democratic winds and waves, and resist the effect of our corroding political atmosphere, consolidate our interests, and

prove the legitimacy of our origin. (Loud cheering) (Quoted in P.B. Waite, *The Life and Times of Confederation* [1962], p. 99.)

More perhaps for the pro-British attitude he represented than for his pomposity, McGee was assassinated in Ottawa by a Fenian in April 1868. This was the occasion for bringing together the little group of nationalists dedicating themselves to Canada First. Charles Mair, William Foster, George Denison, Robert Haliburton, and Henry Morgan were five young intellectuals among the thousands who felt wounded by the loss of the "prophet of Confederation". As a result, they resolved to carry on where McGee had fallen, to infuse some spirit into a country that seemed "to crawl into existence in a humdrum, common place, matter-of-fact way" rather than by "fiery ordeals".

The Canada Firsters felt that the path of glory could yet be trod if only they could reveal to Canadians the full potential of the superiority of their race in North America. The people needed to be shown that all Canadians, regardless of province, were descended from the "Aryan tribes" of Northern Europe and were therefore of good stock for starting a virile new land. Unlike the United States which had sprung from similar origins, the Canadians were sturdier for their having been nursed on "the icy bosom of the frozen North." They, the "Northmen of the New World," were destined for greatness, a destiny which would be fully realized one day in a great "rattling war" with the then "weak and effeminate" Americans. At that appointed hour, the "defensively warlike" Canadians would emerge triumphant, "a single nation of brothers." Here, then, was the appearance of the myth of "The True North Strong and Free," no more racist or jejune than the other myths born of the other movements for national consolidation at the same time. What was unusual about the Canadian case is the subsequent failure of racist nationalism to infect a significant portion of the population outside Ontario.

The failure of the ideological nationalism propagated by Mair, Foster, Denison, Haliburton, and Morgan is all the more interesting since the ideal opportunity to impress the message on the national consciousness appeared to have arrived near the end of 1869. By November, everything seemed set to complete the transfer of Rupert's Land from the control of the Hudson's Bay Company to Canada. In the spring, negotiations with the HBC had led to the drafting of an agreement covering the acquisition of the West. In summary, for £300 000 and one twentieth of all the land in Henry Hind's "fertile belt", the HBC agreed to relinquish all rights to governance and colonization in the territory. What remained as of November was the disbursement of the money and the proclamation of the transfer by the Queen, set to take place on December 1. Then Canada would administer the region as something like a Crown colony. Someday, in the remote and hazy future after the conquest of all its western primitivism, provinces would emerge in Rupert's Land. But provincial status could only occur after the influx of "actual settlers". Provincial status could not be accorded even a part of Rupert's Land as it was then constituted, a land of people who were Indian or partly Indian, not "settlers" in the Canadian understanding of the term.

Unexpectedly, the semi-agricultural people in the vicinity of Red River resented the Canadian government's conspicuous disregard of their wishes. They had not been consulted and they were disturbed by the appearance of Canadian government land surveyors, even before the transfer. Fear developed that the population of the Red River settlement was to be driven back from the river (see map 12.1) and the land given to others. At first, the Métis people of the district felt rather helpless to influence these developments. But with the leadership of the parish priest of St. Norbert and one of their own (a promising scholar sent to the seminaries of Quebec for an education), a protest movement had developed over the summer of 1869. Father Ritchot and Louis Riel were the very antithesis of Canada First nationalism, especially Riel. Moreover, Riel was no less inclined to celebrate his race than were the Canada Firsters to boast of theirs. In Riel's case, however, the material lending itself to this sort of treatment was even more romantic since he and his compatriots could trace their origins to a mingling of European paternal ancestors and Indian maternal forebears joined by the fur trade and the buffalo hunt. Truly, Riel's "Métis nation" was a distinct New World type which lent itself to romanticization even more easily than the myth of Canada as the home of a special mingling of the "Aryan tribes" of Europe.

Riel himself felt a mission to defend the life of the hunt, the river lot farms, and the barter economy of Red River. He saw these activities as ordained by God along with the cyclical round of seasons and the Roman Catholic sacraments. Even more than this (since the Red River settlement was by no means entirely Catholic), Riel could be followed simply because he was an attractive political leader. Despite his youth of twenty-five years, he might help bring Red River through its crisis of the transfer and prevent it from becoming a colony of a colony.

After Riel and his followers interrupted the apparently inexorable transfer of Rupert's Land to Canada on November 16, 1869 by barring at the border the would-be governor, William McDougall, the Government of Canada faced a real dilemma. Two courses of action were open. Macdonald could work with his Minister of the Militia, George Cartier, to plan a war, or he could work with the same person as his principal partner in Confederation to negotiate a settlement with the unruly cousins of French Canada on the prairies. From the standpoint of Canada First, a show of force was justified, indeed, desirable. But Macdonald chose negotiation, and for more reasons than the humanitarianism of this alternative. First, the Red River insurgents had not violated any Canadian law. To be sure,

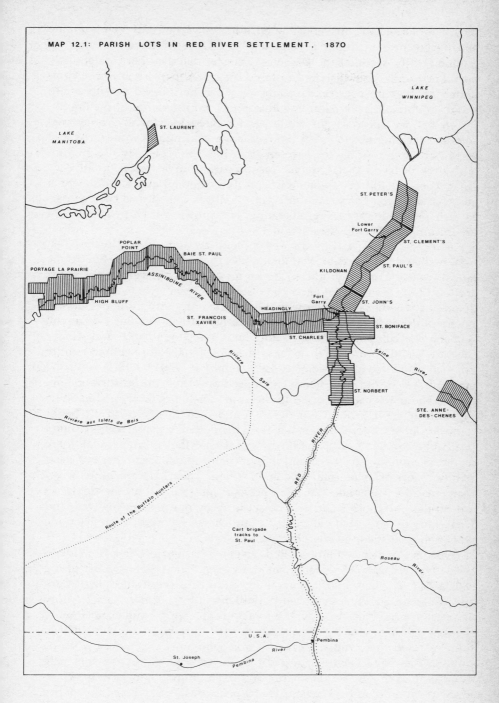

MAP 12.1: PARISH LOTS IN RED RIVER SETTLEMENT, 1870

they had blocked the arrival of the territorial governor, but technically he had no business in Rupert's Land until the Queen ratified the transfer. Ignorant of the fact that the December transfer date had been indefinitely postponed until the British had restored order, the hapless governor committed another trespass on December 1 when he crossed the border to shout the formality prematurely into the unheeding silence of the empty, frozen prairie. The onset of winter underscored Macdonald's other reasons for deciding not to crush the resistance. During the winter it would be physically impossible to move an army into the region. In the interim, if it were believed that Canada was preparing an invasion of Rupert's Land, there would be preparations by its defenders and their potential allies. It was even conceivable that the Americans might use such a crisis as their pretext for annexing, liberating, and protecting the people of Red River from Canadian invasion.

For these reasons, it was decided to send an ambassador to the West first, to give the impression that justice was to be done. Donald Smith, the Hudson's Bay Company official chosen for the task, arrived on the scene at the end of December and an extraordinary series of events unfolded. To determine whether Red River would negotiate entry into Confederation or pursue an independent course like the other provinces which were still refusing to compromise their autonomy (Newfoundland and Prince Edward Island, principally), a mass meeting took place with the entire population invited to participate. On January 19 and 20, 1870, with the temperature so cold that breath condensed and froze on beards and eyebrows, about 1000 adults stood in the snow for hours under a china blue sky to hear speeches on Confederation and their own version of "better terms". Donald Smith persuaded the crowd that Canada sought union peaceably and without prejudice. Then Louis Riel affirmed that there would be no entry to the union without appropriate assurances of basic rights. "Most of us are half-breeds," he said. Then he went on to assert that "we all have rights. We claim no half rights, ... but all the rights we are entitled to. Those rights will be set forth by our respresentatives, and what is more ... we will get them." Loud cheers followed, then everyone went home satisfied the crisis had passed.

Two developments followed Red River's decision to enter Confederation. One was growing resentment in Ontario. The other was increasing satisfaction in Quebec. Ontario was resentful because the people of Canada West had grown accustomed to thinking of the northwestern territory as their birthright and the revolt seemed to threaten the full acquisition of their patrimony. The legislation which was introduced in May 1870 to bring the Red River settlement into Confederation as a province with the Indian name of *Manitoba* suggested that the new province was not going to develop in the image of Ontario. Although "inferior" in race, the existing population of approximately 12 000 people was guaranteed a superior position on the land by promises of secure tenure of the river lots they already occupied and a reserve of 1.4 million acres apparently to be allotted to individuals of the next generation. Similarly, Roman Catholicism was to be protected by assurances of support from the public treasury for denominational schools; and the French language was to be a language of record as well as debate.

What bothered Ontario most, however, was that the insurgents appeared to be getting away with murder. On March 4, 1870, the "rebel government" quartered at Fort Garry had executed one Thomas Scott in the courtyard of the fort for resisting Métis authority. Although Scott was certainly a troublemaker, he probably did not deserve death by firing squad for his crimes. At least, that was the consensus in Ontario when two Canadians fled Red River early in 1870 to spread the word across their home province that a brother in the Loyal Orange Lodge, therefore a pure flower of Ontario youth, had been brutally slain on orders from a half-breed papist usurping Canada's destiny. For this reason, many people in Ontario were anxious for a bit of a war against Manitoba.

The demands for "Riel's head in a sack" were so strident that Macdonald appeared to bow to irresistible pressure to send a military expedition to Red River even though there was no real disorder to suppress there. In fact, he had been planning the military assault at the same time that the ambassadorial ruse had been devised. In this force of 1200 volunteers, led by the British Colonel Wolseley, two thirds of the troops were from Ontario and anxious for blood, especially after their gruelling trek over the fur trade route from the head of navigation on Lake Superior to the vicinity of Lake Winnipeg. Every portage, each fresh swarm of mosquitoes and black flies whetted their thirst for revenge. But when Wolseley's force arrived at Fort Garry in August 1870, Riel was no longer on the scene and there was no resistance of any kind from the people who did remain. So there was no bloodbath, only quiet resentment by the Métis. Canada had broken its assurance of an amicable settlement of the affair. What other promises were to be repudiated?

## III   Further Territorial Acquisitions

Despite Macdonald's double-dealing with the Red River insurgents, the basic settlement of the episode by negotiation rather than by war reflected one more aspect of successful national consolidation by prosaic methods rather than by the "fiery ordeals" demanded by such persons as the Canada Firsters. A similar business approach was also to be seen in the case of

British Columbia, the next area to be caught up in the Canadian merger movement. In 1870, British Columbia encompassed more territory than that covered by all four of the original provinces in Confederation, but only 36 000 people lived in this vast mountainous expanse. Approximately 21 000 of the population were Indian, perhaps the most prosperous Native People of North America, blessed as they were with apparently inexhaustible resources and a climate that was as mild as the rest of nature was bountiful. Moreover, very few white people trespassed upon their land. Of the Europeans that did live there, about half lived on Vancouver Island (most at Victoria). On the mainland, a small population occupied the capital that was then New Westminster, and several thousand other white people remained in the gold mining regions around Barkerville, the Cariboo, and up the Fraser River (see map 12.2). The rest were scattered over the vast expanse of the province which remained in its nearly pristine state. Gold was still the major attraction. Newcomers did not yet mine base metals, or cut the forests or fish for salmon. For this reason, BC lurched from one tide of gold discovery to the next, the most recent being a rush and decline of prospectors to the Cariboo country in the 1860s. Aside from the native people, the most stable part of the British Columbia population in 1870 was probably Victoria, developed first by the Hudson's Bay Company in the trade for sea otter skins, and expanded in the 1840s (as was mentioned in the previous chapter) to check American expansion. Since the gold prospectors were primarily Americans and since the Victoria settlers were decidedly British — indeed, English — this gave the province an interesting ethnic as well as a geographical split. Looking to the future, some people — especially mainlanders — anticipated annexation by the United States, sandwiched as they were between Alaska to the north and Washington to the south with nothing side to side except oceans of salt water beyond the islands and prairie beyond the mountains. For the present, however, a volatile situation was kept in check by maintaining the province as a Crown colony. The governor, Frederick Seymour, reigned with an English entourage above and apart from the others. A partly elected Legislative Council served as a surrogate for representative government.

One of the councilors, a Nova Scotia-born Smith named William, lately of California and there renamed "Amor de Cosmos", was the most outspoken proponent of unity with the Dominion once Confederation had been partly achieved in the East in 1867. In May of 1868, de Cosmos succeeded in forming a group called the Confederation League, the first organization in the province to resemble a political party. Its declared aims were "to effect Confederation as speedily as possible and secure representative institutions for the colony, and thus get rid of the present one-man government, with its huge staff of overpaid and do-nothing officials." As the League developed momentum, Seymour dissolved the elec-

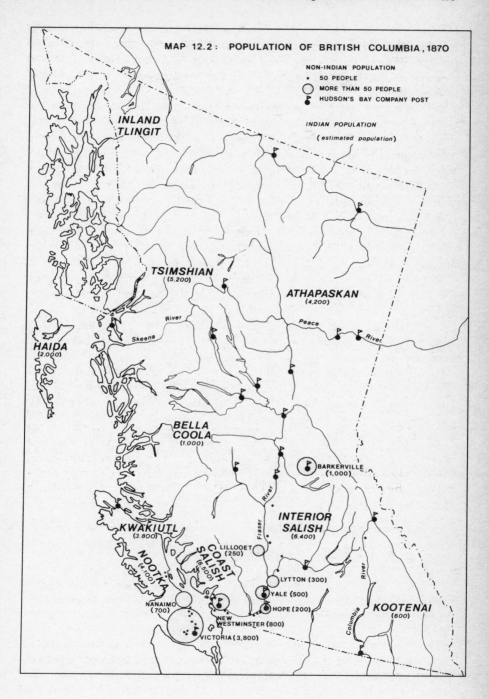

MAP 12.2 :  POPULATION OF BRITISH COLUMBIA, 1870

NON-INDIAN POPULATION
- • 50 PEOPLE
- ○ MORE THAN 50 PEOPLE
- HUDSON'S BAY COMPANY POST

INDIAN POPULATION
( estimated population )

INLAND
TLINGIT

TSIMSHIAN
(5,200)

ATHAPASKAN
(4,200)

Skeena River

Peace River

HAIDA
(2,000)

BELLA
COOLA
(1,000)

BARKERVILLE
(1,000)

KWAKIUTL
(3,800)

INTERIOR
SALISH
(6,400)

NOOTKA
(4,100)

COAST
SALISH
(6,500)

LILLOOET
(250)

Fraser River

LYTTON (300)

YALE (500)

HOPE (200)

KOOTENAI
(600)

Columbia River

NANAIMO
(700)

NEW
WESTMINSTER (800)

VICTORIA (3,800)

ted part of the Legislative Council and enfranchised the Americans to elect a body opposed to annexation by Canada. Seymour was not willing to promote annexation by the United States, but his tactic did serve nicely to defeat the Confederation League. Then Governor Seymour died suddenly in June 1869.

Seymour's replacement, Anthony Musgrave, had instructions from the Colonial Office to promote, rather than to retard, the Confederation project. Having failed in this mission at his previous posting to Newfoundland, Musgrave moved cautiously. Still, with his encouragement, on March 12, 1870, the Legislative Council did adopt the terms for Confederation that had been agitated by de Cosmos's party over the last year. If Canada would assume the colony's debt and agree to some rather lavish transportation schemes, they would join the federation. But their transportation improvement demands were large: they wanted a carriage road all the way to the head of navigation on Lake Superior and assurances that a railway would soon replace the wagon trail.

The committee which took BC's terms to Ottawa, a group of three men not including de Cosmos, also did not bring the demand for responsible government. This the governor and his party were able to defeat in council. Still, the demands the delegation did make were substantial, so they expected tough negotiations. The Prime Minister might have been expected to participate in the bargaining but Macdonald was too exhausted from illness in the midst of the debate on the Manitoba Act to deal with British Columbia. Cartier did most of the bargaining for Canada. His bargain was assumption of BC's debt, subsidies for local public works, and a railway from eastern Canada over the north shore of the lakes, across the prairies, through the mountains, and terminating on the Pacific coast. The railway was to be started within two years of British Columbia's entrance into the union and to be completed in a decade.

At the same time, parallel negotiations with de Cosmos's party had led to the inclusion of the rather vague assurance that

the Government of the Dominion will readily consent to the introduction of Responsible Government when desired by the inhabitants of British Columbia, and it being likewise understood that it is the intention of the Government of British Columbia under the authority of the Secretary of State for the Colonies, to amend the existing constitution of the Legislature by providing that a majority of the members shall be elective. (Quoted in G. Woodcock, *Amor de Cosmos* [1975], p. 128.)

The responsible government proviso was inoffensive, and the rest was "outstandingly better... than what we asked for," one delegate reported. The British Columbians were especially pleased about the railway because it was "*guaranteed* without a reservation!!" Understandably, the Legislative

Council ratified the agreement unanimously on the delegation's return to New Westminster, and the province entered the union officially on July 20, 1871.

With British Columbia set to join the union, the Macdonald government could claim to have completed most of the tasks of territorial consolidation by the end of 1870. Section 146 of the BNA Act empowered the central govenment to add "other colonies" to the Dominion and this had certainly been done — even more successfully than might have been predicted at the height of the Nova Scotia pacification crisis. In 1867, Canada extended only halfway to the Pacific and the hold on the Atlantic shore was uncertain at best. Nova Scotia had cost $800 000 in additional subsidy. Rupert's Land was bought for £300 000 and land promises to the Hudson's Bay Company and half-breeds. British Columbia would cost a railway. But all of this Macdonald could turn to the political advantage of his party. Since there would have to be a general election in 1872, the railway might be launched in time to provide the sort of focus to make the union seem worthwhile and positive and to confirm Macdonald's party as the indispensable coalition for its continuation. For this reason, Macdonald was uneasy with the old name of his party. After all, it was not a principle or a philosophy that united his group, but a program: "going in for union with England against all annexationists and independents, and for the union of all the Provinces ... against all anti-Confederates ...." Wondering about possible alternatives to the label *Conservatives*, Macdonald asked one political friend, "What think you of such a name as 'the Constitutional Union Party'?"

## IV    Political Ingenuity

Macdonald's anticipation of future success was rudely interrupted at the end of 1870, however, by a problem that threatened to be as perplexing as anything that had arisen to date. The difficulty was an invitation to particiate in a treaty-making conference to be held in Washington in the spring of 1871 to resolve the tangle of diplomatic loose ends which had complicated Anglo-American relations since the War Between the States. In one sense, the agenda involved the United States and Great Britain alone. But those two countries had shown before that they could settle disputes between themselves at the expense of Canada; therefore, Macdonald could hardly refuse the invitation to participate. His dilemma was imagining how he might affect the course of negotiations as only one commissioner in a group of ten — five Americans, four British, one Canadian.

From the outset, Macdonald was quite embarrassed by the assignment. If he accepted, he was sure to be denounced for any unreasonable compromise of Canadian interests; but if he refused, he was certain to be criticized for cowardice. Either way, an ordinary politician would have emerged a loser.

John A. Macdonald's political enemies called him an ingratiating deceiver, and knew that he was prone to great binges of drinking; but even his worst enemies never regarded him as ordinary. Macdonald was brilliant in politics, a genuine magician. He could not turn water into wine but he had shown himself fully capable of giving a rude assembly of provinces the appearance of nationality. In 1871, his challenge was to make humiliation appear to be a triumph because the negotiations were almost certainly going to be humiliating. When they concluded in May, the Americans had gained assurances of compensation for the *Alabama* claims and free access to the inshore fisheries of the Atlantic provinces from which they had been excluded since the United States had abrogated the reciprocity agreement in 1866. Great Britain, for her part, won recognition of the principle that the settlement of the *Alabama* claims would involve nothing more than a monetary award, and the amount would be determined by a board of arbitration. Having conceded the fisheries of New Brunswick and Nova Scotia, the country's best bargaining chip, what had Canada gained? Macdonald had dared to hope that the British might join him to secure reparations for the Fenian raids and restoration of reciprocal free trade with the United States. In the end, the British did neither, but Macdonald was instructed to sign the treaty in which his country conceded a great deal and gained nothing more than free navigation of several obscure Alaskan rivers. Macdonald could hardly bear to put pen to paper as he did his duty for Britain. "Here go the fisheries," he muttered.

"You get a good equivalent for them," Hamilton Fish, the American Secretary of State, said in reply.

Not wanting to say what he must have felt, the Canadian Prime Minister simply finished his signature and repeated himself by way of denial: "They are gone." Once back in Canada, the Prime Minister privately complained that the country had been disgraced by the "squeezeable" British. Publicly, however, he said not a word.

The opposition press was not so reticent and moved immediately to publicize the Treaty of Washington for the disgraceful humiliation it had been. For an entire year, the opposition newspapers denounced the government's latest blunder in the context of all the other errors, formulating what amounted to a comprehensive critique of the business merger approach to national consolidation. The Intercolonial Railway was costing too much and there were needless delays in construction. The railway promise to British Columbia was only so many miles of empty fantasy. Negotiations with the half-breed murderers was a national insult; and now the capstone, the ocean treasury of the Atlantic region had been traded for nothing. At least the other extravagance had bought provinces.

In the face of all criticism, Macdonald did not break his silence, and he avoided as long as possible the call for the last session of the first parliament. Finally the session began almost a year after the Treaty of Washington had been signed, and the opposition joined the debate enthusiastically thirsting for Macdonald's blood after sitting impatiently through a Speech from the Throne which called, among other things, for the ratification of the impossible agreement. As the debate reached its full fury, Macdonald still said not a word. Then, at last, everyone discovered the reason for his near smugness in silence. When he finally spoke, it was revealed that in consideration for Canada's ratification of the Washington treaty, the British would agree to guarantee the financing of the Pacific Railway to the extent of two million, five hundred thousand British pounds sterling. Moreover, the fisheries were not to be thrown away for nothing. Only the system of licenses in effect since 1866 was abandoned. Canada was to receive a lump sum rather than a payment per ton for American vessels fishing in Canadian waters. In this way, the Prime Minister seemed to have played a pivotal role in solving two problems at once. He had contributed to the resolution of difficult Anglo-American relations and at the same time he had significantly diminished the risks in financing the Pacific Railway. Seen in this light, the conference in Washington had been a triumph, not a humiliation. As Macdonald was reported to have asserted later in one exhuberant speech, "If he wished to have any record on his tombstone, it was this, that he had been a party in the making of the Treaty of Washington."

Privately, however, Macdonald continued to feel humiliated even though he knew that he had played the most stealthy game possible. He had signed the treaty but informed his British colleagues at the time that his signature was meaningless without ratification by the Canadian Parliament, and that, he said, was impossible without something to sweeten the poison. Originally Macdonald had demanded four million for the railway but settled in the end for about half of his original demand. From the British point of view, his behavior was pure "treachery". In the House of Commons, however, the whole business was a parliamentary coup.

Another nice maneuvre that was intended to prove that Macdonald's leadership was not only competent, but completely nonideological, was Canada's first labor legislation enacted in the last session of the initial Parliament. A nine-hour day movement had developed in the leading manufacturing centers of Montreal, Hamilton, and Toronto. In Toronto, the typographical union, the oldest and probably the best organized in Canada, went on strike against George Brown's paper, the *Globe*. When Brown took the union to court on grounds that they were a criminal conspiracy in restraint of trade, and when he won his case, Macdonald seized the moment for his own party's advantage. The year before, a similar case in England had led the Gladstone government to change the criminal code with Trade Union and Criminal Law Amendment Acts defining labor unions as legal combinations. Interestingly, the motto of the Toronto Typographical Society since its formation in 1844 had been "United to support, not combined to injure", indicating how sensitive the organizations themselves were to the fine line drawn in common law between lawful association and criminal conspiracy. Hurriedly adapting the two British statutes of 1871 to suit Canadian conditions, Macdonald was able to work a Trades Union Act into the legislative program of 1872. Since no genius was greater in George Brown's eyes than William Ewart Gladstone, Macdonald was thus able to quiet the apprentice with the latest enactment of the master.

Understandably, Macdonald's Gladstonian labor legislation made him quite popular with workers, one indication of which was the Toronto Trades Assembly's inviting him to a celebration on July 11 for the purpose of making a presentation, an ornamental box for Agnes Macdonald "as a slight token" of their appreciation for Macdonald's "timely efforts in the interests of the operatives of this Dominion." Accepting the gift for his wife, Macdonald joked about the nine-hours movement in a way that revealed his true interest in the workers and their cause. "I am a working man myself," he said, adding that "I work more than nine hours every day" and went on to suggest that he was particularly skillful in his craft. "If you look at the Confederation Act, in the framing of I had some hand, you will admit that I am a pretty good joiner; and, as for cabinet making," he claimed that there were none better than himself. Given the applause and cheers that followed, the audience of tradesmen did not seem offended by their Prime Minister's tending to trivialize their cause and to divert their attention to the nation-making theme. But the "operatives" class in Canada with which Macdonald was momentarily so popular was hardly 20 percent of the population overall. Other voters — especially rural Protestant Ontario farmers — were far less willing to support the old "joiner" in 1872 than they had been in 1867.

# V    Scandal

The election of 1867 had been four local plebiscites on Confederation, and, with the exception of Nova Scotia, most voters seemed to have approved the accomplished fact which confronted them. Understandably, given the way he had worked the national consolidation theme over the previous four years, Macdonald attempted to stage the same kind of contest in 1872. The Prime Minister claimed that he wanted nothing more than another term to round out the great work launched in 1867, carried forward to date but not yet quite complete. Confederation was still only "in the gristle," he said, more of his kind of leadership was needed before the union would have "hardened into bone, and ... taken such root as to be able to stand the storm."

The buffeting of Macdonald's Union Party was not directed against Confederation, however. It was the government of that federation and its latest project, the railway, which came under attack. One of the major reasons was the alleged extravagance of constructing so long a line so far in advance of demand. On the other hand, the very enormity of the project made it attractive to some businessmen, all land speculators, and those workers who would benefit directly from building the line to British Columbia in ten years. Others were more inclined to regard the scheme as a public work which should be undertaken over a longer period and with less direct association between government and profiteers. The first two railways with significant government involvement, the Grand Trunk and the Intercolonial, were bad enough, it was argued. The potential for corruption with the latest proposal seemed even more monumental. In George Brown's opinion, building the Pacific Railway in such a hurry was a "rash and maybe disastrous step."

Criticism notwithstanding, Macdonald had pushed his railway bill through Parliament just before dissolution. The act promised 30 million dollars and 50 million acres to the private company which would complete the work from a point about 200 miles directly north of Toronto to the Pacific Ocean within ten years of July 20, 1871. Another interesting feature of the legislation was the discretion left to the cabinet in awarding the charter. Parliament left it to the cabinet alone to dispense the award, the greatest piece of patronage in Canadian history.

By 1872, there were two rivals contending for the prize. The Grand Trunk Railway, in one sense the firm most likely to receive the reward, was not one of the contenders. Most of the directors of the Grand Trunk were skeptical about the feasibility of blasting a railway through the Shield and, supposing it were possible to do the work, they doubted the wisdom of building a line through so much unsettled territory. But there were some Grand Trunk directors who liked the project because of the enormity of its government backing and they gathered around Senator D.L. Macpherson in Toronto. Their rivals were located in the other commercial capital of Canada, in Montreal, around Sir Hugh Allan who was allied with American railway promoters in Chicago and Minneapolis.

Macdonald wanted the Allan group to jettison its American affiliation and combine with Macpherson to make one Canadian firm. For obvious political reasons merger was far more attractive than picking one group over the other. When they refused to look beyond their own narrow interests, the Prime Minister hesitated to award the charter to either, and the particulars in the award of the contract were postponed until after the election of the new House of Commons.

In the context of the election, however, the anticipation of would-be promoters was exploited to full advantage by Macdonald in order to defray his party's campaign expenses. It is not clear how much cash was raised from the Macpherson group. But, after the victory, his party's dealings with Allan came out in lurid detail because the Government of Canada betrayed an implicit trust by awarding the charter to a forced conglomeration of Canadians with Sir Hugh Allan shorn of his American backers. Then, American informants began to provide the opposition with all the necessary detail to destroy Macdonald's government.

In the episode that followed, the Pacific Scandal (which raged nearly unabated from April through October of 1873), there were two major issues. One was nationalism in the sense that Sir John A. Macdonald, "the founder and father of Canada", had been caught accepting campaign contributions apparently from American as well as Canadian favorites. The other issue was the question of corruption, the morality of soliciting favors from expectant recipients of government patronage. Parliament and the country had become exceedingly sensitive on both matters by 1873. In the summer, Macdonald diverted attention somewhat by charming Prince Edward Island into Confederation (with the promise of a railway, of course). But the scandal kept resurfacing. By November, the Prime Minister lost control of his majority.

Heightened sensitivity on matters of national and political integrity brought about Macdonald's resignation in the first week of November 1873. Ironically, in large part this was the final confirmation of the reality of his and Cartier's successes in the ten years before. In 1867, there had been no national integrity to violate. At best, the country was four provinces agreeing to disagree on the somewhat neutral ground of Ottawa. Six years later, there was at least the shadow of a sense of national purpose, and thus a basis on which to assert that the present government had behaved scandalously. Virtue triumphed and the ministry led by John A. Macdonald resigned on November 5.

Lord Dufferin, the Governor General, believed that there was "no one in the country capable of administering its affairs to greater advantage" than Macdonald; but in 1873, "John A." did not inspire sufficient confidence as the preceptor of national morality, and that, precisely, was what the Parliament and the country seemed to demand.

A new government, that of the Reformers led by Alexander Mackenzie, assumed control of the House and in the subsequent general election that was held in January of 1874, Macdonald's party was routed. But it remained to be seen how successfully a party could govern by the other approach of strict adherence to principle. It did not take long to learn, and the lesson was learned very well indeed. Once Mackenzie was defeated, almost a century passed before another government was elected on the same barren ground of "Canadian virtue".

# Bibliography

The volume in the Canadian Centenary Series that covers the achievement of Confederation, W.L. Morton's book, *The Critical Years: The Union of British North America, 1857-1873* (1964), also treats the period of the consolidation of the union covered by this chapter. In addition, several biographies serve as good general introductions to the theme of the first six years of national consolidation. Donald Creighton's *John A. Macdonald: The Old Chieftain* (1955) tends to identify Canada with whatever Macdonald was doing and Alastair Sweeney's *George-Etienne Cartier: A Biography* (1976) advances the same claim for his hero. J.M.S. Careless has written two volumes on the life of the figure who was Macdonald's greatest critic throughout this period; his *Brown of the Globe: Statesman of Confederation* (1963) is thus a useful counterweight to both Creighton and Sweeney. A general history that takes a more critical approach to the subject than any of the above is Stanley Ryerson's impassioned critique, *Unequal Union* (1968).

More specialized studies of the more important facets of the general theme considered in this chapter are also available. For the pacification of Nova Scotia, readers should consult Kenneth G. Pryke, *Nova Scotia and Confederation* (1979). An equally detailed account of the seduction of Prince Edward Island is F.W.P. Bolger's *Prince Edward Island and Confederation, 1863-1873* (1964).

Since the case of Rupert's Land is rather more glamorous than that of the Maritime Provinces (because of the Riel resistance), this subject has attracted far more of the historians' attention, and therefore interpretations abound. A delightfully romantic treatment of the affair is J.K. Howard's, *Strange Empire* (1952). More scholarly is W.L. Morton's booklength introduction to *Alexander Begg's Red River Journal* (1950). Morton tells the story as an episode in the history of French-English relations. G.F.G. Stanley emphasizes a theme of "primitives" versus the expansion of a "civilized" people in his *Birth of Western Canada* (1936) and biography of *Louis Riel* (1963). More recently, Frits Pannekoek has seized upon the divisions within Red River society itself in a brief but provocative interpretation which is revealed clearly by the title, "The Rev. Griffiths Owen Corbett and the Red River Civil War of 1869-70," CHA (1976). Other historians have projected their interest in the Red River episode — or of the early West in general — upon the rest of the country. In his article, "French Canada and the Prairie Frontier, 1870- 1890," CHA (1969), Arthur Silver has argued that sentiment toward the West in Quebec was and continued to be one of indifference, while David Gagan, in "The Relevance of 'Canada First'," JCS (1970), has shown that Ontario was not only keenly interested but pursued its regional ambition as if it were identical with the national interest. A synthesis of these diverse threads with what they imply for the nature of the Canadian federation itself is the extraordinarily judicious essay by D.J. Hall, entitled "'The Spirit of Confederation: Ralph Heintzman, Professor Creighton and the Bicultural Compact Theory," JCS (1976).

The works on Manitoba's entrance to Confederation, unlike those on Nova Scotia and PEI, have been concerned with the society in question as much as with the political sequence involved, perhaps because the Manitoba case was indeed a society so unlike the others. Similarly, the materials which have appeared in recent years on British Columbia's joining the union have also shown this concern. The work which is addressed most specifically to the political theme is H. Robert Kendrick's, *British Columbia and Confederation* (1967), and the biography of Amor de Cosmos, *Amor de Cosmos: Journalist and Reformer* (1975), by George Woodcock also covers this aspect of the story well. But since two thirds of BC's population consisted of Native People in 1870, and since this population continued to be relatively prosperous despite a century of contact with Europeans, readers interested in this aspect of the social history of British Columbia should read Robin Fisher's *Contact and Conflict: Indian European Relations in British Columbia, 1774-1890* (1977) along with the material which is focused more specifically on the Europeans, such works as "The Character of the British Columbia Frontier," by Barry M. Gough, *BC Studies* (1976-77).

Finally, since consolidation of the union implied changed relations with the United States and Great Britain as well as bringing additional provinces into Confederation, readers might wish to consult additional material on the subject of Canada's relations with both countries between 1864 and 1873. Robin Winks has written on *Canada and the United States: The*

*Civil War Years* (1960) and C.P. Stacey covers "Britain's Withdrawal from North America, 1864-71," CHR (1955). The settlement of the three countries' differences in 1871 is described by Goldwin Smith in *The Treaty of Washington* (1941), but the best account of this episode is Creighton's "Fish and Diplomacy" in his biography of Macdonald cited above.

"Canadian virtue came in many different
denominations . . ."

# CHAPTER 13

# *Their Principles Were Their Politics*

---

I    Liberals with "Sound Principles"

---

Soon after John A. Macdonald resigned in disgrace over the Pacific Scandal, the new government, that of Alexander Mackenzie, went to the people in a general election in January 1874. The voting for Canada's third Parliament was more significant than either previous election (from the standpoint of the history of political parties) because for the first time there were contestants standing for something resembling national political organizations. Macdonald's group had been well organized from the start, but the other factions — Repealers, Anti-Ministerialists, Reformers, etc. — were simply the opposition. It was not until the Pacific Scandal that all elements found unity in adversity and chose a leader. Alexander Mackenzie then emerged at the head of one nominal party called the *Reformer-Liberals,* and therefore it was Mackenzie who was called upon by Lord Dufferin to form a new government when Macdonald resigned on November 5. It was also Mackenzie who was chiefly responsible for dramatizing the differences between those on his side of the House and the other group in the election of 1874.

When Mackenzie addressed his own electors in Lambton County, Ontario, he suggested that the main difference between the two parties was morality rather than ideology. Both professed similar truths, he said, but the previous government was distinctive because it was immoral. Its "members were elected by the corrupt use of Sir Hugh Allan's money." His Reformer-Liberals, in contrast to the "corruptionists," were the ones who were true to "sound principles." They could be counted upon to "elevate the standard of public morality ... and ... conduct public affairs upon principles of which honest men can approve, and by practices which will bear the light of day." Macdonald's method of promoting national consolidation was to give bribes to provinces with public money and to take bribes for his party from private contractors. Not surprisingly, the new Prime Minister promised to dismantle the main bribe of his predecessor. He would renegotiate the "impossible" gift of a railway to British Columbia. Instead of proceeding with overly expensive public projects, Mackenzie's party would institute reforms that would cost the public almost nothing and benefit the country a great deal. In this sense, his program was to be the purity of the government itself.

Three kinds of reform were promised. One was electoral reform. The second was reform of the constitution. The third was fiscal stringency. With regard to the first, cleaner elections were pledged by changing the Elections Act to require simultaneous voting on the assumption that if everyone voted on the same day an incumbent government would be less able to resort to the corrupt practice of bowling over critical constituencies, one by one, as was the established practice to date. Other reforms of election procedure included abandoning open voting in favor of the secret ballot, trial of controverted elections by a judge instead of by a House of Commons committee, and extension of the franchise beyond property owners.

Mackenzie promised two constitutional reforms. One was a revision of the militia system intended to make it more professional and less vulnerable to domination by political appointees. He proposed a national military college to supply the Canadian army with officers who were more than mere political appointees. The creation of a Canadian officer corps implied a fairly robust nationalism. So also did Mackenzie's proposal to create a Canadian Supreme Court, apparently to eliminate the British Privy Council as the last court of appeal.

The promised fiscal reforms pertained to public and private spending. Mackenzie indicated a need for an "insolvency law" to facilitate the declaration of personal bankruptcy without subsequent imprisonment for debt. But at the same time, to set a good example of the way to avoid bankruptcy in the first place, Mackenzie promised to scale down the level of government spending. He denounced Macdonald's railway plans in this regard as particularly extravagant. These would be cut, and the government's need for revenues could be reduced accordingly. In this way, the voters were led to expect that the government's prime source of income, the tariff, would be lowered significantly below the current rate of 15 percent. Honest and frugal government would relieve everyone — a little. Invigorated honesty and pride would raise Canada in spirit and the constitutional reforms would lessen dependency upon Britain, thus advancing the country among the community of nations. This was Alexander Mackenzie's promise to his own electors, and although it was a slower way to build a country than Macdonald's methods, in the new Prime Minister's opinion it was the only proper method.

The electorate seemed to agree. Mackenzie triumphed in Lambton, and Reformer-Liberals triumphed elsewhere as well, gaining a two to one majority over Macdonald's group with 138 seats in the House of Commons. Since this result occurred in every province except British Columbia ("the spoiled child of Confederation"), Alexander Mackenzie felt justified in voicing strong words of satisfaction with the conquest, saying "the country has pronounced its condemnation of the Pacific Scandal." He said "the old corruptionists are fairly stupefied." With the great victory, everything he had promised in Lambton could be enacted in Ottawa because Canada seemed completely united behind Mackenzie and the party that promised to stand uncompromisingly for "sound principles".

Canadian virtue came in many different denominations in 1874, however. Among Mackenzie's Reformers, there were no fewer than four different strains of reform-minded politicians pulling at the unity of one nominal party. From Ontario, the oldest and most outspoken of the reformer-moralists were those of the old Clear Grit persuasion such as the leader himself, and George Brown, out of Parliament but still active in politics through his ownership of the most formidable newspaper in Canada, the Toronto *Globe*. The distinguishing characteristic of this sort of reformer was his assumption that society was nothing more than an agglomeration of individuals and an ideal government was primarily nothing more than an impartial referee in disputes as they might arise between individuals in pursuit of their private interests. The power of government was thus seen as an essentially negative force preventing combinations of wage earners, for instance, from forcing their will upon the individuals who employed them. Nor was the state to favor combinations of businessmen in their projects, for example, railways. Government was to play limited, self-denying frugal roles; it was not to be an active, ambitious power on its own. As Mackenzie expressed his philosophy on a visit to his Scottish homeland in 1875: "I have believed... and I now believe, in the extinction of all class legislation, and of all legislation that tends to promote any body of men or any class of men from the mere fact of their belonging to a class of higher position... in the community." In Canada, he continued, "we take the ground simply and completely that every man stands equal in the eye of the law, and every man has the same opportunity by exercise of the talent with which God has blessed him to rise in the world, in the confidence of his fellow-citizens, the one quite as much as the other."

Another strain of the reform persuasion was the Quebec variety which A.A. Dorion represented. This was the old *Rouge* position, more temperate in its republicanism in 1874, but only slightly more compatible with the ancients of the Clear Grit turn of mind. The *Rouges* were still ardently anti-

Protestant and hypersensitive to insults from Protestant nationalists. But their chief enmity in this period was the clergy for the *Rouges* demanded that the Church must play nothing more than a neutral role in the politics of the day. To the clerical hierarchy such a stance would have been totally irresponsible, however. Moreover, the Holy Father himself, Pope Pius IX, had issued an encyclical as recently as 1864 in which the clergy was ordered to commit itself to fighting an appended list of eighty errors which included the notion of the separation of church and state, and denounced pantheism, naturalism, absolute rationalism, moderate rationalism, indifferentism, latitudinarianism, socialism, communism, and secret societies. To make all the foregoing more emphatic, in July 1870, the Church proclaimed the Dogma of Papal Infallibility. The freshly reasserted position of spiritual authority made certain Bishops in Quebec even more militant than they had been in the past, even more committed to what they perceived as their special mission in North America.

Clerical ascendancy and ultramontanism (orientation more to Rome than to local secular or clerical leaders), led to open conflict between the Church and the anticlericals. The most outspoken young anticlericals were associated in a literary society called the *Institut Canadien*. The Bishop of Montreal, Ignace Bourget, denounced them for propagating errors the Pope had recently condemned, and when the *Institut* reciprocated by denouncing the bishop as a meddler, Bourget brandished threats of excommunication. The animosity reached crisis proportions in 1874 when an excommunicated Liberal and member of the *Institut* who had been dead for five years, was awarded Catholic burial by court order. Backed by the law and English units of the militia, Joseph Guibord was entombed in reinforced concrete where his relatives wished. When Bishop Bourget then ruled that Guibord's plot in the cemetary was profane, he seemed to have the last word in the dispute and the alliance between the Church and the *Bleus* emerged the stronger. The central problem for Quebec Liberals was to draw a distinction between liberal Catholicism (condemned by the Pope) and Catholic liberalism (theoretically not inimical to the ultramontane doctrines of the Quebec Church). The first evident steps in this direction were not apparent until 1877 when the young Wilfrid Laurier proclaimed his liberalism was nothing more than his being "one of those who think that everywhere, in human things, there are abuses to be remedied, new horizons to be opened up, and new forces to be developed." Such pronouncments placed Laurier more in the tradition of utilitarian liberalism than *Rouge* anticlericalism or the Grit Protestant individualism affirmed by such persons as Mackenzie and Brown, but it did not win many friends in Quebec — not in the 1870s. In the meantime, Mackenzie was left with three *Rouge* reformers in his cabinet — persons who were even less popular than Laurier with the Quebec Church and traditionally despised by the Grit reformers of Ontario.

Two other kinds of partisans in Mackenzie's Reformer party were even more evidently on his side by reason of circumstance than the *Parti Rouge*. The first were those independent nationalists espousing Canada First, calling themselves a "movement" in 1874. They were with Mackenzie then because of their revulsion at Macdonald's "sordid and mercenary" means of national consolidation. Still, it had to be admitted that the first Prime Minister was an active builder between 1867 and 1873. As soon as it would become evident that Mackenzie intended nothing more than the few reforms he promised at Lambton, they would oppose him just as they had criticized Macdonald on other grounds. Thus, Edward Blake — perhaps the most delicately temperamental politician in Canada — emerged as the leader of such criticism as early as October of 1874 when he hinted that Mackenzie was far too cautious in the reforms he was willing to pursue. "How long is this talk ... of the desirability, aye, of the necessity of fostering a national spirit among the people of Canada, to be mere talk?", he asked his audience in Aurora, Ontario on October 3. "It is impossible to foster a national spirit unless you have national interests to attend to ...," he continued, and concluded with the prophesy that "The time will come ... when we shall realize that we are four millions of Britons who are not free ... ."

George Brown was inclined to dismiss such talk as empty, "juvenile" rhetoric. In response to the demand for Canada First, Brown snorted, "God save the grand old British race first." So also did the last of the remaining groups in the Reformer party, amounting to about half the membership of Mackenzie's Cabinet. They were the turncoat ministerialists, persons formerly associated with Macdonald's party. They accepted few, if any, of the doctrines of "Canada First" or dogmatic Grit liberalism, and coming from Nova Scotia, New Brunswick, or Ontario, they had nothing to do with *Rouge* liberalism. But they were with Mackenzie in 1874 because, along with much of the rest of the country, they could not approve what Macdonald had formerly done with his majority. The "loose fish," as Macdonald called them, or "shaky fellows" in George Brown's description, waited to see what Mackenzie would do with his majority.

## II    A Railway in Principle

The mix of contradictory liberalisms and commitment to rigid adherence to principle meant that Mackenzie was never able to develop a strong team of ministers and enjoy the luxury of distributing responsibility among a competent crew of trusted lieutenants. To a remarkable degree, Alexander

Mackenzie attempted to look after all the important affairs of government entirely on his own. Ostensibly, he was the Minister of Public Works, a crushing job in itself given the work of superintending the railway projects. But he also retained the initiative in preparing most of nearly one hundred pieces of legislation for introduction in the first session of Parliament. Remarkably, by November 1875, he had launched all he believed needed launching. Not everything had been completed as promised in his Lambton address, but "not one promise ... has been left to rust or die out," he said. The election reforms, reform of the militia and a military college, bankruptcy legislation, the supreme court, and the railway had all been pursued more or less as promised. Mackenzie continued to believe that the need for reform would "never cease as long as this world is peopled by sinners," but he did feel in 1875 that the most flagrantly wicked of his generation were in retreat. Thus, he settled into what Canada Firsters had been denouncing since October 1874 as a cautious, unimaginative, and penny-pinching administration.

Mackenzie's railway policy was the prime illustration of his alleged inaction and penury. The Prime Minister abandoned Macdonald's promise of building a through-line from British Columbia to eastern Canada over a period of ten years. It was a railway ahead of demand, and he also believed that it was beyond the means of a small country like Canada, then sliding into the worst trade depression since 1857. What he advocated instead, in principle, was piecemeal construction to follow rather than advance settlement. Also, in principle, his would be a railway to supplement rather than to supersede navigable "water stretches". Transport would move by boat over the Great Lakes as far as Port Arthur. There a railway would run to the chain of lakes fifty miles west. Then it was back to boats for the two hundred and seventy miles over Shebandowan Lake, Lac de Milles Lacs, Rainy Lake, Rainy River and the Lake of the Woods (see map 13.1). At the northeast corner of the last lake, the railway would resume and by this means cargo would be transported the remaining 115 miles to Red River. For the forseeable future, that terminus, roughly the site of present-day Winnipeg, would be the western terminus of the Pacific Railway as well. As soon as possible, there would be a through-line built from Port Arthur to Winnipeg, and also from Winnipeg south along the east side of the Red River to the United States border. Mackenzie did not believe, however, that the country could afford, in his lifetime, to build the expensive line over the mountains to British Columbia, and the astronomically expensive section traversing the north shore of Lake Superior. The project Alexander Mackenzie would approve was a transcontinental railway only in principle. His biographer, Dale Thomson, has argued that Mackenzie's was the only feasible alternative given the reduced government revenue in the depressed years between 1873 and 1878. Even with the truncated system supported by Mackenzie, Thomson

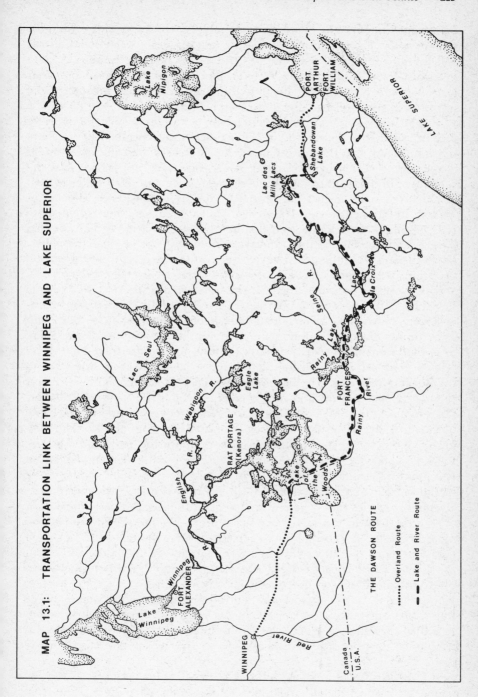

MAP 13.1: TRANSPORTATION LINK BETWEEN WINNIPEG AND LAKE SUPERIOR

THE DAWSON ROUTE

Overland Route
Lake and River Route

points out, roughly one quarter of the entire federal expenditure went for public works. The implication is that the railway was not neglected, it was still the government's first priority. With more revenue to spend, more miles of railway would have been built. But Pierre Berton, and most other historians are convinced that "it is doubtful that, given prosperity, he would have accomplished any more than he did."

Despite their apparent disagreement on what Mackenzie might have accomplished with the railway in better times, historians do seem to share the assumption that the railway had to be built — and as quickly as possible. Recent research in the United States, however, has shown that the settlement of that country was quite feasible using improved water routes, in much the same fashion advocated by the Canadian Prime Minister in 1874. Had Mackenzie developed his "water stretches" alternative more fully he might have pointed out that as late as 1870, in the already settled part of Canada, the existing railways carried less freight than the water-borne carriers. Then he might have asserted that the North West posessed a system of natural waterways almost as attractive as the St. Lawrence, and pointed the accusing finger at the other side of the House to argue that those "members elected by the corrupt use of Sir Hugh Allan's money" were railway promoters first, fathers of Confederation second, and opportunists always. His Reformers, he might have continued, were going to pursue Canada's western destiny through her northern waters. Mackenzie's party would make the St. Lawrence navigable from tidewater to the Rocky Mountains. The big project would be a canal from Port Arthur to Lake Shebandowan, and improvements around the seventy-odd portages to Lake of the Woods. Then, rather than moving overland, the route of the fur traders over the Winnipeg River to Lake Winnipeg would be followed. From there, north was the Nelson, south the Red, and westerly the Saskatchewan and the Assiniboine. Later, as settlement advanced west and as capital accumulated in enterprising private hands, there would be railway connections as well, but not with the extravagant government subsidies that were required to build them ahead of demand.

The one flaw in the scenario was its impossibility. Mackenzie was no more interested in Liberal seaways than Conservative railways. Nor were many of his party any less infected with the railway mania than the Conservatives. What concerned Mackenzie, and mightily, was expenditure. That was the basis for his "water stretches" railway policy in the first place. Since it could not work without improvements to the waterways as they were, and since such improvements were only relatively less expensive than the railways (not cheap in absolute terms), in the end, Mackenzie's government had to admit that its water-stretches policy was primarily just a tactic to avoid more extravagant action.

To establish *some* transportation link with Manitoba, Mackenzie decided in the last year of his administration to accelerate the route leading from

Port Arthur toward Winnipeg, and the line south along the Red River to the United States. The Pembina Branch, as the second line was called, was far shorter and since it ran over loamy, level ground for the entire distance, it was more or less operational by the end of 1878 and linked up with the St. Paul and Pacific Railroad at the US border. From this date the Pembina Branch functioned as the main link between Manitoba and the rest of the world until the other line to Port Arthur came into service in 1882, four years after Mackenzie had been turned out of office.

In the meantime, intending settlers and their freight traveled west from Ontario by ship as far as Duluth, Minnesota, then by train through the United States to the Pembina Branch. Once in Winnipeg they could, if they intended to settle in the West beyond Manitoba, board the steamer *Northcote* and travel in high-water seasons west via the Saskatchewan River, in its unimproved state, nearly as far as Edmonton. In a sense, that was a transportation system assisted by water stretches, but it was not the one which might have been, nor the scheme Alexander Mackenzie espoused in principle.

## III    Extinguishment of Aboriginal Title

Mackenzie was more successful in clearing Canadian title to the West than in promoting transportation improvements for its settlement. Earlier, Macdonald's government had purchased title to Rupert's Land from the Hudson's Bay Company, but the HBC was only one claimant. The people actually in possession of the land were the Indians and Métis. In 1869, they had no intention of relinquishing their claims.

In the previous chapter, it was shown that the Métis settlers around Red River had effectively dissuaded the government from annexing their region as a colony of the Dominion. At the same time, they won assurances that their land, religion, and language would also be secure under the new regime. It is not clear whether Macdonald and his associates had made promises they intended to honor once Rupert's Land was securely in their grasp, but it is clear that the opposition despised all the major provisions of the Manitoba Act from the time of its introduction to the House of Commons in May of 1870. Not surprisingly, once in power, Mackenzie took important steps to vitiate what were regarded as the most objectionable features of the Manitoba Act — the land promises. The assurance of continuity in the occupancy of riverfront lots, an unqualified guarantee in Section 32 of the law, was changed in 1874 into a less definite opportunity. In the new act, "persons satisfactorily establishing undisturbed occupancy ... and peaceable possession" of their riverfront homes were assured confirmation of ownership by the Dominion. In practice, the proof that was demanded was documentation of ownership by deed from the Hudson's Bay Company or improvements of the land in the sense of fenced and cultivated acreage, the construction of houses and outbuildings. But the HBC had given very few deeds to its settlers in the years between 1835 and 1869, and since the Métis tended to "ranch" the buffalo more than they "farmed" the land, less than 20 percent of the original population were able to pass the homestead test. The "Old Settlement Belt" of Manitoba was thus cleared of its original population at almost no cost to the Government of Canada. The other benefit of this policy (from the standpoint of officialdom in Ottawa) was that it freed the reserve of the 1.4 million acres promised to the children of the half-breed heads of families in Section 31 of the Manitoba Act. Having lost their riverfront homes, the Métis tended to leave Manitoba, of course taking their children with them. Enterprising "land agents" tracked them to their new locations and obtained assignments of the children's allotments of land, or, having failed to find such persons in preliminary searches, simply forged fraudulent transfers. The irregularities in such practices were so complicated that the Legislative Assembly of Manitoba (predominantly Ontario-born by 1878), enacted a special code of property law concerning the "estates" of "half-breed infants". Not surprisingly, the Dominion government did not disallow such legislation even though there were good grounds for doing so in Section 91 (24) of the BNA Act.

Government policy was to clear the land of Métis and Indians, to make way for "actual settlers" and to do so as economically as possible. At first, the Indians seemed even less moveable than the Métis had been in 1869. At Fort Frances in 1870, for instance, Colonel Wolseley offered gaudy presents to one chief who rejected them on the spot, saying: "Am I a pike to be caught with such bait as that? Shall I sell my land for a bit of red cloth? We will let the palefaces pass through our country, but we will sell them none of our land, nor have any of them to live amongst us." Similarly, another chief further west rejected comparable offerings on the same logic: "We want none of the Queen's presents; when we set a fox-trap we scatter pieces of meat all round, but when the fox gets into the trap, we knock him on the head."

Still, it was in the period of Alexander Mackenzie's administration, between 1874 and 1877, that most of the Indian lands between Manitoba and the Rocky Mountains (south of 60 degrees North latitude) were transferred by treaty from the Native People to the Government of Canada and at almost no immediate cost to the Dominion (see map 13.2). Military force was not the reason. In fact, the only soldiers Canada sent West were paramilitary constables, the North West Mounted Police, whom the Indian chiefs tended to welcome because they were a force to discipline the whis-

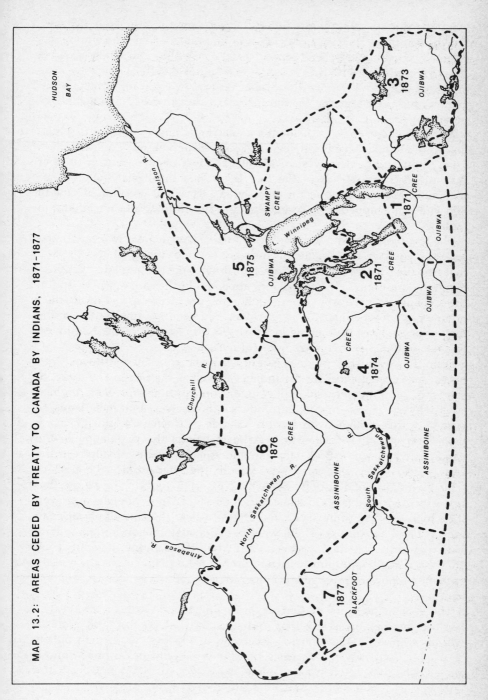

MAP 13.2: AREAS CEDED BY TREATY TO CANADA BY INDIANS, 1871–1877

key traders and wolf hunters — interlopers mainly from the United States. But the Mounties were not present in large numbers. The force as it was originally constituted in 1873 was only 150 constables, and when Mackenzie's government sent them west from Manitoba in 1874 the force was increased only to 300 since the Prime Minister was no more inclined to extravagance in budgeting for the national police than for national transportation.

Nor was encroaching settlement the reason behind the Indian capitulation. In the whole decade between 1870 and 1880 there were no more than a few thousand settlers west of Manitoba. Most people went no further than the rich farm lands of the Red River area that began to prove its potential for wheat production as early as 1876 when the first surplus of Red Fife was shipped from Manitoba by way of Minnesota for milling in Ontario.

The few pioneers who did ride the *Northcote* west tended to locate themselves in compact settlements on the very shore of the great river system that was their highway. Thus Protestant Prince Albert came into existence. Similarly, a number of Métis villages appeared in the same vicinity and in the Qu'appelle valley by the migration of people displaced from their home province (see map 13.3). The Métis had been hunting buffalo in the region for generations. Having lost their place in Manitoba, the Northwest was a logical place to which they might retreat.

Soon, however, the buffalo began to disappear from the Northwest with disastrous consequences for the Indians as well as the Métis. The threat of starvation, and the decimation of Native People by smallpox, were the reasons why so many Indians surrendered themselves and their lands to become wards of the Government of Canada between 1874 and 1877. Pestilence came to the Indians first. At least half of the population of the bands in what is now Saskatchewan and Alberta died of smallpox in the early 1870s. Those who survived epidemic then had to face the crisis of their dwindling food supply. Systematic extermination of the beasts that had provided the Plains Indians with their sustenance, shelter, and even their fuel, was begun in the United States to clear the land of obstacles to railways and agriculture. There were perhaps sixty million buffalo milling back and forth over the invisible border when the slaughtering started. By 1875 the herds had diminished enough to threaten famine. As the specter of famine followed the experience of empidemic, the will to resist was broken.

There were no wars in Canada preceding the making of the treaties because decimation by smallpox and threatened starvation "did more to win an empire for the whites," according to J.K. Howard, "than bullets could." In fact, Howard suggests that "bullets could never have done it alone." The final result was the same as military conquest, however. The once proud rulers of the Prairies surrendered without invasion. In all,

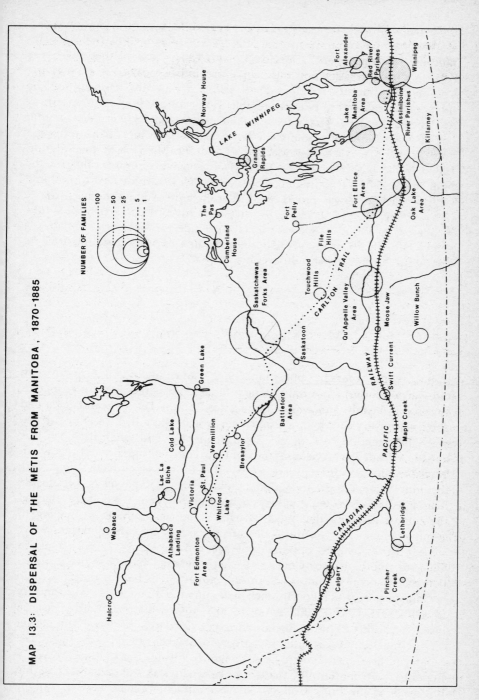

MAP 13.3: DISPERSAL OF THE MÉTIS FROM MANITOBA, 1870-1885

NUMBER OF FAMILIES

100
50
25
5
1

Halcro

Wabasca

Athabasca Landing

Lac La Biche

Cold Lake

Green Lake

Fort Edmonton Area

Victoria

St. Paul

Whitford Lake

Vermillion

Bresaylor

Battleford Area

Saskatchewan Forks Area

Cumberland House

The Pas

Grand Rapids

Norway House

LAKE WINNIPEG

Fort Alexander

Red River Parishes

Winnipeg

Assiniboine River Parishes

Lake Manitoba Area

Killarney

Oak Lake Area

Fort Ellice Area

Fort Pelly

File Hills

Touchwood Hills

Qu'Appelle Valley Area

Willow Bunch

Saskatoon

Moose Jaw

CARLTON TRAIL

Swift Current

Maple Creek

CANADIAN PACIFIC RAILWAY

Calgary

Pincher Creek

Lethbridge

there were four treaties negotiated between 1874 and 1877, one per year. The last two were the most difficult to negotiate as well as the most significant in achievement. The two final treaties were settled with the Alberta Cree and Blackfoot, the people previously most adverse to giving up their land to the whites. Their price, apparently minimal for the moment, threatened to be considerable in the future, however, since they demanded the usual guarantees of land reserves and government annuities but also a promise from Canada to secure them forever from hunger and disease. To Alexander Mackenzie and the Minister of the Interior, David Mills, both seemed dangerously expensive promises. But for the moment, it had to be admitted that the land was won for next to nothing. Of this Mackenzie was proud. And Mackenzie needed all the reassurance he could get in 1877 because by that year Macdonald's party had fully recovered its voice in opposition. Non-confidence motions, normally "a somewhat solemn or grand matter," according to Mackenzie, were being served up "for breakfast, dinner, and supper".

## IV   Mackenzie's Opposition

In his first two years in opposition, John A. Macdonald languished like an old warrior suffering mortal wounds. Since he was nearly sixty years old, suffered ill health, and was fully disgraced by the Pacific Scandal, he had good reason to think his political career was finished in 1874. Not surprisingly, he attended Parliament only infrequently, and when he did it was not as a leader who seemed anxious to court popularity. Thus, when Mackenzie introduced legislation providing for the secret ballot, defending the innovation on grounds that employees of companies risked losing their jobs if they voted contrary to their employers, Macdonald attacked the reform insisting that when a man voted he ought to be willing to assume responsibility for his actions regardless of the consequences.

The more effective opponent of Mackenzie, before 1876, was Lord Dufferin, the Governor General. Dufferin refused to accept the proposition that the concession of responsible government had made the Crown in Canada a mere symbol. If Mackenzie pursued a policy that ran contrary to Dufferin's Vice-Regal instincts, the interventionist Lord Dufferin insisted that his Prime Minister had to convince him he was wrong. After one of their many disputes he informed Mackenzie that "You said last night you are not a Crown Colony, which is true, but neither are you a Republic." To Dufferin, Canada's in-between status meant that "within the walls of the Privy Council I have as much right to contend for my opinion as any of My Ministers, and in matters of moment they must not expect me to accept their advice merely because they give it, but they must approve it to my understanding and conscience ... .''

When Mackenzie aimed to negotiate a reciprocity agreement with the United States in 1874 using George Brown as Canada's ambassador, Dufferin objected, suggesting that a British dependency should have to work through a commission named by the Colonial Office. When Mackenzie sought legislation creating a Supreme Court in 1875, Dufferin recommended disallowance in London on grounds that it conflicted with every British subject's right to appeal to the Crown (meaning the Judicial Committee of the Privy Council) as the final arbiter of disputes. And when Mackenzie pursued a railway policy that brought British Columbia to the brink of separation in 1876, Dufferin insisted that the Government of Canada would have to live with the bargain that had been struck in 1870. In each dispute, the nationalist Prime Minister and the interventionist Governor General both eventually compromised: George Brown did indeed negotiate (but every near-agreement had to be referred to London for Colonial Office approval until the talks ultimately failed); a Canadian Supreme Court was created (but only in principle, since appeals to the British Privy Council were allowed to continue); and Mackenzie did agree to abide by the spirit if not the letter of the Pacific Railway promise. Thus, the two strong-minded leaders had been able to moderate their differences. Perhaps the telephone installed between the offices of the two leaders in September 1877 (the first in Canada), was the important link facilitating such communication. As the advertisement for the new instrument explained, ''When converstation is carried on in the ordinary tone and the words are clearly enunciated intercourse can be kept up with as much ease as if the two individuals were in the same room.''

Macdonald resented Mackenzie's nationalist stance vis-à-vis Great Britain, calling such measures as the Supreme Court ''veiled treason''. He preferred to avoid such constitutional matters and focus attention on policies that did not appear to erode the old imperial tie. For two years, however, he did not have an appropriate issue on which to focus his limited energy. But in 1876, the tariff appeared to be the question on which Mackenzie might be most effectively criticized, and an alternative affirmed which seemed to out-distance Mackenzie's own nationalism without ruffling British patriotism.

Until the introduction of the personal income tax, the tariff was the most important source of funds for the Government of Canada, accounting for about three quarters of the government's revenue. Because of the continuing depression, however, imports had diminished, government revenue declined, and the administration was thus limited in all its other projects. Local growth in manufacturing did not help. For example, a number of manufacturers had taken advantage of the Canadian Patent Act which did not honor foreign patents unless inventors agreed to establish branch manufacturing capacity in Canada itself. Some manufacturers prospered by copying American designs for products for which there were already markets in the Dominion. One agricultural implement maker reported that "wherever" he expanded "the American manufacturers have retired from the field for the reason that we can undersell them. They make a very nice machine; it is the same machine... that we sell." But where Americans charged $100 for their product, this Canadian sold it for $75. In other words, the treasury of Canada lost $15 every time a farmer bought an implement from the Canadian rather than the American supplier.

There were two conventional methods for Mackenzie's government to solve the problem of declining revenue. One was to increase the excise tax on domestic manufacturing. The other was increasing the rate of taxation on the dwindling volume of imports. Richard Cartwright, the Minister of Finance, had already compromised his free trade scruples more than he had intended by raising the 15 percent tariff of the previous government to 17.5 percent and he would not stand for any other tax on trade given the generally weak state of the economy. But how was he to cope with the $134 million national debt he had inherited from Macdonald? The interest charges alone were $6 million, which represented about one third of all receipts projected for 1876. In Cartwright's view, the problem was essentially a moral issue. The evil was the "past extravagance and folly" of Macdonald's party. The cure was "prudence and economy until this present trial is passed."

Cartwright's moralism was just the opportunity Macdonald needed to bring about his revival. In 1876, it appeared that the Reformers were espousing yet another policy of inaction because of the rigidity of their principles, and wrong principles at that, said Macdonald. Even though he had never declared a dogmatic position on tariff policy publicly before, once that it became clear that the Reformers would keep the tariff low regardless of the consequences, Macdonald stood unequivocally on the side of a dramatic increase. He produced a motion in mid-March of 1876 calling for a much higher tariff, not simply for revenue to subsidize projects, for instance railways, but also like the patent law, to encourage manufacturing in Canada.

Canadian firms were not clamoring for such protection, but the wider profit margin a higher tariff assured was not cause for complaint, either. Moreover, those would-be manufacturers intending to start a business with costs in excess of world prices could find encouragement in a tariff subsidy just as labor might be presuaded to support a fiscal policy that promised to protect them from the unfair competition of workers who were supposed to be employed at starvation wages in Europe. Even farmers could develop an interest in a scheme that would tend to encourage greater consumption of their own produce. Appropriately, Macdonald called his panacea the "National Policy".

The convenient vehicle for selling the high tariff to the public was the political picnic, meetings of voters and their families on sunny summer afternoons to feast upon sandwiches, lemonade, other beverages, and politics. Other politicians would eventually come to denounce the custom as "nothing but a lot of people walking about a field and some nasty provisions spoiling on a long table in the sun." For John A. Macdonald, however, the picnic device was a lovely way to build support through conviviality rather than by angry harangues or mountains of newsprint. He was "a happy soul whom everybody likes." Mackenzie lamely responded with picnics of his own, "But he could never be taught these little arts ... There was no gin and talk about Mac."

Mackenzie preferred to remain true to his promises of delivering reform. Consequently, in the last session before dissolution, he delivered one last cleansing measure by introducing a local-option prohibition law permitting local authorites to impose complete abstinence on the picnickers, drunks, and tipplers of a whole district.

Then in September 1878, after the third summer of political picnicking, the electorate defeated the party whose politics were mainly their principles. John A. Macdonald and his party had a clear program. Moreover, unlike Macdonald's previous matter-of-fact, even crass, consolidation of national boundaries by cash promises and railway schemes, the new program, no less tangible, was calculated to arouse a "national sentiment." "There has arisen in this country a Canadian Party," he said in reference to his own, "which declares we must have Canada for the Canadians." This was not the ideological, racial nationalism of Canada First, nor the anticolonial nationalism of Alexander Mackenzie. Macdonald's brand was economic nationalism repudiating nothing more than reciprocity with the Americans. "You cannot get anything by kissing the feet of the people of the United States," he said. In Macdonald's view, the way to the bright future was where Great Britain had pioneered. "England, gentlemen, was the greatest Protectionist country in the world until she got possession of the markets of the world ... ." The tariff would work this magic for Canada, he promised. Like Britain before, Canada would "give a sprat to catch a mackerel."

The Reformers denounced Macdonald's economic nationalism as so much "humbug" and "bunkum". Cartwright ridiculed the proposition saying that it benefitted only the rich, "the poor and needy manufacturers who occupy those squalid hovels which adorn the suburbs of Montreal, Hamilton, and every city of the Dominion." It was a tax upon 95 percent of the people chiefly to benefit the top five. But the electorate was tired of depression and pious inactivity. In September of 1878, the Reformers were routed. "Nothing has happened in my time so astonishing," Mackenzie complained. There was also bitterness in his complaint that "Canada does not care for rigid adherence to principle in government."

# Bibliography

The volume in the Canadian Centenary Series that covers the Mackenzie years is P.B. Waite, *Canada 1874-1896: Arduous Destiny* (1971). Equally useful is Dale Thomson's biography of the Prime Minister, *Alexander Mackenzie: Clear Grit* (1960). Other important Grits have also received full biographical treatment. George Brown's attempts to negotiate reciprocity are found in J.M.S. Careless, *Brown of the Globe: Statesman of Confederation, 1860-1880* (1963) and Joseph Schull's account of Edward Blake's unwillingness to lead or be led, *Edward Blake: The Man of the Other Way* (1975). Generally, however, the Mackenzie "interlude" has been rather undeservedly neglected by historians. Only certain aspects of the period have received serious attention.

The make-up of Mackenzie's group as a party has been described by Escott Reid in "The Rise of National Parties in Canada," *Papers and Proceedings of the Canadian Political Science Association* (1932) and F.H. Underhill, "The Development of National Political Parties in Canada," CHR (1935). Here, however, the Liberals' *Rouge* component has received the greatest attention, especially in more recent work. English readers have M. Ayearst, "The *Parti Rouge* and the Clergy," CHR (1937) and Lovell Clark, *The Guibord Affair* (1971). Two book-length works on the subject in French are Jean-Paul Bernard, *Les Rouges: Libéralisme, Nationalisme et Anticléricalisme au Milieu du XIXe siècle* (1971) and Pierre Savard, *Aspects du Catholicisme canadien-francais au XIXe siècle* (1980).

Mackenzie's railway policy has recieved a great deal of attention — especially criticism. Harold Innis, *A History of the Canadian Pacific Railway* (1923) and Pierre Berton, *The National Dream: The Great Railway, 1871-1881* both described Mackenzie's railway policy primarily to condemn it. But Peter George's twenty-page forward to a 1971 reprint of Innis raises a minority report on the matter by focusing on the issues of construction ahead of demand and the axiom of indispensibility as both have arisen in the scholarship of Albert Fishlow, *American Railroads and the Transformation of the Ante-Bellum Economy* (1965) and Robert W. Fogel, *Railroads and American Economic Growth: Essays in Econometric History* (1964).

Another aspect of the Mackenzie years that historians have focused on recently is Canada and native people. D.N. Sprague has criticized the administration of the land promises to the Métis in the Manitoba Act. His title, "Government Lawlessness in the Administration of Manitoba Land Claims," *Manitoba Law Journal* (1980) suggests the severity of his criticism. J.K. Howard is equally critical of the government's handling of other groups in *The Strange Empire of Louis Riel* (1952). Less polemical than Sprague or Howard is the section on treaty making by G.F.G. Stanley, *The Birth of Western Canada* (1936). Also useful in understanding the significance of the treaties are Hugh Dempsey's biographical accounts of two leaders, *Crowfoot: Chief of the Blackfeet* (1960) and *Red Crow: Warrior Chief* (1980).

Several important questions concerning the Mackenzie years remain for future scholarship. For example, it is clear from Thomson's biography of the Prime Minister that the period between 1874 and 1878 was an important one in Canadian constitutional history for defining both the place of Canada in the British Empire and also for clarifying the role of the Governor General in Canadian domestic politics. But fuller studies of both issues remain to be done. Similarly, it is clear from Waite's outstanding account of national politics and general economic themes that the depression that began in 1873 had important consequences for reductions in both workers' wages and national revenue, but in other respects (particularly concerning banking and manufacturing) the economy continued to grow. Here as well, more research is needed to enlarge understanding of the anomalies of growth in recession. Studies by James Gilmour, *Spatial Evolution of Manufacturing: Southern Ontario, 1851-1891* (1972) and R.T. Naylor, *The History of Canadian Business, 1867-1914* (1975) hardly touch on either subject for the period in question.

"... the CPR's launching resembled mobilization for
national emergency ..."

# CHAPTER 14

# Years of Crisis

## I    A Tariff and a Railway

Although the National Policy had been popularized in rhetorical flourishes that Mackenzie's party called "humbug," the Conservatives' program itself was not a sham. It was not simply an image to be used in an election and then forgotten. For good or ill, the tariff Macdonald promised was the most conspicuous and controversial feature of his first budget, submitted to Parliament on March 14, 1879.

It had taken the Minister of Finance, Leonard Tilley, nearly three months to make all the adjustments for the new schedule of duties. Some items, such as raw cotton and the machinery for manufacturing processes such as textile production, were exempted from any duty at all. Other commodities, without particular pattern, were taxed to the sky. Such chaos was the result of every manufacturer's writing his own order, and the process of endless lobbying made Tilley's work a nightmare since protection seekers were said to have "waylaid him" by night and by day. Ultimately, a statistician skilled in the arts of tariff scheduling had to be called in. Depending upon the article, the final rates ranged from zero to 35 percent, most falling around the 25 percent level.

The new tariff was debated in the House of Commons from mid-March to the end of April 1879 because Macdonald's Conservatives were committing themselves to a policy of permanent indirect subsidies to industry on the stated premise that it was impossible for manufacturing to flourish in the Canadian state under conditions of free trade. It was indeed true that some manufacturers had asserted that the tariff would have to be permanent. If such a need were valid and general, then Macdonald's tariff was truly a National Policy. But in 1879, the issues had not been examined in these terms. At the time of its introduction, the tariff was simply good politics. Protection had been found to be a popular election issue and it seemed to be an even more effective method of assuring continuing support for Macdonald's party from manufacturing interests.

The identification of the national interest with the interests of business, at first so evident in the new tariff, soon became even more clear in Macdonald's resurrection of the Pacific Railway project. Mackenzie's approach had been piecemeal construction on the basis of public works. Contractors bid to build sections Canada owned. Macdonald's was rapid construction of the entire line as a subsidized private corporation. But businessmen did not rush to take advantage of what would appear in retrospect to have been recklessly generous support from the government. Only one syndicate, a group led by the Director of the Bank of Montreal, George Stephen, came forward with a serious offer to take advantage of Macdonald's well publicized willingness to offer tremendous guarantees in the undertaking.

In 1879 Stephen was Canada's clearest living example of the success myth in action. He was the best example anyone could cite to prove the myth that immigrants could rise to lofty pre-eminence by cunning industry. In 1850 Stephen started in the country as a newly arrived clerk from Scotland, working in a dry goods store. Through shrewd dealing and the support of his clan, by 1872 he had become a wealthy textile manufacturer. In 1879, he headed the Bank of Montreal and with his cousin, Donald A. Smith, Stephen was deeply involved in western land speculation and railway construction. It was this pair, with American associates, who were making the St. Paul and Pacific Railroad the first railway link to the east by connecting Winnipeg with Lake Superior over United States territory from Pembina to Duluth.

Stephen and his syndicate agreed to build the Canadian Pacific Railway, but the terms they demanded were so extraordinary that any government agreeing to them would have to persuade the country that Canada faced a do-or-die challenge. The political problem was to make rapid construction of the railway appear to be a genuine national emergency because the syndicate demanded an immediate cash subsidy roughly equivalent to the annual national revenue; that is $25 million. They demanded title to half the arable land in a belt twenty-four miles wide on either side of the CPR mainline from Winnipeg to the Rockies; they demanded title to the three sections of railway already completed or under contract at public expense (in all, 730 miles valued at $31.5 million); they demanded a traffic monopoly for the rest of the century and a perpetual exemption from all taxation. In return, Stephen's syndicate agreed to build 650 miles from Port Arthur to Callender and about 1200 miles from Winnipeg to Kamloops by May 1, 1891.

In December 1880, Macdonald brought the railway contract before Parliament thinking that he could secure ratification before the New Year. But the opposition attacked the railway scheme even more vehemently than the tariff, using every argument and strategy they could in order to persuade the government to revise the terms. The debate raged without end until Christmas recess and resumed in January, running nonstop to the end of the month.

The opposition's arguments — including Edward Blake's five-hour speech — elaborated two propositions. One was that the contract was extravagant. The other was that the arrangement was sinister. Both objections would be met if Macdonald would abandon his obsession with rapid construction, they said. Pressing their preference for building the "prairie section as fast as settlement demands" and indefinite "postponement" of the Rocky Mountain and Lake Superior sections, they argued that the slower pace would permit greater economy and obviate the need to offer the reckless inducements that they predicted would "ruin the public credit" in any case.

The aspects of the arrangement denounced as sinister were the size of the land grant and the implications of the monopoly. The opposition argued that the government was making the Northwest a fief of one syndicate having rescued it so recently from another, because the company which would be the landlord of most of the settlers was also to be their exclusive carrier. Of the two roles, that of transportation monopolist was denounced the more heatedly. Manitobans already complained that Stephen was gouging them with exorbitant freight rates. In 1880, wheat sold in Toronto for $1.10 a bushel and transportation charges consumed about half the price. The first third of the trip, over Stephen's already completed railway, accounted for most of the charges. Manitobans were anxious to see the rail line over Lake Superior operated competitively. To their horror, the government proposed to give it to the same syndicate which owned the other route.

Western hopes that the debate in Parliament might make a difference were dashed in February 1881. None of their proposed amendments was adopted. The most important act of incorporation in the history of Canada was thus presented and debated in Parliament like a controversial treaty with a foreign power. The measure was criticized and alternative wordings were proposed, but in the end the contract was accepted whole. How would the electorate react? Would the resurrected railway and the new departure in tariff policy meet with the approval of the voting public of Canada?

Macdonald was not certain, and he attempted to hedge his uncertainties by taking advantage of the opportunity for redistribution of electoral boundaries that was presented by the results of the 1881 census. Most of the provinces of Canada had shown a 17 percent increase over their 1871 population. The two exceptions were Ontario and Manitoba which had both grown faster than the national average. Manitoba had grown to 62 000 people in 1881 from the 12 000 of 1870. Ontario grew from 1.6 million to just under 2 million people in the same period. According to the

BNA Act, Quebec was always to have 65 members of the House of Commons, and the other provinces would have entitlement to Members of Parliament proportionately. All provinces growing at the same rate, the House of Commons would always have the same number of members, and legislative reapportionment would never be necessary. But Manitoba and Ontario having grown significantly faster than Quebec or the rest of the country, the latter was now entitled to 92 rather than 88 members, and the former could now claim five. In Manitoba, the fifth riding could be drawn on the electoral map without creating a tidal wave of protest. Where, though, would the four new constituencies of Ontario be added? More particularly, how many of the old electoral boundaries would have to be redrawn to accommodate the new? In 1882, all 88 of the old constituencies ceased to exist and 92 new electoral districts were proposed to accommodate Ontario's right to four additional seats in the House of Commons. In Parliament, Macdonald said this was to assure that each constituency was approximately equal in population. In private, he did not hesitate to admit that the purpose of redistribution was to "hive the Grits" since electoral boundaries were run to make each Conservative vote count for more, every Liberal vote a bit less.

Where the tariff had generated a debate, and the railway contract nearly a filibuster, Macdonald's Redistribution Act precipitated what P.B. Waite describes as a "sustained howl". Although the measure affected Ontario most particularly, other provinces joined in the protest with equal indignation. In the end, Macdonald was perhaps outdone by his own cleverness because once the ballots were counted (and there were ballots in this election, thanks to one of Mackenzie's reforms of electoral practices) it was seen that Macdonald's party had done less well in 1882 than in 1878. Even so, the Conservatives did win an overall majority — even from Ontario. Macdonald had spent his last mandate translating the image of a National Policy into the two realities of tariff protection and railway construction. Public opinion seemed to approve. The electorate must have known by 1882 that the tariff would mean higher prices and the CPR would require a mounting national debt. But both inflationary policies had given a boost to the economy when slow growth and deflation were the twin woes of politicians. In the apparent prosperity that followed tariff protection and national mobilization for the construction of the CPR, Canadians may have glimpsed a vision of the nation Macdonald and his supporters claimed they were building, but they also doubtless perceived a tangible benefit in the form of higher profits, steadier employment, and a faster pace of economic and population growth than would have been the case with lower government spending and freer trade.

## II     Mobilization for the CPR

If the CPR's launching resembled a mobilization for national emergency, the frenzied construction that followed was the appropriate continuation. Two hundred and seventy-five miles of track were laid in 1881 and William Cornelius Van Horne, an American railway builder, was recruited from his superintendency of an American railroad to fill the position of Engineer-in-Chief to make the distance covered in 1882 an even 500 miles. He succeeded. By the end of the 1882 construction season, the crews were pushed to within 75 miles of Medicine Hat. Thus, they crossed the prairies. The other sections, one over the Rocky Mountains and the other over the north shore of Lake Superior, were infinitely more costly in both time and money.

Building all sections of the railway at a frantic pace demanded logistics of supply similar to those employed in modern world wars. With the construction of the Canadian transcontinental railway, however, the enemy was nature and the allies included Germany (supplying steel rails), the United States and England (providing capital), and China and Ireland (contributing manpower). In such a pattern of international cooperation, Chinese, Irish, and Canadian laborers forced the wilderness first into armistice and finally into unconditional surrender.

While noting that the Canadian railway served national and international purposes, it is also well to remember that the CPR was the instrument of a commercial company's path to profits as much as the means of realizing John A. Macdonald's "National Dream". In this aspect, the syndicate which received the public's money looked after themselves first and the public later. The best indication of the self-serving nature of the railway owners is, perhaps, their decision to change the common-sense choice of a route through the fertile, rolling agricultural land in the Saskatchewan river system in favor of a more southerly route close to the American border through the near desert of Palliser's Triangle (see map 14.1). Since settlement was bound to follow where the railway led, the decision had dire consequences for the future of Canadian agriculture. Why, then, was the southerly route preferred? There are two obvious reasons — both related to profits. First, they wanted their mainline as close to the American border as possible in anticipation of the future competition with the Northern Pacific Railroad also under construction (through Montana, bound for Seattle). The monopoly clause would run for just twenty years. After that time, the NP might have branch lines running north across the border like pickets in a fence. The greater the distance between the two mainlines, the more threatening the branches.

The other reason pertained to the CPR's status as landowner. Since the Canadian railway was to receive half the arable land along 24 miles on

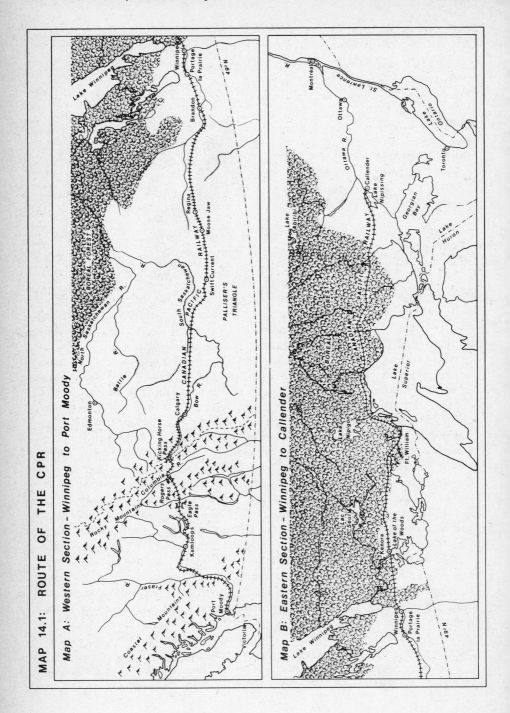

MAP 14.1: ROUTE OF THE CPR

Map A: Western Section – Winnipeg to Port Moody

Map B: Eastern Section – Winnipeg to Callender

either side of the right of way (with substitute acreage where the immediate territory was not fairly fit for settlement), if the chosen route were utterly uninhabited, the CPR would own the future townsites as well as most of the farm land. By opting for the southerly course, they bypassed existing settlement and were thus able to run their railway through the most empty, i.e., the most exclusively CPR, country possible. Their own branch lines would take care of the northern settlements in due course. The strategy meant longer hauls for future settlers in the Saskatchewan Valley, but insofar as revenue was a function of the distance freight traveled before reaching the mainline, more profits were assured by the same stroke.

It appears from such indications as their choice of the route that the CPR's directors were careful to assure future maximum income, and in this sense they were farsighted, cautious managers. But for the present, they were reckless in rushing construction of new lines and buying ready-made railways in the East to connect with Atlantic ports. Stephen knew that Macdonald's government could ill afford to see the railway languish should it fail in its attempt to recruit short-term private capital to keep the railway building at the frantic pace. Thus, Van Horne would boast one day that he "never estimated the cost of any work," and Stephen would return unblushing for more government subsidies, loans, or dividend guarantees the next.

In this fashion, the cost escalated in a terrifying way. By 1884 the CPR was demanding $30 million over contract. Rather than declare the railway forfeit, Macdonald somehow found $23 million. But a year later Stephen was back again demanding yet another $30 million. Private capital simply would not come forward to keep pace with the frenzied construction. This time Macdonald balked. He knew that his party would rebel. It looked as though he and his railway would go under. What would save him?

## III    Victory in Defeat

Ironically, the railway and the government were both saved by a crisis that ought to have been even more disturbing than the CPR's passing into receivership. On March 26, 1885, just as the railway was becoming technically bankrupt (having spent fifty-five million dollars of the public's money and thirty-seven million recruited from private investors), rebellion erupted in the North West.

Over the course of the last seven years, neglect and injury had brought three distinct populations in the West to the brink of a war of secession. The first group were white settlers, directly injured by the change of direction by the railway far to the south, in many cases angry and disappointed by frustrated land speculation. But their violence was entirely rhetorical. The actual rebellion was launched by the Métis and Indians of the area.

In the early 1880s, the Indians of the North West faced a period of crisis nearly as awful as the smallpox epidemics earlier in the decade. This time the scourge was famine following the extermination of the buffalo. The last treaties, those of 1876 and 1877, had both promised relief from such catastrophe. But instead of assistance the Government of Canada had responded with a program of moving Indians onto reserves at which places they were starved one day and fed the next on the assumption that this was the appropriate incentive to turn them into self-supporting farmers.

In a particularly well-chosen metaphor, the Indians protested that "you cannot make an ox of a deer." Their point was that they feared that they would no longer be Indians if they were to become farmers — a fear that expressed more than empty culturalism, since they knew that it was impossible to make an ox of a bull without first making him a steer. From their standpoint, they had exchanged title to their land guarantees against famine and pestilence. They were now starving; it was therefore time for the Government of Canada to live up to its side of the bargain. The Superintendant-General of Indian Affairs since 1878, John A. Macdonald himself, did not say yes, nor did he say no. His "vexatious delay" (as one Indian agent described Macdonald's procrastination), changed the Indians' misery first into resentment and finally into hate.

Of course, the disappearance of the buffalo affected the Métis, as well. But they also suffered from competition with the railway in the freighting business since the Red River cart or York boat was no contest against box cars on rails. Moreover, about 80 percent of the Métis population of Manitoba had lost legal ground for claiming riverfront lots in their home province when the Mackenzie government amended the terms of Section 32 of the Manitoba Act. Having lost their homes in the old Red River colony, many attempted to start afresh along various rivers further west and north (see map 13.3, previous chapter). The new difficulty that drove the Métis to war was their problem in obtaining assurances that they would be able to confirm title to the land to which they had retreated after leaving Manitoba.

According to the Dominion Lands Act of 1872, a grid of 36-section townships starting at 95 degrees west longitude and 49 degrees north latitude (the southeast corner of Manitoba), was to be extended westward through

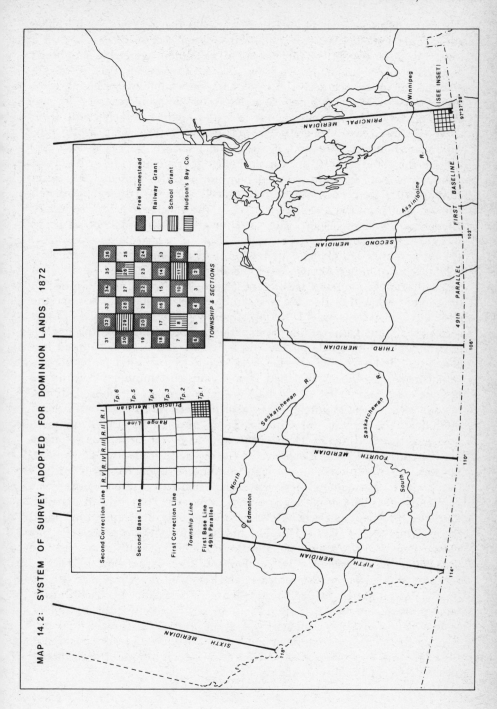

MAP 14.2:   SYSTEM  OF  SURVEY  ADOPTED  FOR  DOMINION  LANDS ,  1872

the fertile belt (see map 14.2). For a ten dollar registration fee, any male adult could enter a claim for a 160-acre quarter section of any part of a township open for settlement. Closed to settlement were odd-numbered sections of every township. Sections 11 and 19 were held back to raise a revenue for future schools. The rest of the odd-numbered sections were reserved for railway purposes. Sections 8 and 26 were reserved for the Hudson's Bay Company. Elsewhere, a settler might enter his claim. If he survived three years on his quarter-section and "proved it up" with cultivation and house construction, it was his in freehold.

From the standpoint of the United States government, the inventors of the system, and from the point of view of the Government of Canada adopting it in 1872, such a pattern of orderly survey assured rapid development. But from the *Métis* point of view, the checkerboard of imaginary townships was unrealistic because such a grid pattern did not take into account the course of the rivers on the banks of which people took root. The *Métis* wanted their land in the form of the familiar riverfront lots. When they petitioned Ottawa to permit this irregularity, they were met at first with only a long and indifferent silence. Having suffered the loss of their land before, they decided to mount another resistance. This time the people were led by Gabriel Dumont, superbly gifted in all the arts of *Métis* society save one: Dumont had no experience negotiating with the English government in Ottawa. Louis Riel did have such credentials. Dumont reasoned that Riel might help his people a second time in the new resistance.

Since 1870, however, Riel had been living as a hunted villain and a haunted visionary. First, there had been no amnesty (promised during negotiations for the Manitoba Act). Instead, there was a price on his head offered by the Province of Ontario. Then, after being elected on three occasions to the Canadian House of Commons by the people of Manitoba between 1870 and 1874, Riel was refused his rightful place in Parliament. Instead, he was offered an amnesty conditional upon his acceptance of five years, banishment. By 1884 the exile period had expired but Riel was comfortably settled among his people in Montana. Here he had married, found employment as a school teacher, and become a citizen of the United States. In June 1884 Gabriel Dumont and his lieutenants appeared in Riel's village personally to persuade the *Métis* leader to return with them to organize a new resistance at the Forks of the Saskatchewan. Having accepted the invitation, he returned and did well the work that needed doing. But on March 19, 1885, support for the resistance by white Protestant sympathisers was lost when Riel took a step they would not follow. Having failed to move Ottawa by petition and verbal threats, Riel proclaimed the *Métis* nation as a separate state with himself in the position of President and Pope. Mosaic laws were its only statutes and the *Métis* cavalry of Gabriel Dumont the sole security.

Had there been a purpose to Macdonald's studied neglect of the North West it was about to be realized because the great railway soon fulfilled its first and most dramatic popular mission in suppressing the second Riel episode, the North West Rebellion.

On March 22, the General Officer Commanding the Canadian militia, Frederick Middleton, was ordered to place a force of 8000 troops on alert for action. Four days later, the same day Macdonald temporarily refused George Stephen's latest loan demand, skirmishing broke out between the *Métis* cavalry and the North West Mounted Police near Fort Carlton (see map 14.3). Then the Indians near Frog Lake also rose in rebellion and the troops were ordered west — by train.

In 1870, Wolseley and his men had had a terrible time getting as far as Red River. A short fifteen years later, a more serious threat much further west was dealt with promptly and easily, thanks to the railway. To be sure, there were still four relatively short gaps in the line over Lake Superior, distances that had to be crossed on foot or by sleigh in the numbing cold of late winter. But in comparison with the trek led by Wolseley, Middleton's troops were whisked to the vicinity of the new disturbance. By May 15, Louis Riel had surrendered. By May 26, the last Indian resistance, that led by Chief Poundmaker, was also silenced. Less than fifty Canadian troops had died in the fighting. They were sewn in their blankets and buried at places with quaintly western names like Fish Creek and Batoche. The other troops went home to heroes' welcomes and arrived in time to help with the 1885 harvest. In the euphoria of speedy victory, there was no difficulty in persuading Parliament and the nation that the railway was worth an additional $15 million to rush on to completion.

## IV    Reaping the Whirlwind

With fresh government support, the CPR moved quickly to completion at the end of the 1885 construction season. The two long lines of steel met in British Columbia and there was a last spike ceremony on November 7. To many people, the completion of the railway was a momentous occasion, a great symbol of the country having been "stitched down". Pushed to an extreme, however, such a view betrays an adherence to the hero theory of history — the view that everything important follows from the actions of a few great individuals — in this case, a corporation rather than a person.

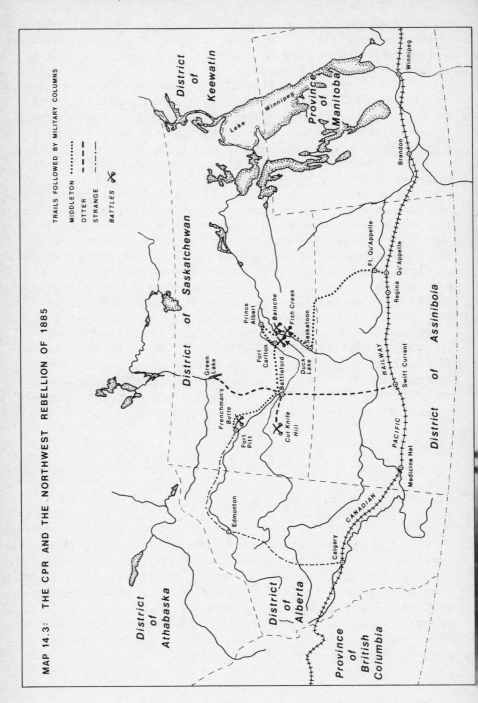

MAP 14.3:  THE CPR AND THE NORTHWEST REBELLION OF 1885

TRAILS FOLLOWED BY MILITARY COLUMNS

MIDDLETON  ··········
OTTER  ----------
STRANGE  —··—··—
BATTLES  ✕

District of Keewatin

Province of Manitoba

Lake Winnipeg

District of Saskatchewan

District of Assiniboia

District of Athabaska

District of Alberta

Province of British Columbia

Winnipeg
Brandon
Ft. Qu'Appelle
Regina  Qu'Appelle
Swift Current
Medicine Hat
Calgary
Edmonton
Green Lake
Frenchman's Butte
Fort Pitt
Cut Knife Hill
Battleford
Fort Carlton
Prince Albert
Batoche
Fish Creek
Duck Lake
Saskatoon

CANADIAN    PACIFIC    RAILWAY

Certainly, the completed railway did bring the provinces into closer physical proximity, a unity that was also symbolized by the adoption of standard time zones in the same year. But in other respects all the regional diversities of the country were still obvious. Indeed, they were reinvigorated by events that developed in the aftermath of the North West Rebellion because the glory of having driven the last spike for the railway was soon darkened by the long shadow cast by a Regina scaffold where an execution occurred on November 16. The minister responsible for Indian affairs, John A. Macdonald, had no intention of assuming responsibility for the rebellion himself even though seven years of procrastination, perhaps studied neglect, had magnified simple questions over land titles and government treaty obligations into monumental frustrations that ultimatedly drove the people to rebellion. The Government of Canada intended to put the burden of villainy entirely upon the shoulders of the rebels, and one rebel in particular, Louis Riel.

A number of leaders were captured, but Riel was the only one charged with high treason as defined by the fourteenth-century English "Statute of Treasons". His life hung on the question whether he did "most wickedly, maliciously, and traitorously ... levy and make war against our said Lady the Queen." Since Riel's participation — indeed his leadership — was beyond doubt, the matter appeared settled even before the court began to hear the case. But the issue at the trial was Riel's sanity. If he was found to be insane, then the government was morally bound to pity rather than to punish him. Riel denied to the end that he was mad. He declared "humbly through the grace of God I believe I am the prophet of the new world." It delighted him that the government found such declarations reasonable. His jury of six white Protestant males was not so easily persuaded. They found him guilty but recommended mercy on account of his mental state. However, the instructions from the Minister of Justice to the stipendiary magistrate trying the case were that he was bound to ignore the recommendation for clemency. Riel must hang. There were appeals, of course, and when they all failed — as they had to fail — the man who was held responsible for the rebellion paid the full price of his life on November 16, 1885.

To many Ontario Protestants, Riel's execution was just punishment for two rebellions. Even if he had not been completely sane in 1885, he was lucid enough in 1870 and Protestant Ontario still considered the Red River Resistance no less a rebellion than the later episode. Consequently, there were few regrets in Protestant Canada over the execution of the troublemaker who kept returning. All rebels had to be equal before the law, it was argued. The Toronto *Mail*, a Conservative party newspaper, asserted it would prefer to "smash Confederation" rather than compromise the legal principle for the sake of Riel's Roman Catholic sympathizers.

Quebec spokesmen were quick to reply that Riel was not the only person involved in the uprising and wondered aloud why he was the only victim of the hangman. Their conclusion was that the real motive for the hanging was Protestant resentment of the compassion Riel had won from French-speaking Catholics in and out of Quebec. Protestant bigotry blinded Ontario to Riel's madness and the jury's recommendation for clemency, they said. The man deserved pity rather than punishment.

The storm of controversy raged for nearly six months before Macdonald felt it was calm enough to seek a resumption of the parliamentary session in the spring of 1886. Then the fury resumed all over again. The Prime Minister kept silent, but he did permit — in fact Macdonald promoted — a demonstration of anger by Quebec Conservatives. As soon as the House began its business, A.G.P.R. Landry, the president of the Quebec Conservative Association, moved a resolution in the House of Commons expressing regret that Louis Riel had been executed.

In the debate that followed, Edward Blake (leader of the Liberal party since 1880 and arch-critic of Riel since 1870) indicated that he did not propose to "construct a political platform out of the Regina Scaffold." Blake's default enabled Wilfrid Laurier to become the rising star of the Liberal party with a speech that was poignant without being maudlin, scathing but not unseemly. He offered an indictment that hinted the government had been playing a political game all along. "Had they taken as much pains to do right, as they have taken to punish wrong," Laurier suggested, "they never would have had any occasion to convince those people that the law cannot be violated with impunity, because the law would never have been violated at all." Laurier's thinly veiled accusation that Macdonald had manipulated the people of the North West into an action that would give him an opportunity to dramatize the usefulness of his railway, was met with complete silence from the Prime Minister. Macdonald said nothing in reply, not one word to confirm or deny the charge.

Ultimately, the Landry motion was defeated. Only 52 members affirmed regret; 146 voted that they approved of the execution. The division was free, not following party lines, and therefore stood as an indication of the politicians' sentiments on the question. About one third of the Liberals voted with Conservatives who approved the hanging. Nearly half of the Quebec Conservatives either abstained or voted with the regretters, in this way censuring the government.

In Quebec itself, opinion was divided in similar proportions, half-approving and half-regretting. Consequently, the controversy offered an ideal opportunity for the rising politician, Honoré Mercier, to complete the work of diverting attention from hated Liberal Catholicism to the more benign Catholic Liberalism of Laurier by taking Laurier's attack on Macdonald one step further and contending that Quebec's integrity in Confederation was challenged. Mercier called for a new centrist coalition, neither Liberal nor Conservative but drawing together in a truly *Parti national* and hammered away at his theme of the insult paid to Quebec by the judicial murder of "notre frère" until he and the *nationalistes* had won control of the provincial legislature early in 1887.

# V    Disunity

The revitalization of Quebec nationalism was consistent with a drive toward provincial autonomy that was general, a trend that led most people in Canada to elect provincial adminstrations dedicated to opposing the central government. In New Brunswick and Nova Scotia, the basis for the revolt against Ottawa was almost entirely economic. The economies of both provinces, oriented so prosperously toward shipbuilding, the fisheries, and transoceanic commerce in the 1860s, had begun to show signs of deep decline in the twenty years since Confederation. During the period of the Golden Age of wooden shipbuilding, 1865-1869, 730 000 tons of shipping had been launched in British North America (compared to 690 000 in the United States or 518 000 in the United Kingdom during the same period). But later, between 1885 and 1890, a mere 148 000 tons of wooden ships were constructed in Canada. Elsewhere, shipbuilding flourished with iron as the new material of construction. But in the Maritimes shipbuilding simply went into decline. At Yarmouth, Nova Scotia, formerly one of the most important maritime centers of Canada, the builders and owners of wooden ships gradually shifted their capital from active promotion of shipbuilding and shipping, to passive investment, mere stockholding in other lines of enterprise, and frequently in other countries or other regions in Canada. Investors who did support local enterprise tended to go into coal mining and sugar refining. In a sense, such growth was dramatic. According to T.W. Acheson, "between 1881 and 1891, the industrial growth rate of Nova Scotia outstripped all other provinces in eastern Canada" and led to the creation of such firms as the Nova Scotia Steel and Coal Company, by 1900 the "most fully integrated industrial company in the country."

Employment in such protected mining and manufacturing appealed to some Maritimers, but thousands of "saw and hatchet men" preferred to continue working in wood and moved south to become housebuilders in such places as Boston's "streetcar suburbs". In the 1880s and 90s, one fifth of all the carpenters in Boston were Nova Scotia-born. In other words, people were being displaced from their old occupations faster than new employment was developing, even though Nova Scotia's pace of industrialization was faster than Ontario's in this period. As a result, populations that had grown between 15 and 20 percent per decade in Nova Scotia and New Brunswick in the 1850s and 60s, shrank to nil or minus rates in the 1880s. Unable to aim alternate industry at the Canadian market, the once prospering Maritimes appeared to be economic backwaters and demographic railway stations, the most valuable export becoming the population itself.

W.S. Fielding, the Premier of Nova Scotia, blamed Confederation for the disturbing trend, arguing that free trade with the United States was preferable to protection in Canada. In 1886, having despaired of persuading Ottawa of such a policy, he argued in the provincial legislature "that the financial and commercial interests of the people of Nova Scotia, New Brunswick, and Prince Edward Island would be advanced by these Provinces withdrawing from the Canadian Federation and uniting under one Government ..." He carried the Assembly with his Maritime Union alternative and then went to the people who awarded his liberals 29 of the 39 seats in the legislature. Subsequently, the Maritime Union idea died away, and however much his critics could legitimately protest that the maneuver was simply a cynical ploy in the first place, the fact remained that an anti-Canadian sentiment did have great appeal with the voters in 1886, just as in 1867.

Ironically, the central government that was criticized for serving "Empire Ontario" best, was only slightly less criticized by Ontario's provincial administration led by Oliver Mowat since 1872. Indeed, Mowat is generally considered the "father of the provincial rights movement in Canada" since he had been quarreling with Macdonald long before Fielding or Mercier. In Mowat's case, however, the primary object was consolidation of an already strong position — confirming coordinate power with Ottawa. Mowat had no quarrel with the National Policy as long as it continued to work toward building Empire Ontario. What Mowat did oppose — and mightily — was Macdonald's wish to whittle down the provinces in the course of realizing his dream of building "Empire Canada". To defend his province from national consolidation, Mowat went to court repeatedly, seeking judicial support for his own understanding of the division of powers. The turning point in the process involved an apparently trivial point of law arising from the licensing of taverns.

According to John A. Macdonald's theory of Confederation, the powers of the provinces and the central government fell in two compartments. Section 91 gave the government in Ottawa authority "to make Laws for the Peace, Order and Good Government of Canada." For "greater Certainty, but not so as to restrict the Generality" of this overarching power, 28 illustrations of such areas of activity were enummerated. What remained for the provinces was a far less numerous list of "subjects" of a "merely local or private nature," such as "shop, Tavern ... and other Licences in order to the raising of a revenue" enummerated in Section 92. In Macdonald's theory, Mowat could seek the enactment of a provincial statute, a kind of municipal by-law, requiring tavern owners to pay a fee to operate in his province. The power Mowat could not exercise, in Macdonald's view, was the regulation of commerce under the guise of raising a revenue.

The theory of Oliver Mowat and other opponents of centralizing administration was that the words of Sections 91 and 92 actually placed legislative powers in three compartments. One compartment was the 28 powers belonging exclusively to the government in Ottawa, the enummerated powers in Section 91. The second compartment was the list of 16 classes of legislation assigned exclusively to the provinces in Section 92. The third compartment was the "Peace, Order and Good Government" preamble to Section 91, words that Macdonald took as his license for unrestricted generality. For Mowat, however, the general power was simply a twenty-ninth subject area — national emergencies.

In the case of tavern licensing, the problem was that the Province of Ontario set regulations for tavern operation at the same time that a fee was collected and the license awarded. John A. Macdonald and a tavern owner named Archibald Hodge perceived the legislation as a dangerous encroachment on federal jurisdiction. Hodge paid his license fee, but he insisted upon waiting for a statute from Ottawa before he would see himself in any way restricted with respect to his hours of operation. In May 1881, because he allowed his billiard-playing patrons to continue at their pool tables after the 7 PM Saturday closing hour set by the Ontario statute, Hodge was prosecuted for a breach of the Ontario Liquor License Act. Subsequently, he appealed his conviction all the way to the Judicial Committee of the Privy Council of Great Britain and there the English Law Lords ruled in favor of Ontario in 1883. In their view, the legislation was "entirely local in its character and operation" and they agreed that it was intended primarily to raise a revenue though the licensing function. The Law Lords might have severed the regulatory aspect of the licensing act from the rest of the statute, but they did not. Instead, they confirmed Oliver Mowat's favorite doctrine of coordinate power:

When the *British North America Act* enacted that there should be a legislature for Ontario and that its Legislative Assembly should have exclusive authority to make laws for the province, and for provincial purposes in relation to the matters enumerated in s. 92, it conferred powers not in any sense to be exercised by delegation, [according to Lord Fitzgerald,] but authority as plenary and as ample within the limits prescribed by s. 92, as the Imperial parliament, in the plenitude of its power, possessed and could bestow. Within these limits of subjects and area the local legislature is supreme, and has the same authority as the Imperial Parliament or the Parliament of the Dominion ... (Quoted in G. Stanley, *Short History of the Canadian Constitution* [1969], pp. 119-120.)

Later, after the Government of Canada argued in another case that the regulation of liquor traffic had to be considered a matter relating to the "Peace, Order and Good Government of Canada," the Law Lords once again ruled in favor of Ontario in 1896. This time, Lord Watson extended the doctrine of coordinate power even further than Lord Fitzgerald had done in 1883, saying "the Dominion Parliament has no authority to encroach upon any class of subjects which is exclusively assigned to provincial legislatures by section 92 ... ." Placing the peace, order, and good government clause in a third compartment, Watson asserted that

If it were conceded that the Parliament of Canada has authority to make laws applicable to the whole Dominion in relation matters which, in each province, are substantially of local or private interest, upon the assumption that these matters also concern peace, order and good government of the Dominion, there is hardly a subject enumerated in section 92 upon which it might not legislate, to the exclusion of the provincial leglislatures. (Quoted in G. Stanley, *Short History of the Canadian Constitution* [1969], pp. 120-121.)

In this way, Macdonald's original theory of Confederation, indeed, his hope of what the union might develop into, had been defeated by the country's most powerful local premier. Since the tide of centralization had obviously begun to turn in the constitutional sense as early as 1883, and politically after 1885, the dissenting premiers thought that they might join forces in 1887 to establish the principle of coordinate power even more broadly than the Law Lords had recently allowed. They and their fellow dissenters gathered for a second Quebec conference in October 1887 to formulate resolutions affirming an even more robust array of provincial powers. Most notably, they demanded changes to give them a greater share of the national revenue, and called for abandonment of the principle that Ottawa might continue to disallow provincial legislation, such as

Mowat's liquor laws or the railway bills that Manitoba's Norquay enacted in defiance of the CPR's monopoly privilege. Predictably, Macdonald denounced the resolutions of the first premiers' conference as the emanations of a party gathering. After all, only one of the attending premiers was from Macdonald's own party. Still, the fact remained that with only Prince Edward Island and British Columbia prepared to stand by Macdonald's conception of Confederation, with five of the most populous provinces having declared against him, a truly remarkable protest against centralism had been made.

What did the electorate prefer? In Nova Scotia (the province that approved Fieldings' separatist resolution overwhelmingly in June 1886), the voters cast their ballots overwhelmingly for Macdonald's party in the federal election of February 1887. Nova Scotia was not unusual in its apparently divided loyalties. Every other province that sent a dissenting premier to the Quebec conference had exhibited the same tendency of preferring Macdonald's centralizing Conservatives for Ottawa even though they were just as clear in their preference for retaining outspoken provincial autonomy advocates locally. It was perverse, in a sense even schizophrenic, but the pattern seemed to be proof that Canadians wanted a clear national as well as a salient regional identification. They wanted a strong country at the same time they were determined to prolong the vitality of each provincial jurisdiction.

## VI    The End of an Era

The issue of national unity was placed in yet another context in 1891 when the general election of that year developed as a plebiscite on economic nationalism versus continentalism. The Liberals, led by Wilfrid Laurier, advocated abandonment of the protective tariff in favor of unrestricted reciprocity with the United States, a free trade position consistent with the provincial autonomy advocated by most premiers. But Conservatives asserted that reciprocity would threaten even provincial autonomy by jeopardizing the country as a whole. Some Ontario Liberals agreed that free trade with the Americans was essentially economic union, a first step to political annexation, as did Edward Blake when he observed with a certain philosophical detachment that "political union with the United States, though becoming more probable, is by no means our ideal, or as yet our inevitable future," and refused to support his party's policy accordingly.

Others asserted that free trade had nothing to do with political independence but they were confounded by the Conservatives who stressed that at the minimum reciprocity with the United States was at least a reduction of the tie to Great Britain. Appealing to the old flag and the old allegiance, they argued that the continuation of the tariff was indispensable for the survival of Canada as a British country. The election was close, but Macdonald's Conservatives were once more victorious.

The last battle of the old champion of national consolidation was a pyrrhic victory in another sense, however, since Sir John A. Macdonald, the seventy-six-year-old chieftain, began to suffer a series of paralytic strokes within weeks of the 1891 election. On the evening of Saturday, June 6, he died and there was no Conservative to replace him. Macdonald's death was thus a crisis for his political party, but also for his country. More than any other single person or project, it was the force of Macdonald's amiable personality and his centralist orientation that had secured the union of diverse provinces in the first instance and promoted their consolidation subsequently. The man who made Canada was mortal; so also perhaps was his creation.

The first to suffer the predictable effects of Macdonald's demise were the leaderless Conservatives who subsequently drifted toward a dangerously militant Ontario Protestantism that Macdonald had done much to dampen. Two years before his death, in March 1889, it had been moved in the House of Commons that the power of the Dominion should be used to disallow a recent provincial statute of Quebec, inimical because it set a precedent for intervention by an authority unknown to the British Crown. The law in question was the Jesuits' Estates Act calling for papal arbitration of $400 000 to be divided among contending claimants for property lost at the time of the cession of New France to Britain. Naturally, to ultra-Protestants the measure appeared to be a kind of repeal of the Conquest itself. But after several days of debate, the motion to disallow the Jesuits' Estates Act was defeated 188 votes to 13.

Here the matter might have remained, but the Toronto *Mail* editorialized that "the abandonment of Quebec to the Ultramontane and the Jesuit will be the death of Canadian nationality ... ." Having struck a sensitive nerve in Ontario, a nerve that the "Noble Thirteen" Members of Parliament had failed to arouse in the House, their most eloquent spokesman, D'Alton McCarthy, then found himself leading an appeal to the people. An Equal Rights Association was formed in Toronto in June 1889 demanding equal rights for all religious denominations and special privileges for none, an old slogan in Ontario, and a liberal-democratic doctrine that sounded lofty in principle. In this case, however, democracy meant repression of minorities on a national scale. First, it involved withdrawal of the long-established public support to Catholic schools, then withdrawal of the customary toleration that was sometimes accorded the French language outside Quebec in New Brunswick, Ottawa, and most recently, by statute, in the West. Ultimately, equal rights would have to mean utilization of Dominion power to coerce the provinces because eventually French-speaking Canadians would seek refuge in a militantly defensive Quebec. There, at the last ditch, they would outnumber English-speaking Protestants, and by the same doctrine of majority rule the French-Canadians would tell the English to attend schools and speak the language that accorded with the majority in Quebec. But since Ottawa could claim that the English-speaking people of Quebec were part of the wider Canadian majority, in this sense not a minority at all, they might say, in McCarthy's words: "No. This is a nation, the provinces have great powers for local govenment, but all these must be subject to unwritten laws which must regulate the whole Dominion." What McCarthy meant was that Canada had to become one centralized British state. Except for his rather extreme position on the Jesuits' Estates question, it should be clear why McCarthy was in every other respect a thoroughly orthodox Conservative, at one time thought to be the most likely successor to Macdonald.

D'Alton McCarthy made himself obnoxious to many people by his position on minority rights, however. For that reason, the person to whom the Tory leadership passed, after an interregnum presided over by J.J.C. Abbott (who admitted that "I am here because I am not particularly obnoxious to anybody"), was Sir John Thompson, a lapsed Methodist and convert to Roman Catholicism. Acutely aware that he was the first Roman Catholic Prime Minister in Canada and that every Protestant in the country (especially those in the Orange Lodge) would be watching for signs that he was favoring his co-religionists, Thompson "bent over backwards to avoid even the appearance" of favoring Catholics. As a result, according to Lovell Clark, "he did them less than justice."

Thompson's overcompensation was well seen in his handling of the Manitoba Schools Question. By the late 1880s, Manitoba had received a fresh influx of new settlers from Ontario, without a balancing contingent from Quebec. Naturally, the people of the province became increasingly uneasy about the anachronistic dualism provided by the Manitoba Act. After two speeches touching on the subject late in the summer of 1889, one by D'Alton McCarthy and the other by the Attorney General, "Fighting Joe" Martin, Premier Thomas Greenway moved quickly to enact legislation that had already been approved in principle. In 1890, Greenway defied the constitution, and abolished the official status of French; at the same time, his government revoked public support for denominational schools.

It was the latter measure that caused the more immediate controversy as an appeal made its tortuous way through the courts in the early 1890s. The basis of the case was that the BNA Act and the Manitoba Act both protected denominational schools. Section 93 (1) of Canada's constitution stipulated that "Nothing ... shall prejudicially affect any right or privilege with respect to denominational schools which any class of persons have by law in the Province at the Union." The safeguard in Section 22 of the Manitoba Act was even more emphatic in assuring that no prejudicial legislation might affect any such right or provision established "by Law or practice in the Province at the Union." But in 1892, it was held by the Judicial Committee of the Privy Council that the system existing in 1870 was not covered by either protection since it was supported by private donations rather than by taxation.

The constitution permitted appeals to the "Governor General in Council" in matters "affecting any right or privilege of the Protestant or Roman Catholic minority" and the aggrieved minority of Manitoba did make such an appeal to Ottawa but Thompson was in no position to support such a step. After his death in 1894, he was succeeded by Mackenzie Bowell, a character even more flaccid than Abbott. Worse, Bowell was a prominent Orangeman as well. When the leadership of the Conservatives passed next to Charles Tupper in 1896, the situation was so far out of hand that even the most pragmatic approach was bound to be ineffective. By this time, the only resort of the embattled minority in Manitoba was to appeal to the Government of Canada in accordance with the provisions of Section 93 (4) permitting Parliament to enact "remedial laws" to preserve "any right or privilege of the Protestant or Roman Catholic minority in relation to education." This much the courts had established: the School Act of 1890 had affected denominational schools, and the central government did have the right to overturn such legislation at its discretion. But such action would antagonize the Protestants and the radical majoritarians and arouse a fresh crisis in provincial-dominion relations. On the other hand, to continue to withold the remedial bill was to confirm Quebec's worst fear that they had no future beyond their own province.

It was against this background that the next general election occurred. Here, after nearly twenty years in power, the Conservative party went down to defeat. One dynasty ended and another was about to begin.

# Bibliography

The volume in the Canadian Centenary Series that covers the politics of the critical years from 1878 to 1896, the period from Macdonald's return to power to his death and the subsequent disarray of the Conservative Party, is P.B. Waite, *Canada, 1874-1896: Arduous Destiny* (1971). Another general account of somewhat more limited scope is R.C. Brown, *Canada's National Policy, 1883-1900: A Study in Canadian-American Relations* (1964). As the title suggests, Brown's book tends to focus more on the implications of commercial policy for Canada's relations with the United States.

For the railway, readers are directed to Pierre Berton's second volume on the CPR, *The Last Spike* (1971). The other works on the railway cited in the bibliography of the previous chapter are also appropriate but two additional works are recommended to readers interested in criticism of the implications of the CPR's contract approved by Parliament in 1881, the route choice in the same period, and the company's enormous power then and later. One is the harshly critical book by Robert Chodos, *The CPR: A Century of Corporate Welfare* (1973). The other is the more balanced *History of the Canadian Pacific Railway* (1977) by W. Kaye Lamb.

Since the building of the railway is closely associated with the dislocation of Native People and the Northwest Rebellion in 1885, Berton's book also gives a colorful overview of that crisis. More detailed accounts are also available. The biographies of Riel by Stanley and Howard cited previously cover Riel's activities from 1870 to 1885. More recent work by T. Flanagan has contributed new evidence to the continuing controversy surrounding Riel's sanity. See Flanagan's *Louis 'David' Riel: Prophet of the New World* (1979) or the article-length exposition of the same thesis, "Louis 'David' Riel: Prophet, Priest-King, Infallible Pontiff," *JCS* (1974). Complementing Flanagan's work is a critique by Lewis H. Thomas of the government's approach to Riel's punishment, "A Judicial Murder — The Trial of Louis Riel," in Howard Palmer, ed., *The Settlement of the West* (1977). Readers interested in military aspects of the rebellion should read Desmond Morton, *The Last War Drum: The North West Campaign of 1885* (1972), profusely illustrated with both maps and photographs.

Another body of literature concerning the Northwest Rebellion is new material that puts other people besides Riel and other events besides the military action into the spotlight. For example, George Woodcock has recently published a biography of *Gabriel Dumont* (1975). The book's subtitle, *The Métis Chief and His Lost World*, reveals Woodcock's belief that Dumont was in many respects a more important leader than Riel. Other work tending to shift the focus from Riel and Middleton's forces is D.J. Hall, "The Half Breed Claims Commission," *Alberta History* (1977), and Doug Owram, *Promise of Eden* (1980), particularly the chapter entitled "Disillusionment: Regional Discontent in the 1880s."

Also in recent years, a number of works have been published to shed more light on the revolt of the eastern provinces in the 1880s. Quebec's position in this period is covered briefly but clearly in Ramsay Cook's, *Provincial Autonomy, Minority Rights and the Compact Theory, 1867-1921* (1969). A more detailed account and a book which places Mercier's rise to prominence in a context of many more local issues is *The Dream of Nation: A Social and Intellectual History of Quebec* (1982) by Susan Mann Trofimenkoff.

The economic background to the revolt of the Maritime provinces is found in C.K. Harley, "On the Persistence of Old Techniques: The Case of North American Wooden Shipbuilding," *Journal of Economic History* (1973) and David Alexander and Gerry Panting, "The Mercantile Fleet and its Owners: Yarmouth, Nova Scotia, 1840-1889," *Acadiensis* (1978). The struggle to develop a different economy has been analyzed by T.W. Acheson, "The Maritimes and 'Empire Canada'" in D.J. Bercuson, ed., *Canada and the Burden of Unity* (1977) and also in Acheson's, "The National Policy and the Industrialization of the Maritimes, 1880-1900," *Acadiensis* (1972). The demographic response to the decline in shipbuilding is outlined by Alan A. Brookes, "Outmigration from the Maritime Provinces, 1860-1900," *Acadiensis* (1976). For Fielding's political response, see C. Bruce Fergusson, *The Mantle of Howe* (1970).

Oliver Mowat's revolt against Macdonald's centralist aims are described by Christopher Armstrong, "The Mowat Heritage in Federal-Provincial Relations," in Donald Swainson, ed., *Oliver Mowat's Ontario* (1972) and Armstrong's book-length study, *The Politics of Federalism: Ontario's Relations with the Federal Government, 1867-1942* (1981). The more technical legal aspects of the conflicting interpretations of the BNA Act are summarized for the general reader in G.F.G. Stanley, *A Short History of the Canadian Constitution* (1969). Readers interested in more detail, particularly concerning the opinions of British Law Lords on specific cases, should consult G.P. Browne, *The Judicial Committee and the British North America Act* (1967).

The special case of the Manitoba Schools question is introduced by P.F.W. Rutherford, "The Western Press and Regionalism, 1870-96," CHR (1971), and Robert Painchaud, "French Canadian Historiography and Franco-Catholic Settlement in Western Canada, 1870-1915," CHR (1978). Lovell Clark analyzes the national repercussions of these trends in his brilliant but abrasive "Conservative Party in the 1890s" in B. Hodgins and R.

Page, eds., *Canadian History since Confederation: Essays and Interpretations* (1972). Another statement of Clark's interpretation is found in his *Manitoba Schools Question* (1969). A work that puts less responsibility on D'Alton McCarthy is J.R. Miller, "D'Alton McCarthy, Equal Rights, and the Origins of the Manitoba Scools Question," CHR (1973).

". . . Canada emerged as the world's leading exporter
of wood pulp."

# CHAPTER 15

# *Illusions of Change*

## I    Laurier — a Politician Like Macdonald

The election of 1896 seemed to mark a decisive change in Canadian politics. After an eternity in the wilderness (only five years in office since Confederation) the Liberal party came to power at last and there they stayed for the next fifteen years. But this was primarily a change in names, not of policies or a shift in styles of leadership. Even the election that brought Laurier to power suggested continuity with Macdonald, rather than a break with the past.

The primary issue in the contest of 1896 was the Manitoba Schools Question, in the handling of which it was Laurier, not Charles Tupper, who was seen as the true heir to Macdonald's smiling pragmatism. As far back as 1893, Laurier had indicated privately that he preferred tax-supported schools on nonsectarian lines, but that where Catholic children were already being instructed by Catholic authorities the pattern should be retained. Early in the crisis, Laurier thus espoused something of a middle position, one which avoided an expanding system of denominational schools as much as the Manitoba plan suddenly to impose nonsectarian education.

Laurier's flexibility was revealing; even more significant was his refusal to make his position public. Whereas others, notably Blake (his predecessor as Liberal leader), would have rushed forward with an open avowal of conviction, Laurier preferred to keep quiet. Later (with reference to his reticence between 1893 and 1896) he asserted that "under existing circumstances it was impossible to make a bold and well defined attitude without breaking the unity of the party." He wanted "to keep and maintain party unity, whilst the government was hopelessly divided." Here, too, in the tactic of delay, Laurier had learned from the master. In matters of political

253

style, Laurier and Macdonald were successor and predecessor, not opposites or even contrasts.

In the 1896 election contest itself, however, both parties seemed to be claiming the mantle of Macdonald. At the last minute, Tupper backed a Remedial Bill purporting to restore minority educational rights in Manitoba, forced Parliament to debate the measure in day and night sittings, then withdrew the bill and went to the people. During the campaign, the unpassed Remedial Bill was then treated as a possibility rather than an accomplished fact, and individual Conservative candidates were permitted to tailor the party's preference to whatever seemed popular locally. In a sense, the tactic showed flexibility because the full weight of party discipline was not used to crush those who opposed the proposal furiously. The tactic temporarily saved the Conservative Party, but it lost the election.

More successful was Laurier's handling of the awkward problem. He implied rather than specified. Referring to one of Aesop's fables in which the warming sun rather than the blustering cold is more effective in compelling a traveler to shed his defense of a heavy overcoat, Laurier suggested that a sunny approach was the way to deal with Premier Greenway's actions in Manitoba. Laurier said the Conservatives were "very windy. They have blown and raged and threatened, but the more they have threatened and raged and blown, the more that man Greenway has stuck to his coat. If it were in my power," Laurier said, "I would try the sunny way." Macdonald's style, now the "sunny way" of Wilfrid Laurier, was thus contrasted with the harsh cleverness of Charles Tupper. Naturally, Laurier's glib assertion that cleverness and affability cure all did not please everyone. The Catholic hierarchy and the Ultramontanes in Quebec were especially antagonistic to Laurier's apparent unwillingness to put up a strong fight for minority rights. They preferred Tupper's belated but strongly worded Remedial Bill. Of course, the public declarations of support of Tupper by the Ultramontanes only made Tupper more odious in Protestant Canada, and the official position of Tupper's clerical supporters failed to bring Quebeckers to heal. Finally, there was the question of the Conservative leader's sincerity.

Tupper's cleverness did appeal to the electorate of Manitoba and many voters in Ontario, perhaps because they imagined he would drop the question for good once the Conservatives were returned safely to power. Thus, Manitobans voted for Tupper. In the end, however, a "sunny way" solution was negotiated with Greenway. The agreement provided that an urban school of 40 Catholic pupils and a rural school with 25 could demand a Catholic teacher; heads of families could demand religious instruction by a priest or minister in the last half hour of the school day; and where the pupils spoke a language other than English, the teaching could be bilingual (the last proviso was enacted with French in mind but was to have rather exotic consequences once European migration flooded to Manitoba in the new century). For the moment, however, Laurier's "sunny way" won the support of most Manitoba voters. In the next general election, that of 1900, Manitobans joined the rest of the country in the renewal of Laurier's mandate, so pleased were they with the wily arts of Macdonald pragmatism reaffirmed and continued by Wilfrid Laurier.

## II    Continuing Macdonald's National Policy

Essential continuity rather than abrupt change was to be seen in matters of substance as well as style. With respect to the tariff, for example, such continuity was doubly remarkable because Laurier had been a convinced Free Trader until 1891. But in the election of 1896, the Liberals were conspicuously silent on the matter. Expediency had suppressed the urge to free trade. After coming to power, however, the issue was on the agenda for policy decision rather than campaign strategy. Since expediency still dictated retention of the tariff more or less as inherited, the tariff was retained. In April 1897, the country received Laurier's first budget and was treated with a schedule of duties essentially the same as Macdonald's. As a token gesture toward farmers there were some reductions on their machinery. And as a nod in the direction of the party's free trade past, a five percent reduction was offered to any other country willing to reciprocate. Basically, however, the structure that had risen to 30 percent by 1891 was to remain as Macdonald's government had left it.

Although the tariff was the central feature of Macdonald's strategy for national development, more broadly construed, his national policy also involved federal assistance for railway construction and active encouragement of immigration for rapid settlement of the Prairies. Both additional policies were elaborated by Laurier's government along lines that were perfectly consistent with Macdonald's definitions. An early effort to promote railways was an arrangement with the CPR in 1897 by which the Government of Canada agreed to subsidize construction of a more southerly line through the Rocky Mountains by Crow's Nest pass in order to give the company access to its mineral lands in the Kootenay range. In return for the government guarantee of profit to the railway's mining subsidiary, the CPR agreed to make freight rate concessions that were intended to promote more rapid agricultural development of the Prairies and to benefit manufacturing in central Canada. The company promised to lower freight rates on cereal crops moving east and to provide lower rates on building materials or agricultural machinery shipped west.

With respect to immigration promotion and land distribution, Laurier's Minister of the Interior, Clifford Sifton, worked more imaginatively than any of his predecessors first to advertise Canada in the United States, Great Britain, and Europe, and then to ensure attractive colonization rates of travel for newcomers. To reduce administrative complications, procedures for entering homestead claims and gaining patents were streamlined.

Almost immediately, the old policies pursued with renewed vigor seemed to pay large benefits long withheld. The great depression that had begun in 1873 (abating only briefly between 1879 and 1883), showed unmistakeable signs of lifting completely in the late 1890s. Naturally, the development was a prosperity for which the new Prime Minister and his newly oriented party were only too happy to take full credit.

Several factors explain the surge of growth. First, an infusion of gold from newly opened mines in South Africa in large enough volume to cause inflation on a global scale made the price of Canadian staples rise. Between 1896 and 1914 the index of staple-commodity prices rose 32 percent. Foodstuffs — particularly grains — nearly doubled in price, in the latter case because of the increasingly urban setting of Europe's population and a relative decline in European grain production.

Another factor contributing to the boom was technological change that invited Canadians to exploit completely new staples. There were innovations in hard-rock mining, for instance, that reoriented Canadians to "the land God gave Cain". Previously, the Shield had been exploited as a source of fur or it was simply bypassed as an obstacle to agriculture. In the new era, it became a treasure-trove of minerals such as nickel and silver. Other technological changes led to new uses of the same previously valueless territory. There were beginnings in hydroelectricity generation, for example, but more immediately important was the development of a technique for making paper from ground wood fiber.

Prior to the introduction of the new technology for making paper, nearly all the world's supply was manufactured from cotton and linen rags. The old product was satisfactory in every respect but price. The new paper made from wood pulp was infinitely less durable, but proportionately cheaper. Any country with trees unsuitable for lumbering could lead in its production. For this reason, the jack-pine forests of the Shield began to fall before the pulpmaker's cutters as the larger white pines had once fallen to the British timber buyers. An industry that had not existed at the time of Confederation emerged suddenly as one of the leading sources of economic growth in Canada. In fact, no other country turned to the new staple with the same emphasis. Almost overnight, Canada emerged as the world's leading exporter of wood pulp.

Thus, the typical use of the Shield forest emerged as timber-cutting for papermaking rather than as lumbering for construction. The relative decline in lumbering in the East was more than offset by a spectacular rise in logging in British Columbia where great stands of Douglas Fir and Western Red Cedar on the slopes of mountains rising immediately from navigable coastal water meant that capital – intensive economies of scale were practicable almost as soon as the railway was completed to the west coast. A lumber industry that barely existed in 1870 or 1880 grew to gigantic scale between 1890 and 1910. British Columbia production tripled every decade and continued that pace of development until 1920. By then, more than half of all the large sawmills in Canada were located in BC.

All Canadian staples, new as well as old, were bulky cargoes that were sold thousands of miles from their points of origin, and therefore were highly responsive to even slight changes in shipping charges. A third factor fueling the boom was a dramatic fall in transoceanic freight rates that accompanied the completion of the world's shift from wooden-hulled sailing vessels (leaky and requiring large crews) to the new norm in commerce, the steel-hulled "tramp steamers" (watertight and less heavily manned).

Together, all these factors created and sustained a new trade and a new prosperity. That, in turn, stimulated both immigration and settlement. Earlier, between 1878 and 1891, immigrants had moved into Canada at the rate of about 50 000 per year. After 1896, the rate of immigration was four times that of the earlier period bringing almost 2 million people to Canada between 1897 and 1911. About half settled in cities, the others migrated to the mines, bush camps, or free land of the Prairies. As a result, new farms emerged at the rate of about 30 000 per year.

The vast transfer of population west, coupled with the other factors mentioned above, resulted in spectacular growth in the output of agricultural staples, particularly wheat. The production of grain increased even more rapidly than the output of BC lumbering. In 1896, production stood at 8 million bushels; by 1912, the annual yield of wheat had tripled three times. Then it stood at 232 million. Given the new volume of freight, the CPR groaned under the burden of the annual harvest.

In 1882, critics complained that a transcontinental railway through empty land would not generate enough revenue to pay even for its axle grease. By 1899, many Canadians were saying no amount of railways were sufficient: "We want all the railways we can get," Manitobans asserted.

In 1903, Laurier obliged with yet another program of subsidies to businessmen wishing to make profits building railways. Two firms vied for the privilege of building the one additional transcontinental that was apparently needed. One was the creation of William Mackenzie and Donald Mann, speculators and tycoons who were the very epitome of that reckless optimism that Americans call the "can-do spirit". Their railway, the Canadian Northern, was a hodgepodge of branch lines put together by joining Western areas the CPR had declined to serve. By 1901, Mackenzie and Mann were ready to spring across the Shield from Port Arthur to Montreal. They wanted government sanction. But in the East, the Grand Trunk vied for the same recognition — from the opposite direction. Their problem was building through the West. The reasonable policy in 1903 would have been a forced merger of the Canadian Northern and Grand Trunk with one short and expensive connection north of Lake Superior. The problem with the merger was that neither the directors of the firms nor the leaders in government were willing to create it.

Caught between businessmen and his cabinet, Laurier paled at the thought of attempting to coerce either. But he was just as reluctant to turn down the two firms and confront the public with a least-growth option. As a result, Laurier said yes to everyone but his closest advisors. The Grand Trunk was authorized to strike out across the Prairies as the Grand Trunk Pacific and Mackenzie and Mann were allowed to build the Canadian Northern toward the Atlantic. But there was more. Since the existing eastern railways all ran through southern Canada, a third railway, the National Transcontinental, was to be built from Moncton through northern Quebec and Ontario to Winnipeg (see map 15.1). Since Laurier disliked the idea of government ownership, once completed, the National Transcontinental was to be leased to the Grand Trunk. In this way, two firms had competed for the honor of building the one additional transcontinental that was needed, both received the consent they sought, and Laurier threw in one more 1 800 mile railway for good measure. Another interesting feature of the arrangement was that any government-subsidized construction was required to utilize Canadian rails to encourage the domestic primary steel industry. All this was "national policy" in the grand manner.

Launching such a vast railway scheme was contrary to the judgment of the Minister of Railways and Canals, A.G. Blair, who resigned on the question in 1903. But Laurier knew that he had acted in the style that would win the election coming up in 1904. His policy would be popular because it disappointed the least number of speculators, contractors, and local politicians. Such a bold policy was consistent with the optimism that led Laurier to describe Canada as "the star towards which all men who love progress and freedom shall come for the next hundred years." He said it with such amiable assurance that one Toronto newspaper recognized just how completely he had "that strange and mysterious gift, which Sir John Macdonald possessed in almost equal degree." Like his predecessor, Laurier appreciated that economic nationalism and growth were the two topics which Canadians could almost always be expected to support. Under Macdonald, the national policy was partisan. Under Laurier it became a hallowed tradition.

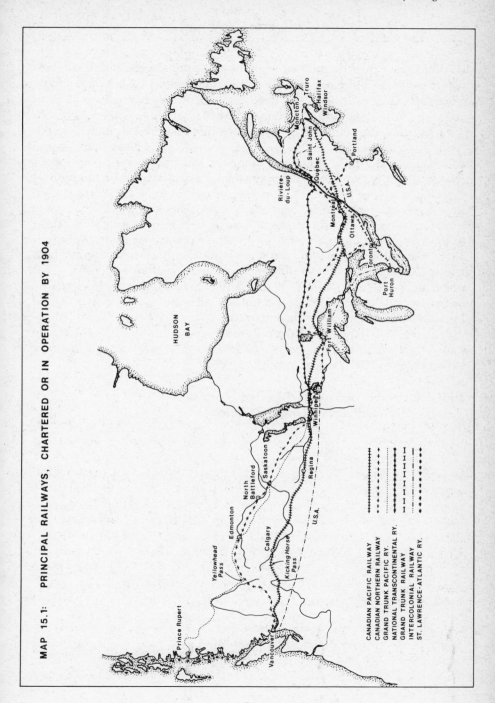

MAP 15.1: PRINCIPAL RAILWAYS, CHARTERED OR IN OPERATION BY 1904

HUDSON BAY

Prince Rupert

Yellowhead Pass

Edmonton

North Battleford

Saskatoon

Calgary

Kicking Horse Pass

Vancouver

Regina

Winnipeg

U.S.A.

William

Port Huron

Toronto

Ottawa

Montreal

Riviere-du-Loup

U.S.A.

Portland

Quebec

Saint John

Moncton

Truro

Halifax

Windsor

CANADIAN PACIFIC RAILWAY
CANADIAN NORTHERN RAILWAY
GRAND TRUNK PACIFIC RY.
NATIONAL TRANSCONTINENTAL RY.
GRAND TRUNK RAILWAY
INTERCOLONIAL RAILWAY
ST. LAWRENCE-ATLANTIC RY.

## III    Economic Change

It would seem that the political significance of the change of prime ministers meant little, but what of the economic developments? It would appear from that which has just been described that there was nothing illusory about the economic transformation of Canada between 1890 and 1910. In the first place, the country had undergone rapid industrialization. Secondly, the development of the Prairie West proceeded at a dizzy pace. As the East was ceasing to be rural and agrarian, and the West was no longer wild and empty, what could demonstrate a sharper break in continuity? The first, and perhaps the most important continuity is that Canada continued to be dangerously dependent upon the sale of a few staple commodities on the world market in raw or semifinished form. The wheat of the West, accounting for one third of the value of Canadian exports by 1911, was only the most important illustration of such dependency. Less well publicized was the continuing dependence of the "industrial" East upon its agricultural exports. Wood pulp, minerals, and hydroelectricity were new glamor staples of central Canada, but dairy products and livestock were even more valuable to the East in the Laurier years. Moreover, table 15.1 shows that livestock, meat, and dairy products (produced mainly in Ontario and Quebec) were actually more important in national exports than Western wheat until after 1905.

**Table 15.1**  Value of Exports, Selected Years
(millions of dollars,  1900 prices)

| Years | Fish | Livestock Meat and Dairy Products | Forest Products | Grain | Iron Ware | Other Exports | Total |
|---|---|---|---|---|---|---|---|
| 1885 | 10.8 | 23.7 | 24.4 | 14.3 | .5 | 14.2 | 87.9 |
| 1890 | 8.4 | 22.5 | 29.1 | .2 | .6 | 30.3 | 91.1 |
| 1895 | 11.8 | 31.0 | 27.3 | 15.9 | 1.1 | 26.2 | 113.3 |
| 1900 | 11.2 | 53.3 | 33.2 | 32.7 | 3.7 | 49.1 | 183.2 |
| 1905 | 9.9 | 55.3 | 35.5 | 23.3 | 5.8 | 61.5 | 191.3 |
| 1910 | 13.2 | 43.9 | 39.7 | 63.6 | 7.8 | 71.2 | 239.4 |

SOURCE: K.W. Taylor, "Statistics of Foreign Trade" in *Statistical Contributions to Canadian Economic History*, vol. 2 (1931), pp. 38-44.

Only in the last years of the "wheat boom" did the value of western staples surpass eastern animal and dairy products. New staples and new regions emerged as sources of supply, but overall, the East continued to be the dominant agricultural region, and staples continued to dominate exports.

Canada was industrializing but the manufacturing sector that had developed between 1890 and 1911 had emerged primarily to serve the domestic market, maintaining remarkable stability from the period of earliest industrialization (see table 15.2). Moreover, the value of the output of these secondary industries in the export sector relative to the value of raw materials exports was almost the same in 1910 as in 1890.

**Table 15.2** Relative Positions of Industry Groups, 1870-1910

| | Years | | |
|---|---|---|---|
| Industry Group* | 1870 | 1890 | 1910 |
| Iron and steel goods | 1 | 1 | 1 |
| Leather products | 2 | 3 | 5 |
| Manufactured food products | 3 | 4 | 3 |
| Transportation equipment | 4 | 5 | 4 |
| Clothing | 5 | 2 | 2 |
| Wood products such as furniture | 6 | 7 | 9 |
| Textiles | 7 | 6 | 6 |
| Dressed building stone | 8 | 8 | 8 |
| Printing and publishing | 9 | 9 | 9 |
| Chemical and drugs | 10 | 11 | 11 |
| *secondary manufacturing only | | | |

SOURCE: Adapted from G.W. Bertram, "Historical Statistics on Growth and Structure of Manufacturing in Canada, 1870-1957" in J. Henripin and A. Asimakopulas, eds., *Conference on Statistics, 1962 and 1963 (1964)*, pp. 104-105.

Why had Canada developed only a truncated manufacturing sector and one oriented overwhelmingly just to the domestic market? One explanation is that there was a fatal flaw in the values and expectations of Canadian entrepreneurship. According to R.T. Naylor, Canada suffered from a deeply entrenched tradition of merchant capitalism (an orientation to trade, activities such as merchandising, land speculation, or simple banking). Naylor thinks such a tradition biased the businessmen of the country against industrial capitalism (relatively higher risk, capital intensive ventures such as secondary industry). L.R. Macdonald has replied to Naylor's argument with evidence showing that merchant ventures demanded equal or higher fixed costs than the early forms of manufacturing: "Entry into and exit from manufacturing was not difficult," says Macdonald. Then why did the manufacturing sector continue to lag behind the primary or staple sector of the economy?

A different version of the "merchants against industry" hypothesis shifts the focus from "weak entrepreneurship" to "colonialism". In this view, the manufacturing sector failed to develop as fully as it might have because too many Canadians waited for foreigners to develop the sector for them, and when foreigners did invest they did not usually develop value-added secondary manufacturing for the world market. The problem was that the foreigners investing in Canada between 1890 and 1910 tended to put their capital in one of several categories: enclave industry linked forward to manufacturing elsewhere, resource-extraction tied to the vertical integration of foreign industry, or tariff-induced branch plant manufacturing intended only to replace imports.

The first category of foreign investment exploited cheap Canadian labor and energy in a form of industrialization that was more closely associated with manufacturing abroad. In the case of aluminum, for example, Americans exploited cheap labor and hydroelectricity in Quebec to refine bauxite mined in the Caribbean. The output of ALCOA's plant at Shawinigan Falls was ingots that might have been used as inputs in Canadian manufacturing and did have something of this effect. By 1910 nonferrous metal products had risen to tenth position among secondary industries in Canada. But most of the output of the Canadian primary aluminum industry was exported to the world in raw ingot form.

In a second kind of direct foreign investment, the product output was not linked forward to Canadian secondary manufacturing at all. In the case of foreign investment in newsprint production, for example, mills were built in Canada for the sole purpose of supplying paper to the investing newspapers of the United States. Canadians were able to reap the benefit of exporting trees in the value-added form of newsprint. But the paper from such mills was not available as an input for secondary manufacturing in Canada.

In the third type of direct foreign investment, foreigners built Canadian branch plants, for one reason: to avoid the tariff. A Singer Sewing machine assembled in the United States was foreign; the same machine assembled in Canada was Canadian. By 1913, according to Michael Bliss, there were more than 400 American branch plant assembly operations located in Canada. In a sense, they produced goods that were "Made in Canada", but each sold for about 30 percent more than in the United States or at the world price, and therefore the product of none was exportable. The rapid growth of such firms between 1880 and 1920 added population and also GNP to the Canadian economy. As far as the Canadian Manufacturers' Association was concerned, that was sufficient justification to continue to encourage their development by way of the protective tariff. From the standpoint of Michael Bliss, however, that was "a particularly self-defeating kind of economic nationalism." Indeed, it was a sad admission by the elite of a small country that they believed they could not have manufacturing by any other means. Does it follow that Canadian businessmen were inhibited by a colonial mentality?

The merchants against industry hypothesis, in its colonial mentality guise, seems to explain too much and to do so on the ground of irrelevant idealism because the profit motive in a capitalist economy is never bashful.

If there were real opportunities for local entrepreneurs, it is unlikely they would have gone unnoticed for long. In this perspective, it is likely that the Laurier boom expanded along the lines of exportable staples more rapidly than in exportable manufactured goods simply because the one was more immediately profitable than the other. To be sure, Canadians did miss the value-added that would have followed from the export of more finished goods, but the harsh reality may have been that such an option was simply not available.

## IV   Population Growth and Change

If continuity characterized Canadian economic growth between 1890 and 1910, it would appear that change was the keynote of population patterns in the same period. In 1891, 44 percent of Canada's population lived in Ontario and 31 percent resided in Quebec. About 20 percent of the country's population lived in the Maritimes and only 5 percent were counted in the West. Just twenty years later, the number of Canadians living in the Atlantic region had fallen below 13 percent of the national total. Quebec's share had fallen to 27 percent and Ontario had declined to 35 percent overall. The reason for the relative decline in the East was the rapid settlement of the West: in 1911, almost one-fourth of all the people in Canada lived west of the Ontario border.

Between 1891 and 1911, the West received about half of the immigration from abroad and much of the migration internal to Canada, growing from 250 000 people to nearly 2 million. Ontario received approximately one third of the immigrants, but lost population to the West and the United States, and therefore Ontario grew only slightly from 2.1 million to 2.5 million between 1891 and 1911. Neither Quebec nor the Maritimes attracted much of the immigrant population and both regions saw a large percentage of their native-born move to the United States rather than to other provinces in Canada. Since Quebec had a higher birth rate than the Maritimes, Quebec's population increased from 1.5 to 2 million; the Atlantic region remained at about 1 million.

The spectacular increase in the population of the West meant that the territory between Manitoba and British Columbia had to be accorded some kind of provincial status in Confederation early in the new century. In 1905, that promotion was granted in the form of Autonomy Bills that created Alberta and Saskatchewan with nearly the same powers as the other "partners" in Confederation. Both new provinces gained local responsible government and additional representation in the House of Commons and

Senate. But neither Alberta nor Saskatchewan was granted control of its natural resources. The Crown lands in both were retained for "Dominion purposes". Retention of the public domain by the central government was one controversial aspect of the Autonomy Bills.

Another and more hotly debated point concerned the issue of language and schools. The statute that first made provision for schools in Alberta and Saskatchewan, the North West Territories Act of 1875, required denominational institutions, and thus the majority and minority languages of central Canada. The Territories, like early Manitoba, were to be French and Catholic as well as English and Protestant. But in the period from 1875 to 1905, emigration from Quebec (or the repatriation of French-speaking Canadians from the United States) had not proceeded as well as the clergy had hoped. Migration from Ontario, the United States, Great Britain, and immigration from Europe after 1896 were the central tendencies. In part, the pattern was the result of government recruitment practices. The most actively recruited newcomers were English-speaking settlers from the United States and the British Isles. It was believed that these sources offered the highest class of immigrants because the British were British and the Americans had money. On average, American immigrants brought $500 cash and $350-worth of settlers' effects, compared with the Europeans who arrived almost penniless — only $15 cash and personal property combined. Balancing their poverty was the European's willingness to settle on empty prairie or work for low wages. They also did not grumble about the necessity of learning English to fit into the emerging society of the West. For this last reason (and also to avoid charges of seeking to depopulate French-Canada), Clifford Sifton's Department of the Interior did little to stimulate a flow of population from Quebec to the Prairies. The principal promotor of French-speaking migration to the West was the Church but even its effort in that direction was not as strong as its attempt to keep Quebeckers in their home province. As a result, the West filled rapidly with newcomers already speaking English or eager to learn. Ironically, the factory towns of New England became less alien to migrating French Canadians than was the Canadian West. In Manchester, New Hampshire, for example, at the largest textile mill in the world in 1900 (the Amoskeag Manufacturing Company), about one third of the labor force was French Canadian. There was more French spoken in New Hampshire, in other words, than in the Canadian West. The largest French-speaking community west of Ontario was St. Boniface, Manitoba, with less than 4000 people. Except for small pockets of rural French Canadians or desperately poor *Métis* communities, the rest of the West was effectively "British" by 1905.

Since the French presence in the West was dwarfed by the English, many Westerners hoped that the Autonomy Bills would erase the dualism of language and education that had been imposed originally by dominion statute in 1875, and diluted by stages through territorial ordinances. But French Canadians and Catholics hoped to restore the principle that all schools would be confessional schools and the French language would have equal status with English. Clifford Sifton, the strongest Western voice ever seated in the cabinet, would tolerate nothing more than a protection for the remnant of the denominational schools that still existed. When the Minister of Justice presented Autonomy Bills that would restore the old principle that all schools were either Protestant or Catholic, rather than basically nonsectarian with only minor parochial exceptions, Sifton resigned from the government in disgust. In the resulting fury over religion and language, Laurier defended the principle of confessional schools, but ultimately had to retreat to Sifton's position without taking him back into the cabinet. Thus, French lost status as an official language, and the only separate schools assured of public support in Alberta and Saskatchewan were those already in operation in 1905.

The larger question raised by the Autonomy Bills was the issue of the kind of country Canada was becoming. Without a moment's hesistation, the Siftons of the Dominion affirmed that Canada was a British country. But looking strictly at the data on population migration, it could have been argued with almost equal force that Canada's ultimate destiny was to be absorbed by the United States. In every period between 1861 and 1900, more people left Canada than arrived, and the country to which they tended to go was most frequently the USA.

There are two theories that explain why so many Canadians moved south. One theory focuses on a phenomenon called "demand pull". In this view, Canadians were attracted to the United States only because higher rewards were offered to skilled workers in that country. They left their homeland because there was more demand for carpenters, for example, in the Boston area than in Lunenburg. The evidence that tends to support the demand pull thesis is the predominance of skilled workers in the stream of emigrants. At the same time, however, there was a large emigration of unskilled people from Quebec who arrived in New England only to tend machines in textile mills or shoe factories.

The theory that accounts for emigration in general is a displacement thesis arguing that the tariff insured that goods manufactured in Canada could be sold at higher prices without ensuring commensurate wage increases. By J.H. Dales' estimate, the 25 percent tariff had driven real wages in Canada about 20 percent below those offered for all types of employment in the United States. Assuming the native-born Canadians were less willing to tolerate such lower wages, the unskilled as well as the skilled moved to the United States in order to take up the higher pay for equivalent work. In the fairly prosperous two decades before 1873 (and before the higher tariff enacted in 1879 as an inducement to manufacturing to keep "our work people" from leaving) American officials recorded the entry of 345 000 immigrants from Canada. If they had not emigrated (all other factors being equal) the population of Canada in 1874 would have been about nine percent higher. In the years of rapid growth in the economy and decline in the standard of living relative to the United States, 1896-1926, more than 1.5 million Canadians became landed immigrants in that country. Had that group remained in the land of their birth, the 1926 population of Canada would have been 16 percent greater. From this crude measure, it would appear that the tariff was not very effective as a means of keeping the population at home. According to Dales it was a powerful inducement for Europeans to enter Canada, however. Canada did not attract as many immigrants as might have been the case were the standard of living comparable to the United States, but the two million immigrants who arrived from Europe in the period may not have known they would have been better paid by American employers. Moreover, they may not have been able to afford that destination since the typical European immigrant to Canada arrived with so little resources. In any case, the newcomer had learned in Europe that there were tremendous opportunities in Canada. The displacement aspect of their arrival from Europe, according to Dales, is that far from being a "national" policy, the tariff actually operated as a kind of foreign aid program: it encouraged the native-born to leave and the vacancies created by their leaving were rapidly filled by newcomers from abroad.

## V    The Rural Ethic in an Urban Setting

About one third of the newcomers from Europe who migrated to Canada between 1891 and 1911 settled in the cities. Here they were joined by an even larger stream of native-born Canadians on the move from rural parts of their homeland. In 1891, only 1.5 million people (or 30 percent of the population) lived in towns of even 1 000 or more persons. The rest was designated rural. Just twenty years later, 46 percent of Canada's population was counted as urban. Of course, much of the "urban" population of 1911 resided in towns that were barely more than country villages. At the time, only four cities held 100 000 or more persons. The largest city in Canada in 1911 was Montreal with a population of 491 000. The next largest was Toronto with 382 000. Then came Winnipeg with 136 000 and Vancouver in fourth place with just over 100 000. Canada's two western cities had grown phenomenally but even the eastern metropolitan areas had doubled in size betwen 1891 and 1911. Most of the increase was by migration, especially internal migration. Of the four, the foreign-born outnumbered the native-born only in Winnipeg. Montreal continued to be 80 percent native-born in the new century and although Toronto was far more attractive to immigrants it remained overwhelmingly "British".

Since the largest part of Canada's metropolitan population had rural Canadian orgins, what can be said about the culture or values they brought with them? What impact did the urban environoment have on their old orientation? In simplest terms, rural life had conditioned Canadians to believe in "honest toil" and the efficacy of individual initiative for gaining a "modest competence" or social advancement. This meant that time spent in leisure was somewhat suspect, indebtedness was considered foolish, and poverty was regarded as the appropriate punishment for slothfulness or folly. There was a social category known as the "deserving poor" but it was not large since it consisted mainly of widows, orphans, or other exceptional "unfortunates". Most poor people, the "sturdy poor", were not entitled to sympathy or "coddling" as this was considered only an inducement to idleness. In the world of rural Canada — Catholic as well as Protestant — the industrious farmhand was supposed to apply his talent, budget his time, and accumulate a surplus to buy his own farm. The fisherman saved for his own schooner and the apprentice was supposed to strive to gain possession of his own shop. In a world of independent producers, poverty was only temporary and success was never definitive.

In the metropolitan environment that emerged by 1911, however, about 40 percent of the population consisted of anything but independent producers. They were the unskilled or barely skilled wage earners newly arrived from the farms of Canada or the fields of Europe. Not surprisingly, they fell to the bottom of the social hierarchy. Were they rewarded well enough to accumulate a surplus eventually to challenge the permanency of their bottom-rung position?

The average low-skilled worker earned about $10 per week in Toronto or Montreal in 1900. Prices were also low, but since employment was both seasonal and cyclical, more than 70 percent of a person's earnings went for housing and food, both of which gave Montreal one of the highest infant mortality rates in the world: 1 in 4 of all newborn children were not likely to survive their first year of infancy in the slums of Canada's largest city.

The cruel reality was that the average working-class family's earnings were not proportional to the hard work of the male head of the household. When he could work, the hours he labored were 10 to 12 per day. The problem was that he could not control either the amount of his employment or the rate of return for his labor. Increasingly, the average worker could not even control the operation of his particular task in a factory. In the first phase of industrialization, factories were defined as workplaces employing five or more persons. Mechanization was quite minimal and labor was still craft-oriented. But with increasing mechanization and the appearance of "scientific management", operations were broken down into simpler tasks and the average factory demanded a great deal more unskilled labor. In Toronto, for example, the average firm employed 11 or 12 people in 1890. By 1900, the typical factory required 50 less-skilled personnel — but hands better disciplined to the monotony of tending a machine.

The wonder is that most workers did not rebel against such conditions. Many may have believed that their low position was only temporary, and indeed some were able to escape the slums. There were instances of social mobility within the ranks of a particular work hierarchy or upward mobility by ruthless underconsumption and the utilization of a whole family's labor.

The reality for most, however, was that more than one family member had to seek an income just to carry the household through the winter months of "short hours" or layoffs. Poverty meant that in most working-class families women and children were vital members of the paid labor force. In the early twentieth century about 20 percent of the total labor force were women and 5 to 10 percent were children, usually boys. Girls do not appear to have worked as frequently in paid employment, nor were they in school as often. They were indispensable unpaid babysitters enabling their mothers to work as domestic servants or in factories earning from $4 to $6 per week. Another pattern of income maintenance was turning the family's five-room, cold-water flat into a home workshop by day, thus enabling women and children to perform many tasks needed to finish garments in the needle trades, for example. The point is that the typical, metropolitan working class family could not hope to weather financial emergencies or "get ahead" unless children and women also generated a cash income. According to Terry Copp, "One income was not sufficient to relieve a family from the most abject poverty" in Montreal and Michael Piva has arrived at substantially the same conclusion on the "condition of the working-class" in Toronto at the same time.

The reality of massive inescapable poverty created by low wages and unemployment meant that a significant number of workers did rebel against the rural ethic of individualism and sought security in collective action. Since the 1880s, two different kinds of labor organization had been forming in Canada — both were continent-wide developments. One, the Knights of Labor, attempted to organize all "producing classes" without barriers to the unskilled. Unlike the Knights of Labor locals, the American Federation of Labor sought to organize only along craft lines. The AF of L was interested in organizing the skilled tradesmen and had arrived in Canada very early in the form of railway unions. Even though they aimed at remarkably different clientele, both groups made rather dramatic headway between 1881 and 1890 with the Canadian Labour Congress forming in 1883. By 1900, however, only the craft unions were left and even they were in trouble. By 1911, only 155 000 workers were organized in unions in Canada.

The failure of the Knights and the near destruction of the craft unions is explained by the comprehensive program employers launched to counter worker attempts to squeeze profits or gain control of work processes. The latter object is particularly interesting because the control issue appears to have been the main cause for about half the strikes by the craft unions between 1900 and 1914. According to C. Heron and B. Palmer, of the 421 strikes in southern Ontario in the period, 181 were attempts by skilled workers to frustrate further debasement of work by managers caught up in the efficiency craze that followed from the importing of "scientific management" to Canada. The other 240 strikes were for higher wages or to thwart wage reductions.

Strikers, especially the unskilled, usually lost their battles with management because their only weapon was the inconvenience to an employer of his having to replace the old staff with strikebreakers. On that account, employers maintained a somewhat ambivalent attitude toward immigration. They feared it because the arrival of large numbers of newcomers meant the infusion of an unknown factor that always included a certain portion of "agitators" and other "dangerous foreigners". On the other hand, experience had shown that there was almost no labor difficulty too powerful to resist the competititon from cheap imported labor from Europe. For this reason, manufacturers' agents advertized thousands of nonexistent vacancies in palatial manufacturing establishments at mythical wages even when hiring was nil in order to maintain a steady stream of new competitors for job slots thus forming a "reserve industrial army".

Manufacturers also enlisted the power of the state in their attempt to maintain control of labor. The newly created urban police was one such mechanism, but increasingly after 1900 other security services were the militia, the Immigration Branch, and the Royal North West Mounted Police. More subtle were "arbitration" devices they obtained from government. In 1902, 200 Toronto manufacturers formed the Employers Association of Toronto to place business more effectively "on a more stable and permanent basis by preventing strikes and providing means of arbitration.. in all matters of dispute between capital and labour." Building on the federal Conciliation Act of 1900, the Government of Canada added the Railway Labour Disputes Act in 1903 and the Industrial Disputes Investigation Act of 1907. All such measures provided government intervention to bring indispensable skilled workers back to work while appointed boards of judges and businessmen embarked on fact-finding missions. Since arbitration boards almost never supported the strikers, "arbitration" emerged as a favorite settlement device of industry.

To prevent strikes from arising in the first place, another control strategy was paternalism, a tactic that required employers to adjust the factory environment to provide pleasant dining and toilet facilities, athletic associations, literary societies, and even complaint departments. The one area not addressed was the fundamental problem of low wages because paternalism was a form of manipulative coercion intended specifically to head off profit squeezing without resort to brutal repression. *Industrial Canada* urged employers to go so far as providing their workers with improved housing, arguing that "Workmen who have comfortable homes are more efficient, contented and reliable ... . Out of the slums stalk the Socialist with his red flag, the Union agitator with the auctioneer's voice, and the Anarchist with his torch." In advocating such amelioration, the manufacturers' journal stressed that no reform sentimentality was involved. The motive was not "civic pride" but "a cold business proposition". Employers invested vast sums to increase the efficiency of their steam-driven machines. "Then why not spend a little time and effort to increase the efficiency of your human machines?"

*Industrial Canada's* dissociation of business paternalism from "civic pride" arose from a conscious rejection of a reform movement that had arisen in every medium to large-size city in Canada since the 1880s, but not as a reaction against business (because the reformers were generally business persons themselves). Initially, the civic reformers of the 1880s had sought merely to *purify* city life in the sense of getting rid of the most glaring symbols of modern sin: the saloon, the "house of ill fame", and poor sanitation. Two other aspects of the purity crusade, the City Beautiful and the Garden City movements (the first promoting green space and zoned development, the other promoting evacuation of the city for suburbs) were even more interesting evidences of rural nostalgia since both were supposed to redeem the city dweller by placing him back in the country without cutting him off from urban employment. All of this was indicative of the potency of rural ideals even after people had moved to town.

A more ambiguous reaction of the rural ethic was that which seemed to recognize that the industrial city was a new kind of society demanding new forms of administration. A large number of the middle-class reformers believed that most of the evils of the new industrialism would disappear if cities were transformed from political communities into model corporations. This meant "nonpartisan" administration of municipal affairs by a Board of Control, a Commission, or City Manager. It also entailed raising a revenue from the sale of a product, and expenditures of derived profits on essential social services.

The product of a "progressive city" was its utility base. Civic reformers across the country founded the Union of Canadian Municipalities under the leadership of O.A. Howland in 1901 with the specific mission of taking over urban transportation, water, and gas. Where utilities had an interurban aspect, such as telephone or hydroelectrical generation, a province might also become involved in the process of the "municipalization" of utilities. From the beginning, there were those who denounced such measures as "gas and water socialism" and effectively resisted the movement, as in Montreal, for example. But in most of the larger cities as early as 1910, reformers had successfully persuaded their communities that cheap and reliable basic utilities were so essential "to induce manufacturing establishments to locate in the city" that such services could not be left in private hands. To do so would hamper a town's "Board of Control" from offering attractive rates to industrial newcomers. The pitch was, "Municipal ownership and industrial progress go hand in hand." Moreover, since small-scale users of the utilities could be charged much higher rates by the city, a well managed municipal corporation could be expected to make a "handsome profit". Incidentally, public ownership also served the public health by guaranteeing pure water, for example, as a special side benefit. But even public health measures tended to be justified on "sound business" rather than humanitarian grounds. In Toronto it was argued that the loss of each child in the infant mortality statistics was $1000 lost in opportunity costs, but a comprehensive public health program (including free innoculation against diptheria, etc.) would require only $5 per person.

Essential social services included more than a public health program, however. A progressive city was also expected to provide a professional uniformed police force, fire protection, and especially a new kind of school system. From the standpoint of typical middle-class reformers there was nothing wrong with paying workers $10 per week; the wage system was not degrading. The evil was that the children of the poor did not appear to have a fair opportunity to develop their talents if parents exploited them for their labor. By focusing on the children, the "civic reform" movement was able to find a central purpose that promised to lead to a better world in the future without challenging any of the basic premises of capitalism in the present.

At the end of the civic reform era, W.J. Hanna laid out the essentials to "launch a generation" for the Civic Improvement League of Canada. His ideal included regulation of the conditions of the employment of women to guarantee that each child had a healthy mother; regulation of the distribution of milk and water to ensure a pure supply of both of those essential commodities; town planning to guarantee access to fresh air and recreational open spaces; and the provision of compulsory graded instruction to assure each child a proper education. Since Hanna's recipe was touted as the minimum to "launch a generation", once such measures were fully enacted it was expected that there would be no excuse for continuing poverty except by sloth or "feeblemindedness". Much of Hanna's formula had been enacted by provinicial and municipal governments in Canada between 1900 and 1910, a trend that was reflected in the rising cost of municipal government and the growth of a "tertiary" sector of the labor force. By 1907, Winnipeg and Toronto both spent as much in their annual budgets as the province in which each city was located. By 1910, the tertiary sector of the work force, meaning the white collar, private and service components (admittedly, still based largely in private industry) had nevertheless grown faster than employment in manufacturing or resource development. The tertiary sector was one third of the entire labor force and reflected the rise to paramountcy of a new bureaucratic middle class, perhaps the most important transformation of Canada and a shift that explains two other phenomena: first, the trust of civic reformers in bureaucratic, managerial talent to deal with social problems, and second, the rather naive faith that there were no fundamental evils in capitalism itself. The middle-class reformers never questioned the notion that people were paid roughly what they were worth and that every person's employment or unemployment was an individual and private responsibility. They did promote schemes for workers' compensation covering disability by industrial accident. What they did not entertain was any idea that wages themselves should be insured against seasonal or cyclical misfortune, or that wages could be held by the state above some socially determined minimum. The rural ethic had moved to town and discovered bureaucracy, but in other respects it remained quite the same. So also had the English-speaking Canadians continued to nurture their old loyalty to Britain and the Empire, as Laurier discovered to his surprise and disappointment in the new century.

# Bibliography

The volume in the Canadian Centenary Series that covers the period of the Laurier boom is *Canada, 1896-1921: A Nation Transformed* (1974) by R.C. Brown and R. Cook. The biography of the Prime Minister, *Laurier: The First Canadian* (1965) by Joseph Schull provides a more chronological account of national political development. Equally useful for the politics of the period is the meticulously detailed biography of Clifford Sifton by D.J. Hall, *Clifford Sifton: The Young Napoleon* (1981). For a briefer account of Sifton's impact on the policies of the country, see Hall's article on "Clifford Sifton: Immigration and Settlement Policy, 1896-1905," in H. Palmer, ed., *The Settlement of the West* (1977). For the economic developments of the period, a synthesis for readers with some background in economics is *Canada: An Economic History* (1980) by W.L. Marr and D.G. Paterson.

The monographic literature that pertains to the emergence of particular staples in the period is old but still worth reading. V.C. Fowke's, *National*

*Policy and the Wheat Economy* (1957) is perhaps the classic of the genre. Also useful, especially to correct the tendency to overemphasize the importance of Western agriculture, is H.A. Innis, ed., *The Dairy Industry in Canada* (1937) and H.A. Innis, *Settlement and the Mining Frontier* (1936). For the rise of the pulp and paper industry to the position of dominant product of the forests, see J.A. Guthrie, *The Newsprint Paper Industry* (1941).

More recently, historians have become concerned with the issue of staple development and provincial politics. The book by H.V. Nelles, *The Politics of Development: Forests, Mines and Hydro-Electric Power in Ontario, 1849-1941* (1974) is perhaps the best example of the work on this topic. A more controversial but similar study is Martin Robin's survey of British Columbia resource development, *The Rush for Spoils: The Company Province, 1871-1933* (1972).

The transportation improvements that attended the boom in the new staples are covered by the work on particular railways. A provocative account of the diversification of the CPR into mineral production is found in R. Chodos, *The CPR: A Century of Corporate Welfare* (1973). The same subject and the complex Crow's Nest Pass agreement are covered more thoroughly, however, in the submission of the Province of Saskatchewan to the Royal Commission on Transportation, *An Historical Analysis of the Crow's Nest Pass Agreement on Grain Rates: A Study in National Transportation Policy* (1960). For the building of Laurier's transcontinentals see G.R. Stevens, *Canadian National Railways*, 2 vols. (1973) and T.D. Regehr, *The Canadian Northern Railway: Pioneer Road of the Northern Prairies, 1895-1918* (1976).

The problem of manufacturing development, like that of unlimited railway construction, is very much tied to national policy, particularly policies that encouraged foreign ownership and immigration. R.T. Naylor's "Rise and Fall of the Third Commercial Empire of the St. Lawrence," in Gary Teeple, ed., *Capitalism and the National Question in Canada* (1972) advances the merchants against industry hypothesis; L.R. Macdonald criticizes Naylor's thesis in "Merchants against Industry: An Idea and its Origins," CHR (1975). The work by Michael Bliss that argues the tariff had an early impact on encouraging foreign manufacturing is "Canadianizing American Business: The Roots of the Branch Plant," in Ian Lumsden, ed., *Close the 49th Parallel, etc.: The Americanization of Canada* (1970). The work that focuses on the tariff and immigration is J.H. Dales, *The Protective Tariff in Canada's Development* (1966). A less technical version of Dales' thesis is "Protection, Immigration and Canadian Nationalism," in Peter Russell, ed., *Nationalism in Canada* (1966) or "Some Historical and Theoretical Comment on Canada's National Policies," in B. Hodgins and R. Page, *Canadian History Since Confederation: Essays and Interpretations* (1972).

Urbanization and the conditions of the urban working class are described in urban biographies and social histories. Two comprehensive biographies of metropolitan centers in the period are Peter Goheen, *Victorian Toronto, 1850-1900* (1970) and A.F.J. Artibise, *Winnipeg: A Social History of Urban Growth* (1975). Other excellent studies of the lives of the towns are forthcoming in the *Illustrated History of Canadian Cities* series. A view of the urban working class from the standpoint of ethnic tension is "Divided City: The Immigrant in Winnipeg Society, 1874-1921," by A.F.J. Artibise in G.A. Stelter and Artibise, eds., *The Canadian City: Essays in Urban History* (1977). Studies of the urban working class that focus on the conditions of the poor are Terry Copp, *The Anatomy of Poverty: The Condition of the Working Class in Montreal, 1897-1929* (1974) and Michael J. Piva, *The Condition of the Working Class in Toronto, 1900-1921* (1979). Studies that analyze the Canadian working class in contexts other than Canada's metropolitan centers are Edmund Bradwin, *The Bunkhouse Man* (1972), a reprint of his pioneering study of labor in the bush camps; and T.K. Hareven and R. Langenback, *Amoskeag: Life and Work in an American Factory City* (1978), a study of a large French-Canadian community in New Hampshire.

The story of the early organized rebellion of the working class is introduced in general terms by Desmond Morton and Terry Copp in *Working People: An Illustrated History of Canadian Labour* (1980). More specialized works are D.R. Kennedy's account of the *Knights of Labour in Canada* (1956) and other studies focusing on particular problems. Stuart Jamieson, *Times of Trouble, 1900-1966* (1977) surveys the early industrial disputes in Canada. C. Heron and B.D. Palmer, "Through the Prism of the Strike: Industrial Conflict in Southern Ontario, 1901-14," CHR (1977) analyze the early strikes in the industrial heartland of Canada. Views of early working-class organization in industrial society are Bryan Palmer, *A Culture in Conflict: Skilled Workers and Industrial Capitalism in Hamilton, Ontario, 1860-1914* (1979) and Greg Kealey, *Toronto Workers Respond to Industrial Capitalism, 1867-1892* (1980).

The employers' reactions to worker organization are treated sympathetically by Michael Bliss in *A Living Profit: Studies in the Social History of Canadian Business, 1883-1911* (1974) and in his biography of *A Canadian Millionaire: The Life and Business Times of Sir Joseph Flavelle, Bart., 1858-1939* (1978). Less sympathetic is the latter half of the article by Heron and Palmer, cited above, or the book by Paul Craven, *"An Impartial Umpire": Industrial Relations and the Canadian State* (1980) which explores the partnership of the state and business to neutralize organized labor.

Two articles provide good overviews of the civic reform movement in Canada. Paul Rutherford, "Tomorrow's Metropolis: The Urban Reform Movement in Canada, 1880-1920," is a clear account of the bureaucratic orientation of the new middle class and John C. Weaver, " 'Tomorrow's Metropolis' Revisited: A Critical Assessment of Urban Reform in Canada,

1890-1920," is useful for its characterization of the significance of municipal ownership of the urban utility base. Both articles appear in *The Canadian City: Essays in Urban History*, cited above. A book-length account of the civic reformers that shows how the civic purity crusade came to a focus on "child saving" is Neil Sutherland, *Children in English Canadian Society: Framing the Twentieth-Century Consensus* (1976).

"... Laurier did move slightly toward independence."

# CHAPTER 16

# *Imperialism and the National Policy*

## I    The Beginning of External Affairs

Throughout most of the nineteenth century, Canadians enjoyed a splendid exemption from the crises of the world beyond their own borders. They had little to fear beyond their own continent since Canada enjoyed the security and even some of the prestige of an imperial power. Britain might have withdrawn her garrisons, but the Canadians were not totally abandoned. The later nineteenth century was the time of British naval supremacy, and so long as the mother country maintained the fleet's ascendency, Canada would be protected by it.

Such a state of affairs was particularly attractive to Canadians because British seapower was provided entirely by the British taxpayer; Canada had no tribute to pay, only allegiance. Unfortunately, as the century drew to a close, costs escalated as the English renewed their interest in an expanding empire. The colonies, denounced as "deadweights" in the 1860s, came to be celebrated as the jewels in the imperial crown in the 1880s. Within Europe, however, Germany began to realize industrial and imperial ambitions of its own at the same time. A particularly ambitious German naval program in the 1890s led to a countervailing expansion on the part of Britain. In the face of the costs involved, British politicians began to wonder, as in 1763, if the time had not come for colonials to contribute their mite for the defense of empire.

The issue surfaced in 1897 when colonial leaders were gathered in London to help celebrate the Diamond Jubilee of Queen Victoria. Laurier attended with other representatives of the "self-governing colonies". Together, they heard the British Colonial Secretary, Joseph Chamberlain, make three discreet suggestions. One was to create some "machinery of consultation" in order to discuss the "objects which we shall have in common". Secondly, since with management there must also come responsibility, Chamberlain thought it proper to consider how the colonies might wish to apportion responsibility for such common purposes. Naturally, the second point led Chamberlain to a third "personal suggestion" — the idea that they might wish to make regular cash contributions toward building up the British navy. On the last point, Chamberlain singled out the benefits of British seapower for Canada in particular. He said "if Canada had not behind her today ... the great military and naval power of Great Britain, she would have to make concessions to her neighbours ... ." In his view, the imperial link had enabled Canada "to control all the details of her own destiny." Without imperialism, Chamberlain asserted that Canada "would still be, to a great extent, a dependent country."

Laurier politely replied that Canadians did indeed have reason to cherish and maintain their loyalty to Great Britain. However, the vastness of Canada's public works projects, for instance railways, meant that the Dominion had no surplus for military expenditure, and also the idea of an imperial federation appeared premature. "I am quite satisfied with the condition of things as they are," he said. For the moment, the British initiative was thus stalled. Since Chamberlain's suggestions had been packaged as nothing more than personal hints, and since England was for the moment securely at peace, the conference proceded to a pleasant conclusion without resentment from either side.

Circumstances soon changed. In 1899, the pace of inter-imperial rivalry in Africa brought the tensions of colonial war to Canada and the other Dominions as Britain mounted an effort to put down a rising of the descendants of Dutch settlers in South Africa, a territory claimed by Britain and jealously regarded by Germany. Canada and the self-governing colonies were invited to participate in the defense of British interests. At first, the Canadian Prime Minister responded by pointing out that the conflict posed "no menace to Canada". He said it was a "secondary war" typical of those in which "England is always engaged". A large number of English-speaking Canadians subsequently denounced their leader's refusal as timidity and hypocrisy. What had he meant in 1897 at the imperial conference when he asserted that "We all feel pride in the British empire"? Like Chamberlain, a large number of Canadians had recently found new value in the empire, believing that Canada was developing into a strong country precisely because it was part of a larger imperial system. They perceived no contradiction between "imperialism" and "nationalism", nor were they in any sense bashful on the subject. They protested so loudly that Laurier stated a week after his first announcement that he had recently become aware of a "desire of a great many Canadians who are ready to take service". Within days of arguing that the South African war was none of Canada's business, Laurier announced in mid-October that one thousand volunteers were to be recruited to serve in the war simply because it was British.

Canada's enthusiasm for the Boer War then proved keener than the opportunity their prime minister offered. Before the conflict was over, 8372 Canadians were accepted into service to do their duty for imperial solidarity. This was enough to provoke loud rumblings of protest from anti-imperialists, other Canadian nationalists who suspected that Canada's first official adventure was setting a dangerous precedent for larger, more foolish military action in the future. Laurier attempted to counter such opposition by saying flatly that the South African episode "cannot be regarded as a departure ... nor construed as a precedent for future action." But Henri Bourassa, the major spokesman for the group known as *autonomistes*, replied that "the precedent is the accomplished fact." In Bourassa's opinion, the event marked "a constitutional revolution, the consequences of which no man can calculate." At the very least it did mark the end of what O.D. Skelton, Laurier's friend and official biographer, was to call "passive loyalty". In Skelton's view, however, Canada's participation in the South African War was a forward step, a move toward "responsible partnership" with Britain. If Canada assisted Great Britain more actively abroad, it seemed to follow that the British would be even more helpful in assisting Canada in North America.

## II    Conflict of Empires

The first assistance required of Britain after the South African war concerned the boundary between Alaska and the Northwest Territories. When the United States purchased Alaska from Russia in 1867, it was understood that the boundary between the Russian and British possessions had been settled by treaty in 1825 and that the acquisition included a "panhandle" that ran south to Portland Inlet (see map 16.1). The problem was that the treaty did not seem to specify a clear width for the coastal zone and it also left the division of Portland Inlet unclear. British Columbians wanted the matter settled almost as soon as they entered Confederation but there was no pressing reason for Great Britain or the United States to be concerned with such a trivial matter until July 1897. It was then that ships arrived in Seattle and San Francisco with literally tons of gold washed from the gravel of creeks draining into the Klondike river. An American adventurer, George Washington Carmack, had made the discovery in August of the previous year and the first haul was the fruit of the labor of just a few hundred people who rushed to the scene as news

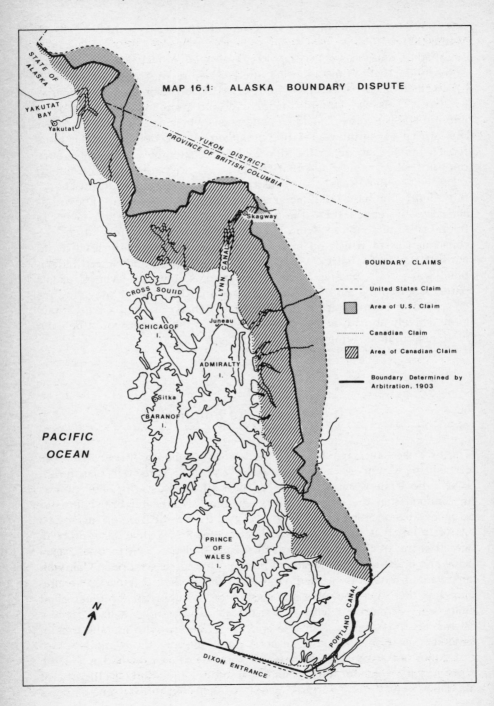

MAP 16.1: ALASKA BOUNDARY DISPUTE

STATE OF ALASKA

YAKUTAT BAY

Yakutat

YUKON DISTRICT
PROVINCE OF BRITISH COLUMBIA

Skagway

BOUNDARY CLAIMS

- - - - - United States Claim

Area of U.S. Claim

· · · · · · · Canadian Claim

Area of Canadian Claim

Boundary Determined by
Arbitration, 1903

CROSS SOUND

LYNN CANAL

CHICAGOF
I.

Juneau

ADMIRALTY
I.

Sitka

BARANOF
I.

PACIFIC
OCEAN

PRINCE
OF
WALES
I.

PORTLAND CANAL

N

DIXON ENTRANCE

of Carmack's luck spread through the north. Instantly the importance of the region of the upper reaches of the Yukon River was transformed from that of a fur reserve to lucrative mining frontier — but of what country?

The Klondike itself was indisputably Canadian. It was access to the gold that was likely to lead to trouble. By the American reading of the old treaty, the Alaskan panhandle extended eastward as far as the summit of the coastal range. Canada and the British contended that it did indeed run parallel to the height of land but at no point did the American zone extend further inland than "ten marine leagues" from the Ocean. In the Americans' interpretation, the Yukon territory was landlocked. In the other, it had an outlet to the sea at Skagway.

Naturally, gold seekers did not wait for a boundary settlement. They followed the most direct routes despite the interruption of disputed boundaries. Most people landed at Skagway where they saw the American flag snapping in the crisp coastal breeze. Later, they saw Union Jacks flying over the first point of undeniable Canadian jurisdiction — the summits of the mountain passes leading inland. One route led to the headwaters of the Yukon River by way of Chilcoot Pass. The other was a steeper climb over White Pass, then a different descent to the same headwaters of the Yukon.

The police at their mountaintop stations did more than show the flag. Every intending prospector had to have "at least 1150 pounds of solid food" and the necessary "tents, cooking utensils, prospectors' and carpenters' tools." Moreover, every newcomer had to pay various fees and duties on his effects before admission to the territory. In 1898 and 1899 the North West Mounted Police inspected more than 30 000 arrivals and collected over $150 000 in taxes. At the same time, they turned back persons whose equipment or other resources were deemed unsatisfatory.

After clearing customs, newcomers made their descent to the Yukon and followed the river downstream to the point at which it met the Klondike. In 1896 the site of the confluence of the two rivers was an uninhabited swampy plain. Predictably, however, the area quickly became the busiest riverine intersection in the North and soon developed the appearance of a town. By 1899 the place had been named Dawson City and held a population of 20 000. Dawson was indeed a city. Such phenomenal growth was not uncommon in similar circumstances elsewhere. What was surprising, in the case of Dawson, was the degree of order that was maintained in the otherwise typical boom town. Dawson City saloons closed every week day from 2:00 to 6:00 AM and closed entirely every weekend from midnight Saturday to 6:00 AM Monday. There were thirteen reported murders on the Klondike during the gold rush period; all but one led to a conviction and an execution. Thus, it is possible that Dawson City was more orderly than Winnipeg. Certainly there were more police on the Klondike — almost 300 constables — and they had broader discretionary powers than any other place in North America. Recognized as a special district in 1898, the Yukon still did not have normal institutions of representative government. According to Morris Zaslow, it was "virtually a police state" but he hastens to add that the all-powerful appointed officals "exercised their power in exemplary fashion." The result was that the Yukon's metropolitan center was forced to behave even more decorously than a typical, medium-sized Canadian town, despite its being populated mainly by Americans who were on the move and on the make.

With the completion of a railway between Skagway and Whitehorse in 1901 and with the elaboration of steam navigation on the Yukon river between Whitehorse and Dawson, the way was well open for capital-intensive exploitation of the gold fields. Mechanization did follow the railway but the peak of placer mining was reached in 1903. Geologists continued to search for the mother lode, the supposed source of the alluvial gold washed down into the creek beds but they never found it. Still, expectations for better things to come from the Yukon were high at the turn of the century.

In 1903, the parties to the boundary dispute agreed to submit the treaty of 1825 to a judicial opinion from a panel of six judges: three American, one British, and two Canadian. Unfortunately, it was naive of Canadians to think that the Americans would allow the matter to be decided on strictly legal grounds, or to believe the British would stand with them in an attempt to overwhelm the United States. Britain had sacrificed Canadian interests in the past to placate American ambition, and such compromise was all the more essential in 1903 because the American President was unusually belligerent in asserting his country's interests. Regarding Alaska, Roosevelt instructed his agents in Britain to convey the message to the British that only one decision would be acceptable from the arbitration panel. If the tribunal did not uphold the American claim, Roosevelt said, "I am going to send a brigade of American regulars up to Skagway and take possession of the disputed territory and hold it by all the power and force of the United States." The result was that the British judge, Lord Alverstone, sided with the Americans, the award went to the United States, and the two Canadians not only refused to sign the document, they also issued a public statement condemning the decision.

Across Canada, newspapers joined in a general condemnation of the affair as another instance of the British sacrificing the interests of a "loyal colony" for the sake of pleasing the appetites of a greedy, upstart republic. Laurier himself criticized the Americans for their "grasping" behavior and wondered in Parliament whether the time had not come for Canada to behave less like "a small colony, a growing colony, but still a colony ...." In Laurier's view, "The difficulty is that as long as Canada remains a dependency of the British Crown the present powers that we have are not sufficient for the maintenance of our rights." This was certainly true. Laurier continued, however, to utter a statement that most historians have come to regard as recklessly naive. "It is important," he added, "that we should ask the British Parliament for more extensive power, so that if ever we have to deal with matters of a similar nature again, we shall deal with them in our own way, in our own fashion, according to the best light that we have." What Laurier seemed to ignore in the temper of the moment was that the Alaskan Boundary dispute — in its ultimate resolution in 1903 — was not a matter of who had the better right, but which country had the greater might.

## III  National Defense

No loosening of ties with Britain immediately followed the souring of Anglo-Canadian relations by Lord Alverstone's behavior even though Laurier did move slightly toward greater independence in 1904 by nationalizing the militia. Previous to the change, the General Officer Commanding had to be a British soldier of command rank, colonel or better. Henceforth, he was to be a native of the Dominion. To some, even this small symbolic step was provocative and repugnant, a sentiment that was appealed to by the retiring GOC, D.D. Dundonald, the Earl of Cochrane, who said: "Men of Canada, keep both hands on the Union Jack".

Another influence that gave Laurier second thoughts about pursuing independence further was the Governor General, Lord Minto, who pointed out shortly after the Alaska boundary arbitration that "if Canada wishes to possess complete treaty-making powers she must be prepared to back her claims with her own forces." But how would the 6 million Canadians of 1903 win anything against the 81 million Americans of the time in an all-out confrontation of force? For that matter, how would Britain? The reality was that Theodore Roosevelt wielded a "big stick", and Canada's best option was to join Britain in sensibly ducking whenever it was swung in their direction. Consequently, national support for imperialism and the inability of Canada to oppose the Americans effectively on their own, combined to check Laurier from making Canada more independent of Britain, but neither factor settled the issue of how much Canada should pay to maintain British friendship.

Then, in 1909, the issue of the dollar value of imperialism surfaced more urgently than ever before. The First Lord of the Admiralty announced in Britain that naval supremacy was being lost again to Germany. He advocated an immediate crash program for building the latest ultimate weapon — specially armored, big-gun battleships like the *Dreadnought*. The cheerleaders in the new arms race chanted "We want eight and we won't wait." Were the Canadians ready to contribute?

It was moved in Parliament by George Foster that the country "should no longer delay in assuming her proper share of responsibility and financial burden incidental to the suitable protection of her exposed coast line and sea ports." Foster advocated an immediate cash contribution like one recently granted to Britain by New Zealand.

Laurier responded with a substitute motion that embraced the response of Australia. He repudiated the notion of cash tribute and advocated, instead, the launching of a Canadian navy to relieve the British of North American responsibilities. After consulting later with the leader of the opposition, Robert Borden (leader of the Conservatives since Tupper's retirement in 1901), the substitute motion hinted that cash support of the Royal Navy might also be possible in exceptional circumstances. For a time, with the emphasis falling on the creation of a small Canadian navy intended for coastal defense, the House of Commons was united, and the Laurier-Borden compromise received unanimous support late in 1909.

Canadians were deeply divided, however, on the question of a local coast guard. On one side, nationalists whose concept of the nation placed them squarely within the British Empire could not imagine any navy but *the* navy, the naval service of Britain "Whose flag had braved a thousand years/The battle and the breeze." By comparison, any naval service in Canada would be a "tin pot navy". Imperialists preferred to make a direct cash contibution to England to the extent of a dreadnought or two, as the Admiralty saw fit.

On the other side, centered largely in Quebec, were the nationalists whose hopes for a more autonomous Canada remained undaunted. For them, autonomy dictated neither tribute nor armament, since they believed that even a limited Canadian navy would invite future jumps on the imperial bandwagon in an endless succession of secondary wars like the South African affair.

Since Laurier's strength in Parliament was largely dependent upon support from Quebec (54 of Quebec's 65 seats were Liberal in the most recent election, that of 1908), the government was extremely cautious in framing the Naval Service Bill presented to the House of Commons in mid-January of 1910. The proposed legislation would make it legal for the government to create a naval service and naval college for the training of officers. But the force that was described to the House was clearly nothing more than a coast guard to consist eventually of five light cruisers and six destroyers. Moreover, like the militia, the navy was to be commanded by personnel answerable to Canada. Laurier emphasized that in times of "emergency" the Canadian navy would not automatically come to the assistance of the Royal Navy. "The position which we take," Laurier explained, "is that it is for the Parliament of Canada, which created the navy, to say when and where it shall go to war."

For Robert Borden, Laurier's proposal showed but halfhearted support for the empire. In his opinion, the British were already "confronted with an emergency which may rend this empire assunder before the proposed service is worthy of the name." Borden therefore chose to disregard the previous unanimity and advocated a "free and loyal contribution" to the mother country instead.

In the end, it was Laurier's compromise that prevailed, but it pleased no one. Imperialists ridiculed the idea of a "tin pot navy" and *autonomistes* warned that its creation was the greatest "backward step" in fifty years. Since the split between imperialism and autonomy was also one of English versus French, the country showed signs of beginning to break along lines of its primary antithesis, a division that was particularly dangerous because both sides were equally patriotic. What divided the imperialists from the *autonomistes* was not concern for Canada, but the method of acquiring a more powerful national existence and at the same time defining purposes for which the new powers would be used.

## IV    A New Direction in Tariff Policy

After the navy controversy, Laurier was ready for relaxation and escape. The aging Prime Minister went west in the hope of gaining some approval if not unqualified recognition for the fruits of his other policies. The Prairies had come into prominence since he had come to power and the recent award of provincial status was well received in Alberta and Saskatchewan. The West was therefore the one region outside Quebec in which Laurier was still likely to receive something of a hero's welcome. The crowds did cheer Sir Wilfrid from June to September as he paraded from Winnipeg to Vancouver and back. It was just the tonic the old politician needed.

But all was not approval and recognition. At nearly every stop along his regal progression there were also angry petitioners, especially farmers who were convinced that the share of the bonanza that was theirs was not all that it might or ought to have been. Since a Prairie farmer was a kind of businessman, and since no group was as likely to complain as loudly or as sharply as businessmen with expectations that were not being realized as fast or as fully as they hoped, the farmers of western Canada did complain and mightily. Not complaining of hardship, they still asserted that their present prosperity was only a shadow of what was possible if government would only accord them better freight rates and more rational storage and marketing of their staple grains. Above all, they wanted exemption from the tariff.

At Saskatoon, one farmer asked Laurier directly what had happened to the Grit in the old Liberal party. He reminded the Prime Minister that it was Laurier who once promised "to skin the Tory bear of protection." This Liberal wanted to know "what you have done with the hide." Such a question put Laurier completely off balance. He could only say that his "blood is a little cooler now." But such a disclaimer only confirmed what Westerners suspected, and they were not pleased with the confirmation that they had little to choose between Liberals and Conservatives.

Having returned to Ottawa in September with angry protests as well as the crowds' cheering still ringing in his ears, the Prime Minister then had to face evidence of faltering popularity in his home province. Quebec had cast the majority of its vote for Liberals for the first time in 1896 on the strength of the popularity of Laurier's approach to the Manitoba Schools Question, and had given him steadily more of the total in each election since. But in November 1910, the voters had their first opportunity to express displeasure with imperialism in a by-election where Liberals had previously won with ease. This time the Liberal candidate was defeated by an *autonomiste* critic of Laurier's navy, by an unknown politician supported only by the powerful pen of Henri Bourassa and his newspaper, *Le Devoir*.

Soon after the defeat in Drummond-Arthabaska, the farm protest resumed. This time a thousand protestors representing the Canadian Council of Agriculture, a group representing every region of the country, descended upon Ottawa demanding more formally all the action that had been called for in a less organized fashion during the prime ministerial tour of the past summer.

Laurier's response was cordial, yet evasive. He found demands for such action as government encouragement of farmers' cooperatives and public ownership of grain elevators "too radical", but there was one concession he might make. Although Laurier announced nothing definite at the time, negotiations were underway and at an advanced stage by December 1910 for a general relaxing of the tariff, particularly as it related to the interests of agriculture.

Earlier, the Americans had proposed full-scale discussion of the question of reciprocal free trade between the two countries and Laurier had been hesitant at first. He became progressively more interested as such a bold new policy seemed likely to divert public attention from the imperialism controversy and to bolster support for Laurier's Liberals in those regions in which they were faltering and most dependent — the West, Quebec, and the Maritimes.

By mid-January, face-to-face negotiations resulted in an agreement to be implemented by concurrent legislation from Congress and the Canadian Parliament. W.S. Fielding, the long-time Finance Minister and erstwhile advocate of free trade, was positively giddy when he reported the proposal to Parliament on January 26. As soon as the legislatures of the Unites States and Canada enacted it into law, there would be free trade in a wide range of natural products (particularly agricultural produce), and certain manufactured goods useful in farming (barbed wire and cream separators, for example). In addition, reciprocal reductions were also to be allowed on a few other trade goods in the future.

At first, the opposition was stunned and stupefied. Anticipating an election soon, Borden observed that there was "the deepest dejection" among Conservatives since they feared that "the government's proposals... would give it another term in office" — Laurier's fifth. It was true that Liberals and Conservatives alike had welcomed the idea of a restoration of that reciprocity which was supposed to have made the decade after 1854 so prosperous. Renewal of reciprocal free trade had been a shared goal of every political leader at one time or another since the expiration of the original agreement in 1866. Even John A. Macdonald, the father and guardian of the National Policy, had explored the possibility of freer trade with the United States as late as 1891 in order to blunt the Liberals' war cry that year. But when he found the Americans unresponsive, Macdonald decided protectionism was still patriotic. The cry of patriotism in 1891 foreshadowed what was to follow in 1911. Still, the Conservatives' initial reaction was to rejoice in the agreement for its economic implications. Their only lament on the day of its announcement was that reciprocity was a Liberal rather than a Conservative coup.

## V    "Borden and King George, or Laurier and Taft?"

The lead of Toronto businessmen proved decisively important in finding good ground on which to oppose reciprocity. Sir Edmund Walker, the President of the Canadian Bank of Commerce, led the way on February 16 when he addressed the Toronto Board of Trade to criticize the tariff agreement because it put continentalism ahead of the British connection. Four days later, eighteen prominent businessmen (identifying themselves as Liberals) echoed the same theme when they issued an open letter to the public denouncing the agreement because it would tend "to weaken the ties which bind Canada to the Empire." Thus, Ontario businessmen who had little to fear from a relaxation of trade restrictions on commodities covered by the proposed change opposed it anyway because they may have feared that one relaxation of the tariff was only the first of many to follow until the principle of protection were entirely repudiated. For them, it was convenient to place freer trade on a higher level of principle (imperialism), then, after drawing attention to the naval service bill, suggest that the two issues together pointed to a sinister "inner meaning" (dissolution of empire). In this way, reciprocity became entangled inextricably with imperial relations and the ground was well prepared for opposition politicians to follow.

Clifford Sifton, the maverick Liberal who left the ministry in 1905 to oppose minority rights, now left the party to fight reciprocity. Other Liberals — ready to make the same move over the militia bill of 1904, or the naval service bill of 1910, or the host of little personal grudges bound to accumulate around a government fifteen years in power — took the occasion of the controversy that developed around reciprocity to get well out of Laurier's trouble and contribute, if possible, to his downfall.

Robert Borden's mood of defeat steadily shifted to one of quiet confidence and the Conservatives decided to filibuster the passage of the trade bill, thus forcing the government into an election that Borden thought he was bound to win. The debate therefore dragged through March and April, then adjourned for two months so that Laurier could attend still another of those increasingly regular conferences in Britain. Upon his return, the debate resumed and continued even after the passage of the measure through the American Congress near the end of July. Since there seemed no end to the Canadian filibuster, the Prime Minister decided to challenge the opposition to a September election and Parliament was dissolved on July 29.

Laurier did not fear the outcome. From an economic standpoint, the case for free trade in natural products was strong. No abrupt repudiation of protected industry was contemplated so the branch plant factories would not shut down. More importantly, there appeared to be substantial benefits for fishermen, miners, forest workers, and most cash crop farmers. These, however, were hypothetical benefits and they looked to the long term. In elections, it is perhaps a truism that the short run is always more important. In that of 1911, voters were told that fruit growers would face immediate and stiff competition from American producers; railway workers were warned that there would be instant and massive layoffs from the east-west transcontinentals because all trade would suddenly start running north-south; and Roblin of Manitoba told the grain producers of his province that Minneapolis was going to become a buyer's market even more than Port Arthur if Canadian and American producers suddenly marketed their produce in the same place. One way or another, all critical points seemed to suggest that the country was tolerably prosperous in 1911. Why disturb the *status quo?*

If the short-term argument against modifying the tariff was more persuasive than the long-term hypothetical benefit, appeals to loyalty were probably even more telling. Ironically, the Americans themselves did the most to assist imperialists in their campaign by some remarkably stupid speeches in support of the proposal. The most quoted man in Canada was the Speaker of the House of Representatives, "Champ" Clark, who said that he was "for it" because of his "hope to see the day when the American flag will float over every square foot of the British North American possessions, clear to the North Pole."

This was precisely the point the Conservatives and former Liberals such as Clifford Sifton were making. They said that closer trade relations would not only weaken the empire, but that reciprocity would probably mean the end of Canada as well. Premier Walter Scott of Saskatchewan attempted to answer that free trade was simply good economics and ridiculed the loyalty issue saying: "We may remain loyal while sending our flax crop over a high tariff wall into the United States but if the wall be removed and we obtain consequent higher prices for our flax we become disloyal." Yes, replied George Foster. He appealed to a vision of a country strengthened by independence in North America and unity with Britain, saying: "Canadian natural resources for the purposes of Canadian development, Canadian markets for Canadian producers, Canadian traffic for Canadian carriers, and a Canadian nation with complete freedom of self-government and the closest possible union and cooperation with the British empire."

On the basis of the optimistic projection of the *status quo*, the rising tide of British imperialism, and a deeply rooted distrust of the United States, the country outside Quebec repudiated Laurier. To have a majority in the House of Commons, however, Borden's Conservatives needed some representation from Quebec. But that which made them so popular in Ontario should have made them all the more odious to French Canada. While Laurier's naval policy was mildly imperialist, Borden's was brazenly so. Assuming the *autonomistes* were more interested in defeating imperialism than Laurier, they should have united behind the Liberal leader as the lesser of two evils once it became apparent how strong the Conservatives were outside Quebec. They did not; and that fact gave the election of 1911 an especially interesting as well as an important twist.

Henri Bourassa, probably the most influential individual in Quebec, thought that he might defeat Laurier's naval policy without furthering Borden's. His plan was to work for the election of a block of *autonomiste* candidates who would be independent of the Conservatives as well as of the Liberals, yet a large enough force to deny either party a majority. Holding the balance of power in the House of Commons, they might then force revisions to the hated naval service bill.

Bourassa's strategy was plausible early in the campaign. The evidence for its success was Borden's willingness to cooperate in the scheme by refusing to run candidates in opposition to Bourassa's. The Conservatives ran only in the Eastern Townships and the few English-speaking ridings of Montreal. The rest was left as a clear field for *autonomistes* and Liberals.

By mid-September, however, it had become evident that Laurier's strength outside Quebec was even less than Bourassa originally expected. By that time, it should have been clear to the powerful editor of *Le Devoir* that votes for the third party were simply, in the words of *La Presse*, "a vote for imperialism with a vengeance." But Bourassa stubbornly refused to throw his support behind his one-time friend. Two days before the election, Laurier knew he had been beaten. But so had Bourassa because it was a Borden *majority* government that took the seals of office. The 16 *autonomistes* elected were still short of commanding the balance of power — even if they sided solidly with the 87 Liberals. Borden's party with 118 seats had a free rein, and they came to power owing no favors to Quebec. What followed was government for the "progressive" imperialist majority, and majoritarianism with a vengeance.

## Bibliography

The volume in the Canadian Centenary Series that covers the period from 1896 to 1921, R.C. Brown and R. Cook, *Canada: A Nation Transformed* (1974), includes material on all aspects of this chapter. A fuller account, however, of relations between Canada, the United States, and Great Britain in these years is C.P. Stacey, *Canada and the Age of Conflict: A History of Canadian External Policies*, Vol. I, 1867-1921 (1977).

A number of specialized works examine the imperialist thrust of English-speaking Canadian nationalists. Carl Berger's *Imperialism and Nationalism, 1884-1914: A Conflict in Canadian Thought* (1969) and his *Sense of Power: Studies in the Ideas of Canadian Imperialism, 1867-1914* (1970) are the two most important works on the theme. A narrower but similar subject with a longer history, the idea of imperial federation, is covered by John Kendle, *The Round Table Movement* (1975).

The *autonomiste* reaction to imperialism is described in Berger's work. But more detailed studies of Henri Bourassa are also available. See Joseph Levitt, *Henri Bourassa on Imperialism and Bi-culturalism, 1900-1918* (1970). For the domestic purposes for which Bourassa hoped to see greater autonomy applied see Levitt's, "Henri Bourassa and Modern Industrial Society, 1900-1914," CHR (1969) or his book-length treatment of the same subject, *Henri Bourassa and the Golden Calf: The Social Program of the Nationalists, 1900-1914* (1969).

North American disputes that were not well served by imperialism are illustrated best, perhaps, by the Alaska Boundary dispute. Morris Zaslow, *The Opening of the Canadian North, 1870-1914* (1971) has excellent chapters on the Klondike gold rush. Pierre Berton's popular account, *Klondike: The Last Great Gold Rush, 1896-1899,* revised edition (1972) is a detailed rendition of the more colorful aspects. Norman Penlington, *The Alaska Boundary Dispute: A Critical Reappraisal* (1972) concludes that the British position was the only reasonable course. Desmond Morton, *Ministers and Generals: Politics and the Canadian Militia, 1868-1904* (1970) provides another perspective, not on the boundary dispute simply, but on the blend of British imperial interests and Canadian domestic political concerns as they came into conflict over control of the militia.

For Laurier's defeat in 1911, the biography by Schull cited in the bibliography to the previous chapter is useful for the sequence of events. More specialized studies include an article by W.M. Baker, "A Case Study of Anti-Americanism in English-speaking Canada: The Election Campaign of 1911," CHR (1970) or the volume by Paul Stevens, *The 1911 General Election: A Study in Canadian Politics* (1970).

". . . no one knows why they fought so well."

# CHAPTER 17

# *The Imperial Tragedy*

## I    Attempted Reform at the National Level

The change from Laurier to Borden in 1911 was reminiscent of the shift from Macdonald to Mackenzie in 1874 in the sense that both new prime ministers were swept into power on a wave of moral indignation. In Borden's case, however, there were broader intentions at stake than the simple vindication of Canadian virtue. Unlike Mackenzie, who professed to be nothing more than an honest version of John A. Macdonald, Borden claimed he was a new leader for a new era. Laurier's reluctance to accept a broader role in the empire and his renewed willingness to lower the tariff barrier against the United States were both denounced by Borden and the Conservatives as a "Little Canada" policy. On the domestic level, Borden said Laurier's administration was equally inappropriate because it was outmoded.

Robert Laird Borden was one of those Canadians who was born in the country (rural Nova Scotia in his case) and subsequently moved to town to profit from the new industrial society that was taking shape. The town that drew Borden off the farm was Halifax and the career he chose was law, not criminal or private civil disputes, but the proceedings of trade and corporate liability. As a corporation lawyer, Borden developed a spectator's admiration for business that was close to religious zeal. Like many other members of the new middle class, Borden had come to believe that a "progressive" state might profitably imitate business models in all its administrative operations.

Borden had no taste for old-fashioned politics, the artful deception and judicious dispensation of patronage that occupied John A. Macdonald and Wilfrid Laurier at least 50 percent of their time in office. For Borden, old-style politics was corrupt and the "machinery" of government was hopelessly inefficient. Too frequently, departments overlapped in operations and they were run by amateurs holding their positions as political favors.

In 1911, Borden thought that he had an opportunity to make a good start in changing all this.

Borden's political education had not prepared him, however, for the tasks he wished to perform. It began late, at age 42 when Charles Tupper dealt him a seat in the House of Commons in 1896. But five years later, the pace of Borden's education admittedly quickened when the same person handed him the leadership of the Conservative party, an award the Tory caucus subsequently approved (in 1901, leadership conventions were still a foreign custom avoided in Canada). In the next five years, Borden struggled to develop as an alternative to Laurier. By 1907, Borden decided that it was time for a national party to promote that which other civic-minded people were advocating on a more local level. Like the other middle-class reformers, Borden saw tangible benefits in public ownership of the utility base; and he believed there was a real need for government to exercise more vigorous "police" powers and provide a broader range of social services by a more efficient bureaucracy. On a national level, the utilities were the railways, the police were the armed forces or various regulatory commissions, and the new social services were operations such as free rural delivery of mail to that half of the country that had not yet moved to town.

Once he was prime minister, Borden dissociated himself from the old-fashioned considerations of patronage and party organization, and tried to devote his twelve-hour working days to more uplifting considerations of how to fulfill the reform promises he had been making since 1907. In 1912 and 1913, the civil service was examined for ways to increase its efficiency; farmers were given free rural mail delivery; and innovations were attempted in federal-provincial cooperation to share the costs of improving country roads and agricultural education. Finally, preliminary and somewhat halting steps were taken toward nationalizing the as yet uncompleted and faltering transcontinental railways authorized by Laurier in 1903. Thus Borden moved to reorganize the political superstructure, but like the other middle-class reformers of his day, he did not believe that there were any fundamental defects in the economic system.

According to Borden's biographer, R.C. Brown, the new prime minister did achieve a "respectable record of legislative accomplishment" within the rather narrow limits in which he thought reform was needed. But Borden was impeded by the Liberal-dominated Senate which kept recommending amendments to his reform proposals. For this reason, Brown suggests that it was Senate obstructionism that prevented Borden from achieving more. John English offers a slightly different explanation. In his view, there was more to Borden's legislative failures than Liberal partisanship in the Senate. According to English, Borden's conviction that there was "an objective and definable general interest" (the validity of which was unquestionable) and Borden's contempt for old-fashioned "brokerage politics" meant that "compromises came grudgingly from him and were abandoned hastily if opportunity arose." In other words, Borden was inclined to believe there was only one truth — it was his — and he attempted to pursue it without due regard for accommodating opposing points of view unless that were absolutely necessary. This, according to English, is what derailed his domestic policies, and what led to even greater failure in his insistence upon an imperialist defense policy.

## II    Imperialism with a Vengeance

Borden came to power intending to bring Canada closer to Great Britain by contributing in some meaningful way to imperial defense and also by gaining a voice in the determination of the objectives for which such strengthened imperial forces might be used. In this sense, Robert Borden offered precisely the kind of cooperation in 1911 that Joseph Chamberlain had sought in 1897. But six months after coming to power, in March 1912, Borden was still not certain of the kind of defense policy that would be most mutually beneficial for Britain and for Canada. He did not wish to create the coast guard Laurier wanted. At the same time, he was reluctant to make a cash contribution to Britain without assurances of shared control. As a result of both considerations, Borden announced on March 18, 1912 that the government was suspending the implementation of the Naval Service Act but did not yet have a permanent policy to replace it. When a permanent policy was determined, he said, it would be submitted to the people for their approval prior to implementation.

On the same day that Borden made his defense policy announcement, the First Lord of the Admiralty, Winston Churchill, announced that a renewed naval crisis was forcing Britain to proceed with yet another crash program of dreadnought construction. Since this was an emergency situation, Borden thought that the appropriate response of Canada would be a cash contribution to the Admiralty. The leader of the anti-Laurier French-Canadian contingent in Parliament, Frederick Monk, refused to consider Churchill's announcement sufficient justification, however. Borden did concede that it would be possible to obtain more substantial confirmation before acting and urged Monk to accompany him to England for this purpose. When Monk demurred, another anti-Laurier French Canadian, Louis-Philippe Pelletier, agreed to go in Monk's place. Thus, a party of Canadian officials boarded ship for England on June 26, 1912.

The important meetings in England were private conferences between Borden and Churchill. In these meetings, Churchill confirmed that the situation was "very serious" and agreed to put his opinion in writing for presentation to key personnel in Canada. "He is quite willing to play the game," Borden noted later in his diary. "Will give assurance in writing as to necessity."

Upon Borden's return to Canada, he confronted Monk with the letter signed by Churchill. Monk was impressed. In his view, the Prime Minister would be wholly justified in setting a policy and presenting it to the electorate in the form of a plebiscite. If the proposed contribution did not divide the country, Monk promised to support it. Without such prior consultation, however, he said he would "retire" and, by implication, take the rest of the French-Canadian, anti-Laurier contingent with him.

Borden wanted — but did not need — the support of the French-Canadians. Moreover, he believed that a plebiscite would be "fatal to us in the English provinces" because it would be too readily apparent that the issue was a problem only in Quebec. Why, then, had Borden suggested earlier that his policy would be submitted to the people before implementation? It would appear that the earlier assurance was a gesture to Quebec, grudgingly offered, and applied only to the permanent policy rather than an emergency expedient. Since the present crisis was apparently a passing phenomenon, it gave Borden the opportunity to abandon his previous commitment. Thus it was suddenly dropped.

Borden's resolve to proceed without a plebiscite (or a general election) was reinforced by his discovery that the "variable" and "unstable" French Canadians were not going to follow Monk. Only seven in the sixteen were willing to join Laurier to oppose Borden. The rest stood with the government like any other kind of Conservative. Bourassa's *autonomistes* thus reverted back to their *Parti Bleu* origins. Their anti-Laurier, anti-Liberal sentiments proved stronger than their anti-imperialist orientation. Since they had their hatreds out of order, Bourassa himself eventually denounced the group he had done so much to create, and it was Laurier's party almost alone that fought Borden's naval aid bill once it was introduced to Parliament in December 1912.

The proposed law would authorize the Government of Canada to spend $35 million for the "construction and equipment of battleships or armoured cruisers of the most modern and powerful type" to be used by "His Majesty for the common defense of the Empire." Laurier opposed the contribution because it did nothing for the Canadian navy. Were he in power, Laurier said, he would proceed in accordance with the Naval Service Act and construct two small fleets to defend Canada's Atlantic and Pacific coasts.

In the end, Borden did neither. Having suspended the Naval Service Act, he refused to reinstate it and the interim policy of aid to Britain failed to pass the Canadian Houses of Parliament. Laurier's opposition to the naval aid bill was the longest, most acrimonious, in the nation's history.

The acrimony began early in December and did not cease until six months later on May 15, 1913. That day, the government ended the debate with a device rather common in the proceedings of the British Parliament but new to the Canadian House of Commons. A new rule empowered the majority to terminate debate and bring a matter to a vote once opposition proved to be "merely obstructionist".

For those, like Borden, who viewed Parliament as a kind of factory whose product was legislation, closure was a sensible streamlining of outmoded procedures. Without it, a howling minority could stop the assembly line by sheer talk and delay the "business" of the House perhaps to the point of dissolution. In an election thus forced, if the voters agreed that the opposition had been merely obstructionist, there could be severe punishment for the "filibuster". On the other hand, an appeal to the people could also defeat a ministry. In this sense, the process of debate could be a great equalizer in parliamentary politics. It was how Laurier prepared the way for his grand entrance in 1896 and Borden for his in 1911.

The problem for Borden was that he was not certain that he could win an election in the spring of 1913; hence the "gag rule". But Laurier had another weapon under the old system, a weapon not yet neutralized by Borden. The Constitution of Canada required passage by both "Houses of Parliament" before any measure could receive royal assent and come into force. By convention, the upper house had developed into a "chamber of sober second thought" offering amendments to measures that the House of Commons would sometimes accept. But the Senate never imposed its will on the Commons by insisting upon a course unacceptable to the lower house. The chamber of sober second thought was not also "a house of partisan second chance" — not until its outright rejection of Borden's naval aid bill. At the end of May 1913, the Senate returned the measure to the House of Commons, stating that it refused to concur: "This House is not justified in giving its assent to the Bill until it is submitted to the judgement of the country."

Here was another direct challenge to Borden for a general election and he refused the bait then as previously. Rather than get caught in Laurier's net, Borden turned away from defense policy and pushed his domestic "equality of opportunity" program with renewed vigor, particularly those measures that were intended to rescue farmers from their rural isolation. By the spring of 1914, it appeared that Borden was well prepared to meet Laurier's challenge for an early election in the sense that he was ready to confront the electorate with a list of reforms achieved and intentions obstructed, claiming the Liberal Senate was to blame for the latter. Here, consistent with the more general call for reform Borden might also demand a restructuring of the upper house of Parliament.

Other developments deflected Borden from seeking a dissolution, however. One was an economic recession, a downturn that was striking in

1913 and worsening in 1914. The acreage of crops sown was lower in 1914 than in any year since 1910 because expected prices were so low. In town, factories were working at only 50 to 75 percent capacity. There were also political discouragements since the Conservatives' organizations in both Ontario and Manitoba had fallen into disarray. In Quebec, of course, the situation was even more hopeless for the Tories. Consequently, Borden decided to take a long vacation rather than to call an election. He took leave from Ottawa and went with his wife, Laura, to the lake country northwest of Toronto to enjoy the pleasant company of Canada's wealthiest cottagers: the Eatons, Sanfords, and the Macleans. Only the daily press found its way to Borden's Port Carling retreat. In this way, he learned on July 27 that as a result of the Austrian heir presumptive's having been killed by a Serbian nationalist, Austria was declaring war on Serbia. The news did not deter Borden from playing golf that day. Soon, however, he was urgently requested to return to Ottawa because it appeared that the rest of Europe, including Great Britain, was also going to war, and therefore Canada, too, was on the brink of adventure. Instantly, the crisis of the present moment dissolved all others and Borden knew that his government was saved — at least for the duration.

## III    The Unifying Impact of the War

As with the response to the call for volunteers to fight in the Boer War, there were far more recruits, initially, than places in the ranks of the contingent to be sent. Nobody suspected that the 1914 adventure was going to be any less exciting than the South African affair. Nobody could tell that Canada was plunging into the most tragic episode in the country's history.

Participation in the Great War led to two kinds of tragedy, quite different in their results. The first was the tragedy of the sacrifice itself, the numbing effect of the slaughter that kept up for over four years. From collective injury it was possible to extract a "sense of power" and national achievement: Canada had made a distinguished contribution to an important moment in the history of the world, the contribution had been at the limit of the country's ability, and Canada survived. The other pattern of tragedy was not so positive in its consequences, but consider the first, more commemorative disaster in greater detail.

At the beginning, mobilization had the effect of unifying the country around a sense of common danger that was far less artificial than anything Canada had experienced in the past. Earlier, in the case of John A. Macdonald's attempt to create an atmosphere of national urgency around the building of the CPR, for example, the artificiality of the effort was only too apparent. Or later, with the South African war, the episode was only English Canada's adventure. In 1914, however, Germany attacked France through neutral Belgium; Russia, Britain, and eventually Italy, joined the conflict. It was clear that there was nothing "secondary" about this war. Borden pledged "every effort and... every sacrifice." He believed that "the manhood of Canada stands ready to fight beyond the seas" to the last individual if necessary. Laurier also affirmed that "when the call goes out, our answer goes at once, and it goes in the classical language of the British answer to the call of Duty: 'Ready, Aye Ready'." The leader of the opposition promised to support the government fully. Laurier said there would be "no criticism so long as there is danger at the front."

It could be charged that both affirmations were reckless or hollow in light of what eventually followed, but no one knew then that they were embarking upon the bloodiest infantry war in human history. Later, even as the brutal reality became dreadfully evident, the spontaneous enthusiasm still held up through the most bloodstained year in the history of warfare. The major signs of disintegration did not become fully apparent until 1917. From this standpoint, there were three years of remarkable unity to pursue a war that demanded more of the country than any struggle before. Surely this was worthy of commemoration.

The self-sacrifice involved more than young, adventuresome men joining the army. It also engaged civilians for voluntary contributions of both time and money for the war effort at home. Every association from the IODE to the YMCA had wartime projects. The most important instance of such voluntarism was perhaps the work of the Canadian Patriotic Fund, an association chartered in 1914 for the purpose of "preserving the families' economic status in comfort and decency, as a partial recognition of the services of the soldiers overseas." The idea was to raise and distribute money to the families of enlisted men in the hope of bridging the discrepancy between what a man could expect from his peacetime work and what he received as his soldier's pay. Although the project was ambitious to the point of pretension, the volunteer workers and contributors almost realized their goal. Before the war, the average pay for a factory worker was about $80 per month. This was the minimum that the Canadian Patriotic Fund did nearly succeed in guaranteeing to the dependent families of men overseas.

Voluntary contributions were enormous at home because the sacrifices of the men in the war were indescribable. In a sense, the war that began in 1914 was a new kind of conflict but since no struggle like it has occurred since, it is deservedly called the Great War. Men on horseback attempted cavalry charges, and infantry units attempted to march against opposing forces as in the days of Napoleon. But in 1914 there were new weapons such as the machine gun, poison gas, and improved artillery. Their killing power was horrendous. It forced men to dig miles of trenches for the protective cover of earth, but to the commanders, whose brilliance stopped at their boot tops, deadlock was demoralizing. Periodically they would order their forces to rush the other side on the bizarre assumption that decimation was less discouraging than stalemate. During such suicidal frontal assaults, the men were frequently cut down by machine-gun fire even before they had cleared their own defenses, but the troops who refused to go "over the top" were shot by their own side for the crime of "cowardice". Such were the conditions Canadians encountered as "civilians in uniform" in April 1915 when the first contingent, organized into a division, was ordered to counter a German attack. In one day, 60 percent of the First Division was killed or wounded. They did gain their objective, however, and no one knows why they fought so well. Their training was slight. They did not come from a country with a strong military tradition. Their equipment was defective (especially their rifles, superb target weapons, but devices that invariably jammed in the gritty conditions of trench war in France). Despite everything that should have led to mutiny or total annihilation, everyone agreed that Canadians fought "second to none" and quickly earned a reputation for being an elite corps of shock troops. Indeed, for this reason, their movements had to be carefully concealed because the Germans knew that whenever the Canadian Corps was moved from one part of the line to another, a big push was imminent from their new location.

By September 1915, the second contingent arrived in Europe and Canada was able to field two divisions, a force of about 42 000 men in combat. Since the ranks could be depleted by as much as 50 percent in a single day's fighting, the Army attempted to maintain one soldier in reserve nearby in England for every two in the line. As soon as it appeared that Canada could maintain two divisions easily even with a high level of reserve forces, the War Office asked for a third division. Recruiting in Canada proceeded better than expected, and by the end of the year, it was thought that a Canadian Corps of four divisions was quite feasible. Altogether, a four-division corps represented a manpower commitment well in excess of 100 000 men in France and England, with another group of approximately the same size in the pipeline from the points of recruitment in Canada. On the eve of 1916, Borden announced that he thought the country might do even better, and perhaps double the number of men in uniform. His goal of one-half million was never reached but the number was a good indication of Borden's faith in the durability of the spirit of voluntarism that had been attained. Moreover, since the announcement was met with surprise but not outrage, the declaration and its reception was also a good gauge to the reality of the degree of unity that had persisted through the first year of the war.

Bloody though the fighting had been in 1915, that of 1916 was worse. In the protracted "battle" of the Somme, a period of two and one half months of mass slaughter, three million men were engaged on the two sides and one million of the combatants were killed, wounded, or disappeared into the ooze of the battle field. In one engagement of the Canadians, 77 000 men were ordered to advance their part of the line 3000 yards. They did, but this one small gain cost the Canadian Corps 24 029 casualties. Such were the victories in the Great War: one side ground at the other and was itself consumed in the process.

It was not until the spring of 1917 that the opponents of Germany gained a breakthrough in the traditional sense. Since the event was planned and executed by the Canadians led by their own Sir Arthur Currie, the victory was doubly rewarding. Currie called it "the grandest day the corps has ever had." The objective was to seize a low four-mile ridge with a commanding view of the British army. The Germans, because of its strategic importance, had fortified the spot with three lines of trenches and gun emplacements in reinforced concrete. Underground, a subterranean railway supplied the largest of the guns with their ammunition.

Currie devised a plan suited to the circumstances — the first such exercise since the war began. All previous attacks were frontal assaults as the military textbooks decreed. But for this action, Currie studied the terrain, the strong points of the enemy, the resources of his own side, and planned accordingly. Every officer and each member of the "other ranks" had a specific task. All were prepared for Easter Monday, 1917. Just before light, 1000 artillery pieces (almost four hundred of which were guns hurling shells weighing nearly a ton) aimed their fire on this one concentration of enemy strength. At 5:30 AM the artillery stopped and all four divisions of the Canadian Corp ran 100 yards toward their first objective. Then at 5:33 everyone fell to the ground and the most colossal artillery bombardment ever let loose on a battle front resumed. Soon it lifted and the Canadians shivering in the sleet and from the proximity of the explosions, continued their uphill rush, occupying the ground the artillery just cleared. They fought their way successfully through the system of trenches, and seized the guns at the top two hours after having begun the assault. At 7:30, looking down at the other side of Vimy Ridge they saw a peaceful scene of green pastures and picturesque farmers' cottages. Behind them, the ground over which the Canadians had just advanced was strewn with more than 3000 comrades in the "awkward humpbacked posture of death" and the terrain itself "looked like nothing so much as a rich plum-pudding before it goes to boiling."

Relative to other encounters, the casualties at Vimy Ridge were light. More striking than the losses were the gains that included the Ridge and also 54 guns, 104 mortars, 124 machine guns, and more than 4000 prisoners. All of which made the victory of Vimy Ridge one of the most dramatic successes of the war. As such, it was a source of enormous pride for everyone who believed that the athletic accomplishments of war can have deep meaning. To those who find poetry in the achievement, the success at Vimy Ridge symbolized Canada's coming of age. The war was a global play-off in which Canadians demonstrated that their country could field a winning major league team. D.L. Goodspeed (and a score of others) have affirmed that "it was on Easter Monday, April 9, 1917, and not on any other date, that Canada became a nation." Vimy was a fiery ordeal such as the Canada Firsters had wanted, and it worked some of the magic such action was supposed to engender. As one veteran put it: "We went up Vimy Ridge as Albertans and Nova Scotians. We came down as Canadians."

Vimy was not the last battle, however. Another even more costly offensive followed in 1917. Inevitably, casualties began to outnumber enlistments. Conscription was imposed. As criticism of that policy accelerated, and as scandals in war profiteering were revealed, the government moved to head off those who might claim that the country was involved in a rich man's war but a poor man's fight. For the first time in Canadian history, schemes were introduced to tax business profits and to "conscript" personal income on an ability-to-pay basis. The  Minister of Finance, Sir Thomas White, introduced Canada to the idea of a personal income tax in 1917, saying: "There has arisen ... a very natural and, in my view a very just, sentiment that those who are in the enjoyment of substantial incomes should substantially and directly contribute to the growing war expenditure ... ." Persons with average incomes were not to be affected but middle-class persons receiving $10 000 per year were to pay $420 of their yearly income and the upper-most group receiving $200 000, for example, were expected to pay about one fourth of their income in direct taxation.

The shift from voluntary enlistment and voluntary cash contributions to conscription and the income tax signified a weakening of spontaneous support. The income tax did nothing to mend other tension, but for a brief moment, since it was a revolution in Canadian fiscal policy, it did tend to blunt some of the class antagonism that conscription had triggered. Obviously, the progressive income tax was too small a gesture to be cathartic for long, but at the time of its implementation, the war was drawing toward its final awful phase.

In the spring of 1918, the German command launched one last desperate offensive and the Allies were driven back nearly to Paris. Then they counterattacked. By early August, they had so thoroughly exhausted the German reserves that they knew they were beaten. Germany initiated proceedings for an armistice and the guns finally fell silent without ceremony on November 11. At an appointed hour, 11.00 AM, the game was simply over.

For a few returned soldiers the experience was totally soul-destroying; "the things that were glorious had no glory," and the sacrifices were like those of stockyards "if nothing was done with the meat except to bury it." For most of the others, however, too much had been expended to dwell on the essential meaninglessness of the struggle. Simpler truths were more reassuring. A country of less than eight million people had placed perhaps 40 percent of its able-bodied, fighting-age men in uniform and 61 326 had been killed. Another 172 950 did return, but with empty sleeves or other signs of permanent disability. No country can sacrifice so much and call it meaningless.

Canadians in 1918, and the country's historians since, have affirmed and reaffirmed every 11th of November that the tragic death of the 61 000 and the inestimable ruin of the lives of the others was a price that was paid for the equally immeasurable, valuable prize of international recognition. Having fought so well and having contibuted so generously, Canada was no longer a colony in fact or in image. Canada was a nation among the others and worthy of every honor to be accorded a nation-state. In 1919, it was thus proper and uncontroversial for Canada to join the new international body called the League of Nations and to do so as a full and independent member.

In this sense, the Great War was "Canada's equivalent of the War of Independence." The struggle "gave a nation its soul." But this is only half the story. There was another less widely publicized pattern of tragedies that contributed nothing positive to even the most imaginative of the nation's myth-makers. Indeed the other record of tragedies tends to impugn the somewhat boastful conclusion of the first because the impact of the second class of disasters was the near destruction of the precarious balance which was the basis for Confederation itself.

## IV    National Disunity

Among the first to experience disillusionment with the cause was Prime Minister Borden himself when he was forced to realize that Canada had chosen to participate as a principal without receiving a proportionate share of the war's direction. In the summer of 1915, Borden went to England to attempt to resolve this and other matters. Rather than resolution, the Canadian Prime Minister found even more problems. Overall, there seemed a frustrating lack of apparent direction in the British approach to the war and in their supercilious evasion of his questions. Borden returned to Canada hurt and angered but his subsequent actions were curious if not childish in light of what went before. Rather than deciding to curtail Canada's involvement on grounds that limited control warranted nothing more than limited liability, Borden decided to double the commitment that had already grown about ten times over the original call to arms. The first call in August 1914 was for 25 000 volunteers (three times more than the Canadian Contingent in the South African War). But even before Borden's trip abroad the call was rising to the 250 000 mark. Then, at the end of 1915, the Prime Minister made his promise of raising a 500 000-man army. By this tragic pledge, Sir Robert hoped to prove that Canada was too important to be treated lightly. He would show Britain — and the world — that his country was no mere colony.

It has already been indicated that Canada never attained the manpower objective set by the Prime Minister. The reason is simple: it defied reality. The total population then was just under 8 million. The total number of seventeen- to forty-year-old males was probably no more than one and one-half million. If half of these men were engaged in essential services such as food production, running the transportation network, and producing munitions (1500 such factories in 90 different towns were created between 1915 and 1918), then there were barely 700 000 left for military service. Since it took 620 000 to maintain the four-division Canadian Corps in France between 1915 and 1918, the unreality of a rhetorical eight-division force should be readily apparent.

The numbers that impressed Borden and many others were the levels of enlistments before New Year's day, 1916. Even these numbers provided ample reason for caution, however. Most of the early enlistments were unmarried immigrants from the British Isles. Less than one third of the first volunteers were Canadian-born, nor was the Canadian portion evenly distributed over the whole country. The Canadians who were most likely to volunteer were the unemployed single men of urban Ontario. Thus, the unity that was apparent in the first rush to enlist was somewhat illusory. The principle that Canada was involved to the maximum, however, remained a commitment that Borden refused to compromise.

Eventually, the need for replacements exhausted the number of able-bodied volunteers. Urban Ontario began to wonder about the rest of the country, and this distress was echoed by Winnipeggers who expressed concern that "enemy aliens" seemed only to have developed a love of Canada and no proportionate affection for the British Empire. Consequently, the Laurier-Greenway compromise of the Manitoba School's question was abandoned by the recently elected government of T.C. Norris in 1916. In the new system, the guiding premise was that "in an English-speaking country, as this is, a knowledge of English is more necessary than a knowledge of arithmetic … ." Earlier, at the height of prewar enthusiasm for imperialism, in 1912, a similar step had been taken in Ontario to eliminate French as a language of instruction, notwithstanding

Section 93 of the BNA Act. In 1916 the wartime Judicial Committee of the Privy Council upheld "Regulation 17" and in the same year, Robert Seller, an Ontario newspaper editor, reiterated the rationale for unilingualism in the fourth edition of his book called *The Tragedy of Quebec*. In the 1916 printing, Seller asserted:

> The issue ... is fundamental and admits of no compromise, it is one that is not local but affects the future of the entire Dominion. It is simply whether this Canada of ours is to be British, and nothing else than British, or whether it is to be a mongrel land, with two official languages and ruled by a divided authority. (Quoted in R.C. Brown and R. Cook, *Canada, 1896-1921: A Nation Transformed* [1974], p. 259.)

Such bigotry — inflamed by the passion of war — was bound to provoke a fight with those who envisioned a different country. French-speaking Canadians in particular questioned the fundamental premise on which unlimited involvement was supposed to have found its ultimate and unanswerable justification. Borden and his party had gone to war initially because Britain was at war. Later, somewhat lamely, it was asserted that the cause was just — a holy war of the civilized nations of the world standing together to resist "Prussianism", meaning belligerent, autocratic, and repressive government. French Canadians began to wonder in 1916 whether the overt discrimination against minorities and a War Measures Act that sanctioned dictatorship so long as the struggle continued did not prove that "Prussianism" was also rampant in Canada.

Another reason for minorities to approach the war with something less than enthusiasm was the absence of anything but English-speaking units in the Canadian Corps. The Royal 22nd Regiment was created, ostensibly to fill this need for Quebeckers, but there were few French-speaking officers and thus it was simply a unit like the others. The crowning insult to Quebec was commissioning a Protestant clergyman to supervise recruiting in that province.

Not having units of their own, and skeptical that the war aims touched them directly, French-speaking Canadians launched an informal boycott of enlistments in 1916. By 1917, the number of volunteers elsewhere had fallen sharply as well. The result was that the number of recruits fell sadly behind the record of casualties in each month of the first half of 1917. Borden then faced a difficult choice. He could reduce the level of Canada's commitment proportionate to what was possible given the new rate of enlistments, or he could respond to British pressure and resort to further "Prussianism" by imposing conscription. The Prime Minister opted for the more tragic of the two alternatives.

On May 18, 1917, Borden announced the necessity of conscription to the House of Commons and anti-conscriptionists in Montreal rioted in protest on May 24. The next day Borden tried to make conscription less bitter by bringing Laurier into a coalition government. But Sir Wilfrid believed that unlimited liability was unwise and conscription worse. Sir Robert was therefore left to pursue his tragic course without the Liberal leader's assistance.

Laurier also made it plain that he thought it was time for the voters of Canada to pass their judgment on Borden's record since 1911. An election should have been held in 1916, but the life of Parliament had been extended one year by consent of the opposition. As the extension was running out, Borden sought another, but was refused.

Political parties usually believe the country's survival hangs upon the defeat of their rivals. This was especially the case in 1917. The heart of the matter was the conscription issue. Borden accepted it because he fervently believed that "the country could not set any limits to its exertions that fell short of the totality of its powers." Laurier agreed. In his view, however, it was unreasonable to see this totality as anything other than the utmost of voluntarism. To the totally committed, such a qualification meant "the virtual withdrawal of Canada from the war, the desertion of her soldiers overseas, the abject surrender of her honour, and the utter loss of her pride." Thus, Borden decided that the election that could not be avoided had to be rigged so that it could not be lost. "Our first duty is to win," he confided to his diary. Since this domestic victory had to be won regardless of cost, the election could not be called "until the ground has been carefully and completely prepared."

Borden's spadework was done by the architect of closure, the Solicitor General, Arthur Meighen of Manitoba. The first preparation was a Military Voters Act that provided means for people in uniform to vote overseas. Service personnel would vote by indicating a simple yes or no to record their support or opposition to the government. Voters who knew the names of individual candidates could also vote for them by entering their names in space provided on the ballots. Since lists of government candidates were taken to the soldiers along with the ballots, in practice the one kind of vote was as portable as the other. By this means, the government was given the power to manipulate approximately 25 percent of the vote to its own best advantage.

There was more. The Military Voters Act broke an old tradition by enfranchising women — the army nurses. Another "reform", the Wartime Elections Act, made even more sweeping changes in the franchise. For the purpose of the coming election, the wives, mothers, sisters and widows of military personnel were given voting privileges. Conversely, all conscientious objectors and all newcomers who took the oath of allegiance after 1902 — regardless of sex — had their voting rights withdrawn if they were natives of one of the countries fighting with the enemy and if they were not themselves in uniform for Canada or women related to soldiers overseas. The purpose of the bill, according to Arthur Meighen, was to "shift the franchise from the doubtful British or anti-British of the male sex and to extend it at the same time to our partiotic women.... ." On this basis, Meighen thought it a "splendid stroke".

Most of the Liberals did not agree, of course. "It would have been more direct and at the same time more honest," one critic observed, "if the bill simply stated that all who did not pledge themselves to vote Conservative would be disfranchised." Not surprisingly, closure was needed to end the debate. Then, since the Senate had been enlarged with Conservatives in 1915, the manipulation of the franchise received assent from that body too. Borden's spade work convinced many Liberals that they could not survive opposition and stampeded to join in a coalition called a Unionist Government, leaving Laurier and a handful of anti-conscriptionists on the outside.

By mid-November of 1917 everything was apparently in order for a Unionist victory, so Borden called the election for December 17. He appealed for unity and harmony on grounds that he led a nonpartisan coalition dedicated to goals that every "red-blooded" Canadian wanted. There was thus a conscious attempt to stigmatize the opposition as seditious. Although it was too bold to arrest the former prime minister on the charge of giving aid and comfort to the enemy, that did not stop Sir George Foster, Laurier's old defense critic, from telling an approving Toronto audience that "Every alien sympathizer, every man of alien blood born in an alien country with few exceptions, is with Sir Wilfrid Laurier, and every Hun sypathizer from Berlin to the trenches, from Berlin to the Cameroons, wishes success to Laurier, with his anti-conscriptionist campaign."

Since the outcome of the election had been cooked in advance, it was a foregone conclusion that Borden's Unionist party would win. But even so, the results did underscore the extent to which the country was divided over the question of unlimited involvement in the war. Three quarters of the electorate in Quebec voted one way, 64 percent of the electorate in the rest of Canada voted the other. The enormous discrepancy on such a vital issue led Henri Bourassa to wonder whether Canada would ever develop a sense of national interest. "So long as English Canadians remain more British than Canadian," Bourassa predicted that "these differences are bound to happen every time there is a conflict between the demands of British imperialism and the resistance of Canadian nationalism."

Of course Borden's supporters considered themselves no less patriotic than Bourassa. But their patriotism stood on the other nationalism, the notion that Canada's strength was realized best by close alliance with Britain. In 1917, the demand of the British connection seemed to be conscription regardless of cost and Canada paid a very high price indeed. There was rioting, Quebec was brought near to secession, civil rights were systematically suspended by the War Measures Act, and the oath of allegiance of the non-British immigrants was cynically disregarded by the War-time Elections Act. These were the tragedies that were bitter, the experience of the war that English-speaking Canadians wanted quickly forgotten.

# Bibliography

The volume in the Canadian Centenary Series that covers the period from Laurier's defeat in 1911 to the end of the Great War is R.C. Brown and R. Cook, *Canada, 1896-1921: A Nation transformed* (1974). Another general work that advances conventional interpretations of the same period but with particular emphasis upon the "advances" in external affairs is the book by the soldier-historian C.P. Stacey, *Canada and the Age of Conflict: A History of Canadian External Policies*, Vol. I: 1867-1921 (1977).

Two works provide useful interpretations of Borden's prewar reform program. One is the biography by R.C. Brown, *Robert Laird Borden: A Biography*, Vol. I: 1854-1914 (1975). More analytical is the interpretation of Borden's departure from traditional political style in John English, *The Decline of Politics: The Conservatives and the Party System* (1977).

Readers wishing to learn more about the agonies of the actual fighting in France and Flanders will find a vast reservoir of material in which to immerse themselves. Two works are especially worthy of mention because they provide evocative portraits of the sacrifices of the fighting men without at the same time seeking to glorify the war. L. Macdonald's *They Called it Passchendaele* (1978) is a history of the fighting in the Ypres Salient, perhaps the least militarily sound choice for a battlefield in the history of the world since it was a low-lying, poorly drained delta that quickly became a sea of mud affording no cover. The story of this blunder and the others is told by D.L. Goodspeed as well in *The Road Past Vimy: The Canadian Corps, 1914-1918* (1969). Goodspeed's brief account (only 174 pages of text) is a masterpiece of condensation showing that history need not be verbose to be comprehensive. He closes his work by suggesting that the "futilities" of the war are no sound justification for neglecting its study since "futilities are not dissipated by ignoring them."

Of course, futility affected the people who remained in Canada almost as much as it touched the lives (and deaths) of those who fought abroad. Several works have appeared recently to signal that there is a serious attempt being mounted to understand the war in its domestic impact. Graham Metson's edition of Archibald MacMechan, *The Halifax Explosion,*

*December 6, 1917* (1978) describes what was perhaps the most dramatic incident on the domestic front. On this day, there was an explosion that leveled much of the town as a result of a collision of two ships in the harbor. No other part of Canada suffered the same kind of destruction, but other wounds were inflicted that were in a sense even less reparable. Barbara M. Wilson, ed., *Ontario and the First World War* (1977) offers a book-length introduction to the development of war fever in the most British province and J.H. Thompson, *The Harvests of War: the Prairie West, 1914-1918* (1978) surveys the impact of the war on the region that was most ethnically diverse. J.M. Hitsman and J.L. Granatstein, *Broken Promises: A History of Conscription in Canada* (1977) is the latest of several works on the "pointless" attempt to bring Quebec to heel by force. For the election that followed, see Desmond Morton, "Polling the Soldier Vote: The Overseas Campaign in the Canadian General Election of 1917," *JCS* (1975).

"What kind of war was this?"

# CHAPTER 18

# Social Ferment

## I   War Fever as a Reform Impulse

Canadians went to war in 1914, initially, because Britain was at war. That was sufficient justification for raising the First Contingent of volunteers. By 1916, however, after the liability was proclaimed to be total, such a justification, by itself, was vulnerable to the charge of jingoism. There had to be more at stake than duty to the mother country. Consequently, two other war aims came to the fore, sometimes separately, sometimes together. One was proving to the rest of the world that Canada was an equal among nations. The other was vindicating the cause of liberty and democracy. Thus, Clifford Sifton asserted that the experience was a baptism in "nationhood with the blood of our sons ... shed for the greatest struggle the world has ever seen and in the noblest cause for which men have ever fought." It was a struggle that was supposed to bring international recognition to Canada individually and to advance the world as a whole.

Where the population was sufficiently British there was no need to overemphasize the disinterested advancement of mankind as a war aim. In provinces such as Ontario, it was nearly sufficient just to stress the "needs of the Empire" and keep "British patriotism and loyalty" running high. In Ontario, the main purpose was to demonstrate that Canada was a strong "self-governing state of the Empire". The emphasis was upon Canada's character as a dedicated part of the wider British nation. Illustrating the mood was the Chief Inspector of Schools in Toronto, Robert Crowley, in his justification for censoring the children's music books. Referring to some melodies by German authors, Cowley said:

> The music reader contains at least some selections that should never be sung in a British school, and whatever may have been the opinion as to their general merit at the time they were introduced, they cannot be regarded as a medium fit to develop the high moral and patriotic ideals of British citizen-

311

ship. (Quoted in B.M. Wilson, ed., *Ontario and the First World War* [1977], p. xciv.)

In the West, by contrast, because of the different ethnic mix, it was necessary to stress the international reform aspect. Illustrating this theme was the work of a Winnipeg clergyman, C.W. Gordon (writing novels under the name of Ralph Connor). One of his characters in *The Sky Pilot in No Man's Land* made plain that "the biggest thing... is not that the motherland is in need of help, though, of course, we all feel that, but that the freedom of the world is threatened, and that Canada, as one of the free nations of the world, must do her part in its defence." Conveniently ignoring that one of the Allies was Russia, every bit as autocratic as Germany, the people who stressed that the war would make mankind free focused only on Germany. By force of arms, the civilized nations of the world (on the Western front) were in a great crusade to make certain that "when the war is over Germany will become a democracy... instead of being ruled by a wicked Emperor." Since such sentiment was also a reform impulse, it was natural that there would be a domestic as well as an international focus for that energy and that the zeal would outlast the fighting in Europe.

But just as there was a lack of national unity on the issue of unlimited involvement in military action and the degree to which the war was aimed at reform in the first place, so also was there a lack of national consensus on the proper direction for the nonmilitary domestic crusades. In the West, where the struggle was perhaps most frequently advertised as an international purification ritual, the demand for other "uplifting" reforms was strongest. Ontario and the Maritime provinces, the most British parts of Canada, were less keen to embrace the other crusades. And in Quebec, the prevailing mood was resentment of social change in general and reforms initiated from the rest of Canada in particular.

## II    Postwar Quebec

Early in 1918, the Legislative Assembly of Quebec debated a resolution to the effect that "this House... would be disposed to accept the breaking of the Confederation Pact of 1867 if, in the other provinces, it is believed that she is an obstacle to the union, progress and development of Canada." The debate provided an opportunity for many speakers to air their dissatisfaction with conscription, the Manitoba and Ontario schools questions, and the manipulated franchise in the recent general election. Eventually, however, the motion was withdrawn before it came to a vote, and in this retreat, fear of change became more visible than dissatisfaction with Confederation.

The sudden emergence of a separatism that was only rhetorical suggested that French-Canadian nationalism had changed a great deal since the days of Papineau and Dorion. In the previous century, before Confederation, there were always republicans willing to defend the integrity of their province by direct action out-of-doors as well as in the Legislative Assembly. At the same time, of course, there were clerical spokesmen no less nationalist but who were less keen to lead the people to the barricades in the name of republicanism and liberty. The clerical leaders usually preferred a quieter — at times almost a passive — resistance as the sounder course, and so also, it seemed, did the general public. Consequently, on the occasions of the most strident nationalism, the Papineau-Dorion style of nationalists trumpeted anti-clerical denunciations as well as their anti-British slogans, and each time the Church emerged the stronger voice of *survivance*. By 1917, French-Canadian nationalism still had its spokesmen, but its main pivot and its dominant style was that of passive ultra-clericalism. Since anti-clerical firebrands were no longer of any consequence, the French-Canadian nationalism that arose from the wake of domestic war injuries was quietly inward-turning, not poised for a mass movement for direct action along the lines that Papineau and Dorion had pioneered. But the resentment was real and the consciousness Quebeckers had as a people unto themselves could be gauged by the manner in which they held on to their memory of the past even as they tried all the harder to promote modern capitalism.

One clear indication of Quebec's sense that its refuge was the past was the new romanticization of agrarianism that came from its writers living in Montreal and Quebec City. This was the sentiment, expressed many times before, that the rural life was morally superior to that of the cities. Such a notion was also expressed at the same time by farmers' movements in western Canada. The peculiar twist in the Quebec case, however, was the idea that the cultural survival of the nation depended upon pastoral simplicity. When Lionel Groulx said "we must sow or go jobless, our people must be agricultural or perish" he was saying a great deal more than that the farmer's vocation was the most noble. Groulx fervently believed that Quebecker's language and religion would perish in the industrial cauldrons of such places as Montreal. He therefore called his people back to the land even though most had already fled to town. Moreover, the new government that came to power in 1920 did so on the strength of the popularity of its promising to promote yet more industrialism.

Alexandre Taschereau said he could make Quebec a leader in the competition for foreign capital investment, but even with Taschereau there was a rural thrust to the industrialism that was promised. He appeared to promote a happy compromise of the rural ideal since his stated motive was to gain development that would create employment opportunities to keep people in the villages of their birth, to spare them migration and the deracination that was expected to follow. Taschereau's program was promoted as a means of preserving the character of traditional society while progressing beyond the old means of production; in the transition from agricultural village to company town the parish priest would care for his parishioners as always. The populations affected would see their pattern of employment shift from agricultural to industrial work, their incomes would rise, and all such benefits would occur without their leaving home. Here was industrialization that posed less of a threat to "our doctrine".

In a similar clerically led manner, there might also be labor organization without militancy or radicalism. Prior to 1920, the unions that had arisen were English-Canadian or American in origin, and clerical authorities had not looked upon either with favor. When a bitter strike at the Thetford Mines in 1915 raised the specter of radical unionism, the Church moved to head off such a development. A Catholic, more quiescent union was organized in its place. The initiative was extended and in 1921 the *Confédération de travailleurs catholiques du Canada* (CTCC), a primarily Quebec labor movement, was promoted. But even this moderate development left the majority of Quebec's workers unorganized.

Having been reviled by the rest of Canada and horrified by Ontario's "effervescence of jingoism", Quebec drew inward and sought refuge under an ultra-clerical, corporate conception of their political community. Whether in the country or in the factory, Quebeckers were told that they had a purpose that transcended materialism or individual well-being. Henri Bourassa, the politician turned editor of *Le Devoir*, expressed this ideal perhaps better than any other spokesman in 1918, saying:

> Our special task, as French Canadians, is to insert into America the spirit of Christian France. It is to defend against all comers, perhaps even against France herself, our religious and national heritage. This heritage does not belong to us alone. It belongs to all Catholic America. It is the inspiring and shining hearth of America. It belongs to the whole Church, and it is the basic foundation of the Church in this part of the world. It belongs to all French civilization of which it is the refuge and fortress and anchor amid the immense sea of saxonizing Americanism. (Quoted in George Grant, *Lament for a Nation* [1965], pp. 80-81.)

Like the rhetorical separatism that surfaced at the same time — or the rural industrialism promoted later by Taschereau — Bourassa's nationalism translated more easily into affirmations of tradition than innovation. The discontent generated by the war in Quebec thus heightened a nationalism that romanticized the past even as it embraced and promoted greater industrialism and the further destruction of the traditional material basis of Quebec society.

## III    Nostalgia in the Maritimes

A similar retreat occurred after the war in the Maritime provinces, although its origins were not to be found in disenchantment with the war or disgruntlement over the fanaticism with which the conflict had been supported by Ontario. Indeed, the people of Halifax, for example, had sacrificed more for the cause than any other community in the country. In addition to the loss of its fighting men, Halifax also suffered thousands of civilian casualties. On December 6, 1917, two ships collided in the harbor. One, the *Mont Blanc*, a munitions ship loaded with highly explosive gun cotton (the propellant for heavy artillery), caught fire. Once the flames reached the explosive cargo, the entire vessel ignited in a split second reducing the ship to atoms, and leveled about one third of the nearby town with casualties comparable to those of a major engagement of the Canadian Corps. Except in the Halifax explosion, more than 400 of the dead were so completely consumed by the force of the blast they vanished without a trace. Weeks later, in the election that was also a plebiscite on the war, a majority of the Maritimers supported the Unionist Government, conscription, and a continuation of the struggle on the level of total commitment. Moreover, they did so without any large promises that the war would bring wholesale reforms. According to C.M. Wallace, it was enough that the conflict was an important "imperial event". Like most of the people of Ontario, the majority of Maritimers saw their Canadian citizenship in British terms.

Another reason that the war appeared to be supported almost without question was that it sustained a level of prosperity in little factory towns such as Amherst, Nova Scotia, towns that otherwise were beginning to suffer from a process of deindustrialization that followed the consolidation of industry in Central Canada. At war's end, with the imminent loss of munitions works, some factories that were on the verge of closing in 1914 faced the prospect of a complete shutdown in 1919. At the same time, however, it was clear that the rest of the country anticipated a "new era" of prosperity. Once postwar recession hit the Maritimes in the summer of 1920, mass protest developed as local politicians urged everyone to forget parochial differences and unite in demanding relief from Ottawa.

The "Maritime Rights" movement of the 1920s resembled at least two other such exercises since 1867. In both preceeding movements, the impulse to preserve or restore a prosperity that was imagined to have depended upon independence from Upper Canadian interference motivated Maritimers to protest. Since their complaints arose from national-political causes, the remedy was also expected from the same source. Rhetoricians skilled in projecting their frustrations as public issues established prominence by tapping a reservoir of resentment, arousing the electorate with accusations that everyone's status was imperiled, and if better terms were not forthcoming, they warned that a separate union of the Maritime provinces would be preferable to continuing the Canadian arrangement. Such protest was defensive nationalism that was nearly as strident as Quebec's. Moreover, unity in resistance was sufficiently cathartic. Little did the voters seem to notice or to care that their saviors made little difference once they were elected. Thus it was with Joseph Howe and his "Repealers" and with W.S. Fielding and the "Secessionists".

In the new movement, however, the cycle of protest unfolded with a special twist because in Nova Scotia and New Brunswick there were specific and local socioeconomic definitions of public problems that were leading thousands of workers into a labor movement that was both militant and political. On Cape Breton Island, the great coal mining part of the region, the miners had successfully formed the largest cohesive body of organized labor in Canada. Local District No. 26 of the United Mine Workers boasted more than 13 000 members. Other workers, for instance the factory hands of the numerous manufacturing establishments in Amherst (a small Nova Scotia town of 10 000) were also organizing "one great union".

The Amherst Federation of Labour was intended as a union of all industrial workers in the community. Whether they worked in Stanfield's textile mill or Robb's machinery works, they recognized that they shared similar grievances concerning conditions of work and rates of pay. Their common interest led them to strike in May 1919 to secure a reduction of hours with no reduction in wages. In the face of such a solid resistance, strikebreakers could not be brought in to replace them. Still, Stanfield refused to talk to the union. Eventually, other owners did make concessions. Consequently, the Amherst General Strike was a partial success.

Elsewhere in the Maritimes, labor made similar gains. At the same time, the new labor movement became openly political in its goals. Labor conventions in New Brunswick and Nova Scotia declared that they would attempt to influence the two established political parties but they also indicated that their greater hope was with independent labor parties. In this trend, Amherst, the same community that successfully struck in 1919, elected a labor candidate to the provincial legislature in 1920. Since there were a number of other Amhersts in Nova Scotia, and since the politically active farmers also defined themselves as a special class (unrepresented by the two old parties) the Conservatives found themselves in third-place position behind a Farmer-Labour coalition in Nova Scotia.

Unfortunately for the labor movement, the war-sustained prosperity collapsed soon after the election. With the rate of unemployment running at 10 percent by 1921 and some plants closing permanently, union membership fell almost 50 percent at once. The Liberal governments in Nova Scotia and New Brunswick groped for recovery measures by blaming the depression on recent tariff and freight rate policies of the Conservatives in Ottawa, but once that party was defeated and replaced by a Liberal government it became more difficult for the Liberal premiers to continue the same line of denunciation. At this point, according to one prominent Liberal, the Conservatives broke into "our pantry and stole our prize bone." The Nova Scotia Conservative House Leader, H.W. Corning, demanded better terms from Ottawa and if they were not forthcoming he claimed that the Maritimers would be justified in separating from the rest of Canada. By the spring of 1923, with such sentiment widespread in New Brunswick and Nova Scotia, Corning proposed a referendum to pull his province out of Confederation to become an "independent, self-governing British dominion" like Newfoundland. Of course, no such referendum was taken and subsequently Corning was displaced by a new Conservative leader who sounded the same note without proposing such specific action. In this way, the Maritime Rights movement was born.

In Nova Scotia and New Brunswick, the rights that were demanded had to do with federal fiscal and transportation policy mainly. No local government had to alter its policies. Moreover, since everyone was urged to forget all local fights in the struggle against the common enemy, and since such persuasion was effective, the third party movements of both provinces were swallowed up by a restored faith in the Conservatives who led in the demand for better terms from Ottawa. In 1925, the Liberal governments of both provinces were defeated. Since the Conservatives attracted 60 percent of the popular vote in Nova Scotia, they won 40 of the 43 seats in the legislature and the Farmer-Labour coalition was wiped out completely. In New Brunswick the margin of victory was almost as complete (37 of 48 seats), with the same devastating impact on the labor party. Thus, a genuine radical protest in the region was absorbed by a more facile, old-style provincial rights crusade.

According to George Rawlyk, the election results of 1925 signified the success of another movement by Maritimers to express their disenchantment "in words rather than effective action." Answering that the region did suffer from Ottawa's adverse fiscal and transportation policies, E.R. Forbes has been less harsh in his judgment and suggests that the movement "went much deeper than mere political maneuvering or... the attempt by the local 'Establishment' to undercut other forms of social protest." Forbes argues that since all "classes" had reason to be discontented, and since the "Maritime rights agitation ... saw all classes united in their demands upon the rest of the country" the Maritime Rights movement was a positive development. That the rest of Canada was unwilling to grant sufficient tariff protection to Maritime products or subsidize freight rates to give Maritimers better access to the wider Canadian market is no fault of the Conservative leaders of the movement, according to Forbes.

Forbes does leave a major question unanswered, however, because he does not explain why the Conservatives did not take more radical action once they lost their war of words with Ottawa. The possibility remains that, notwithstanding E.R. Forbes' assertions to the contrary, the greater enemy all along may have been the more local group that humiliated the Conservatives in 1920 because against labor the victory was total. In communities such as Amherst, according to Nolan Reilly, "by the middle of the 1920s, the formal presence of a trade union movement ... had all but disappeared." Having been checked first by recession and then co-opted into a larger movement that brought the people of the region only slight tangible benefits, the ordinary voters of the Maritimes, like those of Quebec in the same decade, were left stunned by apathy and cynicism. With lower wages and higher levels of unemployment, they also had the highest rate of outmigration. In the meantime, it was managers and mill owners, newspaper editors and "responsible" leaders of labor who continued to sit on Boards of Trade and to talk of "Maritime Rights".

## IV    The Purification of the Prairies

The Prairie provinces were more successful in the reform movement that the war encouraged in their region. In the war years, they accumulated several significant reform victories that were an inspiration for the middle class to embark upon a program of vaster "progressivism" in the 1920s. Since the Prairie progressives had an important impact upon the alignment of political parties nationally, that movement is described in more detail in the next chapter, along with the Maritime Rights movement (insofar as that regional protest also affected the maneuvering of politicians in Ottawa). Here, however, the focus is upon wartime reform victories that were the special concern of middle-class reformers before the war, and matters on which they not only achieved success locally but also led the nation between 1914 and 1918.

Three causes were central to the wartime demand to cleanse and purify the political community engaged in what was advertized as a similar struggle abroad. One was prohibition of the importation and sale of alcoholic beverages. Another was the enfranchisement of women. The third was expulsion of unassimilable "foreigners".

The first to succeed was prohibition on grounds that it hampered the war effort. Intoxication threatened productivity and grains consumed by breweries or disilleries were believed to be better diverted to human or even livestock consumption. On this rationale, and also because a growing minority simply believed alcohol was the root of all evil, the Prairie provinces took the lead in outlawing alcoholic beverages in 1915. The other provinces (except Quebec) followed thereafter. Ultimately, in April 1918, the Government of Canada also issued an order in council prohibiting the importation of liquor for the duration of the war. After the armistice, importation resumed and one by one the provinces relaxed their prohibitions. By 1924, the three western provinces that led the way in abstinence also led the way in temperance by establishing provincial "dispensaries" that carefully regulated amounts and hours of sale. Since temperance — rather than total prohibition — was all that many reformers had sought in the first place, prohibition exemplified a reform that was tested in the extreme for temporary wartime conditions and applied permanently on a somewhat more modest scale later.

The same pattern is evident in an examination of the two other reforms. Female suffrage had been actively agitated in the West since 1912 when a mainly Protestant, English-speaking middle-class women's movement established the Political Equality League in Manitoba and recruited almost 1200 members at once. Over the course of the next several years, they politely petitioned the Manitoba legislature demanding to be enfranchised since they met every qualification to vote except that of sex. In January 1916, in large part simply to prepare the way to neutralize the vote of the "unCanadian influence" of naturalized "foreigners", the legislature of Manitoba granted Nellie McClung's group the vote. Alberta and Saskatchewan followed in March for much the same reason. Thus, on the provincial level in 1916, and on the national level one year later (with the manipulation of the franchise by the Wartime Elections Act), the important, if not the deciding consideration was that the most likely women to vote were those who could be counted upon to support the war. For this reason, it was logical that the region with the most exotic (least British) ethnic mixture was also the part of the country that was first to enfranchise women and that the reform was achieved in wartime.

Similarly, the western elite was also the most interested in the assimilation or expulsion of newcomers. Here was another cause that predated the war but flourished in the context of national mobilization. Moreover, the Government of Canada was also interested and cooperative in the cause. The Department of Justice went to considerable trouble to monitor the activities of persons from central Europe, the "enemy aliens". Since the people of Austro-Hungarian origin were tolerated before the war only as farmers or "guest workers", they were never completely accepted as an appropriate stock from which to build a new country. Predictably, the war intensified such prejudice and prompted action against them.

Shortly after the armistice, indicative of the ill feeling sustained by the war, Borden received a deluge of petitions demanding the expulsion of the "enemy aliens". At about the same time, a Methodist minister in Winnipeg published a history of western settlement that purportedly documented the preceeding twenty years of western development to expose the mistaken faith that had been placed in central Europeans even as "guest workers". Wellington Bridgman's *Breaking Prairie Sod* asserted that the central Europeans were a violent and disruptive group before the war and a disloyal population during the conflict. With "returned men" coming home to Canada by the thousands in 1919, many were finding it difficult to secure peacetime employment. Bridgman argued that the "enemy aliens" should be expelled from the country and their property turned over to war veterans. The procedure he recommended was as follows: "We would ask the Dominion government to appoint a commission of returned soldiers in each province to adjudicate and settle the amount that will be allowed each enemy alien and enemy alien family" before they were returned to Europe. Suggesting that such a policy was consistent with government action to date, referring to the Wartime Elections Act in particular, Bridgman pointed out that the government already "claimed the right and the authority to disfranchise all the enemy aliens in the Dominion ... and on appealing to the country, were endorsed by the largest majorities that ever sent men to Parliament." Since harsh measures were obviously popular, he suggested his scheme would also receive wide acceptance and the returning veterans were the ideal persons to dispossess the disfranchised because "the returned soldier ... knows the Austro-Hun, our enemy over the sea, and he knows the enemy alien better than any other man. His judgement will not be spoiled by prejudice, nor can he ever be tempted to show favoritism." The returned man would have no scruples against the expropriation of the aliens' property at "one fourth of its value or less" — just enough to pay their return passage to Europe.

Bridgman's scheme was seriously considered but ultimately dropped because the Government of Canada was too preoccupied with the problems of demobilization, acccording to Donald Avery. The solution by default was to defer to the provinces and rely on the education panacea, the assimilation cure. Assimilationists shared Bridgman's zeal for making "this Dominion mainly British in spirit" but they were somewhat more optimistic in that they thought that the "inferior races" could be trained, eventually, to develop an "attachment to British ideals and institutions". What the assimilationists shared with the expulsionists was the same sinister distrust of the consequences of Canada's developing into a "mongrel" country.

The new, strident affirmation that Canada was one population or it was nothing was, in a sense, simply a harsher, broader repudiation of minority rights such as the earlier repudiation of dualism in Manitoba in 1890 and the other two Prairie provinces in 1905. There was nothing new in the distrust of minorities, and in the suspicion that minority rights meant unnecessary weakness and expense. The novelty of the new bigotry was its virulence; even the Ku Klux Klan was popular in the 1920s.

## V    The Winnipeg General Strike

The moral fervor behind the nonmilitary domestic crusades was bound to generate conflict between regions, nationalities, and classes. But the first and most dramatic clash after the war was not among regions or the native-born versus the "enemy aliens". The big confrontation involved industry and labor in Winnipeg, at the time Canada's third largest city. Enough has already been shown by the description of labor unrest in the Maritimes and the formation of Catholic unions in Quebec to suggest that labor unrest was universal in Canada immediately after the war. The basic problem was inflation. Everywhere it took at least $1.60 in 1919 to buy what one dollar could purchase in 1913. Some workers such as farm laborers and some railway employees had enjoyed proportionate wage increases, but most workers had not. For most people, the rate of inflation between 1916 and 1919 was about twice that of wage increases. To remedy the situation, people resorted to organized action — twice as many workers were unionized in 1919 as in 1914. But here the universality of the response ended. In some places, the form and methods of organization were remarkably radical. Moreover, there was considerable difference between the kinds of response by government.

A radical union was one that attempted to organize the unskilled as well as the skilled and to organize such workers along the lines of an entire industry or community with one council operating as the exclusive bargaining agent for all the workers thus joined. By this test, the organization of the Amherst Federation of Labour and the "general strike" in that small community of 10 000 were both radical. But the Amherst action involved no more than 3000 workers and the Mayor of the town stepped forward to play the role of honest broker to mediate the dispute. In Winnipeg, ten times as many workers were involved and although every level of jurisdiction played a part, all government action was repressive. This raises two problems. First, why did Maritime and Western Canadian workers appear to be more radical than their equally restive counterparts elsewhere in

Canada? Secondly, what accounts for the different responses of the authorities?

The major key to the first problem may be that the workers of the Maritimes and the West, having missed the demoralizing experience of the defeat of the Knights of Labor in Central Canada in the 1890s, were less willing to consider such action as inherently futile. In this sense, the "one great union" concept found an enthusiastic reception where it had not been tried before. Government's reaction to such industrial unionism, turning to the second problem, may have been most dependent upon how polarized the political community was at the time of the action. Certainly this is illustated by the Amherst and Winnipeg cases. In Amherst, the mayor could intervene with an olive branch, and prepare the way for the traditional leaders to come forward and persuade workers that they should make common cause against the real enemy in Ottawa. In Winnipeg, by contrast, the government had no such subtle control devices. The community was divided and distrustful before the strike, and more so after the dispute.

There were indications that the Winnipeg working class was turning away from the traditional governing elite in favor of its own leaders and political organization as early as 1913. That year, despite a property franchise, R.A. Rigg, the business agent for the Winnipeg Trades and Labour Council, was elected to office as a city alderman. Then in 1914, W.B. Simpson, a mere truck driver, was also elected to the body that was supposed to be eighteen governing businessmen.

By 1915, it was possible to imagine that men of property might someday lose control of the government of Winnipeg completely if they did not set aside their differences and defeat the democracy that put labor's bookkeeper and a socialist teamster in the sanctity of City Hall. Hard measures, if necessary, would be justified to preserve the proper social boundaries between workers and managers. In this spirit, the Winnipeg business community joined to move a variety of issues, significant as well as petty. One of the latter, during the war, was a proposal to start a military flying school on the justification that "Winnipeg could help the cause in no better way than in training pilots for air scouting." To this end, $5000 of public revenue was voted to be added to $40 000 to be raised by private subscription. Tuition for the entrants to the flying school was $400. When labor members of council denounced the scheme for its obvious elitism, businessmen voted in a block to override their objections.

With each subsequent election an additional one or two labor members were added to the growing labor party on Winnipeg City Council. By 1918, the labor group consisted of five members, roughly one third of the whole. Then, they seized the initiative. They moved, for instance, that the high fee for a peddlar's license ought to be reduced, making it easier for someone to hawk merchandise in the streets to the possible disadvantage of established merchants. All but one of the businessmen on council opposed them and the labor initiative on the matter was defeated 11 to 6. But on another issue, curiously, a labor motion passed.

Winnipeg's police force had recently formed a union and the city hesitated to recognize it as their collective bargaining agent. The labor members of council took up the cause with a motion to "recognize and deal with the newly formed Policemen's Union, following a policy that employees in the service of the public shall have the right to form unions." The motion carried, but Alderman Frank Fowler spoke for the business minority in opposition when he said that the police were the ultimate security of property. If they had a union, the middle class would lose its last defense. Fowler asserted that the constables had to decide whether they were on the side of their "sworn duty" or organized labor because, in his view, "they cannot serve both trade unions and the persons whose property they protect." Perhaps the other businessmen on council felt that since the police were so important to their protection they deserved special consideration and this explains why they found it easier to oppose cheaper peddlars' licenses than collective bargaining for the police force. But the incident did show that there was an interesting dichotomy developing between labor and property, and that the city was well polarized and poised for a dramatic confrontation by 1918.

When representatives of Winnipeg's labor unions attended the annual meeting of the Trades and Labour Congress of Canada at Quebec shortly thereafter, westerners discovered that there was almost as much difference between themselves and the eastern representatives as between themselves and the Frank Fowlers of Winnipeg. They complained that the "labour movement of the east is reactionary and servile to its core," committed to old strategies and outmoded policies. The westerners decided that their best interest would be served by divorcing west from east and pursuing an independent course altogether. Subsequently, the western labor leaders met separately at Calgary and enthusiastically endorsed the concept of industrial unionism employing the weapon of the general strike if necessary.

The first test of the new strategy came two months later in Winnipeg. A dispute in the building trades for improved wages and hours joined with a far more fundamental struggle by iron workers to win recognition for the Metal Trades Council as their bargaining agent. Soon these unions appealed to the seventy others in the city for sympathetic action. Under the auspices of the Winnipeg Trades and Labour Council the unions were polled one by one and the membership indicated overwhelming support for calling a general strike.

At midday on May 15, 1919, the business of Canada's third largest city came to a halt when about 30 000 workers walked off their jobs. Everything from movie houses to bakeries closed. No streetcars ran. The telegraph and telephone services were halted. Even toilets stopped flushing since water pressure was kept too low to rise above the first floor of most buildings.

Although the regular institutions of city government continued to function, the actual day-to-day government of Winnipeg passed to the strike committee in a broad variety of matters. For instance, even though the city police had voted to strike, they stayed on the job because they were ordered to do so by the committee. Similarly, milk and bread deliveries were also permitted, again, "by authority of the strike committee".

To Winnipeg's business elite, the issue was no longer one of collective bargaining and the legitimacy of industrial unionism. What was at stake was the larger question of the control of the community. They reacted to the strike committee's extra-legal action by forming a body of their own, a kind of vigilante organization called the Committee of One Thousand — "Citizens' Committee" for short. It was their aim to unite the people still loyal to the two old political parties and thus break the strike through "nonpartisan" action. They duly deputized "special" firemen, then police. Given this array of competing extra-legal authorities — and the explosiveness of the control issue — it would have been understandable if the situation rapidly disintegrated into generalized disorder. But the strikers were careful to prevent any appearance of anarchy and violence because they expected that even a small disturbance would be met with force and martial law. For three weeks, the strike committee worked with a cooperative regular police force to prevent any such pretext from occurring. For three weeks there was uneasy peace.

As soon as the strike began, however, there were unrelenting calls for government intervention from newspapers across the country on grounds that the strike resembled a revolution. "Canada must not become a second Russia," they warned. On the same theme, it was also asserted that the "revolutionary agitators" who were taking over Winnipeg were mainly "enemy aliens". Judging by their surnames, however, the most prominent leaders in the movement were eminently Anglo-Saxon. Indeed, some of the strike leaders were prominent Protestant clergymen such as J.S. Woodsworth and William Ivens who found the strike a glorious outpouring of what they called the social gospel, a Christianity that was concerned with life on earth and the "Brotherhood of Man", rather than with theology or creed.

Far from being an attempt to take over Winnipeg by foreign (or native-born) communists, the strike in simplest description was nothing more than an attempt by the Metal Trades Council to win recognition from three large metal fabricating companies that the Metal Trades Council was the exclusive bargaining agent for all the employees in their type of work. The companies, on the other hand, had not yet adjusted even to the notion that the several different classes of skilled workers in their firms (let alone the unskilled) might bargain collectively. The companies' idea of bargaining was strictly individual or by *ad hoc* committee: "We ... believe that any man has a right to make a living whether he is a member of a union or not ... We have agreed to meet with any of our Employees that have any grievance, or with a committee of our Employees if they desire to discuss any conditions that may not be satisfactory." What the companies would not condone was a formal labor organization — especially the idea of one large union for their industry.

The Government of Canada shared the employers' fear of industrial unionism. The Minister of Labour, Gideon Robertson, had previously approved of groups of craft unions negotiating for a whole industry, for instance railways. But the Winnipeg development was industrial unionism on too vast a scale. He also believed that the general strike, as a weapon, was simply social revolution by another name. Arthur Meighen agreed: "If collective bargaining is to be granted as a principle," he said, "there must be some unit to which the principle ... is to apply, and beyond which it cannot go." Meighen attacked directly the idea that there could be "unlimited and heterogeneous collection of all classes of labor that may get together ... *ad infinitum* ..." What Meighen feared most was the possibility of a united front of all labor with the collective power of universal strike action: One Big Union. This level of organization and industrial action was no less than "seditious conspiracy", a crime in his opinion.

On June 6, 1919, after just twenty minutes of debate, the House of Commons approved amendments to the criminal code providing appropriate penalties for the new offense. The Immigration Act was also changed to provide summary deportation of foreigners guilty of "seditious conspiracy". In the meantime, the mayor of Winnipeg took steps to break the strike by putting the Citizens' Committee in charge of civil order. He dismissed the regular police and replaced them with the citizens' "specials". Within days there was a violent confrontation between "citizens" and strikers and the federal government had its pretext for intervention. In the middle of the night of June 16-17, the strike leaders were rousted from their homes, charged with the new crimes, and jailed in the federal penitentiary at nearby Stony Mountain. Leaderless, the strike collapsed.

As people began to drift back to work, a group of war veterans called upon other "returned men" to parade in protest against the partiality of Ottawa's action. The mayor responded by reiterating a warning that there was a total ban on all parades, but the veterans decided to make their protest regardless. On Saturday morning, June 21, 1919, they gathered at Winnipeg's corner of Portage Avenue and Main Street and began to march. Then specials and the Royal North West Mounted Police attacked the marchers from horseback with revolvers blazing and clubs swinging. Men who had survived years of war in Flanders fell wounded on the pavement of their home town. Thirty-four of the marchers were injured, one fell dead on the spot with a bullet through his head. Another died later in hospital. Eighty were arrested.

On Monday morning, June 23, Winnipeggers went to work in the shadow of thirty-caliber machine guns mounted on trucks ready to silence any recurrence of protest. It was not a pleasant sight even for the "citizens". Not since the conscription riots in Montreal the previous Easter had a popular demonstration been put down with such brutal swiftness and determination. Then, however, action was justified as upholding the war effort. What kind of war was this?

# Bibliography

The volume in the Canadian Centenary Series that covers the social ferment of the war and its immediate aftermath is R.C. Craig and R. Cook, *Canada, 1896-1921: A Nation Transformed* (1974). Other works describe the domestic aspect of the war relative to developments in particular regions (see bibliography to the previous chapter). However, there is no book that attempts to describe the domestic impact of the war upon the entire country. This, by itself, is perhaps additional confirmation of the severe disunity that developed as a consequence of four years' participation in the struggle.

Several works besides the material addressed to the conscription crisis (cited in the bibliography for the previous chapter) focus on social ferment in Quebec. General issues are covered by S.M. Trofimenkoff in the relevant chapters of *The Dream of nation: A Social and Intellectual History of Quebec* (1982). A good assessment of Bourassa's corporatism is Joseph Levitt, "Henri Bourassa and Modern Industrial Society, 1900-1914," CHR (1969). There is a similar study of Lionel Groulx and the content of his thought also by S.M. Trofimenkoff, *Action Francaise: French Canadian Nationalism in the Twenties* (1975).

For the Maritimes, the most comprehensive recent work is that of E.R. Forbes, *The Maritime Rights Movement, 1919-1927: A Study in Canadian Regionalism* (1979). An article by Forbes on "The Origins of the Maritime Rights Movement," *Acadiensis* (1975) dismisses too readily the overall interpretation suggested by George Rawlyk, "Nova Scotia's Regional Protest, 1867-1967," *Queen's Quarterly* (1968), particularly in light of the aftermath of the episode described by Nolan Reilly, "The General Strike in Amherst, Nova Scotia, 1919" *Acadiensis* (1980). For the enduring "British" outlook of Maritimers see C.M. Wallace, "The Nationalization of the Maritimes," in J.M. Bumsted, ed., *Documentary Problems in Canadian History* (1969).

Two works are addressed to wartime reforms initiated from the Prairies. C.L. Cleverdon, *The Woman Suffrage Movement in Canada* (1950) surveys the subject from a national perspective but emphasizes the Prairie provinces as the pioneers in the development. John Herd Thompson's, *The Harvests of War: The Prairie West, 1914-1918* (1978) also surveys the same topic but places suffrage more clearly in the context of other developments. Indeed, his volume is a model for the concise treatment of complex issues. Less brief, but certainly comprehensive on the subject of the development of the "social gospel" (mainly on the Prairies) is Richard Allen, *The Social Passion: Religion and Social Reform in Canada, 1914-1928* (1971).

The social ferment theme that has received the greatest attention of historians to date, however, is in the area of labor history, particularly as it came to a focus in the Winnipeg General Strike. The intellectual background to western radicalism is described by A.R. McCormack, *Reformers, Rebels and Revolutionaries: The Western Canadian Radical Movement, 1899-1919* (1977). Donald Avery, *"Dangerous Foreigners": European Immigrant Workers and Labour Radicalism in Canada,* (1979) analyzes the immigrant contribution and shows how the Immigration Branch and the RNWMP developed special roles as security services in the attempt to eradicate radicalism from foreign sources. For the Winnipeg strike itself, a series of recent volumes have appeared, primarily from the work of D.J. Bercuson. A survey by Bercuson with Kenneth McNaught, *The Winnipeg Strike: 1919* (1974) is a brief and nicely illustrated overview. Two other books and an article by Bercuson provide rather complete proof that the revolutionary aspect of the strike was more in the reactions of the governments involved than from the aims of the strikers. See Bercuson's, "Winnipeg General Strike, Collective Bargaining and the One Big Union Issue," CHR (1970); *Confrontation at Winnipeg: Labour, Industrial Relations and the General Strike* (1974); and *Fools and Wise Men: The Rise and Fall of the One Big Union* (1978).

"... King posed always as the friend of humanity."

# CHAPTER 19

# The Disintegration of National Politics

## I    The Illusion of Union

In the last year of the war, Robert Borden imagined that he was launching a new era of national politics. A wartime union of the Conservatives and many Liberals was a coalition that he and some other Canadians believed might survive the armistice. At the same time, some reformers imagined that the Union Government's electoral triumph in 1917 was a victory for the cause of reform because the platform of the government contained a great deal more than the conscription plank. At westerners' insistence, there were references as well to prohibition, women's suffrage, and a civil service commission to eliminate political patronage from government. Some visionaries speculated that the old days of two-party bickering might be coming to an end and that Canada was moving like a progressive city toward nonpartisan rule. Indeed, the country had not divided on party lines in the election of 1917. The electorate returned a parliament that was not divided as Liberals and Conservatives but as Quebeckers against the rest.

After the Unionist victory, Borden did implement many of the reforms that were promised along with conscription. In 1918 and 1919, a broad range of innovations was enacted by legislation or order in council. Civil service reform made it more difficult for politicians to reward the party faithful; prohibition banned the bar; women were accepted into the franchise for future federal elections; the transcontinental railways (except the CPR) were transformed into a public utility; and legislation was enacted to assist "soldier settlement". These and other innovations in business-government relations (discussed in the next chapter), showed that Borden's

Unionist Government was interested in domestic innovation as well as conscription.

But all of the Unionist tinkerings with the political superstructure contributed nothing to settle the unrest of labor in 1919. On the contrary, the reforms that pertained to labor unrest were all intended to secure the manufacturers and the middle class rather than to protect organized workers. The amendments to the Criminal Code and the Immigration Act (along with long-standing Militia Act provisions) made it relatively simple to break strikes by equating such action with sedition, jailing the leaders, and calling out the army to intimidate the rank and file. In this sense, the nonpartisan quality of the coalition that governed in Ottawa was even more illusory than for the reasons the Quebeckers asserted. The Union was partial in the sense that it failed to comprehend labor as much as it isolated Quebec. For this reason, anyone in 1918 who sincerely believed that a period of party strife was not about to resume more violently than before was sadly deluded.

The Liberal Party might have been expected to be the instrument for defeating the Conservatives' Unionist Party in the postwar period. But such a victory was not possible until Laurier passed from the Liberal leadership. As long as he continued to lead, his party would be identified with opposition to conscription, and therefore with weak patriotism in English Canada. By the same token, Laurier could not be dropped from the leadership without alienating Quebec. Conveniently, he died in February 1919. The problem of finding a replacement leader was so grave that the Liberals held a convention to choose a successor — the first such gathering in Canadian history. At the meeting in August 1919, 1200 delegates from across the country sought a candidate who had been loyal to Laurier and therefore Quebec but not outspokenly anti-conscriptionist and therefore unpatriotic in the sight of the rest of Canada. At the same time, the delegates appeared to seek a leader who might win the affection of the Canadian working class without too severely offending the anti-radical supporters of the Unionist coalition. The man they chose was William Lyon Mackenzie King, grandson of the rebel of 1837, former Minister of Labour in 1909, and published author in 1918.

King's book was a vaguely utopian inquiry into *Industry and Humanity*, more philosophical than factual, and more Christian than either Socialist or Capitalist. For anyone bothering to read the work, it seemed to establish that the forty-three-year-old bachelor who assumed the leadership of the Liberal Party was a genuine lover of humanity, at least in principle. Perhaps for this reason, the Liberals built some interesting reform propositions into their 1919 platform. They called for a living wage for workers, unemployment insurance, old age pensions, mothers' allowances, and the eight-hour day. For King, it was grand evidence that a great party had a clear course to steer in the future. For Borden and other Conservatives, the platform only provided further proof that "the world is in ferment" and there were "doctors and quacks innumerable" to cure its ills.

## II Repudiation of Union in the Heartland of Canadian Conservatism

Since the Conservatives imagined theirs was the legitimate voice of "real democracy" rather than demagogic appeals for class domination, and since they tended to regard Ontario as the most sensible as well as the dominant province in the nation, they were understandably shaken by the outcome of a provincial election in Canada's largest province on October 20, 1919 because it appeared that the voters rejected political sanity and opted for class rule. Except in this case, the "class" that came to power was that of the farmers. Their party, the United Farmers of Ontario (UFO), ran 63 candidates for the 83 seat legislature. Forty-five were elected.

Ironically, the farmers of Ontario took over the government of their province because they feared that they were no longer strong enough to influence the government by other means. Since 1880, most of the rural counties had been losing population to the Prairies and the cities faster than they were being replaced by immigration or reproduction. In the decade before the war, two thirds of the counties experienced an absolute decline in total population. As the rural parts of Ontario diminished and the urban areas grew, did it not follow that the once dominant part of the still dominant province would be subordinated to the cities and governed by politicians who cared little about agriculture and its problems?

Agrarian status anxiety was apparent as early as 1911 but increased during the war in the face of Premier William Hearst's oft-repeated assertion that "the full strength of every arm and heart and brain is demanded in the Empire's cause." The farmers were quite willing to comply but they could not be two places at once. The problem was that the demands on their service seemed to require two roles simultaneously. They were asked to produce more and more butter and cheese to feed the forces in the field and industry. But at the same time, they were constantly being urged to send all their sons into military service. Pinched by the manpower shortage and pained at the suggestion that farm folk were less completely willing to do their share in the fighting at the front, one farmer complained that he and his class were "suffering ... a diarrhoea of advice and a particularly acute constipation in the matter of help." Hearst's government seemed more "carried away with the interested cry of uplift" (keeping up with western reformers and their impractical innovations, such as women's suffrage and prohibition) than in looking after the more immediate difficulties of the wartime labor shortage or reversing rural depopulation. As a result, they formed their own party to defeat the "big interests".

The Conservative premier thought that the farmers' revolt was futile as well as unreasonable. In Hearst's view, all was being done that could be reasonably expected of a responsible administration. He was promoting a program to develop rural amenities, such as better roads. He was also behind a program to replace horse and manpower with more machinery, gasoline tractors in particular. The policy he refused to consider was exemption of farm workers from military service on grounds that such a policy would result in a stampede of young men to the country. Moreover, the exemption question was a federal matter. For this reason, Hearst suggested that even if the UFO captured every seat in Ontario's legislature, "they could not retain one boy on the farm." They did try, however: every county that was losing population ran a UFO candidate and in two thirds of such places they were elected. Nobody was clear how they might "restore agriculture to its former Canadian supremacy" but they were elected for precisely that cause.

## III    The Carcass of Union

Ontario's evident degeneration to class domination and the dementia of the rest of the Canadian domestic scene led Robert Borden to spend more and more time looking for order in international politics. Wearied by domestic issues, he spent most of his time abroad in 1919 and 1920 and few instructions were left for colleagues in his absence. By default, ministers left behind filled prime ministerial functions as well as a growing number of portfolios coming vacant by a plague of resignations beginning in 1919.

The Conservative politician who rose to the top of the cauldron of trouble was Arthur Meighen. He was the same age as Mackenzie King (both were born in 1874 and both first entered Parliament in 1908). In nearly every other respect, however, the two politicians were almost perfect opposites. Where King tended to utter only vague generalities, generally accepted, Meighen stated his positions with stark clarity and unapologetic dogmatism. Where King was indecisive and, like Laurier or Macdonald, appeared to believe that most problems would simply dissolve if delayed long enough, Meighen "could turn a corner so fast you could hear his shirt tails snap." Meighen was openly ruthless. King's ruthlessness was secretive. Meighen, more open in his dealings, acted as if he wanted to be feared; King posed always as the friend of humanity.

The many contrasts between King and Meighen were fully evident in the two politicians' differing attitudes toward radicalism. With regard to the Russian Revolution, for example, King suggested that there was a theme of humanity struggling to become free evident in the epic drama, but Meighen said: "There is nothing there but a disordered, dishevelled, suffering, seething chaos of humanity, with assassination on top and starvation underneath." There was certainly no reason to approve any such "Socialistic, Bolshevik, and Soviet nonsense" for inclusion in the platform of a Canadian political party: "Thousands of people are mentally chasing rainbows, striving for the unattainable, anxious to better their lot and seemingly unwilling to do it in the old-fashioned way by hard, honest intelligent effort," he complained. "Dangerous doctrines taught by dangerous men, enemies of the State, poison and pollute the air."

Arthur Meighen sincerely believed that the atmosphere was dangerously full of insidious doctrines taught by absurd, hypocritical and contemptible teachers, not the least of whom was Mackenzie King. By Meighen's mathematician's logic and his lawyer's skill in argument, he had demonstrated in Parliament that he was the party's best defender of the "old-fashioned way". Consequently, despite his severe political liabilities (his close identification with closure, conscription, disfranchisement of immigrants, and strike-breaking) it was to Meighen that the carcass of the Unionist Government was handed by the Tories when Robert Borden finally said enough and resigned from public life on July 10, 1920.

Technically, it was the leadership of the Liberal-Conservative coalition that Meighen took over. The union was long dead, of course. Still, to maintain the fiction that some nonpartisan organization continued, the group called itself the "National Liberal-Conservative Party". But just as the government's nonpartisanship was hollow, so also — according to King — was the propriety of its continuing in power after the transfer of the leadership to Meighen. In King's view, the Unionist government was a wartime creation elected by an extraordinary franchise; therefore, its right to continue in office expired the day the war was won. Since King did not yet have a seat in the House of Commons, Meighen dismissed King's criticism as the raving of "the outside leader of the outside party". But eventually, in September 1921, he did grant the Liberal leader his chance. An election was set for December.

In the autumn of 1921, as Meighen began to campaign, he realized just how small was his popularity but he did not resign himself to defeat even though he sensed that he had called an election that no Conservative could win. The line of groups seeking revenge in 1921 was simply too long: Quebec was anxious to punish the "blood-stained" author of conscription, the disfranchised voters of 1917 were eager to punish the "usurper" of their voting rights (and they were able to strike in 1921 with double vengeance because their wives were voting with them). Then there were other groups — farmers and workers — whose grievances were economic, either because Meighen had broken their strikes, or controlled the price of grain, or allowed freight and interest rates to float to higher, more profitable levels for the owners of the banks and the CPR. The wonder of the election of 1921 is not that Arthur Meighen was defeated; the shocking outcome was that Mackenzie King was also denied victory.

## IV    The Revolt of the Prairies

In the election of 1921, the Liberals took every seat in Quebec. They also swept the Maritimes taking 25 of their 31 seats. If they had captured the anti-Meighen vote in Ontario and the Prairies they would have won a stunning majority of 184 seats in a 235 member House of Commons. But the Liberals did not win what the Conservatives lost. In this election, a popular third option was available and many people in the West and rural Ontario took it.

The new organization was called the National Progressive Party and grew out of the farmer movements that had developed in every province but especially in Ontario and on the Prairies. The person who was primarily responsible for giving them a national focus was Thomas Crerar, a Manitoba Liberal with a long-standing interest in innovations having to do with direct democracy and tax reform. In 1917 he became the Minister of Agriculture in the Unionist Government and was quite pleased with Borden's wartime fiscal and governmental reforms. Other activities of the Unionists pleased him less, particularly the repressive labor policies and postwar fiscal adjustments. Consequently, in the spring of 1919, when the government refused to implement dramatic reductions in the tariff along with a sharp increase in the business profits tax, Crerar resigned from the cabinet and joined the opposition.

Since the farmers' organizations were calling for a New National Policy that touched on all the reform causes that were dear to Crerar, it was natural that he was the person they would seek when they looked for a national leader. At first, Crerar was skeptical about independent action and hoped to realize his aims through the Liberal Party. By March 1920, however, he reconciled himself to a third party option, but insisted that the farmers' revolt must seek a broader base of support. "Our appeal is not class, not sectional, not religious," he claimed. Crerar said the National Progressive Party was for "all ... who desire to see purity in the government restored, who desire to see public morality supplant public corruption, who desire to sweep away abuse of the function of government for the advancement of the interest of the privileged few."

Affirmations of general principles notwithstanding, there was a distinct agrarianism to the specific policies the Progressives advocated. They stressed the need for reform in the system for marketing grain, restoration of the Crow's Nest Pass freight rates agreed to by Laurier and the CPR in 1897 (but suspended by Meighen after the war), easier credit for farmers, free trade, and concession of provincial control of the natural resources of the three Prairie provinces. Since they also opposed use of the militia for strike-breaking and advocated electoral reforms consistent with the direct democracy demand, there was some appeal of the progressives to urban voters. But the unmistakable fact, no matter what Crerar said to the contrary, was that the National Progressive Party was primarily the national face of the four separate farmer revolts that had developed in Ontario and the West.

Arthur Meighen gambled that most people, including many farmers, had approved of his handling of radicals in the strikes of 1919. More importantly, he knew that most people, including some farmers, regarded opposition to the tariff as tantamount to treason. "If I can get the people of this country to see that the issue is protection or no protection," he believed, "the battle will be won." Crerar was willing to fight over the tariff, but King was afraid that such a debate would divide the protectionist eastern wing of his party from the free trade West. Consequently, the Liberal leader replied that "the issue is the Prime Minister himself and what he and his colleagues represent of autocracy and extravagance in the management of public affairs." King's focus on Meighen was an excellent way of furthering everyone's discontent with the reigning Tories, but how would it convince voters that King's confusion was preferable? Meighen kept bringing the voters' attention back to the tariff and saying King's policy was "Protection on apples in British Columbia, Free Trade in the Prairie provinces and the rural parts of Ontario, Protection in the industrial centres in Ontario, Conscription in Quebec and humbug in the Maritime Provinces."

In the end, the electorate repudiated both of the old parties. Seventy percent of all votes cast went against Meighen's party. Sixty percent were votes against King's Liberals. Arthur Meighen's Conservatives were reduced to a mere 50 seats, and Mackenzie King's Liberals were hardly victorious with their plurality of 116 — two members short of a majority. There were 64 Progressives who could be expected to oppose the Conservatives more often than the Liberals, but the outcome on any question would be uncertain. For the first time in Canadian political history, no party received a majority. Thus, a new dynamic entered into the affairs of the House of Commons.

Like federalism, multi-party politics was something that Canadians discovered they had after it appeared; it was not a pattern that they particularly liked or planned. For the first few years of its operation an effort was made to deny its reality — ironically, by the Progressives themselves. Crerar tended to see the movement as a revolt by people whose true political home was in the Liberal party. As soon as King's Liberals would "come to their senses" on such key issues as the tariff, Crerar expected that the Progressive Party would cease to exist, much like the Populist Party of the United States in the 1890s. But another faction within the Progressives, the Alberta group, was opposed to the very idea of political parties. Henry Wise Wood, the chief spokesman for this point of view (but not himself a Member of Parliament) saw a legislator as a delegate representing an interest group (such as farmers, labor, and so on). He refused to endorse the idea that any coalition should be a permanent party voting monolithically on all questions. Wood's preference was for a constant shifting of allegiances among loosely integrated groups as they voted on the merits of each issue. Yet another faction (mainly from Saskatchewan and less than one third of the whole Progressive contingent), saw the movement as a party in the sense of a solid bloc permanently offering a fresh flow of alternatives acceptable to the special interests of Westerners. But since they were only one of three factions and a minority at that, Meighen's Conservatives formed the official opposition because the number two group was not willing to call itself a political party.

The unwillingness of the Progressives to play the game of party politics at first frustrated the dynamics of minority government, and gave Mackenzie King an ideal opportunity to dismiss the farmers' protest as nothing more than a lot of Liberals in a hurry. Building policy bridges for the Progressives to cross home to Liberalism, he reinstated the Crow's Nest Pass rates and tinkered with the tariff to eliminate the duties on farm machinery. As early as 1923, the strategy began to show signs of success. By the end of the first session of Parliament, it seemed that most Progressives were snugly back where King and their nominal leader thought they belonged. Crerar retired from the party's leadership and King began to speculate about his coming "back into power by getting the Progressive forces and ours united." Interestingly, he also believed that the minor changes that reconciled Crerar-type Progressives were "true to the platform of the 1919 convention, true to the pledges I gave the electors in 1921 ... ."

Angered by King's responsiveness to the Progressives, Arthur Meighen denounced the government for having no policy of its own. In 1922, he complained that the government "listens for the threats and growls ... then all these noises are gathered together, fused into one and the conglomerate emission becomes the tune that he calls the government policy." From a less critical point of view, such commentary only confirms what King's principal biographers suggest was a major strength of his leadership — that King was a pragmatist, like Macdonald or Laurier, but all the more so because of the necessities of minority government. How wide, though, was his audible range?

# V    Missed Opportunities

It is clear that Mackenzie King heard some of the Progressives' demands, but ignored other Members of Parliament even though they advocated policies in social reform that were closer to his party's 1919 platform. The principal spokesman for the new members who were most interested in social reform was J.S. Woodsworth, a Labour member elected because of working-class outrage in Winnipeg. In his first speech in Parliament in 1922, Woodsworth asserted that "we have come to a period in the history of our country when we must decide once and for all which shall prevail, profits or human welfare." Knowing that there was more to Progressivism than what Crerar would promise, Woodsworth went further and asserted that "there is a group of men here, new Members of the House ... who have clearly made up their minds that, insofar as they can decide it, human welfare is to be given precedence." The kinds of action that followed from Woodsworth's reform impulse pertained to tax reform that went beyond the tariff, enlargement of the public utility sector beyond the existing national railway system, and the provision of social security by national policy.

The tax reform Woodsworth advocated was increased personal income and business profits taxes to replace the tariff. Spending for the Great War had added more than $2 billion to the national debt. So great was the burden of war expenditure that roughly one third of the government's $350 million budgets in the 1920s was expended just to cover the interest on the debt. Existing profit and income taxes generated only 10 percent of the annual revenue, and therefore the rest of the government's income came mainly from the tariff. Since Woodsworth claimed that the people who benefited most by the wartime expenditure were Canada's rich, he suggested that they should play a larger role in retiring the debt, thus his steeper income and business profits taxes to "recover from the profiteers the blood money which they laid up during the time of the war."

Woodsworth regarded the leading industrialists as a new "family compact" that controlled the economy for their private benefit rather than the public interest. Pursuing the issue one step further, Woodsworth criticized the government for not including the Canadian Pacific in the Canadian

National system. Reasoning that other monopolies or near monopolies ought to operate for the promotion of the general welfare rather than private greed, he advocated nationalization of other basic industries as well.

To guarantee individual welfare, Woodsworth claimed that public insurance schemes were justified as protection against poverty in old age or privation in the event of unemployment.

Naturally, Meighen's group tended to dismiss all of Woodsworth's proposals as "socialist nonsense". The Tory member for Saint John was so angered to hear socialism in the Canadian House of Commons he demanded a vote on the question so that everyone could "stand up either for the reds or against them." The reds lost 47 to 108, suggesting that 1922 was not a year to expect the enactment of a great deal of Woodsworth's program. But with so many "reds" in the House, was it not possible for King to have enacted at least part of the Liberal platform of 1919?

Bolder action may have been possible given the mix of parties in Parliament, but it was not feasible given the personality of Mackenzie King, a compulsive avoider of unnessary risks. Necessity was that which would keep the Liberal Party in power. A risk was anything that might lead to controversy. All of which was well illustrated by his reluctance to provide the protection to organized labor in 1922 that he had promised before the election — even though such protection was manifestly needed. In January 1922, the British Empire Steel Company (BESCO) announced radical reductions in the wages of workers in the mines and mills of Cape Breton Island. The cut was by one third with the effect that the average Cape Breton miner's income would fall to about three quarters of an Alberta coal miner's even though the cost of living was significantly higher on Cape Breton Island. The matter attracted national attention because near famine conditions resulted. Clearly, if the living wage plank in the Liberal Party platform of 1919 meant anything at all, the Cape Breton miners were workers worthy of the Liberal government's attention. Woodsworth raised the issue in the House of Commons but King pleaded constitutional inability to act. The only coercive power he claimed he could provide was of the workers under the provisions of the Militia Act. He was unwilling to enact legislation that would make federal conciliation reports binding. As a result, after conciliators agreed that the workers were underpaid and BESCO ignored their report, the workers struck, BESCO demanded protection, and the army was sent in to maintain order. In August 1922, the miners finally agreed to the new wage schedule, but "under the muzzle of rifles, machine guns and gleaming bayonets," according to the union president.

King's handling of the Cape Breton miners' dispute was confirmation that King listened only to the bloc whose support was provided at the lowest cost. It was cheaper for him to buy the support of the conservative Progressives with tariff concessions and restoration of the Crow's Nest Pass rates than to "hear" anything the more radical Progressives demanded. As a result, Woodsworth was frustrated by the timidity of most Progressives. To dramatize their conservatism in 1924, he proposed an amendment that the Progressives should have initiated since it called for the kind of tax reform that was supposed to be the main reason for their election. But the Progressives' leader, Robert Forke (successor to Crerar in 1923), did not wish to reveal how many of his ranks had been reconciled with King. As a result, he dared not support further reductions in the tariff or higher taxes on unearned incomes. When Woodsworth did propose precisely such changes, he forced the Progressives to vote against their own declared principles or support him against King and Forke. On May 16, 1924, fifteen Progressives defied their leader and voted with Woodsworth. At the time, Forke indicated that "there will be a certain amount of what I may call unholy glee on the part of some who think this places the Progressives in a rather difficult position." Actually, Forke's apology was a gross understatement of his embarrassment. The Toronto *Telegram* cynically but correctly described the vote as an "explosion" that destroyed the party. Progressives had to decide "whether they should vote for the principles they pretend to love or for the government that has bought them at a price." Most voted with the Liberals and for all practical future electoral purposes, they killed the Progressive Party.

## VI    The Revolt of the Maritimes

In the election of 1925, the Progressive contingent from Ontario and the Prairies was reduced by more than half, to just 24 members. Of this group, most were the "co-operating independents" working with J.S. Woodsworth. By shifting most of the Prairie Progressive vote back to the Liberal Party, Mackenzie King had expected to return to power with a comfortable majority. His party did recover on the Prairies. But King still failed to win a majority overall because in 1925 the Maritimes denied him victory.

In the previous chapter it was suggested that the immediate enemy of the leaders of the Maritime Rights movement was the local Farmer-Labour revolt that had reduced the Conservatives to third-place position in Nova Scotia by 1920. Since the main task of the Maritime Tories was to show that they were more credible than the Farmer-Labour coalition and eventually also the Liberals, they were fortunate in having Liberal governments in power on the provincial and national levels in the period of their most energetic action, 1921-1925. Persuading most Maritimers that the root of their troubles was government by personnel who shunned the truth as preached by Arthur Meighen, they fancied they were about to shake a lethargic federation to its foundations.

The Maritime Conservatives' main demand was for a national policy to develop their region just as the "so-called National Policy" of Macdonald had promoted Ontario and the Prairies. The consistency of the logic was simply too much for Meighen, who was insisting upon the tariff in 1925 exactly as he had earlier. The accommodation he would grant the Maritimes was higher duties on coal and steel since almost half of both commodities consumed in Ontario were imported from the United States. The idea that the Maritimes could be Ontario's alternate supplier prompted yeasty visions of empire-building in Nova Scotia. Meighen nurtured them further by suggesting that he was prepared to adjust freight rates for the Maritimes the way King had recently restored subsidized transportation of grain for the Prairies.

Coal and steel made more expensive by tariff increases were bound to be unpopular in Ontario, the province that gave the Conservatives the largest number of their seats in Parliament, however. For this reason, it remained unclear how Meighen would accommodate the Maritime Rights movement without arousing the ire of Ontario. Mackenzie King attempted to avoid any such embarrassment by asking questions rather than promising solutions. His approach was to suggest that the Maritimers had failed to make clear their grievances over the previous four years. "What are Maritime Rights?," he asked. "Let us know and we will fight for them," he promised. Since Meighen acknowledged that the Maritimers already had a legitimate case and agreed to implement that which local Conservatives said they needed, the Conservatives swept Nova Scotia and New Brunswick with record majorities in both provinces in the voting on October 29, 1925.

The Maritime Rights Conservatives then encountered two problems. One was that they were a bloc of about twenty members in a caucus of 116. How were they to persuade 68 members from Ontario that Maritime Rights required that they give up their cheap American coal and steel? But the first problem was not as frustrating as the second: King held onto power even though his party had only 99 seats in the new Parliament. It was the support from the Progressives and Woodsworth's Ginger Group of "co-operating independents" that kept King's government from falling.

Sustaining King was not Woodsworth's preferred alternative. He tried to get the party leaders to form a new council in lieu of the old cabinet, a council that would not represent any party in particular but would nonetheless be responsible to a parliamentary majority. Of course, King would not consent to such an arrangement. As a result, Woodsworth and Forke each presented King and Meighen with shopping lists of issues to decide which was the lesser of two evils. Meighen responded to his letter from Forke by telling him that "the stand of the Conservative Party has been fully and repeatedly outlined by myself in the House of Commons .... So far as I know it has never been charged that my attitude as Leader on any of these subjects has been equivocal or obscure." In other words, he was not interested in any kind of a trade. Similarly, Meighen replied to Woodsworth's offer of support for unemployment insurance and old age pensions with the assertion that "the thing to do for the unemployed is to get them work" and this could be accomplished by stiff tariff increases. To be sure, the aged would not be well served by Meighen's unemployment cure, but he thought other matters "more pressing" than federal assistance to pensioners.

Woodsworth and Forke received a friendlier reception from King. In Woodsworth's case, the letter led to a dinner invitation, at which occasion Woodsworth was offered the position of Minister of Labour. Woodsworth declined, indicating he would prefer to see the social legislation he mentioned in his letter and also some law reform removing the Meighen amendments to the Criminal Code and the Immigration Act. King protested that the country could ill afford unemployment insurance but would Woodsworth settle for the rest of the package? Yes, said Woodsworth, but he wanted the arrangement in writing. Then, after the first session of the new Parliament opened late in January 1926, Woodsworth read the text of King's letter into Hansard, in a sense as an appendix to the Throne Speech. For Meighen, the bargain was "a shameless brutal assault not only on the most sacred principles of British constitutional government but on common honesty."

It was not, however, Meighen's attack that shook the new government. Much more serious was the allegation made by the Conservative, H.H. Stevens, that the Department of Customs was rife with corruption. He demanded an all-party committee to investigate his specific charges.

The Liberal strategy for dealing with the threat of scandal and also their legislative unpreparedness was to seek a six-week adjournment. Naturally, Meighen denounced the maneuver for being "without parallel or approach in the history of this most extraordinary administration." Meighen's complaint was that "the government comes to Parliament, convened at its own instance, brought here under its own auspices and before any business is despatched suggests that we go to our homes for six weeks because it is not in a position to carry on ... ." Meighen's complaint nothwithstanding, the House did adjourn for the period requested.

Six weeks later, the ramshackle government reconvened and King unveiled his program for making peace not only with the "co-operating independents" but also with the Maritimes. In addition to the old age pension scheme and law reforms promised to Woodsworth, there was the completely free gift of a royal commission to investigate Maritime claims. For anyone who did not have a special sectional or economic interest, there were many other favors of a more general nature: reductions in the income tax, lower tariffs on many items including automobiles, and a lowering of postal rates. When at last the whole package was opened,

Meighen wanted to know what it would cost. He said sarcastically that he did not expect a precise figure but would be satisfied with even a rough estimate, "say, within a hundred million dollars."

Apparently, King expected one short session and then an election, perhaps as early as September, the date the report was demanded from the Maritime claims commission (soon known as the Duncan Commission after its principle commissioner, Sir Andrew Rae Duncan). King's timetable was interrupted in June, however, when the Parliamentary Committee reported on the customs matters Stevens had raised before the adjournment. The evidence was unmistakeable. It appeared that every port in Canada was staffed by customs officers who were cooperating with smugglers, especially those engaged in the illegal liquor traffic with the United States (where prohibition was still in force). In Lunenburg, Nova Scotia, for example, schooners loaded with whiskey would leave for the Carribean or South America and return home from their south Atlantic destinations 48 hours later, only to depart again with the same cargo for the same customers. For the port officials not to have taken action against such fraud there would have to be active connivance between themselves and the smugglers. But was the corruption a function of the system or the government of the day?

Meighen's party claimed that the abuses were the unique result of an especially corrupt Liberal patronage machine. Woodsworth argued that a fuller investigation would show that the real fault lay with the system itself, and recommended that a royal commission should investigate more fully to recommend practicable remedies in the same way that such a body was investigating Maritime rights. Clearly, Woodsworth believed that the Liberals were beginning to embark upon a worthwhile program and should be kept in office until their work was finished. Other members of Woodsworth's group were not so pragmatic, however. M.N. Campbell of Saskatchewan denounced the Liberal government for its responsibility in "one of the worst scandals in the whole history of Canada." He, for one, would not condone its continuation "on the ground of political expediency." Naturally, Meighen's party agreed with Campbell. Attacked by the independents as well as the Tories, it was clear that King's government was going to be defeated on a non-confidence motion late in June.

King hoped to avoid the humiliation of defeat by asking that the House be dissolved before the vote could be taken, but the Governor General, Lord Byng, refused to grant his request and King resigned on June 28. Since a general election had occurred quite recently, and since the Conservatives, the plurality party in the House, had not yet had a chance to govern, Byng turned to Meighen. Once in power, Meighen could not retain enough third party backing and was soon defeated. Then Parliament had to be dissolved and King rejoiced in the alleged constitutional crisis that launched his campaign because the Governor General's action amounted to a breach of responsible government, he said. Of course, nothing of the sort had taken place. Byng had operated within the bounds of the royal prerogative as it was defined in 1926. Byng's real crime was that he was English and an aristocrat; that allowed King to claim that the country's recently-won independence was in jeopardy and to articulate a novel but popular principle when he went into the election saying that the matter was "for Parliament to decide." When Meighen attempted to neutralize King's position with the assertion that "the Governor General acted correctly ... the hysterical platform utterances of Mackenzie King ... should only serve to amuse", it could be argued that his laughter was directed at the country's aspirations for fuller autonomy as much as at King himself. In this sense, the constitutional issue was more genuine than Meighen perceived, as King rejoiced in his diary: "I go into the battle of another election believing we have an issue that the people will respond to." Where the alleged constitutional crisis did not have an effect, King still had his sunshine budget and the just completed report of the Duncan Commission with several practical remedies bound to be popular in the Maritimes. The result (in September 1926) was the voters gave King the majority they had withheld since 1921.

## VII   Return to Politics as Usual

King's victory in 1926 could be interpreted as a return to politics as usual in the sense that it enabled him to govern within the context of his own disciplined party. His period of listening was over. In another sense, King's success marked the completion of a transformation more than a return to normal; it marked the completion of a transition process that had begun in 1911 with the repudiation of the old Macdonald-Laurier tradition of broker politics. Under the old system, the parties articulated national policies that were supposed to represent an accommodation of diverse regional and class interests. By 1911, however, the majority consensus was that such compromises bound the country to "Little Canada" policies. Borden's Conservatives gained popularity in their promise of furthering government that was progressive, nationalizing, and majoritarian. But by 1919, it was only too clear that Borden's nation was Empire Ontario and its satellites. Worse still, the satellites were in revolt and special interest groups were adding their independent voice to national politics. By their 1919 platform it appeared that the Liberals were attempting to create a national party oriented especially to Quebec and the discontented working class, endorsing the living wage, unemployment compensation, the eight-hour day, and more. Meighen for his part, responded by appealing to Canadians' sense of tradition and asked them to join him in returning to first principles: "the National Policy as Macdonald had shaped it, and as it has since endured." But King would not be caught. Instead of posing an alternative tariff policy, or insisting upon his party's 1919 platform, he retreated, as Roger Graham has argued, into "soft, shapeless, confusing, meaningless verbiage". It is not correct, however, to conclude with Graham that King had "nothing to offer but confusion."

To be sure, King did lay down a verbal smoke screen where national policies were concerned, but he sensed better than Meighen — or any other politician — that the key to success was broker politics in which the transactions took place on a purely regional level. Thus, he pacified the Prairies with the restoration of lower freight rates on grain and minor tinkering with the tariff; he hung on to a fragment of Ontario by asserting that his revenue tariff also provided a measure of industrial protection; he kept Quebec support by keeping strong their resentment of conscription and Meighen's autocracy; finally (after 1926) he pacified the Maritimes by conceding some of the recommendations of the Duncan Commission (freight rate reductions, subsidy increases, and regional development schemes) — all of which indicated a return to the politics of accommodation without bothering to develop national policies. The nearest he came to that exercise was the pension scheme that Woodsworth demanded in 1926. But even here, the little that was conceded involved provincial cooperation. The pension plan established in 1927 was a national policy contingent upon provincial acquiescence. The new brokerage politics was thus a positive step in the sense that some real issues were addressed and in a manner that did not further destroy the federation. But the new accommodation was unfortunate in the sense that pressing national problems were shelved by an approach to politics that made the country more regional than ever. In the 1920s, the government in Ottawa became no more than a clearing house for the aspirations of regional principalities. Had the provinces shown concern with the social issues that had first impelled such persons as J.S. Woodsworth into politics, the devolution of authority would have been a harmless trade-off. But they were no more prepared than Ottawa to implement provincial unemployment insurance schemes, for example. Consequently, the country fared all the more poorly with the problems of the Great Depression of the 1930s.

# Bibliography

The volume in the Canadian Centenary Series that covers the subject of national politics in the 1920s is not yet published. The last chapters of R.C. Brown and R. Cook, *Canada, 1896-1921: A Nation Transformed* (1974) does cover the subject through the first election of the decade and J.M. Beck, *Pendulum of Power: Canada's Federal Elections* (1968) has useful chapters on the other contests of the decade. Moreover, although John English, *The Decline of Politics: The Conservatives and the Party System* (1977) concludes with 1921, the book does offer a number of useful insights into the later years with reference to King's political style.

Until more general studies become available, the most comprehensive works on national politics in the 1920s must continue to be the multi-volume biographical accounts of the most important leaders of the decade. Roger Graham's *Arthur Meighen: Vol II, And Fortune Fled* (1963) is a sympathetic account of the leader who has received perhaps the least sympathy of the three. R.M. Dawson and H.B. Neatby have done the commemorative work on Mackenzie King. Dawson's *Volume I* (1958) ends in 1923. Neatby's *Volume II* (1963) covers the period from 1924 to 1932. The comprehensive work on J.S. Woodsworth — and a masterpiece in intellectual history — is Kenneth McNaught, *A Prophet in Politics* (1959). Part II of McNaught's work, covering Woodworth's activity between 1922 and 1927, is indispensable reading for anyone interested in the origins of the multiparty system.

For readers who tire of Graham's partisan defense of Meighen or Neatby's meticulous unraveling of King's tedium, shorter biographies are available by other scholars. *Arthur Meighen* (1977) by John English and *Mackenzie King* (1976) by J.L. Granatstein are both readable accounts and profusely illustrated.

Although biographies are the present, most accessible approaches to the study of national politics in the 1920s, the regional protests that had such an important impact on the national scene have received great attention from historians interested in mass movements. The farmers' revolt in Ontario, for example, is well covered by Peter Oliver, "Sir William Hearst and the Collapse of the Ontario Conservative Party," CHR (1972) and W.R. Young, "Conscription, Rural Depopulation and the Farmers of Ontario, 1917-1919," CHR (1972). W.L. Morton, *The Progressive Party in Canada* (1950) examines the national expression of the farmers' revolt not only for its regional origins but also for its operation in the House of Commons. Some readers, however, will dislike Morton's conclusions since he tends to assume that third parties are inherently ephemeral and irresponsible. Thus, Morton would consider that the Maritimers launched a more reasonable protest since theirs was a regional movement that was content to express itself through the national Conservative organization. To test such an assertion, readers may wish to compare the *Maritime Rights Movement, 1919-1927: A Study in Canadian Regionalism* (1979) by E.R. Forbes with the preliminary section of W. Young's, *Democracy and Discontent* (1969), a view of the Progressives that challenges Morton's.

"... nearly half of the Canadian people were not very interested in innovative approaches to the problems of the unemployed."

# CHAPTER 20

# *Prosperity, Depression, and the Quest for Restoration*

## I    Slide Into Depression

The emergence of multi-party politics in the 1920s was a source of consid-erable anxiety to businessmen who preferred the simpler, apparently more stable two-party state. The new pattern was alarming because the prime minister (or his alternate, the leader of the opposition), was vulnerable to newly organized interests in Parliament. Since the new party groups had enough representation to win concessions from the old, and since the new groups tended to be hostile to the traditional partner relationship between business and the state, the problems for businessmen in influencing policy became exceedingly more complicated in the 1920s. And that disturbing development appeared just as business groups became extraordinarily active in seeking new favors from government.

The basic anxiety of business was overextension in prosperity, and cutthroat competition in recession. In the 1909-13 period, the strategy had been to pursue mergers that might regulate supply in relation to demand by sheer domination of the market. More than 200 firms were involved in 97 mergers in the half-decade before 1913. Such conglomerates as the Steel Company of Canada, Dominion Canners, and Canada Cement were the result. But the trend toward bigness had not prevented the recession of 1913-15, nor did its continuation through the war years disguise the problem that a return to peace would jeopardize prosperity and lead to a renewed period of instability.

To curb "unfair trade practices" in the period of postwar recession, the Borden government created a regulatory agency called the Board of Commerce (BOC) in the autumn of 1919. Since the BOC also had authority to regulate profits and prices, there was a theoretical possibility that it would not serve business as well as the public. Still, the Canadian Manufacturers Association was satisfied that if it were "administered sanely there can be no great objection." The first requirement was that the agency had to be run by personnel with "business experience" rather than by "visionaries and theorists". Properly staffed, the agency could be the culmination of the search for security through regulation, and thus an escape from "destructive" competition. But almost half of the economy still consisted of small-scale or old-fashioned businessmen who regarded any kind of regulation as unnecessary interference. Consequently, the Board of Commerce rapidly disintegrated into symbolic actions rather than real control over prices or allocation of the market. When it collapsed in 1920, it marked a clear failure, according to Tom Traves, of "political and business leaders' attempts to create a regulatory state at the end of the First World War."

Another remarkable failure at the same time pertained to an abortive experiment in business-government labor management. Clearly, the unemployed in the 1913-15 recession had suffered even more than the manufacturers. Equally important, the potential discontent of massive numbers of unemployed affected the security of the whole economic system. Consequently, the Employment Service of Canada (ESC) was created in 1918, even before the Board of Commerce. In one sense, the agency was a temporary body just to monitor employment patterns and provide labor exchanges to utilize labor more effectively in the last days of the war and to facilitate a smoother transition to peacetime employment especially by thousands of returned men. In both ways, the ESC reflected the idea that government responsibility for unemployment was a passing phenomenon. But the director of the agency, Bryce Stewart, imagined that his office could be permanent and eventually could extend its activities to include industrial training, immigration policy, and even unemployment insurance. Stewart was not alone in such hope. Even some businessmen could see the ESC as a valuable aid to industry by managing labor more rationally. Even unemployment insurance made sense to them as long as it did not compromise their interests by exerting an upward pressure on wages, or require their cooperation in contributing premiums.

In 1919, a Royal Commission on Industrial Relations recommended adoption of a state-sponsored unemployment insurance scheme, a plan in which workers would contribute premiums while they were employed and draw benefits considerably below normal wage levels when they were laid off. The concept was reviewed by the Department of Justice in 1920 and found to be well within the "peace, order and good government powers" of the Dominion. But Arthur Meighen and Gideon Robertson rejected the propriety of the plan. After 1921, Mackenzie King rejected its expediency.

The problem for King was that most farmers considered industrialization to have created a rural labor problem, and they believed that urban unemployment was their best hope for recovering cheap labor on the farms. From the standpoint of Thomas Crerar (and other agrarians in Parliament), farmers had not been able to compete with factories in recent years because of the abnormally high demand for unskilled labor during the war. The result was that country producers were left with only "one quarter of the labour needed," according to Crerar. It followed, from his reasoning, that if people were out of work, it was because "they will not do the work which is to be done." The Canadian Council of Agriculture demanded that the government "shovel" the unskilled "back into the country" rather than putting a "premium on idleness". They were thus opposed to the continuation of the Employment Service of Canada and the extension of Stewart's larger ambitions. The parliamentary spokesmen for the farmers of Canada said that they wanted to "make conditions more difficult in the cities." Otherwise, they said, "we cannot hope to hold our people on the farms."

Since Mackenzie King's first priority after 1921 was to attempt to solidify "an alliance with the rural elements," the author of *Industry and Humanity* oversaw the destruction of the ESC on grounds that it represented too much of that "centralizing tendency" that had accompanied the war. To those who persisted in the demand for unemployment insurance as an indispensable amelioration of a serious problem that was a continuing by-product of industrialization, King pleaded constitutional inability to act. Here, however, the BNA Act was his shield from criticism more than his barrier to action. As his own Minister of Labour, James Murdock, reminded King in 1924, there were sound legal reasons for thinking that the "Dominion Parliament has power to enact a national system of unemployment insurance should it desire to do so." But Murdock agreed with King that there were better political reasons to reject such a course. By this time, the agrarians had been tamed. The new fear was simply the cost: better to leave the municipalities with the responsibility for "relief" in "normal times". But what was normal?

Municipal officials claimed in the 1920s that every year was critical since unemployment reached levels of about 16 percent in winter. The Government of Canada insisted that for federal authorities to assume more responsibility for relief, there would have to be evidence that "unemployment was to be permanent." In that event, they asserted they would "sit down ... and work for years until we have found a remedy." But "temporary" difficulties had to be met by the cities themselves. To do otherwise would "shelve responsibility which for fifty years has been theirs."

The consensus that prevailed on the unemployment of the 1920s was thus the "rugged individualism" of small business and farmers and the "fiscal responsibility" of government. As a result, workers were left to shift for themselves — in the traditional way of attempting to gain more than one source of income per family. At the managerial level, corporations sought their security in a second merger movement which led Canada Cement, Canadian General Electric, Canadian Industries Limited, and Imperial Tobacco to develop "near monopolies" in their fields. But neither the trend to monopoly nor the abandonment of the unemployed was considered generally dangerous since the years between 1925 and 1928 appeared to "boom" like those of Laurier.

In the Laurier boom, the developments that attracted attention were the settlement of the West, the building of the railways, and the rise of the metropolitan industrial centers. In the short boom of the later 1920s, the dramatic development was that of the automobile and of building a system of roads on which the middle class might operate their new method of personal transportation. In the short period from 1925 to 1929, the mileage of surfaced roads almost doubled, increasing from 47 to 80 000 miles and accommodating about one million motor vehicles by the end of the decade. Naturally, the country's ability to produce the new machines grew at an even faster rate. By 1929, the plants at Oshawa and Windsor were capable of assembling roughly 500 000 autos per year, even though the market at its most bouyant was less than 300 000 per year. Since the most inexpensive models cost almost as much as a factory worker's entire annual income, a new car was not yet affordable by most of the population. Prosperous city dwellers and farmers were the most likely buyers of automobiles. In the cities, the working class continued to ride the "street railways". But the automobile was still an important factor in the economy of the period because one fourth of the population was able to buy them. For this minority, the whole country was prepared to lay down pavement, the better to operate the new symbol of freedom and affluence.

To improve the transportation of railway passengers over longer distances, and also to improve the movement of staples for export, an additional 5000 miles of railroads were also constructed in the 1920s. The new rail construction reflected a surge in the production of pulp and paper, metals, and grain. In 1928, the wheat farmers of Canada brought in their largest crop to date, almost 600 million bushels. But that was 127 million bushels more than the world market would absorb. Moreover, Canadian mines and paper mills were also beginning to outrun world demand for non-ferrous metals and newsprint at the same time. Prices declined and volume traded diminished. Since the trade in staples accounted for more than half the value of all exports, the work for the country's largest employers, the railways, also declined. The two shocks beginning in 1928 — the one to the staple trades, the other to the transportation system — were then transmitted to the rest of the economy and the automobile manufacturers found it more difficult to sell their cars, builders started fewer houses, and the rest of the domestic manufacturing sector followed in recession. By 1930, unemployment was greater than during the "hard times of 1921-22" and one third of the people who were classified with the employed, the farmers, were so trapped between fixed debts and low prices that they suffered as much as the industrial unemployed. Thus began the worst economic crisis since 1873, a depression that unfolded as a ten-year-long object lesson in the vulnerability of an economy overcommitted to the production of a few staple products and ill-prepared to cope with industrial unemployment.

## II   Apparent Need for a "New Deal"

For the first time in the history of Canada, farmers as well as industrial workers had to ask for "relief" and go through the degrading process by which the heads of households swore that they had utterly failed in their attempts to provide for their families and to swear also that all relatives were equally incompetent to serve as alternate providers. For families thus proving that they were absolutely destitute, a rural or urban municipality would provide rations and housing to prevent death by starvation or exposure. But even with such a minimal level of support, local institutions rapidly exhausted their available resources and sought help from the provinces. Provincial jurisdictions, in their turn, appealed for help from Ottawa.

All but two of the provincial premiers were Conservatives. Since Mackenzie King did not wish to aid or comfort the enemy by shouldering his financial burden, he indicated that he "might be prepared to go a certain length possibly in meeting one or two western provinces that have progressive premiers at the head of their governments, but I would not give a single cent to any Tory government." Thus, at the federal level in 1930, it would be more than fair to describe Mackenzie King as attempting to avoid the crisis rather than confronting it with a broad program of action. He claimed consititutional inability to innovate, but refused to propose amendments to the BNA Act. He knew the provinces needed larger subsidies, but did nothing in that regard either.

Despite the possible unpopularity of King's obstinacy, the Prime Minister chose the summer of 1930 as the most propitious moment for calling a federal election. King was hopeful that most voters wanted their central government to meet the crisis cautiously since most people were not unemployed, and all people could hope that the downturn was only temporary. Perhaps for these reasons, in 1930 his party was only one percent behind its 1926 total when the Liberals won a parliamentary majority with 46 percent of the vote. Then, however, the minor parties still attracted a significant number of votes; this time they were nearly wiped out and their loss appeared to be the Conservatives' gain. With 49 percent of the vote, they won 137 or 56 percent of the seats.

The key to the Tories' success may have been that they appeared even more traditional than King because the Conservatives' leader, R.B. Bennett (successor to Arthur Meighen in 1927), gave the impression that he would restore lost prosperity by taking bold action with tradional means. Bennett said, "Mackenzie King promises you conferences; I promise you action. He promises consideration of the problem of unemployment, I promise to end unemployment." The pledge of a quick solution was all the more appealing because it was supposed to be achieved simply, by a heavier dose of that policy that Canadians were no longer holding as dear as they ought, according to Bennett. He said: "You have been taught to mock at tariffs and to applaud free trade." But he challenged the voters to tell him, "when did free trade fight for you? Tell me, when did free trade fight for you? You say our tariffs are only for our manufacturers; I will make them fight for you as well. I will use them to blast a way into the markets that have been closed to you."

After the election, Bennett kept his promise with two measures submitted to a special session of Parliament. One provided $20 million for emergency relief. The other increased the tariff by 50 percent, the sharpest increase since Macdonald's imposition of the National Policy in 1879. Although Bennett's medicine was no more than what he had promised (in this sense, what the electorate expected), one policy tended to cancel the effect of the other. The disbursement of funds for relief was supposed to ease hardship, but the tariff provisions that prevented dumping of cheap foreign goods stabilized falling prices and thus increased the deprivation of those who were unemployed or living on drastically reduced incomes.

When Bennett's "blasting" failed him, and the worsening crisis continued to worsen (not reaching rock bottom until 1933), Bennett began to feel that he was struggling against a conspiracy of impossible forces. When he increased aid to the provinces, King denounced him for "fiscal irresponsibility." When he refused to go further, other critics complained of his heartlessness. Bennett complained that too many people were looking to government to "take care of them". He said that the "fibre of some of our people has grown softer and they are not willing to turn in and save themselves." But what could they do? It was clear from Bennett's own mail that a large number of people — independent producers — were completely powerless to avoid the utter destitution into which they had fallen. A man wrote from New Brunswick that the family fishing schooner had been sold because the price of fish had fallen too low to repay the cost of fishing.

Another sufferer from Saskatchewan said he had to grow six times the wheat in 1932 to get the same dollar return as in the 1920s. But in the 1930s, because of continuing drought, he grew nothing at all. For such personal reports of hardship, there was a note of sympathy and a $5 bill from Bennett's own pocket as a token of consolation.

Bennett did care. He did feel pain whenever he heard that people were holding him personally responsible for the Depression. He was hurt by farmers who called their horse-drawn Fords "Bennett buggies" because they could not afford the price of gasoline. He was also angered because the urban unemployed were naming their shanty towns in garbage dumps "Bennett boroughs". But Bennett continued to believe that he was doing everything possible. The problem was that unscrupulous opportunists were exaggerating the trouble for their own advantage.

By 1932, Bennett was thus ready to change his strategy from "blasting a way into the markets that have been closed" to blasting radicals. When 3000 unemployed protesters descended on Ottawa, they were met by city police, the RCMP , and a military armored car. So excessive was the reaction, even Conservative newspapers such as the Ottawa *Journal* described the encounter as a "scene that smacks more of fascism than of Canadian constitutional authority." But the repression of radicalism did not diminish.

The single unemployed men of Canada were recruited for removal from the cities to bush camps. There they were put under military discipline and worked for 20 cents a day, sometimes at meaningless tasks such as building roads that ran nowhere, or airstrips for aircraft that never landed. In 1935, an army of the "Royal Twenty Centers" left the camps in droves and gathered in Vancouver demanding work for 50 cents a day. Failing in this demand, they boarded eastbound freight trains to take their complaints to Ottawa. On Dominion Day, the "on to Ottawa" trek was stopped at Regina. There, in an enormous confrontation with police, hundreds were arrested with an approving public calling them "Reds" or "Bums". Bennett called them "criminals".

Fear of communism was leading the federal government to resume the wartime censorship of books, and increase the postwar deportation of "dangerous foreigners". The Department of National Revenue looked for subversive literature; the RCMP monitored the declining labor movement for vulnerable aliens or seditious native-born leaders. When domestic socialists such J.S. Woodsworth attacked the government's anti-radical campaign and demanded repeal of the relevant provisions of the Criminal Code and the Immigration Act, the Conservatives at first refused to debate the justice of repression, then answered that the laws on sedition were "not in any sense a hindrance to any right-thinking person."

But a growing minority of Canadians were not "right-thinking". They viewed the Depression as the final proof that capitalism had failed and that the country needed a different kind of system, one in which all "means of production and distribution, including land, are socially owned and controlled either by voluntarily organized groups of producers and consumers, or ... by public corporations responsible to the peoples' elected representatives." Repudiating the basic premise of acquisitive individualism, they demanded an economy geared toward "the supplying of human needs instead of the making of profits."

Such criticism was common in the 1920s, as was shown in the previous chapter. But in that more prosperous decade, radicals struck at a system that was better able to withstand the assault. Then, the critics of capitalism were more likely to be denounced as "visionaries" and their organizations were endured if not tolerated. In Toronto alone there were a dozen such groups. British Columbia supported three. But in the Depression, the possibility of proscription of radicals loomed ever larger as growing numbers of the middle class demanded that attacks on the economic system should be postponed until the economy recovered.

Fear of repression as much as hope of recouping losses prompted the leaders of the various radical groups to agree that their survival depended upon forgetting their many past differences and working together in a federation of the whole noncommunist left. J.S. Woodsworth played the leading role in the initiative from his office in Ottawa. By August of 1932 he had persuaded delegates from most of the radical farmer and labor groups to meet in Calgary and discuss federation in more detail. One observer of the Calgary gathering commented that the delegates "oozed idealism to the detriment of practical experience." What bothered him was their commitment to a political philosophy. No national party in Canada had ever subordinated a program to a stated philosophy so completely (even Mackenzie King, always unctuous about his "Liberalism", was guided more by caution and opportunism than by principle). Moreover, the name that most of the delegates gave to their philosophy was *socialism.*

Over the winter of 1932-33 the idea of bringing radical groups together proceeded to specific consideration of particular proposals. A draft platform was acquired when Frank Underhill, a Toronto university professor, drafted a document to present to a convention to be held in Regina in August 1933. In final form, the platform of the new Co-operative Commonwealth Federation began with a ringing affirmation that capitalism was bankrupt:

> We aim to replace the present capitalist system, with its inherent injustice and inhumanity, by a social order from which the domination and exploitation of one class by another will be eliminated, in which economic planning will supersede unregulated private enterprise and competition, and in which genuine democratic self-government, based on economic equality will be

possible. (Quoted in K. McNaught, *A Prophet in Politics: A Biography of J.S. Woodsworth* [1959], p. 321.)

The platform closed with the lofty promise that "No CCF government will rest content until it has eradicated capitalism and put into operation the full programme of socialized planning which will lead to the establishment in Canada of the Co-operative Commonwealth."

Subsequently, the CCF was denounced by unrepentant capitalists for naked communism. But the CCF's clear commitment to democracy made it difficult to prosecute its leaders for "seditious conspiracy". More importantly, the National Chairman of the party was J.S. Woodsworth, a member of the House of Commons of twelve years' standing. Saint or subversive, Woodsworth was too prominent to turn into a martyr. For this reason, his presence in the leadership of the CCF gave democratic socialism a legitimizing focus that it had lacked before.

But it was one thing to launch a radical movement that was not vulnerable to criminal prosecution, and quite another to persuade a majority of the people to vote for it. On the other hand, the 1930s were so economically depressed it might have been expected that the Depression was the most likely occasion for the mass of the people to have responded to radical criticism of their former employers' economic system. By the year that the CCF came into existence, perhaps as much as half of the *industrial* labor force was unemployed. Workers who did have jobs, found that their average hourly pay had fallen by roughly two thirds, but the tariff had stabilized prices at about 70 percent of pre-Depression levels. To survive, the unskilled who could find work were employed longer hours (the sixty-five hour week of thirteen hour days was not uncommon). Then there was the plight of fishermen and farmers, supposedly better off because they were classified with the "employed". But prices of their commodities were so low, their work was almost totally unremunerative. No wonder, therefore, that hundreds of CCF associations were formed across the country within a few months of the establishment of the party that promised to eliminate economic hardship completely and forever. Before the end of 1934, the CCF had become the number two party in British Columbia and also Saskatchewan. There were CCF members sitting in most of the other provincial legislatures and the CCF was winning municipal elections.

R.B. Bennett feared that a CCF snowball would develop into a socialist avalanche, and decided to halt its momentum by movng his own party in the direction of reform. He had already taken a few short steps toward reform by launching some reorganization of banking and promoting a new system for marketing natural products that was reminiscent of that which had been employed during the war to sell wheat through a government board. But both measures signified a piecemeal approach and avoided the wage-price spread that had become an issue in Bennett's own party and some Conservatives (led by H.H. Stevens) were preparing to abandon the Tories in the name of securing a more thorough "Social Reconstruction".

Bennett made his move in January 1935 by taking to the air waves without prior consultation with cabinet or caucus to announce "The old order is gone." He said, "It will not return... I am for reform." With the loftiness of a Woodsworth, Bennett asserted that "There can be no permanent recovery without reform." Then came his messages describing a fresh deal of the cards for the Canadian people: unemployment insurance, minimum wages, and a promise of tax reform.

Some of Bennett's party thought their leader had converted to socialism, but the Prime Minister was careful to make clear that he was trying to free capitalism of its "harmful imperfections", to preserve the system, not to repudiate it. Unconvinced by Bennett's recent conversion, Liberals denounced Bennett's New Deal as nothing more than a pre-election ploy, legislation to charm the voters and regain a mandate, followed by an apology later and that it was all unconstitutional. Thus, Mackenzie King — in his usual indirect manner — asked Bennett to

> tell this House whether as leader of the government, knowing that a question will come up immediately as to the jurisdiction of this Parliament and of the provincial legislatures in matters of social legislation, he has secured an opinion from the law officers of the Crown or from the Supreme Court of Canada which will be a sufficient guarantee to this House to proceed with these measures as being without question within its jurisdiction. (Quoted in J.M.S. Careless and R.C. Brown, eds., *The Canadians* [1968], p. 262.)

The question of constitutionality nothwithstanding, five measures covering unemployment insurance, minimum wages, maximum hours, and marketing boards limped through Parliament before dissolution.

The election that followed in October was one of the most interesting — and revealing — in all of Canadian history. The electorate was asked to pass judgment on the question of reform after nearly six years of some of the most harrowing deprivation ever experienced. There was a full spectrum of alternatives. On an innovation continuum, the four leading national organizations ranged from the CCF on the left which promised to "eradicate capitalism", through Stevens' Reconstruction Party that would champion small business, through the Conservatives advocating moderate reform, to the Liberals on the right who pledged themselves to "no precipitate action". In this sense, the election of 1935 was a public opinion poll on how much change the Canadian people thought that the country needed.

The CCF was the largest of the reform parties that advocated radical change. In general terms, they stood on Underhill's two-year-old Regina Manifesto. Their timetable for implementing the program was the novelty of 1935. They promised to nationalize the country's banking institutions first, then use the government's financial power to initiate public works that would end unemployment. The rest of the nationalization of industry would follow gradually thereafter. But such a summary misses the dimension of vengeance with which Canada's socialists advocated their reforms. In one pamphlet, bankers were compared to thieves with the assertion that "Bank Robbers get millions, but the BIG SHOT BANKER IS A BIGGER CRIMINAL THAN THE GUNMAN because the banker's greed hurts all the people all the time." Another was even more blunt in its call to "Smash the Big Shots' Slave Camps and Sweat Shops." In other words, the CCF called on the masses to avenge their hardships as much as to vote positively for economic transformation.

Less vengeful than the CCF was the splinter of the Conservative Party that aimed to reform the system in order to save it but proposed a program of changes that went far beyond Bennett's New Deal. This was the faction that rallied around H.H. Stevens in 1934 and formed their own independent group after dissolution in July 1935. Calling themselves the Reconstruction Party, they proposed a fifteen-point manifesto "to help reconstruct Canada's shattered national policy, to wage war with poverty, and to abolish involuntary idleness." But they stopped short of repudiating acquisitive individualism and advocated a revitalization of small business. Seeing government as an agency to step in when free enterprise faltered, they denounced all notions of centralized planning as "schemes of rigid control of life and organization."

Mackenzie King's Liberals were conspicuous for their dissociation from all reform. Privately, King knew that he was affirming a "policy of having no policy" but publicly his position was assurances for "no precipitate action" saying he refused to institute reforms that were likely to be declared beyond the power of Parliament. But King did not advocate any changes in the BNA Act either. Attempting to appear unruffled by the fact that the capitalist system was in trouble, King said he was for caution. Liberal advertisements stated his position well in four words: "It's King or Chaos."

Here then were the major alternatives for the electorate in 1935: the eradication of capitalism by the CCF; major changes in the organization of large-scale capitalism by the Reconstruction Party; moderate reform with more of Bennett's New Deal; or no change at all in King without chaos. Given the voting behavior of the 1920s, and given the desire for action that might have been inherent in the length and severity of the Depression to 1935, the most understandable prospect was for a minority government headed by King or Bennett. But such did not occur. The more outspoken the party for reform, the more repugnant it was to the electorate. The CCF and Reconstruction groups each received less than 10 percent of the popular vote, the CCF electing only seven members (none east of

Manitoba). Bennett won 30 percent. King's Liberals received 45 percent. The rest went to other minor parties, some to the left of the CCF, some to the right of the Liberals. But the 2 million votes polled for King's party translated into 173 of the 245 seats in the House of Commons — one of the widest majorities in Canadian history.

What can be inferred most easily from the 1935 election results (interpreting them as a public opinion poll) is that nearly half of the Canadian people were not very interested in innovative approaches to the problems of the unemployed. If nearly half of the people were in dire straits, the other half had jobs and perhaps it was these who returned the party that promised to do nothing. In 1935, as in 1930, the Canadian people, in common with most of the Western World, showed little support for innovation. The point was evident in the drift of national politics. On the provincial level, the voters were even more interested in parties that promised hard restoratives, that is, a way to get back to the good old days rather than in experimentation to make a break with the past.

## III    The Restoration Theme in Alberta

One of the most interesting variations of the restoration theme in provincial politics was the enthusiastic response of Albertans to something called Social Credit, an economic theory developed in the 1920s by a British engineer, Major C.H. Douglas. His doctrine was a conscious repudiation of socialist collectivism, while at the same time promising to cure capitalism by providing the solution to the problem of poverty amidst plenty. The great gear that Douglas said was askew was the tendency of cash incomes to individuals always to be less than the aggregate cost of goods for sale, a flaw that he expressed in his "A plus B theorem". Douglas divided (theoretically) all of the cash flows of society into A payments (the payment of money to individuals in the form of wages, salaries, and dividends) and B payments (the flow of cash to organizations for raw materials, bank charges, and other costs). Then he reasoned that "The rate of flow of purchasing power to individuals is represented by A, but since *all* payments go into prices, the rate of flow of prices cannot be less than A plus B." The solution seemed equally clear: "a portion of the product at least equivalent to B must be distributed by a form of purchasing power which is not comprised in the description grouped under A." These were the social credits, the dividends that producers had earned for producing more than they were able to consume.

There was a seductive common sense logic to Social Credit theory from the standpoint of the middle class in the context of the Depression. It was a point that another British theorist, the economist John Maynard Keynes, appreciated when he argued that the fiscal pump of capitalism could be primed by increased government spending to employ people on massive public works, thus restoring their purchasing power. In fact, it was Keynesian theory through the back door that finally brought about recovery through the vast public works project that was the Second World War.

But five years before the war it was Albertans who were singularly attracted to Social Credit, and it was a panacea that they embraced with all the enthusiasm usually associated with religious revival. In part, this was because Major Douglas and his economic theories were woven into the sacred texts of an already influential radio preacher, "Bible Bill" Aberhart.

In the 1930s, Alberta was unusually rural, uniformly Protestant, and remarkably homogeneous since it was the most recently settled, and so many of the newcomers to the province were farmers and ranchers from the United States. Since Alberta was also one of the provinces most hard-hit by the Depression, the Alberta agrarians were doubly troubled by their fixed indebtedness and drastically falling prices. Thus, Alberta was a devoutly Protestant, predominantly rural and agrarian society deeply in trouble. The first impulse was to renew the faith in the old-time religion: if they promised to forsake drink, dancing, and movies, then the Lord might do his part by improving the weather and the price of wheat and beef. But no miracles followed.

Then over the winter of 1932-33, "Bible Bill" began to expound Social Credit doctrine along with his fundamentalist Christianity from the radio studio at the Calgary Prophetic Bible Institute. In this way, the word spread to thousands of listeners. Study groups were organized, and Aberhart became an inspiring teacher as well as the spiritual leader of everyone in radio range — southern Alberta, part of Saskatchewan, and some of Montana.

Throughout 1933, however, Social Credit was still no more than an object of study, not a political movement. The first entry into formal politics did not come until January 1934. At that time, the governing party of Alberta held a convention at which delegates presented the new theory and urged the government to give it careful consideration as a program for recovery. Several months later, the Committee of the Whole House did consider the idea of social dividends. Aberhart testified. Even Major Douglas made an appearance. But the leaders of the United Farmers of Alberta remained skeptical. This, and the involvement of the premier in a sex scandal, convinced the star of the Prophetic Bible Institute that it was time to launch a Social Credit movement with the government of the province as its goal. Aberhart announced in December 1934 that in the next election "reliable, honourable, bribe-proof businessmen who have definitely laid aside their party political affiliations, will be asked to represent Social Credit in every constituency."

Aberhart's announcement was a significant revelation because it showed his conception of the political undertaking as a nonpartisan crusade. Rather than creating a political party in the conventional sense, Aberhart intended to strike a holy alliance of all right-thinking Albertans to purge the province of the political professionals, raise the standard of public morality, and bring about recovery. It was time for "reliable, honourable, bribe-proof businessmen" to succeed where lesser mortals had faltered.

Once Aberhart set his course toward the winning of political power, he dropped the style of the evangelist teacher and stressed his intentions more than the details of the "A plus B theorem" or other doctrinal nice-ties. "You don't have to know all about Social Credit before you vote for it," he said. Aberhart urged his followers to have faith and trust in the authorities. Reasoning by analogy, Aberhart suggested that "you don't have to understand electricity to use it, for you know that the experts have put the system in, and all you have to do is push the button and you get the light." So also with political decision-making, "all you have to do about Social Credit is to cast your vote for it, and we will get the experts to put the system in."

Many people felt that "Bible Bill" would not knowingly deceive them. He was an authority they could trust. Others, the ones who decided to read his pamphlet, the *Social Credit Manual*, discovered that there were even more attractions than the economic promise. They found a wonder-ful instrument for abolishing poverty without compromising the purity of the rural ethic. Every adult was going to receive a monthly $25 dividend but any citizen who "persisted in refusing work" would have his divi-dends "cut off or temporarily suspended." Since the credits were not a premium on idleness, they were touted as a powerful bulwark for the enforcement of the full system of middle-class standards of propriety. Any person who "squandered his dividends... or was improperly clothed" would receive first a warning from his inspector, and the offender would reform his habits and shine his shoes or he would lose his dividends.

The end of poverty without repudiating capitalism and a greater con-formity to the old standards of manners and morals were promised within eighteen months of the election. For some Albertans, the soft totalitarian-ism in Social Credit was a major attraction. For others, it was the $25 per month. For still more, Aberhart was simply an attractive novelty. What-ever the precise combination of motives, the electorate awarded his group of "bribe-proof businessmen" a stunning majority of nearly 90 percent of the seats in the legislature. Two months later in the federal election, Alberta returned a similar proportion of Social Credit members to Ottawa.

On the day after the provincial triumph, a number of people called at Calgary City Hall for their first $25 dividend. But it was not forthcoming then or later. By 1936, Aberhart was ready to regret that he had ever heard of Major C.H. Douglas and his "impractical" theories. "Bible Bill" had discovered that there was simply no way to follow social credit doctrine without simultaneously freezing prices and repudiating the existing debt of the province. This Aberhart considered immoral. But there were a number of insurgents in "his" legislature who demanded a trial of social dividends regardless of the consequences. Thus emerged the Alberta Social Credit Act of 1937 that provided dividends to the amount of "the unused capacity of industries and people." Later in the year, a variety of other such measures followed. But since most of them pertained to banking, an area beyond provincial jurisdiction, the spurt of Social Credit legislation was subsequently referred to the Courts by Ottawa and found to be *ultra vires* before the measures could be implemented. What carried permanence was fiscal orthodoxy and Protestant fundamentalism. On this basis, in the words of Aberhart's chief lieutenant and eventual successor, E.C. Manning, Social Credit provided Alberta with "one of the most genuinely conservative governments in Canada."

## IV   The Restoration Theme in Quebec and Ontario

Conservatism in the sense of aiming to restore and preserve a pre-1929 status quo was the main emphasis of other provincial governments that came to power at the same time as Aberhart's. Quebec and Ontario, two provinces that together included 60 percent of the country's population, provided variations of the restoration theme that were as striking as the Alberta case. In Quebec, the province in which social strife was ethnic as much as economic, the impulse to escape the Depression by restoring the simplicity of the vanishing past gave rise to a pattern of resentment that was nationalist more than reformist. By 1935, a nonpartisan Catholic social action group called *Ecole sociale populaire* proposed a *Programme de restauration sociale* to meet the cisis with diverse restoratives emphasizing the need to encourage a movement of people from the cities back to the land (correcting the alleged evil of overindustrialization) and restoring public credit by funneling the profits of the private utility companies to the public purse through nationalization. When the incumbent Liberal administration of Alexandre Taschereau did not rush to adopt such a program of social restoration, a dissident group rallied to Paul Gouin and formed a third party called the *Action libérale nationale*. Since Gouin was himself the son of a former Liberal premier, the movement could not be ignored. But the politician who observed the disintegration of the Liberals with the keenest interest was the leader of the minority Conservatives, Maurice Duplessis. Carefully, step by step, he maneuvered the Catholic social action group and the dissident Liberals into an alliance with himself, working like Honoré Mercier to unite Liberals and Conservatives under one nationalist banner. Late in 1935 the *Union nationale*, emerged — a party with no pretensions beyond Quebec and no program other than to govern for the people rather than the "trusts". The leader of the new party, Maurice Duplessis, promised to fight nepotism, patronage, and corruption, and he used anti-trust rhetoric but without making any specific proposals for nationalization of particular firms. Once in office in 1936, it was therefore easy for "le chef" to set his own course without taking action against the privately owned utility monopoly, Montreal Light, Heat and Power (as some had expected) or to further any other program of social democracy. Duplessis proved to be as good a friend of enterprise — foreign and free — as any businessman could want. The premier did spend a good deal of money promoting new agricultural settlement in keeping with the theme that "our salvation is rooted to the soil." Also consistent with the idea that "we must sow or go jobless, our people will be agricultural or perish," he turned his back on the problems of the urban poor, especially the suffering unemployed in Montreal, still Canada's largest city.

From another point of view it could be argued that the *Union nationale* paid a great deal of attention to the urban proletariat because it saved them from Godless Socialism. In 1937, Quebec's legislature passed an "Act Respecting Communistic Propaganda" — a measure that empowered the police to lock up any establishment that was used for "propagating Communism or Bolshevism," terms that were left undefined, and which, therefore, were completely dependent upon the interpretive discretion of law enforcement officers. Defenders of "le chef" such as Lionel Groulx applauded his action asserting that the happiest people are those who have "found their dictator," but civil libertarians argued that Quebec's "Padlock Law" was thought control. People were being prosecuted for the content of their ideas rather than for the violence of their behavior.

At the time the Padlock Law was passed in Quebec, Mitchell F. Hepburn in Ontario moved with similar zeal against radicalism after having come to power in 1934 as a maverick Liberal defender of "the little guys" against the "big shots". The people "Mitch" promised to help were still businessmen, however. It was to the small, independent producers — especially farmers — that Hepburn pledged his deepest devotion. Addressing one typical audience in 1934, a group of dairymen, Hepburn asserted that they had to live by one set of rules but the "big shots" lived by another. "If any of you farmers water your milk you go to jail. But if you water your stock you get to be Premier of Ontario." Mitch said he would change that as soon as he was in charge.

Hepburn was not elected to make it legal for dairy farmers to water milk, but a dismantling of privilege was expected and in several superficial ways did follow. The new premier auctioned off some government limousines and he fired all the civil servants hired in the year before his election. He reduced the salaries of the personnel in the remaining civil service and cancelled a number of contracts with hydroelectric companies. All such stunts were bold theatrics, but none of it assisted "little guys" in the sense of industrial workers or the unemployed. Later, when labor attempted to help itself, Hepburn struck with the same vengeance as Duplessis fighting radicals in Quebec.

The specific episode that provoked Hepburn's rage was the contest that developed in 1937 between the emerging Congress of Industrial Organizations (CIO) and the well established firm of General Motors. Both were American organizations, one a militant federation of industrial unions, the other a branch plant auto maker. But when a labor dispute began in Oshawa over management's refusal to recognize the connection of the United Auto Workers with the CIO, Hepburn came to the side of General Motors in the name of Canadian nationalism. He said that Canada's troubles had never been as bad as outside agitators had made them appear and denounced the tactic of "sit-down" strikes. Then, despite assurances from the leaders of the union and the mayor of Oshawa that there would be neither sit-down occupation of the plants nor violence at the gates (as had happened recently in Detroit), Hepburn requested a battalion of RCMP from Ottawa and recruited four hundred of his own special police, soon called "Hepburn's Hussars", to break the CIO in Oshawa. Thus, in Ontario, as in much of the rest of the country, the specter of radical action prompted repression; in this case it was repression of a crisis that did not even exist.

## V    Ten Lost Years

Here, then, were some of the more striking aspects of Canada's responses to the Great Depression. It was a period of hardship that generated enormous concern. But the flamboyant characters who commanded the greatest popularity had two attributes in common: they saw the economic crisis as a temporary setback in the development of capitalism, and believed that no recovery could be valid or permanent if it violated the fundamentals of possessive individualism. The dissenters from orthodoxy were a minority without a hope of gaining power as long as the paranoid fear that was a function of hard times held Canadians in its icy grip. The radical leaders of the 1920s not only lost ground in the 1930s, some even lost their freedom. The period was a time when Canadians, especially the unemployed, had to think very seriously about the structure of their society and the role of their institutions. Some reasoned their way to radical criticism. But most people never lost their jobs, and although they were not unaffected by the crisis, they preferred to escape into the wonderful world of the Dionne quintuplets, Walt Disney's *Snow White and the Seven Dwarfs*, Hollywood musicals, or radio entertainments that were designed to soothe a troubled world. Most Canadians remained "right-thinking" people who hoped for a return of the good old days even though the old days had not been particularly good or easy to recover. Everywhere but on the silver screen, the past was irretrievably *Gone With the Wind*.

# Bibliography

The volume in the Canadian Centenary Series that covers the period of the Great Depression is not yet published. Other general works are available, however. H.B. Neatby, *The Politics of Chaos: Canada and the Thirties* (1972) is a brief but comprehensive overview, too sympathetic, perhaps, to Mackenzie King. Less general, but more thorough on economic issues, is A.E. Safarian, *The Canadian Economy in the Great Depression* (1959), particularly useful for the relationships that are established between the staple trades and secondary manufacturing. For the general human impact of the Depression, James Gray, *The Winter Years* (1966), L.M. Grayson and M. Bliss, eds., *The Wretched of Canada: Letters to R.B. Bennett, 1930-35* (1971), and M. Horn, *The Dirty Thirties* (1972), all provide richly evocative autobiographical material.

On the subject of business-government relations, Tom Traves, *The State and Enterprise: Canadian Manufacturers and the Federal Government* (1979) and James Struthers, "Prelude to Depression: The Federal Government and Unemployment, 1918-29," CHR (1977) both provide useful background to the Depression — Traves on the failure to create the regulatory state and Struthers on the abortive attempt to implement unemployment insurance. After 1929, of course, there were new pressures for both kinds of reform to save capitalism. This theme is developed fully by Alvin Finkel in *Business and Social Reform in the Thirties* (1979). For material on Bennett's "New Deal" in particular, see Donald Forster and Colin Read, "The Politics of Opportunism: The New Deal Broadcasts," CHR (1979) and J.R.H. Wilbur, *The Bennett New Deal* (1968).

On the development of radical alternatives, Michiel Horn, "The League for Social Reconstruction and the Development of a Canadian Socialism, 1932-1936," JCS (1972) discusses the formation and development of the group that has been called the "brains trust" of the CCF. *Anatomy of a Party* (1969) by W. Young examines the larger aspects of the CCF and its program during the thirties. For the story of radicals to the left of Woodsworth's group, see Irving Abella, *Nationalism, Communism and Canadian Labour: The CIO, the Communist Party and the Canadian Congress of Labour, 1935-1956* (1973).

For radicalism on the other side of the political spectrum, the most useful works are those that are addressed to the appeal of the flamboyant right-wing premiers of the period. C.B. Macpherson, *Democracy in Alberta: Social Credit and the Party System* (1953) is the most penetrating in his analysis of the reasons for Aberhart's success. Dupplessis is examined by C. Nish, *Quebec in the Duplessis Era: Dictatorship or Democracy?* (1970) and H.F. Quinn, *The Union nationale*, revised edition (1979). M.F. McKenty, *Mitch Hepburn* (1967) although less analytical than either Nish or Mapherson, is still addressed to the subject of right-wing populism, in this case, in Ontario. M. Ormsby describes the British Columbia variant in "T. Dufferin Patullo and the Little New Deal," CHR (1962). The exceptional case was Manitoba where the government of John Bracken was able to enjoy a unique continuity from the twenties through the thirties. Since Bracken enjoyed political success without resort to the right-wing demagoguery of the others, it is worth comparing the Manitoba case with Alberta, Ontario, Quebec, or British Columbia. See John Kendle, *John Bracken: A Political Biography* (1979).

"... an industrial worker in 1941 earned twice as much
as in 1939, and he or she was twice as likely to be a
member of a union."

# CHAPTER 21

# Recovery by War

## I   Twilight of Depression

Although the economic crisis of the 1930s made Canadians more acutely aware of the insecurities of life in an industrial society, most people continued to think that an individual's privation or prosperity was his own responsibility. Thus, there was no consensus for the social insurance Bennett proposed. Nor was much credence given to the view that massive government spending on public works was an appropriate means of controlling the fluctuations of the business cycle. Between 1930 and 1937, the interesting legislation pertained to banking, broadcasting, and transportation — the creation of the Canadian Broadcasting Corporation (1932), the Bank of Canada (1935), and a national airline (1937) — not social welfare.

After his return to power late in 1935, Mackenzie King kept his promise of "no precipitate action." This meant no social legislation and limited government expenditure. In keeping with both promises, his budgets were restrained and the Bennett New Deal (repudiated at the polls) was referred to the courts. At the same time, immediately after the election, King appointed a National Employment Commission to find means of reducing the burden of subsidizing the relief payments by provinces to the unemployed. The law officers reported before the unemployment commissioners, and the court decisions reinforced the principle that social legislation fell under provincial jurisdiction. The "peace, order and good government" clause in Section 91 was interpreted as an emergency power preventing the Dominion from legislating in areas already allotted to the provinces except in time of war, pestilence, or famine, and therefore the Bennett New Deal was deemed to be almost entirely unconstitutional. Instead of proceeding directly to change the BNA Act, King appointed a commission to study the matter. Headed by N.W. Rowell (who was soon succeeded by Joseph Sirois because of Rowell's failing health), the Royal

Commission on Dominion-Provincial Relations was to examine "the economic and financial basis of Confederation and the distribution of legislative powers in light of the economic and social developments of the last seventy years." With such a broad mandate, their work could not be completed in a matter of a few months. Thus, the Prime Minister gained a period of years, perhaps, in which he was excused from proceeding further with constitutional changes.

Unfortunately for King, the National Employment Commission made fiscal recommendations that demanded immediate attention. Cutting themselves free of traditional economic theory, they espoused recovery remedies advocated by John Maynard Keynes. The Keynesian formula for dealing with recession was tax cuts and deficit spending on the assumption that a modern government should concern itself with balancing the whole economy rather than the budget. A wise government would spend more when private investors invested less and recover such deficits by tax increases and budget surpluses as the economy recovered. When the National Employment Commission endorsed Keynesian economics, the recommendation led to a dangerous split in the government over the budget of 1938.

Norman Rogers, the Minister of Labour, demanded a minimum of $40 million for public works and threatened to resign if the advice of the National Employment Commission were ignored. But Charles Dunning, the Minister of Finance, was equally insistent in his defense of the traditional theory that demanded budgetary restraint in recession. With two ministers thus threatening to quit if his own will did not prevail, others took sides and Mackenzie King faced a crisis that he eventually resolved in the manner of a biblical patriarch: Rogers' demand was cut in half, giving him $25 million to spend in the way that the Employment Commission had recommended, but since the resulting deficit was only half the original minimum, Dunning and his side were not utterly defeated.

The budget compromise of 1938 emerged thus as a significant step from traditional practice. According to H.B. Neatby, "it was the most radical and most constructive innovation of that depression decade." But the half-step toward deficit spending for recovery purposes was soon dwarfed into insignificance by enormously greater borrowing for an infinitely vaster, more startling emergency — that of World War II.

## II    Mobilization for War

Canada's participation in the Second World War from  September 1939 was somewhat anomalous from a combat standpoint. In the beginning, as a matter of policy, the country's liability was said to be "limited". The Prime Minister declared that no "great expeditionary forces of infantry" would be sent to Europe as in the Great War before. It was hoped — and expected — that the allies would be content to make use of Canada's food and industrial resources more than the country's manpower. At first, Britain made little use of either. The British responded to the Canadian offer of help in the autumn of 1939 with a modest request for a program to train aviation personnel and token orders for military equipment. But in the spring of 1940, after the Germans' lightning advance across the Low Countries, the fall of France, and the nearly total abandonment of the British Expeditionary Forces' equipment at Dunkirk, orders for replacement material poured into Canada, and the single division sent to England at Canada's initiative in 1939 was reinforced with several more before the end of the year. To facilitate the growing involvement of Canada in the war, a National Resources Mobilization Act provided for complete planning of the economy by the Department of Munitions and Supply headed by C.D. Howe. The economic control extended to the rationalization of labor, of course, to assure that adequate manpower was available for essential industries and the armed forces. With regard to military recruitment, the NRMA permitted conscription, but for home defense purposes only. The manpower going overseas was to consist of volunteers exclusively.

The voluntary system was expected to be adequate for overseas combat because the troops were not going to be utilized on a full-scale basis. Canada did have approximately the same percentage of the population in uniform as did Britain but a significantly smaller percentage of Canada's forces were committed to fighting. The bulk of the army spent most of the war in England as a "dagger pointed at the heart of Berlin," according to their commander, Major-General A.G.L. McNaughton. But the army was a dagger drawn rather than a weapon bloodied. The personnel trained and retrained while the fighting went on elsewhere without them.

In the early years of the war, Canadian combat personnel were to be seen most frequently in the air or escorting convoys across the Atlantic. The two major exceptions were the nearly 2000 infantrymen killed or captured in the defense of Hong Kong late in 1941 and a similar number who met the same fate in the reconaissance raid on Dieppe in August 1942. Thus, Canada had mobilized for total war without seeming to fight accordingly. The result was that just one third of Canadian war production was utilized by Canadian forces. Britain was the consumer of two thirds of the tanks, artillery, and rifles made in Canada. To imperialists such as Arthur Meighen, it was disgraceful that Canada had not turned immediately to wholehearted commitment of the infantry to fight with the "Tommies" in North Africa, for instance. In Meighen's view, the reservation of the Canadian army in England demonstrated that the Prime Minister was driven by a cowardly fear of the domestic consequences of imposing conscription for overseas service.

King's avoidance of large-scale infantry combat until the end was in sight was a judicious way of avoiding civil war with Quebec, but King's commitment to total effort in war-production demanded a measure of centralization and control of the economy that did create unrest in dominion-provincial relations, and led to maneuvering that reflected anything but cowardice on King's part. In 1940, the Rowell-Sirois Commission submitted its report with the chief recommendation that Ottawa should assume full responsibility for unemployment compensation in order to ensure a uniform standard of relief in every province. Since the assumption of such a responsibility would cost a great deal, it was also recommended that the provinces should surrender their power of direct taxation to Ottawa, with the central government transferring back sufficient funds to maintain provincial administration and other social services. In this way, each province would retain control over its cultural, civil, and educational matters, but in social security each would become an administrative district of a unitary state. King recommended acceptance of the proposition for the sake of the war.

The unity proposed in 1940 proved no more forthcoming than in Macdonald's day, however. Consequently, King exploited the wartime emergency to circumvent the disappointing rejection of the Rowell-Sirois Report by the provincial premiers at a conference early in 1941 that broke down after only three days' discussion. The Minister of Finance, J.L. Ilsley, simply implemented the direct-taxation recommendation on his own — provincial objections notwithstanding. Federal, corporate and personal income taxes were raised so high no province would dare to superimpose its own taxation on top of the new national levels. Having forced them out of the field, Ilsley then offered the premiers two kinds of compensation: they might receive back from Ottawa the amount collected in direct taxation the year before, or claim an amount sufficient to pay the net cost of servicing the provincial debt plus a special subsidy. In this way, the first taxation "rental" agreement emerged as a federal imposition with the provinces settling for what they were given, rather than as a negotiated settlement. The consolation to objecting premiers was the knowledge that the central government's monopolization of direct taxation was temporary, for it was supposed to terminate one year after the war's end.

The recommendation of the Rowell-Sirois Commission regarding unemployment compensation was implemented through the back door with similar dispatch. King's problem was that the adverse court decisions of the previous decade meant that the BNA Act would have to be changed before the unemployment insurance scheme could be implemented, and the change was desired in 1940 because employment was nearly full and the recently re-employed were developing a renewed interest in labor organization, exactly as during the previous war boom. The question was whether they would become equally restive in the next postwar slump. To prepare for such a development, unemployment insurance was to be instituted during the period of full employment to accumulate a large fund in preparation for the expected "hard times" ahead. To this end, the provincial premiers were polled one by one in private correspondence. Then having obtained the premiers' consent for the sake of the war, a joint address of the Senate and House of Commons was submitted to the Government of Great Britain and a new power was added to Section 91 in 1940. With the BNA Act amended, the appropriate legislation went through the Canadian Parliament without controversy in the summer of 1940.

## III    Left Turn

Reform and recovery were proving embarrassingly simple. Between 1939 and 1941, the GNP increased 47 percent as the output of primary commodities doubled and levels of secondary manufacturing trebled. All was directly attributable to federal spending. The government that had spent $322 million on relief during the entire decade of the Depression, spent the same amount in an average month for the war between 1941 and 1943. Thanks to the war, an industrial worker in 1941 earned twice as much as in 1939, and he or she was twice as likely to be a member of a union. Should such persons suffer the misfortune of layoff in the future, earnings after 1940 were at least partially insured.

The war bonanza seemed conclusive evidence that a modern government could orchestrate the peaks and troughs out of the business cycle. There was full employment, a blanket price freeze prevented inflation, and rationing moderated scarcities in such commodities as gasoline and tires. There was also a kind of austerity that followed from shortages of imported liquor and cotton. But such privations affected everyone, not just the jobless or farmers as in the Depression. The important point was the apparent efficiency with which government took control of collective resources and seemed to manage them competently for the shared goal of victory. Naturally, many people came to the conclusion that if a country could spend billions fighting wars and plan the economy for the good of that cause, the same bureaucracy might also control production to ensure peacetime prosperity and promote the general welfare by adding other social security programs to unemployment insurance.

There was a dramatic indication that such opinion had grown to major proportions by 1942 when Arthur Meighen stepped down from the Senate, assumed the leadership of the Conservative party, and sought support from an Ontario riding that had voted Tory in every election since its creation in 1904. Meighen staked his fortunes on his supposition of widespread resentment over King's having mobilized the country for total war without fighting accordingly. He demanded conscription and coalition government. His opponent, a socialist highschool teacher named Joseph Noseworthy, suggested that Meighen wanted the same kind of war as in 1914 and would probably administer the same transition to peace that he had presided over in the 1919 postwar period. Noseworthy countered Meighen's manpower demand with a call for "conscription of wealth" and won 159 of 212 polls in York South — the first CCF victory east of the Prairies and in Toronto of all places.

Meighen's initial reaction to his defeat was to denounce his opponent for unfairly smearing him as a defender of predatory capitalism. Meighen felt he had been "pilloried as a cold and burnt-out reactionary." But once he recovered from his sense of personal injury, Meighen speculated that the York South contest was a fair indicator of the future. Meighen predicted even more success for the CCF in industrial areas after the war. He reasoned that if the Liberals could be confined to Quebec, the Conservatives might command the plurality of Parliament by sweeping the West and the rural East. In order for the strategy to succeed, however, he would have to resign from the leadership in deference to someone with a proven record in the West, and that someone might be John Bracken, Premier of Manitoba since 1922.

Other Conservatives feared that Meighen's strategy would turn their party into little more than a voice of rural protest, and met in an unofficial and unauthorized gathering at Port Hope, Ontario to discuss policies that would enable the Conservatives to lay claim to a middle position between the CCF and the Liberals. Affirming their faith in capitalism, they mapped out a program of reforms that went beyond King's accomplishments to date in assuring every Canadian "a gainful occupation and sufficient income to maintain himself and a family." More specifically, the "Port Hopefuls" went beyond unemployment insurance and called for more "social legislation" in areas such as low-cost housing, collective bargaining, and medical care.

Arthur Meighen subsequently denounced such thinking as the "main cause of the progressive decrepitude of nations", but in a matter of weeks the new eastern Conservatism was being endorsed by Bracken himself, an old-time agrarian. Since Meighen continued to believe that Bracken was the only leader who might fulfill his Western strategy, Bracken's evident romance with social legislation would have to be tolerated. But the Manitoba premier laid down other conditions that were equally disturbing. He said that the party would have to change its name and Bracken also insisted that his nomination would have to flow from harmonious general consent rather than from a bloody convention battle. Meighen dreaded adopting a platform "merely for the sake of votes" and he also disliked a change of name that suggested that the Tories were joining Bracken more than he was coming over to them. Meighen's dilemma was that Bracken remained the only potential leader who seemed likely to sweep the West. For this reason, all of Bracken's demands were more or less conceded and a newly labeled *Progressive* Conservative party was born.

## IV    A Comprehensive Strategy

Meighen's defeat in Toronto, the emergence of Progressive Conservatism, and two other influences prompted Mackenzie King to move his Liberals with the evident leftward swing of public opinion. The two other incentives were external factors, one British and the other American. The British influence was a plan for postwar social reconstruction that the government commissioned from Sir William Beveridge. The Beveridge Report recommended a complete system of public insurance to protect all aspects of Britons' health, employment, and retirement "from the cradle to the grave".

Since the public seemed manifestly receptive to the concept, Mackenzie King received the Beveridge Report as an echo of his own book, *Industry and Humanity*. There, he believed, one would find "pretty much the whole program that now is being suggested for postwar purposes." It was enormously satisfying for King to believe that his earlier work was finding a rendezvous with destiny.

The other influence in making up King's mind to push social security legislation arose from a conversation he had with the American President in December 1942. Somehow the two old politicians wandered onto the subject of the probable future of postwar domestic politics and Roosevelt speculated that "The thought of insurance from the cradle to the grave ... seems to be a line that will appeal." Then, as one pro to another, FDR intimated to King that the two of them should "take that up strongly."

Before the end of the year, a social scientist from McGill University was given the assignment of preparing a Beveridge Report for Canada. Leonard Marsh and his team worked as if they had no time to spare and completed a first draft of their *Report on Social Security for Canada* in mid-January of 1943. They summarized the main features of existing social programs, suggested refinements of the pension and unemployment insurance acts, and outlined new schemes including a health insurance plan and the idea of cash allowances for families of so much per child. Altogether, the Marsh Report was truly a "charter of social security for the whole of Canada" and created a stir of controversy on publication in mid-March of 1943.

Some of the critics of the plan considered it "socialistic". Indeed, the League for Social Reconstruction (sometimes called the "brains trust" of the CCF) had issued a similar report in 1935 under the title of *Social Planning for Canada*. But there were vast differences evident in the two approaches to planned intervention for social welfare. The assumption that ran through the Marsh Report was the idea that there was enough wealth in Canada to deal the whole population into certain securities that were at present limited to the wealthy and the middle class. Only they had the individual resources to protect themselves against unemployment, sickness, and old age. Marsh contended that a minimum standard could be assured to everyone if the government of Canada were willing to administer "properly integrated" schemes of insurance and public works to protect well-being and "purchasing power". In the Marsh approach to planning, the maldistribution of income and production for profit were both left undisturbed in the sense that there was no declaration of intent to impose a ceiling on incomes (as *Social Planning for Canada* had proposed in 1935) nor was public ownership endorsed as a more efficient means of maintaining levels of investment and therefore employment (another LSR-CCF position in 1935). Since both omissions were painfully evident to the socialists of the country, *Canadian Forum* suggested that the Liberals' endorsement of social security on the Marsh plan was simply "the price that Liberalism is willing to pay in order to prevent socialism."

It was well that King did preoccupy himself with socialism in 1943, however, because the "CCFers" — not Progressive Conservatives — appeared to be the Liberals' main rival for popularity. Early in August, the CCF won 34 of the 87 seats in Ontario's legislature. One month later, Canada's socialist party appeared even more popular and the trend appeared to be growing right across the country. In the first Gallup Poll in Canada, in 1943, the CCF appeared to be one percent ahead of the other two parties with 29 per cent of the decided votes.

Mackenzie King responded to the leftward swing of public opinion by writing in his diary that he was satisfied that "the mass of the people" seemed to be "coming a little more into their own." His only "regret" was that "it is not the Liberal party that is winning the position for them." But he imagined that the defect could be rectified if he enacted the right sort of social security legislation before the next general election. He might yet prove to "the great numbers of people ... that I have been true to them from the beginning of my public life." With that intent, he drafted a Throne Speech in December proclaiming that "a national minimum of social security and human welfare should be advanced as rapidly as possible."

Having pledged his party to specific action, something was needed for the new session of Parliament beginning in January 1944. King's problem was where to start. At first he favored legislation for a national health insurance scheme. But such an innovation would require the cooperation of provincial governments and the medical profession. Its implementation meant negotiation and controversy, and King dreaded both. One by one, other items of social legislation were ruled out for the same reason. Ultimately, he seized upon the family allowances scheme even though it had seemed "sheer folly" at first thought.

One attraction of family allowances was that it could be implemented without any cooperation from the provinces since the grants would be direct payments to individuals at so much per head. Other attractions were that it provided several ways of confounding the Tory and socialist opposition. Since the family allowance was to be paid on a per child basis, socialists could be expected to support it as a suitable method for adjusting incomes by need. But since organized labor, like business, insisted that workers should be paid according to skill — a principle that the Liberals also supported — it was possible that the debate over the family allowance might confuse the left by provoking divisions between socialists and organized labor. Equally important, the scheme was certain to anger the Tories because families were to be rewarded in proportion to size. Quebec was still the province with the highest birthrate, and the Tories could be expected to denounce the plan as a bribe to keep Quebeckers solidly Liberal.

Quebec's loyalty to the Liberal party needed additional support because the continuing threat of conscription for overseas service loomed ever larger as the final months of the war approached and the government at last committed the whole army to combat. The invasion of Europe was expected at any moment in the spring of 1944. Once the army was commited to such a bold adventure, casualties would mount and it would be difficult to withdraw forces simply because volunteer reinforcements were not forthcoming. If conscription proved necessary to maintain the strength of the army in Europe, a chain of promises extending back to 1939 would collapse and Quebec would surely hold Mackenzie King responsible for betrayal. Thus, a special gift for the province with the largest families might have been expected to make the difference between success or failure at the next election.

The event that caused King finally to introduce his family allowance scheme was not a crisis in Quebec, however. The determinant of King's timing was disaster in Saskatchewan. On June 11, 1944 — five days after the allies invaded Europe — the CCF won a clear majority in the province hardest hit by the Depression and Saskatchewan emerged with the first socialist government in Canada. Three days later, King brought the family allowance scheme before cabinet for presentation to Parliament in July. In this way, he hoped to provide a dramatic demonstration that his party's commitment to social security was genuine before conscription was imposed and before there were any more dramatic advances by the CCF.

The opposition — especially the Conservatives — were completely cornered. To oppose the scheme seemed to deny commitment to social reform on their own part, but to approve the bill would virtually guarantee the Liberals' re-election. On one line, they lamely asserted with John Diefenbaker that "We believe in social legislation ... . No political party has a monopoly in that direction." But on another line, they had to denounce the measure as "legal bribery". A Toronto Conservative, Herbert Bruce, went furthest in denouncing the proposal by accusing King of "bonusing families who have been unwilling to defend their country." The scheme was a "bribe of the most brazen character," said Bruce, "made chiefly to one province and paid for by the rest."

While it was true that Quebec did have a higher birthrate than the rest of Canada, the government produced evidence showing that Quebec's expected receipts of the family allowance would not be out of proportion to their contributions of federal revenue. Quebec contributed 34 percent of the taxes, and was expected to collect just 33 percent of the family allowance benefits. The government did admit that Ontario, contributing 47 percent of the revenue was likely to collect only 29 percent of the allowances but the difference was to subsidize the Maritimes and the Prairies, not Quebec. In the end, the real issue seemed to be the rectitude of subsidizing motherhood and a happy childhood, and since Herbert Bruce absented himself from the House of Commons the day the crucial vote was taken, the family allowances bill passed unanimously.

The first payments of from $5 to $8 per month (depending upon the age of the child) were scheduled to begin on July 1, 1945 because a general election was expected in the interim. King explained in his diary that he "did not like the idea of spending public money immediately before an election ... People were likely to be more grateful for what they were about to receive than anything they might be given in advance."

## V    Right Turn

Canada's twentieth general election was set for June 11, 1945 once it was clear that the war had reached its final days. King knew that if the election occurred before the defeat of Hitler, the Conservatives' one issue, conscription, would do serious damage to the Liberals' chances of success outside Quebec. King's timing could not have been better. Hitler shot himself in his Berlin bunker on April 29 and the German High Command surrendered unconditionally on May 7. By election day, the war in Europe was thus already history. The Liberals had a great deal about which they might have claimed credit for their successful handling of Canada's war effort. One year longer in duration than the Great War, the Second World War involved a Canada with 50 percent more population but cost 66 percent fewer infantry casualties. Surely that was an achievement worthy of recognition. But the Liberals turned their backs on the war issue and went with a slogan that was incongruous as well as audacious, King asked everyone to forget about the last ten years and "Vote Liberal for a New Social Order".

True to prediction, the Tories backed away from their earlier advocacy of the social security state and posed "opportunity and prosperity" as the preferred alternative to the "rationed scarcity of the socialistic state, or the elaborate and burdensome system of social security which the Liberal party is seeking to create." Their big issue was still conscription since the Conservatives guessed that the vast majority of Canadians wanted one last burst of mobilization to avenge the humiliation of the defenders of Hong Kong by working wholeheartedly with the Americans in the war that was still being fought against Japan. As the election unfolded, the PC's stand on conscription proved to be the greatest miscalculation in their party's history since they sank to 27.4 percent of the vote — their lowest ever.

But the CCF performed even more poorly, winning just 15.6 percent of the votes. What had ruined their fortunes since their apparent lead in September 1943? According to J.L. Granatstein, the CCF was defeated by King's successful reinstatement of the Liberals as the credible center party. King was the experienced leader, and it was he "who had pushed through the great social reform program that more than anything else secured the Liberals their majority." In large part, however, the program was but one measure, the family allowances scheme. Since the promise of the Throne Speech of 1944 was still quite unfulfilled, how could the electorate trust King to finish that which he had first promised in 1919, completely forgotten during the last postwar period, and also through the Depression?

Gerald Caplan suggests that the evident preference for King developed *despite* his past record. In Caplan's view, the CCF was defeated because it was victimized by the "most formidable and devastating campaign in Canadian history." In the autumn of 1943, Canadian business began an expensive and well organized advertising blitz to convince Canada that the CCF was a party completely unlike the others. Canada's socialists were depicted as advocates of "the sort of system they have in Germany and Russia, where the government takes everything away from you and tells everybody what to do." The climate of fear they generated was so all-pervasive that even *Maclean's* magazine began to hint editorially that the CCFers were totalitarians in disguise. Voters could switch from one legitimate party to another but, in the case of the CCF, *Maclean's* warned that "you can't 'try' socialism" on the same basis because "it can work only when socialists are permanently in power which means that opposition couldn't be tolerated." Because of such propaganda, Caplan argues that the voters were systematically frightened away from the CCF without truly knowing what they were rejecting.

The irony of the smear campaign is that the CCF was far more moderate in 1945 than in any of the previous elections in which the party was a factor. There was no rhetoric of "eradicating capitalism" as in 1935. Indeed, the socialism of the CCF was so muted by its own version of the social security state, some voters might have wondered whether it mattered to vote for them. For this reason, the CCF may have been as damaged by its own voices of moderation as by the "nonpartisan" critics who called them Canadian Nazis. The end result is that half of the people who said they were going to vote CCF in 1943 voted Liberal in 1945, and the author of *Industry and Humanity* was returned to power with a clear majority.

Subsequently, King did not complete the work that was outlined in the Throne Speech of 1944; no system of cradle-to-grave social security was forthcoming in 1946 or in King's lifetime. Moreover, King's new evasiveness was accomplished without criticism except from the CCF. This fact suggests that the country may have been leaning far less left than the polls of 1943 seemed to indicate. It may be that the apparent preference for the CCF only indicated a conservative desire to preserve the wartime prosperity that seemed implicit in the social security promise. By 1945 the vast majority of Canadians were probably sick of military discipline, wartime control, high taxes, and enormous government expenditure. Most voters looked forward to a new era of unregulated bonanza. Had the Tories stressed their opportunity and prosperity platform more (remaining completely silent on the issue of conscription for the war against Japan) it is possible that the results of the election would have been remarkably different because after 1945 it was the Tories' platform that the Liberals in fact gave the country. The unfinished aspects of the social security state continued to haunt the electorate for the next generation, but each time it was the CCF that expressed the demand, and in each election after 1945 they lost popularity, slipping to 9.5 percent by 1958. The vast majority of the country seemed content with random prospertiy and each individual's finding his or her own security. The Liberal promise of a new social order was thus quietly forgotten and forgiven as everyone scrambled for a share of the postwar boom. What survived the war better than the concept of a comprehensive social security state was a pattern of wartime alliances, particularly those which led to renewed dependence upon an imperial power.

# Bibliography

The volume in the Canadian Centenary Series that covers the domestic impact of the Second World War is Donald Creighton, *The Forked Road: Canada, 1939-1957* (1976). Another comprehensive general work, well illustrated but emphasizing the military history is W.A.B. Douglas and Brereton Greenhouse, *Out of the Shadows: Canada in the Second World War* (1977).

Works addressed to the prewar consititutional dilemma and the wartime breakthrough are Frank Scott, *Essays on the Constitution: Aspects of Canadian Law and Politics* (1977) and G.F.G. Stanley, *A Short History of the Canadian Constitution* (1969). Scott's volume contains a particularly excellent essay on "centralization and decentralization" and Stanley's offers a useful summary of the Rowell-Sirois Commission's recommendations and the utility of the war in promoting this position despite the premiers' offical rejection of it.

For the emergence of *Progressive* Conservatism, J.L. Granatstein's *Politics of Survival: The Conservative Party of Canada, 1939-45* (1967) is an account that covers both the background and the futile aftermath. John Kendle's study of *John Bracken: A Political Biography* (1979) tells substantially the same story, but from the point of view of the groom in the marriage of convenience.

Mackenzie King's drive to restore the Liberal Party to the center position is developed in another book by Granatstein, *Canada's War: The Politics of the Mackenzie King Government, 1939-45* (1975). Granatstein argues that the triumph of the Liberals in the election of 1945 was largely the product of King's personal skill in directing the war and his timely promotion of the social security state. Gerald Caplan attributes more importance to the two-year anti-CCF campaign promoted by business in *The Dilemma of Canadian Socialism: The CCF in Ontario* (1973). Two works that confront the issue of the postwar decline of the CCF are Walter Young, *The Anatomy of a Party: The National CCF, 1932-61* (1969) and L. Zakuta, *A Protest Movement Becalmed* (1964).

"... Churchill, Roosevelt, and King were photographed as a controlling threesome."

# CHAPTER 22

# Continental Solidarity

## I   A New Relationship with Uncle Sam

The Second World War prompted the implementation of social insurance programs welcomed by many as signs of "social progress". But the emergency that facilitated social development led to regression in external relations in the sense that the country traded sovereignty for security and the new dependence outlasted the war since the "Nazi threat" was almost immediately followed by the new danger of "Soviet expansion". Because resistance to both enemies was almost universally agreed to in Canada, the new colonialism tended to be advertized as international cooperation rather than subordination. But such celebration had to be rather muted because the security obtained in a world of balanced terror after 1945 was more illusory than real. Moreover, Canadians had recently prided themselves on being at the forefront of that development that had led the "autonomous colonies" of Great Britain to become partners in a community of nations. And since Canada had led in the erosion of the old colonialism without repudiating Great Britain, a nice fiction of a British Commonwealth of Nations survived.

In 1917, Prime Minister Borden had insisted that the Imperial War Conference of the Great War change its nature to recognize the constituent members as the equals rather than the subordinates of Britain. It was Borden again who, at the peace talks in Paris, had led in the campaign to have the Dominions sign the Treaties in their own right. And it was Borden's successor, Arthur Meighen, who played the leading role at the Imperial Conference of 1921, causing Britain to abandon the renewal of a treaty between Japan and Britain dating from 1902 that was a pact between countries as empires.

Nor were the Liberals less hesitant in the further development of Canadian autonomy between 1921 and 1939. It was under Mackenzie King that the Chanack incident took place in 1922. In that year a clash between Turkey and Greece in Asia Minor threatened to provoke British intervention, and Britain simply assumed, as in 1914, that Canada would automatically become involved. King decided otherwise and let it be known that his country saw no reason for involvement. A year later autonomy went one degree further when Canada signed a fisheries treaty with the United States without any imperial input at all. And by 1927 an independent Canadian diplomatic presence had been established in Washington as a first step toward making wider ambassadorial links with the world at large.

Such initiatives were not unacceptable to the former mother country. In 1926, in the wake of the King-Byng affair, the Imperial Conference produced the Balfour Report in which the Dominions were defined as "autonomous communities..., equal in status, in no way subordinate one to another in any aspect of their domestic or external affairs ... ." As if that were not sufficient declaration of independence, the words were embodied in law in 1931 by the Statute of Westminster. In this way, Canada and the other autonomous Dominions won their right to an independent foreign policy having already established their right to independence in every other respect.

As the likelihood of a second Great War in Europe loomed after 1935, Mackenzie King used the newly won Canadian autonomy to avoid "entanglements"; he made it particularly clear that in any future war Canada would be "at Britain's side" but not necessarily in the trenches. As a result, in 1938, when Britain recommended that Canada cooperate in a joint program for training aviators in anticipation of possible war, King refused. Canada acknowledged a formal liability if the British were to find themselves entangled in another struggle with Germany but the Canadian Prime Minister meant to imply passive belligerence, not participation as a principal as in the 1914 war. It came as no surprise, therefore, that Canada hesitated before joining Britain and France when they declared war on Germany on September 3, 1939.

Four days elapsed before the Canadian Parliament convened to debate a war resolution of its own. And when Parliament did agree to participate, King announced it would be Canada's policy to provide "effective cooperation" within stated limits. The primary military effort would be home defense.

Soon, however, Canada's liability was extended as King responded to popular pressure for greater involvement. He announced on September 16 that one division would be sent to England. Three months later, on December 17, King announced the program that was supposed to be Canada's major contribution to the war — the British Commonwealth Air Training Plan.

As was shown in the previous chapter, the war was most important to Canada for its usefulness in bringing about recovery from the Great Depression. For some, particularly those Canadians who continued to cling to a strong British orientation and loyalty, the lack of a more robust militarism was regrettable, even cowardly. The first such critic of Mackenzie King was Mitchell Hepburn, the Premier of Ontario, who thought he was speaking for the vast majority of his province when he moved his legislature in January 1940 to condemn the central government for not joining the war in "the vigorous manner the people of Canada desire to see." King responded to Hepburn's jingoism by noting in his diary that it was "just what is needed." Parliament was dissolved on January 24, 1940 and the nineteenth general election unfolded as a plebiscite on King's policy of limited liability. To Hepburn's surprise, the electorate confirmed King's rather than the opposition's position. It appeared that the voters wanted no repetition of the 1914 war. The Liberals won 52 percent of the popular vote and three quarters of the seats in Parliament.

But within months of the 1940 election, the nature of the conflict changed dramatically. The "Phoney War" during which few hostile acts had occurred was suddenly succeeded by the *Blitzkrieg* and the total collapse of France and the evacuation of the British Army from Dunkirk. As German bombs rained down upon British cities, an expectation of defeat developed as the island seemed incapable of holding out for long. It was against such a background that Canada became abruptly receptive to overtures from the United States. On a Friday afternoon in August 1940, Franklin Roosevelt telephoned Mackenzie King and arranged a meeting of the two leaders to take place in Roosevelt's private railway car on the next day in nearby Ogdensburg, New York. In their one meeting on August 17 the two chiefs decided that they would form a joint defense for North America. The purpose was supposed to be self-evident so no rationale was elaborated. Similarly, since it was so manifestly advantageous for the defense of the whole continent then and forever its duration was also left open.

Despite the informality of its inception, the Ogdensburg Agreement was of momentous importance. According to Donald Creighton, one single step taken by a Canadian prime minister without consultation with cabinet or consent of Parliament "effectively bound Canada to a continental system and largely determined Canadian foreign and defense policy for the next thirty years." Under the circumstances, however, such a consolidation seemed eminently sensible — at least for the duration of the present crisis. For the same reason, less than one year later — but still before the United States entered the war actively — there was another accord between King and Roosevelt that was just as sweeping; the second was to cover economic consolidation. The Hyde Park Declaration of April 1941 was the economic corollary to the Ogdensburg Agreement because it stated that "each country should provide the other with the defence articles which it is best able to produce." By this means, Canadian arms producers could bid on American contracts just as if they were firms in the United States and provide "certain kinds of munitions, strategic materials, aluminum, and ships" for the Pentagon with access accorded to no "foreign" country. For the purposes of defense production, King and Roosevelt agreed to pretend that the border between the two countries simply did not exist. In effect, Mackenzie King was elevated to the status of governor of an American State. Here, also, King has been accused of reckless surrender while his defenders suggest that the step was as necessary as it was bold. In this case, the necessity was a balance of payments crisis.

By late 1940, Canada was producing hundreds of millions of dollars worth of arms per month for shipment to Britain. Since approximately one third of the components for war materials had to be imported from the United States, and since Britain was completely unable to obtain its arms on a cash and carry basis from Canada, Canada's loans (later gifts) created a dreadful drain on Canadian dollars to the United States. The solution to the problem was for the Americans to meet many of their own defense needs by purchases in Canada. Since the Hyde Park Declaration solved the balance of payments problem, J.L. Granatstein has argued that the agreement "saved Canada's bacon." Still, the continentalism of the arrangement was undeniable.

If King had fought like Borden to win a measure of control in the councils of war after the United States entered the conflict as an active belligerent (in December 1941), the subordination inherent in the continentalism of the Ogdensburg Agreement and the Hyde Park Declaration might have been considerably muted. But since Churchill and Roosevelt found it difficult to make even the merest of counsultative gestures toward Russia, France, or China, and regarded such consultation with the junior governments of North America as patently absurd as well as unnecessary, the State governments and that of Canada were thus excluded from the Combined Munitions Assignment Board as well as from the Combined Chiefs of Staff. For this reason, the North American part of the alliance emerged as a merger rather than a partnership. Canada was treated as a subordinate more than an autonomous country and Canadians themselves began to speak of "our leaders, Churchill and the President."

Mackenzie King made pathetic gestures to assert Canadian independence but they were more theatrical than real. Thus, there was a conference at Quebec in 1943 with the flags of the three attending leaders all flying side by side, and Churchill, Roosevelt, and King were photographed as a controlling threesome. But insofar as any conferring occurred, it involved the American and the British leaders, not the Canadian. King's role was that of a person who "lent his house for a party. The guests take hardly any notice of him, but just before leaving they remember he is their host and say pleasant things." Still, the meeting was "good theatre" and King was well satisfied that a second such exercise would be "quite sufficient to make clear that all three are in conference together." The result was that the show was rerun in 1944. There was no need for a third performance. By the spring of 1945, the war ended in Europe, and in the summer American atomic bombs — with plutonium refined from Canadian uranium — ended the struggle against Japan in the Pacific.

## II    A Bolder Repression of Minorities

Despite their subordinate status, Canadians emerged from the Second World War imagining that they had become "a power in the world". In the Great War they were told that they had acquired the spirit of a nation; by 1945 they were supposed to have acquired international stature. A country with relatively small population had emerged in the number three position by industrial production and number four by the strength of its armed forces. Both achievements were a source of great satisfaction tending to obscure the less pleasant subordination and proximity to the number one industrial and military power. Another consolation was that Canada had suffered relatively lighter losses than those sustained in the 1914 war. In round numbers, 17 000 airmen, 22 000 soldiers, and 2000 sailors died in the Second War. For a country of nearly twelve million people such losses were not large: about one third of one percent of the population overall. But here as well, satisfaction over one fact obscured a less pleasant reality, in this case, that there were losses on a larger scale that were not included in the battle casualties, and the other class of injuries were not inflicted by the enemy.

Perhaps the best illustration of the self-inflicted wounds in the Second World War is what Canada did to its own people of Japanese descent. For generations, the British Columbians had been looking for a means of eliminating "Orientals" from their province. Asian newcomers were the objects of mob violence in the nineteenth century and legal discrimination in the twentieth. First there were immigration restrictions and for those already in the country there was a denial of basic civil rights, such as the right to vote. Consequently, when war broke out against Japan in December 1941, racism became "patriotic" and a golden opportunity was seized for the complete elimination of the hated minority. The first steps toward that goal were almost reasonable. Thirty-eight persons suspected of being potential subversives were arrested by the RCMP and interned in accordance with the provisions of the War Measures Act. In each case of detention there were individual causes for confinement. The authorities had obtained certain evidence prior to the arrest of each person involved. But local politicians wanted a broader round-up leading to the internment of the entire population. The army was reluctant to act on such an extreme demand since 13 000 of the 22 000 people of Japanese ancestry in BC were British subjects. To the Chief of the General Staff, Ken Stuart, wholesale internment was unnecessary. "I cannot see that they constitute the slightest menace to national security," Stuart explained. The RCMP agreed. The navy also argued that all persons of Japanese origin were militarily neutralized once they were barred from fishing. But political use of racist extremism prevailed. Beginning in January 1942, the "evacuation" began and the lives of 22 000 people were totally disrupted. Families were divided, friendships ended. Householders lost their freedom and their property and the hearts of children were broken by the authorities who seized and destroyed all family pets. From 1942 until 1945 the detainees languished in camps that were far inland from the coast. Finally, in the spring of 1945, the prisoners were given the choice of settling "east of the Rockies" or "repatriation" to Japan. Understandably, almost half chose exile to the shattered land of their ancestors.

Later, British Columbians paid a measure of penance for their racism by offering reparations for confiscated property to those who had the stamina to go through the elaborate procedures for processing claims. And in 1949, those who returned to BC under relaxation of the previous exclusion order could do so in the knowledge that they would also be able to vote for the first time in the history of British Columbia. In this way, a kind of truce was offered to one injured segment of the population — four years after the war had ended abroad.

No such settlement occurred after another episode of self-inflicted injury involving the two founding nationalities of Canada. The trouble was conscription. King had worked desperately through the summer of 1944 to avoid such a confrontation but in September of that year Conn Smyth, a popular sports personality, then an army officer, returned to his home in Toronto to convalesce from combat injuries. Newspapers naturally seized on the event for its human interest value. At the same time, they printed the hero's explanation why he and so many others were getting wounded. Smyth was quoted to the effect that the General Service troops were being reinforced by other volunteers who had very little training. He said, "large numbers of unnecessary casualties result from this greenness both to the rookie and to the older soldiers who have the added task of trying to look after the newcomers as well as themselves." There were soldiers with more training than the green recruits but they were not being sent overseas. The alternate replacements were NRMA men — troops conscripted for home defense since 1940 (under the provisions of the National Resources Mobilization Act). Since the NRMA men were legally exempt from service outside the Western Hemisphere, they were literally half-conscripts and in the view of a growing number of people in English-speaking Canada they were only half-alive, the real-world embodiment of the characters in Hollywood horror movies called "Zombies". On September 18, 1944, Conn Smyth suggested that the time had come to send the "Zombies" overseas.

Other people joined in the suggestion that the NRMA men were less than "real Canadians". As the country brooded over the dichotomous results of a plebiscite on conscription in 1942 (three quarters of Quebec rejecting, a similar portion of the rest of Canada approving), the French-Canadians were identified as the prime Zombies and a furor developed over the renewed demand to send NRMA men to fight in Europe. The army cooperated by making the number of General Service reinforcements seem dangerously low since the Prime Minister had said repeatedly that there would be no conscription for overseas duty unless it were necessary. When the cabinet divided on the question of current necessity, Mackenzie King replaced the pro-conscriptionist Minister of Defence, J.L. Ralston, with a former commander of the army, then retired. But General McNaughton was soon persuaded by district commanders that his predecessor was correct in his conclusion that the supply of General Service replacements was impossible to maintain by volunteers. When NcNaughton said conscription was necessary, King agreed. By the end of 1944, conscripts were on their way to Europe.

Actually, the necessity was entirely political. It had been estimated that 15 000 reinforcements were needed and there were more than 30 000 available in England and Canada by what Douglas and Greenhouse call "energetic remustering" and "cuts in headquarters personnel" (four percent of American combat troops were assigned to generals' staffs with such duties as running the mimeograph machines, while Canadian generals used 13.6 percent of their men for the same purpose). From this standpoint, the necessity was more artificial than real. But one general suggested that "the troops would not feel that the government and country was supporting them wholeheartedly if ... [it allowed them the NRMA soldiers] to sit comfortably in Canada." Judging by public opinion polls in 1944, the majority of the English-speaking electorate agreed. Consequently, King reluctantly gave them what they wanted. In this way, emotionalism determined military necessity and a chain of promises that ran back to 1939 was broken. Civil war did not erupt, but Quebec did emerge from the crisis more distrustful than ever. Subsequently, voters were offered a rich array of extraordinarily resentful politicians for elections in 1944. The most extreme group was a coalition more nationalist than the *Union nationale,* and more reformist than the *Action libérale nationale.* The new group, called the *Bloc populaire* was led by Maxime Raymond, a former Liberal Member of Parliament. But in 1944 nationalism was more popular than radicalism and the

Liberal administration of Adélard Godbout, elected in 1940 to prevent conscription, was rejected (having granted the vote to women in 1940 and having imposed compulsory elementary education in 1943). The most popular nationalist was Maurice Duplessis, an eloquent proponent of Quebec's autonomy and one who could appear to fight the foreigners without disturbing the established order of the Church and the corporations in Quebec itself. After the return of Duplessis as premier (and Camillien Houde as mayor of Montreal) the most colorful anti-Ottawa champions were thus once again in charge. Of course, the rest of the country reciprocated with a resentment that was equally anti-Quebec if not pro-Ottawa. For this reason, it might be said that the war did irreparable harm at home as well as causing a loss of independence in external affairs. In fact, it might further be said, that the English-speaking Canadians emerged from the war feeling closer to the Americans than to the people of their own federation in Quebec.


## III    Continuing Continentalism in External Affairs

Under normal circumstances it might have been expected that with the end of the war, Canada would have worked to restore the independence that had been lost in the alliance to defeat Hitler. For one reason, Prime Minister King had grown increasingly ill at ease with Americans involving themselves in projects on Canadian soil. A prime example was an authorization by the United States Army for the Imperial Oil Company to construct a pipeline from Norman Wells, Northwest Territories to Whitehorse in the Yukon without prior consent from the Government of Canada or the Native People in the area. King understood the disregard of the Indians, but not of his government. Later, after the Americans sent Canada a bill for 60 million dollars to cover the cost of the pipeline, King told Vincent Massey that he thought the "Canadians were looked upon by Americans as a lot of Eskimos." It was King's opinion that "We ought to get the Americans out of further development there and keep control in our own hands." He believed that the "long-range policy of the Americans was to absorb Canada." King asserted that he "would rather have Canada kept within the orbit of the British Commonwealth."

The implications of King's preference for affiliation with the British Dominions were not clear at the time he expressed this view, however, nor were they clarified in the years that followed because a new emergency kept Canada snugly in the orbit of the United States. On September 6, 1945, a cipher clerk from the Soviet embassy, Igor Gouzenko, turned up on the steps of the Government of Canada with a great wad of documents that proved that the Russians had worked tirelessly to obtain secrets of North American high technology almost from the moment the Russian embassy was opened in Ottawa. The documentation also demonstrated that the spy network included Canadian collaborators. Gouzenko's revelations led to a host of arrests and interrogations in the months that followed, all in secrecy under the authority of the War Measures Act. The United States was alerted and a Royal Commission was struck as a modern-day inquisition. Subsequently, the lives of many people were ruined in the course of investigations that implied guilt. A few, having been released to the secular arm for prosecution and punishment, were sent to jail for their crimes. The convicted spies included a nuclear physicist, clerks and secretaries, and a Member of Parliament (Fred Rose, the one communist in the House of Commons).

The exposure of Soviet espionage in Canada was not the sole cause for the cooling in relations with the Russians. Nor was it the earliest sign of impending tension. But the Gouzenko affair was certainly the most dramatic indication to Canadians that a new era of international crisis was beginning. For this reason, officials had serious second thoughts about weakening solidarity with the Americans.

Mackenzie King did continue to be sensitive about Canadian independence, however. Curiously, he displaced his unease about the loss of independence onto the British by attacking the last "badges of colonialism" from that source. King rallied the country to adopt a "distinctive" flag, to define Canadian citizenship distinct from British "subjecthood", to drop references to Canada as a "Dominion" in public documents, and to end appeals from the Supreme Court to the British Privy Council. All were assertions of nationalism that could be interpreted as long overdue but not all were fulfilled in King's lifetime (the flag, for example, was postponed until 1964, and patriation of the Constitution did not occur until 1982). Moreover, none compensated for the loss of sovereignty by continuing dependence on the United States. In the postwar climate of fear of Soviet treachery and imperialism, however, there were few politicians who were willing to identify American influence as colonialism. The proof that such was the case came in 1947 with acquiescence to an American request to exempt its service personnel in Canada from Canadian law. In statutory form, the favor was the Visiting Forces Act. In effect, the law defined American bases in northern Canada as extensions of the United States itself. Stanley Knowles, a CCF member from Winnipeg, wanted to know why the Americans had not been told that the war was over and it was time for them to go home. Spokesmen on the government side solemnly replied that the President had reason to suspect that the Soviet Union was planning to invade North America sometime before 1950; therefore, the Canadian Arctic was the first line of defense. For this reason, the Joint

Board of Defence was being continued and American personnel were also remaining to watch for the Russians. Knowles persisted: "I think this country at this moment has a supreme opportunity." The chance for Canada was to assert neutrality in the face of bi-polarity. "We can say that we are not going to have United States troops in Canada in peacetime. That would be the first move of any small power against the Truman policy or the Stalin policy." But the CCF and the Conservative members who joined Knowles in neutralism were a small minority. Parliament approved the Visiting Forces Act overwhelmingly and thus conceded to the United States in 1947 what had been properly denied to Britain in 1938. The fear of Soviet aggression was stronger than the wish to regain independence.

But Mackenzie King continued to dread even the appearance of any surrender except that which was deemed necessary for defense purposes. For this reason, he killed a project that Canadian civil servants and their opposite numbers in the United States had brought close to fulfillment in 1948. The idea was to establish something close to North American free trade. When the story leaked to the American press, *Life* magazine reported in mid-March that a "Customs Union With Canada" was likely and endorsed the idea saying that "Canada needs us and we need Canada in a violently contracting World." The *Globe and Mail* snorted "Not on Your Life" in prompt reply. Then King began to fear that the opposition might denounce him in the twilight of his career, in much the same way that Laurier had been condemned near the end of his days in 1911. For this reason, the Prime Minister backed away from the free trade scheme he had previously encouraged.

The defense of the tariff, like the flurry of activity to purge the country of the "badges" of British colonialism, implied a robust nationalism but the demand for independence was not nearly as salient as the dread fear of communism and the willingness to defer to the United States as imperial leader in the "cold war" that Canadians wanted won. For this reason, exactly one year after the Canadian opinion makers had denounced free trade because it was supposed to be a prelude to absorption by the United States, Parliament took a giant step toward surrendering Canada's remaining diplomatic neutrality when it ratified the country's membership in the North Atlantic Treaty Organization.

The *Globe and Mail* and the rest of Canada approved NATO because everyone pretended that the treaty was more than a military security pact. Article 2, proposed by Canada, pledged the signers to "make every effort, individually, and collectively, to promote the economic well-being of their peoples and to achieve social justice." A few visionaries in Canada interpreted the clause as the first step toward general acceptance of "Atlanticism", the notion of a North Atlantic community of nations that might formally federate in the future. Thus, membership in NATO was not denounced as a furthering of subordination to the United States. All parties — including the CCF — approved Canada's joining.

The Canadian pretension that NATO was a United Nations on a smaller scale was not shared by the Americans, however. Their sole concern was for NATO's military effectiveness. Since the United States was also the dominant member, NATO emerged as the military security pact that was wanted and expected, and all participating countries were badgered to perform duties as determined by the Americans. Given the buffer of the Atlantic and the less complete dependence of the European members on the United States economically, the Europeans were in a position to resist or withdraw from such pushiness more successfully than could Canada. As the American Secretary of State, Dean Acheson, explained the facts of life to a stunned Lester Pearson, Acheson had enough trouble with divisions within the United States itself. "If you think that we are going to start all over again with our NATO allies, especially with you moralistic, interfering Canadians, then you're crazy." Pearson did not take Acheson's admission as good reason for Canada to reconsider the NATO affiliation, hoping instead that "quiet diplomacy" — a patient wheedling — might somehow breathe life into the stillborn Article 2. Pretensions to the contrary notwithstanding, a diplomatic revolution had been completed. Canada had traded independence for quiescence in the hope of greater security and the country had fallen dutifully into line as a satellite in the American solar system. Policy regarding China, Korea, the Middle East, and North American air defense between 1949 and 1957 was that of the United States rather than a separate country with independent interests.

## IV    Centralism and Continentalism on the Domestic Scene

The evident continuation of the subordination of Canadian diplomacy to the United States was accompanied by another continuity that was almost equally revolutionary. The other wartime expedient that was continued in the postwar period was the centralization of administration in Ottawa, a change that transformed the provinces from alleged partners in Confederation to "junior governments" of Canada. In large part, the change was nothing more than adjustment to conditions under Canada's emergency constitution, the War Measures Act, a statute that was passed in 1914 but whose potential was not fully realized until the Second World War when the government's planning and control powers were exercised to the maximum. Without needing to worry about provincial obstruction or parliamentary delay, the typical instrument of government became the order in council rather than a statute. More than 6 000 such executive orders were approved by cabinet between 1939 and 1945. They revolutionized the scope of the federal government's activity and led to an explosive growth in the Ottawa establishment. The Government of Canada employed 46 000 people in 1939. By 1945, 116 000 were on the federal payroll. As a result, the new strongholds of Confederation were government departments (Finance, Munitions and Supply, and External Affairs) and the new strongmen were several flamboyant ministers and their deputies — the Ottawa ''Mandarins''.

The problem for the Liberal Party and the national bureaucracy in 1945 was that the sleeping dogs of provincial power were awakening from their wartime slumber. After an extremely short period of yawning and stretching, they soon began to bark and also to bite. Since the civil service elite and the Liberal cabinet fervently believed that centralism was the only way to maintain a rapid rate of postwar economic growth because the control of government expenditure was believed to be the main regulator of the economy, the first task was to persuade the premiers that the Ottawa technocrats should continue to collect three quarters of the revenue and control most of the expenditure. How else could the Keynesian recipe succeed? If provinces and municipalities taxed and spent on the same scale as the government in Ottawa, there was a real danger that fiscal policies would work at cross purposes.

What the Mandarins needed was a constitutional conference to establish in peacetime that which had been grudgingly conceded for the sake of the war. Since the aging Mackenzie King was still prime minister he would preside at the meeting, supported by the wisdom of the nation (arrayed in the row of advisors seated behind him). Even with such high-powered support, could he prevent the conference on ''reconstruction'' from ending in disaster? King was frightened by the political implications of his assignment. To be sure, he had started his own career as a would-be Mandarin, but as King matured he became ever less the wizard and ever more a politician. In 1945, he knew that the premiers would not willingly concede that which was offered in a little green book prepared by the wizards on his adminstrative team. Ontario and Quebec were particularly adamant in their refusal to consider the centralist design. Not surprisingly, the first conference ended in failure. After a nine-month recess, a second such meeting was held in the spring of 1946. When the second attempt also ended in failure, the Department of Finance proposed reimplementation of the Ilsley scheme of 1941. Quebec and Ontario refused to join the new rental arrangement until 1952, at which time Ontario accepted a ''rent'' in return for its power of direct taxation. Quebec joined in 1957 after the carrot of ''equalization'' was implemented as an additional incentive. By the latter scheme, any province could collect up to 10 percent of the federal income-tax for its own purposes. Then, having determined the per capita take in the two wealthiest provinces, the others would receive grants from Ottawa to bring the "have not" group up to standard. In this way, Ottawa was able to maintain its control — or at least to channel — the bulk of the public revenue.

The desire to dominate taxation in the postwar period reflected a renewed resolve by the central government to create a prosperous and united country by the force of national policy, a resolve that survived the transition to peace despite Mackenzie King's continuation in the prime ministerial office. In 1948 King retired to be replaced by Louis St. Laurent, a complete believer in the technocratic gospel that government was more administrative than political, more a matter of developing programs than making platitudinous or visionary pronouncements. The ideal government reacted day to day and developed what needed promotion, or solved the administrative difficulty of the moment. Under St. Laurent, government unfolded in essentially managerial functions in which power was distributed broadly throughout a committee of ministers and leading civil servants. C.D. Howe, the Minister of Trade and Commerce, was hardly less prominent than the Prime Minister himself. Douglas Abbott was supreme in Finance and Lester Pearson won a Nobel Prize for his service in External Affairs. Behind such elected leaders were the less conspicuous but equally important near-ministers: J.W. Pickersgill, Clerk of the Privy Council, Clifford Clark in Finance, and Mitchell Sharp in Trade and Commerce.

The major purpose of the St. Laurent Team domestically was to continue the vigorous, centralizing administration that seemed to have won so much favor during the war. Unruffled by premiers' objections, St. Laurent believed that governments with a tangible presence inspired confidence and loyalty. He believed that Quebeckers, for instance, would judge centralism by the successes of specific projects — gargantuan undertakings such as the Trans-Canada Highway begun in 1948 and the St. Lawrence Seaway (a new system of locks and canals) begun in 1954. Both were intended as major arteries of a new prosperity, the final benefit of centralism. During the war, the economy had grown and changed in ways that the government wished to encourage after "reconversion" to peacetime production. Secondary manufacturing had developed to produce synthetic rubber, sophisticated electronic apparatus, and a vast array of plastics where nothing of the kind had been produced in Canada before. A million newly formed families needed housing and everyone wanted automobiles. Since there was an enormous surge in all areas of manufacturing and construction as well as a rush to develop natural resources such as oil in Alberta, and iron ore from Newfoundland (after the last hold-out from Confederation entered the union in 1949), there was full employment, a doubling of the number of households owning automobiles, and by the mid-1950s massive improvement in housing. Canada sustained the highest birthrate of any industrial country in the world, and immigration reached record levels as 30 percent of all the newcomers attracted since 1867 poured into the country between 1945 and 1955. Surely such indicators of growth, along with the nearly annual inflation-fighting budget surpluses and the yearly net increase of the unemployment insurance fund, suggested that Liberal management had led to tangible benefits indeed.

It was in the midst of a mood of somewhat smug satisfaction that Vincent Massey was commissioned in 1949 to survey Canadian attainments in arts and letters with the purpose of recommending adjustments so that Canadian achievements in the cultural field might blossom proportionately to the country's recent attainments in economic development and population growth. Conducted with the assistance of three academic scholars and a Montreal engineer over the course of two years, the survey was less than encouraging, however. In 1951, the Massey Report provided a vast amount of evidence for the hundreds of ways that Canadian culture was derivative and subordinate rather than distinctive and thriving: no national library (or systematic preservation of public records), no national support for universities, museums, theater, and all popular entertainments such as radio and cinema were almost entirely American in content, theme, and origin.

The Massey Commissioners predicted that Canadian culture would be a lost cause without major and immediate support for the country's authors and cultural institutions. Consequently, they recommended financial assistance for the provincial universities and the endowment of a council to provide grants to individual scholars or institutions such as the Winnipeg Ballet Company. From their recommendations it was clear that the Commissioners were most interested in "high" culture. Nothing they recommended touched directly on "mass" culture. Nor was there much demand for such promotion. Canadians seemed completely satisfied with their Hollywood movies and Ellery Queen mystery stories. As for the higher sort, three cities did maintain symphony orchestras and two supported permanent ballet companies. Louis St. Laurent was skeptical that the performing arts were resources that needed developing; as he put it, the Government of Canada had no business "subsidizing ballet dancing".

Grants to the universities were another matter since they emerged in the postwar period as trade schools for various professions and served an obvious purpose in economic development. Consequently, the Massey Commission's funding proposal for higher education was adopted at once. But six years passed before the central government decided to take an interest in "ballet dancing" as well. By then, with an election approaching, Canadians were alerted to American dominance of another sort.

In 1955 a leading accountant, Walter Gordon, decided to publish his thoughts on the continentalist cost of the policies pursued since the war.

Later, Gordon said he had been "worrying about the government's economic policies and particularly the complacency with which Canadians were witnessing the sellout of our resources and business enterprises to Americans and other enterprising foreigners." In such skepticism, Gordon ran against a well established tradition because foreign investment had been actively encouraged by every government since Confederation. The only prior lament of ruling parties was made in the 1930s, and this was that the inflowing stream of capital was never enough. At the time Gordon began to be bothered about the volume of incoming foreign capital, the stream was a flood, greater than ever before. Since most of the investment was American — the same people to whom diplomatic autonomy had been conceded — Gordon decided that unregulated foreign ownership posed an unnecessary risk to whatever sovereignty remained.

He sent a draft of an article on the subject to a Liberal friend in the government. Gordon's thesis was not markedly different from that expounded by spokesperson for various minor parties since the 1920s. The novelty of the warning in 1955 was the source of the alarm: Gordon was an Ontario aristocrat, not a Western populist; he was part of the same circle that had always sought to foster foreign investment; he was a respectable businessman, not a socialist Jeremiah. On this account, Gordon's yet unpublished article was reviewed with considerable interest. He was asked if he "would mind very much if the government took over" his idea that Parliament should concern itself with regulating foreign ownership. To do so intelligently, however, Canada would need another Massey Commission, this one to look at economic rather than cultural prospects. Naturally, Walter Gordon seemed the ideal person to take charge of the new commission in 1955.

Later, when Gordon tabled a preliminary report in time for the 1957 election, the Government found it was once again on the defensive because even the preliminary findings made clear that the economy was under American domination almost as complete as that of diplomacy or culture. Gordon showed that 70 percent of oil and gas, 50 percent of mining, and 43 percent of secondary manufacturing was then controlled by foreigners. To critics of the Liberal management of Canada, such findings were particularly interesting when taken in conjunction with the survey of the Massey Commission and what was common knowledge in external affairs. The evidence seemed to prove that Canada had been "betrayed" by an administration whose approach to national develpment was so piecemeal that the country was emerging more North American than Canadian. What had gone wrong?

One group of critics suggested that Canada had blundered by turning its back on Britain, diplomatically and economically. Another group had no illusions about the British Commonwealth or diverting attention to England, but they did insist that it made sense to develop a greater measure of independence from the United States for the same reasons that it had been worthwhile to sever the colonial ties to the British.

The Liberal establishment denied that they were promoting any kind of "colonialism", arguing that the evident subordination in external affairs arose from mutual interest rather than domination and the apparent "sell-out" of the economy was purely a matter of market conditions rather than policy preferences. American investment followed from thousands of private choices as Canadians sought to develop the largest possible economy in the shortest time. The problem with the Liberal defense was that it seemed to apologize for imperialism in much the same way that the imperialists of an earlier era had rationalized the ties to Britain. The difference was that the new imperialists made their apology more by negating the nation than by identifying it on a higher level. The turn-of-the-century imperialists had argued that Canada was a stronger country for its developing within a larger imperial system and they asserted that every Canadian felt "pride in the British Empire". The latest generation advanced the same major premise (that Canada was stronger for its integration into the larger system), but no one suggested that a Canadian should be proud to be almost American. Unable to provide a remedy for the growing national identity malaise, by 1957 the Liberals were vulnerable to critics who claimed to know how to nurture Canada's integrity without jeopardizing the postwar prosperity.

# Bibliography

The volume in the Canadian Centenary Series that covers the subject of Canadian-American relations and centralism in domestic affairs is Donald Creighton, *The Forked Road: Canada, 1939-1957* (1976). Another general work that addresses the same themes is R. Bothwell, *et al., Canada since 1945: Power, Politics, and Provincialism* (1981). Readers seeking a less tendentious approach will find relief in C.P. Stacey, *Canada and the Age of Conflict: A History of Canadian External Policies, Volume 2: 1921-1948, The Mackenzie King Era* (1981).

Detailed accounts of particular episodes in external affairs are also available. J.L. Granatstein and R.D. Cuff have published articles on "The Hyde Park Declaration," CHR (1977) and "The Rise and Fall of Canadian-American Free Trade, 1947-48," CHR (1977). Other essays by the same authors (including an excellent article on the formation of NATO) appear in the collection edited by Granatstein and Cuff, *Ties That Bind: Canadian American Relations in Wartime From the Great War to the Cold War* (1977). Their treatment of NATO, and also the account by Escott Reid, *Time of Fear and Hope: The Making of the North Atlantic Treaty* (1977), is far less critical than the version presented in this chapter.

On the subject of the repression of minorities during the war, the accounts of the imposition of conscription on Quebec and the internment of the Canadians of Japanese ancestry in W.A.B. Douglas and Brereton Greenhouse, *Out of the Shadows: Canada in the Second World War* (1977) are brief but comprehensive. The more detailed work on conscription is the book by J.M. Hitsman and J.L. Granatstein, *Broken Promises: A History of Conscription in Canada* (1977). S.M. Trofimenkoff's relevant chapter in *The Dream of Nation: A Social and Intellectual History of Quebec* (1982) relates conscription (and feminism) to the postwar political ferment in Quebec. For the background to the "oriental issue" in British Columbia, see Donald Avery and Peter Neary, "Laurier, Borden, and a White British Columbia," JCS (1977). The same subject through the 1940s is treated briefly by W.P. Ward, "British Columbia and the Japanese Evacuation," CHR (1975) and at greater length in Ward's, *White Canada Forever: Popular Attitudes and Public Policy Toward Orientals in British Columbia* (1978), and Ann Sunahara, *The Politics of Racism* (1981).

A wealth of material is also available on the subject of foreign ownership of the Canadian economy. Works that purport to describe without seeking to alarm are Harry G. Johnson, *The Canadian Quandary* (1963) and A.E. Safarian, "Foreign Investment in Canada: Some Myths," JCS (1971). Works that interpret the issue as a serious national problem are D. Godfrey and M. Watkins, eds., *Gordon to Watkins to You* (1970) and Kari Levitt, *Silent Surrender: The Multi-National Corporation in Canada* (1970).

"What went wrong?"

# CHAPTER 23

# *The Diefenbaker Phenomenon*

---

### I    Televised Sell-Out

---

Critics of Liberal continentalism received a dramatic rallying point in March 1956 when the Minister of Trade and Commerce, C.D. Howe, presented Parliament with a project that was to be the crowning achievement in his long career of projects. He announced that the time had come for a pipeline to conduct natural gas from the oil fields of Alberta to Ontario. The route was all-Canadian across the Prairies and over the Shield, but the private company that was to undertake the task was half-American. In 1954, a Canadian firm had come forward but they balked at the cost of bridging the Shield. Consequently, they proposed a line that would run east as far as Winnipeg, then turn south to the lucrative and easily serviced market of the American Midwest. Central Canada would be more economically served by suppliers running lines north from the United States, they said. Howe objected to the continentalism of the Canadian proposal. He preferred to see Alberta gas exported to Ontario but refused to use the local private sector's reluctance as sufficient justification to develop the Canadian gas utility through a Crown corporation. Instead, he forced a merger of the Canadian with an American firm. In this way, Trans-Canada Pipelines came into existence in 1954 — 50 percent American in ownership, but east-west in mission.

In 1955 a problem arose when the company informed Howe that they were unable to raise enough capital to finance the most expensive section across the rugged and sparsely populated Shield. The solution was to create a Crown corporation just for this third of the project (see map 23.1).

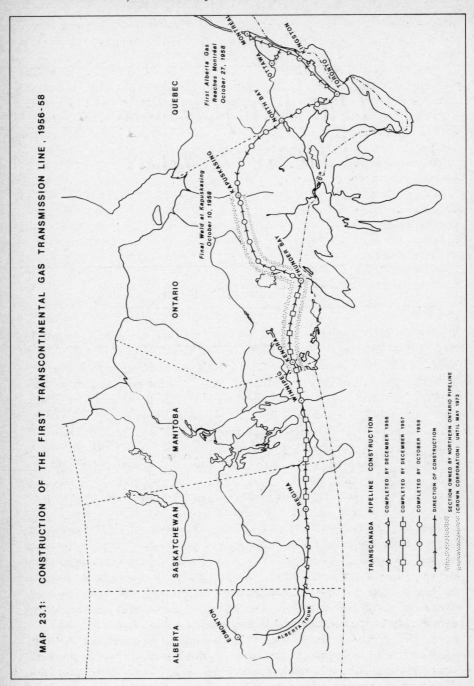

MAP 23.1: CONSTRUCTION OF THE FIRST TRANSCONTINENTAL GAS TRANSMISSION LINE, 1956-58

QUEBEC

ONTARIO

MANITOBA

SASKATCHEWAN

ALBERTA

EDMONTON

First Alberta Gas
Reaches Montréal
October 27, 1958

Final Weld at Kapuskasing
October 10, 1958

KAPUSKASING

MONTREAL

OTTAWA

KINGSTON

TORONTO

NORTH BAY

THUNDER BAY

WINNIPEG

KENORA

REGINA

ALBERTA TRUNK

TRANSCANADA PIPELINE CONSTRUCTION

⟶  COMPLETED BY DECEMBER 1956

⟶  COMPLETED BY DECEMBER 1957

⟶  COMPLETED BY OCTOBER 1958

▲  DIRECTION OF CONSTRUCTION

SECTION OWNED BY NORTHERN ONTARIO PIPELINE
(CROWN CORPORATION) UNTIL MAY 1973

Later, once Trans-Canada was on a better footing financially, the government-owned section was to be sold to the private developers. To create such a firm, parliamentary approval was required.

For C.D. Howe, the ceremonial appeal to Parliament was always the most tedious part of any project since the opposition behaved as if they had the power to influence decisions that were already made. In Howe's view, all their tactics only served to delay the inevitable and it was regrettable to have to waste valuable time in "useless chit chat". Since he was incapable of disguising his contempt, Howe was the chief (but unintentional) contributor to the myth that the Liberals were a group of centralizers, contemptuous of Parliament.

The pipeline was handicapped in the House by the substance of the proposal as much as by the impatience of its principal promotor, however. On the March 9, John Diefenbaker went on the air to condemn a scheme that reserved the "profitable end of the project" to the company and piled the unprofitable part of the undertaking "on the backs of the Canadian taxpayers." On this basis, the project was vulnerable to criticism. And Howe soon gave the opposition even more powerful ammunition.

Just as the proposal was coming up for debate in the House of Commons, the directors of Trans-Canada informed the Minister of Trade and Commerce that their credit was not sufficient to buy the quantity of steel pipe they needed to build the Prairie section in the summer of 1956, but if Howe would agree to the Americans' taking a controlling interest in the company and if he would also agree to an $80 million loan from the Government of Canada to the reorganized firm, the obstacle would disappear. Howe consented and threats of his resignation brought the outraged "Junior League" of the cabinet into line. The greater difficulty was persuading Parliament that the newly complicated proposal was reasonable.

The CCF insisted that the proposed Crown corporation should have control of the entire pipeline and forever. The Tories placed their emphasis on the nationality of the company, arguing that Trans-Canada was analogous to the CPR and ought to be wholly Canadian-owned. Clearly, the two opposition parties had plenty to dislike about the new proposal, but their only unity was a common hatred of Howe's scheme. Still, they could unite to kill the project by talking it to death. In March 1956, a filibuster seemed a reasonable tactic since there were barely three weeks of sitting days left before Trans-Canada's option to purchase pipe from American steel mills ran out on June 7. Surely a matter almost as important as the debate on the award of the contract for the CPR was worthy of this much consideration. What the opposition parties did not know was that Howe was determined to commence construction in 1956 — whatever the cost. To this end, he decided to impose closure at each stage of the legislative process. What Howe and the Liberals failed to keep in mind was the established tradition in Canada of using time limitation only after all details of a measure had been exhaustively debated and it had become clear that further talk was merely obstructionist. In this case, notice was served even before the discussion began. "This isn't the way to run a peanut stand, let alone Parliament!" one Conservative shouted. But all the harangues and points of order availed nothing. The pipeline bill did pass on the June 6, cleared the Senate, and received royal assent with hours to spare.

Howe's triumph was a hollow victory, however, because there was a strike in the American steel industry in the summer of 1956. Without pipe, the progress of the pipeline also halted. When gas did not reach Winnipeg in the autumn as promised, the Liberals were left all the more vulnerable to the charge that their methods were reckless and ineffective. Not only had Howe failed, he had abused Parliament and sold out a valuable resource for the sake of an arbitrary and useless saving of time. In the end, it appeared that a few months were unimportant after all.

The charge of selling out was complicated, and involved more than the nationality of the owners of Trans-Canada. It pertained also to the notion that public utilities ought to be provided as a service by the state. In this case, however (probably because large profits were anticipated), public ownership was considered inappropriate. The *Financial Post* tried to explain that public ownership meant political influence and that would lead to "spur lines to Point Pot Corner and Osmosis Centre" (without indicating why small communities were any less entitled to natural gas than to electricity and why public ownership was suitable for some utilities but not for others). Since C.D. Howe appeared indistinguishable from any other businessman on the public ownership issue, a nagging suspicion lingered that Parliament had been treated with contempt, and something valuable had been given away rather too readily for private advantage. Worst of all, even the people of Osmosis Centre had seen the affair unfold day to day on the nightly news as if they were in Ottawa themselves because they were able to watch reports of the world's events in 1956 almost as they happened over the medium of television. On the stage of the country's electronic boxes, the critics of the government were a main attraction and a sympathetic public sensed that the Liberals had begun to grow old and arrogant in power.

## II   Continentalism on Trial

In the course of the pipeline debate, the Conservative leader, George Drew, exhausted himself and retired from politics on doctor's orders. At the leadership convention that followed in December 1956, the party elected John Diefenbaker, a Saskatchewan lawyer whose Western populism made him seem radical to the Tory faithful that had elected Drew. Diefenbaker was no opponent of capitalism, but the ideal government, in his eyes, dispensed no special favors (even to millionaires), looked after the downtrodden, and defended Canada's British heritage. In a number of ways, Diefenbaker was the man Arthur Meighen had wanted in 1942: exactly the person who might have built the Conservatives' strength in the West, rural Ontario, and in the Maritimes. At the convention, Diefenbaker won grass-roots support from all peripheral sections of Canada. He owed no debts to "eastern politicians or rich men from Bay Street and St. James Street." Nor did he owe anything to Conservatives from Quebec. His supporters were almost exclusively rural or from the urban centers of the West and the Maritimes. To bridge the gap in between, Diefenbaker spoke spaciously about a new spirit of unity, "one unhyphenated Canada". Rather like a prophet for the by-passed individuals or regions of the country, he called his people to a standard that central Canada had forsaken.

Diefenbaker did not have long to wait to launch a crusade to carry his message to the country at large. By the spring of 1957, four years had passed since the last rejuvenation of the government party's mandate. Thus, it was time for another application by St. Laurent's team for a renewal of their lease on power. For the sake of the election, St. Laurent posed once again as "Uncle Louis", the elderly patriarch, lover of children and lecturer on the promise of Canadian development. Any question of an alternate approach to government was dismissed out of hand on the grounds that no other party could develop anything that "we are not already developing." The Liberals' slogan in 1957 was "Unity, Security, Freedom". It directed attention to the material achievements of the recent past and the promise of the immediate future. Like the Conservatives of the early 1870s, the Liberals of the 1950s suggested that their politics were their projects.

In most sections of Canada, the Liberals' projects had worked rather well. C.D. Howe never tired of telling the country that Canada's overall standard of living was second only to that of the United States. Since 1945, the country had slipped from fourth to sixth position in the world of industrial production, but Canada was still number four in the volume of its import-export trade given the booming development of Canadian staples that had followed the war. Ontario and British Columbia garnered the greatest wealth from the new staple exports. Quebec, the Prairies, and the Maritimes were left behind — in the case of the Atlantic provinces and the agricultural West, very far behind. For this reason, many people in Nova Scotia, for example, may have wondered why the Liberals did not help them develop their steel industry before rushing to build the pipeline with thousands of miles of pipe imported from the United States. Similarly, Prairie grain farmers whose net income had dropped by more than 50 percent between 1953 and 1955 probably wondered why the government party (claiming to be developing everything possible) had not devised a plan, along the lines of the Americans', to support the price of wheat domestically, or to support some of Lester Pearson's declarations of good intentions in external affairs with the gift of wheat that was surplus, relative to price, but in desperately short supply given the reality of starvation in the poorest countries of the world.

The Liberals were thus vulnerable to attack for their rather smug assertion that nothing warranted action except that on which they were already working. Diefenbaker did attack them for their smugness, but like Alexander Mackenzie who attacked Macdonald's corruption in 1874, Diefenbaker attacked the Liberals as if their shortcomings were essentially moral and could be corrected by more rigid adherence to right principles. The values on which Diefenbaker placed particular stress were the rights of Parliament (forgotten or systematically abused) and the principle of Canadian autonomy (also violated). The pipeline debate was Diefenbaker's great symbolic issue: "Parliament was made a mockery of at the behest of a few American millionaires." Diefenbaker warned that if the Liberals were returned, "don't ask the opposition to stand up for your rights, because there will be no rights left."

In this sense, Diefenbaker's campaign was strongly negative. He played the role of a Crown attorney seeking the conviction of an especially odious group of offenders. At the same time, Diefenbaker offered redemption as well as retribution. He did speak of a new sense of purpose and revived the image of the "New National Policy". There would be "subventions" (cash grants) for Nova Scotia coal miners, cash advances to farmers for farm-stored grain, significant increases in old age pensions, and government encouragement for greater foreign investment which, under his direction, was promised to return greater benefits to Canada. There was no overall coherence to the package and some commentators suggested that it was dangerously piecemeal, addressed to symptoms rather than to causes. With regard to foreign investment, for example, it was clear that Diefenbaker considered the Liberals' deals dangerous, but he failed to clarify how his own arrangements with "American millionaires" would be different.

What did become clear between April and June of 1957 was the intensity of Diefenbaker's indignation and a growing tendency of the voters outside Quebec to share his sense of outrage. The degradation of Parliament was the theme that Diefenbaker developed with enormous effectiveness over the course of a speaking tour that covered more than 20 000 miles and led him to make approximately the same speech to over one hundred different audiences. The enthusiastic crowds and Diefenbaker's phenomenal sincerity looked especially genuine in film excerpts on television; there was just enough on the nightly news to convey the intensity without the incoherence. In this way, people who saw Diefenbaker only on their television screens might have been even more susceptible to his message than those who saw him in person.

The voters to whom Diefenbaker appealed most were English-speaking Canadians of moderate incomes who wanted rapid development of the country's resources without compromising either the national integrity or democratic processes. Such voters were to be found almost everywhere, though Diefenbaker ignored Quebec. The attitude tended to be reciprocal since the premier of that province professed apathy concerning the outcome even as the election developed momentum elsewhere. When asked to comment on the relative strengths of the parties in Quebec, Duplessis would only say that "the party that wins the largest number of seats will win."

In the rest of Canada, excitement developed over the possibility that the winners might not be the Liberals. Diefenbaker felt confident that he had scored something of a moral victory by the end of the campaign, even though he doubted he would win the election. Similarly, the Liberals expected to lose some of their previously overwhelming majority, but having won the last five general elections in succession they, too, had come to imagine that their return was more or less inevitable. Indeed, they did win the largest share of the votes on June 10, and the CCF did continue its apparently inexorable decline. But the Liberals' share of the seats in the new Parliament fell from 65 to 40 percent: nine Liberal cabinet ministers were defeated, including C.D. Howe. One explained that the "electorate got bored. St. Laurent made it seem so easy to govern Canada that the electorate decided that anybody could do it. And so the people elected anybody." Such smug assurances disguised the more important fact that Liberal representation on the Prairies and in the Maritimes fell from one half to one fifth of their Members of Parliament. Such dissatisfaction in the regions that had benefitted least from the postwar boom had to indicate more than boredom. The question in the summer of 1957 was whether the Parliament of minorities led by John Diefenbaker could implement policies that would serve the forgotten regions better than C.D. Howe's leadership for the business community.

## III    Government Party Vanquished

The Conservatives had been in opposition for over a generation. No member of the new cabinet had shared in the government of Canada before; there was much for everyone to learn about the exercise of power. But two things helped ease the transition from opposition to government. First, the economic situation aided the Tories since the enormous expansion of the economy that had followed the Second World War had begun to decelerate by 1957. The Keynesian recipe for recovery called for tax cuts and increases in government spending. The Tories provided both — not because they were committed to the new economics, but because they had promised to spend more on the disadvantaged and to provide tax relief for the able. Taxes were cut by $178 million; old age pensions were increased from $40 to $55 per month; and farmers were granted a $150 million advance on the sale of farm-stored grain.

The second strength of the new government was the ineptness of the Liberals in opposition. The old team was largely defeated or retired; a new group of younger members that Howe called the "Junior League" remained. Lester Pearson had succeeded St. Laurent in the leadership and soon bungled his new role. Once unemployment took a sharp rise in January 1958, Pearson said that it was no time for government by amateurs. He moved that "in view of the desirability at this time of having a government pledged to implement Liberal policies, His Excellency's advisors should ... submit their resignations forthwith." There would be no need for a dissolution and another campaign. Diefenbaker could yield to Pearson much as King had given way to Meighen in 1926. Diefenbaker responded to Pearson's motion by working himself into a lather on the subject of Liberal arrogance. First, he attacked the Liberals for their apparent desire to govern without the bother of winning support at the polls: "Don't have an election but give us back our jobs" was, he insisted, the Liberal demand. By the time Diefenbaker had finished on his favorite theme, one Member of Parliament was moved to "wonder if the Prime Minister believes in the humane slaughter of animals." But then Diefenbaker followed the first attack with a second revealing that a "hidden report" had been produced by civil servants in the Department of Trade and Commerce while the Liberals were still in power. The document warned that unemployment was the danger facing the country before the previous election. Since the Minister of Finance, Walter Harris, had insisted that inflation was the continuing danger and budgeted for restraint in expenditure, Diefenbaker asserted that Pearson's claims notwithstanding, the Liberals were far from omnicompetent.

With apparent proof of Liberal incompetence as well as arrogance, Diefenbaker had no fear in challenging them to another election. Subsequently, Parliament was dissolved and Diefenbaker returned in February 1958 to the work he loved best. Once again, he confronted the country eyeball to eyeball in what developed as the most emotional campaign in Canada's history. After generations of measuring national health by growth of the Gross National Product, Diefenbaker asked Canadians to strive for more than their country's material expansion. He invited them "to create a new sense of a national purpose and national destiny." Diefenbaker claimed to know the way to a more unified, self aware, and independent Canada. He made cash promises that also conveyed a sense of cosmic purpose: "Jobs! Jobs for hundreds of thousands of Canadians. A new vision! A new hope! A new soul for Canada!" The nation could save its character and reap the material promise of unlimited development. "Catch the vision of the kind of Canada this can be! I've seen this vision; I've seen this future of Canada. I ask you to have faith in this land and faith in our people." Elect a few more Conservatives. "We need a clear majority to carry out this long-range plan, this great design, this blue print for the Canada which her resources make possible."

Of course, some skeptics said that there was no plan, no coherent blueprint, only — in Pearson's words — "quivering clichés or evangelistic exhortations". But others agreed with the Ottawa *Journal* which called the Diefenbaker "vision" an "homage to imagination which makes democracy exciting." They saw a prime minister asking his electorate if they wished to have "one country" developed by themselves in accordance with their own destiny. If so, he was the one to lead them there. It was possible — and in the immediate future through the magic of a Diefenbaker majority. Not since the days of the restoration promises of the 1930s or the zeal of Alexander Mackenzie in 1874 had the electorate been promised so much for so little. Eighty percent of the eligible voters turned out, and 54 percent voted for Diefenbaker's Conservatives. Even Quebec seemed to approve the new nationalism by awarding "Dief the Chief" 50 of its 75 seats. The rest of Canada was even more generous. Overall, 208 of the 265-member House were to sit on Diefenbaker's side. The Liberals and the minor parties were absolutely routed.

## IV     Continentalism Continued

It soon became obvious, however, that the high priest of Canadian nationalism could arouse the people to moral indignation more effectively than he could enact the kind of integrated program he asserted without defining. In the 46 days of campaigning, four central intentions had been indicated: northern development, revitalization of federalism, reduction of continentalism, and restoration of closer relations with Great Britain and the Commonwealth. But in the years that followed, despite his commanding the largest majority in Canadian history, Diefenbaker made measurable headway only with the first of his four declared purposes. There was a promotion of mineral exploration in the Arctic, and road and railway development aiming north. But no northern boom followed. Useful and expensive facilities were provided, but they neither transformed nor significantly altered the shape of the Canadian economy.

Other successes were symbolic or the results of good fortune. In the first category was the Canadian Bill of Rights, a statute of the Parliament of Canada enacted in 1960 and advertised as a guarantee of basic freedoms. The guarantee only applied to matters under federal jurisdiction, however, and the protection provided was indirect to say the least. All persons were said to have certain rights unless Parliament declared otherwise. Future discrimination on the basis of religion, sex, or race, for example, would have to be enacted "notwithstanding the Canadian Bill of Rights." The presumption was that Parliament would find it so embarrassing to include such a declaration in future statutes, everyone would be virtually free from violation. As a Bill of Rights that placed certain freedoms beyond legislative trespass, however, the law was meaningless. In this sense, Diefenbaker's achievement was more symbolic than real.

Another notable success of Diefenbaker after 1958 was a windfall benefit in foreign trade. After two years of crop failure in China, the government of that country sought cereal grains on the world market in 1960. Since the United States neither recognized nor traded with China, Canada was approached. Subsequently, the Government of Canada permitted the Wheat Board to negotiate with the Chinese, even though the Canadians also refused to recognize the Communists as the legitimate government of China. Political differences notwithstanding, the two countries agreed to trade with one another and the bargaining led to the sale of 240 million bushels of wheat and barley in 1961 and 1962. Canada continued to withhold diplomatic recognition, but the $450 million grain deal transformed China into one of Canada's most important customers. The Wheat Board sold all surplus stocks during the Diefenbaker years and net farm income trebled in the same period. Diefenbaker was not responsible for the crop failure in China or the embargo that forced the Chinese to seek supplies outside the United States. To his credit, however, he did agree to guarantee the sale, and Diefenbaker did protest when the United States attempted to intervene to prevent subsidiaries of American firms (such as Imperial Oil) from doing business with the Chinese ships when they called at Canadian ports.

Diefenbaker's successes were more than balanced by actions in areas where government initiatives had been promised but none taken, or areas in which one line of action was indicated but the opposite was pursued. Nothing illustrates such tendencies better than the difference between what was promised and what was done in relations with the United States and Great Britain. Out of a genuine attachment to Britain and because of genuine distress over the recent increasing integration of Canadian trade with the United States (see table 23.1), Diefenbaker proposed in July of

1957 to divert 15 percent of Canadian imports from the Americans to the British. Britain responded immediately with a proposal for free trade between the two countries, but Diefenbaker did not take up their offer then — or later.

**Table 23.1** US-British Shares of Canadian Trade,* 1874-1954

|  | Canadian Imports | | Canadian Exports | |
|  | *From* | *From* | *To* | *To* |
| *Years* | *UK* | *US* | *UK* | *US* |
| 1874 | 49.9 | 42.0 | 46.6 | 43.3 |
| 1894 | 34.0 | 46.5 | 58.6 | 31.4 |
| 1914 | 21.4 | 64.0 | 49.9 | 37.9 |
| 1934 | 24.2 | 54.9 | 43.3 | 33.0 |
| 1954 | 9.6 | 72.3 | 16.7 | 60.0 |

*Values are percentages.

SOURCE: See Appendix A, Tables 6 and 7.

Rather than attempting to reorient Canada to Britain and the Commonwealth, Diefenbaker furthered the continentalist policies of the Liberals. In 1957, the air forces of the two countries were consolidated under one joint command located under a mountain in Colorado. The NORAD (North American Air Defense) arrangement resembled the Ogdensburg agreement of 1940, except in 1957 neither country was at war. Nevertheless, one year later, the Diefenbaker government approved another understanding — the new one resembling the Hyde Park Declaration of 1941. The Development and Production Sharing Program, approved in 1958, enabled companies in Canada to bid on American defense contracts on the same basis as the firms that were under the jurisdiction of a junior government of the United States. From the standpoint of the rationalization of the manufacturing of the continent, and also to improve Canada's balance of payments with the Americans, the agreement made economic sense. Moreover, the firms most likely to take advantage of the program were already American with respect to ownership. But further integration of the two economies reduced Canada's freedom of action in external affairs. How could the Government of Canada ever claim impartiality in future wars involving the United States and third parties if Canada was a significant supplier to the Pentagon, or operated as a branch of the United States Air Force? In this sense, Canada's acceptance of the new arrangement contradicted Diefenbaker's promise that he would lead the country along a more independent course.

Other examples of the same contradiction involved the joint utilization of Canadian energy resources. In 1960, the first exports of natural gas to the United States were permitted, and in 1961 Diefenbaker signed a treaty that permitted the Americans to exploit the hydroelectric potential of the Columbia by damming the river near the border and flooding land in BC. The compensation for Canada was a cash settlement. Thus, Diefenbaker not only failed to act as he had promised; his continentalism was even more advanced than the Liberals'. What went wrong?

Diefenbaker's problem — the problem of his country in microcosm — was the handicap of cross purposes. Anticommunism neutralized ardent nationalism. A dogmatic commitment to private enterprise and individual liberty was blunted by an equally strong commitment to maintaining public welfare and vigorous government. A fervent desire to promote humanitarian idealism was cancelled by an impulse to maintain fiscal orthodoxy. Thus, Diefenbaker professed do-it-yourself development but acquiesced in subservience to the United States for the sake of a more vigorous stand against communism. He would act one way to promote exploration of the north, but sell out Canadian resources to the Americans as quickly as possible in the south. Or more frequently, Diefenbaker would find himself and his party locked between alternatives and they would not act at all.

Since Diefenbaker had campaigned in 1958 for bold initiatives, and since he had won the largest majority in Canadian history, he became especially vulnerable to ridicule on grounds of indecision and incompetence. The *Globe and Mail* dubbed his majority the "idle Parliament." He was far from idle. Indeed, his own estimate of his accomplishments since 1957 was that he had made dramatic headway toward the fulfillment of his promises. Campaigning in 1962 for a renewal of his majority, he made no apologies. Diefenbaker said: "Vast as our program has been in the last five years, it will be even greater in the five years ahead." He repeated the vision, but the magic was gone.

The Liberals posed as the "professional team", a group of experts who were well trained in the technique of government and anxious to win power in order to make the machinery of administration hum. Their image was that of a completely nonideological party, a group that was completely unencumbered by visions or antiquated moral purposes. They were technicians who promised to get everything moving again and to put an end to "indecision and fumbling".

Given the choice between Diefenbaker's demagoguery and Pearson's espousal of expediency under the banner of professionalism, many voters turned to minor parties. In Quebec, a new version of Social Credit under the tutelage of Real Caouette appeared especially interesting to voters there and won almost half of the Quebec representation. Elsewhere, the CCF (repackaged and relabelled as the New Democratic Party in order to minimize even the barest hint of socialism) looked more attractive and recovered slightly from its slide into oblivion: 15.6 percent in 1945, 13.4 in 1949, 11.3 in 1953, 10.7 in 1957, and 9.5 in 1958. In 1962, the NDP attracted 13.5 percent of the votes, winning 19 seats in Parliament. What remained for Diefenbaker was the rural vote of English-speaking Canada; his majority of 208 was reduced to a plurality of 116.

## V    Defeat in Defense of Canada

The return to minority government did not make Diefenbaker more decisive, but it did make him vulnerable to defeat in a crisis of indecision that was already six months old at the time of the 1962 election. The problem was deciding upon a defense policy that was anticommunist without being subserviently pro-American. It has already been mentioned that Diefenbaker's anticommunism led him to accept an extension of continentalist collective security by the NORAD agreement of 1957. Since Canada would need more sophisticated weaponry for its role in the new arrangement, the same anticommunism led Diefenbaker to seek the latest weaponry with which to equip the Royal Canadian Air Force. His nationalism encouraged him to think such hardware might be produced in Canada itself.

Since 1952 the Liberals had encouraged the A.V. Roe Company of Malton, Ontario to develop sophisticated military jet aircraft. More particularly, they were encouraged to develop one airplane, a supersonic fighter called the *Arrow*. By 1957, however, the Liberals decided that the project was not cost effective and it was determined that all further development would be cancelled after the election. Diefenbaker's cabinet was less willing to abandon the Arrow — not until 1959 when it became clear that each plane would cost approximately $8 million. Diefenbaker's sense of fiscal conservatism rebelled at the billion dollars it might cost to equip the RCAF with Arrows. Despite its technical sophistication and the loss of 14 000 jobs in Malton, the Arrow was scrapped and a partial substitute was found in the BOMARC interceptor (an unmanned missile manufactured by the Boeing Corporation of the United States). The attraction of the BOMARC was that it was cheap. Canada would pay for the installation sites, the Americans would provide the missiles.

Soon a snag developed as it became clear that the BOMARC was available with nuclear warheads only. Since American law prohibited the release of atomic bombs to foreign powers, if the BOMARCs were not to be elegant blank cartridges the installations would have to be manned by Americans as well as Canadians.

Diefenbaker's sense of national pride rebelled at the idea of further subordination of Canada to the United States — even at the best of times. But the years after 1960 were not the best. John F. Kennedy had succeeded

Eisenhower like a handsome prince to the throne of an aging monarch. In some respects, he seemed youthful and idealistic, beckoning his people to follow him forward to a "New Frontier". Beyond the rhetoric of humanitarian idealism, however, Kennedy was simply a younger caesar. Diefenbaker and Kennedy developed a deep and mutual dislike of one another, a dislike that increased enormously in the autumn of 1962. On October 22, Kennedy declared naval war on Cuba and the Soviet Union to prevent the installation of Russian missiles so close to American territory. Part of the emergency was to order the RCAF onto alert in accordance with Canada's NORAD commitment, but Diefenbaker insisted upon his own assessment of the situation and kept the Canadian Air Force out of action for nearly two days. In this way, Diefenbaker supported the principle of Canadian independence by refusing immediate and unquestioning compliance. Then, as a further gesture toward an independent Canada, Diefenbaker dug in his heels at accepting nuclear bombs for the BOMARCs or the Canadian NATO forces in Europe.

The issue of defense, and the BOMARCs in particular, revealed Diefenbaker caught in an agony of indecision. He wanted nuclear weapons in order to have a more terrifying saber to rattle at the Russian dictator, Nikita Kruschev. Thus, he did not find it easy to refuse them. But since he loathed the idea of American controls he did not find it easy to accept them, either. Diefenbaker was thus paralyzed between YES and NO from February of 1962 (the date of completing the first BOMARC site in Canada) to February 1963 (when all parties united to defeat Diefenbaker in the House of Commons).

The beginning of the end was Lester Pearson's announcement on January 12 that the expedient course was to accept the warheads. Pearson said it was more important to maintain international commitments than any other principle. He also asserted that the BOMARCs and other bits of military hardware were useless without the bombs and wondered why the government accepted the delivery devices in the first place if there was no intention of taking the warheads as well.

Diefenbaker tried to answer Pearson when the House reconvened on January 25. He repeated his reservations about accepting the warheads immediately, and asked for time, saying that a decision would follow from the next meeting of the NATO allies in May 1963. In the meantime, he suggested that everyone should pray for divine guidance in the matter, adding that "Some may ridicule that belief on my part." Still, the Prime Minister insisted that "the Western World has been directed by God in the last few years..." and he wanted to leave the Government of Canada to the Lord for another several months.

Prayer was not enough for the opposition or Diefenbaker's cabinet, however. On February 3 the Minister of Defence resigned and Lester Pearson moved his non-confidence motion the next day, accusing the government of "lack of leadership, the breakdown of unity in the cabinet, and confusion and indecision in dealing with national and international problems ... ." In the judgment of Parliament, the charge was valid since the NDP and Social Credit members joined the Liberals to defeat the government on February 5th.

Diefenbaker's defeat in the House of Commons was followed two months later by a defeat at the polls. The humiliation by the electorate seemed even more significant than the repudiation by Parliament since other prime ministers had suffered a similar fate in the House. But the election of 1963 was the first time in Canadian history that a dramatic appeal to nationalism failed. Diefenbaker compared the Liberals to the promoters of the Annexation Manifesto of 1849, and taunted them as wantonly unprincipled pursuers of expediency. They were the tools of the Americans and the "sinister interests" while he was simply "trying to help others," attempting to fulfill the vow that he had made in 1956 when he accepted the Conservative leadership: "I hope it will be said of me when I give up the highest honour that you can confer on any man, as was said of another in public service: 'He wasn't always right; sometimes he was on the wrong side, but never on the side of wrong.' That is my dedication; that is my humble declaration." Diefenbaker was still making the same affirmation in 1963: "I'm not asking for the support of the powerful, the strong and the mighty, but of the average Canadian — the group to which I belong."

In the election of 1963, the old affirmations and paranoid accusations did not work well enough to return even the plurality he had won the year before. Since the defense question was the central issue, to some observers, the defeat of Diefenbaker signified the defeat of Canadian nationalism; and, a "lament for a nation" was called for. But this point of view, expressed most eloquently by George Grant, failed to appreciate that previous popular nationalists offered more than "rigid adherence to principle". They were also proponents of some wonderful policy to make the nation as well as to affirm it. In that tradition, Diefenbaker was defeated because Canadians still expected that a nation would follow from actions rather than words. The voter in Halifax who said "he's not the man I thought he was," expressed disappointment similar to the *Globe and Mail* when that paper charged that "there never was a programme ... . Mr. Diefenbaker is barren of constructive ideas and incapable of action."

Nationalism versus continentalism was thus only the surface issue. The other, broader question in the election of 1963 was whether Canada would have a government whose politics was its principles, or an administration whose politics was its program. The two questions tended to blur, of course. But on both matters public opinion was quite clear. Only 40 percent of the electorate voted for the Liberals, the party that advocated acceptance of the nuclear warheads and the wider continentalism that implied. Diefenbaker's Conservatives, the NDP, and the Social Credit Party were all relatively clear in their opposition to nuclear proliferation and these three parties together received nearly 60 percent of the popular vote. But the nuclear question was only the most obvious issue. The other question, the matter of Diefenbaker's indecisiveness (his seven-year failure to advance a legislative program consistent with his declared intentions) was even more relevant to his defeat. In this sense, it was perhaps the promise of "Sixty Days of Decision" and the slogan of "Pearson or Paralysis" that made the Liberals more attractive than the Tories. Diefenbaker's was the only party that stood entirely upon the ground of pious nationalism in defense policy and rigid adherence to principle in other matters. On that basis, they received a mere 30 percent of the vote. The other 70 percent went to the Liberals, the NDP, and Social Credit, groups that differed on what they promised, but united in their opinion that principles and pious intentions were not enough. It was time to return to government by projects.

By 1963, in short, most of the electorate appeared to be thoroughly sick of John Diefenbaker and his pious platitudes. As a result, "Dief the Chief" was returned to oppose a government rather than to lead one, in much the same way as Alexander Mackenzie in 1878 — piously to oppose an administration that asked to be judged in accordance with the projects it completed, rather than by the principles it professed.

# Bibliography

The coverage of Canadian history by the Centenary Series does not extend beyond 1957. A general work of comparable detail, but without the same level of annotation, is Robert Bothwell, *et al.*, *Canada since 1945: Power, Politics, and Provincialism* (1981). Less comprehensive and now somewhat dated but still eminently readable is Blair Fraser, *The Search for Identity: Canada, 1945-67* (1967). A tract for the times, but still useful, is Peter Newman, *Renegade in Power* (1963). All of these works are rather sympathetic to the Liberals and their purposes. A version that is far more sympathetic to Diefenbaker's intentions if not his accomplishments is found in Donald Creighton, *Canada's First Century, 1867-1967* (1970).

Some specialized works have appeared recently on select aspects of the period. The biography of *C.D. Howe* (1979) by Robert Bothwell and William Kilbourn, for example, provides excellent material on the twilight of the St. Laurent period; and William Kilbourn's, *Pipeline* (1970) offers a comprehensive account of the pipeline debate. For the elections of the period, John Meisel's studies of *The Canadian General Election of 1957* (1962) and *Papers on the 1962 Election* (1964) contain useful survey data. James Dow's book on *The Arrow* (1979) analyzes that interesting chapter in the history of Canadian technology. George Grant's *Lament for a Nation* (1965) is a brilliant, poetic post-mortem on Canadian nationalism written in the aftermath of Diefenbaker's defeat in 1963.

Clearly, most of the important questions on the period await the research of future historians. In the meantime, the works that are likely to be important source material for such investigators (as well as material to perpetuate the battles of the partisans themselves) are the memoirs of the leaders of the two major parties: Diefenbaker's, *One Canada*, 3 volumes (1975-7) and Pearson's, *Mike*, 2 volumes (1972-5).

". . . diplomacy set the tone of Pearson's
government . . ."

# CHAPTER 24

# *Tenth-Decade Diplomacy*

I Decisions and Doubts in Canadian-American
Relations

When Pearson's "professional team" returned to power in the spring of
1963, they promised "sixty days of decision". The principal area of indicated activity was in external relations: arming the BOMARC missiles and
accepting American control of the nuclear warheads thus taken. Other
areas in which action could be expected concerned health insurance,
improved old age pensions, federal assistance to municipalities, federal
programs to moderate regional disparities, and government discouragement of further foreign investment. Diplomacy was a factor in the domestic areas as well, however, because the regulation of foreign ownership
had serious implications for relations with the United States, and because
new circumstances in Canada itself meant that social legislation planned in
Ottawa was no longer easily imposed on the provinces by shared cost programs. Moreover, that which was acceptable to other governments still
had to be presented to Parliament with considerable diplomacy because
Pearson and his colleagues were four members short of a majority in 1963,
and two members short in 1965. For all reasons — the nature of the Liberals' policy intentions, a new assertiveness of the provinces, and the lack of
a majority in the House of Commons — diplomatic issues and a diplomatic style of administration were central to the Pearson years, the period
from 1963 through 1968.

Another reason why diplomacy set the tone of Pearson's government is
that the Prime Minister himself was one of Canada's first and finest professional diplomats. In the 1920s (after a stint in the army and the comple-

tion of a bachelor degree in history at the University of Toronto), Pearson rejected a career in business or law, traveled to Oxford for more advanced study of history, and settled into his first living as a lecturer at his *alma mater* in Toronto. In 1928 Pearson abandoned his teaching career to join the small but elite group of diplomat-trainees that had gravitated to the new Department of External Affairs in the decade when Canada's autonomy expanded most dramatically. Pearson continued in that department until the autumn of 1948, then made the move that was so easy for several other Mandarins at the same time: he accepted a Liberal nomination for a safe seat in Parliament. Following his by-election victory, Pearson then appeared in the House of Commons but as a member more interested in government than politics. Even after he accepted the leadership of the Liberal Party in January 1958, Pearson in no way retired from diplomacy. As he later expressed it: "My whole career, my deepest instincts, have been dedicated to the resolution of disputes ... ." In his chosen profession, Pearson was remarkably successful, indeed, his helping settle the seemingly endless succession of wars that broke out in the Middle East won him the Nobel Prize in 1957. But the task of mediation is ever a thankless one. To some, the mediator is simply a person who fears saying anything unpleasant face to face; he is never in control; he only reacts moving one way and another in the continuous search for common ground between adversaries.

Like Diefenbaker, Pearson was often caught between cross purposes. Also like Diefenbaker, Pearson reacted more than he led with his own initiatives. But unlike Diefenbaker, Pearson appeared always to be in motion, cheerfully going about his diplomat's work because he was truly "dedicated to the resolution of disputes, to the search for agreement, to the avoidance of controversy, and the finding of solutions to difficult problems." His first such effort after the election of 1963 was to give the Minister of Finance, Walter Gordon, a free rein to develop a budget to discourage foreign investment while he personally visited the American President to assure him that the new Government of Canada would honor its commitments internationally and would continue to cherish its fraternal association with the United States.

In the visit to President Kennedy, Pearson chatted about baseball, NATO commitments, and further development of shared resources such as the Columbia River. Canadian-American relations, strained in the Diefenbaker years, were thus repaired almost immediately in the first weeks of the Pearson administration. "He'll do!", Kennedy remarked afterwards, but what Pearson agreed to "do" was nothing Walter Gordon would accept with approving smiles. Still, a rift in Canadian-American relations had been closed by Pearson's affirmation that the BOMARCs would be armed and Canadian NATO forces bolstered. In this manner, there was relief in the ending of the crisis if not in the substance of its resolution.

Walter Gordon's experimentation with economic nationalism unfolded less facilely or cheerfully. The budget, introduced on June 13, included two revolutionary proposals. One was a 30 percent tax on the value of Canadian firms purchased by American corporations. The other was a tax on dividends that varied according to the amount that a firm was foreign owned. For the first time in Canadian history, a government proposed specific measures to discourage foreign investment. There were no loud objections from the Americans, but the Canadian business community (potential sellers of manufacturing plant) denounced the budget so persuasively that the "takeover" tax was withdrawn for "further study" on June 19. Early in July it was dropped entirely, and the tax on dividends was significantly modified. All that remained was the record of the attempt.

For the next two years, continentalism appeared to be a stronger current than economic nationalism. A ripple of continental disharmony did develop in 1964 over Canada's refusal to permit foreign ownership of the chartered banks, but the rest seemed to be goodwill and solidarity, symbolized best, perhaps, by the announcement of an arrangement for quasi free trade in automobiles. By the "Auto Pact", announced in January 1965, domestic car manufacturers were permitted to treat North America as one market. The agreement permitted greater rationalization of production by the big three auto makers, but the limited import-export freedoms applied to manufacturers only. As far as consumers were concerned, North America continued divided. The greater rationalization enabled manufacturers to reduce production costs, but because the final product continued to be "priced to the separate markets", relative prices changed very little. What was gained besides greater profits for the companies? From the standpoint of the Government of Canada, the Auto Pact was worthwhile because minimum levels of Canadian production relative to sales were assured without conceding a maximum level of Canadian output. In this way, the agreement appeared to be a ticket to increased exports without conceding any protection on domestic manufacturing — a real triumph in "quiet diplomacy".

By 1965 it seemed that Canada had resolved its fitful doubts concerning the advantages of continentalism. Shortly after the achievement of the auto agreement, two senior diplomats issued a report two years in the making on procedures for assuring the compatibility of policies in the two countries. Pearson and the President had commissioned the study by Arnold Heeney (for Canada) and Livingston Merchant (for the United States) in 1963. In that year, both leaders were agreed that it was important to find ways to "make it easier to avoid divergencies in economic and other policies." Appearing in July 1965, the Heeney-Merchant *Principles for Partnership* was an unqualified endorsement of "the practice of quiet diplomacy", an approach considered more "neighbourly" and also "far more effective than the alternative of raising a row and being unpleasant in public." The assumption was that the two countries lived similar collective lives on one continent and hoped for the same future in a difficult and troubled world. Such a view seemed wise in 1940 when the world's villains were perfectly villainous; it was also popular in 1948, in the face of the new menace of Stalinism and the new fear that an irresponsible dictator might plunge the world into a nuclear holocaust. But by 1965, many Canadians were beginning to believe that the United States was no longer the chief proponent of peace and international sobriety. By 1965 the American Commander in Chief seemed so obsessed with communism, he was willing to support any kind of noncommunist regime by any means. On the American domestic scene, images of the Americans were equally unreassuring. The televised assassination of President Kennedy in 1963 and pictures of Americans violently resisting the civil rights movement for blacks in 1964 were two shocks. Then the air war against the people of Vietnam that was launched in 1965 caused even deeper questioning of American leadership of the "free world".

For Lester Pearson, the American war against Vietnam was another crisis to mediate. In an invited address to students at Temple University in Philadelphia in April 1965, Pearson suggested that a pause in the bombing of North Vietnam might be an effective invitation to the other side to negotiate a settlement that might lead to unification and peace. Going immediately from Philadelphia to a meeting with President Lyndon Johnson at his retreat near Washington D.C., Pearson discovered that Johnson was outraged by Pearson's clumsy attempt at mediation. The President grabbed the Prime Minister by the lapels and raked him over the coals for telling the Americans how to carry their burden of defending world freedom when the Canadians did so little to shoulder any share of it themselves. Too shocked to reply coherently, Pearson fumbled an answer. From that moment, according to Robert Bothwell, Pearson knew that Johnson was a "bully who threatened, a vulgar manipulator... ." From that moment, the United States came to be regarded less as a senior partner, and more as a country to be regarded from afar.

The Vietnam War was thus as important for Canada's relations with the United States as the Great War had been in Canada's view of Britain. Both wars convinced the country that a greater measure of independence was both warranted and worthwhile. Robert Fulford, normally a critic of art and literature, thought that he was speaking for a generation of North American Canadians when he suggested that persons born of the Second World War "baby boom" had grown up believing that "if we were very good or very smart, or both, we would surely graduate from Canada." They had learned to look beyond Canada much as the imperialists had looked beyond their country between 1900 and 1914. This is what made Diefenbaker so phenomenal: 1958 excepted, most of the time, most people seemed to accept the popular notion that a Canadian was a North American who had not yet accepted a job in the States. But in 1965 — in the face of assassination, race riots, and an obscene war — new critics of continentalism seemed to have tangible proof that greater political distance from the American Empire was necessary. They asserted — they pleaded — that Canada had to be different from and independent of the Americans. The national preoccupation with the Canadian identity resumed.

After France pulled out of NATO, in 1965, critics of American-dominated collective security questioned Canada's membership in NATO and especially NORAD. Suggesting that independence was nothing more than the exercise of the right to say "no", one observer, Stephen Clarkson, asserted that a more negative Canada might even receive greater material advantages from the United States, pointing out that "the more truculent General de Gaulle has become, the gentler has been the Americans' treatment of France. With so much direct investment in Canada, it is unlikely that the Americans... would want to get rid of a blemish on the finger by amputating the arm." Disenchantment with American foreign policy and domestic leadership after 1963 thus led Canadians to contemplate the desirability of greater independence in their own affairs, and also to consider more deeply what sort of country they were creating. Especially did the people of Quebec address themselves to such considerations.

## II   Autonomy With New Purposes in Quebec

Normally, Canadians outside Quebec tended to regard dependence upon Britain or (later) the United States as benevolent associations between senior and junior partners. For a country not yet mature, such relations yielded gains significant enough to offset the unpleasant chores. Quebec, however, was always quick to denounce such colonialism, particularly in defense and diplomatic matters. For throughout the ages, Quebeckers had been told continually by their leaders that they were a people with a special character and mission, one that had to be preserved from cultural contamination or extinction, a mission to preserve the faith, the language, and the pastoral way of life.

During the crises of the Great Depression and wartime conscription (discussed in previous chapters), Quebeckers took refuge in defensive nationalism. But the way of life that the race was called upon to defend was already largely extinct. By 1941, the population was still overwhelmingly Catholic and French-speaking, but the rural-farm aspect had not been dominant for decades, and it continued to decline despite persistent assertions of clerical and governmental authorities that French Canadians had to be agricultural or perish. Ignoring the growing importance of urban living in Quebec, nationalists such as Richard Arès continued to insist in the 1940s that "By tradition, vocation as well as necessity, we are a people of peasants. Everything that takes us away from the land diminishes and weakens us as a people...." More than a decade later, the Tremblay Commission reporting on cultural survival, echoed the same theme, even though by 1956, the year of the Tremblay Report, almost 75 percent of all French-origin Quebeckers were neither farmers nor country dwellers (see table 24.1).

**Table 24.1**  Rural-Urban Characteristics of Quebec Population, 1941-1971

|  | Origins* | | | | |
| --- | --- | --- | --- | --- | --- |
|  | French | | | Other | |
|  | Rural | Rural | | | Overall |
| Years | Non farm | Farm | Total | All locations | total |
| 1941 | 1 107 | 105 | 271 | 1 849 | 3 332 |
| 1951 | 714 | 522 | 855 | 1 965 | 4 056 |
| 1961 | 533 | 699 | 1 777 | 2 250 | 5 259 |
| *Values are in thousands | | | | | |

SOURCE: Adapted from data in D. Posgate and K. McRoberts, *Quebec: Social Change and Political Crisis* (1976), pp. 48-49.

The persistence of the myth of the pastoral French Canadian was thus an indicator of the intensity of a belief rather than a mirror of reality. But so long as the myth remained strong, governments were excused from developing complicated strategies for promoting industrial development, or paying much attention to the problems of industrial workers in an urban context. The winning electoral formula developed by Maurice Duplessis in the 1930s — the formula that kept his *Union nationale* in power almost continuously to 1960 — involved local favors rather than sweeping policies. In the 1940s and 50s, just before an election, advertisements would appear in local newspapers recounting the funds that the government had recently expended on public works in the district. If the incumbent candidate happened to be a Liberal, the favors were attributed to the local UN organizer. Otherwise, the benefits were listed as the achievement of the local legislative patron. Since the UN was also touted as the party most likely to win the upcoming election, voters were advised to make certain that they elected a member of the ruling party to assure them an even larger share of future patronage. On this basis, as well as by demagogic appeals to elect a government that was "closer to the people", the UN usually won large majorities and maintained the support of the working class even though Duplessis was demonstrably opposed to militant organized labor.

Workers or organizers who troubled the political scene were vulnerable to harassment under the old Padlock Law that survived the 1930s, and aggressive unions felt the pressure of a labor code that empowered the Minister of Labour to take bold action against strikes deemed to be illegal or turbulent. The most dramatic such repression occurred in the spring of 1949 when the workers employed in the asbestos mines of the Eastern Townships decided to go on strike without waiting for cumbersome conciliation proceedings to run their time-consuming course to an inevitable denial of the union's demands. Duplessis came to the aid of the workers' American employers with police protection for strikebreakers, and enlisted the Church to join him in denouncing the union. Had the event followed the pattern established in previous strikes, the three authorities of Church, state, and company would have been sufficient to dictate terms to the workers. But in 1949 the archbishop of Montreal, Joseph Charbonneau, sided with the Catholic union. The strikers were emboldened by their unexpected support and the strike became violent before it was ended with the mediation efforts of the archbishop of Quebec. The five-month dispute won the workers a 10-cent raise and assurances of re-employment. But scores of the more outspoken leaders of the strike were not re-employed and Charbonneau found that his superiors thought that he would be more effective in another diocese, transferring him to Victoria, British Columbia. Other clergy were warned to drop their labor activism in 1950 and in 1954 the Duplessis government added a new power to its antiradical weaponry with a law that empowered the Minister of Labour to decertify unions if they even "tolerated communists" or "threatened to strike public services".

In a number of ways, the Asbestos strike seemed nothing more than a minor setback for the companies and the Government of Quebec. In the longer term, however, the episode proved to be a major turning point because it accelerated the tendency of the secular intelligentsia and the reform-minded clergy to think along lines of a new ideology, one that would preclude a government from preaching agrarian nationalism to an industrial society, or from posing as a major defender of Quebec's autonomy while leaving the initiative in social and economic development to the

traditionalist Church or foreign-dominated corporations. The new nationalists held that it was time to "unshackle the superstructures, desanctify
civil society, democratize politics, break into economic life, relearn French,
get inessentials out of the university, open the borders to culture and
minds to progress."

The breakthrough for reformers came in 1960. Duplessis died in 1959;
his successor, Paul Sauvé, also died in office, just four months after succeeding his predecessor. The loss of both leaders in such rapid succession
left the *Union nationale* disorganized and vulnerable to defeat by the
reform-oriented Liberals.

The electoral victory of the reformers led by Jean Lesage indicated the
desire for change in 1960 as much as the weakness of the UN, however.
The slogan, "Things must change" *(Il faut que ça change)* indicated more
than an electoral stance. The Liberals were determined to move boldly to
"catch up" with the rest of the world. So dramatic was the difference
between the new and the old government, in this respect, that one
reporter of events in Quebec for the *Globe and Mail* called the change of
government a "Quiet Revolution". The break with the past was particularly dramatic in the attitudes of the new politicians toward the role of
the state in shaping society. Replacing the agrarian myth that justified
limited government was the notion that Quebec had to refine its technological proficiency and look to the state to set the pace and direction of
such refinement.

Nowhere was the effect of the new ideology more evident than in the
Liberals' reforms of education. Under the old system, there was one set of
institutions controlled by what was, in effect, a committee of the Catholic
church for the children of Catholic parents. All others went to "Protestant" schools controlled by a different religious body. Church and state
were thus inseparable since the preceding governments had delegated all
responsibility for the social development of human resources to religious
authorities. The new government operated from the premise that education had to be directed by secular institutions because education was
regarded as job training more than catechism; the schools were to transfer
skills more than beliefs. One of the first official acts of the Liberals was,
therefore, to appoint a commission — of secular as well as clerical educa-
tors — to survey the existing pattern of schools and recommend changes.
The Parent Commission (reporting in 1963) gave the Minister of Youth,
Paul Gérin-Lajoie, precisely the information he wanted. In May 1964, the
government assumed responsibility for schooling by creating a Ministry of
Education under Gérin-Lajoie, and the expensive work of transforming
the schools into training grounds for manipulators of technology began.

Equally ambitious — and expensive — were the projects for the decolonization and development of Quebec's economy. Here, too, the new government operated from an assumption that was radically different from its predecessors who assumed that economic growth was an entirely private matter, and who left the initiative in the hands of individual farmers and businessmen. The new regime assumed that the state had an active role to play, particularly in the promotion of French Canadians to the managerial level of the Quebec economy. The most outspoken advocate of such active statism was René Lévesque, the Minister of Natural Resources and, after Gérin-Lajoie, the most important person in the government.

Although Lévesque was outspoken in his affirmations of economic nationalism (and considerably left of center in his economic philosophy), the program he implemented was striking for its pragmatism. Consider, for example, the great headline-maker of 1962-63, the "nationalization" of electrical utilities. Critics of the campaign called it socialist or insanely nationalist because privately owned companies were taken over by the government, and French Canadians appeared promptly in the management of the new public conglomerate, Hydro-Québec. But only one third of the private firms were taken over, and the process of acquisition employed a pragmatic principle of selection as well as compensation for the owners. A truly radical approach would have insisted upon the takeover of all firms and expropriation without payment. To Lévesque, however, the important goals were improving a service that was either unavailable or too expensive. The private companies in the northwestern part of the province were thus one target because they provided 25-cycle power in a 60-cycle world. They were nationalized to make the conversion. The other large target, on the Gaspé Peninsula, came under the public utility umbrella to reduce rates from five times those of Montreal to the same standard. But the private companies that produced cheap, sixty-cycle power for the American corporations in the Lac St. Jean region were left as they were. In this way, public ownership was instrumental in solving specific problems, not an end in itself.

A similar pragmatism characterized two other initiatives in the area of economic policy, the creation of the Quebec Advisory Council (*Conseil d'orientation economique*) and the establishment of the General Investment Corporation (*La Société générale de financement*). The first was a planning agency to study "the economic organization of the province with a view to the most complete utilization of its material and human resources...", a body to "indicate" the way to a rationalized economy with French Canadian participation above the level of "cheap and docile labour". The role of the other institution was to offer financial assistance enabling private enterprise to follow the "indicative planning" of the Advisory Council. The

General Investment Corporation was supposed to provide funds (in the form of loans or actual investment) for small firms to consolidate into larger operations and thus achieve economies of scale.

Accepting the state as the principal power to promote economic and social development led to enormous growth in the civil service and an astronomical increase in the scale of government expenditure. Between 1960 and 1965, the Liberals created six new ministries and eight public enterprises to begin to deliver a broad spectrum of social services available elsewhere in Canada but unknown in Quebec because Duplessis refused to participate in federal shared-cost programs. Under the old regime of Duplessis, Quebec was short on services but taxes were also low. In 1959, the Government of Quebec collected only $556 million in revenue and finished the year with a $23 million surplus. The provincial income tax was so low it exempted one fifth of all wage earners completely. By 1966, the Liberals had imposed a six percent sales tax and had increased the personal income tax so greatly that the government collected nearly $1 billion in revenue, but still completed the year with an enormous deficit.

A reorganized *Union nationale* seized on the contrast and suggested that the Quiet Revolution was starting to cost a great deal more than people ought to be willing to pay. Many voters began to agree with the UN that the Liberals were a "government of taxers" and other critics suggested that many of the new programs on which so much revenue was lavished benefitted the middle class more than the population as a whole. Consequently, the Quiet Revolution led to a quiet reaction. In 1966, the Lesage Liberals were turned out of office as the UN, led by Daniel Johnson, came to power, promising a slower pace of social innovation and scaled down expenditure. At the same time, however, pointing to severe strains that had developed in federal-provincial relations since Quebec had started to exercise its full powers under the Constitution, Johnson promised to forge ahead and secure a new relation between Quebec and Canada. Here was a policy thrust that was completely consistent with the popular autonomy theme, and a program with low cost implications. But there was little in the diplomacy of Quebec-Ottawa relations between 1960 and 1966 to suggest that Johnson was going to be very successful in winning the significant concessions he claimed were needed.

## III    Federal-Provincial Diplomacy

Traditionally, the Quebec autonomy demand had meant nothing more than defending the powers assigned to the provinces by the BNA Act. For Duplessis, the best defense in the struggle was to denounce each federal encroachment and refuse to participate in each "shared cost" program as Ottawa put up funds to confront problems that Duplessis maintained were exclusively provincial. Thus, Quebec was the only province in 1959 that did not take federal money to maintain hospitals and universities, for example. Since the Government of Quebec did not choose to launch programs of its own in these fields, Duplessis always seemed to win his little wars with Ottawa and no blood was shed in the fighting. Moreover, the Government of Canada also emerged a winner because the centralization process was not interrupted. Canada continued to develop its social security programs (but without Quebec whenever provincial cooperation was called for).

An enormous problem developed once the Government of Quebec chose to develop the same social services as Canada without sacrificing any of the autonomy Duplessis had defended. At the first federal-provincial conference attended by the Lesage government in July 1960, the "Prime Minister" of Quebec proposed an end of the shared cost programs, with compensation for the revenue thus lost to be covered by the federal government's abatement of 25 percent of its income tax, 25 percent of its tax on corporate income, and all inheritance duties. Diefenbaker conceded some room for Quebec to raise revenue for universities by direct taxation but the overall 25-25-100 formula was rejected because Diefenbaker refused to see the central government impoverished, claiming the Canadian nation would be transformed into an agglomeration of associate states. In the case of Quebec's aspirations for fuller autonomy, Diefenbaker's nationalism was stronger than his other declared commitment to provincial autonomy and fiscal conservatism.

If all provinces had presented a united front behind the abatement formula advanced by Lesage, it is possible that one of Diefenbaker's other principles would have led to a different outcome in 1960. But the only point on which all were agreed was that every province needed more revenue. They could not agree on the method. Demanding greater equalization payments or federal assumption of a larger share of the shared cost programs were both markedly different from the idea that the central government should make room for the provinces to impose higher personal and corporate income taxes of their own. That preoccupation was peculiar to Quebec. Since Lesage refused to back away from his new concept of autonomy, for Canada the Quiet Revolution developed rapidly into the "Quebec Problem".

Diefenbaker seemed insensitive to Quebec's new aspirations. Equally important, he did not seem to know how to respond except to ignore them. In 1962, for instance, one of the few French Canadian members of the cabinet, Paul Martineau, asked Diefenbaker how he should respond to reporters' persistent questions on the government's policy regarding Quebec. "Look," Diefenbaker replied, "you didn't make too much trouble before you were in the cabinet: I hope you're not going to start making trouble now." For Diefenbaker, the issue of Quebec versus Ottawa was inherently troublesome, too complicated for day-to-day government.

Lester Pearson viewed the conflict from a diplomat's perspective and also with a completely different concept of Canada itself. While Diefenbaker insisted that Canada was one "unhyphenated" nation, Pearson believed that the facts of the French-English past had made the country binational. In December 1962, he therefore called for a commission to investigate not only the realities of the past and present but also "the means of developing the bicultural character of Canada" in the future. The country, in his opinion, had to grow beyond the "narrow vision" that promoted bilingualism in Quebec and tolerated English-only for the rest. At the same time, Pearson suggested that Canadians would have to recognize that Quebeckers were "determined to become directors of their economic and cultural destiny in their own changed and changing society ... ." For this reason, "the greatest possible constitutional decentralization" was needed, said Pearson, "to strengthen, indeed to establish and maintain unity."

Lesage did not take Pearson's pronouncements on bilingualism and biculturalism seriously, but he did intend to hold the leader of the Liberal Party to his implied repudiation of centralism. Three days before the election that defeated Diefenbaker in 1963, Lesage claimed that he wanted nothing more than the "full exercise" of the powers that every province had under the Constitution. If the federal government did not make room for the provinces in the field of direct taxation, Lesage implied that the local taxes on corporate and personal incomes would be raised regardless of the uproar. "Twelve months will go by before the next budget speech," said Lesage. "Either the federal government ... will have made use of the 12 months to make allowance for Quebec's needs, or else we in Quebec will have taken steps on our own side to make the required decisions in fiscal policy."

Once elected, Pearson indicated that he was "prepared to make substantial concessions to Quebec (and to the other provinces) in the interest of national unity." But the first concessions showed a commitment to bilingual unity more than fiscal or constitutional decentralization. French became a language of caucus and cabinet discussion. Bilingualism was encouraged in the federal civil service, and in July 1963, Pearson announced the membership of the Royal Commission on Bilingualism and Biculturalism that he had called for the previous December. None of Pearson's steps to accommodate Quebec addressed the more pressing issue of Quebec's demand for room in the field of direct taxation, however. On the revenue issue, there was every indication that the Pearson government intended to advance its occupation of the field yet further with new levies to support a new pension plan.

The problem with the 1963 pension proposal was that Quebec had been working on a scheme of its own at the same time that the federal initiative was undertaken. That detail was enormously important because the constitutional amendment that gave the federal government power to legislate in the area (Section 94A, adopted in 1951), declared that "no law made by the Parliament of Canada in relation to old age pensions shall affect the operation of any law present or future of a Provincial Legislature in relation to old age pensions." The wording of the BNA Act raised two issues. First, there was the matter of provincial paramountcy in the field. The other was that the federal proposal was more than an old age pension. It was also a method of providing security in the form of "supplementary benefits" to the disabled and to the survivors of deceased contributors to the pension fund. On either point, the federal government faced defeat by any province that might withold acquiescence. Ontario had reservations. But the Quebec legislature voted unanimously to reject the federal plan as soon as it became public in 1963.

Having cornered the Government of Canada with the prospect of defeat, the Government of Quebec invited the Premiers and Pearson to meet in Quebec City to find an opening in the apparent impasse. The conference that followed from March 31 to April 3, 1964 was extremely effective in creating a united front against Ottawa as Lesage unveiled the Quebec plan in lavish detail. It was more generous to contributors in benefits and, equally important from the standpoint of the leaders of the provincial governments, the fund that accrued in the Quebec scheme was a pool of capital that the province could use to finance its own development schemes — just as private insurance companies invested the money held in trust for their policy holders. The effect on Ottawa was devastating. According to one member of the Pearson delegation, "the federal government position was destroyed."

In the diplomacy that followed, Quebec agreed to a constitutional amendment that gave the Government of Canada power to make laws in relation to old age pensions and supplementary benefits, "including survivors' and disability benefits irrespective of age". The reasons for Quebec's apparent concession were varied. In the first place, the text of the new version of Section 94A still left the provinces paramount in the field since the amendment declared that "no such law shall affect the operation of any law present or future of a provincial legislature in relation to any such matter." In this light, Quebec's power to enact its own scheme was not jeopardized. The other provinces were also pleased with the arrangement because the plan Ottawa took to them in March 1965 was essentially the same as Quebec's: employers and employees each were to contribute 1.8 percent of the the first $5000 of earnings and the fund (estimated to grow to $5 billion by 1970) was to be shared by the provinces in proportion to their contributions. But most important, in return for Quebec's willingness to accept the new Section 94A, Ottawa agreed to negotiate "opt out" privileges with respect to the shared cost programs and to vacate a significant portion of the field of personal and corporate income taxes.

Defenders of Pearsons's diplomacy called it "cooperative federalism" and argued that the "opt out" arrangement was proof that Quebec's aspirations could be accommodated within Confederation. In Quebec, however, it was argued by Claude Morin (the Deputy Minister of Intergovernmental Affairs), that "In setting up the Quebec Pension Plan ... Quebec conquered no new constitutional territory, but simply occupied a field of its own that Ottawa had been preparing to mine." Similarly, in the other complicated negotiations by which Quebec "won the right to collect 20 additional tax points instead of getting federal subsidies" there was no concession of new power to the province. In Morin's view, here as well, "Quebec was simply repossessing some of its own territory," a power that was defined clearly in Section 92 of the BNA Act. But since Quebec's repossession was still Ottawa's loss, critics of Pearson who thought he had conceded too much, feared that the retreat from the fiscal field would jeopardize the ability of the central legislature to respond to complicated issues with national policies. By 1965, the consensus — even within Pearson's Liberal Party — was that too much had been yielded to Lesage. In the future, Quebec would have to be content with the economic benefits of equalizing federalism or to find satisfaction with symbolic changes. The first involved federal programs to insure economic development in the less wealthy provinces, the group of "have nots" in which Quebec was usually classified. To avoid the stigma of paternalism, such initiatives were usually summed up simply as "paying federalism". The other area of possible concessions was a program of gestures such as a new flag and unified armed forces devoid of British symbolism, and a language program that was supposed to enhance the status of French-speaking Canadians outside Quebec.

This is where Daniel Johnson entered the scene — just as the Government of Canada decided to hold a firmer line on constitutional concessions. Johnson would settle for neither federal substitute for he had decided to increase the demand from the recovery of what was constitutionally Quebec's own legal territory to the extension of its authority over a number of powers that were clearly within Ottawa's exclusive jurisdiction under Section 91 of the BNA Act.

---

IV     Separatism

---

The government of Daniel Johnson was more cautious than that of Jean Lesage in social and economic policies, but Johnson was clearly more daring with respect to Quebec's status in Confederation. In September 1966, Johnson suggested that his constitutional objectives were to achieve complete mastery of cultural affairs and human development issues. Theoretically, both goals were attainable under the powers enumerated in Section 92 of the BNA Act, but Johnson also demanded the right to establish regional banks and a special role in external relations — both areas reserved to the central government.

The insistence upon the right to enter into agreements with foreign countries (French-speaking states, in particular) developed as the most contentious attempt by Quebec to assert full autonomy, and reached crisis proportions in 1967. The issue was made all the more complicated because France under General Charles de Gaulle fully supported Quebec's attempt to establish quasi-sovereign status in the field of foreign affairs. Thus, when "Prime Minister" Johnson personally invited de Gaulle to visit Quebec to take part in Canada's centennial celebrations in 1967, the invitation was accepted in 1966 without consulting Canada. There was no question that de Gaulle would be invited (all heads of state with the remotest ties to Canada attended). The problem was that de Gaulle accepted his invitation from Johnson rather than Pearson. Subsequently, each attempted to outmaneuvre the other in planning the visit and setting de Gaulle's itinerary. Ultimately, it was clear that the winner was Johnson.

De Gaulle crossed the Atlantic on a French warship, the *Colbert*, arriving at Quebec City on July 23, 1967. As he stepped ashore, the welcome was thunderous with an enormous crowd chanting *"de Gaulle"* and *"Vive la France"*. The next day, over the course of de Gaulle's regal progression from Quebec to Montreal, the people who lined the roadway were no less enthusiastic. Finally, the welcome reached a crescendo once de Gaulle arrived at Montreal City Hall and began to address the adoring populace from a balcony. The old man began his address by telling everyone that his welcome by a half-million persons representing the survival of the French fact in North America moved him nearly as much as the welcome he received from the Parisiens who greeted him in 1944 on their liberation from Nazi occupation. Then came the climactic phrases whose impact was made all the greater by the pause and roar of approval that followed each salutation: "*Vive Montréal! Vive le Québec! Vive le Québec libre.*"

Predictably, the government in Ottawa reacted to de Gaulle's utterances with less than the adoration of Quebeckers. Pearson declared in the evening that the "people of Canada are free. Every province is free. Canadians do not need to be liberated." Then the English-language newspapers rallied to their prime minister and openly questioned de Gaulle's sanity. De Gaulle, for his part, was unruffled and unrepentant. Having cut short his visit, he returned home to France and faced criticism from his own countrymen for meddling in delicate Canadian issues, but insisted to his dying day that the welcome he received on July 23 and 24 was "a unanimous and indescribable will for emancipation".

The French-language press in Quebec tended to agree with de Gaulle. They agreed that Quebec was not as free as it wished to be, and denied that de Gaulle's affirmation of good will to Quebec was sufficient cause for the fear and hysteria that had developed in Canada. Claude Ryan refused to condemn de Gaulle's visit in *Le Devoir*. "Prime Minister" Johnson also refused to denounce de Gaulle's remarks. A public opinion poll revealed that Ryan and Johnson reflected sentiments of the majority of Quebeckers, as well. Almost three quarters thought that the visit had been worthwhile. Only one fifth believed that de Gaulle had intended to encourage separatism.

For another part of the Quebec population, the reaction to the de Gaulle visit had a different meaning. Agreeing with Ryan that Canadian resentment was unjustifiable, they also agreed with the English press that de Gaulle encouraged separatism but asserted that such was a worthwhile goal. Any further experimentation with federalist association was a waste of energy, they asserted. Then dramatic policital developments followed. François Aquin, a backbench Liberal member of the legislature, declared in the autumn that, henceforth, he was a separatist. Soon, others joined him. The cause gained its greatest convert when René Lévesque announced that he, too, was leaving the Liberal Party because Confederation was hopeless: "the two majorities would only continue to collide, always harder…." Independence was the only solution, said Lévesque, because it promised "the chance to live life in one's own way according to one's needs and priorities" with the least interference from outsiders.

Lévesque's separatist "option" appeared at greater length in January of 1968 in book form and became an instant best-seller. Less notorious, but equally important, was the Canadian rejoinder, a White Paper of the Government of Canada called *Federalism for the Future*. Nothing illustrated better the rift that had developed in conceptions of Canada than the two documents side by side. Lévesque's Canada of the future was an association of sovereign states in economic community — a North American echo of the European Economic Community. Ottawa's image was of a national entity with a strong central administration and ten complementary junior administrations. "There are central areas of responsibility to the apparatus of a modern sovereign state", the report declared. Enumerating minimum powers for establishing the necessary central focus, the report mentioned control of "economic policy, the equalization of opportunity, technological and cultural development, and international affairs." Although the report admitted that some "central areas of responsibility" could be "shared with the provinces", *Federalism for the Future* asserted that no provincial power could be construed as an exclusive right. "We question whether it is any longer realistic to expect that some neat compartmentalization of powers can be found ... ."

Clearly, no common ground was immediately evident between separatism and centralizing federalism. But in 1968, there was no reason to think that Lévesque's position was particularly threatening since it represented the preference of no more than 10 percent of the population, characteristically the new middle class that had profited most from the politics of the Lesage government and perceived an obstacle-strewn future in 1967 because of Johnson's unimaginative economic policies and the hardening of Quebec-Ottawa diplomacy.

The more important threat to the Ottawa Mandarins' centralism in 1968 was Daniel Johnson's demand for special status within Confederation, a Constitution that would make the "Canada of ten into a Canada of two." In the special status scheme, Ottawa could have its version of federalism for the other nine, but Quebec would occupy the paramount position in social policy and local economic development for itself, Johnson insisted. The Government of Quebec and its Mandarins (Claude Morin, most notably), had become keenly aware that governments were then ubiquitous and interventionist — legislating on the environment, unemployment, housing, income maintenance, and health in ways that no one had foreseen in 1867 or imagined was possible in Quebec as late as the 1950s. Quebeckers also appreciated that the government that retained the initiative in the new areas of growing responsibility also had the power to mold society and was the only body legitimately entitled to call itself the *national* government. How long would Quebec survive as an entity unlike the others if Quebec's "National Assembly" fell behind Ottawa? The central grievance with Ottawa was thus still running in a rather narrow culturalist channel. As long as this continued to be the case, Quebec was bound to be isolated on the issue of consititutional change because for the others the *nation* was then — at least ceremoniously — Canada. Still the other provinces were beginning to show signs of growing dissatisfaction with the consequences of apparently inexorable centralist growth. For the disenchanted the issue was less a matter of competing allegiances than regional disparities and the inability of a provincial administration to raise an adequate revenue to deal with such matters after paying the federal tax collector. Since that position was the starting point for Quebec in the federal-provincial diplomacy of the 1960s, it was possible that a common front against Ottawa could yet develop, but not as long as economic development and fiscal arrangements were entangeled with competing nationalisms.

## Bibliography

An excellent brief introduction to the Pearson years is the biography of the Prime Minister by Robert Bothwell, *Pearson: His Life and World* (1978). Another general work, more detailed and more concerned with the social history of the period, is Robert Bothwell, *et al.*, *Canada since 1945: Power, Politics, and Provincialism* (1981). A dated but interesting treatment of select political episodes (particularly those that reflect the obsession with the Canadian identity in the period) is Blair Fraser, *The Search for Identity: Canada, 1945-1967* (1967).

For the diplomacy of the Pearson years, the debate on Canadian-American relations is treated — and reflected — in Stephen Clarkson, ed., *An Independent Foreign Policy for Canada?* (1973). The other aspect of the diplomacy of the 1960s, the internal relations between Ottawa and the provinces, is covered by Richard Simeon, *Federal Provincial Diplomacy* (1972). The special concerns of Quebec are elaborated by Claude Morin in *Quebec versus Ottawa* (1976). For the sake of comparison, readers may wish to consult Christopher Armstrong, *The Politics of Federalism: Ontario's Relations with the Federal Government, 1867-1942* (1981) for the story of an earlier attempt by a strong province to challenge "Empire Canada".

The phenomenon that led Quebec to resist centralism in new ways is the Quiet Revolution. Excellent background to this development is in Pierre Trudeau, "Quebec on the Eve of the Asbestos Strike," in Ramsay Cook, ed., *French Canadian Nationalism* (1967). For developments in the

Lesage years, see Richard Jones, *Community in Crisis: French Canadian Nationalism in Perspective* (1967) and Edward M. Corbett, *Quebec Confronts Canada* (1967). More analytical and written from a longer historical perspective is Dale Posgate and Kenneth McRoberts, *Quebec: Social Change and Political Crisis* (1976).

"Such enthusiasm had not been seen since
Diefenbaker's 1958 vision speeches."

# CHAPTER 25

# New Era of Confrontation

## I    New Century, New Leaders

By 1965, Quebec's Quiet Revolution had reached its full pace and Lester Pearson was fast approaching (some said he had already exceeded) the limit of propriety in the autonomy that the federal government would yield in giving the newly energetic province room to exercise its full powers under the BNA Act. A new strategy emphasizing the presence and power of French Canadians in the Government of Canada itself then unfolded to convince Quebeckers that their future was as much with the federal as the provincial structure. Thus, personalities who were themselves architects of the new Quebec were recruited by the Liberals for participation in federal politics.

Maurice Lamontagne, perhaps the most prominent Quebecker already in the federal cabinet, approached Jean Marchand (the head of the largest branch of the Quebec labor movement) to join the government. Marchand accepted the challenge in 1965, but insisted that two friends must do the same. One of Marchand's associates was Gérard Pelletier, a Quebec journalist. Like Marchand, Pelletier's career was very much part of the recent history of organized labor in Quebec. In Pelletier's case, revulsion at Duplessis had led to journalism and the founding of *Cité Libre*, a quarterly magazine of social criticism in which Pelletier and his fellows were as inclined to criticize the reigning Liberal Party in Ottawa as they were the *Union nationale* in Quebec.

A frequent contributor to *Cité Libre* was Marchand's second friend, Pierre Trudeau. Unlike Pelletier or Marchand, Trudeau had known the advantages of wealth and position all his life. Educated at the best schools, well traveled, then — even in his mid-forties — Trudeau was (as Marchand politely put it) "under employed". He wrote a little, lectured in law at the Universtiy of Montreal, and still seemed to enjoy travel more than any other activity. In 1965, Trudeau was a wealthy dilettante who had won the respect of Pelletier and Marchand for his role in social criticism. But like the other writers in *Cité Libre*, Trudeau had not limited his scorn to local enemies. In 1963, for example, Trudeau had called Pearson a "Defrocked Priest of Peace" for arming the BOMARC missiles with nuclear warheads. On the more positive side (from the standpoint of Ottawa), Trudeau had denounced the racist nationalism of Quebec (even after the Quiet Revolution), and thus embraced federalism as the appropriate counterweight to such irrationalism. Pelletier had done the same and that made both more acceptable to the federal Liberal Party. It was the tie to Marchand, however, that was most important initially. To get the big fish the Liberals had to take the lesser fry as well. Ironically, it was Trudeau — not Marchand — who subsequently had the greatest impact on national politics.

After successful election to the safe seats for which the "three wise men" were recruited, all were given important positions in the government late in 1965. But in 1966 the spotlight was on other personalities and priorities as the government moved finally to honor the social security cheque the Liberals first wrote in 1919. Old age pensions, unemployment insurance, and family allowances had been implemented decades earlier. Little headway had been made with health insurance. A national scheme for hospital assistance had been enacted in 1957 but comprehensive medical insurance had been left to the provinces. Saskatchewan, the one province with a CCF government (since 1944), was the lone actor on comprehensive health insurance — and not until 1963. Three others subsidized the premiums of "poor risks" with private companies. The rest left medical care to individuals to provide for themselves.

In 1961, Diefenbaker had appointed a Royal Commission on Health Services under Emmett Hall, Chief Justice of Saskatchewan. After an extensive three-year study of the matter, the Hall Commission endorsed the Saskatchewan model in 1964 to "make all the fruits of the health sciences available to all our residents without hindrance of any kind." One year later, Pearson put the proposal before the premiers. Then, in the spring of 1966, Allan MacEachen, Minister of Health and Welfare, introduced the legislation to Parliament.

In the development of the health insurance scheme, great care had been taken to find an approach that would not give rise to another monolithic shared cost program. In the diplomacy of 1965, Pearson declared that the federal government had no intention of designing a specific scheme for the provinces to join or ignore. The particulars of medicare were to be planned province by province. Wherever a provincial scheme conformed to certain broad criteria, Pearson said it would be eligible for a federal grant, adjusted from time to time at the federal government's discretion. The criteria were indeed broad: any publicly administered, comprehensive scheme covering all residents could be eligible for the grants.

It was hoped by Pearson and MacEachen that the enabling legislation introduced in 1966 could be passed and the program inaugurated on July 1, 1967 because Pearson liked the symbolism of completing the fundamentals of the social security state on the one-hundredth anniversary of the federation itself. Pearson's target was missed, however, because Mitchell Sharp, the Minister of Finance, was more interested in controlling government expenditure. Sharp convinced the cabinet that medicare would be inflationary in 1967 but less so in 1968. For fiscal reasons, the inaugural day for the program was postponed twelve months even though the legislation passed before the end of 1966. Thus, the provinces gained an additional year to devise qualifying plans, but even with the additional time only two — Saskatchewan and British Columbia — had qualifying schemes on July 1, 1968. Five more provinces followed in 1969. Prince Edward Island, and Quebec inaugurated their plans in 1970. New Brunswick and the Territories followed in 1971-72.

By Canada's centennial year, medicare was thus at least partially fulfilled — something like the country itself. Since centennial celebrations tend to amplify the positive *ad nauseum*, cynics were happily surprised that the twelve months of 1967 provoked nothing more nauseating than smug satisfaction. For one reason, Canada appeared to be better led than the United States, then at the height of the agony of Vietnam and racial violence in its cities. Another reason was "Expo '67", Canada's first World's Fair. Fifty million visitors toured the site on a man-made island off Montreal, gawking at the sights and marveling at the mood of the place. Elsewhere, centennial celebrations were also neither as dull nor as crass as might have been expected. For example, the citizenry of Bowsman, Manitoba, got a federal grant to install a new sewer system and celebrated its inauguration by staging a "Centennial Privy Parade" with all the outhouses in town borne festively to the flames. Everywhere an enthusiasm for change was evident. The symbolic sign of the times became the new flag adopted officially in great parliamentary rancor in 1964. In 1967, a whole population made it sentimentally their own. Nearly one million of the red maple leaf flags were sold and given away. They showed up everywhere, especially on the packsacks of young Canadians trooping across the country and Europe (anxious to distinguish themselves from other North Americans).

John Diefenbaker (and many others) never reconciled themselves to the "Pearson Pennant" or the other dizziness of 1967. Increasingly, it became evident to Diefenbaker's party that the Chief was a liability as well as an embarrassment. By 1967, the Tories had fallen behind even the NDP in the Gallup polls. That was persuasive evidence to nearly everyone but Diefenbaker that a change in direction was called for. There was a convention in September. Still, Diefenbaker refused to resign gracefully, standing for re-election and finishing fifth on the first ballot. Ultimately, Robert Stanfield, the premier of Nova Scotia was elected. Diefenbaker congratulated the new leader, asked the delegates to unite behind him, and then left the convention pouting about his party's ingratitude and subsequently ignored his own advice about unity.

Diefenbaker's hurt pride notwithstanding, the change of leaders did prove immediately beneficial to the Tories who rapidly moved ahead of both the NDP and the Liberals in just two months. By December, Pearson knew that his time had come; politely he announced his retirement, and called for a leadership convention to take place the following April.

Since the Liberals observed a tradition of alternating between French-Canadian and English leaders, Pearson's successor had to be a Quebecker. Pearson tried to convince Jean Marchand to accept the challenge, but Marchand refused since he thought that he lacked the administrative talent and an adequate command of English. Pearson then turned to the Quebec Liberal who lacked Marchand's political skills but who was perfectly bilingual and had developed a remarkable media persona since his appearance in Ottawa in 1965. Pierre Trudeau had also achieved a following by proclaiming himself a "new guy with new ideas". While MacEachen was working on medicare, Trudeau was promoting reforms in Canada's divorce law and the criminal code to broaden the grounds for marriage dissolution, and to legalize lotteries, therapeutic abortions, and homosexuality between consenting adults. According to Richard Gwyn, "if Expo had been a person, that person would have been Trudeau." The Liberals elected him leader.

Three days after becoming leader of the Liberal Party and Prime Minister of Canada, Trudeau plunged the country into a general election. Because it was called so suddenly, Trudeau was free to run against the record of his own party as well as his major opponent, Robert Stanfield. Since Stanfield was also relatively new in his job, Canada then faced the kind of contest that the Americans confront every four or eight years. The election of 1968 was a kind of presidential contest between two leaders unknown except by personality. Moreover, the two major candidates were almost perfect opposites from the standpoint of the personas that appeared on television. Stanfield wanted to tour the country making major policy addresses. He loathed the informality of newsmen rushing up to politicians to "shove a bunch of microphones in your face and in thirty seconds you're expected to produce a profound and intelligent answer to an extremely complicated national issue."

Neither the informality nor the 30-second bit parts seemed to bother

Pierre Trudeau who plunged into a crowd on foot, in the daytime at a shopping plaza, uttered a few compelling words about the "Just Society" he hoped to build and warned that there would be no giveaways. "It is more important to have a sound dollar than to satisfy this or that particular interest," he said. Such boldness was provocation for heckling, of course. Once that began Trudeau's quick wit usually turned criticism to his own advantage. Even skeptics warmed to his style. At the end, without having developed any particular point elaborately, Trudeau simply dared people to vote for him: "If Canadians want to take a bit of a risk, if they want to take a chance on the future, then we're asking them to vote for us." Wherever he went — even in Calgary — Canadians seemed to respond positively to his style. Such enthusiasm had not been seen since Diefenbaker's 1958 vision speeches. The press called the enthusiasm "Trudeau-mania". Richard Gwyn suggests that post-Expo "Canada-mania" sums up the reaction more accurately.

Stanfield harrumphed that the Trudeau style was nothing more than theatrics and, forgetting Diefenbaker, asserted that "for the first time in Canadian history a prime minister has asked the people for a blank cheque." Similarly, the leader of the NDP, T.C. Douglas, warned Canadians that beyond the image of the innovator was "the orthodoxy of the 1930s." Thus, Stanfield and Douglas both attempted to call the electorate down to specific issues in 1968. Stanfield began to make proposals "by the bucketful". He proposed innovations in public housing, agriculture, regional development — even a guaranteed annual income. Striking the same note, Douglas proposed a "Minimum Program for a New Canadian Society" that included proposals to deal with foreign ownership, iniquities in tax law and corporate power, as well as social welfare innovations. But in the end, on June 25, 45 percent of the voters gave their nod to Trudeau candidates. For the first time in a decade, Canadians elected a majority government.

## II   Trudeau in Power

Even as the 1968 election euphoria was at its height, some observers were predicting that the voters' enthusiasm for their new prime minister was going to be short lived. Dalton Camp suggested that Trudeau's arousal of enthusiastic support from Canadians with "opposite views and conflicting interests" would lead to trouble as soon as it was discovered that they admired the same leader from contradictory standpoints. For the moment, however, Pierre Trudeau said simply that he was a "new guy with new ideas" and everyone waited eagerly to see what he meant.

Trudeau did have intentions to pursue bold policies for promoting bilingualism, advancing French Canadians in the public service, reducing regional disparities, and adjusting government priorities to reduce defense commitments so that greater resources would be freed for domestic programs. All were areas in which the government subsequently did move. Language legislation and a lavish regional development program were introduced in 1968. A 50 percent phased reduction of the NATO commitment was announced in 1969. Other dramatic initiatives were attempted in native affairs, tax reform, and augmented unemployment insurance benefits. In 1970, the Government of Canada established diplomatic relations with China (the second country in the West to do so, following France). Finally, there was an effort to coordinate the activities of more than 100 provincial marketing boards in order to assure continuing prosperity for farmers whose collective position continued to improve despite falling world prices and transportation problems.

The Trudeau record between 1968 and 1972 was thus broad-ranging. But few successes were achieved. Like Diefenbaker, Trudeau had created expectations that were unfulfilled. Also like Diefenbaker, Trudeau's lack of fulfillment was said to have arisen from a fatal flaw of character. Where Diefenbaker was criticized for his "indecision", Trudeau's weakness was called "arrogance". Observors seized upon the alleged characteristic because many imagined that it described not only his own personality but also the leading quality of the administration he molded in Ottawa. Trudeau's personal staff was the largest ever — a "Supergroup", according to Walter Stewart, that seemed to matter more than the cabinet. Parliamentary power was said to have all but vanished, and the federal bureaucracy grew three times faster than the rate of population increase. Under Trudeau, the technocrats seemed to have taken charge as never before. The "arrogance" of the government was thus more than a personality foible of its leading personage, for the term referred as well to the overbearing aloofness of an entire administration.

The mood of the Mandarins following the 1968 election was that the real work of making a Canadian nation was only then beginning. The Official Languages Act was perhaps the first indication that Trudeau thought he was a nation-builder, a leader like John A. Macdonald attempting to fashion a continent-wide country out of a culturally fragmented federation. In the case of Macdonald's CPR, however, there was general agreement that the railway was needed. The consensus was less clear on Trudeau's proposed measure to grant more meaningful equality to the French and English languages in Canada. Introduced in October 1968, passed in July 1969, the Official Languages Act extended the minimal guarantees already in the BNA Act and asserted that Canada was one nation with two languages, rather than a federation of two national entities in splendid linguistic isolation.

A Gallup poll showed that most Canadians supported the new language law in principle. But in the West, 70 percent of the population did not favor even the idea of two official languages. With one region solidly opposed, it was suggested that the policy promoted division rather than unity. Trudeau's reply was that he was providing insurance against Quebec separatism by showing Quebeckers that French-speaking Canadians could feel at home anywhere in Canada.

One year after enacting the Official Languages Act, Trudeau showed that he was willing to employ even more dramatic discouragements to separatism. On October 5, 1970, two men took the British Trade Commissioner, James Cross, from his Montreal home at gunpoint. On the way to their car, one of the kidnappers announced that they were the FLQ *(Front de Libération du Québec,* a separatist group that pursued independence as part of a broader impulse toward social revolution). At first, the Cross kidnapping was treated as just another local police matter, but the ransom demanded was extraordinary. Among other things, the kidnappers wanted the release of twenty-three "political prisoners" (other terrorists convicted of less spectacular deeds than the Cross abduction), $500 000 in gold, and safe conduct and transportation to Cuba or Algeria. When it appeared that none of the major demands was going to be met, rather than killing Cross, another abduction occurred. On October 10, a different FLQ cell seized another dignatary, the Quebec Minister of Labour, Pierre Laporte. Local government then became frantic lest more kidnappings follow. The first minister was moved into a guarded suite in downtown Montreal. Troops were posted outside the homes of federal cabinet ministers in Ottawa, and Prime Minister Trudeau began to talk about doing whatever was necessary to preserve public order.

"How far would you be willing to go?" a reporter asked on October 12.

"Just watch me," Trudeau replied.

On October 16, the Government of Canada invoked the War Measures Act to give the police special powers to undertake "ceaseless pursuit" of the FLQ. Two days later, Laporte was strangled by his captors and Cross continued to be held by persons unknown. Eventually, the location of Cross and the murderers of Laporte were both uncovered by routine police work. By that time, however, a debate had developed not only on the wisdom of invoking the emergency powers but also over the motives of the government in doing so.

Uncritical observers such as Robert Bothwell claim that the jailing of everyone remotely sympathetic to the FLQ "made plain that those who played at parlour revolution faced real and immediate sanctions." Consequently, the "enthusiasm for a day at the barricades ... noticeably diminished." It is also suggested that bold action was vindicated completely in the court of public opinion since 87 percent of the population — in Quebec as well as the rest of Canada — approved the government's course.

Critics of the action suggest that the use of a cannon to swat a fly did irreparable harm to the cause of civil liberties in Canada. It was also suggested that since most of the 500 persons detained without charge had not the remotest connection with terrorism, there were actually two targets in the round-up: separatism in general as well as the FLQ in particular even though the government repeatedly asserted that nonviolent separatists had every right to pursue their objective by democratic means. Such affirmations notwithstanding, there were no fine distinctions drawn between separatism and terrorism in the general round-up in October. Moreover, after the crisis had passed, rather than issuing an apology for such overzealous police work, the Prime Minister boasted that separatism was "dead". Other leading Liberals agreed: the FLQ crisis had been an opportunity to "smash separatism" and the government had taken it.

Before and after the crisis, the cabinet approved other extraordinary measures in its fight against separatism. Under John Starnes, its Director-General of Security and Intelligence, the RCMP prepared a special memorandum in 1970 on groups "likely to promote violent confrontation with authority". At the head of the list was the *Parti québécois*. Despite the inclusion of such peaceful and democratic organizations on the Starnes subversives list, Trudeau praised the review as a "damn fine piece of work", gave the RCMP a long leash, and did not prevent the force from indulging in gestapo-like activities to disrupt all kinds of radicals across Canada. Here again, the arrogance was not simply Trudeau's, but the smug assumption of the bureaucracy that the liberal-democratic, centralized state was superior to any other and that superiority jusitified a heavy hand from the controlling center even if the actions included theft, arson, invasions of privacy, and the defamation of character.

So all-pervading was the arrogance of the Ottawa Mandarins that even potentially useful programs in equalization and economic development became subtle — and not so subtle — devices for expanding federal power in areas hitherto exclusively reserved to the provinces. Thus "education" became "training"; "municipal affairs" became "problems of urban growth"; and "community development" emerged in the guise of the "fight against unemployment". Rather than pursuing the medicare approach devised by Pearson, the Trudeau government created a Department of Regional Economic Expansion (DREE) to engage in flag-raising contests with the provinces as much as to make headway in the areas that were spending priorities.

By 1972, most of the electorate had decided that the "new guy with new ideas" was not offering a fresh approach to old problems so much as a new push of centralism upon a country that was not prepared to accept an expanded federal power. In the context of a general election, the government was thus on trial for its arrogance. Trudeau attempted to counter the criticism that his administration was aloof and overbearing by telling Maritimers how much DREE was doing to correct their economic backwardness; by telling Quebeckers that their status had been enhanced by their becoming more influential in Ottawa; and by warning British Columbians that Canada needed a strong leader to keep Quebec in place.

Sixty-two percent of the voters were unconvinced that Trudeau was the right leader to continue in power but since a significant number of voters shifted from the Liberals to the NDP, the result was a Parliament of minorities with the largest New Democratic caucus ever elected: NDP 31, Liberals 109, and Conservatives 107. David Lewis (the successor to T.C. Douglas) was thus in roughly the same position in 1972 as J.S. Woodsworth in 1926; and Pierre Trudeau responded to Lewis in approximately the same way as King had dealt with Woodsworth. For 18 months, Trudeau was as progressive as he said he was, but far more innovative than he ever managed with his own majority.

The record of Trudeau's minority government was impressive. Acting finally on the Watkins report on foreign ownership (submitted in 1968), a Foreign Investment Review Agency (FIRA) was created to monitor foreign takeovers of Canadian business. There were tax reforms including the indexing of income tax rates to the rate of inflation; improvements in pension and family allowance benefits; and the century-old Elections Act was reformed to require disclosure of the sources of large campaign contributions. A number of conferences and inquiries (such as the Western Economic Opportunities Conference and the Berger inquiry into the social and environomental impact of a petroleum pipeline down the Mackenzie Valley) showed a more consultative approach to development issues. But most importantly, a bold policy to cope with a sudden and unexpected rise in the price of oil was announced at the end of 1973.

A few months before the oil crisis, the Energy Minister, Donald Macdonald, forecast a price of $5 per barrel for the year 2000. Then on October 6, war broke out in the Middle East, raged for less than one month, and led the Arab suppliers to the West to boycott the supporters of Israel. The success of the embargo led to the first successful escalation of prices by a thirteen-year-old cartel of Oil Producing Exporting Countries (OPEC), and the oil that sold for $3 per barrel before the war, reached $10 by year's end.

The acute shortage and the dramatic rise in price caused Prime Minister Trudeau to announce a complex program for meeting the emergency. The five eastern provinces dependent on imported oil were to receive a subsidy on imports derived from a tax on oil and gas still to be exported from the producing provinces in Western Canada. In this way, a controlled single price was assured. To make the east less dependent on imports, pipelines were to be extended as quickly as possible, and to cope with the increased demands on domestic production the government announced a new program of incentives to encourage exploration and development of hitherto unexploited deposits of heavy oil and tar sands. One of the vehicles for the new production was to be a national petroleum corporation — Petro-Canada.

Largely due to the program announced in December, Canadians weathered the winter of 1973-74 without oil shortages and without the wild rise in prices that continued elsewhere. But an inflation scare soon replaced the oil scare. Robert Stanfield's Conservatives demanded wage and price controls. Trudeau refused. Instead, his finance minister introduced a budget loaded with tax concessions to corporations — bound to be intolerable to the NDP. In this way, Trudeau engineered defeat in the House of Commons at a time of his own choosing, and went to the people heaping abuse on Stanfield's proposed incomes policy. The Prime Minister called controls a "proven disaster looking for a new place to happen" and suggested that since Canada imported one third of what the country consumed, controlling prices was absurd. "The only thing controls will control will be your wages," he told the working people of Canada. With such condemnation of the Tories, and having shown that "when he wanted to, he could be the best Prime Minister around," according to Richard Gwyn, the electorate restored Trudeau's majority on July 8, 1974. But having gone after controls "like a terrier after a rat" he had left little room to maneuvre subsequently. By 1975, most Canadians wanted an incomes policy. By 1975 according to a Gallup poll, the leading difficulty was excessive wage demands extorted by overpowerful unions.

## III    Organized Labor and the Economic Malaise

"Big labor" had come relatively late to Canada, long after big business and big government. At the outbreak of the Second World War, the percentage of the nonagricultural work force in unions was about the same as in 1914. But in the context of full employment for war production (and wartime wage controls), labor organizers made enormous gains. In 1943 and 1944, several provincial governments adopted labor laws that protected workers in their organizational drive and also required employers to negotiate with unions certified as the chosen agent of a majority of the employees. The Government of Canada followed in 1944 with a wartime regulation of its own that universalized such rights. Under the protection of an order in council (PC 1003) first agreements were negotiated by workers in hundreds of companies that had resisted unionization for decades. Such recognition did not usually take the form of the "closed shop" — employees were not required to join a union as a condition of employment. But to give labor organizations some measure of security once certified, Ontario endorsed a device known as the Rand Formula (after its author, Justice Ivan Rand), by which employees could join or refuse to join, but nonjoiners would find the equivalent of union dues deducted from their wages. After the war, the Government of Canada grafted its wartime labor policies onto the Industrial Disputes Investigation Act renaming the amended law the Industrial Relations and Disputes Investigation Act. Since the IRDI Act was a regular statute (rather than a wartime order, such as PC 1003), its provisions applied only to workers under federal jurisdiction. Subsequently, however, the provinces that did not already have labor relations acts did adopt such laws, usually patterned after the IRDI Act. The result was that the wartime gains were not lost in the postwar period.

By the 1950s, organized labor had grown to nearly one million persons and included most of the work force in major manufacturing, mining and forest products. But small industry was still largely unorganized, and even those who were in unions were not part of a unified movement. One division was regional since the unionized labor of Quebec tended to be organized in unions of the Canadian and Catholic Confederation of Labour (CCCL) separate from the rest of Canada and systematically intimidated by the government of Maurice Duplessis. Elsewhere, the situation was similarly weakened by division but of a different sort. The largest group of organized labor in English-speaking Canada consisted of 522 000 workers affiliated with the Trades and Labour Congress of Canada (TLC). Like the American Federation of Labor, TLC unions tended to be craft-oriented and limited in their objectives to narrow wages and hours issues. Like the profit maximizers who owned the means of production, their goal was "more and more".

A competing group sought industrial organization to promote broader issues of social change and consciously repudiated the "business unionism" of the conservative TLC. The Canadian Congress of Labour (CCL), like the Congress of Industrial Organizations (CIO) in the United States, was a breakaway group promoting more massive organization and broader political aims. But since its appearance in 1939, the Canadian Congress of Labour was as divided within its own ranks as from the TLC. In the 1940s, approximately one third of CCL leaders called themselves Communists, the others supported the CCF. By 1950 (due to government repression and opposition from the rank and file), the once significant Communist presence in the CCL all but disappeared. In the same period, the CIO in the United States went even further toward the right and converted to business unionism. When merger inevitably followed with the AFL in 1955, the CCL in Canada almost immediately united with the TLC, emerging as the Canadian Labour Congress (CLC), also in 1955.

The reason that the divisions and alliances between the AFL-CIO and TLC-CCL were so parallel is that nearly 70 percent of the organized workers in English-speaking Canada were members of "international" (meaning *American)* unions. In this sense, the CLC was largely a northern echo of the AFL-CIO. But the Canadian group did harbor a stronger commitment to "political unionism", a fact that was particularly evident in 1961 when the New Democratic Party emerged from a convention of 710 delegates from the CCF, 613 delegates from unions, and 318 representatives of "New Party Clubs". Since the leaders of the CLC claimed to speak for all working people of Canada, there were great expectations that a Canadian Labour Party might be emerging. But less than one third of the nonagricultural work force was unionized in 1961, and three quarters of the persons who did belong to unions continued to vote for the Liberals or Conservatives.

Nothing developed between 1961 and 1974 to suggest that workers were finding a keener interest in political unionism, but there was a dramatic surge in the number of persons unionized after 1965. The year before, the Government of Quebec unveiled a new labor code that conceded collective bargaining rights to all public service employees except firemen and policemen. Prior to Quebec's move to permit meaningful organization of civil servants, only Saskatchewan had given civil servants collective bargaining rights (in 1944 after the election of the CCF). In the Quebec code of 1964, there was a catch, however, since a clause prevented any public employee from joining a union that endorsed a political party. Thus, the CLC was effectively barred from organizing the public service of Quebec because it still endorsed the NDP. The old confessional unions, secularized and renamed the Confederation of National Trade Unions (CNTU) thus had privileged access to the growth sector of the labor movement in French Canada. After the Government of Canada and the other provinces granted similar rights to their civil servants (the federal government leading the way in 1967) the CLC was also able to take advantage of the boom in public service organization. By 1970, the public service unions emerged as rivals to all but the largest internationals and the portion of the nonagricultural work force that was unionized grew to 40 percent of the total.

By the 1970s, organized labor in Canada had thus reached its own centennial and could point with pride to many accomplishments — especially in the period since 1940. From a minority movement of less than 10 percent of the work force, organized labor appeared to be edging toward majority status with a membership of 2.2 million persons contributing $100 million in dues in 1970. Since the Second World War, wages had quadrupled. Workers' purchasing power had doubled. But organized labor was almost as divided as ever with leaders of the CLC continuing to talk politics as if they spoke for all when in fact they could barely unite conventions of a thousand committed delegates. More importantly, most workers (organized or not) had begun to think that strikes were becoming too common and wages (except their own) too high.

In 1974 and 1975, time lost in strikes, levels of wage settlements, and the rate of inflation were higher than anytime before in Canadian history. Many commentators concluded that the fault lay with the demands of organized labor, a conclusion that was seized upon especially firmly in the summer of 1975 when the inside postal workers struck and won a 71 percent wage increase with a thirty-hour week. But overall, Canadian wage settlements were considerablly behind those of West Germany and Japan, the two countries that were frequently mentioned as models of restraint in wage demands.

The more basic problem in Canada was the systematic relation between businessmen's demands for high profits, workers desire to keep up with rising prices, and the cost of government programs to support workers who were laid off as businessmen exercised their only effective defense against profit squeezing — unemployment. In the years between 1971 and 1974, profits of the largest corporations increased rapidly, while wages, salaries, and the incomes of smaller businesses did not grow at nearly the same pace. When workers raced to catch up in 1974 and 1975, two record years of strikes resulted, and negotiated wage settlements averaged 17 percent. Facing recessionary prospects, large corporations imposed massive layoffs. Government programs automatically injected enormous amounts of public spending into the economy in the form of such payments as unemployment benefits. Then public sector deficits inevitably reached record levels in their turn. The result was stagnation with high inflation — "stagflation" in the jargon of the panic of 1975.

In the face of 14 percent inflation, rising unemployment, and a fiscal situation that seemed totally out of control, the Minister of Finance, John Turner, was forced to formulate some appropriate new policy. The Conservative opposition said that if their controls program had been implemented as they had demanded in 1974, no such crisis would be developing. Turner, however, refused to implement mandatory controls, and asked labor to observe voluntary restraint. Once voluntarism failed, Turner knew that the government's options were narrowing and asked to be relieved of the finance portfolio. When Trudeau refused to consider Turner's release from his politically disastrous post, Turner resigned. After a cabinet shuffle that put the former energy minister, Donald Macdonald, in the position of Minister of Finance, a crash program of compulsory wage and price controls was designed for implementation in October.

On Thanksgiving Day, October 13, 1975, Prime Minister Trudeau appeared on television to announce that the country had to swallow "strong medicine". He announced that any private company with more than 500 employees, and all public service workers would be subject to three years of wage and price controls effective immediately. The limit for the first years was 10 percent, 8 in year two, and 6 percent in the final year of the program. All provinces agreed to cooperate, even Saskatchewan and Manitoba (their NDP premiers explaining that an "incomes policy" was a necessary feature of any truly planned economy). Equally interesting, a Gallup poll showed that 62 percent of the general population endorsed controls at the time of their inauguration, and the endorsement did not drop dramatically in most provinces over the next three years. Business also favored at least the wage controls aspect of the scheme. But they did grow increasingly nervous about the economic planning that Premiers Blakeney and Schreyer had advocated, especially as Prime Minister Trudeau also seemed determined to embark in the same direction.

At the end of 1975, Trudeau suggested that the controls program was no long-term solution to Canada's economic malaise, only a short breathing space. Looking to the post-controls period, he warned that if Canadians did not "change their social structure and values ... then the same economic mainsprings will create inflation and unemployment all over again." Trudeau said that controls were only the beginning of a much vaster, overdue intervention by the government in the economy. The Prime Minister knew that the country faced real panic. He knew that his policy had been accepted despite the obligatory grumbling from the leaders of the unions. He also seemed to sense that basic structural changes in the Canadian economy might have been accepted during the inflation crisis, just as basic changes had been implemented at the time of the energy panic in 1973. But in the earlier emergency he faced the daily possibility of defeat in the House of Commons. In 1975 his majority was restored. As was his custom in the comfort of power, Trudeau dithered and wandered in abstractions rather than taking effective action. In the end, the rhetoric of basic change proved to be nothing more than prime ministerial mutterings aloud.

The kinds of reforms that Trudeau had the opportunity to launch early in 1976 (but ultimately avoided) pertained to the fundamental underdevelopment of the Canadian economy, an underdevelopment that meant two thirds of the country's exports continued to be resource products shipped out of Canada in a raw or semi-finished form while the value of manufactured goods imported exceeded those exported by about $10 billion. What was needed was an ambitious program to encourage import-replacing manufacturing to provide high productivity jobs for Canadians making, for example, the $6 billion-worth of equipment used in mining and agriculture that continued to be imported. Alternatively, initiatives might have been taken to promote selective development of high technology industries not already dominated by another country. The time was right, in other words, for the government to implement an ambitious "industrial strategy". Instead, Trudeau and his ministers offered homilies about the need to change "attitudes" and hoped that a world recovery might promote another boom in Canada's raw materials in the near future. In the meantime, the government counted on the many divisions within organized labor and more generally within the Canadian working class to keep opposition to a minimum. But workers became less willing to forego increases once it became apparent that the only purpose of the program was to make them worried about their jobs, less prone to strike, and to tolerate wage increases that were lower than the rate of inflation. The first such workers to mount an effective opposition on this account were in Quebec with the apparent triumph of separatism on November 15, 1976.

# IV    Quebec Separatism

The first significant separatist movement in twentieth-century Quebec was that led by René Lévesque, the disgruntled Liberal who bolted his party in October 1967 to publish his *Option for Quebec* in January 1968, and who eight months later organized a movement, the *Parti québécois*, dedicated to political independence. At its founding convention in the middle of October, the PQ promised a unilateral declaration of separation from Canada followed by negotiations to establish a common market. Then, sweeping changes would follow at "home". The proposed domestic reforms included establishment of French as the official language of the province, and regulations to control the export of profits by foreigners. As a palliative to the English-speaking minority, there was a promise to continue English-language schools, thus repeating the experiment in dualism to the extent that it was first launched in 1867, but on a smaller scale and with the English rather than the French in the subordinate, at least minority, position.

Lévesque's party was not as immediately popular as his book, however. The manifesto that had been an instant success (a popularity that can be interpreted as an incentive to form the party in the first place), did not spill over immediately to the political movement. A Gallup poll indicated that only 10 percent of Quebeckers considered themselves separatists in 1968. Still, almost 20 percent were undecided. Lévesque reasoned that if they could be won over, and if the *Union nationale* and Liberals continued to be roughly similar in their popularity, there was hope for a PQ victory even with a minority movement given the winner-take-all system for counting ballots. It was even possible that a 34 percent vote could yield 100 percent of the seats in the legislature if the UN and Liberals each received 33 percent in every riding.

The two established parties anticipated such a split as well. Still, both had cause for greater optimism than Lévesque. Over the next two years, the UN and Liberals adjusted their images for maximum effect at the much anticipated next election. The Liberals leaned right in the expectation that most Quebeckers had no interest in separatism and were even sick of hearing the demand for "special status". They advocated a "paying federalism" *(un fédéralisme rentable)* that would go hand-in-hand with the promotion of economic development without sacrificing cultural sovereignty. Such was their luxury of opposition. The UN was still the party in power (following the previous defeat of the Liberals in 1966). The UN aimed to appear moderate (by repudiating separatism) but at the same time they took dramatic steps to affirm the symbols of national status. Before the end of 1968, for example, the UN abolished the Upper House of the legislature and changed the name of the lower chamber from the Legislative Assembly to the National Assembly.

The three parties thus prepared Quebeckers for an election that was to unfold as a *de facto* referendum on separatism. When the showdown came in April 1970, the results seemed to indicate a clear preference for the party that promised economic development without constitutional wrangling. The Liberals received 42 percent of the vote, almost twice as much as the PQ with 23 percent, or the UN with 20 (the other 15 percent was divided among a plethora of splinter parties, the largest of which was the *Ralliement créditiste* with 11 percent of the vote). But the electoral system translated the distribution of opinion into a pattern of representation that was far less kind to the PQ than they expected. The Liberals' 42 percent gave them a majority government with 72 of the 108 seats. The UN became the official opposition, and the *Créditistes* came away with nearly twice as many representatives in the Assembly as the PQ (whose 23 percent elected only seven members).

Lévesque had hoped that the UN would be more uniformly popular. But in the 1970 election there were only pockets of *Creditiste* and UN support. The main show emerged as a contest between Liberals and *Péquistes* with the PQ running as a significant, but distant, minority movement nearly everywhere. Lévesque himself failed in the riding in which he had run successfully before as a Liberal. To some separatists, the irony was infuriating. They lost interest in the movement or became more radical. Indeed, one frequently cited explanation for the timing of the FLQ kidnappings in October was the depth of bitterness that resulted from democratic separatists winning one fourth of the vote but only one twentieth of the representation in the legislature.

Lévesque disassociated himself completely from the violent separatists, calling the FLQ "sewer rats". He also began to emphasize the social reform intentions of his group more than its aspirations for independence. After 1970, the PQ developed as a Quebec social democratic party with separatism somewhat incidental to its larger program.

In the next provincial election, that of 1973, voters polarized more than in 1970 — without the PQ having gained enough strength to offer a signficant challenge to the Liberals. The PQ did increase in popularity to about 30 percent, but since the increase was so uniformly distributed and since the UN deterioration was also widespread, the *Péquistes* actually lost strength in the legislature. In 1973, 30 percent of the votes elected only six members. In the new National Assembly, the Liberals occupied nearly every seat.

Once again, Lévesque responded by downplaying separatism. Independence — the PQ's ostensible reason for being — was shelved by a device that Wilfrid Laurier or Mackenzie King would have recognzied as his own style of accommodation and evasion. Claude Morin championed a pledge that any PQ government would hold a referendum before moving toward independence; it was the ideal way to disassociate the party from the separatist issue without seeming hypocritical or flaccid. What remained was the party's still strong advocacy of social democracy, especially popular with the increasingly militant Quebec labor movement. Working class support was widely regarded as the PQ's essential ticket for crossing the magical 40 percent threshold in popular vote and gaining the government. To retain the allegiance of the older *Péquistes*, there would have to be a referendum on separatism, but not necessarily independence.

In the meantime, the reigning Liberals moved from one crisis to another exhibiting opportunism more than competence. In Quebec, as in the rest of the country, the most difficult problems were economic. Bourassa's Lib-

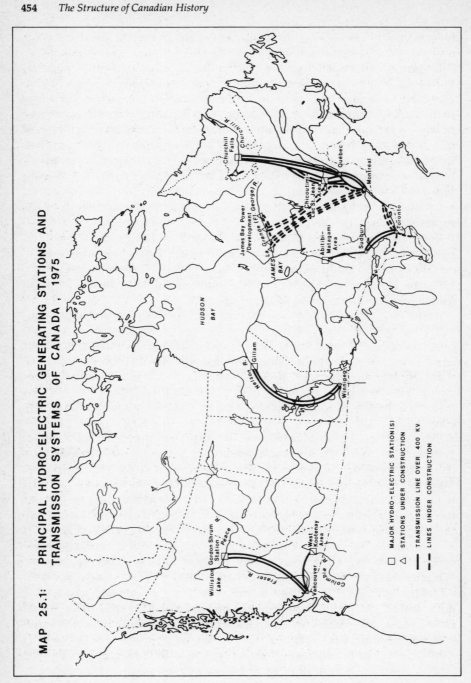

MAP 25.1:    PRINCIPAL HYDRO-ELECTRIC GENERATING STATIONS AND
TRANSMISSION SYSTEMS OF CANADA, 1975

erals appeared particularly inept in dealing with the most militant unions and in controlling expenditures for worthwhile projects such as a gigantic hydroelectric development on James Bay (see map 25.1), or frivolous projects such as the installations for the billion-dollar Olympic Games held in Montreal in 1976. Then, too, there was anger over language legislation that English-speaking Quebeckers regarded as discriminatory, Trudeau called "politically stupid", and the *Péquistes* dismissed as too little too late. Additional disasters were a nine-day strike over the use of French between pilots and air traffic controllers in Quebec, and growing resentment over Ottawa's incomes policy. Everything was set for a strong protest vote once Bourassa called an election for late in the autumn of 1976.

Given the problems of the moment, and the PQ's almost complete disassociation from separatism, the PQ looked especially attractive to the middle- and lower-class French-speaking Quebeckers. Lévesque's party promised to reform labor law, elaborate existing social programs, and stand against Ottawa. A slightly reinvigorated *Union nationale* and a significantly less popular Liberal Party meant that the electoral system finally worked as Lévesque had hoped. On November 15, its evenly distributed 41 percent of the vote gave the *Parti québécois* almost three quarters of the seats in the legislature.

The rest of Canada was stunned by the victory that was the proudest day in Lévesque's life. Nearly everyone but Trudeau seemed to be thrown into a momentary panic. The Prime Minister went on television to congratulate the PQ on their spectacular success and promised the same cooperation with Lévesque's government as Canada extended to any other province while stressing that the country did face a grave crisis. Trudeau seemed to have every confidence that appropriate constitutional reforms would demonstate that it was "possible to be at one and the same time, a good Canadian and a good Quebecker." Should the process fail, however, Trudeau stressed that no military or police action would be used to keep Quebec within Canada. "Canada cannot, Canada must not, survive by force," he affirmed. The bond that would hold the country together had to be that of "fraternity, of hope and of charity in the scriptural sense, for if the Canadian nation is to survive, it will only survive in mutual respect and in love for one another."

Trudeau's message of November 24 seemed to close an era of confrontation with conciliation. More than a decade earlier, in January 1965, Daniel Johnson had said that if a government in Quebec were "to lay the ground immediately for independence," the rest of the country would come round quickly "to grant equality for the French-Canadian nation in a truly bi-national Canada." In the spring of 1977, something of a spirit of accommodation seemed to develop as Canadians affirmed faith in their country from coast to coast. Even Lévesque began to talk about building "a true Confederation" instead of simply abandoning the old one. It seemed that Canada might yet resolve its constitutional difficulties, and then, having achieved a new accommodation in that area, make headway on the more serious economic problems.

# Bibliography

The most comprehensive general work on the Trudeau-Lévesque period from 1968 through 1976 is Robert Bothwell, *et al.*, *Canada since 1945: Power, Politics, and Provincialism* (1981). Unfortunately, Bothwell's work tends merely to chronicle events or to defend Trudeau from his critics rather than attempt a balanced assessment of the period. Much more satisfactory as an analysis of Trudeau in power is Richard Gwyn, *The Northern Magus: Pierre Trudeau and Canadians* (1980). Other provocative biographical accounts are Geoffrey Stevens, *Robert Stanfield* (1973) which offers an excellent account of Trudeau's language policy, and Walter Stewart, *Shrug: Trudeau in Power* (1971), too harshly critical in most respects but still useful in its analysis of the parliamentary and administrative reforms that tended to concentrate power in the Prime Minister's Office.

The important development that the meteoric rise of Trudeau obscured and upstaged was the advent of medicare between 1965 and 1968, described fully by Malcom G. Taylor, *Health Insurance and Canadian Public Policy: The Seven Decisions that Created the Canadian Health Insurance System* (1978).

The event that generated the greatest notoriety for Trudeau once in power was the October crisis, criticized from the standpoint of a civil libertarian, Denis Smith, in *Bleeding Hearts ... Bleeding Country: Canada and the Quebec Crisis* (1971) and described from the inside by Gérard Pelletier in *The October Crisis* (1971).

The event that was most notable in Trudeau's second majority, wage and price controls, is unintelligible without background in labor history and labor economics. The first is provided by Desmond Morton and Terry Copp in *Working People: An Illustrated History of Canadian Labour* (1980). The second is found in Cy Gonick, *Out of Work: Why There's So Much Unemployment and Why It's Getting Worse* (1978).

For understanding the capstone of the first Trudeau period, the development of separatism in Quebec, a biographical account of Lévesque by Peter Desbarat and a chronicle of events by John Saywell are both useful. Desbarat's biogaphy is called *René: A Canadian in Search of a Country* (1976). Saywell's narrative is *The Rise of the Parti Québécois* (1977).

"... the scheme that finally passed bore little resemblance to Trudeau's original proposal ..."

# CHAPTER 26

# Constitutional Draw

I   Decline and Fall of the Liberal Party
_____

The election of the *Parti québécois* in November 1976 had a tonic effect on
Prime Minister Trudeau's popularity. A majority of the country took his
November 24 address promising constitutional innovation seriously, and
many thousands of Canadians appeared willing to accept bold innovation
to hold the country together. The government did appoint a Task Force on
Canadian Unity (headed by Jean Luc Pépin, former administrator of wage
and price controls, and John Robarts, former Premier of Ontario). The
Pépin-Robarts Commission toured the country gathering constitutional
wisdom and there was no shortage of submissions to its proceedings. But
to Trudeau's displeasure, most called for palpable recognition that Canada
was a federation of two — or more — national entities, rather than one
people that happened to speak two languages. Trudeau warned against a
hasty rush to the "panacea of decentralization". Curiously, however, his
own proposals were not immediately forthcoming, and did not appear
until nearly two years after the election of the PQ.

Appearing in June 1978, Trudeau's package was anti-climatic. Ironically,
the Trudeau approach to "Constitutional renewal" was called *A Time for
Action*. The title was ironic because the document was so late and offered
so little. The national acceptance of the need for constitutional reform had
peaked the year before between April and September. Had *A Time for
Action* offered more, its tardy appearance might not have mattered. But
instead of presenting an imaginative approach to restructuring the Canadian federation, Trudeau's document, according to Robert Bothwell, was
"a badly written and worse-conceived potpourri of Senate reform and
Supreme Court fiddlings." Literally too little too late, it "fell with a dull
thud before an astonished and somewhat bemused populace."

By the early summer of 1978, the main preoccupation of Canadians was
not the unity issue, but the state of the economy once again. The dollar

had begun a day-by-day slide from parity with American currency (reaching 86 cents by May). Unemployment was up to 8.6 percent. Inflation rose to 10 percent, and the federal budget deficit approached the record level of $12 billion (the equivalent of one fourth of Ottawa's total revenue, or 5 percent of the entire GNP). Many economists (and almost all Tories) claimed that the apparently uncontrolled spending was the leading factor in the whole malaise because it eroded business confidence and discouraged investment, and that led to unemployment.

After attending an economic conference with other heads of governments in July (and receiving public opinion data that showed more and more voters were blaming expensive government for their woes), Trudeau and his advisors decided that the deficit was the top priority and aimed to trim in the summer of 1978 in preparation for an election.

The problem of the federal deficit was far too complicated, however, for the government simply — and suddenly — to decide to spend a great deal less. Some payments were fixed and uncontrollable: unemployment insurance, pension benefits, and the oil price subsidy for the eastern provinces, for example, were determined by statute and the amounts payable varied by eligible applicants rather than budget decisions. There was no way to reduce expenditures on such fixed costs except to change the law establishing regional equality in oil prices, or lowering pension benefits, or turning away from the unemployed. The only area that the federal government could cut and hurt only itself, in a sense, was the $12.6 billion spent on maintaining the federal bureaucracy. Since Trudeau and his advisors were not about to reduce the Government of Canada to a cipher, and since they were equally loathe to reduce subsidies and grants that pinched individual taxpayers (also voters), the bold program announced in mid-August to "ensure our continued prosperity", in the end, was largely cosmetic, trimming no more than one fifth of the anticipated deficit.

The more important policy was adoption of a gimmick advocated by an American economist, Milton Friedman. In Friedman's approach, the trendsetting central bank of a country was to increase its interest rates to unheard-of levels in the expectation that tighter credit would offset the inflationary impact of larger government deficits, thus reducing the rate of inflation generally. Higher returns to lenders would bring in a rush of foreign investment, thus increasing the value of the currency of the country with the highest interest rates. With falling inflation and a rising dollar, general investor confidence was also supposed to grow, ultimately affecting unemployment as general investment levels increased. The new orthodoxy (called *monetarism*) caused some excitement because it seemed to go beyond old-fashioned Keynesian economics. Moreover, the new orthodoxy claimed to be capable of accomplishing a great deal more by the vastly simpler manipulation of interest rates. To be sure, the potential for international "beggar thy neighbor" and internal suffering caused by increased bankruptcy and unemployment was much greater than the hurt that might have followed from the 30 percent tax increase that was needed to cover the deficit (or the suffering that would follow from cancelled subsidies and grants that would enable government the better to live within existing revenues). But in the summer of 1978, monetarism and neoconservative rhetoric about balancing the budget, "deregulation", and returning certain functions of government back to the private sector seemed more politically opportune than tax increases or greater intervention to restructure Canada's truncated economy.

Unfortunately for Trudeau, his modest budget cuts and rising interest rates were denounced by the left as "fighting inflation on the backs of the poor" and from the right as trivial "tinkering" that left the budget and the civil service still "out of control".

A series of by-elections in the autumn of 1978 underscored the depth of the dissatisfaction, and foretold defeat for the Liberals in a general election that would have to occur in the summer of 1979 at the latest. Trudeau responded by attempting to divert attention from economic problems to the unity issue — by suggesting that the country needed a prime minister who was a strong leader and not afraid to stand up to the premiers. "Who shall speak for Canada?" he asked late in 1978. He warned that the business cycle would rise and fall, but if the central government did not look to the long term and insist upon the welfare of the country as a constitutional entity, "we'll have a piece of geography with ten principalities with semi-sovereign states, and a federal government that can't do anything."

The leaders of the opposition parties (Joe Clark of the Conservatives and Ed Broadbent of the NDP) answered that the unity problem was largely of Trudeau's own making. Both agreed that Trudeau seemed to prefer confrontation to negotiation, and Joe Clark asserted that Trudeau's concept of Canada was unrealistic. Clark suggested that the government in Ottawa had to recognize that the country was "a community of communities". Insistence upon centralism would lead to further trouble, and he called for greater flexibility to put a "fresh face on federalism".

Dismissing Clark as a "puppet of the Premiers", Trudeau called the election for May 22. Then, shoulders back, head held high, he strode directly into disaster. His campaign style was that of a warrior in single-champion combat saying the issue was leadership. But the opposition parties — and most of the electorate — put economic concerns uppermost. The NDP went after "cut-backs" and made its alliance with the Canadian Labour Congress more explicit than ever in the hope of rallying workers in the industrial heartland of Ontario. The Conservatives went after interest rates and promised a balanced budget and mortgage relief to homebuyers in order to rally the middle class of the country.

The Liberal Party was defeated, of course, but the curious aspect of the election of 1979 is that the Liberals went down to defeat even though they won more seats than in 1972 (114 to 109), and they won 4 percentage points more of the votes than did the Conservatives. Unfortunately for the Liberals, too many of their votes were in Quebec where they won nearly every seat with huge majorities, and in 1979 the NDP fared less well against the Tories. The Tories did especially well in the West where the Liberals were defeated almost totally. Trudeau's inability to win seats in the West was the special disaster in the election because the four western provinces were a region that had undergone a quiet revolution of its own in the 1970s, a revolution the Government of Canada at first ignored and then opposed. In this way, the already complex constitutional problems were further complicated.

## II    Quiet Revolution in Alberta and Saskatchewan

The western provinces, like Quebec, complained of a long history of colonization. In the case of the West, however, colonialism in the sense of political and financial hegemony was constitutionally entrenched by section 109 of the BNA Act, a clause that conspicuously excluded the west from provincial control of natural resources. It was not until 1930 that the law was amended to provide official equality. Then, it was not until the post-Second World War period that substantial benefits began to be realized from provincial resources in the form of royalties. Manitoba and British Columbia gained from mining, hydroelectric development, and the exploitation of forest products. Alberta and Saskatchewan had oil. Saskatchewan also began to develop its potash, a mineral fertilizer occurring more abundantly west of Regina than anywhere else on earth. But not all western provinces prospered equally from their resource development in the 1950s and 60s, and (as another indicator of the effects of long standing colonialism) all tended to trade low "rents" for rapid development. Thus, the terms of resource exploitation were more advantageous to investors (normally foreign corporations) than to the resident population.

Beginning in the 1970s, however, a remarkable trend toward reversing what John Richards and Larry Pratt have called "the inglorious rentier traditions" became evident in all four western provinces, but especially clear in the cases of Alberta and Saskatchewan. Another fact that made Saskatchewan and Alberta particularly interesting in the 1970s is that the governments of both provinces adopted bold strategies for promoting local entrepreneurship in the resource sector — but from remarkably different ideological perspectives. The agency of change in Saskatchewan was a bureaucratic elite wedded to socialist approaches to economic development. In Alberta, by contrast, the government elite had its origins in business, retained those connections, and aimed to use the power of the state to promote and encourage a more aggressive local capitalism.

The leading figure in the quiet revolution in Alberta was Peter Lougheed, grandson of James A. Lougheed (one of Alberta's pioneers and perhaps the greatest land speculator in the history of the province). Lougheed was thus a part of Alberta's established society. He was also an important figure in the business community by his association with the Loram Company, a huge Calgary-based construction and engineering conglomerate. In 1962, Lougheed added a political career to his interest in business and accepted the leadership of Alberta's Conservatives in 1965, when the Alberta Tories were still "only one step from outright decrepitude."

The reigning party of Alberta was Social Credit, still as fundamentalist as when it came to power in the mid-1930s under "Bible Bill" Aberhart. Aberhart's successor and protégé, Ernest Manning, was himself a radio preacher in the tradition of his mentor. Lougheed, schooled in the new North American traditions of image politics, thus found it easy to call Manning and his party "reactionary". While Manning continued to broadcast calls for Christian regeneration on his weekly Back to the Bible Hour, Lougheed studied *The Making of the President 1960*, and refined his television image as a handsome and athletic, young and dynamic scion of Alberta's best (or near-best) family.

To Alberta's growing urban middle class, the product of the oil boom, Social Credit had been tolerable because it was dependably friendly to business. But it was still something of an embarrassment because Manning and his Protestant fundamentalism was almost totally lacking in swank. Lougheed was ostentatiously smart and urbane. Moreover, he offered a plausible critique of Manning that was still safely right of center. Lougheed claimed that the province was too dependent on oil and gas extraction and the old staples of agriculture. He warned that the oil was running out, as also was Alberta's prosperity. Assuming there was considerable unrealized potential for manfuacturing in the West, Lougheed criticized Manning's government for "coasting" and for failing to realize sufficient "capital revenues" from oil to promote such development. Lougheed also suggested that the outside forces that would strive to keep manufacturing in central Canada needed to be neutralized, and on the anti-Ottawa ground the Manning regime was also found wanting, since Lougheed said Social Credit had been consistently "out-negotiated by the Federal government".

Lougheed's critique of the Manning government appealed to Alberta's urban voters, the dominant part of the electorate by 1970. As a result, they ended the twenty-five year dynasty of Social Credit in August 1971 by electing 49 Tories to the 75-member legislature. In the years that followed, the new government provided substantial change as well as the image of dynamism.

The first evident change was a growing competence and expertise in the government bureaucracy, which was enlarged and upgraded to foster a provincial economic nationalism, promoting Alberta business over the "Toronto-Montreal establishment" and "its" federal government. Ironically, foreign capital was perceived as a powerful ally. The result was a perpetuation of foreign influences, but also what Richards and Pratt have called a "break with marginality" meaning a "new consciousness" and "growing restlessness with the West's hinterland status".

After OPEC dramatically increased the price of oil at the end of 1973, the Government of Canada imposed price controls along with the export tax and subsidy regime discussed in the previous chapter. Such protection of Canadian consumers was interpreted in Alberta as simply the latest instance of central Canadian arrogance. One popular Alberta counter to the national oil policy was an offer to trade their oil at fixed prices if Ottawa would compel Ontario to sell the produce of its gold mines at half or one fourth of the world price. Angered by the forced sale of a nonrenewable resource at artificially low prices, the Government of Alberta doubled the *rate* of its royalty between 1973 and 1975 because the price of Canadian produced oil was held by the federal government to about half of the world price. Then, in 1976, the Government of Alberta created a Heritage Savings Trust Fund with an initial balance of $1.5 billion and the statutory assurance that one third of the royalties from all nonrenewable resources would be added to the fund in the future. The purpose of 85 percent of the huge and growing savings account was to provide development capital for infrastructure or outright loans to local investors; only 15 percent was available to worthy borrowers outside Alberta.

A similar activism developed at the same time in Saskatchewan, except the boom staple was potash as well as oil, and the development strategy was socialism as well as corporatism on the Alberta model. The leading encouragement for the alternate approach was Allan Blakeney, a Nova Scotia-born Rhodes Scholar and former civil servant who entered politics in 1958 on the side of the CCF. Blakeney's philosophy was that the state should own the most important industries, especially in the resource sector.

Although active in politics for over a decade, most of Blakeney's career before 1971 was in opposition, the CCF having been defeated by the Liberals in 1964. Notorious for his denunciations of the CCF experiments in public ownership, the Liberal Premier, Ross Thatcher, asserted that the usual practice was for the CCF to put "some teacher or preacher or someone who knows nothing about business ... in charge of an enterprise" and the result was failure even where success was certain because, according to Thatcher, "the CCF can't sell nuts to chimps." Thus, one problem for

Blakeney, stepping into the leadership of the NDP and easily winning the election of 1971, was to change the image of incompetent management in public enterprise.

Blakeney's other problem was to mediate a deep split within his own party. A troublesome group known as the "Waffle" faction had emerged in 1969 to turn not only the Saskatchewan party but also the NDP nationally onto a more frankly socialist platform. Having been badly beaten at the national level in 1971 (and after facing outright expulsion from the British Columbia and Ontario provincial parties), the Waffle still maintained some degree of influence in Saskatchewan. The question after Blakeney's electoral success in 1971 was whether he would prove more accommodating than NDP leaders elsewhere. Blakeney did move cautiously, but his caution only exhausted the patience of the radicals who withdrew voluntarily from the Saskatchewan NDP in 1973 (ironically, just as the events that led to a new Alberta began to have even more radical consequences for Saskatchewan).

Following Lougheed, Blakeney dramatically increased royalties on oil — and also on potash. Unlike the resource industries of Alberta, however, those that faced similar increases in Saskatchewan staged a dramatic rebellion in 1974. The potash industry led by launching a series of legal actions challenging the authority of Saskatchewan to impose such taxation. Blakeney went to the electorate for a renewal of his mandate and confronted the companies with the nationalization of the industry in 1975. In the meantime, the oil companies mounted their own legal battle with Saskatchewan.

In the important case of *CIGOL versus the Government of Saskatchewan* it was claimed by the plaintiff (Canadian Industrial Gas and Oil Limited) that the new levy they had to pay was not a royalty at all, but a tax, and since it imposed costs that were passed on to the consumer, the form of taxation was indirect, and therefore not within the power of a provincial government. On the face of the issues at stake, it appeared that the dispute involved just one company and the province. But since the case also had implications for the federal government's ability to tax resources, or the royalties that other provinces might levy on their resources, a long line of interveners fell in behind CIGOL and Saskatchewan. Most conspicuously, the Government of Canada intervened on the side of CIGOL, and Alberta sided with Saskatchewan. Finally, in 1977, the Supreme Court of Canada supported the companies and the Government of Canada by declaring that the Saskatchewan royalty scheme was unconstitutional because it amounted to indirect taxation. Clearly, the CIGOL case posed an equal threat to Alberta's ability to extract higher rents from its resources.

By the end of 1977, it had become clear that the provinces that retained ownership of their natural resources and developed them through Crown corporations were likely to enjoy the more secure return for two reasons. First, public ownership by-passed the royalty versus tax and direct versus indirect taxation issues. Secondly, a provincial Crown corporation was exempt from taxation by the federal government. Both points were not lost on Alberta, where dedication to private entreprise had become a secular religion. One result was a position paper on the constitution issued in 1978, *Harmony in Diversity*, in which the Government of Alberta demanded broader powers of taxation and clarification of provincial paramountcy in resource development.

Thus, the events of the 1970s led to the discovery of new justifications for public ownership in the case of Saskatchewan, and a new stridency for constitutional special status — this time from Alberta. Like the Government of Quebec, that of Alberta sought a new division of power, but just the reverse of what Quebec demanded: Alberta's ideal was for ten economic sovereignties in one political association, rather than ten political sovereignties in an economic union.

By intervention in the constitutional cases on control of resources, the Government of Canada showed resistance to the Western autonomy demand that was as strong as its opposition to Quebec separatism. But by Trudeau's constant striving to preserve and protect the French fact in a wider context, he had been able to resist the autonomy aspirations of Quebec without seeming anti-French. No such positive counterweight balanced Trudeau's dismissal of the Westerners' position on resources, or Maritimers' desire to control the development of their offshore oil potential. Since the West was completely united on the resource question — and since western Canada returned more members to Parliament than Quebec — Trudeau's government was defeated in 1979 by the quiet revolutions the Liberals had ignored as much as they had previously been saved by the earlier revolution in which Pierre Trudeau had taken part.

## III    Resurrection and Referendum

With Pierre Trudeau out of power in 1979, some observers imagined that new leadership might put new life into federalism. Trudeau had developed a deep personal antipathy to René Lévesque, in particular, and Westerners in general. It seemed, ironically, that Trudeau had become a cause as much as a master of Canada's national unity problems. The new government of Joe Clark, having denounced the "confrontation" tactics exhibited by Canada in recent years, began to deliver on its promise of "flexibility" with Quebec, concession of offshore resources to Newfoundland, and negotiation of resource issues with the West.

Pierre Trudeau was discouraged by the apparent popularity of what he continued to call the "panacea of decentralization". Moreover, since he had always been in power (one way or another) after his entry onto the federal political stage in 1965, functioning in opposition was a role he did not know or wish to learn. On November 21, roughly six months after his electoral defeat, Trudeau therefore resigned. "It's all over," he told the Liberal caucus. Then the news of the end of an era was bestowed on the nation. Naturally, the newspapers were filled with assessments of Trudeau's career. Most were critical, agreeing with Geoffrey Stevens of the *Globe and Mail:* "He controlled the political system absolutely but he could not make it work." Most also agreed that the country was worse off in 1979 than in 1968, and that much of Canada's constitutional "disarray" was Trudeau's own making. Would the Tories do better?

Trudeau's resignation seemed to give Joe Clark the free rein he wanted to behave as though he led a comfortable majority in the House of Commons. It was certainly unthinkable that the Liberals would unite with the other opposition parties to defeat the plurality Tories while they were still leaderless. It seemed safe, in other words, for the Conservatives to pursue domestic economic policies that were known to be unpopular, but nevertheless correct from the standpoint of the Minister of Finance, John Crosbie. Consequently, Crosbie imposed a budget of "short term pains for long term gains" on December 11. Taxes were to go up, expenditures relative to revenues would come down. By significant increases in federal sales taxes — especially that on gasoline — and by limiting the growth of government spending, Crosbie claimed that the federal budget would be in balance by 1984.

The feature of the Crosbie budget that was especially unpopular was the proposed 18 cent per gallon tax on gasoline, denounced by all opposition parties because it bore proportionally more heavily on low-income Canadians. On December 12, Trudeau told reporters that the Liberals would vote against the budget, and the next day the unthinkable did happen: the leaderless Liberals joined the rest of the opposition to show non-confidence in the Crosbie budget.

As the country prepared for a general election in February, the Liberals resurrected their old leader. Polls showed that they were 20 percentage points ahead of the Tories. The same surveys also confirmed that Trudeau was the most suitable Liberal to fill the role of leader. Naturally, the caucus wanted him back, and the former leader was willing but he waited nearly one week before making his announcement on December 18, saying "It is my duty to accept the draft of the party." Then, as if making his first election promise, Trudeau asserted that the 1980 campaign would be his last. He promised to resign again "well before" the next election.

The event that Trudeau wished to see through before his final resignation was the referendum on separatism promised by the *Parti québecois* after their election in 1976. The date for the referendum was still not set, however, and before Trudeau could shepherd the country through that crisis he had still to win the general election of 18 February. In campaign speeches, Trudeau denounced the Tories for making excessive provision for the oil producing western provinces, and promised cheaper gasoline by imposing a "blended price" on the Canadian petroleum industry. He promised to continue, in other words, the policy that he had launched late in 1973. When Premier Lougheed replied that such a continued imposition on Alberta was intolerable, the impression that was left in the minds of eastern voters was that the national unity prime minister could subdue the West as well as the Quebec separatists. Since French-speaking Quebeckers continued to believe that Trudeau was their champion as much as their opponent, the unity stance produced continued good feeling there. Liberals won every seat but one in Trudeau's home province. In the West, by contrast, they lost every seat but two. Still, his Quebec and Ontario support was enough to prevent disaster, indeed sufficient for a Parliamentary majority.

Within days of the reappearance of Pierre Trudeau in the prime ministerial office, René Lévesque announced the question to be posed in the coming referendum:

> The Government of Québec has made public its proposal to negotiate a new agreement with the rest of Canada, based on the equality of nations; this agreement would enable Québec to acquire exclusive power to make its laws, levy its taxes and establish relations abroad — in other words, sovereignty — and at the same time, to maintain with Canada an economic association including a common currency; no change in political status resulting from these negotiations will be effected without approval from the people through another referendum; on these terms, do you give the Government of Québec the mandate to negotiate the proposed agreement between Québec and Canada? (Quoted in R. Bothwell, *et al.*, *Canada since 1945* [1981], p. 403.)

The "public" proposal cited in the first clause of the rambling question was a White Paper issued the previous November to elaborate the association that the PQ sought to obtain from Canada. Four links were proposed: one, a kind of parliament in which the two countries would share "fundamental legal equality"; the second was a standing commission of inquiry, a body of experts providing a basis for informed action; the third would be a supreme court; and the last was a monetary authority analogous to the Bank of Canada. In this way, Quebec was supposed to obtain its full political sovereignty while developing a new association based on mutual economic interest.

The provincial opposition led by Claude Ryan (former editor of *Le Devoir*), responded with proposals of its own in January. Ryan's "beige paper" was a complex package advocating the kind of decentalization Trudeau had been denouncing since the mid-70s but falling considerably short of Lévesque's "sovereignty association". Consequently, Lévesque was able to campaign for a YES answer without organized or coherent opposition. Moreover, the question itself seemed to have little more effect than to underscore the power the PQ already enjoyed as the legitimate government of Quebec.

All circumstances — and the question itself — seemed configured for an easy YES victory. Early in the spring of 1980, Lévesque announced that the vote would take place on May 20, and began a tour of the province to tell Quebeckers they were witnessing the first stages of the birth of the nation. It was "a question of honour," said Lévesque. A resounding YES vote would not lead to independence immediately, but it would say "this is the direction we want to go in."

Gradually, however, it became clear that much of the equality Lévesque said Quebeckers should begin to demand had, in fact, already been achieved. A significant omission from the referendum campaign was the assertion that Quebec had to separate from the rest of Canada to preserve its own language and culture. The main reason was that the Government of Quebec had already asserted its cultural sovereignty without truculence from the rest of the country. After the 1976 election, the first bill the new government introduced (in April 1977) affirmed the full and unequivocally French character of Quebec. Bill 101 banned English from most governmental and legal proceedings; from businesses of fifty or more employees; and all children except Anglo-Quebeckers henceforth were to enrol in French-language schools. The one and only official language of Quebec was thus French. The rest of the country was stunned. But the first most vocal critics of Bill 101 were the stalwart admirers of Trudeau's one-people-two-languages vision of Canada and archmonarchists who still gloated over the conquest and questioned whether French should be permitted anywhere in the Kingdom of Canada. Those in between considered the measure narrow and chauvinistic. Indeed, Camille Laurin (the minister in charge of language in Quebec) admitted that Bill 101 was "ethnocentric", adding that "All nations are founded on the principle of ethnocentricity." Most Canadians were skeptical that Laurin and his party were founding a nation so much as taking steps to preserve and protect a well established society catering to a majority in the same way that the governments of New Brunswick, Ontario, and Manitoba had supported theirs — in accordance with well established principles of ethnocentricity (not to say bigotry). Consequently, few people in Canada demanded action by the federal government to strike Bill 101 down, and the government was ill-disposed to act on its own. The result several years later, in the context of the referendum campaign, was that Lévesque's claim that a YES would begin a process of "clearing away" (déblocage) did not ring true because the process was already too well advanced to seem frustrated. On that account, the referendum campaign lost steam even as it began.

Near the end, both leaders of the major national parties made excursions into Quebec. Joe Clark, on behalf of the Tories, asserted that "The Canada that Mr. Lévesque wants to separate from no longer exists." Trudeau sounded the same note and made a "solemn declaration" that a NO vote would not be taken as an endorsement of the status quo and promised that it would begin a process of substantial constitutional change. Such an affirmation may have convinced many Quebeckers that they could vote "no thanks" without self-humiliation. Clark's assertion that the fight had already been won may also have been in accord with a sentiment of most of the population. In any case, when the votes were counted on May 20, 60 percent of the electorate did vote NO. Then, as emotional as he was on November 15 four years before, Lévesque went on televison to hold Trudeau to his pledge saying that the ball was back in the federal court.

## IV   Patriation versus Reform

Prime Minister Trudeau began a new round of discussions on the constitution saying "Everything is negotiable." His assertion was consistent with other affirmations of good will that followed the referendum, but even the most optimistic observers qualified their hopes with memories that the federal government and the provinces had conceded little on consititutional issues in the past. Basically, there were two sets of constitutional questions confronting Canadians in 1980. One problem had been on the agenda since 1926; another, far more important set of issues had arisen only since the 1960s.

The long-standing, relatively unimportant matter was "patriation". Since Canada's Constitution was a statute of Great Britain, every time it was amended the amendments had to be enacted by the Parliament of that country. Once Canada had been declared equal and in no way subordinate to Britain, continuing to call upon the British for amendments was anomolous to say the least. But before the constitution could be patriated to Canada (thus relieving the British of their amending role), an alternative procedure had to be invented. Past practice was too complicated to offer easy guidance for the future. Occasionally the federal government acted unilaterally (as in the case of the BNA Act of 1871, for example), but usually the Government of Canada obtained unanimous consent from the provinces before passing a joint resolution of the two houses of Parliament asking Britain for an amendment. The subtle variety of approaches meant that the federal government and the provinces could never agree on one certain procedure to be observed in every case in the future; therefore, it had become convenient to leave the BNA Act in British custody and expend governmental energy on the more important problems of the day.

In the 1960s, however, constitutional questions surfaced in a new, more urgent form. When Quebec attempted to exercise its full powers under the BNA Act it found them wanting, because so much of the control it sought over taxation and social policy had developed as shared areas of jurisdiction. By the mid-1960s, it seemed that the country had outgrown the latest form of federalism that had emerged under the general umbrella of the BNA Act. The first federalism, lasting from 1867 to about 1885, was hardly federal at all since the central government attempted to rule the constituent parts as subordinate jurisdictions. But after the successful rebellion of Ontario and reversals for Canada in the courts, a more classical form of federalism did emerge by the end of the century; it was recognized that each level of government had exclusive powers that had to be respected. Consequently, Canada developed between 1885 and 1914 more as an association of provinces than the unitary state Macdonald had wanted. But with the coming of the Great War, and the passage of the War Measures Act, closer union developed in the guise of emergency federalism. In the new formula, the federal government trespassed upon provincial powers the better to deal with emergencies. The problem in the 1920s and 30s, however, was to define *peacetime* emergencies. With the new undoubted emergency of the Second World War, the Government of Canada reinstated the War Measures Act and consolidated power more completely than ever before. The benefits of such consolidation seemed so manifestly obvious to many, perhaps most, Canadians, they did not want the powers abandoned in 1945. Consequently, emergency federalism was redefined as cooperative federalism. In the new formula, provinces were nominally still powerful in the area of social policy and direct taxation, but by "renting" their power of direct taxation to the federal government, authority was conveyed to Ottawa to rule the country by means of shared-cost programs. After 1960, the nub of the problem with Quebec was its demand for the restoration of the old powers, and the return process was expected to take the form of an explicit revision of the BNA Act defining more clearly the areas in which a province was paramount.

Having yielded about one third of the field of direct taxation, and admitted broad areas of "concurrent" power in the field of social legislation, the Government of Canada believed that Ottawa's ability to behave as a "national" government would dangerously diminish if the federal level were no longer able to speak for Canada in foreign affairs, work to maintain a national minimum in social welfare, or play a role in lessening regional disparities by raising a revenue  for equalization payments to the poorer provinces. Quebec, however, refused to consider concurrent power in the field of social legislation and called equalization a sham. Acording to Claude Morin, the so-called have not provinces (Quebec included) gained no more from federal expenditures than the taxation contributed. Eventually, Westerners joined in the same denunciation. George Woodcock (a Manitoban transplanted to British Columbia by way of Great Britain), called equalization a "charity system" imposed by the federal government's "right hand giving crusts from the loaves which the left hand still takes away by sustaining an economy that continues to benefit the central provinces." Eventually, Westerners and Quebeckers would agree (more or less) with Woodcock's observation that what was needed was "a genuine confederation in which no region profits to the detriment of the rest, and in which every region has an equal political voice," a regime, according to Morin, that "lets Quebec function as a true government" rather than as "a mere regional administration bereft of meaningful prerogative." The four western provinces, Newfoundland, and Quebec eventually agreed that any meaningful discussion of the Constitution had to include a clarification of the distribution of powers. The federal politicians — supported by the Mandarins anxious to defend their bureaucratic empires — insisted that any further devolution would either weaken the country beyond repair, or jeopardize flexible responses to unanticipated problems by imposing a constitutional strait jacket upon future generations. In this way, the two orders of government both appeared anxious to resolve the constitutional malaise, but they approached the problem from irreconcilable positions. Ottawa consistently sought to preserve powers recently won *de facto*. The provinces increasingly wanted a clarification of the distribution in order to undo the centralization that had arisen from the first vaguely written BNA Act.

Initially, Quebec was the most outspoken in demanding a new definition of provincial powers, and Ottawa used Quebec's isolation effectively to defeat Quebec's demand for "special status". Another advantage of the federal position was the election of an outspokenly federalist government in Quebec in April 1970 when Robert Bourassa came to power promising to ease federal-provincial tensions by emphasizing economic issues rather than consitutional matters. Almost immediately after his election, the Government of Canada brought a package of proposals to Quebec City, a package that contained an amending formula (giving Quebec and Ontario veto powers), entrenchment of certain civil rights, and some tinkering with concurrent powers in the field of taxation and social policy. When Bourassa did not reject the package out of hand, it was taken to the other provinces one by one with the assertion that "substantial agreement" had already been secured with Quebec. Then all governments agreed to consider the federal proposals more seriously at a meeting to be held in Victoria in June 1971.

By the time arrangements for the Victoria conference had been made, the new Government of Quebec was informed that Bourassa had endorsed a constitutional position that two preceding governments had already rejected. Moreover, Bourassa was convinced that he had blundered in doing so. Consequently, just before the Victoria meeting, the Government of Quebec informed the other premiers and the Government of Canada that provincial paramountcy in social policy would have to be included in any package acceptable to Quebec. The federal government responded with advice to the premiers of the poorer provinces that such a change might lead to wholesale opting-out from existing national programs, and the federal government would no longer have any reason to participate with the rest. The success of Quebec's position would thus lead to a costly transfer of responsibilities, they said. Predictably, Quebec lost practically all support from the other provinces for changing the BNA Act to establish provincial paramountcy in social policy.

The Victoria conference unfolded then as a closed-door marathon concerned with partriation, an amending formula, and Quebec's concern with social policy. Despite the full agenda, "tentative" agreement was established on a package that included the federal government's conceding clarification of the sections of the BNA Act pertaining to social policy. Then Trudeau announced that the provinces had ten days officially to accept or reject Ottawa's final offer. "If there isn't agreement, then that is the end of the matter for now ... ."

On his return to Quebec, Bourassa came under heavy pressure to withhold agreement until the actual clarification had been achieved. Consequently, Bourassa anounced on June 23 that his government would suspend compliance for the present because of "the need to reach as complete agreement as possible on clear and precise constitutional texts." To do otherwise would lead to endless court battles and "transfer to the judiciary power ... of a responsibility that belongs pre-eminently to the political power ... ." Although the Government of Quebec thus left the way open for further discussion to develop appropriate "texts" in the area, Prime Minister Trudeau, true to his word, decided that Quebec's second thoughts were final, and the June 23 announcement ended the matter for nearly a decade.

Many observers (from fellow Liberals such as Claude Ryan to academic commentators such as Dale Posgate and Kenneth McRoberts) argued subsequently that Trudeau's "intransigence" in refusing to continue negotiations not only blocked the development of a new constitutional accommodation, but by seeming to prove that French Canada could never speak to Ottawa as "equals", gave active encouragement to separatism as well. For that reason, when Lévesque announced that the ball was back in the federal court in May 1980, Trudeau's assertion that everything was negotiable seemed to have special significance indeed.

## V     Patriation

In the summer of 1980, Jean Chrétien functioned as Trudeau's ambassador to the provinces, preparing the way for a constitutional conference in the early autumn. Unlike preparations for the Victoria conference, ten years earlier, there was more than one wild card in the deck, however. Newfoundland and the four western provinces also sought clarification of their powers, in particular, their paramountcy over natural resources, just as Quebec had insisted earlier upon establishing its superiority in the field of social development. Consequently, Chrétien found his summer perambulations disappointing. He discovered that all provinces were willing to listen to the federal proposal for patriation, an amending formula, and a Charter of Canadian Rights and Freedoms, but for their concession of exclusive jurisdiction over civil rights, they wanted something in return from Ottawa. Various provinces mentioned natural resources, family law, communications, and other aspects of social and economic development. Chrétien complained that it was "depressing bargaining rights against administrative advantages for the provinces." In fact, the federal government was as anxious about the distribution of powers as the provincial governments. The difference was that Chrétien sought to defend a balance that already favored Ottawa. In this sense, the federal government was no less power-hungry than the provinces.

It was not surprising that the summer's meetings proved inconclusive and that vast differences appeared once the two orders of govenment met in full conference in September. Prime Minister Trudeau continued to insist upon what Murray Beck has called his "splendid, if idealistic and impracticable, concept of ... an open society all of whose citizens would be protected by an entrenched bill of rights guaranteeing, among other things, their linguistic rights ... ." Trudeau viewed Canada as "an association of people", in short. But nearly all of the premiers contended that Canada was an "association of provinces". In their view, it did not matter a great deal that a Canadian might migrate from one province to another and discover that he had moved to a remarkably different society, different economy, social policies, and a new language. Naturally, between the two concepts of Canada no agreement was possible. The conference had to end in failure.

Less than one month after the "First Ministers" failed to agree on a constitutional package, Prime Minister Trudeau added fuel to an already inflamed situation by announcing on October 2 that he intended to patriate the BNA Act unilaterally — and with a charter of rights. He said that the amending formula and rights charter were interim arrangements subject to revision at conferences to take place later. Then, if agreement were still impossible, that which was to be temporary would become permanent. Charles Lynch, the senior journalist in Ottawa, declared that the "method is shocking" but having reported on so many previous failures, he agreed that there was "no other way" to break the impasse.

Conspicuously absent in the Trudeau patriation scheme was any clarification of provincial power in social policy or resource ownership. Here the second shock was a federal announcement on October 28 that a National Energy Policy (NEP) would come into effect immediately to use the power of the national government to effect 50 percent Canadian ownership and self-sufficiency in the petroleum industry by 1990. To that end, Ottawa was expanding its "rent" on oil and gas from 10 to 23 percent, reducing the return to the producing provinces by 2 percentage points, and to the companies by nearly one fifth. Premier Lougheed denounced the scheme as "an outright attempt to take over the resources" of the provinces, and warned that Alberta would reduce production by 180 000 barrels per day (in three steps, at three month intervals after the first of the coming year) unless the Government of Canada backed down from its bold assertion of concurrent power in the resource sector.

In the meantime, Trudeau's patriation scheme was referred by Parliament to a joint Senate-Commons committee to hear submissions from the general public; and, in Britain, a similar committee headed by Sir Anthony Kershaw considered the legality of unilateralism. In Canada, civil libertarians generally agreed that the list of rights and liberties to be safeguarded was not sufficiently lengthy and the safeguards were not sufficiently stringent. In Britain, the Kershaw committee concluded that the British Parliament would not have to accept the package unless a substantial number of provinces concurred with the action. Trudeau hinted that Britain's refusal to do his bidding would provoke a grave crisis: "If they're wise they'll get through it quickly and hold their nose while they're doing it ... ." On this basis, Chrétien predicted the whole business would be finished by Easter 1981.

In the end, the package was delayed by one full year and the scheme that finally passed bore little resemblance to Trudeau's original proposal because the role of the Canadian courts in the process proved to be decisive. Early in 1981, the provinces of Manitoba, Quebec, and Newfoundland challenged the consititutionality of Trudeau's unilateral action and five other dissenting premiers immediately joined as interveners. The "gang of eight" lost their appeals in Manitoba and Quebec, but at the end of March the Supreme Court of Newfoundland ruled unanimously that unilateralism was illegal. Then the federal Tories launched a filibuster in the House of Commons demanding postponement of further proceedings until the Supreme Court of Canada could rule on the matter. Imagining that such a concession could only cost him time, Trudeau agreed to wait on the last court of appeal.

In September, the Supreme Court rendered a surprise decision. A majority (seven to two, led by Chief Justice Bora Laskin), ruled that the proposed unilateral patriation process did not contravene any law the courts of Canada had the power to enforce. They said that unilateralism was legal, but only in a narrow, technical sense. Then the court declared unanimously that such a course would be most unwise since it would violate a century-old convention that required the consent of the provinces before requesting any changes that affected their rights.

What followed in October 1981 was a flurry of informal negotiation culminating in an agreement to meet in Ottawa for one last attempt in November. There, nine of the ten provinces and the federal government did find acceptable wording for an amending formula and also a charter of rights. The amending formula jettisoned Ontario and Quebec's traditional right of veto by permitting any seven provinces with at least 50 percent of the population to ratify any change to the constitution. Up to three provinces could thus dissent. They might also enjoy exemption from the provisions ratified by the others and later choose to opt-in, but once accepting the change, such a latecomer would be bound by subsequent ratification forever. Previously, Trudeau had criticized the opt-out provision as "incremental separatism ... a Confederation of 500 shopping centres." Accepting the proviso was, therefore, a massive concession on his part. The premiers also showed flexibility by accepting an entrenched bill of rights, palatable in November 1981 because an override clause permitted provincial legislatures to breach civil rights (the charter "notwithstanding"). In this respect, the new charter was no more binding than the old Diefenbaker bill of rights had been on the Parliament of Canada. In the new charter, however, certain rights such as the equality of the sexes and the two official languages were deeply entrenched in the sense that neither could be overridden by the "notwithstanding clause".

Because the rights of English- and French-speaking minorities ("where numbers warrant") were among the more deeply entrenched freedoms, the Government of Quebec witheld its consent and claimed the patriation scheme was illegal because it violated the "fundamental duality" of Canada by ignoring Quebec's veto. On the last day of the conference, perhaps because he was anticipating future challenges to his Bill 101, Premier Lévesque growled prophetically that the proceedings would have "incalculable consequences".

Subsequently, the patriation scheme passed by the Canadian Parliament in the first week of December was approved by the British early in 1982. Both issues of the amending formula and the charter of rights seemed at last settled. But the manner of the settlement invited future difficulty by what was accomplished as well as by what was ignored. At best, the new Canada Act (see text in Appendix B), was only peripheral to the major questions raised in the previous decade. The settlement inflamed and isolated Quebec, and no clarification of the distribution of powers for dealing with the economy was obtained. For the moment, the latter defect was the more telling because the problems of declining manufacturing, rising unemployment, high inflation, and staggering interest rates placed Canada among the most economically crippled countries of the industrialized world in 1982.

The economic adversities, the apparently interminable jurisdictional squabblings, and Canada's overwhelming geography and harsh climate served as proofs to outside observers that the country was in some respects still "the land God gave Cain." But for those inhabitants of Canada in 1982 who continued to find the meaning of their individual lives more in the development of their particular place than in some national or regional myth, the challenges of a hostile climate, geography, and capitalism, would continue to invite association to promote their mutual survival. In 1982, as earlier, Canada was not — perhaps never would be — a nation in the nineteenth-century meaning of one people with a unified sense of cosmic purpose. Instead, Canada held together by the more prosaic bonds of propinquity, friendship, and loose political affiliation. There, in the diversity of Canada's 5 million households was the ultimate value of the politicians' failure ever to have articulated a "common Canadianism", the critical point in the structure of past Canadian experience and the chief pointer to the country's future.

# Bibliography

Trudeau's decline and resurrection is decribed by Robert Bothwell, *et al.*, *Canada since 1945: Power, Politics, and Provincialism* (1981); analysis of developments is offered by Richard Gwyn in *The Northern Magus: Pierre Trudeau and Canadians* (1980). The same contrast applies to Trudeau's role in the constitutional initiatives of the period: the Bothwell volume is hardly more than a chronicle; Gwyn (despite his proximity to the events as both observer and actor) offers an analysis that is singular for both its depth and balance.

Since the subjects treated in this chapter are still of quite recent developmnent, the more specialized history remains to be written. Still, a surprising number of works of considerable use and interest have appeared. On the subject of the development of the new West, for example, rather antiseptic treatments of the themes of urbanization, urban politics, and the decline of the Liberal Party are available. Roger Gibbins, *Prairie Politics and Society: Regionalism in Decline* (1980) contends that the west's politics have become progressively more like those of the east, a contention that contrasts considerably with another recent work on Prairie politics by David

Smith, *The Regional Decline of a National Party: Liberals on the Prairies* (1981).

By far the most interesting works on the new west, however, are those that focus on its struggle for decolonization. David Jay Bercuson, ed., *Canada and the Burden of Unity* (1977) and Martin Robins' two-volume work on British Columbia, *The Company Province* (1972-73) provide background for understanding what John Richards and Larry Pratt call the "rentier tradition". Richards' and Pratt's own work, *Prairie Capitalism: Power and Influence in the New West* (1979) is a brilliant analysis of the developments in the 1970s that have promoted decolonization in Saskatchewan and Alberta.

Richards and Pratt also offer a useful discussion of the constitutional position of the west in the same work. A more strident, yet interesting, tract for the times is George Woodcock's, *Confederation Betrayed!: The Case Against Trudeau's Canada* (1981). More sober views than Woodcock's are found in R.B. Byers and R.W. Reford, *Canada Challenged: The Viability of Confederation* (1979). Here, the essay by J. Murray Beck, "Overlapping and Divided Jurisdictions: The Nub of the Debate" is particularly helpful to readers seeking a brief summary of complex issues. Finally, a speculative essay on the kind of people Canadians are and what sets them apart, is David Bell and Lorne Tepperman, *The Roots of Disunity: A Look at Canadian Political Culture* (1979).

## General Bibliographical Note

No form of historical literature becomes obsolete more rapidly than lists or essays covering "recent publications". Such material is necessarily serialized. On a quarterly basis, *The Canadian Historical Review* (CHR) and *The Journal of Canadian Studies* (JCS) both publish extensive reviews of new books, and cumulative lists of materials not reviewed. For periodical essays that relate new developments to preceeding scholarship the most useful material appears in *Acadiensis,* a journal that specializes in the history of the Atlantic region but has achieved national importance in recent years for its historiographical essays on topics of general significance. More comprehensive, but less analytical, are the essays in *A Reader's Guide to Canadian History,* 2 vols. (1982). Volume one, D.A. Muise, ed., covers *Beginnings to Confederation.* The second volume, edited by J.L. Granatstein and Paul Stevens, covers *Confederation to the Present.* But the Muise and Granatstein volumes are already out of date and neither is well indexed. The guide that fills the need of quarterly updating the reader with new material while providing more than a mere listing of recent works is *America: History and Life* because it seems to cover subjects in Canadian' history almost as thoroughly as does the CHR's "Recent Publications Relating to Canada". But items are indexed (by author, title, and subject) and described more fully in brief abstracts. Thus, *America: History and Life* is perhaps the most useful guide to current books and articles for students of Canadian history.

# APPENDIX I:  Statistical Tables

**TABLE 1  Population of Canada, by province, census dates, 1851 to 1981**

| Year | Canada | Newfoundland | Prince Edward Island | Nova Scotia | New Brunswick | Quebec | Ontario | Manitoba | Saskatchewan | Alberta | British Columbia | Yukon | Northwest Territories |
|---|---|---|---|---|---|---|---|---|---|---|---|---|---|
| 1981 | 24 498 900 | 570 500 | 123 000 | 850 000 | 698 600 | 6 455 700 | 8 664 700 | 1 029 900 | 977 400 | 2 287 400 | 2 771 300 | 23 800 | 46 500 |
| 1971 | 21 731 000 | 528 000 | 112 000 | 793 000 | 640 000 | 6 047 000 | 7 777 000 | 989 000 | 919 000 | 1 644 000 | 2 227 000 | 19 000 | 36 000 |
| 1961 | 18 238 247 | 457 853 | 104 629 | 737 007 | 597 936 | 5 259 211 | 6 236 092 | 921 686 | 925 181 | 1 331 944 | 1 629 082 | 14 628 | 22 998 |
| 1956 | 16 080 791 | 415 074 | 99 285 | 694 717 | 554 616 | 4 628 378 | 5 404 933 | 850 040 | 880 665 | 1 123 116 | 1 398 464 | 12 190 | 19 313 |
| 1951 | 14 009 429 | 361 416 | 98 429 | 642 584 | 515 697 | 4 055 681 | 4 597 542 | 776 541 | 831 728 | 939 501 | 1 165 210 | 9 096 | 16 004 |
| 1941 | 11 506 655 | — | 95 047 | 577 962 | 457 401 | 3 331 882 | 3 787 655 | 729 744 | 895 992 | 796 169 | 817 861 | 4 914 | 12 028 |
| 1931 | 10 376 786 | — | 88 038 | 512 846 | 408 219 | 2 874 662 | 3 431 683 | 700 139 | 921 785 | 731 605 | 694 263 | 4 230 | 9 316 |
| 1921 | 8 787 949 | — | 88 615 | 523 837 | 387 876 | 2 360 510 | 2 933 662 | 610 118 | 757 510 | 588 454 | 524 582 | 4 157 | 8 143 |
| 1911 | 7 206 643 | — | 93 728 | 492 338 | 351 889 | 2 005 776 | 2 527 292 | 461 394 | 492 432 | 374 295 | 392 480 | 8 512 | 6 507 |
| 1901 | 5 371 315 | — | 103 259 | 459 574 | 331 120 | 1 648 898 | 2 182 947 | 255 211 | 91 279 | 73 022 | 178 657 | 27 219 | 20 129 |
| 1891 | 4 833 239 | — | 109 078 | 450 396 | 321 263 | 1 488 535 | 2 114 321 | 152 506 | — | — | 98 173 | — | 98 967 |
| 1881 | 4 324 810 | — | 108 891 | 440 572 | 321 233 | 1 359 027 | 1 926 922 | 62 260 | — | — | 49 459 | — | 56 446 |
| 1871 | 3 689 257 | — | 94 021 | 387 800 | 285 594 | 1 191 516 | 1 620 851 | 25 228 | — | — | 36 247 | — | 48 000 |
| 1861 | 3 229 633 | — | 80 857 | 330 857 | 252 047 | 1 111 566 | 1 396 091 | — | — | — | 51 524 | — | 6 691[3] |
| 1851 | 2 436 297 | — | 62 678 | 276 854 | 193 800 | 890 261 | 952 004 | — | — | — | 55 000 | — | 5 700[3] |

SOURCES:  M. C. Urquhart and K. A. H. Buckley, eds., *Historical Statistics of Canada* (Toronto, 1965), p. 14, and, *Canadian Statistical Review*, 1971, 1982.

**TABLE 2    Urban Population of Canada, 1871-1951**

| Year | 100 000 persons and over | 30 000-99 999 persons | 5 000-29 999 persons | 1 000-4 999 persons | Urban Total |
|------|-------------------------|-----------------------|----------------------|---------------------|-------------|
| 1951 | 3 260 939 | 1 147 888 | 1 947 128 | 1 155 584 | 7 511 539 |
| 1941 | 2 645 133 | 928 367 | 1 370 375 | 909 728 | 5 853 603 |
| 1931 | 2 328 175 | 696 680 | 1 305 304 | 830 742 | 5 160 901 |
| 1921 | 1 658 697 | 495 566 | 1 057 965 | 764 836 | 3 977 064 |
| 1911 | 1 080 960 | 488 748 | 782 771 | 655 097 | 3 007 576 |
| 1901 | 475 770 | 343 266 | 503 187 | 545 037 | 1 867 260 |
| 1891 | 397 865 | 224 760 | 390 670 | 427 310 | 1 440 605 |
| 1881 | 140 747 | 220 922 | 298 371 | 316 000 | 976 040 |
| 1871 | 107 225 | 115 791 | 228 354 | 196 000 | 647 370 |

SOURCE:   Urquhart and Buckley, *Historical Statistics*, p. 15.

**TABLE 3    Immigrant arrivals in Canada, 1852 to 1960**

| Year | Numbers | Year | Numbers | Year | Numbers | Year | Numbers | Year | Numbers | Year | Numbers |
|------|---------|------|---------|------|---------|------|---------|------|---------|------|---------|
| 1960 | 104 111 | 1940 | 11 324 | 1920 | 138 824 | 1900 | 41 681 | 1880 | 38 505 | 1860 | 6 276 |
| 1959 | 106 928 | 1939 | 16 994 | 1919 | 107 698 | 1899 | 44 543 | 1879 | 40 492 | 1859 | 6 300 |
| 1958 | 124 851 | 1938 | 17 244 | 1918 | 41 845 | 1898 | 31 900 | 1878 | 29 807 | 1858 | 12 339 |
| 1957 | 282 164 | 1937 | 15 101 | 1917 | 72 910 | 1897 | 21 716 | 1877 | 27 082 | 1857 | 33 854 |
| 1956 | 164 857 | 1936 | 11 643 | 1916 | 55 914 | 1896 | 16 835 | 1876 | 25 633 | 1856 | 22 544 |
| 1955 | 109 946 | 1935 | 11 277 | 1915 | 36 665 | 1895 | 18 790 | 1875 | 27 382 | 1855 | 25 296 |
| 1954 | 154 227 | 1934 | 12 476 | 1914 | 150 484 | 1894 | 20 829 | 1874 | 39 373 | 1854 | 37 263 |
| 1953 | 168 868 | 1933 | 14 382 | 1913 | 400 870 | 1893 | 29 633 | 1873 | 50 050 | 1853 | 29 464 |
| 1952 | 164 498 | 1932 | 20 591 | 1912 | 375 756 | 1892 | 30 996 | 1872 | 36 578 | 1852 | 29 307 |
| 1951 | 194 391 | 1931 | 27 530 | 1911 | 331 288 | 1891 | 82 165 | 1871 | 27 773 | — | — |
| 1950 | 73 912 | 1930 | 104 806 | 1910 | 286 839 | 1890 | 75 067 | 1870 | 24 706 | — | — |
| 1949 | 95 217 | 1929 | 164 993 | 1909 | 173 694 | 1889 | 91 600 | 1869 | 18 630 | — | — |
| 1948 | 125 414 | 1928 | 166 783 | 1908 | 143 326 | 1888 | 88 766 | 1868 | 12 765 | — | — |
| 1947 | 64 127 | 1927 | 158 886 | 1907 | 272 409 | 1887 | 84 526 | 1867 | 10 666 | — | — |
| 1946 | 71 719 | 1926 | 135 982 | 1906 | 211 653 | 1886 | 69 152 | 1866 | 11 427 | — | — |
| 1945 | 22 722 | 1925 | 84 907 | 1905 | 141 465 | 1885 | 79 169 | 1865 | 18 958 | — | — |
| 1944 | 12 801 | 1924 | 124 164 | 1904 | 131 252 | 1884 | 103 824 | 1864 | 24 779 | — | — |
| 1943 | 8 504 | 1923 | 133 729 | 1903 | 138 660 | 1883 | 133 624 | 1863 | 21 000 | — | — |
| 1942 | 7 576 | 1922 | 64 224 | 1902 | 89 102 | 1882 | 112 458 | 1862 | 18 294 | — | — |
| 1941 | 9 329 | 1921 | 91 728 | 1901 | 55 747 | 1881 | 47 991 | 1861 | 13 589 | — | — |

SOURCE:   Urquhart and Buckley, *Historical Statistics*, p. 23.

**TABLE 4** Estimates of changes in the population ten years and over of the provinces through natural increase and migration, by decades, 1881 to 1941 (thousands)

| Decade | Population and changes | Canada | Prince Edward Island | Nova Scotia | New Brunswick | Quebec | Ontario | Manitoba | Saskatchewan | Alberta | British Columbia | Yukon | Northwest Territories |
|---|---|---|---|---|---|---|---|---|---|---|---|---|---|
| 1901-41 | Natural increase | 4 488 | 39 | 243 | 219 | 1 600 | 1 137 | 335 | 440 | 304 | 162 | - 1 | 9 |
|  | Net migration | +819 | -42 | -133 | -111 | -170 | +324 | + 84 | +218 | +290 | +395 | -21 | -15 |
| 1941 | Population 10+ | 9 409 | 76 | 464 | 359 | 2 631 | 3 188 | 606 | 723 | 646 | 703 | 4 | 9 |
| 1931-41 | Natural increase | 1 352 | 9 | 60 | 62 | 495 | 322 | 89 | 156 | 109 | 48 | — | 2 |
|  | Net migration | -112 | - 2 | + 2 | - 13 | - 32 | + 75 | - 41 | -138 | - 35 | + 72 | — | — |
| 1931 | Population 10 + | 8 169 | 69 | 402 | 310 | 2 168 | 2 791 | 558 | 705 | 572 | 583 | 4 | 7 |
| 1921-31 | Natural increase | 1 389 | 9 | 69 | 61 | 443 | 338 | 116 | 173 | 116 | 62 | — | 2 |
|  | Net migration | +103 | - 9 | - 70 | - 43 | - 10 | +129 | - 10 | - 5 | + 22 | +101 | — | - 1 |
| 1921 | Population 10+ | 6 677 | 69 | 403 | 292 | 1 735 | 2 324 | 452 | 537 | 434 | 420 | 4 | 6 |
| 1911-21 | Natural increase | 1 036 | 9 | 62 | 52 | 378 | 259 | 82 | 93 | 64 | 36 | — | 1 |
|  | Net migration | +113 | -14 | - 37 | - 25 | - 99 | + 46 | + 24 | + 78 | + 85 | + 58 | - 4 | — |
| 1911 | Population 10+ | 5 528 | 74 | 378 | 265 | 1 456 | 2 019 | 346 | 366 | 285 | 326 | 8 | 5 |
| 1901-11 | Natural increase | 711 | 12 | 52 | 44 | 284 | 218 | 48 | 18 | 15 | 16 | - 1 | 4 |
|  | Net migration | +715 | -17 | - 28 | - 30 | - 29 | + 74 | +111 | +283 | +218 | +164 | -17 | -14 |
| 1901 | Population 10+ | 4 101 | 79 | 354 | 251 | 1 201 | 1 727 | 187 | 65 | 52 | 146 | 26 | 15 |
| 1891-1901 | Natural increase | 654 | 14 | 50 | 43 | 249 | 245 | 30 | — | — | 8 | — | 17 |
|  | Net migration | -181 | -17 | - 40 | - 32 | -121 | -144 | + 48 | — | — | + 58 | — | +68 |
| 1891 | Population 10+ | 3 628 | 82 | 344 | 240 | 1 073 | 1 626 | 109 | — | — | 80 | — | 73 |
| 1881-91 | Natural increase | 669 | 16 | 60 | 48 | 235 | 282 | 13 | — | — | 5 | — | 13 |
|  | Net migration | -205 | -14 | - 43 | - 44 | -132 | - 84 | + 52 | — | — | + 37 | — | +21 |
| 1881 | Population 10+ | 3 164 | 80 | 327 | 236 | 970 | 1 428 | 44 | — | — | 38 | — | 39 |

SOURCE: Urquhart and Buckley, *Historical Statistics*, p. 22.

### TABLE 5    Population and Economic Development, US and Canada, 1870-1955

| Year | Population in millions | | Gross national product in billions of 1929 dollars | |
|------|------|------|------|------|
| | Can. | U.S. | Can. | U.S. |
| 1870 | 3.63 | 39.91 | .88 | 9.40 |
| 1880 | 4.26 | 50.26 | 1.13 | 17.45 |
| 1890 | 4.78 | 63.06 | 1.57 | 26.20 |
| 1900 | 5.30 | 76.09 | 2.16 | 38.20 |
| 1910 | 6.99 | 92.41 | 3.55 | 56.50 |
| 1915 | 7.98 | 100.55 | 4.15 | 60.42 |
| 1916 | 8.00 | 101.97 | 4.32 | 68.87 |
| 1917 | 8.06 | 103.27 | 4.40 | 67.26 |
| 1918 | 8.15 | 103.20 | 4.45 | 73.36 |
| 1919 | 8.31 | 104.51 | 4.55 | 74.16 |
| 1920 | 8.56 | 106.47 | 4.42 | 73.31 |
| 1921 | 8.79 | 108.54 | 4.03 | 71.58 |
| 1922 | 8.92 | 110.06 | 4.35 | 75.79 |
| 1923 | 9.01 | 111.95 | 4.51 | 85.82 |
| 1924 | 9.14 | 114.11 | 4.51 | 88.36 |
| 1925 | 9.29 | 115.83 | 4.82 | 90.53 |
| 1926 | 9.45 | 117.4 | 5.13 | 96.4 |
| 1927 | 9.64 | 119.0 | 5.60 | 97.3 |
| 1928 | 9.84 | 120.5 | 6.12 | 98.5 |
| 1929 | 10.03 | 121.8 | 6.13 | 104.4 |
| 1930 | 10.21 | 123.1 | 5.88 | 95.1 |
| 1931 | 10.38 | 124.0 | 5.12 | 89.5 |
| 1932 | 10.51 | 124.8 | 4.60 | 76.4 |
| 1933 | 10.63 | 125.6 | 4.31 | 74.2 |
| 1934 | 10.74 | 126.4 | 4.83 | 80.8 |
| 1935 | 10.85 | 127.3 | 5.20 | 91.4 |
| 1936 | 10.95 | 128.1 | 5.43 | 100.9 |
| 1937 | 11.05 | 128.8 | 5.97 | 109.1 |
| 1938 | 11.15 | 129.8 | 6.01 | 103.2 |
| 1939 | 11.27 | 130.9 | 6.46 | 111.0 |
| 1940 | 11.38 | 132.0 | 7.39 | 121.0 |
| 1941 | 11.51 | 133.1 | 8.45 | 138.7 |
| 1942 | 11.65 | 133.9 | 10.36 | 154.7 |
| 1943 | 11.80 | 134.2 | 10.44 | 170.2 |
| 1944 | 11.95 | 132.9 | 10.8 | 183.6 |
| 1945 | 12.07 | 132.5 | 10.5 | 180.9 |
| 1946 | 12.29 | 140.1 | 10.3 | 165.6 |
| 1947 | 12.55 | 143.4 | 10.5 | 164.1 |
| 1948 | 12.82 | 146.1 | 10.7 | 173.0 |
| 1949 | 13.45 | 148.7 | 11.1 | 170.6 |
| 1950 | 13.71 | 151.2 | 11.8 | 187.4 |
| 1951 | 14.01 | 153.4 | 12.6 | 199.4 |
| 1952 | 14.46 | 155.8 | 13.6 | 205.8 |
| 1953 | 14.85 | 158.3 | 14.1 | 214.0 |
| 1954 | 15.29 | 161.2 | 13.7 | 208.6 |
| 1955 | 15.70 | 164.3 | 14.8 | 225.6 |

SOURCE:    J. H. Dales, *The Protective Tariff in Canada's Development* (Toronto: University of Toronto Press), pp. 136-137.

**TABLE 6    Canadian Export Trade, selective years, 1869-1959 (thousands of dollars)**

| Year | *A.* Exports to United Kingdom | *A/D* *(%)* | *B.* Exports to United States | *B/D* *(%)* | *C.* Exports to Other Countries | *D.* Value of Total Exports |
|---|---|---|---|---|---|---|
| 1869 | 20 486 | 39.1 | 26 718 | 51.0 | 5 197 | 52 401 |
| 1874 | 35 769 | 46.6 | 33 196 | 43.3 | 7 777 | 76 742 |
| 1879 | 29 393 | 47.1 | 25 491 | 40.8 | 7 546 | 62 431 |
| 1884 | 37 411 | 46.9 | 34 333 | 43.0 | 8 090 | 79 833 |
| 1889 | 33 504 | 41.7 | 39 520 | 49.2 | 7 248 | 80 272 |
| 1894 | 60 878 | 58.6 | 32 563 | 31.4 | 10 411 | 103 852 |
| 1899 | 85 114 | 62.0 | 39 327 | 29.0 | 12 921 | 137 361 |
| 1904 | 110 121 | 55.5 | 66 857 | 33.7 | 21 437 | 198 414 |
| 1909 | 126 385 | 52.1 | 85 335 | 35.2 | 30 884 | 242 604 |
| 1914 | 215 254 | 49.9 | 163 373 | 37.9 | 52 962 | 431 588 |
| 1919 | 540 751 | 44.5 | 454 873 | 37.4 | 220 820 | 1 216 444 |
| 1924 | 360 057 | 34.4 | 430 707 | 41.2 | 254 585 | 1 045 351 |
| 1929 | 429 730 | 31.4 | 504 161 | 36.8 | 434 367 | 1 368 259 |
| 1934 | 288 582 | 43.3 | 220 072 | 33.0 | 157 298 | 665 954 |
| 1939 | 325 465 | 36.0 | 375 939 | 39.9 | 225 557 | 926 962 |
| 1944 | 1 235 030 | 35.9 | 1 301 322 | 37.8 | 903 601 | 3 439 953 |
| 1949 | 709 261 | 23.5 | 1 524 024 | 50.4 | 789 168 | 3 022 453 |
| 1954 | 658 315 | 16.7 | 2 367 439 | 60.0 | 921 163 | 3 946 917 |
| 1959 | 797 098 | 15.4 | 3 206 543 | 62.0 | 1 175 737 | 5 179 378 |

SOURCE: C. P. Stacey, *Canada and the Age of Conflict,* Vol. I (Toronto: Macmillan, 1977), p. 356-357, Vol. II (Toronto: University of Toronto Press, 1981), p. 434-435; and Urquhart and Buckley, *Historical Statistics,* p. 183.

**TABLE 7**  **Canadian Import Trade, selected years, 1869-1959 (thousands of dollars)**

| Year | A.<br>Imports from<br>United Kingdom | A/D<br>(%) | B.<br>Imports from<br>United States | B/D<br>(%) | C.<br>Imports from<br>Other Countries | D.<br>Value of<br>Total Imports |
|------|------|------|------|------|------|------|
| 1869 | 35 497 | 56.2 | 21 497 | 34.0 | 6 161 | 63 155 |
| 1874 | 61 424 | 49.9 | 51 707 | 42.0 | 10 050 | 123 181 |
| 1879 | 30 968 | 39.3 | 42 170 | 53.6 | 5 564 | 78 703 |
| 1884 | 41 925 | 39.6 | 49 786 | 47.0 | 14 262 | 105 973 |
| 1889 | 42 251 | 38.7 | 50 029 | 46.0 | 16 818 | 109 098 |
| 1894 | 37 036 | 34.0 | 50 746 | 46.5 | 21 289 | 109 071 |
| 1899 | 36 967 | 24.7 | 88 507 | 59.2 | 23 949 | 149 422 |
| 1904 | 61 725 | 25.3 | 143 330 | 58.7 | 38 855 | 243 909 |
| 1909 | 70 683 | 24.5 | 170 432 | 59.0 | 47 479 | 288 594 |
| 1914 | 132 070 | 21.4 | 396 302 | 64.0 | 90 821 | 619 194 |
| 1919 | 73 035 | 8.0 | 750 203 | 81.6 | 96 474 | 919 712 |
| 1924 | 153 586 | 17.2 | 601 256 | 67.3 | 138 523 | 893 366 |
| 1929 | 194 041 | 15.3 | 868 012 | 68.6 | 203 625 | 1 265 679 |
| 1934 | 105 100 | 24.2 | 238 187 | 54.9 | 90 510 | 433 789 |
| 1939 | 115 636 | 17.6 | 412 476 | 62.7 | 130 115 | 658 228 |
| 1944 | 110 599 | 6.3 | 1 447 226 | 82.3 | 201 073 | 1 758 898 |
| 1949 | 307 450 | 11.1 | 1 951 860 | 70.7 | 501 897 | 2 761 207 |
| 1954 | 392 472 | 9.6 | 2 961 380 | 72.3 | 739 344 | 4 093 196 |
| 1959 | 596 562 | 10.6 | 3 829 438 | 67.7 | 1 228 423 | 5 654 423 |

SOURCE: C. P. Stacey, *Canada and the Age of Conflict*, Vol. I (Toronto: Macmillan, 1977), p. 356-357, Vol. II (Toronto: University of Toronto Press, 1981), p. 434-435; and Urquhart and Buckley, *Historical Statistics*, p. 183.

**TABLE 8  Tax Revenues of the Federal Government, 1867 to 1960 (millions of dollars)**

| | Direct taxes | | | | | | Indirect taxes | | | | | | |
| | Income tax | | | | | | | | | | | | |
| Year[1] | Corporation | Individual | Non-resident | Estate tax[2] | Excess profits tax | Total direct taxes | Net sales tax | Other excise taxes | Excise duties | Customs import duties | Miscellaneous indirect taxes | Total indirect taxes | Total tax revenue |
|---|---|---|---|---|---|---|---|---|---|---|---|---|---|
| 1960 | 1 276.6 | 1 711.2 | 88.2 | 84.9 | — | 3 160.9 | 720.6 | 290.7 | 344.9 | 498.7 | — | 1 854.9 | 5 015.8 |
| 1959 | 1 142.9 | 1 566.6 | 73.3 | 88.4 | — | 2 871.2 | 732.7 | 286.6 | 335.2 | 525.7 | .9 | 1 881.1 | 4 752.3 |
| 1958 | 1 020.6 | 1 353.5 | 61.2 | 72.6 | — | 2 507.9 | 694.5 | 240.6 | 316.7 | 486.5 | 1.2 | 1 739.5 | 4 247.4 |
| 1957 | 1 234.8 | 1 499.8 | 64.3 | 71.6 | — | 2 870.5 | 703.2 | 249.4 | 300.1 | 498.1 | 1.5 | 1 752.3 | 4 622.8 |
| 1956 | 1 268.3 | 1 400.5 | 76.4 | 79.7 | — | 2 824.9 | 717.1 | 267.1 | 271.4 | 549.1 | 18.3 | 1 823.0 | 4 647.9 |
| 1955 | 1 027.7 | 1 185.6 | 66.2 | 66.6 | — | 2 346.1 | 641.5 | 260.7 | 240.4 | 481.2 | 16.8 | 1 640.6 | 3 995.7 |
| 1954 | 1 020.6 | 1 183.4 | 61.3 | 44.8 | — | 2 310.1 | 572.2 | 252.0 | 226.5 | 397.2 | 15.5 | 1 463.4 | 3 773.5 |
| 1953 | 1 191.2 | 1 187.7 | 53.8 | 39.1 | — | 2 471.8 | 587.3 | 296.0 | 226.7 | 407.3 | 14.5 | 1 531.8 | 4 003.6 |
| 1952 | 1 240.1 | 1 180.0 | 53.7 | 38.1 | — | 2 511.9 | 566.2 | 275.7 | 241.4 | 389.4 | 13.0 | 1 485.7 | 3 997.6 |
| 1951 | 1 130.7 | 975.7 | 55.0 | 38.2 | 2.3 | 2 201.9 | 573.5 | 312.4 | 217.9 | 346.4 | 5.7 | 1 455.9 | 3 657.8 |
| 1950 | 799.2 | 652.3 | 61.6 | 33.6 | 10.1 | 1 556.8 | 460.1 | 226.7 | 241.1 | 295.7 | 4.9 | 1 228.5 | 2 785.3 |
| 1949 | 603.2 | 622.0 | 47.5 | 29.9 | -1.8 | 1 300.8 | 403.4 | 168.0 | 220.6 | 225.9 | 4.4 | 1 022.3 | 2 323.1 |
| 1948 | 492.0 | 762.6 | 43.4 | 25.5 | 44.8 | 1 368.3 | 377.3 | 258.8 | 204.6 | 223.0 | 4.1 | 1 067.8 | 2 436.1 |
| 1947 | 364.2 | 659.8 | 35.9 | 30.8 | 227.0 | 1 317.7 | 372.3 | 268.5 | 196.8 | 293.0 | 3.8 | 1 134.4 | 2 452.1 |
| 1946 | 238.8 | 670.5 | 30.1 | 23.6 | 442.5 | 1 405.5 | 298.2 | 280.8 | 196.0 | 237.4 | 9.7 | 1 022.1 | 2 427.6 |
| 1945 | 217.8 | 686.6 | 28.3 | 21.5 | 426.7 | 1 380.9 | 212.2 | 284.7 | 186.7 | 128.9 | 9.0 | 821.5 | 2 202.4 |
| 1944 | 276.4 | 672.8 | 28.5 | 17.3 | 341.3 | 1 336.3 | 209.4 | 333.7 | 151.9 | 115.1 | 8.2 | 818.3 | 2 154.6 |
| 1943 | 311.4 | 698.4 | 26.9 | 15.1 | 428.7 | 1 480.5 | 304.9 | 333.8 | 142.1 | 167.8 | 7.7 | 956.3 | 2 436.8 |
| 1942 | 348.0 | 484.2 | 28.0 | 13.3 | 434.6 | 1 308.1 | 232.9 | 255.8 | 138.7 | 119.0 | 12.2 | 758.6 | 2 066.7 |
| 1941 | 185.8 | 296.2 | 28.2 | 7.0 | 135.2 | 652.4 | 236.2 | 217.2 | 110.1 | 142.4 | 2.6 | 708.5 | 1 360.9 |
| 1940 | 131.6 | 103.5 | 13.0 | — | 24.0 | 272.1 | 179.7 | 104.4 | 88.6 | 130.8 | 2.5 | 506.0 | 778.1 |
| 1939 | 77.9 | 45.4 | 11.1 | — | — | 134.4 | 137.4 | 28.6 | 61.1 | 104.3 | 2.4 | 333.8 | 468.2 |
| 1938 | 85.2 | 46.9 | 9.9 | — | — | 142.0 | 122.1 | 39.6 | 51.3 | 78.8 | 2.4 | 294.2 | 436.2 |
| 1937 | 69.8 | 40.4 | 10.2 | — | — | 120.4 | 138.0 | 42.8 | 52.0 | 93.5 | 2.5 | 328.8 | 449.2 |
| 1936 | 58.0 | 35.5 | 8.9 | — | — | 102.4 | 112.8 | 39.7 | 45.9 | 83.8 | 2.4 | 284.6 | 387.0 |
| 1935 | 42.5 | 33.0 | 7.2 | — | — | 82.7 | 77.6 | 35.1 | 44.4 | 74.0 | 3.8 | 234.9 | 317.6 |
| 1934 | 35.8 | 25.2 | 5.8 | — | — | 66.8 | 72.4 | 39.8 | 43.2 | 76.6 | 6.1 | 238.1 | 304.9 |
| 1933 | 27.4 | 29.2 | 4.8 | — | — | 61.4 | 61.4 | 45.2 | 35.5 | 66.3 | 2.3 | 210.7 | 272.1 |
| 1932 | 36.0 | 26.0 | — | — | — | 62.0 | 56.8 | 25.4 | 37.8 | 70.1 | 2.4 | 192.5 | 254.5 |

TABLE 8    Tax Revenues of the Federal Government, 1867 to 1960 (millions of dollars) (continuation)

| Year[1] | Income tax | | Non-resident | Estate tax[2] | Excess profits tax | Total direct taxes | Net sales tax | Other excise taxes | Excise duties | Customs import duties | Miscellaneous indirect taxes | Total indirect taxes | Total tax revenue |
|---|---|---|---|---|---|---|---|---|---|---|---|---|---|
| | Corporation | Individual | | | | | | | | | | | |
| 1931 | 36.5 | 24.8 | — | — | — | 61.3 | 41.7 | 17.9 | 48.7 | 104.1 | 1.7 | 214.1 | 275.4 |
| 1930 | 44.4 | 26.6 | — | — | — | 71.0 | 20.2 | 14.5 | 57.7 | 131.2 | 2.1 | 225.7 | 296.7 |
| 1929 | 41.8 | 27.2 | — | — | .2 | 69.2 | 44.1 | 19.3 | 65.0 | 179.4 | 1.8 | 309.6 | 378.8 |
| 1928 | 34.6 | 24.8 | — | — | .5 | 59.9 | 62.6 | 20.4 | 63.7 | 187.2 | 2.4 | 336.3 | 396.2 |
| 1927 | 33.4 | 23.2 | — | — | .9 | 57.5 | 70.6 | 19.6 | 57.4 | 157.0 | 2.9 | 307.5 | 365.0 |
| 1926 | 29.3 | 18.1 | — | — | .7 | 48.1 | 81.2 | 24.4 | 48.5 | 141.9 | 2.9 | 298.9 | 347.0 |
| 1925 | 31.7 | 23.9 | — | — | 1.2 | 56.8 | 72.9 | 25.2 | 42.9 | 127.3 | 2.8 | 271.1 | 327.9 |
| 1924 | 31.0 | 25.2 | — | — | 2.7 | 58.9 | 63.2 | 22.6 | 38.6 | 108.1 | 2.5 | 235.0 | 293.0 |
| 1923 | 28.5 | 25.7 | — | — | 4.7 | 58.9 | 98.0 | 22.7 | 38.2 | 121.5 | 2.4 | 282.8 | 341.7 |
| 1922 | 28.0 | 31.7 | — | — | 13.0 | 72.7 | 89.8 | 16.7 | 35.8 | 118.0 | 2.4 | 262.7 | 335.4 |
| 1921 | 38.9 | 39.8 | — | — | 22.8 | 101.5 | 61.3 | 12.4 | 36.7 | 105.7 | 2.3 | 218.4 | 319.9 |
| 1920 | 13.9 | 32.5 | — | — | 40.8 | 87.2 | 37.6 | 41.2 | 37.1 | 163.3 | 2.4 | 281.4 | 368.8 |
| 1919 | 7.1 | 13.2 | — | — | 44.1 | 64.4 | — | 15.6 | 42.7 | 168.8 | 2.1 | 229.2 | 293.6 |
| 1918 | 1.4 | 8.0 | — | — | 32.9 | 42.3 | — | 11.8 | 30.3 | 147.1 | 2.2 | 191.4 | 233.7 |
| 1917 | — | — | — | — | 21.2 | 21.2 | — | 2.2 | 27.2 | 144.2 | 1.9 | 175.5 | 196.7 |
| 1916 | — | — | — | — | 12.5 | 12.5 | — | 2.1 | 24.4 | 134.1 | 1.7 | 162.3 | 174.8 |
| 1915 | — | — | — | — | — | — | — | 1.6 | 22.4 | 98.6 | 2.1 | 124.7 | 124.7 |
| 1914 | — | — | — | — | — | — | — | .1 | 21.5 | 75.9 | — | 97.5 | 97.5 |
| 1913 | — | — | — | — | — | — | — | — | 21.4 | 104.7 | — | 126.1 | 126.1 |
| 1912 | — | — | — | — | — | — | — | — | 21.4 | 111.8 | — | 133.2 | 133.2 |
| 1911 | — | — | — | — | — | — | — | — | 19.3 | 85.0 | — | 104.3 | 104.3 |
| 1910 | — | — | — | — | — | — | — | — | 16.9 | 71.8 | — | 88.7 | 88.7 |
| 1909 | — | — | — | — | — | — | — | — | 15.2 | 59.8 | — | 75.0 | 75.0 |
| 1908 | — | — | — | — | — | — | — | — | 14.9 | 47.1 | — | 62.0 | 62.0 |
| 1907 | — | — | — | — | — | — | — | — | 15.8 | 57.2 | — | 73.0 | 73.0 |
| 1906 | — | — | — | — | — | — | — | — | 11.8 | 39.7 | — | 51.5 | 51.5 |
| 1905 | — | — | — | — | — | — | — | — | 14.0 | 46.1 | — | 60.1 | 60.1 |
| 1904 | — | — | — | — | — | — | — | — | 12.6 | 41.5 | — | 54.1 | 54.1 |
| 1903 | — | — | — | — | — | — | — | — | 12.9 | 40.5 | — | 53.4 | 53.4 |

| Year | | | | | | | | | | |
|------|------|------|---|------|------|---|---|---|---|---|
| 1902 | 48.7 | 48.7 | — | 36.7 | 12.0 | — | — | — | — | — |
| 1901 | 43.1 | 43.1 | — | 31.9 | 11.2 | — | — | — | — | — |
| 1900 | 38.6 | 38.6 | — | 28.3 | 10.3 | — | — | — | — | — |
| 1899 | 38.1 | 38.1 | — | 28.2 | 9.9 | — | — | — | — | — |
| 1898 | 34.8 | 34.8 | — | 25.2 | 9.6 | — | — | — | — | — |
| 1897 | 29.5 | 29.5 | — | 21.6 | 7.9 | — | — | — | — | — |
| 1896 | 28.6 | 28.6 | — | 19.4 | 9.2 | — | — | — | — | — |
| 1895 | 27.7 | 27.7 | — | 19.8 | 7.9 | — | — | — | — | — |
| 1894 | 25.4 | 25.4 | — | 17.6 | 7.8 | — | — | — | — | — |
| 1893 | 27.5 | 27.5 | — | 19.1 | 8.4 | — | — | — | — | — |
| 1892 | 29.3 | 29.3 | — | 20.9 | 8.4 | — | — | — | — | — |
| 1891 | 28.4 | 28.4 | — | 20.5 | 7.9 | — | — | — | — | — |
| 1890 | 30.3 | 30.3 | — | 23.4 | 6.9 | — | — | — | — | — |
| 1889 | 31.5 | 31.5 | — | 23.9 | 7.6 | — | — | — | — | — |
| 1888 | 30.6 | 30.6 | — | 23.7 | 6.9 | — | — | — | — | — |
| 1887 | 28.2 | 28.2 | — | 22.1 | 6.1 | — | — | — | — | — |
| 1886 | 28.7 | 28.7 | — | 22.4 | 6.3 | — | — | — | — | — |
| 1885 | 25.2 | 25.2 | — | 19.4 | 5.8 | — | — | — | — | — |
| 1884 | 25.4 | 25.4 | — | 18.9 | 6.5 | — | — | — | — | — |
| 1883 | 25.5 | 25.5 | — | 20.0 | 5.5 | — | — | — | — | — |
| 1882 | 29.3 | 29.3 | — | 23.0 | 6.3 | — | — | — | — | — |
| 1881 | 27.5 | 27.5 | — | 21.6 | 5.9 | — | — | — | — | — |
| 1880 | 23.7 | 23.7 | — | 18.4 | 5.3 | — | — | — | — | — |
| 1879 | 18.3 | 18.3 | — | 14.1 | 4.2 | — | — | — | — | — |
| 1878 | 18.3 | 18.3 | — | 12.9 | 5.4 | — | — | — | — | — |
| 1877 | 17.6 | 17.6 | — | 12.8 | 4.8 | — | — | — | — | — |
| 1876 | 17.5 | 17.5 | — | 12.6 | 4.9 | — | — | — | — | — |
| 1875 | 18.4 | 18.4 | — | 12.8 | 5.6 | — | — | — | — | — |
| 1874 | 20.4 | 20.4 | — | 15.3 | 5.1 | — | — | — | — | — |
| 1873 | 19.9 | 19.9 | — | 14.3 | 5.6 | — | — | — | — | — |
| 1872 | 17.4 | 17.4 | — | 12.9 | 4.5 | — | — | — | — | — |
| 1871 | 17.5 | 17.5 | — | 12.8 | 4.7 | — | — | — | — | — |
| 1870 | 16.1 | 16.1 | — | 11.8 | 4.3 | — | — | — | — | — |
| 1869 | 12.9 | 12.9 | — | 9.3 | 3.6 | — | — | — | — | — |
| 1868 | 11.1 | 11.1 | — | 8.4 | 2.7 | — | — | — | — | — |
| 1867 | 11.6 | 11.6 | — | 8.6 | 3.0 | — | — | — | — | — |

SOURCE: Urquhart and Buckley, *Historical Statistics*, pp. 197-198.

**TABLE 9   Expenditures of the Federal Government, 1867 to 1960 (millions of dollars)**

| Year | Defence and mutual aid | Health | Family allowances | Unemployment assistance and relief projects | Old age assistance, blind and disabled persons' allowances | Public debt charges | General government | Payments to provincial and municipal governments | budgetary expenditure |
|---|---|---|---|---|---|---|---|---|---|
| 1960 | 1 537.9 | 269.8 | 506.2 | 51.5 | 51.3 | 797.6 | 386.9 | 563.4 | 5 958.1 |
| 1959 | 1 536.8 | 227.2 | 491.2 | 40.2 | 50.6 | 783.5 | 368.0 | 542.5 | 5 702.9 |
| 1958 | 1 442.4 | 132.1 | 474.8 | 23.9 | 49.7 | 648.0 | 378.4 | 490.0 | 5 364.0 |
| 1957 | 1 687.4 | 64.6 | 437.9 | 8.2 | 39.8 | 567.4 | 405.8 | 401.2 | 5 087.4 |
| 1956 | 1 783.8 | 62.0 | 397.5 | 7.9 | 30.5 | 534.1 | 410.6 | 405.7 | 4 849.0 |
| 1955 | 1 768.6 | 56.4 | 382.5 | — | 29.5 | 514.3 | 291.9 | 358.5 | 4 433.1 |
| 1954 | 1 687.9 | 53.1 | 366.5 | — | 24.3 | 502.3 | 286.5 | 362.6 | 4 275.3 |
| 1953 | 1 857.8 | 49.5 | 350.1 | — | 23.2 | 495.7 | 279.4 | 344.6 | 4 350.5 |
| 1952 | 1 972.9 | 44.9 | 334.2 | — | 22.1 | 464.9 | 236.9 | 341.7 | 4 337.3 |
| 1951 | 1 446.5 | 41.0 | 320.5 | — | 83.2 | 531.0 | 299.6 | 129.5 | 3 732.9 |
| 1950 | 787.3 | 33.1 | 309.5 | 2.9 | 103.2 | 439.0 | 221.8 | 125.5 | 2 901.2 |
| 1949 | 387.2 | 29.5 | 297.5 | 3.6 | 93.2 | 450.8 | 170.0 | 104.6 | 2 448.6 |
| 1948 | 268.8 | 19.1 | 270.9 | — | 66.8 | 475.2 | 150.3 | 101.7 | 2 175.9 |
| 1947 | 196.0 | 8.4 | 263.2 | — | 59.1 | 466.7 | 156.4 | 155.9 | 2 195.6 |
| 1946 | 387.6 | 6.0 | 245.1 | — | 45.4 | 477.2 | 165.1 | 108.8 | 2 634.2 |
| 1945 | 2 942.1 | 2.3 | 172.6 | — | 42.8 | 437.6 | 129.9 | 112.7 | 5 136.2 |
| 1944 | 3 999.9 | 1.1 | — | — | 41.0 | 339.8 | 138.6 | 108.2 | 5 245.6 |
| 1943 | 4 241.6 | .7 | — | — | 33.5 | 262.1 | 66.7 | 109.8 | 5 322.2 |
| 1942 | 2 563.3 | 1.1 | — | — | 31.0 | 202.5 | 69.5 | 109.1 | 4 387.1 |
| 1941 | 1 267.7 | 1.1 | — | 2.0 | 29.6 | 171.6 | 90.0 | 35.5 | 1 885.0 |
| 1940 | 730.1 | 1.0 | — | 19.7 | 29.9 | 145.7 | 66.7 | 19.4 | 1 249.6 |
| 1939 | 125.7 | .9 | — | 39.7 | 30.0 | 134.6 | 38.3 | 19.4 | 680.8 |
| 1938 | 34.8 | .9 | — | 42.8 | 29.1 | 133.1 | 45.1 | 21.4 | 553.1 |
| 1937 | 32.7 | .1 | — | 68.5 | 28.7 | 132.1 | 41.7 | 21.3 | 534.4 |
| 1936 | 22.9 | .1 | — | 78.0 | 21.1 | 137.4 | 37.3 | 16.9 | 532.0 |
| 1935 | 17.2 | .6 | — | 79.4 | 16.7 | 134.5 | 36.5 | 17.8 | 532.6 |
| 1934 | 13.9 | .5 | — | 61.0 | 14.9 | 138.5 | 26.0 | 15.4 | 478.1 |
| 1933 | 13.2 | .5 | — | 36.0 | 12.3 | 139.7 | 30.4 | 15.3 | 458.2 |
| 1932 | 13.5 | .6 | — | 36.7 | 11.5 | 135.0 | 33.1 | 15.3 | 532.4 |
| 1931 | 17.9 | .9 | — | 38.3 | 10.1 | 121.1 | 33.5 | 14.0 | 448.7 |

| Year | | | | | | | | | |
|------|------|-----|---|-----|-----|-------|------|------|-------|
| 1930 | 23.4 | .9 | — | 4.4 | 5.6 | 121.3 | 29.3 | 19.2 | 441.6 |
| 1929 | 21.8 | 1.0 | — | — | 1.5 | 121.6 | 28.9 | 14.4 | 405.3 |
| 1928 | 19.6 | .9 | — | 2.0 | .8 | 125.0 | 28.4 | 14.2 | 394.1 |
| 1927 | 17.6 | .8 | — | — | .2 | 128.9 | 22.7 | 14.4 | 379.8 |
| 1926 | 14.8 | .7 | — | — | .1 | 129.7 | 20.7 | 12.7 | 359.2 |
| 1925 | 14.1 | .6 | — | — | — | 130.7 | 19.5 | 12.7 | 355.6 |
| 1924 | 13.2 | .6 | — | — | — | 134.8 | 16.6 | 12.6 | 352.2 |
| 1923 | 13.4 | .6 | — | .9 | — | 136.2 | 18.8 | 12.7 | 371.8 |
| 1922 | 14.2 | .7 | — | .5 | — | 137.9 | 19.5 | 12.2 | 441.2 |
| 1921 | 17.5 | .7 | — | — | — | 135.2 | 23.4 | 12.2 | 476.3 |
| 1920 | 30.2 | .7 | — | 1.5 | — | 139.5 | 20.2 | 11.5 | 528.9 |
| 1919 | 346.6 | .5 | — | — | — | 125.4 | 23.2 | 11.5 | 740.1 |
| 1918 | 438.7 | .4 | — | — | — | 77.4 | 8.0 | 11.3 | 695.6 |
| 1917 | 343.8 | .4 | — | — | — | 47.8 | 16.3 | 11.3 | 573.5 |
| 1916 | 312.0 | .4 | — | — | — | 35.8 | 14.4 | 11.5 | 496.7 |
| 1915 | 172.5 | .3 | — | — | — | 21.4 | 9.5 | 11.5 | 337.9 |
| 1914 | 72.4 | .4 | — | — | — | 15.7 | 13.2 | 11.5 | 246.4 |
| 1913 | 13.5 | .2 | — | — | — | 12.9 | 14.6 | 11.4 | 184.9 |
| 1912 | 11.4 | .1 | — | — | — | 12.6 | 9.8 | 13.2 | 143.1 |
| 1911 | 9.7 | .1 | — | — | — | 12.3 | 7.5 | 10.3 | 136.0 |
| 1910 | 9.2 | .1 | — | — | — | 12.5 | 8.2 | 9.1 | 121.6 |
| 1909 | 6.1 | — | — | — | — | 13.1 | 8.1 | 9.4 | 113.9 |
| 1908 | 6.5 | — | — | — | — | 11.6 | 7.1 | 9.1 | 131.5 |
| 1907 | 6.9 | — | — | — | — | 11.0 | 6.0 | 9.1 | 110.3 |
| 1906[1] | 4.4 | — | — | — | — | 6.7 | 4.1 | 9.7 | 64.6 |
| 1905 | 5.7 | — | — | — | — | 10.8 | 5.3 | 6.7 | 81.0 |
| 1904 | 4.2 | — | — | — | — | 10.6 | 5.6 | 4.5 | 76.5 |
| 1903 | 3.7 | — | — | — | — | 11.1 | 5.1 | 9.8 | 69.9 |
| 1902 | 2.6 | — | — | — | — | 11.1 | 4.3 | 4.4 | 59.1 |
| 1901 | 2.8 | — | — | — | — | 11.0 | 4.2 | 4.4 | 61.4 |
| 1900 | 3.2 | — | — | — | — | 10.8 | 4.1 | 4.3 | 55.5 |
| 1899 | 3.6 | — | — | — | — | 10.7 | 4.2 | 4.3 | 50.2 |
| 1898 | 2.6 | — | — | — | — | 10.8 | 4.1 | 4.2 | 49.0 |
| 1897 | 1.8 | — | — | — | — | 10.5 | 4.2 | 4.2 | 43.0 |
| 1896 | 2.6 | — | — | — | — | 10.6 | 4.3 | 4.2 | 40.9 |
| 1895 | 2.2 | — | — | — | — | 10.5 | 4.4 | 4.2 | 42.0 |
| 1894 | 1.7 | — | — | — | — | 10.5 | 4.5 | 4.2 | 40.9 |
| 1893 | 1.4 | — | — | — | — | 10.2 | 4.1 | 4.2 | 40.9 |

TABLE 9    Expenditures of the Federal Government, 1867 to 1960 (millions of dollars) (continuation)

| Year | Defence and mutual aid | Health | Family allowances | Unemployment assistance and relief projects | Old age assistance, blind and disabled persons' allowances | Public debt charges | General government | Payments to provincial and municipal governments | budgetary expenditure |
|---|---|---|---|---|---|---|---|---|---|
| 1892 | 1.5 | — | — | — | — | 9.8 | 4.0 | 3.9 | 38.7 |
| 1891 | 1.4 | — | — | — | — | 9.8 | 3.9 | 3.9 | 40.2 |
| 1890 | 1.4 | — | — | — | — | 9.6 | 3.9 | 3.9 | 38.9 |
| 1889 | 1.4 | — | — | — | — | 9.7 | 3.5 | 3.9 | 39.9 |
| 1888 | 1.4 | — | — | — | — | 10.1 | 3.7 | 4.1 | 41.8 |
| 1887 | 1.9 | — | — | — | — | 9.8 | 3.5 | 4.2 | 43.1 |
| 1886 | 1.6 | — | — | — | — | 9.7 | 2.3 | 4.2 | 39.9 |
| 1885 | 4.5 | — | — | — | — | 10.1 | 4.4 | 4.2 | 60.2 |
| 1884 | 2.8 | — | — | — | — | 9.4 | 2.8 | 4.0 | 47.6 |
| 1883 | 1.1 | — | — | — | — | 7.7 | 3.0 | 3.6 | 56.5 |
| 1882 | .8 | — | — | — | — | 7.7 | 2.8 | 3.6 | 41.6 |
| 1881 | .9 | — | — | — | — | 7.7 | 2.6 | 3.5 | 33.4 |
| 1880 | .8 | — | — | — | — | 7.6 | 2.6 | 3.5 | 32.6 |
| 1879 | .8 | — | — | — | — | 7.8 | 2.3 | 3.4 | 32.8 |
| 1878 | .8 | — | — | — | — | 7.2 | 2.4 | 3.4 | 29.6 |
| 1877 | .6 | — | — | — | — | 7.0 | 2.5 | 3.5 | 29.5 |
| 1876 | .6 | — | — | — | — | 6.8 | 2.3 | 3.6 | 31.6 |
| 1875 | 1.1 | — | — | — | — | 6.4 | 2.4 | 3.7 | 31.1 |
| 1874 | 1.1 | — | — | — | — | 6.6 | 2.5 | 3.8 | 32.3 |
| 1873 | 1.3 | — | — | — | — | 5.7 | 2.5 | 3.8 | 33.0 |
| 1872 | 1.3 | — | — | — | — | 5.2 | 2.6 | 2.9 | 38.6 |
| 1871 | 1.7 | — | — | — | — | 5.2 | 1.6 | 2.9 | 25.2 |
| 1870 | .9 | — | — | — | — | 5.1 | 1.4 | 2.6 | 18.9 |
| 1869 | 1.2 | — | — | — | — | 5.0 | 1.4 | 2.6 | 17.9 |
| 1868 | .9 | — | — | — | — | 4.9 | 1.6 | 2.6 | 14.5 |
| 1867 | .8 | — | — | — | — | 4.1 | 1.5 | 2.6 | 13.7 |

SOURCE:   Urquhart and Buckley, *Historical Statistics*, pp. 200-203.

**TABLE 10** Revenues of the Provinces, selected years, 1933-1960 (millions of dollars)

| | Taxes | | | | | | Privileges, licences and permits | | | | | | | | Transfers from other governments | | | | |
| | Income tax | | | | | | | | | | | Govern-ment enter-prises | Other revenue | Sub-total | Federal-provincial tax sharing | Federal-provincial tax rentals | Subsidies etc. | Sub-total | Total net revenues |
| Year[1] | Corporate | Individual | Total | General sales | Motor fuel | Total taxes | Liquor control | Motor vehicles | Natural resources | Other | Total | | | | | | | | |
|---|---|---|---|---|---|---|---|---|---|---|---|---|---|---|---|---|---|---|---|
| 1960[2] | 269 | 61 | 330 | 212 | 402 | 1 246 | 47 | 172 | 277 | 28 | 524 | 191 | 53 | 2 014 | 480 | — | 58 | 538 | 2 552 |
| 1959 | 249 | 54 | 303 | 209 | 382 | 1 168 | 45 | 164 | 303 | 27 | 539 | 186 | 52 | 1 945 | 460 | — | 58 | 518 | 2 463 |
| 1958 | 226 | 48 | 274 | 187 | 364 | 1 010 | 38 | 146 | 259 | 23 | 466 | 180 | 53 | 1 709 | 398 | — | 69 | 467 | 2 176 |
| 1957 | 214 | 41 | 255 | 183 | 347 | 955 | 40 | 140 | 278 | 20 | 478 | 167 | 40 | 1 640 | 353 | — | 29 | 382 | 2 022 |
| 1956 | 62 | 36 | 98 | 178 | 300 | 732 | 33 | 128 | 288 | 20 | 469 | 157 | 37 | 1 395 | — | 366 | 29 | 395 | 1 790 |
| 1955 | 54 | 30 | 84 | 149 | 269 | 664 | 33 | 114 | 257 | 18 | 422 | 141 | 32 | 1 259 | — | 320 | 32 | 352 | 1 611 |
| 1954 | 49 | 25 | 74 | 129 | 240 | 566 | 31 | 94 | 185 | 17 | 327 | 130 | 30 | 1 053 | — | 327 | 32 | 359 | 1 412 |
| 1953 | 49 | — | 49 | 108 | 224 | 506 | 32 | 88 | 195 | 16 | 331 | 128 | 28 | 993 | — | 309 | 32 | 341 | 1 334 |
| 1952 | 65 | — | 65 | 101 | 200 | 487 | 31 | 81 | —[2] | 170 | 282 | 130 | 25 | 924 | — | 303 | 31 | 334 | 1 258 |
| 1951 | 163 | — | 163 | 91 | 182 | 566 | 28 | 73 | —[2] | 139 | 240 | 118 | 25 | 949 | — | 96 | 31 | 127 | 1 076 |
| 1950 | 127 | — | 127 | 76 | 157 | 478 | 27 | 67 | 99 | 14 | 207 | 115 | 28 | 828 | — | 93 | 30 | 123 | 951 |
| 1949 | 106 | — | 106 | 62 | 139 | 418 | 26 | 58 | 82 | 12 | 178 | 111 | 26 | 733 | — | 80 | 28 | 108 | 841 |
| 1948 | 88 | — | 88 | 48 | 125 | 363 | 25 | 50 | 59 | 11 | 145 | 107 | 27 | 642 | — | 84 | 19 | 103 | 745 |
| 1947 | 62 | — | 62 | 31 | 112 | 287 | 24 | 46 | 42 | 11 | 123 | 103 | 27 | 540 | — | 131 | 19 | 150 | 690 |
| 1946 | 1 | — | 1 | 25 | 74 | 165 | 21 | 38 | 42 | 10 | 111 | 104 | 21 | 401 | — | 84 | 17 | 101 | 502 |
| 1945 | — | — | — | 21 | 59 | 131 | 20 | 32 | —[2] | 47 | 99 | 80 | 12 | 322 | — | 88 | 19 | 107 | 429 |
| 1943 | — | 1 | 1 | 18 | 46 | 108 | —[3] | 30 | 33 | 10 | — | —[3] | 70 | 251 | — | 93 | 17 | 110 | 361 |
| 1941 | 31 | 11 | 42 | 16 | 60 | 178 | —[3] | 32 | 34 | 9 | — | —[3] | 49 | 302 | — | 20 | 17 | 37 | 339 |
| 1939 | 11 | 12 | 23 | 3 | 53 | 139 | —[3] | 28 | 24 | 9 | — | —[3] | 36 | 236 | — | — | 22 | 22 | 258 |
| 1937 | 9 | 12 | 21 | 2 | 39 | 129 | —[3] | 26 | 25 | 9 | — | —[3] | 32 | 221 | — | — | 24 | 24 | 245 |
| 1933 | 3 | 5 | 8 | — | 26 | 73 | —[3] | 20 | 13 | 8 | — | —[3] | 19 | 133 | — | — | 19 | 19 | 152 |

[1] Figures are for fiscal year ending nearest 31 December of year named.
[2] Included in 'other privileges, licences and permits'.
[3] Included in 'other revenue'.

SOURCE: Urquhart and Buckley, *Historical Statistics*, pp. 200-209.

**TABLE 11   Expenditures of the Provinces, selected years, 1933-1960 (millions of dollars)**

| Year[1] | Health | Social welfare | Education | Transportation and communication | Natural resources and primary industries | Debt charges | General | Protection of persons and property | Other | Sub-total | Subsidies to municipalities | Total net expenditure |
|---|---|---|---|---|---|---|---|---|---|---|---|---|
| 1960 | 508 | 257 | 698 | 713 | 201 | 67 | 125 | 136 | 93 | 2 798 | 70 | 2 868 |
| 1959 | 436 | 206 | 602 | 680 | 174 | 57 | 110 | 126 | 86 | 2 477 | 66 | 2 543 |
| 1958 | 330 | 191 | 521 | 622 | 158 | 55 | 95 | 116 | 76 | 2 164 | 61 | 2 225 |
| 1957 | 301 | 168 | 452 | 587 | 147 | 55 | 83 | 108 | 78 | 1 979 | 54 | 2 033 |
| 1956 | 261 | 143 | 362 | 561 | 132 | 55 | 70 | 92 | 54 | 1 730 | 41 | 1 771 |
| 1955 | 246 | 134 | 333 | 447 | 122 | 55 | 65 | 82 | 53 | 1 537 | 36 | 1 573 |
| 1954 | 234 | 124 | 274 | 371 | 107 | 57 | 55 | 78 | 47 | 1 347 | 37 | 1 384 |
| 1953 | 209 | 103 | 234 | 353 | 102 | 53 | 52 | 77 | 44 | 1 227 | 30 | 1 257 |
| 1952 | 192 | 95 | 221 | 367 | 94 | 57 | 48 | 67 | 39 | 1 180 | 27 | 1 207 |
| 1951 | 174 | 92 | 196 | 299 | 85 | 57 | 45 | 61 | 41 | 1 050 | 23 | 1 073 |
| 1950 | 158 | 87 | 183 | 250 | 72 | 52 | 37 | 51 | 35 | 925 | 16 | 941 |
| 1949 | 143 | 80 | 160 | 254 | 60 | 53 | 33 | 46 | 33 | 862 | 14 | 876 |
| 1948 | 102 | 62 | 142 | 255 | 75 | 52 | 34 | 35 | 28 | 785 | 13 | 798 |
| 1947 | 78 | 54 | 124 | 207 | 60 | 49 | 28 | 29 | 19 | 648 | 8 | 656 |
| 1946 | 57 | 44 | 88 | 135 | 46 | 51 | 21 | 24 | 12 | 478 | 9 | 487 |
| 1945 | 42 | 41 | 70 | 78 | 37 | 56 | 22 | 21 | 9 | 376 | 9 | 385 |
| 1943 | 35 | 33 | 50 | 55 | 30 | 60 | —² | —² | 38 | 301 | 3 | 304 |
| 1941 | 30 | 34 | 43 | 71 | 32 | 63 | —² | —² | 38 | 311 | 3 | 314 |
| 1939 | 30 | 68 | 38 | 89 | 30 | 61 | —² | —² | 39 | 355 | 5 | 360 |
| 1937 | 26 | 82 | 33 | 101 | 29 | 54 | —² | —² | 35 | 360 | 3 | 363 |
| 1933 | 19 | 46 | 28 | 34 | 17 | 50 | —² | —² | 25 | 219 | — | 219 |

[1] Figures are for fiscal year ending nearest to 31 December of year named.
[2] Included in 'other expenditure'.
SOURCE:   Urquhart and Buckley, *Historical Statistics*, p. 209.

## TABLE 12   Canadian Ministries, 1867-1980

| Year | Number | Prime Minister | Dates of Ministry | Party[1] |
|------|--------|----------------|-------------------|----------|
| 1980- | 22 | Rt. Hon. Pierre Elliott Trudeau | 3 March 1980 | Lib. |
| 1979-1980 | 21 | Rt. Hon. Charles Joseph Clark | 4 June 1979-<br>3 March 1980 | Cons. |
| 1968-1979 | 20 | Rt. Hon. Pierre Elliott Trudeau | 20 April 1968-<br>4 June 1979 | Lib. |
| 1963-1968 | 19 | Rt. Hon. Lester Bowles Pearson | 22 April 1963-<br>20 April 1968 | Lib. |
| 1957-1963 | 18 | Rt. Hon. John George Diefenbaker | 21 June 1957-<br>22 April 1963 | Cons. |
| 1948-1957 | 17 | Rt. Hon. Louis Stephen St. Laurent | 15 November 1948-<br>21 June 1957 | Lib. |
| 1935-1948 | 16 | Rt. Hon. William Lyon Mackenzie King | 23 Octrober 1935-<br>15 November 1948 | Lib. |
| 1930-1935 | 15 | Rt. Hon. Richard Bedford Bennett | 7 August 1930-<br>23 October 1935 | Cons. |
| 1926-1930 | 14 | Rt. Hon. William Lyon Mackenzie King | 25 September 1926-<br>6 August 1930 | Lib. |
| 1926 | 13 | Rt. Hon. Arthur Meighen | 29 June 1926-<br>25 September 1926 | Cons. |
| 1921-1926 | 12 | Rt. Hon. William Lyon Mackenzie King | 29 December 1921-<br>28 June 1926 | Lib. |
| 1920-1921 | 11 | Rt. Hon. Arthur Meighen | 10 July 1920-<br>29 December 1921 | Unionist |
| 1917-1920 | 10 | Rt. Hon. Sir Robert Laird Borden | 12 October 1917-<br>10 July 1920 | Unionist |
| 1911-1917 | 9 | Rt. Hon. Sir Robert Laird Borden | 10 October 1911-<br>12 October 1917 | Cons. |
| 1896-1911 | 8 | Rt. Hon. Sir Wilfrid Laurier | 11 July 1896-<br>6 October 1911 | Lib. |
| 1896 | 7 | Hon. Sir Charles Tupper | 1 May 1896-<br>8 July 1896 | Cons. |
| 1894-1896 | 6 | Hon. Sir. Mackenzie Bowell | 21 December 1894-<br>27 April 1896 | Cons. |
| 1892-1894 | 5 | Rt. Hon. Sir John Sparrow David Thompson | 5 December 1892-<br>12 December 1894 | Cons. |
| 1891-1892 | 4 | Hon. Sir John Joseph Caldwell Abbott | 16 June 1891-<br>24 November 1892 | Cons. |
| 1878-1891 | 3 | Rt. Hon. Sir John Alexander Macdonald | 17 October 1878-<br>6 June 1891 | Cons. |
| 1873-1878 | 2 | Hon. Alexander Mackenzie | 7 November 1873-<br>9 October 1878 | Lib. |
| 1867-1873 | 1 | Rt. Hon. Sir John Alexander Macdonald | 1 July 1867-<br>5 November 1873 | Cons. |

SOURCE:   Urquhart and Buckley, *Historical Statistics,* p. 613; and *Canadian Parliamentray Guide,* 1981.

**TABLE 13**   **Votes Polled in Federal General Elections, 1867-1980**

*18 February 1980*

| Province | Progressive Conservative | Liberal | New Democratic Party | Social Credit | Ralliement des Créditistes de Québec | Others |
|---|---|---|---|---|---|---|
| Newfoundland | 72 999 | 95 354 | 33 943 | — | — | 749 |
| Nova Scotia | 163 459 | 168 304 | 88 052 | — | — | 2 427 |
| New Brunswick | 109 056 | 168 316 | 54 517 | — | — | 3 841 |
| Prince Edward Island | 30 653 | 31 005 | 4 339 | — | — | 208 |
| Quebec | 373 317 | 2 017 156 | 268 409 | — | 174 583 | 123 577 |
| Ontario | 1 420 436 | 1 675 519 | 874 229 | 804 | — | 29 853 |
| Manitoba | 179 607 | 133 253 | 159 434 | — | — | 3 610 |
| Saskatchewan | 177 376 | 110 517 | 165 308 | 178 | — | 2 395 |
| Alberta | 516 079 | 176 601 | 81 755 | 8 158 | — | 12 852 |
| British Columbia | 502 088 | 268 262 | 426 858 | 1 763 | — | 10 841 |
| Yukon and NWT | 7 924 | 9 627 | 8 143 | — | — | 180 |
| Totals for Canada | 3 552 994 | 4 853 914 | 2 164 987 | 10 903 | 174 583 | 190 533 |

*22 May 1979*

| Province | Progressive Conservative | Liberal | New Democratic Party | Social Credit | Ralliement des Créditistes de Québec | Others |
|---|---|---|---|---|---|---|
| Newfoundland | 59 893 | 81 861 | 59 978 | — | — | — |
| Nova Scotia | 193 099 | 151 078 | 76 603 | — | — | 1 829 |
| New Brunswick | 134 998 | 150 634 | 51 642 | — | — | 258 |
| Prince Edward Island | 34 147 | 26 231 | 4 181 | — | 512 995 | 54 |
| Quebec | 432 199 | 1 975 526 | 163 492 | — | — | 119 817 |
| Ontario | 1 732 717 | 1 509 926 | 873 182 | 1 002 | — | 26 168 |
| Manitoba | 222 787 | 120 493 | 167 850 | 1 044 | — | 1 599 |
| Saskatchewan | 201 803 | 106 550 | 175 011 | 2 514 | — | 3 526 |
| Alberta | 559 588 | 188 295 | 84 236 | 8 164 | — | 12 894 |
| British Columbia | 530 678 | 274 946 | 381 678 | 1 885 | — | 6 923 |
| Yukon and NWT | 9 948 | 8 779 | 7 926 | — | — | 273 |
| Totals for Canada | 4 111 559 | 4 594 319 | 2 048 779 | 14 609 | 512 995 | 173 341 |

**TABLE 13  Votes Polled in Federal General Elections (continuation)**

*8 July 1974*

| Province | Progressive Conservative | Liberal | New Democratic Party | Social Credit | Ralliement des Créditistes de Québec | Others |
|---|---|---|---|---|---|---|
| Newfoundland | 75 816 | 81 299 | 16 445 | 143 | — | 242 |
| Nova Scotia | 183 897 | 157 582 | 43 470 | 1 457 | — | 458 |
| New Brunswick | 94 934 | 135 723 | 24 869 | — | 8 407 | 23 417 |
| Prince Edward Island | 28 578 | 26 932 | 2 666 | — | — | 77 |
| Quebec | 520 632 | 1 330 337 | 162 080 | — | 420 018 | 25 608 |
| Ontario | 1 252 082 | 1 609 786 | 680 113 | 6 575 | — | 16 981 |
| Manitoba | 212 990 | 122 470 | 104 829 | 4 750 | — | 1 692 |
| Saskatchewan | 150 846 | 127 282 | 130 391 | 4 539 | — | 876 |
| Alberta | 417 422 | 168 973 | 63 310 | 22 909 | — | 9 955 |
| British Columbia | 423 954 | 336 435 | 232 547 | 12 453 | — | 5 512 |
| Yukon and NWT | 8 184 | 5 957 | 7 028 | — | — | — |
| Totals for Canada | 3 369 335 | 4 102 776 | 1 467 748 | 52 806 | 428 425 | 84 818 |

*30 October 1972*

| Province | Progressive Conservative | Liberal | New Democratic Party | Social Credit | Ralliement des Créditistes de Québec | Others |
|---|---|---|---|---|---|---|
| Newfoundland | 85 857 | 78 505 | 8 165 | 266 | — | 2 253 |
| Nova Scotia | 204 460 | 129 738 | 47 072 | 1 316 | — | 501 |
| New Brunswick | 131 455 | 125 935 | 16 703 | — | 16 450 | 1 948 |
| Prince Edward Island | 29 419 | 22 950 | 4 229 | 55 | — | — |
| Quebec | 457 418 | 1 289 139 | 168 910 | — | 639 207 | 70 362 |
| Ontario | 1 399 148 | 1 366 922 | 768 076 | 12 937 | — | 30 969 |
| Manitoba | 184 363 | 136 906 | 116 474 | 3 228 | — | 2 183 |
| Saskatchewan | 159 629 | 109 342 | 155 195 | 7 717 | — | 621 |
| Alberta | 409 857 | 177 599 | 89 811 | 31 689 | — | 1 996 |
| British Columbia | 313 253 | 274 468 | 332 345 | 25 107 | — | 3 116 |
| Yukon and NWT | 8 671 | 6 754 | 6 548 | — | — | — |
| Totals for Canada | 3 383 530 | 3 718 258 | 1 713 528 | 82 315 | 655 657 | 114 201 |

**TABLE 13   Votes Polled in Federal General Elections (continuation)**

| Province | Progressive Conservative | Liberal | New Democratic Party | Social Credit | Ralliement des Créditistes de Québec | Others |
|---|---|---|---|---|---|---|
| | | | *25 June 1968* | | | |
| Newfoundland | 84 521 | 68 492 | 7 035 | 126 | — | — |
| Nova Scotia | 186 071 | 127 920 | 22 683 | — | — | 294 |
| New Brunswick | 125 263 | 111 847 | 12 262 | — | 1 769 | 821 |
| Prince Edward Island | 26 283 | 22 786 | 1 639 | — | — | — |
| Quebec | 466 259 | 1 170 610 | 164 363 | — | 358 116 | 24 574 |
| Ontario | 942 755 | 1 372 612 | 607 019 | 889 | — | 24 715 |
| Manitoba | 125 713 | 166 022 | 99 974 | 5 969 | — | 2 708 |
| Saskatchewan | 153 228 | 112 333 | 147 950 | — | — | 919 |
| Alberta | 283 997 | 201 015 | 52 688 | 10 940 | — | 15 139 |
| British Columbia | 155 350 | 334 171 | 261 253 | 46 105 | — | 2 725 |
| Yukon and NWT | 5 325 | 9 067 | 1 523 | — | — | — |
| Totals for Canada | 2 554 765 | 3 696 875 | 1 378 389 | 64 029 | 359 885 | 71 895 |

| Province | Progressive Conservative | Liberal | New Democratic Party | Social Credit | Ralliement des Créditistes de Québec | Others |
|---|---|---|---|---|---|---|
| | | | *8 November 1965* | | | |
| Newfoundland | 47 638 | 94 291 | 1 742 | 2 352 | — | 1 022 |
| Nova Scotia | 203 123 | 175 415 | 38 043 | — | — | 1 249 |
| New Brunswick | 102 714 | 114 781 | 22 759 | 352 | 1 081 | — |
| Prince Edward Island | 38 566 | 31 532 | 1 463 | — | — | — |
| Quebec | 432 901 | 928 530 | 244 339 | — | 357 153 | 74 389 |
| Ontario | 933 753 | 1 196 308 | 594 112 | 9 791 | 1 204 | 8 615 |
| Manitoba | 154 253 | 117 442 | 91 193 | 16 315 | — | 237 |
| Saskatchewan | 193 254 | 96 740 | 104 626 | 7 526 | — | 179 |
| Alberta | 247 734 | 119 014 | 43 818 | 119 586 | — | 1 275 |
| British Columbia | 139 226 | 217 726 | 239 132 | 126 532 | — | 3 368 |
| Yukon and NWT | 6 751 | 7 740 | 431 | — | — | — |
| Totals for Canada | 2 499 913 | 3 099 519 | 1 381 658 | 282 454 | 359 438 | 90 334 |

**TABLE 13** **Votes Polled in Federal General Elections (continuation)**

| Province | Progressive Conservative | Liberal | 8 April 1963 New Democratic Party | Social Credit | Others |
|---|---|---|---|---|---|
| Newfoundland | 45 491 | 97 576 | 6 364 | — | 1 943 |
| Nova Scotia | 195 711 | 195 007 | 26 617 | 401 | — |
| New Brunswick | 98 462 | 115 036 | 8 899 | 21 050 | — |
| Prince Edward Island | 35 965 | 32 073 | 1 140 | — | — |
| Quebec | 413 562 | 966 172 | 151 061 | 578 347 | 8 903 |
| Ontario | 979 359 | 1 286 791 | 442 340 | 56 276 | 11 896 |
| Manitoba | 169 013 | 134 905 | 66 652 | 28 157 | 826 |
| Saskatchewan | 224 700 | 100 747 | 76 126 | 16 110 | 443 |
| Alberta | 249 067 | 121 473 | 35 775 | 141 956 | 1 255 |
| British Columbia | 172 501 | 237 896 | 222 883 | 97 846 | 4 846 |
| Yukon Territory | 2 969 | 2 455 | — | 560 | — |
| Northwest Territories | 4 814 | 3 659 | — | — | — |
| Totals for Canada | 2 591 614 | 3 293 790 | 1 037 857 | 940 703 | 30 112 |

| Province | Progressive Conservative | Liberal | 18 June 1962 New Democratic Party | Social Credit | Others |
|---|---|---|---|---|---|
| Newfoundland | 55 396 | 90 896 | 7 590 | 158 | — |
| Nova Scotia | 198 902 | 178 520 | 39 689 | 3 764 | — |
| New Brunswick | 115 973 | 110 850 | 13 220 | 9 016 | 441 |
| Prince Edward Island | 37 388 | 31 603 | 3 802 | 153 | — |
| Quebec | 617 762 | 818 760 | 91 795 | 542 433 | 19 173 |
| Ontario | 1 056 095 | 1 122 222 | 456 459 | 49 734 | 3 135 |
| Manitoba | 161 824 | 121 041 | 76 514 | 26 662 | 3 297 |
| Saskatchewan | 213 385 | 96 676 | 93 444 | 19 648 | 317 |
| Alberta | 214 699 | 97 322 | 42 305 | 146 662 | 997 |
| British Columbia | 187 389 | 187 438 | 212 035 | 97 396 | 1 931 |
| Yukon and NWT | 6 769 | 6 506 | — | 948 | — |
| Totals for Canada | 2 865 582 | 2 861 834 | 1 036 853 | 896 574 | 29 291 |

## TABLE 13   Votes Polled in Federal General Elections (continuation)

| | 31 March 1958 | | | | | | 10 June 1957 | | | | | |
| Province | Progressive Conservative | Liberal | Cooperative Commonwealth Federation | Social Credit | Labour Progressive Party | Others | Liberal | Progressive Conservative | Cooperative Commonwealth Federation | Social Credit[3] | Labour Progressive Party | Others |
|---|---|---|---|---|---|---|---|---|---|---|---|---|
| Newfoundland | 72 282 | 86 960 | 240 | — | — | 263 | 56 993 | 34 795 | 321 | — | — | — |
| Prince Edward Island | 42 911 | 25 847 | 215 | — | — | — | 31 162 | 34 965 | 680 | 473 | — | — |
| Nova Scotia | 237 422 | 160 026 | 18 911 | — | — | — | 176 891 | 197 676 | 17 117 | — | — | — |
| New Brunswick | 133 935 | 107 297 | 4 541 | 1 711 | — | — | 112 518 | 114 060 | 2 001 | 2 420 | — | 3 159 |
| Quebec | 1 005 120 | 935 881 | 45 594 | 12 858 | 1 162 | 23 634 | 1 116 028 | 562 133 | 31 780 | 3 877 | 2 377 | 73 865 |
| Ontario | 1 413 730 | 815 524 | 262 120 | 8 386 | 3 035 | 1 718 | 845 308 | 1 104 366 | 274 069 | 38 418 | 1 432 | 978 |
| Manitoba | 216 948 | 82 450 | 74 906 | 6 753 | 1 503 | — | 93 258 | 124 867 | 82 398 | 45 803 | 1 579 | 205 |
| Saskatchewan | 204 442 | 78 121 | 112 800 | 1 745 | 458 | 146 | 118 282 | 90 359 | 140 293 | 40 830 | 212 | 122 |
| Alberta | 269 942 | 61 583 | 19 666 | 97 502 | 1 196 | — | 119 190 | 118 225 | 27 127 | 162 083 | 815 | 212 |
| British Columbia | 308 971 | 100 889 | 153 405 | 59 762 | 2 515 | — | 121 301 | 192 988 | 131 873 | 143 145 | 1 345 | 887 |
| Yukon | 3 069 | 2 340 | — | — | — | — | 2 422 | 2 358 | — | — | — | — |
| Mackenzie River | 2 080 | 2 782 | — | — | — | — | 2 686 | 1 253 | — | — | — | — |
| Totals for Canada | 3 910 852 | 2 459 700 | 692 398 | 188 717 | 9 869 | 25 761 | 2 796 039 | 2 578 045 | 707 659 | 437 049 | 7 760 | 79 428 |

## TABLE 13   Votes Polled in Federal General Elections (continuation)

### 10 August 1953

| Province | Liberal | Progressive Conservative | Cooperative Commonwealth Federation | Social Credit | Labour Progressive Party | Others |
|---|---|---|---|---|---|---|
| Newfoundland | 74 357 | 31 060 | 707 | — | — | 4 459 |
| Prince Edward Island | 33 874 | 31 836 | 552 | — | — | — |
| Nova Scotia | 176 554 | 133 498 | 22 357 | — | 794 | — |
| New Brunswick | 121 936 | 93 450 | 6 769 | 931 | — | — |
| Quebec | 1 001 655 | 455 688 | 23 833 | — | 10 819 | 54 778 |
| Ontario | 898 692 | 772 691 | 212 224 | 5 427 | 18 414 | 7 972 |
| Manitoba | 110 843 | 73 644 | 64 402 | 17 260 | 6 194 | 434 |
| Saskatchewan | 133 493 | 41 538 | 156 406 | 18 810 | 3 906 | — |
| Alberta | 118 941 | 49 450 | 23 573 | 138 847 | 9 155 | 275 |
| British Columbia | 145 570 | 66 426 | 125 487 | 123 700 | 10 340 | — |
| Yukon | 2 176 | 590 | — | 998 | — | — |
| Mackenzie River | 1 722 | 1 344 | — | — | — | 421 |
| Totals for Canada | 2 819 813 | 1 751 215 | 636 310 | 305 973 | 59 622 | 68 339 |

### 27 June 1949

| Province | Liberal | Progressive Conservative | Cooperative Commonwealth Federation | Social Credit[3] | Union des Electeurs | Labour Progressive Party | Others |
|---|---|---|---|---|---|---|---|
| Newfoundland | 75 235 | 29 203 | 197 | — | — | — | — |
| Prince Edward Island | 33 480 | 32 989 | 1 626 | — | — | — | — |
| Nova Scotia | 177 680 | 126 365 | 33 333 | — | — | — | — |
| New Brunswick | 123 453 | 88 049 | 9 450 | — | 2 172 | — | 533 |
| Quebec | 984 131 | 397 803 | 17 767 | — | 80 990 | 4 868 | 107 741 |
| Ontario | 930 719 | 757 987 | 306 551 | 3 225 | 2 036 | 13 613 | 8 043 |
| Manitoba | 153 857 | 70 689 | 83 176 | — | — | 6 523 | 6 666 |
| Saskatchewan | 161 887 | 53 624 | 152 399 | 3 474 | — | 1 531 | — |
| Alberta | 116 647 | 56 947 | 31 329 | 131 007 | — | 2 201 | — |
| British Columbia | 169 018 | 128 620 | 145 442 | 2 109 | — | 3 887 | 11 992 |
| Yukon | 3 284 | — | 1 140 | — | — | — | 2 283 |
| Mackenzie River | — | — | — | — | — | — | — |
| Totals for Canada | 2 929 391 | 1 742 276 | 782 410 | 139 815 | 85 198 | 32 623 | 137 258 |

**TABLE 13  Votes Polled in Federal General Elections (continuation)**

| Province | 11 June 1945 | | | | | | | 26 March 1940 | | | | |
|---|---|---|---|---|---|---|---|---|---|---|---|---|
| | Liberal | Progressive Conservative | Cooperative Commonwealth Federation | Social Credit | Bloc Populaire | Labour Progressive Party | Others | Liberal | Conservative | Cooperative Commonwealth Federation | New Democrat | Others |
| Prince Edward Island | 30 696 | 30 025 | 2 685 | — | — | — | — | 34 664 | 28 028 | — | — | — |
| Nova Scotia | 141 911 | 114 214 | 51 892 | — | — | 1 800 | 850 | 151 731 | 112 206 | 17 715 | — | — |
| New Brunswick | 100 939 | 77 225 | 14 999 | 2 300 | — | — | 6 423 | 97 062 | 74 970 | 761 | — | — |
| Quebec | 722 707 | 138 344 | 33 729 | 63 310 | 168 389 | 14 641 | 273 049 | 868 663 | 231 851 | 7 610 | 11 191 | 52 182 |
| Ontario | 745 571 | 757 057 | 260 502 | 3 906 | 5 038 | 36 333 | 6 560 | 834 166 | 687 816 | 61 166 | 786 | 25 480 |
| Manitoba | 111 863 | 80 303 | 101 892 | 10 322 | — | 15 984 | 2 451 | 151 480 | 82 240 | 61 448 | 5 831 | 15 884 |
| Saskatchewan | 124 191 | 70 830 | 167 233 | 11 449 | — | 3 183 | — | 159 530 | 52 496 | 106 267 | 12 106 | 40 735 |
| Alberta | 67 662 | 58 077 | 57 077 | 113 821 | — | 14 136 | — | 102 060 | 35 116 | 35 082 | 93 023 | 4 062 |
| British Columbia | 125 085 | 128 529 | 132 068 | 9 890 | — | 25 128 | 7 741 | 136 065 | 110 619 | 103 181 | 506 | 12 773 |
| Yukon | — | 849 | 584 | — | — | 687 | — | 793 | 915 | — | — | — |
| Totals for Canada | 2 170 625 | 1 455 453 | 822 661 | 214 998 | 173 427 | 111 892 | 297 074 | 2 536 514 | 1 416 257 | 393 230 | 123 443 | 151 116 |

**TABLE 13   Votes Polled in Federal General Elections (continuation)**

14 October 1935

| Province | Liberal | Conservative | Re-construction | Cooperative Commonwealth Federation | Social Credit | Independent Liberal | Communist | Others | Rejected Ballots |
|---|---|---|---|---|---|---|---|---|---|
| Prince Edward Island | 35 757 | 23 602 | 2 089 | — | — | — | — | — | 193 |
| Nova Scotia | 142 334 | 87 893 | 38 175 | — | — | — | 5 365 | — | 1 756 |
| New Brunswick | 100 537 | 56 145 | 18 408 | — | — | 672 | — | — | 1 723 |
| Quebec | 623 579 | 323 177 | 103 857 | 7 326 | — | 70 504 | 3 385 | 14 693 | 16 341 |
| Ontario | 675 803 | 562 513 | 181 981 | 129 457 | — | 14 459 | 8 945 | 21 089 | 13 997 |
| Manitoba | 100 535 | 75 574 | 16 439 | 54 491 | 5 751 | 18 973 | 9 229 | — | 3 597 |
| Saskatchewan | 134 914 | 71 285 | 2 273 | 73 505 | 63 593 | — | — | — | 1 966 |
| Alberta | 50 539 | 40 236 | 1 785 | 29 066 | 111 627 | — | 2 672 | 2 588 | 2 594 |
| British Columbia | 91 729 | 71 034 | 19 208 | 97 015 | 1 796 | — | 1 555 | 6 446 | 3 640 |
| Yukon | — | — | — | — | — | 555 | — | 696 | 14 |
| Totals for Canada | 1 955 727 | 1 311 459 | 384 215 | 390 860 | 182 767 | 105 163 | 31 151 | 45 512 | 45 821 |

TABLE 13   Votes Polled in Federal General Elections (continuation)

28 July 1930

| Province | Conservative | Liberal | Progressive | Labour Progressive | Labour | Independent | United Farmers of Alberta | Farmer | Communist |
|---|---|---|---|---|---|---|---|---|---|
| Prince Edward Island | 29 692 | 29 698 | — | — | — | — | — | — | — |
| Nova Scotia | 140 513 | 127 189 | — | — | — | — | — | — | — |
| New Brunswick | 109 839 | 75 221 | — | — | — | — | — | — | — |
| Quebec | 456 037 | 542 135 | — | — | — | 21 776 | — | — | 313 |
| Ontario | 745 414 | 590 071 | 12 815 | — | 992 | 8 785 | — | — | 1 499 |
| Manitoba | 111 312 | 37 234 | — | 59 155 | 19 809 | 2 018 | — | — | — |
| Saskatchewan | 129 420 | 153 673 | 18 178 | — | — | 6 155 | — | 22 766 | 3 873 |
| Alberta | 67 808 | 60 148 | — | — | 8 769 | 2 727 | 60 924 | — | — |
| British Columbia | 119 074 | 98 933 | — | — | 15 732 | 7 894 | — | — | — |
| Yukon | 846 | 558 | — | — | — | — | — | — | — |
| Totals for Canada | 1 909 955 | 1 714 860 | 30 993 | 59 155 | 45 302 | 49 355 | 60 924 | 22 766 | 5 685 |

**TABLE 13  Votes Polled in Federal General Elections (continuation)**

| Province | 14 September 1926 | | | | | | | | 29 October 1925 | | | | |
|---|---|---|---|---|---|---|---|---|---|---|---|---|---|
| | Conservative | Liberal | Progressive | Labour Progressive | Labour | Independent | United Farmers of Alberta | Rejected Ballots | Liberal | Conservative | Progressive | Labour | Independent |
| Prince Edward Island | 26 217 | 29 222 | — | — | — | — | — | 130 | 25 681 | 23 799 | — | — | — |
| Nova Scotia | 122 965 | 99 581 | — | — | 6 412 | — | — | 888 | 92 525 | 124 545 | — | 3 617 | — |
| New Brunswick | 87 080 | 74 465 | — | — | — | — | — | 1 232 | 61 161 | 90 405 | — | — | 84 |
| Quebec | 266 824 | 507 775 | — | 38 112 | — | 8 787 | — | 5 909 | 469 475 | 273 818 | — | 1 685 | 58 588 |
| Ontario | 680 742 | 441 254 | 50 360 | 38 379 | 6 282 | 5 356 | — | 4 161 | 392 039 | 691 365 | 108 051 | 9 552 | 19 104 |
| Manitoba | 83 100 | 36 242 | 22 092 | 13 413 | 17 194 | — | — | 1 021 | 34 538 | 70 264 | 45 859 | 18 335 | — |
| Saskatchewan | 67 524 | 125 849 | 38 324 | — | — | — | — | 1 350 | 82 810 | 51 512 | 62 268 | — | 1 914 |
| Alberta | 49 514 | 38 451 | — | — | 8 148 | 163 | 60 740 | 977 | 44 291 | 51 114 | 50 592 | 8 572 | 6 040 |
| British Columbia | 100 066 | 68 317 | — | — | 11 757 | 4 330 | — | 875 | 63 506 | 90 032 | 15 829 | 11 463 | 888 |
| Yukon | 823 | 648 | — | — | — | — | — | 11 | 508 | 742 | — | — | — |
| Totals for Canada | 1 504 855 | 1 421 804 | 110 776 | 89 904 | 49 793 | 18 636 | 60 740 | 16 554 | 1 266 534 | 1 467 596 | 282 599 | 53 224 | 87 618 |

# TABLE 13   Votes Polled in Federal General Elections (continuation)

| Province | 6 December 1921 | | | | 17 December 1917 | | | | 21 September 1911 | | |
|---|---|---|---|---|---|---|---|---|---|---|---|
| | | | | | Unionist | | Laurier-Liberals | | | | |
| | Liberal | Conservative | Progressive | Independent | Civilian | Soldiers | Civilian | Soldiers | Conservative | Liberal | Other |
| Prince Edward Island | 23 950 | 19 504 | 8 990 | — | 10 450 | 2 775 | 12 224 | 434 | 14 638 | 13 998 | — |
| Nova Scotia | 136 064 | 87 988 | 35 741 | — | 40 985 | 10 699 | 49 831 | 1 474 | 55 209 | 57 462 | 351 |
| New Brunswick | 76 653 | 61 172 | 17 447 | — | 35 871 | 9 934 | 32 397 | 919 | 38 880 | 40 192 | — |
| Quebec | 558 056 | 163 743 | 31 790 | 39 477 | 61 808 | 14 206 | 240 504 | 2 927 | 159 299 | 164 281 | 459 |
| Ontario | 351 717 | 445 150 | 329 502 | 9 003 | 419 928 | 95 212 | 263 300 | 5 793 | 269 930 | 207 078 | 3 564 |
| Manitoba | 29 525 | 46 486 | 83 350 | 13 361 | 83 469 | 23 698 | 26 073 | 1 157 | 40 356 | 34 781 | 2 559 |
| Saskatchewan | 46 447 | 37 345 | 136 486 | 3 610 | 68 424 | 12 996 | 30 829 | 2 672 | 34 700 | 52 924 | 1 419 |
| Alberta | 27 404 | 35 181 | 104 295 | 6 024 | 60 399 | 19 575 | 48 865 | 1 055 | 29 675 | 37 208 | 2 892 |
| British Columbia | 46 249 | 74 226 | 21 786 | 12 739 | 59 944 | 26 461 | 40 050 | 2 059 | 25 622 | 16 350 | 1 587 |
| Yukon | 658 | 707 | — | 18 | 666 | 293 | 776 | 32 | 1 285 | 829 | — |
| Totals for Canada | 1 296 723 | 971 502 | 769 387 | 84 232 | 841 944 | 215 849 | 744 849 | 18 522 | 669 594 | 625 103 | 12 831 |

**TABLE 13**   Votes Polled in Federal General Elections (continuation)

| Province | 26 October 1908 | | | 3 November 1904 | | | 7 November 1900 | | | 23 June 1896 | | |
|---|---|---|---|---|---|---|---|---|---|---|---|---|
| | *Liberal* | *Conservative* | *Other* | *Liberal* | *Conservative* | *Other* | *Liberal* | *Conservative* | *Other* | *Liberal* | *Conservative* | *Other* |
| Prince Edward Island | 14 496 | 14 286 | — | 14 441 | 14 986 | — | 10 887 | 10 139 | — | 9 515 | 9 157 | — |
| Nova Scotia | 56 638 | 54 500 | — | 56 526 | 46 131 | 994 | 54 384 | 50 810 | — | 49 176 | 50 772 | 737 |
| New Brunswick | 40 716 | 34 935 | — | 37 158 | 35 503 | 138 | 35 401 | 32 638 | 228 | 28 383 | 31 399 | 4 318 |
| Quebec | 162 176 | 115 579 | 5 377 | 144 992 | 111 550 | 522 | 133 566 | 103 253 | 501 | 120 321 | 102 884 | 1 485 |
| Ontario | 217 963 | 237 548 | 6 769 | 219 871 | 223 627 | 759 | 212 595 | 212 413 | 2 165 | 169 480 | 189 927 | 62 668 |
| Manitoba | 30 892 | 35 078 | 2 077 | 26 713 | 20 119 | 1 290 | 21 597 | 20 177 | — | 11 519 | 15 459 | 5 906 |
| Saskatchewan | 33 885 | 22 007 | 3 976 | | | | | | | | | |
| Alberta | 23 100 | 20 433 | 2 439 | 27 173 | 19 367 | 136 | 13 012 | 10 606 | — | 8 191 | 7 811 | 1 786 |
| British Columbia | 13 412 | 17 503 | 6 453 | 12 458 | 9 781 | 2 945 | 12 985 | 10 814 | 2 652 | 8 921 | 9 231 | — |
| Yukon | 992 | 265 | 1 208 | 1 495 | 2 113 | — | | | | | | |
| Totals for Canada | 594 270 | 552 134 | 28 299 | 540 827 | 483 177 | 6 784 | 494 427 | 450 790 | 5 546 | 405 506 | 416 640 | 76 900 |

SOURCE: Urquhart and Buckley, *Historical Statistics*, p. 615.

**TABLE 13    Votes Polled in Federal General Elections (continuation)**

| Province | 5 March 1891 | | |
| --- | --- | --- | --- |
| | Conservative | Liberal | Other |
| Nova Scotia | 46 934 | 40 155 | 1 223 |
| New Brunswick | 34 730 | 24 939 | 2 377 |
| Prince Edward Island | 17 892 | 18 966 | — |
| Quebec | 94 837 | 88 711 | 3 097 |
| Ontario | 183 208 | 182 213 | 5 658 |
| Manitoba | 9 369 | 8 281 | — |
| British Columbia | 4 009 | 1 592 | — |
| NWT | 6 752 | 1 960 | 1 619 |
| Totals for Canada | 397 731 | 366 817 | 13 974 |

| Province | 22 February 1887 | | |
| --- | --- | --- | --- |
| | Conservative | Liberal | Other |
| Nova Scotia | 41 411 | 39 255 | 2 584 |
| New Brunswick | 28 884 | 28 994 | 277 |
| Prince Edward Island | 17 145 | 19 733 | — |
| Quebec | 79 155 | 78 098 | 2 383 |
| Ontario | 181 537 | 176 001 | 455 |
| Manitoba | 7 712 | 7 280 | — |
| British Columbia | 2 571 | 603 | 1 424 |
| NWT | 4 217 | 2 220 | 783 |
| Totals for Canada | 362 632 | 352 184 | 7 906 |

| Province | 20 June 1882 | | |
| --- | --- | --- | --- |
| | Conservative | Liberal | Other |
| Nova Scotia | 28 967 | 25 345 | 2 058 |
| New Brunswick | 18 848 | 17 625 | 2 298 |
| Prince Edward Island | 15 188 | 15 270 | — |
| Quebec | 55 476 | 44 801 | 5 790 |
| Ontario | 137 947 | 134 204 | 1 628 |
| Manitoba | 3 305 | 3 855 | 73 |
| British Columbia | 1 562 | 300 | 964 |
| Totals for Canada | 261 293 | 241 400 | 12 811 |

| Province | 17 September 1878 | | |
| --- | --- | --- | --- |
| | Conservative | Liberal | Other |
| Nova Scotia | 33 226 | 28 880 | 2 054 |
| New Brunswick | 17 964 | 20 148 | 1 768 |
| Prince Edward Island | 13 978 | 10 621 | — |
| Quebec | 78 719 | 61 523 | 877 |
| Ontario | 133 633 | 125 316 | 815 |
| Manitoba | 546 | 555 | — |
| British Columbia | 2 158 | — | 1 160 |
| Totals for Canada | 280 224 | 247 043 | 6 674 |

## TABLE 13    Votes Polled in Federal General Elections (continuation)

| Province | 22 January 1874 | | |
| | Conservative | Liberal | Other |
| --- | --- | --- | --- |
| Nova Scotia | 16 466 | 23 377 | — |
| New Brunswick | 10 367 | 13 872 | 30 |
| Prince Edward Island | 2 502 | 7 226 | — |
| Quebec | 31 449 | 34 328 | 576 |
| Ontario | 83 556 | 94 736 | 1 088 |
| Manitoba | 861 | 938 | 264 |
| British Columbia | 1 264 | — | 719 |
| Totals for Canada | 146 465 | 173 477 | 2 677 |

| Province | 20 July 1872-12 October 1872 | | |
| | Conservative | Liberal | Other |
| --- | --- | --- | --- |
| Nova Scotia | 19 939 | 19 974 | — |
| New Brunswick | 11 590 | 12 705 | 684 |
| Quebec | 45 092 | 41 957 | 1 578 |
| Ontario | 80 896 | 81 146 | 520 |
| Manitoba | 646 | 583 | 76 |
| British Columbia | 843 | — | 113 |
| Totals for Canada | 159 006 | 156 365 | 2 971 |

| Province | 7 August 1867-20 September 1867 | | |
| | Government | Opposition | Others |
| --- | --- | --- | --- |
| Nova Scotia | 14 862 | 21 139 | 362 |
| New Brunswick | 9 137 | 9 939 | 505 |
| Quebec | 38 796 | 32 654 | 962 |
| Ontario | 71 474 | 67 632 | 755 |
| Totals for Canada | 134 269 | 131 364 | 2 584 |

SOURCE:  *Report of the Chief Electoral Officer,* 1972, 1974, 1979, and 1980; Urquhart and Buckley, *Historical Statistics,* pp. 616-618; and J. Murray Beck, *Pendulum of Power: Canada's Federal Elections* (Scarborough, Ontario: Prentice-Hall of Canada, 1968).

**TABLE 14**   Members Elected to the House of Commons, 1867–1980

| Year | Party | Totals for Canada | New-foundland | Prince Edward Island | Nova Scotia | New Brunswick | Quebec | Ontario | Manitoba | Saskat-chewan | Alberta | British Columbia | Yukon and Northwest Territories |
|---|---|---|---|---|---|---|---|---|---|---|---|---|---|
| 1980 | Liberal | 147 | 5 | 2 | 5 | 7 | 74 | 52 | 2 | — | — | — | — |
| | Progressive Conservative | 103 | 2 | 2 | 6 | 3 | 1 | 38 | 5 | 7 | 21 | 16 | 2 |
| | New Democratic Party | 32 | — | — | — | — | — | 5 | 7 | 7 | — | 12 | 1 |
| 1979 | Progressive Conservative | 136 | 2 | 4 | 8 | 4 | 2 | 57 | 7 | 10 | 21 | 19 | 2 |
| | Liberal | 114 | 4 | — | 2 | 6 | 67 | 32 | 2 | — | — | 1 | — |
| | New Democratic Party | 26 | 1 | — | 1 | — | — | 6 | 5 | 4 | — | 8 | 1 |
| | Créditiste | 6 | — | — | — | — | 6 | — | — | — | — | — | — |
| 1974 | Liberal | 141 | 4 | 1 | 2 | 6 | 60 | 55 | 2 | 3 | — | 8 | — |
| | Progressive Conservative | 95 | 3 | 3 | 8 | 3 | 3 | 25 | 9 | 8 | 19 | 13 | 1 |
| | New Democratic Party | 16 | — | — | 1 | — | — | 8 | 2 | 2 | — | 2 | 1 |
| | Créditiste | 11 | — | — | — | — | 11 | — | — | — | — | — | — |
| | Independent | 1 | — | — | — | 1 | — | — | — | — | — | — | — |
| 1972 | Liberal | 109 | 3 | 1 | 1 | 5 | 56 | 36 | 2 | 1 | — | 4 | — |
| | Progressive Conservative | 107 | 4 | 3 | 10 | 5 | 2 | 40 | 8 | 7 | 19 | 8 | 1 |
| | New Democratic Party | 31 | — | — | — | — | — | 11 | 3 | 5 | — | 11 | 1 |
| | Créditiste | 15 | — | — | — | — | 15 | — | — | — | — | — | — |
| | Independent | 2 | — | — | — | — | 1 | 1 | — | — | — | — | — |
| 1968 | Liberal | 155 | 1 | — | 1 | 5 | 56 | 64 | 5 | 2 | 4 | 16 | 1 |
| | Progressive Conservative | 72 | 6 | 4 | 10 | 5 | 4 | 17 | 5 | 5 | 15 | — | 1 |
| | New Democratic Party | 22 | — | — | — | — | — | 6 | 3 | 6 | — | 7 | — |
| | Créditiste | 14 | — | — | — | — | 14 | — | — | — | — | — | — |
| | Independent | 1 | — | — | — | — | — | 1 | — | — | — | — | — |
| 1965 | Liberal | 131 | 7 | — | 2 | 6 | 56 | 51 | 1 | — | — | 7 | 1 |
| | Progressive Conservative | 97 | — | 4 | 10 | 4 | 8 | 25 | 10 | 17 | 15 | 3 | 1 |
| | New Democratic Party | 21 | — | — | — | — | — | 9 | 3 | — | — | 9 | — |
| | Créditiste | 9 | — | — | — | — | 9 | — | — | — | — | — | — |

| Year | Party | Total | Nfld | PEI | NS | NB | Que | Ont | Man | Sask | Alta | BC | Yukon | NWT |
|------|-------|-------|------|-----|-----|-----|-----|-----|-----|------|------|-----|-------|-----|
| 1963 | Social Credit | 5 | — | — | — | — | 2 | — | — | — | 2 | 3 | — | 2 |
| | Independent | 2 | — | — | — | — | — | — | — | — | — | — | — | — |
| | Liberal | 129 | 7 | 2 | 5 | 6 | 47 | 52 | 2 | — | 1 | 7 | — | — |
| | Progressive Conservative | 95 | — | 2 | 7 | 4 | 8 | 27 | 10 | 17 | 14 | 4 | — | 2 |
| | Social Credit | 24 | — | — | — | — | 20 | — | 2 | — | 2 | 2 | — | — |
| | New Democratic Party | 17 | — | — | — | — | — | 6 | 2 | — | — | 9 | — | — |
| 1962 | Progressive Conservative | 116 | 1 | 4 | 9 | 4 | 14 | 35 | 11 | 16 | 15 | 6 | 1 | 1 |
| | Liberal | 100 | 6 | — | 2 | 6 | 35 | 43 | 1 | — | — | 4 | — | 1 |
| | Social Credit | 30 | — | — | — | — | 26 | — | — | — | 2 | 2 | — | — |
| | New Democratic Party | 19 | — | 1 | — | — | — | 6 | 2 | — | — | 10 | — | — |
| | Independent | 1 | — | — | — | — | — | 1 | — | — | — | — | — | — |
| 1958 | Progressive Conservative | 208 | 2 | 4 | 12 | 7 | 50 | 67 | 14 | 16 | 17 | 18 | 1 | 1 |
| | Liberal | 48 | 5 | * | * | 3 | 25 | 14 | * | 1 | * | 4 | * | * |
| | Cooperative Commonwealth Federation | 8 | * | * | * | * | * | 3 | * | 1 | * | 4 | * | * |
| | Liberal Labour | 1 | * | * | * | * | 1 | * | * | * | * | * | * | * |
| 1957 | Progressive Conservative | 112 | 2 | 4 | 10 | 5 | 9 | 61 | 8 | 3 | 8 | 7 | 3 | 2 |
| | Liberal | 105 | 5 | * | 2 | 5 | 63 | 20 | 1 | 4 | 1 | 2 | 1 | * |
| | Independent Liberal | 1 | * | * | * | * | 1 | * | * | * | * | * | * | * |
| | Cooperative Commonwealth Federation | 25 | * | * | * | * | * | 3 | 5 | 10 | * | 7 | * | * |
| | Social Credit | 19 | * | * | * | * | * | * | * | * | 13 | 6 | * | * |
| | Liberal Labour | 1 | * | * | * | * | 1 | * | * | * | * | * | * | * |
| | Independent | 2 | * | * | * | * | 2 | * | * | * | * | * | * | * |
| 1953 | Liberal | 170 | 7 | 3 | 10 | 7 | 66 | 50 | 8 | 5 | 4 | 8 | 1 | 2 |
| | Independent Liberal | 2 | * | * | * | * | 2 | * | * | * | * | * | * | * |
| | Progressive Conservative | 51 | 1 | 1 | 3 | 1 | 4 | 33 | 3 | 1 | 2 | 3 | * | * |
| | Cooperative Commonwealth Federation | 23 | * | * | 1 | * | 1 | 1 | 3 | 11 | * | 7 | * | * |
| | Social Credit | 15 | * | * | * | * | * | * | * | * | 11 | 4 | * | * |
| | Independent | 3 | * | * | * | * | 3 | * | * | * | * | * | * | * |
| | Liberal Labour | 1 | * | * | * | * | 1 | * | * | * | * | * | * | * |

**TABLE 14   Members Elected to the House of Commons (continuation)**

| Year | Party | Totals for Canada | Newfoundland | Prince Edward Island | Nova Scotia | New Brunswick | Quebec | Ontario | Manitoba | Saskatchewan | Alberta | British Columbia | Yukon and Northwest Territories |
|---|---|---|---|---|---|---|---|---|---|---|---|---|---|
| 1949 | Liberal | 190 | 5 | 3 | 10 | 7 | 66 | 56 | 12 | 14 | 5 | 11 | 1 |
| | Independent Liberal | 3 | * | * | * | 1 | 1 | 1 | * | * | * | * | * |
| | Progressive Conservative | 41 | 2 | 1 | 2 | 2 | 2 | 25 | 1 | 1 | 2 | 3 | * |
| | Cooperative Commonwealth Federation | 13 | * | * | 1 | * | * | 1 | 3 | 5 | * | 3 | * |
| | Social Credit | 10 | * | * | * | * | * | * | * | * | 10 | * | * |
| | Independent | 5 | * | * | * | * | 4 | * | * | * | * | 1 | * |
| 1945 | Liberal | 125 | — | 3 | 8 | 7 | 54 | 34 | 10 | 2 | 2 | 5 | * |
| | Independent Liberal | 2 | — | * | * | * | 2 | * | * | * | * | * | * |
| | Progressive Conservative | 67 | — | 1 | 3 | 3 | 1 | 48 | 2 | 1 | 2 | 5 | 1 |
| | Independent Conservative | 1 | — | * | * | * | 1 | * | * | * | * | * | * |
| | Cooperative Commonwealth Federation | 28 | — | * | 1 | * | * | * | 5 | 18 | * | 4 | * |
| | Independent Cooperative Commonwealth Federation | 1 | — | * | * | 1 | * | * | * | * | * | * | * |
| | Social Credit | 13 | — | * | * | * | * | * | * | * | 13 | * | * |
| | Independent | 5 | — | * | * | * | 4 | * | * | * | * | 1 | * |
| | Bloc Populaire | 2 | — | * | * | * | 2 | * | * | * | * | * | * |
| | Labour Progressive Party | 1 | — | * | * | * | 1 | * | * | * | * | * | * |
| 1940 | Liberal | 178 | — | 4 | 10 | 5 | 61 | 55 | 14 | 12 | 7 | 10 | * |
| | Independent Liberal | 3 | — | * | * | * | 3 | * | * | * | * | * | * |
| | Conservative | 39 | — | * | 1 | 5 | * | 25 | 1 | 2 | * | 4 | 1 |
| | Independent Conservative | 1 | — | * | * | * | 1 | * | * | * | * | * | * |
| | Social Credit | 10 | — | * | * | * | * | * | * | * | 10 | * | * |
| | Cooperative Commonwealth Federation | 8 | — | * | 1 | * | * | * | 1 | 5 | * | 1 | * |
| | Liberal Progressive | 3 | — | * | * | * | * | 2 | 1 | * | * | * | * |
| | Independent | 1 | — | * | * | * | * | * | * | * | * | 1 | * |
| | Unity | 2 | — | * | * | * | * | * | * | 2 | * | * | * |

| Year | Party | | | | | | | | | | | | |
|---|---|---|---|---|---|---|---|---|---|---|---|---|---|
| 1935 | Liberal | 171 | — | 4 | 12 | 9 | 55 | 56 | 12 | 16 | 1 | 6 | * |
| | Independent Liberal | 5 | — | * | * | * | 5 | * | * | * | * | * | * |
| | Conservative | 39 | — | * | * | 1 | 5 | 25 | 1 | 1 | 1 | 5 | * |
| | Independent Conservative | 1 | — | * | * | * | * | * | * | * | * | * | 1 |
| | Social Credit | 17 | — | * | * | * | * | * | * | 2 | 15 | * | * |
| | Cooperative Commonwealth Federation | 7 | — | * | * | * | * | * | 2 | 2 | * | 3 | * |
| | Liberal Progressive | 2 | — | * | * | * | * | * | 2 | * | * | * | * |
| | Reconstruction | 1 | — | * | * | * | * | * | * | * | * | 1 | * |
| | Independent | 1 | — | * | * | * | * | * | * | * | * | 1 | * |
| | United Farmers of Ontario — Labour | 1 | — | * | * | * | * | 1 | * | * | * | * | * |
| 1930 | Conservative | 137 | — | 3 | 10 | 10 | 24 | 59 | 11 | 8 | 4 | 7 | 1 |
| | Liberal | 88 | — | 1 | 4 | 1 | 40 | 22 | 1 | 11 | 3 | 5 | * |
| | United Farmers | 10 | — | * | * | * | * | * | * | 1 | 9 | * | * |
| | Progressive | 2 | — | * | * | * | * | * | * | 2 | * | * | * |
| | Liberal Progressive | 3 | — | * | * | * | * | * | 3 | * | * | * | * |
| | Labour | 2 | — | * | * | * | * | * | 1 | * | * | 1 | * |
| | Independent Labour | 1 | — | * | * | * | * | * | 1 | * | * | * | * |
| | Independent | 2 | — | * | * | * | 1 | * | * | * | * | 1 | * |
| 1926 | Liberal | 116 | — | 3 | 2 | 4 | 60 | 23 | 4 | 16 | 3 | 1 | * |
| | Conservative | 91 | — | 1 | 12 | 7 | 4 | 53 | ○ | ○ | 1 | 12 | 1 |
| | United Farmers of Alberta | 11 | — | * | * | * | ○ | ○ | * | * | 11 | * | * |
| | Progressive | 13 | — | ○ | ○ | * | ○ | ○ | 4 | 5 | * | 4 | * |
| | Liberal Progressive | 9 | — | ○ | ○ | * | ○ | ○ | 7 | 2 | * | * | * |
| | Labour | 3 | — | * | * | * | * | * | 2 | * | * | 1 | * |
| | Independent | 2 | — | * | * | * | 1 | * | * | * | * | 1 | * |
| 1925 | Liberal | 101 | — | 2 | 3 | 1 | 60 | 12 | 1 | 15 | 4 | 3 | * |
| | Conservative | 116 | — | 2 | 11 | 10 | 4 | 68 | 7 | 7 | 6 | 1 | * |
| | Progressive | 24 | — | ○ | ○ | * | ○ | ○ | 7 | 6 | 9 | 2 | * |
| | Labour | 2 | — | * | * | * | * | * | 1 | * | * | 1 | * |
| | Independent | 2 | — | * | * | * | 1 | * | * | * | * | 1 | * |
| 1921 | Liberal | 117 | — | 4 | 16 | 5 | 65 | 21 | 1 | 2 | * | 3 | * |
| | Conservative | 50 | — | ○ | ○ | 5 | ○ | 37 | ○ | ○ | ○ | 7 | 1 |
| | Progressive | 64 | — | ○ | ○ | 1 | ○ | 24 | 12 | 15 | 10 | 2 | * |
| | Labour | 3 | — | * | * | * | * | * | 2 | * | 1 | * | * |
| | Independent | 1 | — | * | * | * | 1 | * | * | * | * | * | * |

**TABLE 14  Members Elected to the House of Commons (continuation)**

| Year | Party | Totals for Canada | Newfoundland | Prince Edward Island | Nova Scotia | New Brunswick | Quebec | Ontario | Manitoba | Saskatchewan | Alberta | British Columbia | Yukon and Northwest Territories |
|------|-------|------|------|------|------|------|------|------|------|------|------|------|------|
| 1917 | Unionist | 153 | — | 2 | 12 | 7 | 3 | 74 | 14 | 16 | 11 | 13 | 1 |
|  | Liberal | 82 | — | 2 | 4 | 4 | 62 | 8 | 1 | ○ | 1 | ○ | ○ |
| 1911 | Conservative | 133 | — | 2 | 9 | 5 | 27 | 72 | 8 | 1 | 1 | 7 | 1 |
|  | Liberal | 86 | — | 2 | 9 | 8 | 37 | 13 | 2 | 9 | 6 | ○ | ○ |
|  | Independent | 2 | — | * | * | * | 1 | 1 | * | * | * | * | * |
| 1908 | Liberal | 133 | — | 3 | 12 | 11 | 53 | 36 | 2 | 9 | 4 | 2 | 1 |
|  | Conservative | 85 | — | 1 | 6 | 2 | 11 | 48 | 8 | 1 | 3 | 5 | ○ |
|  | Independent | 3 | — | * | * | * | 1 | 2 | * | * | * | * | * |
| 1904 | Liberal | 139 | — | 1 | 18 | 7 | 54 | 38 | 7 | — | — | 7 | 7 |
|  | Conservative | 75 | — | 3 | ○ | 6 | 11 | 48 | 3 | — | — | ○ | 4 |
| 1900 | Liberal | 128 | — | 3 | 15 | 9 | 56 | 35 | 2 | — | — | 3 | 5 |
|  | Conservative | 78 | — | 2 | 5 | 5 | 7 | 54 | 3 | — | — | 3 | ○ |
|  | Other (no details) | 8 | — | — | — | — | — | — | — | — | — | — | — |
| 1896 | Liberal | 117 | — | 2 | 10 | 5 | 49 | 43 | 2 | — | — | 4 | 2 |
|  | Conservative | 89 | — | 3 | 10 | 9 | 16 | 44 | 4 | — | — | 2 | 1 |
|  | Independent | 7 | — | * | * | * | * | 5 | 1 | — | — | * | 1 |
| 1891 | Conservative | 123 | — | 2 | 16 | 13 | 30 | 48 | 4 | — | — | 6 | 4 |
|  | Liberal | 92 | — | 4 | 5 | 3 | 35 | 44 | 1 | — | — | ○ | ○ |
| 1887 | Conservative | 123 | — | ○ | 14 | 10 | 33 | 52 | 4 | — | — | 6 | 4 |
|  | Liberal | 92 | — | 6 | 7 | 6 | 32 | 40 | 1 | — | — | ○ | ○ |
| 1882 | Conservative | 139 | — | 4 | 15 | 10 | 48 | 54 | 2 | — | — | 6 | 4 |
|  | Liberal | 71 | — | 2 | 6 | 6 | 17 | 37 | 3 | — | — | ○ | — |

| Year | Party | | | | | | | | | | | | | |
|---|---|---|---|---|---|---|---|---|---|---|---|---|---|---|
| 1878 | Conservative | 137 | — | 5 | 14 | 5 | 45 | 59 | 3 | — | — | — | — | 6 |
| | Liberal | 69 | — | 1 | 7 | 11 | 20 | 29 | 1 | — | — | — | — | O |
| 1874 | Liberal | 133 | — | 6 | 17 | 11 | 33 | 64 | 2 | — | — | — | — | O |
| | Conservative | 73 | — | O | 4 | 5 | 32 | 24 | 2 | — | — | — | — | 6 |
| 1872 | Conservative | 103 | — | — | 11 | 7 | 38 | 38 | 3 | — | — | — | — | 6 |
| | Liberal | 97 | — | — | 10 | 9 | 27 | 50 | 1 | — | — | — | — | O |
| 1867 | Conservative | 101 | — | — | 3 | 7 | 45 | 46 | — | — | — | — | — | — |
| | Liberal | 80 | — | — | 16 | 8 | 20 | 36 | — | — | — | — | — | — |

SOURCE: *Canadian Parliamentary Guide, 1981*; and, Urquhart and Buckley, *Historical Statistics*, pp. 619-620.

O An open circle indicates that before 1930, as far as the records show, a party ran candidates without success.

\* An asterisk indicates that no candidates were entered in the election.

— A dash indicates that there are no records for that particular election.

## APPENDIX II PART A:  The British North America Act (with amendments to 1975)

The text that follows is the BNA Act (1867) with subsequent amendments to 1975 prepared by Elmes A. Driedger and published by the Canadian Department of Justice as *A Consolidation of the British North America Acts*, 1867 to 1975 (Ottawa: Canadian Government Publishing Centre, 1976). The schedules (covering electoral districts of Ontario and Quebec, public works and assets, and oaths of allegiance and qualification) are not reproduced.

# THE BRITISH NORTH AMERICA ACT, 1867

## 30 & 31 Victoria, c. 3.

### (Consolidated with amendments)

An Act for the Union of Canada, Nova Scotia, and New Brunswick, and the Government thereof; and for Purposes connected therewith.

*(29th March, 1867.)*

WHEREAS the Provinces of Canada, Nova Scotia and New Brunswick have expressed their Desire to be federally united into One Dominion under the Crown of the United Kingdom of Great Britain and Ireland, with a Constitution similar in Principle to that of the United Kingdom:

And whereas such a Union would conduce to the Welfare of the Provinces and promote the Interests of the British Empire:

And whereas on the Establishment of the Union by Authority of Parliament it is expedient, not only that the Constitution of the Legislative Authority in the Dominion be provided for, but also that the Nature of the Executive Government therein be declared:

And whereas it is expedient that Provision be made for the eventual Admission into the Union of other Parts of British North America: (1)

### I.—PRELIMINARY.

**1.** This Act may be cited as The British North America Act, 1867.    Short title.

**2.** Repealed. (2)

---

(1) The enacting clause was repealed by the *Statute Law Revision Act. 1893,* 56-57 Vict., c 14 (U.K). It read as follows:

> Be it therefore enacted and declared by the Queen's Most Excellent Majesty, by and with the Advice and Consent of the Lords Spiritual and Temporal, and Commons, in this present Parliament assembled, and by the Authority of the same, as follows:

(2) Section 2, repealed by the *Statute Law Revision Act, 1893,* 56-57 Vict., c. 14 (U.K.), read as follows:

> **2.** The Provisions of this Act referring to Her Majesty the Queen extend also to the Heirs and Successors of Her Mamesty, Kings and Queens of the United Kingdom of Great Britain and Ireland.

## II.—UNION.

Declaration of
Union.

**3.** It shall be lawful for the Queen, by and with the Advice of Her Majesty's Most Honourable Privy Council, to declare by Proclamation that, on and after a Day therein appointed, not being more than Six Months after the passing of this Act, the Provinces of Canada, Nova Scotia, and New Brunswick shall form and be One Dominion under the Name of Canada; anu on and after that Day those Three Provinces shall form and be One Dominion under that Name accordingly. (3)

Construction of
subsequent
Provisions of
Act.

**4.** Unless it is otherwise expressed or implied, the Name Canada shall be taken to mean Canada as constituted under this Act. (4)

Four Provinces.

**5.** Canada shall be divided into Four Provinces, named Ontario, Quebec, Nova Scotia, and New Brunswick. (5)

---

(3) The first day of July, 1867, was fixed by proclamation dated May 22, 1867.

(4) Partially repealed by the *Statute Law Revision Act, 1893*, 56-57 Vict., c. 14 (U.K.). As originally enacted the section read as follows:

> **4.** The subsequent Provisions of this Act, shall, unless it is otherwise expressed or implied, commence and have effect on and after the Union, that is to say, on and after the Day appointed for the Union taking effect in the Queen's Proclamation; and in the same Provisions, unless it is otherwise expressed or implied, the Name Canada shall be taken to mean Canada as constituted under this Act.

(5) Canada now consists of ten provinces (Ontario, Quebec, Nova Scotia, New Brunswick, Manitoba, British Columbia, Prince Edward Island, Alberta, Saskatchewan and Newfoundland) and two territories (the Yukon Territory and the Northwest Territories).

The first territories added to the Union were Rupert's Land and the North-Western Territory, (subsequently designated the Northwest Territories), which were admitted pursuant to section 146 of the *British North America Act, 1867* and the *Rupert's Land Act, 1868*, 31-32 Vict., c. 105 (U.K.), by Order in Council of June 23, 1870, effective July 15, 1870. Prior to the admission of these territories the Parliament of Canada enacted the *Act for the temporary Government of Rupert's Land and the North-Western Territory when united with Canada* (32-33 Vict., c. 3), and the *Manitoba Act* (33 Vict., c. 3), which provided for the formation of the Province of Manitoba.

British Columbia was admitted into the Union pursuant to section 146 of the *British North America Act, 1867*, by Order in Council of May 16, 1871, effective July 20, 1871.

Prince Edward Island was admitted pursuant to section 146 of the *British North America Act, 1867*, by Order in Council of June 26, 1873, effective July 1, 1873.

On June 29, 1871, the United Kingdom Parliament enacted the *British North America Act, 1871* (34-35 Vict., c. 28) authorizing the creation of additional provinces out of territories not included in any province. Pursuant to this statute, the Parliament of Canada enacted *The Alberta Act*, (July 20, 1905, 4-5 Edw. VII, c. 3) and *The Saskatchewan Act*, (July 20, 1905, 4-5 Edw. VII, c. 42), providing for the creation of the provinces of Alberta and Saskatchewan respectively. Both these Acts came into force on Sept. 1, 1905.

Meanwhile, all remaining British possessions and territories in North America and the islands adjacent thereto, except the colony of Newfoundland and its dependencies, were admitted into the Canadian Confederation by Order in Council dated July 31, 1880.

The Parliament of Canada added portions of the Northwest Territories to the adjoining provinces in 1912 by *The Ontario Boundaries Extension Act*, 2 Geo. V, c. 40, *The Quebec Boundaries Extension Act, 1912*, 2 Geo. V, c. 45 and *The Manitoba Boundaries Extension Act, 1912*, 2 Geo. V, c. 32, and further additions were made to Manitoba by *The Manitoba Boundaries Extension Act, 1930*, 20-21 Geo. V, c. 28.

The Yukon Territory was created out of the Northwest Territories in 1898 by *The Yukon Territory Act*, 61 Vict., c. 6, (Canada).

Newfoundland was added on March 31, 1949, by the *British North America Act, 1949*, (U.K.), 12-13 Geo. VI, c. 22, which ratified the Terms of Union between Canada and Newfoundland.

**6.** The Parts of the Province of Canada (as it exists at the passing of this Act) which formerly constituted respectively the Provinces of Upper Canada and Lower Canada shall be deemed to be severed, and shall form Two separate Provinces. The Part which formerly constituted the Province of Upper Canada shall constitute the Province of Ontario; and the Part which formerly constituted the Province of Lower Canada shall constitute the Province of Quebec.

*Provinces of Ontario and Quebec.*

**7.** The Provinces of Nova Scotia and New Brunswick shall have the same Limits as at the passing of this Act.

*Provinces of Nova Scotia and New Brunswick.*

**8.** In the general Census of the Population of Canada which is hereby required to be taken in the Year One thousand eight hundred and seventy-one, and in every Tenth Year thereafter, the respective Populations of the Four Provinces shall be distinguished.

*Decennial Census.*

### III.—Executive Power.

**9.** The Executive Government and Authority of and over Canada is hereby declared to continue and be vested in the Queen.

*Declaration of Executive Power in the Queen.*

**10.** The Provisions of this Act referring to the Governor General extend and apply to the Governor General for the Time being of Canada, or other the Chief Executive Officer or Administrator for the Time being carrying on the Government of Canada on behalf and in the Name of the Queen, by whatever Title he is designated.

*Application of Provisions referring to Governor General.*

**11.** There shall be a Council to aid and advise in the Government of Canada, to be styled the Queen's Privy Council for Canada; and the Persons who are to be Members of that Council shall be from Time to Time chosen and summoned by the Governor General and sworn in as Privy Councillors, and Members thereof may be from Time to Time removed by the Governor General.

*Constitution of Privy Council for Canada.*

**12.** All Powers, Authorities, and Functions which under any Act of the Parliament of Great Britain, or of the Parliament of the United Kingdom of Great Britain and Ireland, or of the Legislature of Upper Canada, Lower Canada, Canada, Nova Scotia, or New Brunswick, are at the Union vested in or exerciseable by the respective Governors or Lieutenant Governors of those Provinces, with the Advice, or with the Advice and Consent, of the respective Executive Councils thereof, or in conjunction with those Councils, or with any Number of Members thereof, or by those Governors or Lieutenant Governors individually, shall, as far as the same continue in existence and capable of being exercised after the Union in relation to the Government of Canada, be vested in and exerciseable by the Governor General, with the Advice or with the Advice and Consent of or in conjunction with the

*All Powers under Acts to be exercised by Governor General with Advice of Privy Council, or alone.*

Queen's Privy Council for Canada, or any Member thereof, or by the Governor General individually, as the Case requires, subject nevertheless (except with respect to such as exist under Acts of the Parliament of Great Britain or of the Parliament of the United Kingdom of Great Britain and Ireland) to be abolished or altered by the Parliament of Canada. (6)

Application of Provisions referring to Governor General in Council.

**13.** The Provisions of this Act referring to the Governor General in Council shall be construed as referring to the Governor General acting by and with the Advice of the Queen's Privy Council for Canada.

Power to Her Majesty to authorize Governor General to appoint Deputies.

**14.** It shall be lawful for the Queen, if Her Majesty thinks fit, to authorize the Governor General from Time to Time to appoint any Person or any Persons jointly or severally to be his Deputy or Deputies within any Part or Parts of Canada, and in that Capacity to exercise during the Pleasure of the Governor General such of the Powers, Authorities, and Functions of the Governor General as the Governor General deems it necessary or expedient to assign to him or them, subject to any Limitations or Directions expressed or given by the Queen; but the Appointment of such a Deputy or Deputies shall not affect the Exercise by the Governor General himself of any Power, Authority or Function.

Command of armed Forces to continue to be vested in the Queen.

**15.** The Command-in-Chief of the Land and Naval Militia, and of all Naval and Military Forces, of and in Canada, is hereby declared to continue and be vested in the Queen.

Seat of Government of Canada.

**16.** Until the Queen otherwise directs, the Seat of Government of Canada shall be Ottawa.

### IV.—LEGISLATIVE POWER.

Constitution of Parliament of Canada.

**17.** There shall be One Parliament for Canada, consisting of the Queen, an Upper House styled the Senate, and the House of Commons.

Privileges, etc., of Houses.

**18.** The privileges, immunities, and powers to be held, enjoyed, and exercised by the Senate and by the House of Commons, and by the Members thereof respectively, shall be such as are from time to time defined by Act of the Parliament of Canada, but so that any Act of the Parliament of Canada defining such privileges, immunities, and powers shall not confer any privileges, immunities, or powers exceeding those at the passing of such Act held, enjoyed, and exercised by the Commons House of Parliament of the

---

(6) See the notes to section 129, *infra*.

United Kingdom of Great Britain and Ireland, and by the Members thereof. (7)

**19.** The Parliament of Canada shall be called together not later than Six Months after the Union. (8)

First Session of the Parliament of Canada.

**20.** There shall be a Session of the Parliament of Canada once at least in every Year, so that Twelve Months shall not intervene between the last Sitting of the Parliament in one Session and its first Sitting in the next Session. (9)

Yearly Session of the Parliament of Canada.

### The Senate.

**21.** The Senate shall, subject to the Provisions of this Act, consist of One Hundred and four Members, who shall be styled Senators. (10)

Number of Senators.

**22.** In relation to the Constitution of the Senate Canada shall be deemed to consist of Four Divisions:—

Representation of Provinces in Senate.

1. Ontario;
2. Quebec;
3. The Maritime Provinces, Nova Scotia and New Brunswick, and Prince Edward Island;
4. The Western Provinces of Manitoba, British Columbia, Saskatchewan, and Alberta;

which Four Divisions shall (subject to the Provisions of this Act) be equally represented in the Senate as follows: Ontario by twenty-four senators; Quebec by twenty-four senators; the Maritime Provinces and Prince Edward Island by twenty-four senators, ten thereof representing Nova Scotia, ten thereof representing New Brunswick, and four thereof representing Prince Edward Island; the Western Provinces by

---

(7) Repealed and re-enacted by the *Parliament of Canada Act, 1875*, 38-39 Vict., c. 38 (U.K.). The original section read as follows:

> **18.** The Privileges Immunities, and Powers to be held, enjoyed, and exercised by the Senate and by the House of Commons and by the Members thereof respectively shall be such as are from Time to Time defined by Act of the Parliament of Canada, but so that the same shall never exceed those at the passing of this Act held, enjoyed, and exercised by the Commons House of Parliament of the United Kingdom of Great Britain and Ireland and by the Members thereof.

(8) Spent. The first session of the first Parliament began on November 6, 1867.

(9) The term of the twelfth Parliament was extended by the *British North America Act, 1916*, 6-7 Geo. V, c. 19 (U.K.), which Act was repealed by the *Statute Law Revision Act, 1927*, 17-18 Geo. V, c. 42 (U.K.).

(10) As amended by the *British North America Act, 1915*, 5-6 Geo. V, c. 45 (U.K.), and modified by the *British North America Act, 1949*, 12-13 Geo. VI, c. 22 (U.K.), and the *British North America Act, (No. 2) 1975*, S.C. 1974-75-76, c. 53.

The original section read as follows:

> **21.** The Senate shall, subject to the Provisions of this Act, consist of Seventy-two Members, who shall be styled Senators.

The *Manitoba Act* added two for Manitoba; the Order in Council admitting British Columbia added three; upon admission of Prince Edward Island four more were provided by section 147 of the *British North America Act, 1867*; *The Alberta Act* and *The Saskatchewan Act* each added four. The Senate was reconstituted at 96 by the *British North America Act, 1915*, six more Senators were added upon union with Newfoundland, and one Senator each was added for the Yukon Territory and the Northwest Territories by the *British North America Act, (No. 2) 1975*.

twenty-four senators, six thereof representing Manitoba, six thereof representing British Columbia, six thereof representing Saskatchewan, and six thereof representing Alberta; Newfoundland shall be entitled to be represented in the Senate by six members; the Yukon Territory and the Northwest Territories shall be entitled to be represented in the Senate by one member each.

In the Case of Quebec each of the Twenty-four Senators representing that Province shall be appointed for One of the Twenty-four Electoral Divisions of Lower Canada specified in Schedule A. to Chapter One of the Consolidated statutes of Canada. (11)

Qualifications
of Senator.

**23.** The Qualification of a Senator shall be as follows:

(1) He shall be of the full age of Thirty Years:

(2) He shall be either a natural-born Subject of the Queen, or a Subject of the Queen naturalized by an Act of the Parliament of Great Britain, or of the Parliament of the United Kingdom of Great Britain and Ireland, or of the Legislature of One of the Provinces of Upper Canada, Lower Canada, Canada, Nova Scotia, or New Brunswick, before the Union, or of the Parliament of Canada, after the Union:

(3) He shall be legally or equitably seised as of Freehold for his own Use and Benefit of Lands or Tenements held in Free and Common Socage, or seised or possessed for his own Use and Benefit of Lands or Tenements held in Franc-alleu or in Roture, within the Province for which he is appointed, of the Value of Four thousand Dollars, over and above all Rents, Dues, Debts, Charges, Mortgages, and Incumbrances due or payable out of or charged on or affecting the same:

(4) His Real and Personal Property shall be together worth Four thousand Dollars over and above his Debts and Liabilities:

---

(11) As amended by the *British North America Act, 1915,* the *British North America Act, 1949,* 12-13 Geo. VI, c. 22 (U.K.), and the *British North America Act, (No. 2) 1975,* S.C. 1974-75-76, c. 53. The original section read as follows:

22. In relation to the Constitution of the Senate, Canada shall be deemed to consist of Three Divisions:

1. Ontario;

2. Quebec;

3. The Maritime Provinces, Nova Scotia and New Brunswick; which Three Divisions shall (subject to the Provisions of this Act) be equally represented in the Senate as follows: Ontario by Twenty-four Senators; Quebec by Twenty-four Senators; and the Maritime Provinces by Twenty-four Senators, Twelve thereof representing Nova Scotia, and Twelve thereof representing New Brunswick.

In the case of Quebec each of the Twenty-four Senators representing that Province shall be appointed for One of the Twenty-four Electoral Divisions of Lower Canada specified in Schedule A. to Chapter One of the Consolidated Statutes of Canada.

(5) He shall be resident in the Province for which he is appointed:

(6) In the Case of Quebec he shall have his Real Property Qualification in the Electoral Division for which he is appointed, or shall be resident in that Division. (11A)

**24.** The Governor General shall from Time to Time, in the Queen's Name, by Instrument under the Great Seal of Canada, summon qualified Persons to the Senate; and, subject to the Provisions of this Act, every Person so summoned shall become and be a Member of the Senate and a Senator. Summons of Senator.

**25.** Repealed. (12)

**26.** If at any Time on the Recommendation of the Governor General the Queen thinks fit to direct that Four or Eight Members be added to the Senate, the Governor General may by Summons to Four or Eight qualified Persons (as the Case may be), representing equally the Four Divisions of Canada, add to the Senate accordingly. (13) Addition of Senators in certain cases.

**27.** In case of such Addition being at any Time made, the Governor General shall not summon any Person to the Senate, except upon a further like Direction by the Queen on the like Recommendation, to represent one of the Four Divisions until such Division is represented by Twenty-four Senators and no more. (14) Reduction of Senate to normal Number.

---

(11A) Section 2 of the *British North America Act, (No. 2) 1975*, S.C. 1974-75-76, c. 53 provided that for the purposes of that Act (which added one Senator each for the Yukon Territory and the Northwest Territories) the term "Province" in section 23 of the *British North America Act, 1867*, has the same meaning as is assigned to the term "province" by section 28 of the *Interpretation Act*, R.S.C. 1970, c. I-23, which provides that the term "province" means "a province of Canada, and includes the Yukon Territory and the Northwest Territories."

(12) Repealed by the *Statute Law Revision Act, 1893*, 56-57 Vict., 14 (U.K.). The section read as follows:

> **25.** Such Persons shall be first summoned to the Senate as the Queen by Warrant under Her Majesty's Royal Sign Manual thinks fit to approve, and their Names shall be inserted in the Queen's Proclamation of Union.

(13) As amended by the *British North America Act, 1915*, 5-6 Geo. V, c. 45 (U.K.). The original section read as follows:

> **26.** If at any Time on the Recommendation of the Governor General the Queen thinks fit to direct that Three or Six Members be added to the Senate, the Governor General may by Summons to Three or Six qualified Persons (as the Case may be), representing equally the Three Divisions of Canada, add to the Senate accordingly.

(14) As amended by the *British North America Act, 1915*, 5-6 Geo. V, c. 45 (U.K.). The original section read as follows:

> **27.** In case of such Addition being at any Time made the Governor General shall not summon any Person to the Senate, except on a further like Direction by the Queen on the like Recommendation, until each of the Three Divisions of Canada is represented by Twenty-four Senators and no more.

Maximum
Number of
Senators.

**28.** The Number of Senators shall not at any Time exceed One Hundred and twelve. (15)

Tenure of Place
in Senate.

**29.** (1) Subject to subsection (2), a Senator shall, subject to the provisions of this Act, hold his place in the Senate for life.

Retirement
upon attaining
age of
seventy-five
years.

(2) A Senator who is summoned to the Senate after the coming into force of this subsection shall, subject to this Act, hold his place in the Senate until he attains the age of seventy-five years. (15A)

Resignation of
Place in Senate.

**30.** A Senator may by Writing under his Hand addressed to the Governor General resign his Place in the Senate, and thereupon the same shall be vacant.

Disqualification
of Senators.

**31.** The Place of a Senator shall become vacant in any of the following Cases:

(1) If for Two consecutive Sessions of the Parliament he fails to give his Attendance in the Senate:

(2) If he takes an Oath or makes a Declaration or Acknowledgment of Allegiance, Obedience, or Adherence to a Foreign Power, or does an Act whereby he becomes a Subject or Citizen, or entitled to the Rights or Privileges of a Subject or Citizen, of a Foreign Power:

(3) If he is adjudged Bankrupt or Insolvent, or applies for the Benefit of any Law relating to Insolvent Debtors, or becomes a public Defaulter:

(4) If he is attainted of Treason or convicted of Felony or of any infamous Crime:

(5) If he ceases to be qualified in respect of Property or of Residence; provided, that a Senator shall not be deemed to have ceased to be qualified in respect of Residence by reason only of his residing at the Seat of the Government of Canada while holding an Office under that Government requiring his Presence there.

Summons on
Vacancy in
Senate.

**32.** When a Vacancy happens in the Senate by Resignation, Death, or otherwise, the Governor General shall by Summons to a fit and qualified Person fill the Vacancy.

---

(15) As amended by the *British North America Act, 1915,* 5-6 Geo. V, c. 45 (U.K.), and the *British North America Act, (No. 2) 1975,* S.C. 1974-75-76, c. 53. The original section read as follows:

**28.** The Number of Senators shall not at any Time exceed Seventy-eight.

(15A) As enacted by the *British North America Act, 1965,* Statutes of Canada, 1965, c. 4 which came into force on the 1st of June 1965. The original section read as follows:

**29.** A Senator shall, subject to the Provisions of this Act, hold his Place in the Senate for Life.

**33.** If any Question arises respecting the Qualification of a Senator or a Vacancy in the Senate the same shall be heard and determined by the Senate.

**34.** The Governor General may from Time to Time, by Instrument under the Great Seal of Canada, appoint a Senator to be Speaker of the Senate, and may remove him and appoint another in his Stead. (16)

**35.** Until the Parliament of Canada otherwise provides, the Presence of at least Fifteen Senators, including the Speaker, shall be necessary to constitute a Meeting of the Senate for the Exercise of its Powers.

**36.** Questions arising in the Senate shall be decided by a Majority of Voices, and the Speaker shall in all Cases have a Vote, and when the Voices are equal the Decision shall be deemed to be in the Negative.

### *The House of Commons.*

**37.** The House of Commons shall, subject to the Provisions of this Act, consist of two hundred and eighty-two members of whom ninety-five shall be elected for Ontario, seventy-five for Quebec, eleven for Nova Scotia, ten for New Brunswick, fourteen for Manitoba, twenty-eight for British Columbia, four for Prince Edward Island, twenty-one for Alberta, fourteen for Saskatchewan, seven for Newfoundland, one for the Yukon Territory and two for the Northwest Territories. (17)

**38.** The Governor General shall from Time to Time, in the Queen's Name, by Instrument under the Great Seal of Canada, summon and call together the House of Commons.

**39.** A Senator shall not be capable of being elected or of sitting or voting as a Member of the House of Commons.

---

(16) Provision for exercising the functions of Speaker during his absence is made by the *Speaker of the Senate Act*, R.S.C. 1970, c. S-14. Doubts as to the power of Parliament to enact such an Act were removed by the *Canadian Speaker (Appointment of Deputy) Act, 1895*, 59 Vict., c. 3, (U.K.).

(17) The figures given here would result from the application of section 51, as enacted by the *British North America Act, 1974*, S.C. 1974-75-76, c. 13 and amended by the *British North America Act, 1975*, S.C. 1974-75-76, c. 28. At press time effect had not yet been given to this readjustment as contemplated by the *Electoral Boundaries Readjustment Act*, R.S.C. 1970, c. E-2. Section 6 of the *Representation Act, 1974* provides that the number of members of the House of Commons and the representation of the provinces therein on the thirtieth day of December, 1974, remain unchanged until adjusted pursuant to section 51(1). As of that date the number of members was 264, as follows: 88 for Ontario, 74 for Quebec, 11 for Nova Scotia, 10 for New Brunswick, 13 for Manitoba, 23 for British Columbia, 4 for Prince Edward Island, 19 for Alberta, 13 for Saskatchewan, 7 for Newfoundland, 1 for the Yukon Territory, and 1 for the Northwest Territories. The original section (which was altered from time to time as the result of the addition of new provinces and changes in population) read as follows:

> **37.** The House of Commons shall, subject to the Provisions of this Act, consist of one hundred and eighty-one members, of whom Eighty-two shall be elected for Ontario, Sixty-five for Quebec, Nineteen for Nova Scotia, and Fifteen for New Brunswick.

Electoral
districts of the
Four Provinces.

**40.** Until the Parliament of Canada otherwise provides, Ontario, Quebec, Nova Scotia, and New Brunswick shall, for the Purposes of the Election of Members to serve in the House of Commons, be divided into Electoral Districts as follows:

### 1.—ONTARIO.

Ontario shall be divided into the Counties, Ridings of Counties, Cities, Parts of Cities, and Towns enumerated in the First Schedule to this Act, each whereof shall be an Electoral District, each such District as numbered in that Schedule being entitled to return One Member.

### 2.—QUEBEC.

Quebec shall be divided into Sixty-five Electoral Districts, composed of the Sixty-five Electoral Divisions into which Lower Canada is at the passing of this Act divided under Chapter Two of the Consolidated Statutes of Canada, Chapter Seventy-five of the Consolidated Statutes for Lower Canada, and the Act of the Province of Canada of the Twenty-third Year of the Queen, Chapter One, or any other Act amending the same in force at the Union, so that each such Electoral Division shall be for the Purposes of this Act an Electoral District entitled to return One Member.

### 3.—NOVA SCOTIA.

Each of the Eighteen Counties of Nova Scotia shall be an Electoral District. The County of Halifax shall be entitled to return Two Members, and each of the other Counties One Member.

### 4.—NEW BRUNSWICK.

Each of the Fourteen Counties into which New Brunswick is divided, including the City and County of St. John, shall be an Electoral District. The City of St. John shall also be a separate Electoral District. Each of those Fifteen Electoral Districts shall be entitled to return One Member. (18)

Continuance of
existing
Election Laws
until Parlia-
ment of Canada
otherwise
provides.

**41.** Until the Parliament of Canada otherwise provides, all Laws in force in the several Provinces at the Union relative to the following Matters or any of them, namely,— the Qualifications and Disqualifications of Persons to be elected or to sit or vote as Members of the House of Assembly or Legislative Assembly in the several Provinces, the Voters at Elections of such Members, the Oaths to be taken by Voters, the Returning Officers, their Powers and Duties, the Proceedings at Elections, the Periods during

---

(18) Spent. The electoral districts are now established by Proclamations issued from time to time under the *Electoral Boundaries Readjustment Act*, R.S.C., c. 1970, E-2, as amended for particular districts by Acts of Parliament, for which see the most recent Table of Public Statutes.

which Elections may be continued, the Trial of controverted Elections, and Proceedings incident thereto, the vacating of Seats of Members, and the Execution of new Writs in case of Seats vacated otherwise than by Dissolution,—shall respectively apply to Elections of Members to serve in the House of Commons for the same several Provinces.

Provided that, until the Parliament of Canada otherwise provides, at any Election for a Member of the House of Commons for the District of Algoma, in addition to Persons qualified by the Law of the Province of Canada to vote, every Male British Subject, aged Twenty-one Years or upwards, being a Householder, shall have a Vote.(19)

**42.** Repealed. (20)

**43.** Repealed. (21)

**44.** The House of Commons on its first assembling after a General Election shall proceed with all practicable Speed to elect One of its Members to be Speaker.

As to Election of Speaker of House of Commons.

**45.** In case of a Vacancy happening in the Office of Speaker by Death, Resignation, or otherwise, the House of Commons shall with all practicable Speed proceed to elect another of its Members to be Speaker.

As to filling up Vacancy in Office of Speaker.

**46.** The Speaker shall preside at all Meetings of the House of Commons.

Speaker to preside.

**47.** Until the Parliament of Canada otherwise provides, in case of the Absence for any Reason of the Speaker from the Chair of the House of Commons for a Period of Forty-eight

Provision in case of Absence of Speaker.

---

(19) Spent. Elections are now provided for by the *Canada Elections Act*, R.S.C. 1970 (1st Supp.), c. 14; controverted elections by the *Dominion Controverted Elections Act*, R.S.C. 1970, c. C-28; qualifications and disqualifications of members by the *House of Commons Act*, R.S.C. 1970, c. H-9 and the *Senate and House of Commons Act*, R.S.C. 1970, c. S-8.

(20) Repealed by the *Statute Law Revision Act, 1893*, 56-57 Vict., c. 14 (U.K.). The section read as follows:

> **42.** For the First Election of Members to serve in the House of Commons the Governor General shall cause Writs to be issued by such Person, in such Form, and addressed to such Returning Officers as he thinks fit
>
> The Person issuing Writs under this Section shall have the like Powers as are possessed at the Union by the Officers charged with the issuing of Writs for the Election of Members to serve in the respective House of Assembly or Legislative Assembly of the Province of Canada, Nova Scotia, or New Brunswick; and the Returning Officers to whom Writs are directed under this Section shall have the like Powers as are possessed at the Union by the Officers charged with the returning of Writs for the Election of Members to serve in the same respective House of Assembly or Legislative Assembly.

(21) Repealed by the *Statute Law Revision Act, 1893*, 56-57 Vict., c. 14 (U.K.) The section read as follows:

> **43.** In case a Vacancy in the Representation in the House of Commons of any Electoral District happens before the Meeting of the Parliament, or after the Meeting of the Parliament before Provision is made by the Parliament in this Behalf, the Provisions of the last foregoing Section of this Act shall extend and apply to the issuing and returning of a Writ in respect of such vacant District.

consecutive Hours, the House may elect another of its Members to act as Speaker, and the Member so elected shall during the Continuance of such Absence of the Speaker have and execute all the Powers, Privileges, and Duties of Speaker. (22)

Quorum of
House of
Commons.

**48.** The Presence of at least Twenty Members of the House of Commons shall be necessary to constitute a Meeting of the House for the Exercise of its Powers, and for that Purpose the Speaker shall be reckoned as a Member.

Voting in
House of
Commons.

**49.** Questions arising in the House of Commons shall be decided by a Majority of Voices other than that of the Speaker, and when the Voices are equal, but not otherwise, the Speaker shall have a Vote.

Duration of
House of
Commons.

**50.** Every House of Commons shall continue for Five Years from the Day of the Return of the Writs for choosing the House (subject to be sooner dissolved by the Governor General), and no longer.

Readjustment
of representa-
tion in
Commons.

**51.** (1) The number of members of the House of Commons and the representation of the provinces therein shall upon the coming into force of this subsection and thereafter on the completion of each decennial census be readjusted by such authority, in such manner, and from such time as the Parliament of Canada from time to time provides, subject and according to the following Rules:

Rules.

1. There shall be assigned to Quebec seventy-five members in the readjustment following the completion of the decennial census taken in the year 1971, and thereafter four additional members in each subsequent readjustment.

2. Subject to Rules 5(2) and (3), there shall be assigned to a large province a number of members equal to the number obtained by dividing the population of the large province by the electoral quotient of Quebec.

3. Subject to Rules 5(2) and (3), there shall be assigned to a small province a number of members equal to the number obtained by dividing
(a) the sum of the populations, determined according to the results of the penultimate decennial census, of the provinces (other than Quebec) having populations of less than one and a half million, determined according to the results of that census, by the sum of the numbers of members assigned to those provinces in the readjustment following the completion of that census; and

---

(22) Provision for exercising the functions of Speaker during his absence is now made by the *Speaker of the House of Commons Act,* R.S.C. 1970, c. S-13.

(*b*) the population of the small province by the quotient obtained under paragraph (*a*).

4. Subject to Rules 5(1)(*a*), (2) and (3), there shall be assigned to an intermediate province a number of members equal to the number obtained

(*a*) by dividing the sum of the populations of the provinces (other than Quebec) having populations of less than one and a half million by the sum of the number of members assigned to those provinces under any of Rules 3, 5(1)*b*), (2) and (3);

(*b*) by dividing the population of the intermediate province by the quotient obtained under paragraph (*a*); and

(*c*) by adding to the number of members assigned to the intermediate province in the readjustment following the completion of the penultimate decennial census one-half of the difference resulting from the subtraction of that number from the quotient obtained under paragraph (*b*).

5. (1) On any readjustment,

(*a*) if no province (other than Quebec) has a population of less than one and a half million, Rule 4 shall not be applied and, subject to Rules 5(2) and (3), there shall be assigned to an intermediate province a number of members equal to the number obtained by dividing

(i) the sum of the populations, determined according to the results of the penultimate decennial census, of the provinces (other than Quebec) having populations of not less than one and a half million and not more than two and a half million, determined according to the results of that census, by the sum of the numbers of members assigned to those provinces in the readjustment following the completion of that census, and

(ii) the population of the intermediate province by the quotient obtained under subparagraph (i);

(*b*) if a province (other than Quebec) having a population of

(i) less than one and a half million, or

(ii) not less than one and a half million and not more than two and a half million

does not have a population greater than its population determined according to the results of the penultimate decennial census, it shall, subject to Rules 5(2) and (3), be assigned the number of members assigned to it in the readjustment following the completion of that census.

(2) On any readjustment,

(*a*) if, under any of Rules 2 to 5(1), the number of members to be assigned to a province (in this paragraph referred to as "the first province") is smaller than the number of members to be assigned to any other prov-

ince not having a population greater than that of the
first province, those Rules shall not be applied to the
first province and it shall be assigned a number of
members equal to the largest number of members to be
assigned to any other province not having a population
greater than that of the first province;

(*b*) if, under any of Rules 2 to 5(1)(*a*), the number of
members to be assigned to a province is smaller than
the number of members assigned to it in the readjustment following the completion of the penultimate
decennial census, those Rules shall not be applied to it
and it shall be assigned the latter number of members;

(*c*) if both paragraphs (*a*) and (*b*) apply to a province,
it shall be assigned a number of members equal to the
greater of the numbers produced under those
paragraphs.

(3) On any readjustment,

(*a*) if the electoral quotient of a province (in this
paragraph referred to as "the first province") obtained
by dividing its population by the number of members to
be assigned to it under any of Rules 2 to 5(2) is greater
than the electoral quotient of Quebec, those Rules shall
not be applied to the first province and it shall be
assigned a number of members equal to the number
obtained by dividing its population by the electoral
quotient of Quebec;

(*b*) if, as a result of the application of Rule 6(2)(*a*), the
number of members assigned to a province under paragraph (*a*) equals the number of members to be assigned
to it under any of Rules 2 to 5(2), it shall be assigned
that number of members and paragraph (*a*) shall cease
to apply to that province.

6. (1) In these Rules,

"electoral quotient" means, in respect of a province,
the quotient obtained by dividing its population,
determined according to the results of the then most
recent decennial census, by the number of members
to be assigned to it under any of Rules 1 to 5(3) in
the readjustment following the completion of that
census;

"intermediate province" means a province (other than
Quebec) having a population greater than its population determined according to the results of the
penultimate decennial census but not more than two
and a half million and not less than one and a half
million;

"large province" means a province (other than
Quebec) having a population greater than two and a
half million;

"penultimate decennial census" means the decennial census that preceded the then most recent decennial census;

"population" means, except where otherwise specified, the population determined according to the results of the then most recent decennial census;

"small province" means a province (other than Quebec) having a population greater than its population determined according to the results of the penultimate decennial census and less than one and a half million.

(2) For the purposes of these Rules,

(*a*) if any fraction less than one remains upon completion of the final calculation that produces the number of members to be assigned to a province, that number of members shall equal the number so produced disregarding the fraction;

(*b*) if more than one readjustment follows the completion of a decennial census, the most recent of those readjustments shall, upon taking effect, be deemed to be the only readjustment following the completion of that census;

(*c*) a readjustment shall not take effect until the termination of the then existing Parliament. (23)

---

(23) As enacted by the *British North America Act 1974*, S.C. 1974-75-76, c. 13, which came into force on December 31, 1974. The section, as originally enacted, read as follows:

> **51.** On the Completion of the Census in the Year One Thousand eight hundred and seventy-one, and of each subsequent decennial Census, the Representation of the Four Provinces shall be readjusted by such Authority, in such Manner, and from such Time, as the Parliament of Canada from Time to Time provides, subject and according to the following Rules:
>
> > (1) Quebec shall have the fixed Number of Sixty-five Members:
> >
> > (2) There shall be assigned to each of the other Provinces such a Number of Members as will bear the same Proportion to the Number of its Population (ascertained at such Census) as the Number Sixty-five bears to the Number of the Population of Quebec (so ascertained):
> >
> > (3) In the Computation of the Number of Members for a Province a fractional Part not exceeding One Half of the whole Number requisite for entitling the Province to a Member shall be disregarded; but a fractional Part exceeding One Half of that Number shall be equivalent to the whole Number:
> >
> > (4) On any such Re-adjustment the Number of Members for a Province shall not be reduced unless the Proportion which the Number of the Population of the Province bore to the Number of the aggregate Population of Canada at the then last preceding Re-adjustment of the Number of Members for the Province is ascertained at the then latest Census to be diminished by One Twentieth Part or upwards:
> >
> > (5) Such Re-adjustment shall not take effect until the Termination of the then existing Parliament.

The section was amended by the *Statute Law Revision Act, 1893*, 56-57 Vict., c. 14 (U.K.) by repealing the words from "of the census" to "seventy-one and" and the word "subsequent".

By the *British North America Act, 1943*, 6-7 Geo VI, c. 30 (U.K.) redistribution of seats following the 1941 census was postponed until the first session of Parliament after the war. The section was re-enacted by the *British North America Act, 1946*, 9-10 Geo. VI, c. 63 (U.K.) to read as follows:

> **51.** (1) The number of members of the House of Commons shall be two hundred and fifty-five and the representation of the provinces therein shall forthwith upon the coming into force of this section and thereafter on the completion of each decennial

census be readjusted by such authority, in such manner, and from such time as the Parliament of Canada from time to time provides, subject and according to the following rules:—

(1) Subject as hereinafter provided, there shall be assigned to each of the provinces a number of members computed by dividing the total population of the provinces by two hundred and fifty-four and by dividing the population of each province by the quotient so obtained, disregarding, except as hereinafter in this section provided, the remainder, if any, after the said process of division.

(2) If the total number of members assigned to all the provinces pursuant to rule one is less than two hundred and fifty-four, additional members shall be assigned to the provinces (one to a province) having remainders in the computation under rule one commencing with the province having the largest remainder and continuing with the other provinces in the order of the magnitude of their respective remainders until the total number of members assigned is two hundred and fifty-four.

(3) Notwithstanding anything in this section, if upon completion of a computation under rules one and two, the number of members to be assigned to a province is less than the number of senators representing the said province, rules one and two shall cease to apply in respect of the said province, and there shall be assigned to the said province a number of members equal to the said number of senators.

(4) In the event that rules one and two cease to apply in respect of a province then, for the purpose of computing the number of members to be assigned to the provinces in respect of which rules one and two continue to apply, the total population of the provinces shall be reduced by the number of the population of the province in respect of which rules one and two have ceased to apply and the number two hundred and fifty-four shall be reduced by the number of members assigned to such province pursuant to rule three.

(5) Such readjustment shall not take effect until the termination of the then existing Parliament.

(2) The Yukon Territory as constituted by Chapter forty-one of the Statutes of Canada, 1901, together with any Part of Canada not comprised within a province which may from time to time be included therein by the Parliament of Canada for the purposes of representation in Parliament, shall be entitled to one member.

The section was re-enacted by the *British North America Act, 1952,* S.C. 1952, c. 15 as follows:

**51.** (1) Subject as hereinafter provided, the number of members of the House of Commons shall be two hundred and sixty-three and the representation of the provinces therein shall forthwith upon the coming into force of this section and thereafter on the completion of each decennial census be readjusted by such authority, in such manner, and from such time as the Parliament of Canada from time to time provides, subject and according to the following rules:

1. There shall be assigned to each of the provinces a number of members computed by dividing the total population of the provinces by two hundred and sixty-one and by dividing the population of each province by the quotient so obtained, disregarding, except as hereinafter in this section provided, the remainder, if any, after the said process of division.

2. If the total number of members assigned to all the provinces pursuant to rule one is less than two hundred and sixty-one, additional members shall be assigned to the provinces (one to a province) having remainders in the computation under rule one commencing with the province having the largest remainder and continuing with the other provinces in the order of the magnitude of their respective remainders until the total number of members assigned is two hundred and sixty-one.

3. Notwithstanding anything in this section, if upon completion of a computation under rules one and two the number of members to be assigned to a province is less than the number of senators representing the said province, rules one and two shall cease to apply in respect of the said province, and there shall be assigned to the said province a number of members equal to the said number of senators.

4. In the event that rules one and two cease to apply in respect of a province then, for the purposes of computing the number of members to be assigned to the provinces in respect of which rules one and two continue to apply, the total population of the provinces shall be reduced by the number of the population of the province in respect of which rules one and two have ceased to apply and the number two hundred and sixty-one shall be reduced by the number of members assigned to such province pursuant to rule three.

5. On any such readjustment the number of members for any province shall not be reduced by more than fifteen per cent below the representation to which such province was entitled under rules one to four of this subsection at the last preceding readjustment of the representation of that province, and

(2) The Yukon Territory as bounded and described in the schedule to chapter Y-2 of the Revised Statutes of Canada, 1970, shall be entitled to one member, and the Northwest Territories as bounded and described in section 2 of chapter N-22 of the Revised Statutes of Canada, 1970, shall be entitled to two members. (24)

Yukon Territory and Northwest Territories.

**51A.** Notwithstanding anything in this Act a province shall always be entitled to a number of members in the House of Commons not less than the number of senators representing such province. (25)

Constitution of House of Commons.

**52.** The Number of Members of the House of Commons may be from Time to Time increased by the Parliament of Canada, provided the proportionate Representation of the Provinces prescribed by this Act is not thereby disturbed.

Increase of Number of House of Commons.

### *Money Votes; Royal Assent.*

**53.** Bills for appropriating any Part of the Public Revenue, or for imposing any Tax or Impost, shall originate in the House of Commons.

Appropriation and Tax Bills.

**54.** It shall not be lawful for the House of Commons to adopt or pass any Vote, Resolution, Address, or Bill for the Appropriation of any Part of the Public Revenue, or of any Tax or Impost, to any Purpose that has not been first recommended to that House by Message of the Governor General in the Session in which such Vote, Resolution, Address, or Bill is proposed.

Recommendation of Money Votes.

**55.** Where a Bill passed by the Houses of the Parliament is presented to the Governor General for the Queen's Assent, he shall declare, according to his Discretion, but subject to the Provisions of this Act and to Her Majesty's Instructions, either that he assents thereto in the Queen's Name, or that he withholds the Queen's Assent, or that he reserves the Bill for the Signification of the Queen's Pleasure.

Royal Assent to Bills, etc.

---

there shall be no reduction in the representation of any province as a result of which that province would have a smaller number of members than any other province that according to the results of the then last decennial census did not have a larger population; but for the purposes of any subsequent readjustment of representation under this section any increase in the number of members of the House of Commons resulting from the application of this rule shall not be included in the divisor mentioned in rules one to four of this subsection.

6. Such readjustment shall not take effect until the termination of the then existing Parliament.

(2) The Yukon Territory as constituted by chapter forty-one of the statutes of Canada, 1901, shall be entitled to one member, and such other part of Canada not comprised within a province as may from time to time be defined by the Parliament of Canada shall be entitled to one member.

(24) As enacted by the *British North America Act, 1975*, S.C. 1974-75-76, c. 28.

(25) As enacted by the *British North America Act, 1915*, 5-6 Geo. V, c. 45 (U.K.).

**Disallowance by Order in Council of Act assented to by Governor General.**

**56.** Where the Governor General assents to a Bill in the Queen's Name, he shall by the first convenient Opportunity send an authentic Copy of the Act to one of Her Majesty's Principal Secretaries of State, and if the Queen in Council within Two Years after Receipt thereof by the Secretary of State thinks fit to disallow the Act, such Disallowance (with a Certificate of the Secretary of State of the Day on which the Act was received by him) being signified by the Governor General, by Speech or Message to each of the Houses of the Parliament or by Proclamation, shall annul the Act from and after the Day of such Signification.

**Signification of Queen's Pleasure on Bill reserved.**

**57.** A Bill reserved for the Signification of the Queen's Pleasure shall not have any Force unless and until, within Two Years from the Day on which it was presented to the Governor General for the Queen's Assent, the Governor General signifies, by Speech or Message to each of the Houses of the Parliament or by Proclamation, that it has received the Assent of the Queen in Council.

An Entry of every such Speech, Message, or Proclamation shall be made in the Journal of each House, and a Duplicate thereof duly attested shall be delivered to the proper Officer to be kept among the Records of Canada.

### V.—PROVINCIAL CONSTITUTIONS.

#### *Executive Power.*

**Appointment of Lieutenant Governors of Provinces.**

**58.** For each Province there shall be an Officer, styled the Lieutenant Governor, appointed by the Governor General in Council by Instrument under the Great Seal of Canada.

**Tenure of Office of Lieutenant Governor.**

**59.** A Lieutenant Governor shall hold Office during the Pleasure of the Governor General; but any Lieutenant Governor appointed after the Commencement of the First Session of the Parliament of Canada shall not be removeable within Five Years from his Appointment, except for Cause assigned, which shall be communicated to him in Writing within One Month after the Order for his Removal is made, and shall be communicated by Message to the Senate and to the House of Commons within One Week thereafter if the Parliament is then sitting, and if not then within One Week after the Commencement of the next Session of the Parliament.

**Salaries of Lieutenant Governors.**

**60.** The Salaries of the Lieutenant Governors shall be fixed and provided by the Parliament of Canada. (26)

**Oaths, etc., of Lieutenant Governor.**

**61.** Every Lieutenant Governor shall, before assuming the Duties of his Office, make and subscribe before the Governor

---

(26) Provided for by the *Salaries Act*, R.S.C. 1970, c. S-2.

General or some Person authorized by him Oaths of Allegiance and Office similar to those taken by the Governor General.

**62.** The Provisions of this Act referring to the Lieutenant Governor extend and apply to the Lieutenant Governor for the Time being of each Province, or other the Chief Executive Officer or Administrator for the Time being carrying on the Government of the Province, by whatever Title he is designated.

Application of provisions referring to Lieutenant Governor.

**63.** The Executive Council of Ontario and of Quebec shall be composed of such Persons as the Lieutenant Governor from Time to Time thinks fit, and in the first instance of the following Officers, namely,—the Attorney General, the Secretary and Registrar of the Province, the Treasurer of the Province, the Commissioner of Crown Lands, and the Commissioner of Agriculture and Public Works, with in Quebec the Speaker of the Legislative Council and the Solicitor General. (27)

Appointment of Executive Officers for Ontario and Quebec.

**64.** The Constitution of the Executive Authority in each of the Provinces of Nova Scotia and New Brunswick shall, subject to the Provisions of this Act, continue as it exists at the Union until altered under the Authority of this Act. (28)

Executive Government of Nova Scotia and New Brunswick.

**65.** All Powers, Authorities, and Functions which under any Act of the Parliament of Great Britain, or of the Parliament of the United Kingdom of Great Britain and Ireland, or of the Legislature of Upper Canada, Lower Canada, or Canada, were or are before or at the Union vested in or exerciseable by the respective Governors or Lieutenant Governors of those Provinces, with the Advice or with the Advice and Consent of the respective Executive Councils thereof, or in conjunction with those Councils, or with any Number of Members thereof, or by those Governors or Lieutenant Governors individually, shall, as far as the same are capable of being exercised after the Union in relation to the Government of Ontario and Quebec respectively, be vested in and shall or may be exercised by the Lieutenant Governor of Ontario and Quebec respectively, with the Advice or with the Advice and Consent of or in conjunction with the respective Executive Councils, or any Members thereof, or by the Lieutenant Governor individually, as the Case requires, subject nevertheless (except with respect to such as exist under Acts of the Parliament of Great Britain, or of the Parliament of the

Powers to be exercised by Lieutenant Governor of Ontario or Quebec with Advice, or alone.

---

(27) Now provided for in Ontario by the *Executive Council Act,* R.S.O. 1970, c. 153, and in Quebec by the *Executive Power Act,* R.S.Q. 1964, c. 9.

(28) A similar provision was included in each of the instruments admitting British Columbia, Prince Edward Island, and Newfoundland. The Executive Authorities for Manitoba, Alberta and Saskatchewan were established by the statutes creating those provinces. See the footnotes to section 5, *supra.*

United Kingdom of Great Britain and Ireland,) to be abolished or altered by the respective Legislatures of Ontario and Quebec. (29)

Application of Provisions referring to Lieutenant Governor in Council.

**66.** The Provisions of this Act referring to the Lieutenant Governor in Council shall be construed as referring to the Lieutenant Governor of the Province acting by and with the Advice of the Executive Council thereof.

Administration in Absence, etc., of Lieutenant Governor.

**67.** The Governor General in Council may from Time to Time appoint an Administrator to execute the Office and Functions of Lieutenant Governor during his Absence, Illness, or other Inability.

Seats of Provincial Governments.

**68.** Unless and until the Executive Government of any Province otherwise directs with respect to that Province, the Seats of Government of the Provinces shall be as follows, namely,—of Ontario, the City of Toronto; of Quebec, the City of Quebec; of Nova Scotia, the City of Halifax; and of New Brunswick, the City of Fredericton.

*Legislative Power.*

1.—ONTARIO.

Legislature for Ontario.

**69.** There shall be a Legislature for Ontario consisting of the Lieutenant Governor and of One House, styled the Legislative Assembly of Ontario.

Electoral districts.

**70.** The Legislative Assembly of Ontario shall be composed of Eighty-two Members, to be elected to represent the Eighty-two Electoral Districts set forth in the First Schedule to this Act. (30)

2.—QUEBEC.

Legislature for Quebec.

**71.** There shall be a Legislature for Quebec consisting of the Lieutenant Governor and of Two Houses, styled the Legislative Council of Quebec and the Legislative Assembly of Quebec. (31)

Constitution of Legislative Council.

**72.** The Legislative Council of Quebec shall be composed of Twenty-four Members, to be appointed by the Lieutenant Governor, in the Queen's Name, by Instrument under the Great Seal of Quebec, One being appointed to represent each of the Twenty-four Electoral Divisions of Lower Canada in this Act referred to, and each holding Office for the Term of his Life, unless the Legislature of Quebec otherwise provides under the Provisions of this Act.

---

(29) See the notes to section 129, *infra.*

(30) Spent. Now covered by the *Representation Act,* R.S.O. 1970, c. 413.

(31) The Act respecting the Legislative Council of Quebec, S.Q. 1968, c. 9, provided that the Legislature for Quebec shall consist of the Lieutenant Governor and the National Assembly of Quebec, and repealed the provisions of the *Legislature Act,* R.S.Q. 1964, c. 6, relating to the Legislative Council of Quebec. Sections 72 to 79 following are therefore completely spent.

**73.** The Qualifications of the Legislative Councillors of Quebec shall be the same as those of the Senators for Quebec.

**74.** The Place of a Legislative Councillor of Quebec shall become vacant in the Cases, *mutatis mutandis*, in which the Place of Senator becomes vacant.

**75.** When a Vacancy happens in the Legislative Council of Quebec by Resignation, Death, or otherwise, the Lieutenant Governor, in the Queen's Name, by Instrument under the Great Seal of Quebec, shall appoint a fit and qualified Person to fill the Vacancy.

**76.** If any Question arises respecting the Qualification of a Legislative Councillor of Quebec, or a Vacancy in the Legislative Council of Quebec, the same shall be heard and determined by the Legislative Council.

**77.** The Lieutenant Governor may from Time to Time, by Instrument under the Great Seal of Quebec, appoint a Member of the Legislative Council of Quebec to be Speaker thereof, and may remove him and appoint another in his Stead.

**78.** Until the Legislature of Quebec otherwise provides, the Presence of at least Ten Members of the Legislative Council, including the Speaker, shall be necessary to constitute a Meeting for the Exercise of its Powers.

**79.** Questions arising in the Legislative Council of Quebec shall be decided by a Majority of Voices, and the Speaker shall in all Cases have a Vote, and when the Voices are equal the Decision shall be deemed to be in the Negative.

**80.** The Legislative Assembly of Quebec shall be composed of Sixty-five Members, to be elected to represent the Sixty-five Electoral Divisions or Districts of Lower Canada in this Act referred to, subject to Alteration thereof by the Legislature of Quebec: Provided that it shall not be lawful to present to the Lieutenant Governor of Quebec for Assent any Bill for altering the Limits of any of the Electoral Divisions or Districts mentioned in the Second Schedule to this Act, unless the Second and Third Readings of such Bill have been passed in the Legislative Assembly with the Concurrence of the Majority of the Members representing all those Electoral Divisions or Districts, and the Assent shall not be given to such Bill unless an Address has been presented by the Legislative Assembly to the Lieutenant Governor stating that it has been so passed. (32)

---

(32) The Act respecting electoral districts, S.Q. 1970, c. 7, s. 1, provides that this section no longer has effect.

## 3.—ONTARIO AND QUEBEC.

**81.** Repealed. (33)

Summoning of
Legislative
Assemblies.

**82.** The Lieutenant Governor of Ontario and of Quebec shall from Time to Time, in the Queen's Name, by Instrument under the Great Seal of the Province, summon and call together the Legislative Assembly of the Province.

Restriction on
election of
Holders of
offices.

**83.** Until the Legislature of Ontario or of Quebec otherwise provides, a Person accepting or holding in Ontario or in Quebec any Office, Commission, or Employment, permanent or temporary, at the Nomination of the Lieutenant Governor, to which an annual Salary, or any Fee, Allowance, Emolument, or Profit of any Kind or Amount whatever from the Province is attached, shall not be eligible as a Member of the Legislative Assembly of the respective Province, nor shall he sit or vote as such; but nothing in this Section shall make ineligible any Person being a Member of the Executive Council of the respective Province, or holding any of the following Offices, that is to say, the Offices of Attorney General, Secretary and Registrar of the Province, Treasurer of the Province, Commissioner of Crown Lands, and Commissioner of Agriculture and Public Works, and in Quebec Solicitor General, or shall disqualify him to sit or vote in the House for which he is elected, provided he is elected while holding such Office. (34)

Continuance of
existing
Election Laws.

**84.** Until the Legislatures of Ontario and Quebec respectively otherwise provide, all Laws which at the Union are in force in those Provinces respectively, relative to the following Matters, or any of them, namely,—the Qualifications and Disqualifications of Persons to be elected or to sit or vote as Members of the Assembly of Canada, the Qualifications or Disqualifications of Voters, the Oaths to be taken by Voters, the Returning Officers, their Powers and Duties, the Proceedings at Elections, the Periods during which such Elections may be continued, and the Trial of controverted Elections and the Proceedings incident thereto, the vacating of the Seats of Members and the issuing and execution of new Writs in case of Seats vacated otherwise than by Dissolution,—shall respectively apply to Elections of Members to serve in the respective Legislative Assemblies of Ontario and Quebec.

Provided that, until the Legislature of Ontario otherwise provides, at any Election for a Member of the Legislative Assembly of Ontario for the District of Algoma, in addition

---

(33) Repealed by the *Statute Law Revision Act, 1893,* 56-57 Vict., c. 14 (U.K.). The section read as follows:

> **81.** The Legislatures of Ontario and Quebec respectively shall be called together not later than Six Months after the Union.

(34) Probably spent. The subject-matter of this section is now covered in Ontario by the *Legislative Assembly Act,* R.S.O. 1970, c. 240, and in Quebec by the *Legislature Act,* R.S.Q. 1964, c. 6.

to Persons qualified by the Law of the Province of Canada to vote, every male British Subject, aged Twenty-one Years or upwards, being a Householder, shall have a vote. (35)

**85.** Every Legislative Assembly of Ontario and every Legislative Assembly of Quebec shall continue for Four Years from the Day of the Return of the Writs for choosing the same (subject nevertheless to either the Legislative Assembly of Ontario or the Legislative Assembly of Quebec being sooner dissolved by the Lieutenant Governor of the Province), and no longer. (36)

Duration of Legislative Assemblies.

**86.** There shall be a Session of the Legislature of Ontario and of that of Quebec once at least in every Year, so that Twelve Months shall not intervene between the last Sitting of the Legislature in each Province in one Session and its first Sitting in the next Session.

Yearly Session of Legislature.

**87.** The following Provisions of this Act respecting the House of Commons of Canada shall extend and apply to the Legislative Assemblies of Ontario and Quebec, that is to say,—the Provisions relating to the Election of a Speaker originally and on Vacancies, the Duties of the Speaker, the Absence of the Speaker, the Quorum, and the Mode of voting, as if those Provisions were here re-enacted and made applicable in Terms to each such Legislative Assembly.

Speaker, Quorum, etc.

### 4.—NOVA SCOTIA AND NEW BRUNSWICK.

**88.** The Constitution of the Legislature of each of the Provinces of Nova Scotia and New Brunswick shall, subject to the Provisions of this Act, continue as it exists at the Union until altered under the Authority of this Act. (37)

Constitutions of Legislatures of Nova Scotia and New Brunswick.

---

(35) Probably spent. The subject-matter of this section is now covered in Ontario by the *Election Act*, R.S.O. 1970, c. 142, the *Controverted Elections Act*, R.S.O. 1970, c. 84 and the *Legislative Assembly Act*, R.S.O. 1970, c. 240, in Quebec by the *Elections Act*, R.S.Q. 1964, c. 7, the *Provincial Controverted Elections Act*, R.S.Q. 1964, c. 8 and the *Legislature Act*, R.S.Q. 1964, c. 6.

(36) The maximum duration of the Legislative Assembly for Ontario and Quebec has been changed to five years by the *Legislative Assembly Act*, R.S.O. 1970, c. 240, and the *Legislature Act*, R.S.Q. 1964, c. 6 respectively.

(37) Partially repealed by the *Statute Law Revision Act, 1893*, 56-57 Vict., c. 14 (U.K.) which deleted the following concluding words of the original enactment:
> and the House of Assembly of New Brunswick existing at the passing of this Act shall, unless sooner dissolved, continue for the Period for which it was elected.

A similar provision was included in each of the instruments admitting British Columbia, Prince Edward Island, and Newfoundland. The Legislatures of Manitoba, Alberta and Saskatchewan were established by the statutes creating those provinces. See the footnotes to section 5, *supra*.

**89.** Repealed. (38)

### 6.—THE FOUR PROVINCES.

Application to
Legislatures of
Provisions
respecting
Money Votes,
etc.

**90.** The following Provisions of this Act respecting the Parliament of Canada, namely,—the Provisions relating to Appropriation and Tax Bills, the Recommendation of Money Votes, the Assent to Bills, the Disallowance of Acts, and the Signification of Pleasure on Bills reserved,—shall extend and apply to the Legislatures of the several Provinces as if those Provisions were here re-enacted and made applicable in Terms to the respective Provinces and the Legislatures thereof, with the Substitution of the Lieutenant Governor of the Province for the Governor General, of the Governor General for the Queen and for a Secretary of State, of One Year for Two Years, and of the Province for Canada.

### VI.—DISTRIBUTION OF LEGISLATIVE POWERS.

*Powers of the Parliament.*

Legislative
Authority of
Parliament of
Canada.

**91.** It shall be lawful for the Queen, by and with the Advice and Consent of the Senate and House of Commons, to make Laws for the Peace, Order, and good Government of Canada, in relation to all Matters not coming within the Classes of Subjects by this Act assigned exclusively to the Legislatures of the Provinces; and for greater Certainty, but not so as to restrict the Generality of the foregoing Terms of this Section, it is hereby declared that (notwithstanding anything in this Act) the exclusive Legislative Authority of the Parliament of Canada extends to all Matters coming within the Classes of Subjects next herein-after enumerated; that is to say,—

1. The amendment from time to time of the Constitution of Canada, except as regards matters coming within the classes of subjects by this Act assigned exclusively to the Legislatures of the provinces, or as regards rights or privileges by this or any other Constitutional Act granted or secured to the Legislature or the Government of a province, or to any class of persons with respect to

---

(38) Repealed by the *Statute Law Revision Act, 1893,* 56-57 Vict., c. 14 (U.K.). The section read as follows:

### 5.—ONTARIO, QUEBEC, AND NOVA SCOTIA.

**89.** Each of the Lieutenant Governors of Ontario, Quebec and Nova Scotia shall cause Writs to be issued for the First Election of Members of the Legislative Assembly thereof in such Form and by such Person as he thinks fit, and at such Time and addressed to such Returning Officer as the Governor General directs, and so that the First Election of Member of Assembly for any Electoral District or any Subdivision thereof shall be held at the same Time and at the same Places as the Election for a Member to serve in the House of Commons of Canada for the Electoral District.

schools or as regards the use of the English or the French language or as regards the requirements that there shall be a session of the Parliament of Canada at least once each year, and that no House of Commons shall continue for more than five years from the day of the return of the Writs for choosing the House: provided, however, that a House of Commons may in time of real or apprehended war, invasion or insurrection be continued by the Parliament of Canada if such continuation is not opposed by the votes of more than one-third of the members of such House. (39)

1A.  The Public Debt and Property. (40)
 2.  The Regulation of Trade and Commerce.
2A.  Unemployment insurance. (41)
 3.  The raising of Money by any Mode or System of Taxation.
 4.  The borrowing of Money on the Public Credit.
 5.  Postal Service.
 6.  The Census and Statistics.
 7.  Militia, Military and Naval Service, and Defence.
 8.  The fixing of and providing for the Salaries and Allowances of Civil and other Officers of the Government of Canada.
 9.  Beacons, Buoys. Lighthouses, and Sable Island.
10.  Navigation and Shipping.
11.  Quarantine and the Establishment and Maintenance of Marine Hospitals.
12.  Sea Coast and Inland Fisheries.
13.  Ferries between a Province and any British or Foreign Country or between Two Provinces.
14.  Currency and Coinage.
15.  Banking, Incorporation of Banks, and the Issue of Paper Money.
16.  Savings Banks.
17.  Weights and Measures.
18.  Bills of Exchange and Promissory Notes.
19.  Interest.
20.  Legal Tender.
21.  Bankruptcy and Insolvency.
22.  Patents of Invention and Discovery.
23.  Copyrights.
24.  Indians, and Lands reserved for the Indians.
25.  Naturalization and Aliens.
26.  Marriage and Divorce.

---

(39) Added by the *British North America (No. 2) Act, 1949*, 13 Geo. VI, c. 81 (U.K.).

(40) Re-numbered by the *British North America (No. 2) Act, 1949*.

(41) Added by the *British North America Act, 1940*, 3-4 Geo. VI, c. 36 (U.K.).

27.   The Criminal Law, except the Constitution of Courts of Criminal Jurisdiction, but including the Procedure in Criminal Matters.

28.   The Establishment, Maintenance, and Management of Penitentiaries.

29.   Such Classes of Subjects as are expressly excepted in the Enumeration of the Classes of Subjects by this Act assigned exclusively to the Legislatures of the Provinces.

And any Matter coming within any of the Classes of Subjects enumerated in this Section shall not be deemed to come within the Class of Matters of a local or private Nature comprised in the Enumeration of the Classes of Subjects by this Act assigned exclusively to the Legislatures of the Provinces. (42)

---

(42) Legislative authority has been conferred on Parliament by other Acts as follows:

1. The *British North America Act, 1871,* 34-35 Vict., c. 28 (U.K.).

> 2. The Parliament of Canada, may from time to time establish new Provinces in any territories forming for the time being part of the Dominion of Canada, but not included in any Province thereof, and may, at the time of such establishment, make provision for the constitution and administration of any such Province, and for the passing of laws for the peace, order, and good government of such Province, and for its representation in the said Parliament.

> 3. The Parliament of Canada may from time to time, with the consent of the Legislature of any Province of the said Dominion, increase, diminish, or otherwise alter the limits of such Province, upon such terms and conditions as may be agreed to by the said Legislature, and may, with the like consent, make provision respecting the effect and operation of any such increase or diminution or alteration of territory in relation to any Province affected thereby.

> 4. The Parliament of Canada may from time to time make provision for the administration peace, order, and good government of any territory not for the time being included in any Province.

> 5. The following Acts passed by the said Parliament of Canada, and intituled respectively,—"An Act for the temporary government of Rupert's Land and the North Western Territory when united with Canada"; and "An Act to amend and continue the Act thirty-two and thirty-three Victoria, chapter three, and to establish and provide for the government of "the Province of Manitoba," shall be and be deemed to have been valid and effectual for all purposes whatsoever from the date at which they respectively received the assent, in the Queen's name, of the Governor General of the said Dominion of Canada.

> 6. Except as provided by the third section of this Act, it shall not be competent for the Parliament of Canada to alter the provisions of the last-mentioned Act of the said Parliament in so far as it relates to the Province of Manitoba, or of any other Act hereafter establishing new Provinces in the said Dominion, subject always to the right of the Legislature of the Province of Manitoba to alter from time to time the provisions of any law respecting the qualification of electors and members of the Legislative Assembly, and to make laws respecting elections in the said Province.

The *Rupert's Land Act 1868,* 31-32 Vict., c. 105 (U.K.) (repealed by the *Statute Law Revision Act, 1893,* 56-57 Vict., c. 14 (U.K.)) had previously conferred similar authority in relation to Rupert's Land and the North-Western Territory upon admission of those areas.

2. The *British North America Act, 1886,* 49-50 Vict., c. 35, (U.K.).

> 1. The Parliament of Canada may from time to time make provision for the representation in the Senate and House of Commons of Canada, or in either of them, of any territories which for the time being form part of the Dominion of Canada, but are not included in any province thereof.

3. The *Statute of Westminster, 1931,* 22 Geo. V, c. 4, (U.K.).

> 3. It is hereby declared and enacted that the Parliament of a Dominion has full power to make laws having extra-territorial operation.

*Exclusive Powers of Provincial Legislatures.*

**92.** In each Province the Legislature may exclusively make Laws in relation to Matters coming within the Classes of Subject next herein-after enumerated; that is to say,— Subjects of exclusive Provincial Legislation.

1. The Amendment from Time to Time, notwithstanding anything in this Act, of the Constitution of the Province, except as regards the Office of Lieutenant Governor.

2. Direct Taxation within the Province in order to the raising of a Revenue for Provincial Purposes.

3. The borrowing of Money on the sole Credit of the Province.

4. The Establishment and Tenure of Provincial Offices and the Appointment and Payment of Provincial Officers.

5. The Management and Sale of the Public Lands belonging to the Province and of the Timber and Wood thereon.

6. The Establishment, Maintenance, and Management of Public and Reformatory Prisons in and for the Province.

7. The Establishment, Maintenance, and Management of Hospitals, Asylums, Charities, and Eleemosynary Institutions in and for the Province, other than Marine Hospitals.

8. Municipal Institutions in the Province.

9. Shop, Saloon, Tavern, Auctioneer, and other Licences in order to the raising of a Revenue for Provincial, Local, or Municipal Purposes.

10. Local Works and Undertakings other than such as are of the following Classes:—

    (*a*) Lines of Steam or other Ships, Railways, Canals, Telegraphs, and other Works and Undertakings connecting the Province with any other or others of the Provinces, or extending beyond the Limits of the Province;

    (*b*) Lines of Steam Ships between the Province and any British or Foreign Country;

    (*c*) Such Works as, although wholly situate within the Province, are before or after their Execution declared by the Parliament of Canada to be for the general Advantage of Canada or for the Advantage of Two or more of the Provinces.

11. The Incorporation of Companies with Provincial Objects.

12. The Solemnization of Marriage in the Province.

13. Property and Civil Rights in the Province.

14. The Administration of Justice in the Province, including the Constitution, Maintenance, and Organization of Provincial Courts, both of Civil and of Criminal Jurisdiction, and including Procedure in Civil Matters in those Courts.

15. The Imposition of Punishment by Fine, Penalty, or Imprisonment for enforcing any Law of the Province made in relation to any Matter coming within any of the Classes of Subjects enumerated in this Section.

16. Generally all Matters of a merely local or private Nature in the Province.

## *Education.*

Legislation respecting Education.

**93.** In and for each Province the Legislature may exclusively make Laws in relation to Education, subject and according to the following Provisions:—

(1) Nothing in any such Law shall prejudicially affect any Right or Privilege with respect to Denominational Schools which any Class of Persons have by Law in the Province at the Union:

(2) All the Powers, Privileges, and Duties at the Union by Law conferred and imposed in Upper Canada on the Separate Schools and School Trustees of the Queen's Roman Catholic Subjects shall be and the same are hereby extended to the Dissentient Schools of the Queen's Protestant and Roman Catholic Subjects in Quebec:

(3) Where in any Province a System of Separate or Dissentient Schools exists by Law at the Union or is thereafter established by the Legislature of the Province, an Appeal shall lie to the Governor General in Council from any Act or Decision of any Provincial Authority affecting any Right or Privilege of the Protestant or Roman Catholic Minority of the Queen's Subjects in relation to Education:

(4) In case any such Provincial Law as from Time to Time seems to the Governor General in Council requisite for the due Execution of the Provisions of this Section is not made, or in case any Decision of the Governor General in Council on any Appeal under this Section is not duly executed by the proper Provincial Authority in that Behalf, then and in every such Case, and as far only as the Circumstances of each Case require, the Parliament of Canada may make remedial Laws for the due Execution of the

Provisions of this Section and of any Decision of the
Governor General in Council under this Section. (43)

*Uniformity of Laws in Ontario, Nova Scotia and New
Brunswick.*

**94.** Notwithstanding anything in this Act, the Parliament
of Canada may make Provision for the Uniformity of all or

Legislation for
Uniformity of
Laws in Three
Provinces.

---

(43) Altered for Manitoba by section 22 of the *Manitoba Act*, 33 Vict., c. 3 (Canada),
(confirmed by the *British North America Act, 1871*), which reads as follows:

**22.** In and for the Province, the said Legislature may exclusively make Laws in
relation to Education, subject and according to the following provisions:—

(1) Nothing in any such Law shall prejudicially affect any right or privilege with
respect to Denominational Schools which any class of persons have by Law or
practice in the Province at the Union:

(2) An appeal shall lie to the Governor General in Council from any Act or
decision of the Legislature of the Province, or of any Provincial Authority, affecting
any right or privilege, of the Protestant or Roman Catholic minority of the Queen's
subjects in relation to Education:

(3) In case any such Provincial Law, as from time to time seems to the Governor
General in Council requisite for the due execution of the provisions of this section, is
not made, or in case any decision of the Governor General in Council on any appeal
under this section is not duly executed by the proper Provincial Authority in that
behalf, then, and in every such case, and as far only as the circumstances of each
case require, the Parliament of Canada may make remedial Laws for the due
execution of the provisions of this section, and of any decision of the Governor
General in Council under this section.

Altered for Alberta by section 17 of *The Alberta Act*, 4-5 Edw. VII, c. 3 which reads as follows:

**17.** Section 93 of The British North America Act, 1867, shall apply to the said
province, with the substitution for paragraph (1) of the said section 93 of the
following paragraph:—

(1) Nothing in any such law shall prejudicially affect any right or privilege with
respect to separate schools which any class of persons have at the date of the passing
of this Act, under the terms of chapters 29 and 30 of the Ordinances of the
Northwest Territories, passed in the year 1901, or with respect to religious instruction in any public or separate school as provided for in the said ordinances.

**2.** In the appropriation by the Legislature or distribution by the Government of
the province of any moneys for the support of schools organized and carried on in
accordance with the said chapter 29 or any Act passed in amendment thereof, or in
substitution therefor, there shall be no discrimination against schools of any class
described in the said chapter 29.

**3.** Where the expression "by law" is employed in paragraph 3 of the said section
93, it shall be held to mean the law as set out in the said chapters 29 and 30, and
where the expression "at the Union" is employed, in the said paragraph 3, it shall be
held to mean the date at which this Act comes into force.

Altered for Saskatchewan by section 17 of *The Saskatchewan* Act, 4-5 Edw. VII, c. 42, which
reads as follows:

**17.** Section 93 of the British North America Act, 1867, shall apply to the said
province, with the substitution for paragraph (1) of the said section 93, of the
following paragraph:—

(1) Nothing in any such law shall prejudicially affect any right or privilege with
respect to separate schools which any class of persons have at the date of the passing
of this Act, under the terms of chapters 29 and 30 of the Ordinances of the
Northwest Territories, passed in the year 1901, or with respect to religious instruction in any public or separate school as provided for in the said ordinances.

**2.** In the appropriation by the Legislature or distribution by the Government of
the province of any moneys for the support of schools organized and carried on in
accordance with the said chapter 29, or any Act passed in amendment thereof or in
substitution therefor, there shall be no discrimination against schools of any class
described in the said chapter 29.

**3.** Where the expression "by law" is employed in paragraph (3) of the said
section 93, it shall be held to mean the law as set out in the said chapters 29 and 30;
and where the expression "at the Union" is employed in the said paragraph (3), it
shall be held to mean the date at which this Act comes into force.

any of the Laws relative to Property and Civil Rights in Ontario, Nova Scotia, and New Brunswick, and of the Procedure of all or any of the Courts in Those Three Provinces, and from and after the passing of any Act in that Behalf the Power of the Parliament of Canada to make Laws in relation to any Matter comprised in any such Act shall, notwithstanding anything in this Act, be unrestricted; but any Act of the Parliament of Canada making Provision for such Uniformity shall not have effect in any Province unless and until it is adopted and enacted as Law by the Legislature thereof.

### Old Age Pensions.

Legislation respecting old age pensions and supplementary benefits.

**94A.** The Parliament of Canada may make laws in relation to old age pensions and supplementary benefits, including survivors' and disability benefits irrespective of age, but no such law shall affect the operation of any law present or future of a provincial legislature in relation to any such matter. (44)

### Agriculture and Immigration.

Concurrent Powers of Legislation respecting Agriculture, etc.

**95.** In each Province the Legislature may make Laws in relation to Agriculture in the Province, and to Immigration into the Province; and it is hereby declared that the Parliament of Canada may from Time to Time make Laws in relation to Agriculture in all or any of the Provinces, and to Immigration into all or any of the Provinces; and any Law of the Legislature of a Province relative to Agriculture or to Immigration shall have effect in and for the Province as long and as far only as it is not repugnant to any Act of the Parliament of Canada.

---

Altered by Term 17 of the Terms of Union of Newfoundland with Canada (confirmed by the *British North America Act, 1949*, 12-13 Geo. VI, c. 22 (UK.)), which reads as follows:

17. In lieu of section ninety-three of the British North America Act, 1867, the following term shall apply in respect of the Province of Newfoundland:

In and for the Province of Newfoundland the Legislature shall have exclusive authority to make laws in relation to education, but the Legislature will not have authority to make laws prejudicially affecting any right or privilege with respect to denominational schools, common (amalgamated) schools, or denominational colleges, that any class or classes of persons have by law in Newfoundland at the date of Union, and out of public funds of the Province of Newfoundland, provided for education,

(a) all such schools shall receive their share of such funds in accordance with scales determined on a non-discriminatory basis from time to time by the Legislature for all schools then being conducted under authority of the Legislature; and

(b) all such colleges shall receive their share of any grant from time to time voted for all colleges then being conducted under authority of the Legislature, such grant being distributed on a non-discriminatory basis.

(44) Added by the *British North America Act, 1964*, 12-13, Eliz. II, c. 73 (U.K.). Originally enacted by the *British North America Act, 1951*, 14-15 Geo. VI, c. 32 (U.K.), as follows:

94A. It is hereby declared that the Parliament of Canada may from time to time make laws in relation to old age pensions in Canada, but no law made by the Parliament of Canada in relation to old age pensions shall affect the operation of any law present or future of a Provincial Legislature in relation to old age pensions.

## VII.—Judicature.

**96.** The Governor General shall appoint the Judges of the Superior, District, and County Courts in each Province, except those of the Courts of Probate in Nova Scotia and New Brunswick.

Appointment of Judges.

**97.** Until the laws relative to Property and Civil Rights in Ontario, Nova Scotia, and New Brunswick, and the Procedure of the Courts in those Provinces, are made uniform, the Judges of the Courts of those Provinces appointed by the Governor General shall be selected from the respective Bars of those Provinces.

Selection of Judges in Ontario, etc.

**98.** The Judges of the Courts of Quebec shall be selected from the Bar of that Province.

Selection of Judges in Quebec.

**99.** (1) Subject to subsection two of this section, the Judges of the Superior Courts shall hold office during good behaviour, but shall be removable by the Governor General on Address of the Senate and House of Commons.

Tenure of office of Judges.

(2) A Judge of a Superior Court, whether appointed before or after the coming into force of this section, shall cease to hold office upon attaining the age of seventy-five years, or upon the coming into force of this section if at that time he has already attained that age. (44A)

Termination at age 75.

**100.** The Salaries, Allowances, and Pensions of the Judges of the Superior, District, and County Courts (except the Courts of Probate in Nova Scotia and New Brunswick), and of the Admiralty Courts in Cases where the Judges thereof are for the Time being paid by Salary, shall be fixed and provided by the Parliament of Canada. (45)

Salaries etc., of Judges.

**101.** The Parliament of Canada may, notwithstanding anything in this Act, from Time to Time provide for the Constitution, Maintenance, and Organization of a General Court of Appeal for Canada, and for the Establishment of any additional Courts for the better Administration of the Laws of Canada. (46)

General Court of Appeal, etc.

### VIII.—Revenues; Debts; Assets; Taxation

**102.** All Duties and Revenues over which the respective Legislatures of Canada, Nova Scotia, and New Brunswick before and at the Union had and have Power of Appropria-

Creation of Consolidated Revenue Fund.

---

(44A) Repealed and re-enacted by the *British North America Act, 1960,* 9 Eliz. II, c. 2 (U.K.), which came into force on the 1st day of March, 1961. The original section read as follows:

> **99.** The Judges of the Superior Courts shall hold Office during good Behaviour, but shall be removable by the Governor General on Address of the Senate and House of Commons.

(45) Now provided for in the *Judges Act,* R.S.C. 1970, c. J-1.

(46) See the *Supreme Court Act,* R.S.C. 1970, c. S-19, and the *Federal Court Act,* R.S.C. 1970, (2nd Supp.) c. 10.

tion, except such Portions thereof as are by this Act reserved to the respective Legislatures of the Provinces, or are raised by them in accordance with the special Powers conferred on them by this Act, shall form One Consolidated Revenue Fund, to be appropriated for the Public Service of Canada in the Manner and subject to the Charges in this Act provided.

Expenses of Collection, etc.

**103.** The Consolidated Revenue Fund of Canada shall be permanently charged with the Costs, Charges, and Expenses incident to the Collection, Management, and Receipt thereof, and the same shall form the First Charge thereon, subject to be reviewed and audited in such Manner as shall be ordered by the Governor General in Council until the Parliament otherwise provides.

Interest of Provincial Public Debts.

**104.** The annual Interest of the Public Debts of the several Provinces of Canada, Nova Scotia, and New Brunswick at the Union shall form the Second Charge on the Consolidated Revenue Fund of Canada.

Salary of Governor General.

**105.** Unless altered by the Parliament of Canada, the Salary of the Governor General shall be Ten thousand Pounds Sterling Money of the United Kingdom of Great Britain and Ireland, payable out of the Consolidated Revenue Fund of Canada, and the same shall form the Third Charge thereon. (47)

Appropriation from Time to Time.

**106.** Subject to the several Payments by this Act charged on the Consolidated Revenue Fund of Canada, the same shall be appropriated by the Parliament of Canada for the Public Service.

Transfer of Stocks, etc.

**107.** All Stocks, Cash, Banker's Balances, and Securities for Money belonging to each Province at the Time of the Union, except as in this Act mentioned, shall be the Property of Canada, and shall be taken in Reduction of the Amount of the respective Debts of the Provinces at the Union.

Transfer of Property in Schedule.

**108.** The Public Works and Property of each Province, enumerated in the Third Schedule to this Act, shall be the Property of Canada.

Property in Lands, Mines, etc.

**109.** All Lands, Mines, Minerals, and Royalties belonging to the several Provinces of Canada, Nova Scotia, and New Brunswick at the Union, and all Sums then due or payable for such Lands, Mines, Minerals, or Royalties, shall belong to the several Provinces of Ontario, Quebec, Nova Scotia, and New Brunswick in which the same are situate or arise, subject to any Trusts existing in respect thereof, and to any Interest other than that of the Province in the same. (48)

---

(47) Now covered by the *Governor General's Act*, R.S.C. 1970, c. G-14.

(48) The four western provinces were placed in the same position as the original provinces by the *British North America Act, 1930*, 21 Geo. V, c. 26 (U.K.).

**110.** All Assets connected with such Portions of the Public Debt of each Province as are assumed by that Province shall belong to that Province. Assets connected with Provincial Debts.

**111.** Canada shall be liable for the Debts and Liabilities of each Province existing at the Union. Canada to be liable for Provincial Debts.

**112.** Ontario and Quebec conjointly shall be liable to Canada for the Amount (if any) by which the Debt of the Province of Canada exceeds at the Union Sixty-two million five hundred thousand Dollars, and shall be charged with Interest at the Rate of Five per Centum per Annum thereon. Debts of Ontario and Quebec.

**113.** The Assets enumerated in the Fourth Schedule to this Act belonging at the Union to the Province of Canada shall be the Property of Ontario and Quebec conjointly. Assets of Ontario and Quebec.

**114.** Nova Scotia shall be liable to Canada for the Amount (if any) by which its Public Debt exceeds at the Union Eight million Dollars, and shall be charged with Interest at the Rate of Five per Centum per Annum thereon. (49) Debt of Nova Scotia.

**115.** New Brunswick shall be liable to Canada for the Amount (if any) by which its Public Debt exceeds at the Union Seven million Dollars, and shall be charged with Interest at the Rate of Five per Centum per Annum thereon. Debt of New Brunswick.

**116.** In case the Public Debts of Nova Scotia and New Brunswick do not at the Union amount to Eight million and Seven million Dollars respectively, they shall respectively receive by half-yearly Payments in advance from the Government of Canada Interest at Five per Centum per Annum on the Difference between the actual Amounts of their respective Debts and such stipulated Amounts. Payment of interest to Nova Scotia and New Brunswick

**117.** The several Provinces shall retain all their respective Public Property not otherwise disposed of in this Act, subject to the Right of Canada to assume any Lands or Public Property required for Fortifications or for the Defence of the Country. Provincial Public Property.

**118.** Repealed. (50)

---

(49) The obligations imposed by this section, sections 115 and 116, and similar obligations under the instruments creating or admitting other provinces, have been carried into legislation of the Parliament of Canada and are now to be found in the *Provincial Subsidies Act*, R.S.C. 1970, c. P-26.

(50) Repealed by the *Statute Law Revision Act, 1950*, 14 Geo. VI, c. 6 (U.K.). As originally enacted the section read as follows:

> **118.** The following Sums shall be paid yearly by Canada to the several Provinces for the Support of their Governments and Legislatures:
>
> | | Dollars |
> |---|---|
> | Ontario | Eighty thousand. |
> | Quebec | Seventy thousand. |
> | Nova Scotia | Sixty thousand. |
> | New Brunswick | Fifty thousand. |
>
> Two hundred and sixty thousand;
> and an annual Grant in aid of each Province shall be made, equal to Eighty Cents per Head of the Population as ascertained by the Census of One thousand eight

hundred and sixty-one, and in the Case of Nova Scotia and New Brunswick, by each subsequent Decennial Census until the Population of each of those two Provinces amounts to Four hundred thousand Souls, at which Rate such Grant shall thereafter remain. Such Grants shall be in full Settlement of all future Demands on Canada, and shall be paid half-yearly in advance to each Province; but the Government of Canada shall deduct from such Grants, as against any Province, all Sums chargeable as Interest on the Public Debt of that Province in excess of the several Amounts stipulated in this Act.

The section was made obsolete by the *British North America Act, 1907*, 7 Edw. VII, c. 11 (U.K.) which provided:

**1.** (1) The following grants shall be made yearly by Canada to every province, which at the commencement of this Act is a province of the Dominion, for its local purposes and the support of its Government and Legislature:—

(*a*)  A fixed grant—
where the population of the province is under one hundred and fifty thousand, of one hundred thousand dollars;
where the population of the province is one hundred and fifty thousand, but does not exceed two hundred thousand, of one hundred and fifty thousand dollars;
where the population of the province is two hundred thousand, but does not exceed four hundred thousand, of one hundred and eighty thousand dollars;
where the population of the province is four hundred thousand, but does not exceed eight hundred thousand, of one hundred and ninety thousand dollars;
where the population of the province is eight hundred thousand, but does not exceed one million five hundred thousand, of two hundred and twenty thousand dollars;
where the population of the province exceeds one million five hundred thousand, of two hundred and forty thousand dollars; and

(*b*)  Subject to the special provisions of this Act as to the provinces of British Columbia and Prince Edward Island, a grant at the rate of eighty cents per head of the population of the province up to the number of two million five hundred thousand, and at the rate of sixty cents per head of so much of the population as exceeds that number.

(2) An additional grant of one hundred thousand dollars shall be made yearly to the province of British Columbia for a period of ten years from the commencement of this Act.

(3) The population of a province shall be ascertained from time to time in the case of the provinces of Manitoba, Saskatchewan, and Alberta respectively by the last quinquennial census or statutory estimate of population made under the Acts establishing those provinces or any other Act of the Parliament of Canada making provision for the purpose, and in the case of any other province by the last decennial census for the time being.

(4) The grants payable under this Act shall be paid half-yearly in advance to each province.

(5) The grants payable under this Act shall be substituted for the grants or subsidies (in this Act referred to as existing grants) payable for the like purposes at the commencement of this Act to the several provinces of the Dominion under the provisions of section one hundred and eighteen of the British North America Act 1867, or of any Order in Council establishing a province, or of any Act of the Parliament of Canada containing directions for the payment of any such grant or subsidy, and those provisions shall cease to have effect.

(6) The Government of Canada shall have the same power of deducting sums charged against a province on account of the interest on public debt in the case of the grant payable under this Act to the province as they have in the case of the existing grant.

(7) Nothing in this Act shall affect the obligation of the Government of Canada to pay to any province any grant which is payable to that province, other than the existing grant for which the grant under this Act is substituted.

(8) In the case of the provinces of British Columbia and Prince Edward Island, the amount paid on account of the grant payable per head of the population to the provinces under this Act shall not at any time be less than the amount of the corresponding grant payable at the commencement of this Act, and if it is found on any decennial census that the population of the province has decreased since the last decennial census, the amount paid on account of the grant shall not be decreased below the amount then payable, notwithstanding the decrease of the population.

See the *Provincial Subsidies Act*, R.S.C. 1970, c. P-26, *The Maritime Provinces Additional Subsidies Act*, 1942-43, c. 14, and the Terms of Union of Newfoundland with Canada, appended to the *British North America Act, 1949*, and also to *An Act to approve the Terms of Union of Newfoundland with Canada*, chapter 1 of the statutes of Canada, 1949.

**119.** New Brunswick shall receive by half-yearly Payments in advance from Canada for the Period of Ten Years from the Union an additional Allowance of Sixty-three thousand Dollars per Annum; but as long as the Public Debt of that Province remains under Seven million Dollars, a Deduction equal to the Interest at Five per Centum per Annum on such Deficiency shall be made from that Allowance of Sixty-three thousand Dollars. (51)

*Further Grant to New Brunswick.*

**120.** All Payments to be made under this Act, or in discharge of Liabilities created under any Act of the Provinces of Canada, Nova Scotia, and New Brunswick respectively, and assumed by Canada, shall, until the Parliament of Canada otherwise directs, be made in such Form and Manner as may from Time to Time be ordered by the Governor General in Council.

*Form of Payments.*

**121.** All Articles of the Growth, Produce, or Manufacture of any one of the Provinces shall, from and after the Union, be admitted free into each of the other Provinces.

*Canadian Manufactures, etc.*

**122.** The Customs and Excise Laws of each Province shall, subject to the Provisions of this Act, continue in force until altered by the Parliament of Canada. (52)

*Continuance of Customs and Excise Laws.*

**123.** Where Customs Duties are, at the Union, leviable on any Goods, Wares, or Merchandises in any Two Provinces, those Goods, Wares, and Merchandises may, from and after the Union, be imported from one of those Provinces into the other of them on Proof of Payment of the Customs Duty leviable thereon in the Province of Exportation, and on Payment of such further Amount (if any) of Customs Duty as is leviable thereon in the Province of Importation. (53)

*Exportation and Importation as between Two Provinces.*

**124.** Nothing in this Act shall affect the Right of New Brunswick to levy the Lumber Dues provided in Chapter Fifteen of Title Three of the Revised Statutes of New Brunswick, or in any Act amending that Act before or after the Union, and not increasing the Amount of such Dues; but the Lumber of any of the Provinces other than New Brunswick shall not be subject to such Dues. (54)

*Lumber Dues in New Brunswick.*

**125.** No Lands or Property belonging to Canada or any Province shall be liable to Taxation.

*Exemption of Public Lands, etc.*

---

(51) Spent.

(52) Spent. Now covered by the *Customs Act*, R.S.C. 1970, c. C-40, the *Customs Tariff*, R.S.C. 1970, c. C-41, the *Excise Act*, R.S.C. 1970, c. E-12 and the *Excise Tax Act*, R.S.C. 1970, c. E-13.

(53) Spent.

(54) These dues were repealed in 1873 by 36 Vict., c. 16 (N.B.). And see *An Act respecting the Export Duties imposed on Lumber*, etc., (1873) 36 Vict., c. 41 (Canada), and section 2 of the *Provincial Subsidies Act*, R.S.C. 1970, c. P-26.

Provincial
Consolidated
Revenue Fund.

**126.** Such Portions of the Duties and Revenues over which the respective Legislatures of Canada, Nova Scotia, and New Brunswick had before the Union Power of Appropriation as are by this Act reserved to the respective Governments or Legislatures of the Provinces, and all Duties and Revenues raised by them in accordance with the special Powers conferred upon them by this Act, shall in each Province form One Consolidated Revenue Fund to be appropriated for the Public Service of the Province.

IX.—MISCELLANEOUS PROVISIONS.

*General.*

**127.** Repealed. (55)

Oath of
Allegiance, etc.

**128.** Every Member of the Senate or House of Commons of Canada shall before taking his Seat therein take and subscribe before the Governor General or some Person authorized by him, and every Member of a Legislative Council or Legislative Assembly of any Province shall before taking his Seat therein take and subscribe before the Lieutenant Governor of the Province or some Person authorized by him, the Oath of Allegiance contained in the Fifth Schedule to this Act; and every Member of the Senate of Canada and every Member of the Legislative Council of Quebec shall also, before taking his Seat therein, take and subscribe before the Governor General, or some Person authorized by him, the Declaration of Qualification contained in the same Schedule.

Continuance of
existing Laws,
Courts,
Officers, etc.

**129.** Except as otherwise provided by this Act, all Laws in force in Canada, Nova Scotia, or New Brunswick at the Union, and all Courts of Civil and Criminal Jurisdiction, and all legal Commissions, Powers, and Authorities, and all Officers, Judicial, Administrative, and Ministerial, existing therein at the Union, shall continue in Ontario, Quebec, Nova Scotia, and New Brunswick respectively, as if the Union had not been made; subject nevertheless (except with respect to such as are enacted by or exist under Acts of the Parliament of Great Britain or of the Parliament of the United Kingdom of Great Britain and Ireland,) to be repealed, abolished, or altered by the Parliament of Canada, or by the Legislature of

---

(55) Repealed by the *Statute Law Revision Act, 1893*, 56-57 Vict., c. 14 (U.K.). The section read as follows:

> **127.** If any Person being at the passing of this Act a Member of the Legislative Council of Canada, Nova Scotia, or New Brunswick to whom a Place in the Senate is offered, does not within Thirty Days thereafter, by Writing under his Hand addressed to the Governor General of the Province of Canada or to the Lieutenant Governor of Nova Scotia or New Brunswick (as the Case may be), accept the same, he shall be deemed to have declined the same; and any Person who, being at the passing of this Act a Member of the Legislative Council of Nova Scotia or New Brunswick, accepts a Place in the Senate, shall thereby vacate his Seat in such Legislative Council.

the respective Province, according to the Authority of the Parliament or of that Legislature under this Act. (56)

**130.** Until the Parliament of Canada otherwise provides, all Officers of the several Provinces having Duties to discharge in relation to Matters other than those coming within the Classes of Subjects by this Act assigned exclusively to the Legislatures of the Provinces shall be Officers of Canada, and shall continue to discharge the Duties of their respective Offices under the same Liabilities, Responsibilities, and Penalties as if the Union had not been made. (57)

Transfer of Officers to Canada.

**131.** Until the Parliament of Canada otherwise provides, the Governor General in Council may from Time to Time appoint such Officers as the Governor General in Council deems necessary or proper for the effectual Execution of this Act.

Appointment of new Officers.

**132.** The Parliament and Government of Canada shall have all Powers necessary or proper for performing the Obligations of Canada or of any Province thereof, as Part of the British Empire, towards Foreign Countries, arising under Treaties between the Empire and such Foreign Countries.

Treaty Obligations.

**133.** Either the English or the French Language may be used by any Person in the Debates of the Houses of the Parliament of Canada and of the Houses of the Legislature of Quebec; and both those Languages shall be used in the respective Records and Journals of those Houses; and either of those Languages may be used by any Person or in any Pleading or Process in or issuing from any Court of Canada established under this Act, and in or from all or any of the Courts of Quebec.

Use of English and French Languages.

The Acts of the Parliament of Canada and of the Legislature of Quebec shall be printed and published in both those Languages.

### Ontario and Quebec.

**134.** Until the Legislature of Ontario or of Quebec otherwise provides, the Lieutenant Governors of Ontario and Quebec may each appoint under the Great Seal of the Province the following Officers, to hold Office during Pleasure, that is to say,—the Attorney General, the Secretary and Registrar of the Province, the Treasurer of the Province, the Commissioner of Crown Lands, and the Commissioner of Agriculture and Public Works, and in the Case of Quebec the

Appointment of Executive Officers for Ontario and Quebec.

---

(56) The restriction against altering or repealing laws enacted by or existing under statutes of the United Kingdom was removed by the *Statute of Westminster, 1931,* 22 Geo. V, c. 4 (U.K.)

(57) Spent.

Solicitor General, and may, by Order of the Lieutenant Governor in Council, from Time to Time prescribe the Duties of those Officers, and of the several Departments over which they shall preside or to which they shall belong, and of the Officers and Clerks thereof, and may also appoint other and additional Officers to hold Office during Pleasure, and may from Time to Time prescribe the Duties of those Officers, and of the several Departments over which they shall preside or to which they shall belong, and of the Officers and Clerks thereof. (58)

Powers, Duties, etc. of Executive Officers.

**135.** Until the Legislature of Ontario or Quebec otherwise provides, all Rights, Powers, Duties, Functions, Responsibilities, or Authorities at the passing of this Act vested in or imposed on the Attorney General, Solicitor General, Secretary and Registrar of the Province of Canada, Minister of Finance, Commissioner of Crown Lands, Commissioner of Public Works, and Minister of Agriculture and Receiver General, by any Law, Statute, or Ordinance of Upper Canada, Lower Canada, or Canada, and not repugnant to this Act, shall be vested in or imposed on any Officer to be appointed by the Lieutenant Governor for the Discharge of the same or any of them; and the Commissioner of Agriculture and Public Works shall perform the Duties and Functions of the Office of Minister of Agriculture at the passing of this Act imposed by the Law of the Province of Canada, as well as those of the Commissioner of Public Works. (59)

Great Seals.

**136.** Until altered by the Lieutenant Governor in Council, the Great Seals of Ontario and Quebec respectively shall be the same, or of the same Design, as those used in the Provinces of Upper Canada and Lower Canada respectively before their Union as the Province of Canada.

Construction of temporary Acts.

**137.** The words "and from thence to the End of the then next ensuing Session of the Legislature," or Words to the same Effect, used in any temporary Act of the Province of Canada not expired before the Union, shall be construed to extend and apply to the next Session of the Parliament of Canada if the Subject Matter of the Act is within the Powers of the same as defined by this Act, or to the next Sessions of the Legislatures of Ontario and Quebec respectively if the Subject Matter of the Act is within the Powers of the same as defined by this Act.

As to Errors in Names.

**138.** From and after the Union the Use of the Words "Upper Canada" instead of "Ontario," or "Lower Canada" instead of "Quebec," in any Deed, Writ, Process, Pleading, Document, Matter, or Thing, shall not invalidate the same.

---

(58) Spent. Now covered in Ontario by the *Executive Council Act*, R.S.O. 1970, c. 153 and in Quebec by the *Executive Power Act*, R.S.Q. 1964, c. 9.

(59) Probably spent.

**139.** Any Proclamation under the Great Seal of the Province of Canada issued before the Union to take effect at a Time which is subsequent to the Union, whether relating to that Province, or to Upper Canada, or to Lower Canada, and the several Matters and Things therein proclaimed, shall be and continue of like Force and Effect as if the Union had not been made. (60)

As to issue of Proclamations before Union, to commence after Union.

**140.** Any Proclamation which is authorized by any Act of the Legislature of the Province of Canada to be issued under the Great Seal of the Province of Canada, whether relating to that Province, or to Upper Canada, or to Lower Canada, and which is not issued before the Union, may be issued by the Lieutenant Governor of Ontario or of Quebec, as its Subject Matter requires, under the Great Seal thereof; and from and after the Issue of such Proclamation the same and the several Matters and Things therein proclaimed shall be and continue of the like Force and Effect in Ontario or Quebec as if the Union had not been made. (61)

As to issue of Proclamations after Union.

**141.** The Penitentiary of the Province of Canada shall, until the Parliament of Canada otherwise provides, be and continue the Penitentiary of Ontario and of Quebec. (62)

Peniteniary.

**142.** The Division and Adjustment of the Debts, Credits, Liabilities, Properties, and Assets of Upper Canada and Lower Canada shall be referred to the Arbitrament of Three Arbitrators, One chosen by the Government of Ontario, One by the Government of Quebec, and One by the Government of Canada; and the Selection of the Arbitrators shall not be made until the Parliament of Canada and the Legislatures of Ontario and Quebec have met; and the Arbitrator chosen by the Government of Canada shall not be a Resident either in Ontario or in Quebec. (63)

Arbitration respecting Debts, etc.

**143.** The Governor General in Council may from Time to Time order that such and so many of the Records, Books, and Documents of the Province of Canada as he thinks fit shall be appropriated and delivered either to Ontario or to Quebec, and the same shall thenceforth be the Property of that Province; and any Copy thereof or Extract therefrom, duly certified by the Officer having charge of the Original thereof, shall be admitted as Evidence. (64)

Division of Records.

(60) Probably spent.

(61) Probably spent.

(62) Spent. Penitentiaries are now provided for by the *Penitentiary Act*, R.S.C. 1970, c. P-6.

(63) Spent. See pages (xi) and (xii) of the Public Accounts, 1902-03.

(64) Probably spent. Two orders were made under this section on the 24th of January, 1868.

Constitution of
Townships in
Quebec.

**144.** The Lieutenant Governor of Quebec may from Time of Time, by Proclamation under the Great Seal of the Province, to take effect from a Day to be appointed therein, constitute Townships in those Parts of the Province of Quebec in which Townships are not then already constituted, and fix the Metes and Bounds thereof.

**145.** Repealed. (65)

### XI.—Admission of Other Colonies

Power to admit
Newfoundland,
etc., into the
Union.

**146.** It shall be lawful for the Queen, by and with the Advice of Her Majesty's Most Honourable Privy Council, on Addresses from the Houses of the Parliament of Canada, and from the Houses of the respective Legislatures of the Colonies or Provinces of Newfoundland, Prince Edward Island, and British Columbia, to admit those Colonies or Provinces, or any of them, into the Union, and on Address from the Houses of the Parliament of Canada to admit Rupert's Land and the North-western Territory, or either of them, into the Union, on such Terms and Conditions in each Case as are in the Addresses expressed and as the Queen thinks fit to approve, subject to the Provisions of this Act; and the Provisions of any Order in Council in that Behalf shall have effect as if they had been enacted by the Parliament of the United Kingdom of Great Britain and Ireland. (66)

As to Represen-
tation of
Newfoundland
and Prince
Edward Island
in Senate.

**147.** In case of the Admission of Newfoundland and Prince Edward Island, or either of them, each shall be entitled to a Representation in the Senate of Canada of Four Members, and (notwithstanding anything in this Act) in case of the Admission of Newfoundland the normal Number of Senators shall be Seventy-six and their maximum Number shall be Eighty-two; but Prince Edward Island when admitted

---

(65) Repealed by the *Statute Law Revision Act, 1893*, 56-57 Vict., c. 14, (U.K.). The section reads as follows:

#### X.—Intercolonial Railway.

**145.** Inasmuch as the Provinces of Canada, Nova Scotia, and New Brunswick have joined in a Declaration that the Construction of the Intercolonial Railway is essential to the Consolidation of the Union of British North America, and to the Assent thereto of Nova Scotia and New Brunswick, and have consequently agreed that Provision should be made for its immediate Construction by the Government of Canada: Therefore, in order to give effect to that Agreement, it shall be the Duty of the Government and Parliament of Canada to provide for the Commencement, within Six Months after the Union, of a Railway connecting the River St. Lawrence with the City of Halifax in Nova Scotia, and for the Construction thereof without Intermission, and the Completion thereof with all practicable Speed.

(66) All territories mentioned in this section are now part of Canada. See the notes to section 5, *supra.*

shall be deemed to be comprised in the Third of Three Divisions into which Canada is, in relation to the Constitution of the Senate, divided by this Act, and accordingly, after the Admission of Prince Edward Island, whether Newfoundland is admitted or not, the Representation of Nova Scotia and New Brunswick in the Senate shall, as Vacancies occur, be reduced from Twelve to Ten Members respectively, and the Representation of each of those Provinces shall not be increased at any Time beyond Ten, except under the Provisions of this Act for the Appointment of Three or Six additional Senators under the Direction of the Queen. (67)

---

(67) Spent. See the notes to sections 21, 22, 26, 27 and 28, *supra*.

# APPENDIX II PART B:   The Constitution Act, 1982

The text that follows reproduces the statute as published by Supply and Services Canada, *The Constitution Act, 1982* (Ottawa: Canadian Government Publishing Centre, 1982) omitting only the French translation.

CONSTITUTION ACT, 1982

PART I

CANADIAN CHARTER OF RIGHTS
AND FREEDOMS

Whereas Canada is founded upon principles that recognize the supremacy of God and the rule of law:

*Guarantee of Rights and Freedoms*

Rights and freedoms in Canada

**1.** The *Canadian Charter of Rights and Freedoms* guarantees the rights and freedoms set out in it subject only to such reasonable limits prescribed by law as can be demonstrably justified in a free and democratic society.

*Fundamental Freedoms*

Fundamental freedoms

**2.** Everyone has the following fundamental freedoms:

(*a*) freedom of conscience and religion;

(*b*) freedom of thought, belief, opinion and expression, including freedom of the press and other media of communication;

(*c*) freedom of peaceful assembly; and

(*d*) freedom of association.

*Democratic Rights*

Democratic rights of citizens

**3.** Every citizen of Canada has the right to vote in an election of members of the House of Commons or of a legislative assembly and to be qualified for membership therein.

Maximum duration of legislative bodies

**4.** (1) No House of Commons and no legislative assembly shall continue for longer than five years from the date fixed for the return of the writs at a general election of its members.

Continuation in special circumstances

(2) In time of real or apprehended war, invasion or insurrection, a House of Commons may be continued by Parliament and a legislative assembly may be continued by the legislature beyond five years if such continuation is not opposed by the votes of more than one-third of the members of the House of Commons or the legislative assembly, as the case may be.

Annual sitting of legislative bodies

**5.** There shall be a sitting of Parliament and of each legislature at least once every twelve months.

*Mobility Rights*

Mobility of citizens

**6.** (1) Every citizen of Canada has the right to enter, remain in and leave Canada.

Rights to move and gain livelihood

(2) Every citizen of Canada and every person who has the status of a permanent resident of Canada has the right

(*a*) to move to and take up residence in any province; and

(*b*) to pursue the gaining of a livelihood in any province.

Limitation

(3) The rights specified in subsection (2) are subject to

(*a*) any laws or practices of general application in force in a province other than those that discriminate among persons primarily on the basis of province of present or previous residence; and

(*b*) any laws providing for reasonable residency requirements as a qualification for the receipt of publicly provided social services.

Affirmative action programs

(4) Subsections (2) and (3) do not preclude any law, program or activity that has as its object the amelioration in a province of conditions of individuals in that province who are socially or economically disadvantaged if the rate of employment in that province is below the rate of employment in Canada.

*Legal Rights*

Life, liberty and security of person

**7.** Everyone has the right to life, liberty and security of the person and the right not to be deprived thereof except in accordance with the principles of fundamental justice.

Search or seizure

**8.** Everyone has the right to be secure against unreasonable search or seizure.

Detention or imprisonment

**9.** Everyone has the right not to be arbitrarily detained or imprisoned.

Arrest or detention

**10.** Everyone has the right on arrest or detention

(*a*) to be informed promptly of the reasons therefor;

(*b*) to retain and instruct counsel without delay and to be informed of that right; and

(*c*) to have the validity of the detention determined by way of *habeas corpus* and to be released if the detention is not lawful.

Proceedings in criminal and penal matters

**11.** Any person charged with an offence has the right

(*a*) to be informed without unreasonable delay of the specific offence;

(*b*) to be tried within a reasonable time;

(*c*) not to be compelled to be a witness in proceedings against that person in respect of the offence;

(*d*) to be presumed innocent until proven guilty according to law in a fair and public hearing by an independent and impartial tribunal;

(*e*) not to be denied reasonable bail without just cause;

(*f*) except in the case of an offence under military law tried before a military tribunal, to the benefit of trial by jury where the maximum punishment for the offence is imprisonment for five years or a more severe punishment;

(*g*) not to be found guilty on account of any act or omission unless, at the time of the act or omission, it constituted an offence under Canadian or international law or was criminal according to the general principles of law recognized by the community of nations;

(*h*) if finally acquitted of the offence, not to be tried for it again and, if finally found guilty and punished for the offence, not to be tried or punished for it again; and

(*i*) if found guilty of the offence and if the punishment for the offence has been varied between the time of commission and the time of sentencing, to the benefit of the lesser punishment.

Treatment or punishment

**12.** Everyone has the right not to be subjected to any cruel and unusual treatment or punishment.

Self-crimination

**13.** A witness who testifies in any proceedings has the right not to have any incriminating evidence so given used to incriminate that witness in any other proceedings, except in a prosecution for perjury or for the giving of contradictory evidence.

Interpreter

**14.** A party or witness in any proceedings who does not understand or speak the language in which the proceedings are conducted or who is deaf has the right to the assistance of an interpreter.

### Equality Rights

Equality before and under law and equal protection and benefit of law

**15.** (1) Every individual is equal before and under the law and has the right to the equal protection and equal benefit of the law without discrimination and, in particular, without discrimination based on race, national or ethnic origin, colour, religion, sex, age or mental or physical disability.

Affirmative action programs

(2) Subsection (1) does not preclude any law, program or activity that has as its object the amelioration of conditions of disadvantaged individuals or groups including those that are disadvantaged because of

race, national or ethnic origin, colour, religion, sex, age or mental or physical disability.

### Official Languages of Canada

Official languages of Canada

**16.** (1) English and French are the official languages of Canada and have equality of status and equal rights and privileges as to their use in all institutions of the Parliament and government of Canada.

Official languages of New Brunswick

(2) English and French are the official languages of New Brunswick and have equality of status and equal rights and privileges as to their use in all institutions of the legislature and government of New Brunswick.

Advancement of status and use

(3) Nothing in this Charter limits the authority of Parliament or a legislature to advance the equality of status or use of English and French.

Proceedings of Parliament

**17.** (1) Everyone has the right to use English or French in any debates and other proceedings of Parliament.

Proceedings of New Brunswick legislature

(2) Everyone has the right to use English or French in any debates and other proceedings of the legislature of New Brunswick.

Parliamentary statutes and records

**18.** (1) The statutes, records and journals of Parliament shall be printed and published in English and French and both language versions are equally authoritative.

New Brunswick statutes and records

(2) The statutes, records and journals of the legislature of New Brunswick shall be printed and published in English and French and both language versions are equally authoritative.

Proceedings in courts established by Parliament

**19.** (1) Either English or French may be used by any person in, or in any pleading in or process issuing from, any court established by Parliament.

Proceedings in New Brunswick courts

(2) Either English or French may be used by any person in, or in any pleading in or process issuing from, any court of New Brunswick.

Communications by public with federal institutions

**20.** (1) Any member of the public in Canada has the right to communicate with, and to receive available services from, any head or central office of an institution of the Parliament or government of Canada in English or French, and has the same right with respect to any other office of any such institution where

(*a*) there is a significant demand for communications with and services from that office in such language; or

(*b*) due to the nature of the office, it is reasonable that communications with and services from that office be available in both English and French.

Communications by public with New Brunswick institutions

(2) Any member of the public in New Brunswick has the right to communicate with, and to receive available services from, any office of an institution of the legislature or government of New Brunswick in English or French.

Continuation of existing constitutional provisions

**21.** Nothing in sections 16 to 20 abrogates or derogates from any right, privilege or obligation with respect to the English and French languages, or either of them, that exists or is continued by virtue of any other provision of the Constitution of Canada.

Rights and privileges preserved

**22.** Nothing in sections 16 to 20 abrogates or derogates from any legal or customary right or privilege acquired or enjoyed either before or after the coming into force of this Charter with respect to any language that is not English or French.

### Minority Language Educational Rights

Language of instruction

**23.** (1) Citizens of Canada

(*a*) whose first language learned and still understood is that of the English or French linguistic minority population of the province in which they reside, or

(*b*) who have received their primary school instruction in Canada in English or French and reside in a province where the language in which they received that instruction is the language of the English or French linguistic minority population of the province,

have the right to have their children receive primary and secondary school instruction in that language in that province.

**Continuity of language instruction**

(2) Citizens of Canada of whom any child has received or is receiving primary or secondary school instruction in English or French in Canada, have the right to have all their children receive primary and secondary school instruction in the same language.

**Application where numbers warrant**

(3) The right of citizens of Canada under subsections (1) and (2) to have their children receive primary and secondary school instruction in the language of the English or French linguistic minority population of a province

(*a*) applies wherever in the province the number of children of citizens who have such a right is sufficient to warrant the provision to them out of public funds of minority language instruction; and

(*b*) includes, where the number of those children so warrants, the right to have them receive that instruction in minority language educational facilities provided out of public funds.

*Enforcement*

**Enforcement of guaranteed rights and freedoms**

**24.** (1) Anyone whose rights or freedoms, as guaranteed by this Charter, have been infringed or denied may apply to a court of competent jurisdiction to obtain such remedy as the court considers appropriate and just in the circumstances.

**Exclusion of evidence bringing administration of justice into disrepute**

(2) Where, in proceedings under subsection (1), a court concludes that evidence was obtained in a manner

that infringed or denied any rights or freedoms guaranteed by this Charter, the evidence shall be excluded if it is established that, having regard to all the circumstances, the admission of it in the proceedings would bring the administration of justice into disrepute.

*General*

**25.** The guarantee in this Charter of certain rights and freedoms shall not be construed so as to abrogate or derogate from any aboriginal, treaty or other rights or freedoms that pertain to the aboriginal peoples of Canada including

**Aboriginal rights and freedoms not affected by Charter**

(*a*) any rights or freedoms that have been recognized by the Royal Proclamation of October 7, 1763; and

(*b*) any rights or freedoms that may be acquired by the aboriginal peoples of Canada by way of land claims settlement.

**26.** The guarantee in this Charter of certain rights and freedoms shall not be construed as denying the existence of any other rights or freedoms that exist in Canada.

**Other rights and freedoms not affected by Charter**

**27.** This Charter shall be interpreted in a manner consistent with the preservation and enhancement of the multicultural heritage of Canadians.

**Multicultural heritage**

**28.** Notwithstanding anything in this Charter, the rights and freedoms referred to in it are guaranteed equally to male and female persons.

**Rights guaranteed equally to both sexes**

**29.** Nothing in this Charter abrogates or derogates from any rights or privileges guaranteed by or under the Constitution of Canada in respect of denominational, separate or dissentient schools.

**Rights respecting certain schools preserved**

**30.** A reference in this Charter to a province or to the legislative assembly or legislature of a province shall be deemed to include a reference to the Yukon Territory and the Northwest Territories, or to the appropriate legislative authority thereof, as the case may be.

**Application to territories and territorial authorities**

Legislative powers not extended

**31.** Nothing in this Charter extends the legislative powers of any body or authority.

*Application of Charter*

Application of Charter

**32.** (1) This Charter applies

(*a*) to the Parliament and government of Canada in respect of all matters within the authority of Parliament including all matters relating to the Yukon Territory and Northwest Territories; and

(*b*) to the legislature and government of each province in respect of all matters within the authority of the legislature of each province.

Exception

(2) Notwithstanding subsection (1), section 15 shall not have effect until three years after this section comes into force.

Exception where express declaration

**33.** (1) Parliament or the legislature of a province may expressly declare in an Act of Parliament or of the legislature, as the case may be, that the Act or a provision thereof shall operate notwithstanding a provision included in section 2 or sections 7 to 15 of this Charter.

Operation of exception

(2) An Act or a provision of an Act in respect of which a declaration made under this section is in effect shall have such operation as it would have but for the provision of this Charter referred to in the declaration.

Five year limitation

(3) A declaration made under subsection (1) shall cease to have effect five years after it comes into force or on such earlier date as may be specified in the declaration.

Re-enactment

(4) Parliament or the legislature of a province may re-enact a declaration made under subsection (1).

Five year limitation

(5) Subsection (3) applies in respect of a re-enactment made under subsection (4).

*Citation*

Citation

**34.** This Part may be cited as the *Canadian Charter of Rights and Freedoms.*

## PART II

### RIGHTS OF THE ABORIGINAL PEOPLES OF CANADA

Recognition of existing aboriginal and treaty rights

**35.** (1) The existing aboriginal and treaty rights of the aboriginal peoples of Canada are hereby recognized and affirmed.

Definition of "aboriginal peoples of Canada"

(2) In this Act, "aboriginal peoples of Canada" includes the Indian, Inuit and Métis peoples of Canada.

## PART III

### EQUALIZATION AND REGIONAL DISPARITIES

Commitment to promote equal opportunities

**36.** (1) Without altering the legislative authority of Parliament or of the provincial legislatures, or the rights of any of them with respect to the exercise of their legislative authority, Parliament and the legislatures, together with the government of Canada and the provincial governments, are committed to

(*a*) promoting equal opportunities for the well-being of Canadians;

(*b*) furthering economic development to reduce disparity in opportunities; and

(*c*) providing essential public services of reasonable quality to all Canadians.

Commitment respecting public services

(2) Parliament and the government of Canada are committed to the principle of making equalization payments to ensure that provincial governments have sufficient revenues to provide reasonably comparable levels of public services at reasonably comparable levels of taxation.

## PART IV

### CONSTITUTIONAL CONFERENCE

Constitutional conference

**37.** (1) A constitutional conference composed of the Prime Minister of Canada and the first ministers of the provinces shall be convened by the Prime Minister of Canada within one year after this Part comes into force.

Participation of aboriginal peoples

(2) The conference convened under subsection (1) shall have included in its agenda an item respecting constitutional matters that directly affect the aboriginal peoples of Canada, including the identification and definition of the rights of those peoples to be included in the Constitution of Canada, and the Prime Minister of Canada shall invite representatives of those peoples to participate in the discussions on that item.

Participation of territories

(3) The Prime Minister of Canada shall invite elected representatives of the governments of the Yukon Territory and the Northwest Territories to participate in the discussions on any item on the agenda of the conference convened under subsection (1) that, in the opinion of the Prime Minister, directly affects the Yukon Territory and the Northwest Territories.

### PART V

### PROCEDURE FOR AMENDING CONSTITUTION OF CANADA

General procedure for amending Constitution of Canada

**38.** (1) An amendment to the Constitution of Canada may be made by proclamation issued by the Governor General under the Great Seal of Canada where so authorized by

(*a*) resolutions of the Senate and House of Commons; and

(*b*) resolutions of the legislative assemblies of at least two-thirds of the provinces that have, in the aggregate, according to the then latest general census, at least fifty per cent of the population of all the provinces.

Majority of members

(2) An amendment made under subsection (1) that derogates from the legislative powers, the proprietary rights or any other rights or privileges of the legislature or government of a province shall require a resolution supported by a majority of the members of each of the Senate, the House of Commons and the legislative assemblies required under subsection (1).

Expression of dissent

(3) An amendment referred to in subsection (2) shall not have effect in a province the legislative assembly of which has expressed its dissent thereto by resolution supported by a majority of its members prior to the issue of the proclamation to which the amendment relates unless that legislative assembly, subsequently, by resolution supported by a majority of its members, revokes its dissent and authorizes the amendment.

Revocation of dissent

(4) A resolution of dissent made for the purposes of subsection (3) may be revoked at any time before or after the issue of the proclamation to which it relates.

Restriction on proclamation

**39.** (1) A proclamation shall not be issued under subsection 38(1) before the expiration of one year from the adoption of the resolution initiating the amendment procedure thereunder, unless the legislative assembly of each province has previously adopted a resolution of assent or dissent.

Idem

(2) A proclamation shall not be issued under subsection 38(1) after the expiration of three years from the adoption of the resolution initiating the amendment procedure thereunder.

Compensation

**40.** Where an amendment is made under subsection 38(1) that transfers provincial legislative powers relating to education or other cultural matters from provincial legislatures to Parliament, Canada shall provide reasonable compensation to any province to which the amendment does not apply.

Amendment by unanimous consent

**41.** An amendment to the Constitution of Canada in relation to the following matters may be made by proclamation issued by the Governor General under the Great Seal of

Canada only where authorized by resolutions of the Senate and House of Commons and of the legislative assembly of each province:

(*a*) the office of the Queen, the Governor General and the Lieutenant Governor of a province;

(*b*) the right of a province to a number of members in the House of Commons not less than the number of Senators by which the province is entitled to be represented at the time this Part comes into force;

(*c*) subject to section 43, the use of the English or the French language;

(*d*) the composition of the Supreme Court of Canada; and

(*e*) an amendment to this Part.

**Amendment by general procedure**

**42.** (1) An amendment to the Constitution of Canada in relation to the following matters may be made only in accordance with subsection 38(1):

(*a*) the principle of proportionate representation of the provinces in the House of Commons prescribed by the Constitution of Canada;

(*b*) the powers of the Senate and the method of selecting Senators;

(*c*) the number of members by which a province is entitled to be represented in the Senate and the residence qualifications of Senators;

(*d*) subject to paragraph 41(*d*), the Supreme Court of Canada;

(*e*) the extension of existing provinces into the territories; and

(*f*) notwithstanding any other law or practice, the establishment of new provinces.

**Exception**

(2) Subsections 38(2) to (4) do not apply in respect of amendments in relation to matters referred to in subsection (1).

**Amendment of provisions relating to some but not all provinces**

**43.** An amendment to the Constitution of Canada in relation to any provision that applies to one or more, but not all, provinces, including

(*a*) any alteration to boundaries between provinces, and

(*b*) any amendment to any provision that relates to the use of the English or the French language within a province,

may be made by proclamation issued by the Governor General under the Great Seal of Canada only where so authorized by resolutions of the Senate and House of Commons and of the legislative assembly of each province to which the amendment applies.

**44.** Subject to sections 41 and 42, Parliament may exclusively make laws amending the Constitution of Canada in relation to the executive government of Canada or the Senate and House of Commons.

**Amendments by Parliament**

**45.** Subject to section 41, the legislature of each province may exclusively make laws amending the constitution of the province.

**Amendments by provincial legislatures**

**46.** (1) The procedures for amendment under sections 38, 41, 42 and 43 may be initiated either by the Senate or the House of Commons or by the legislative assembly of a province.

**Initiation of amendment procedures**

(2) A resolution of assent made for the purposes of this Part may be revoked at any time before the issue of a proclamation authorized by it.

**Revocation of authorization**

**47.** (1) An amendment to the Constitution of Canada made by proclamation under section 38, 41, 42 or 43 may be made without a resolution of the Senate authorizing the issue of the proclamation if, within one hundred and eighty days after the adoption by the House of Commons of a resolution authorizing its issue, the Senate has not adopted such a resolution and if, at any time after the expiration of that period, the House of Commons again adopts the resolution.

**Amendments without Senate resolution**

(2) Any period when Parliament is prorogued or dissolved shall not be counted in computing the one hundred and eighty day period referred to in subsection (1).

**Computation of period**

Advice to issue
proclamation

**48.** The Queen's Privy Council for Canada shall advise the Governor General to issue a proclamation under this Part forthwith on the adoption of the resolutions required for an amendment made by proclamation under this Part.

Constitutional
conference

**49.** A constitutional conference composed of the Prime Minister of Canada and the first ministers of the provinces shall be convened by the Prime Minister of Canada within fifteen years after this Part comes into force to review the provisions of this Part.

PART VI

AMENDMENT TO THE
CONSTITUTION ACT, 1867

Amendment to
Constitution
Act, 1867

**50.** The *Constitution Act, 1867* (formerly named the *British North America Act, 1867*) is amended by adding thereto, immediately after section 92 thereof, the following heading and section:

*"Non-Renewable Natural
Resources, Forestry Resources and
Electrical Energy*

Laws respecting
non-renewable
natural
resources,
forestry
resources and
electrical
energy

**92A.** (1) In each province, the legislature may exclusively make laws in relation to

(*a*) exploration for non-renewable natural resources in the province;

(*b*) development, conservation and management of non-renewable natural resources and forestry resources in the province, including laws in relation to the rate of primary production therefrom; and

(*c*) development, conservation and management of sites and facilities in the province for the generation and production of electrical energy.

Export from
provinces of
resources

(2) In each province, the legislature may make laws in relation to the export from the province to another part of Canada of the primary production from non-renewable natural resources and forestry resources in the province and the production from facilities in the province for the generation of electrical energy, but such laws may not authorize or provide for discrimination in prices or in supplies exported to another part of Canada.

(3) Nothing in subsection (2) derogates from the authority of Parliament to enact laws in relation to the matters referred to in that subsection and, where such a law of Parliament and a law of a province conflict, the law of Parliament prevails to the extent of the conflict.

Authority of
Parliament

(4) In each province, the legislature may make laws in relation to the raising of money by any mode or system of taxation in respect of

Taxation of
resources

(*a*) non-renewable natural resources and forestry resources in the province and the primary production therefrom, and

(*b*) sites and facilities in the province for the generation of electrical energy and the production therefrom,

whether or not such production is exported in whole or in part from the province, but such laws may not authorize or provide for taxation that differentiates between production exported to another part of Canada and production not exported from the province.

(5) The expression "primary production" has the meaning assigned by the Sixth Schedule.

"Primary
production"

(6) Nothing in subsections (1) to (5) derogates from any powers or rights that a legislature or government of a province had immediately before the coming into force of this section."

Existing powers
or rights

Idem

**51.** The said Act is further amended by adding thereto the following Schedule:

## "THE SIXTH SCHEDULE

### *Primary Production from Non-Renewable Natural Resources and Forestry Resources*

**1.** For the purposes of section 92A of this Act,

(*a*) production from a non-renewable natural resource is primary production therefrom if

(i) it is in the form in which it exists upon its recovery or severance from its natural state, or

(ii) it is a product resulting from processing or refining the resource, and is not a manufactured product or a product resulting from refining crude oil, refining upgraded heavy crude oil, refining gases or liquids derived from coal or refining a synthetic equivalent of crude oil; and

(*b*) production from a forestry resource is primary production therefrom if it consists of sawlogs, poles, lumber, wood chips, sawdust or any other primary wood product, or wood pulp, and is not a product manufactured from wood."

### PART VII

### GENERAL

Primacy of Constitution of Canada

**52.** (1) The Constitution of Canada is the supreme law of Canada, and any law that is inconsistent with the provisions of the Constitution is, to the extent of the inconsistency, of no force or effect.

Constitution of Canada

(2) The Constitution of Canada includes

(*a*) the *Canada Act 1982*, including this Act;

(*b*) the Acts and orders referred to in the schedule; and

(*c*) any amendment to any Act or order referred to in paragraph (*a*) or (*b*).

Amendments to Constitution of Canada

(3) Amendments to the Constitution of Canada shall be made only in accordance with the authority contained in the Constitution of Canada.

Repeals and new names

**53.** (1) The enactments referred to in Column I of the schedule are hereby repealed or amended to the extent indicated in Column II thereof and, unless repealed, shall continue as law in Canada under the names set out in Column III thereof.

Consequential amendments

(2) Every enactment, except the *Canada Act 1982*, that refers to an enactment referred to in the schedule by the name in Column I thereof is hereby amended by substituting for that name the corresponding name in Column III thereof, and any British North America Act not referred to in the schedule may be cited as the *Constitution Act* followed by the year and number, if any, of its enactment.

Repeal and consequential amendments

**54.** Part IV is repealed on the day that is one year after this Part comes into force and this section may be repealed and this Act renumbered, consequentially upon the repeal of Part IV and this section, by proclamation issued by the Governor General under the Great Seal of Canada.

French version of Constitution of Canada

**55.** A French version of the portions of the Constitution of Canada referred to in the schedule shall be prepared by the Minister of Justice of Canada as expeditiously as possible and, when any portion thereof sufficient to warrant action being taken has been so prepared, it shall be put forward for enactment by proclamation issued by the Governor General under the Great Seal of Canada pursuant to the procedure then applicable to an amendment of the same provisions of the Constitution of Canada.

**English and French versions of certain constitutional texts**

**56.** Where any portion of the Constitution of Canada has been or is enacted in English and French or where a French version of any portion of the Constitution is enacted pursuant to section 55, the English and French versions of that portion of the Constitution are equally authoritative.

**English and French versions of this Act**

**57.** The English and French versions of this Act are equally authoritative.

**Commencement**

**58.** Subject to section 59, this Act shall come into force on a day to be fixed by proclamation issued by the Queen or the Governor General under the Great Seal of Canada.

**Commencement of paragraph 23(1)(a) in respect of Quebec**

**59.** (1) Paragraph 23(1)(a) shall come into force in respect of Quebec on a day to be fixed by proclamation issued by the Queen or the Governor General under the Great Seal of Canada.

(2) A proclamation under subsection (1) shall be issued only where authorized by the legislative assembly or government of Quebec.

**Authorization of Quebec**

(3) This section may be repealed on the day paragraph 23(1)(a) comes into force in respect of Quebec and this Act amended and renumbered, consequentially upon the repeal of this section, by proclamation issued by the Queen or the Governor General under the Great Seal of Canada.

**Repeal of this section**

**60.** This Act may be cited as the *Constitution Act, 1982*, and the Constitution Acts 1867 to 1975 (No. 2) and this Act may be cited together as the *Constitution Acts, 1867 to 1982*.

**Short title and citations**

## SCHEDULE

to the

## CONSTITUTION ACT, 1982

## MODERNIZATION OF THE CONSTITUTION

| Item | Column I<br>Act Affected | Column II<br>Amendment | Column III<br>New Name |
|---|---|---|---|
| 1. | British North America Act, 1867, 30-31 Vict., c. 3 (U.K.) | (1) Section 1 is repealed and the following substituted therefor:<br>"1. This Act may be cited as the *Constitution Act, 1867*."<br>(2) Section 20 is repealed.<br>(3) Class 1 of section 91 is repealed.<br>(4) Class 1 of section 92 is repealed. | Constitution Act, 1867 |
| 2. | An Act to amend and continue the Act 32-33 Victoria chapter 3; and to establish and provide for the Government of the Province of Manitoba, 1870, 33 Vict., c. 3 (Can.) | (1) The long title is repealed and the following substituted therefor:<br>"*Manitoba Act, 1870.*"<br>(2) Section 20 is repealed. | Manitoba Act, 1870 |
| 3. | Order of Her Majesty in Council admitting Rupert's Land and the North-Western Territory into the union, dated the 23rd day of June, 1870 | | Rupert's Land and North-Western Territory Order |
| 4. | Order of Her Majesty in Council admitting British Columbia into the Union, dated the 16th day of May, 1871 | | British Columbia Terms of Union |
| 5. | British North America Act, 1871, 34-35 Vict., c. 28 (U.K.) | Section 1 is repealed and the following substituted therefor:<br>"1. This Act may be cited as the *Constitution Act, 1871*." | Constitution Act, 1871 |
| 6. | Order of Her Majesty in Council admitting Prince Edward Island into the Union, dated the 26th day of June, 1873 | | Prince Edward Island Terms of Union |
| 7. | Parliament of Canada Act, 1875, 38-39 Vict., c. 38 (U.K.) | | Parliament of Canada Act, 1875 |
| 8. | Order of Her Majesty in Council admitting all British possessions and Territories in North America and islands adjacent thereto into the Union, dated the 31st day of July, 1880 | | Adjacent Territories Order |

SCHEDULE

to the

CONSTITUTION ACT, 1982—*Continued*

| Item | Column I<br>Act Affected | Column II<br>Amendment | Column III<br>New Name |
|---|---|---|---|
| 9. | British North America Act, 1886, 49-50 Vict., c. 35 (U.K.) | Section 3 is repealed and the following substituted therefor:<br>"3. This Act may be cited as the *Constitution Act, 1886*." | Constitution Act, 1886 |
| 10. | Canada (Ontario Boundary) Act, 1889, 52-53 Vict., c. 28 (U.K.) | | Canada (Ontario Boundary) Act, 1889 |
| 11. | Canadian Speaker (Appointment of Deputy) Act, 1895, 2nd Sess., 59 Vict., c. 3 (U.K.) | The Act is repealed. | |
| 12. | The Alberta Act, 1905, 4-5 Edw. VII, c. 3 (Can.) | | Alberta Act |
| 13. | The Saskatchewan Act, 1905, 4-5 Edw. VII, c. 42 (Can.) | | Saskatchewan Act |
| 14. | British North America Act, 1907, 7 Edw. VII, c. 11 (U.K.) | Section 2 is repealed and the following substituted therefor:<br>"2. This Act may be cited as the *Constitution Act, 1907*." | Constitution Act, 1907 |
| 15. | British North America Act, 1915, 5-6 Geo. V, c. 45 (U.K.) | Section 3 is repealed and the following substituted therefor:<br>"3. This Act may be cited as the *Constitution Act, 1915*." | Constitution Act, 1915 |
| 16. | British North America Act, 1930, 20-21 Geo. V, c. 26 (U.K.) | Section 3 is repealed and the following substituted therefor:<br>"3. This Act may be cited as the *Constitution Act, 1930*." | Constitution Act, 1930 |
| 17. | Statute of Westminster, 1931, 22 Geo. V, c. 4 (U.K.) | In so far as they apply to Canada,<br>(*a*) section 4 is repealed; and<br>(*b*) subsection 7(1) is repealed. | Statute of Westminster, 1931 |

SCHEDULE

to the

CONSTITUTION ACT, 1982— *Continued*

| Item | Column I<br>Act Affected | Column II<br>Amendment | Column III<br>New Name |
|------|--------------------------|------------------------|------------------------|
| 18. | British North America Act, 1940, 3-4 Geo. VI, c. 36 (U.K.) | Section 2 is repealed and the following substituted therefor:<br>"2. This Act may be cited as the *Constitution Act, 1940*." | Constitution Act, 1940 |
| 19. | British North America Act, 1943, 6-7 Geo. VI, c. 30 (U.K.) | The Act is repealed. | |
| 20. | British North America Act, 1946, 9-10 Geo. VI, c. 63 (U.K.) | The Act is repealed. | |
| 21. | British North America Act, 1949, 12-13 Geo. VI, c. 22 (U.K.) | Section 3 is repealed and the following substituted therefor:<br>"3. This Act may be cited as the *Newfoundland Act*." | Newfoundland Act |
| 22. | British North America (No. 2) Act, 1949, 13 Geo. VI, c. 81 (U.K.) | The Act is repealed. | |
| 23. | British North America Act, 1951, 14-15 Geo. VI, c. 32 (U.K.) | The Act is repealed. | |
| 24. | British North America Act, 1952, 1 Eliz. II, c. 15 (Can.) | The Act is repealed. | |
| 25. | British North America Act, 1960, 9 Eliz. II, c. 2 (U.K.) | Section 2 is repealed and the following substituted therefor:<br>"2. This Act may be cited as the *Constitution Act, 1960*." | Constitution Act, 1960 |
| 26. | British North America Act, 1964, 12-13 Eliz. II, c. 73 (U.K.) | Section 2 is repealed and the following substituted therefor:<br>"2. This Act may be cited as the *Constitution Act, 1964*." | Constitution Act, 1964 |

SCHEDULE

to the

CONSTITUTION ACT, 1982—*Concluded*

| Item | Column I<br>Act Affected | Column II<br>Amendment | Column III<br>New Name |
|------|--------------------------|------------------------|------------------------|
| 27. | British North America Act, 1965, 14 Eliz. II, c. 4, Part I (Can.) | Section 2 is repealed and the following substituted therefor:<br>"2. This Part may be cited as the *Constitution Act, 1965*." | Constitution Act, 1965 |
| 28. | British North America Act, 1974, 23 Eliz. II, c. 13, Part I (Can.) | Section 3, as amended by 25-26 Eliz. II, c. 28, s. 38(1) (Can.), is repealed and the following substituted therefor:<br>"3. This Part may be cited as the *Constitution Act, 1974*." | Constitution Act, 1974 |
| 29. | British North America Act, 1975, 23-24 Eliz. II, c. 28, Part I (Can.) | Section 3, as amended by 25-26 Eliz. II, c. 28, s. 31 (Can.), is repealed and the following substituted therefor:<br>"3. This Part may be cited as the *Constitution Act (No. 1), 1975*." | Constitution Act (No. 1), 1975 |
| 30. | British North America Act (No. 2), 1975, 23-24 Eliz. II, c. 53 (Can.) | Section 3 is repealed and the following substituted therefor:<br>"3. This Act may be cited as the *Constitution Act (No. 2), 1975*." | Constitution Act (No. 2), 1975 |

# Photo Credits

Every reasonable effort has been made to find copyright holders of the following material. The publishers would be pleased to have any errors or omissions brought to their attention.

p.xiv Early map of the New World, mid-1500's (Public Archives of Canada—National Map Collection); p. 16 "Abitation de Quebec", engraved after the original published by Samuel de Champlain in Paris, 1613 (APC/PAC C-09711); p. 28 Seventeenth-century parish of Pointe-Clare drawn by James Duncan, 1831 (McCord Museum, Boston); p. 42 Habitant's bedroom with goose feather mattress and pine armoire (National Film Board of Canada); p. 58 Representation of the Battle of the Plains of Abraham, painted by G.B. Campion, 1759 (PAC C-4501); p. 80 Montreal, painted by A. Sheriff Scott, 1826 (Canadian Imperial Bank of Commerce); p. 94 Surrender of Gen. William Hull to Gen. Isaac Brock, Aug. 16, 1812 (PAC C-16404); p. 111 Louis Joseph Papineau (PAC C-66899) and William Lyon Mackenzie (PAC C-1993); p. 128 John Lambton, first Earl of Durham (PAC C-15017); p. 144 Shipbuilding in the fields, near Dorchester, N.S. (PAC C-72924); p. 164 Charlottetown Conference, 1864 (PAC C-733); p. 184 Sir John A. Macdonald (PAC C-8447) and George Etienne Cartier (PAC C-14247); p. 206 Edward Blake (PAC PA-13010) and Alexander Mackenzie (PAC C-96); p. 226 The last spike ceremony staged by the construction crew that missed the original ceremony, 1885 (PAC C-14115); p. 252 Lumbering off Keewatin, Ont. at the end of the nineteenth century (PAC C-11779); p. 276 Wilfrid Laurier campaigning in 1908 (PAC C-463); p. 292 A Canadian battalion going over the top, Oct. 1916 (PAC PA-648); p. 328 William Lyon Mackenzie King; p. 346 Single Men's Unemployment Association parading in Toronto, 1930's (National Photography Collection/PAC C-29397); p. 366 Defense workers during WWII (PAC C-467); p. 380 First Quebec Conference, Aug. 1943 (left to right): W.L. Mackenzie King, Franklin D. Roosevelt and Winston Churchill (PAC C-29466); p. 398 John G. Diefenbaker (PAC C-10434/Copyright: Grand Grip and Batten, Ottawa); p. 416 Charles de Gaulle, Montreal, 1967; p. 436 Pierre Elliott Trudeau at a Liberal (leadership) convention, Ottawa, April 1968 (PAC PR-117472); p. 458 Queen Elizabeth signing the new Canadian Constitution, April 1982.

Maps by Victor Lytwyn

# Index